Strategies for Effective Teaching

Strategies for Effective Teaching

Allan C. Ornstein

Loyola University of Chicago

HarperCollinsPublishers

Sponsoring Editor: Alan McClare
Project Coordination: Publishing Synthesis, Ltd.
Art Direction/Cover Coordination: Heather Ziegler
Cover Design: Lucy Krikorian
Cover Photo: The Stock Market © Palmer/Kane, Inc.
Production: Beth Maglione

Strategies for Effective Teaching

Copyright © 1990 by HarperCollins*Publishers*, Inc.

Library of Congress Cataloging-in-Publication Data

Ornstein, Allan C.
    Strategies for effective teaching / Allan C. Ornstein.
        p.   cm.
    ISBN 0-06-044927-6
    1. Teaching.   2. Classroom management.   3. Lesson planning.
    4. Teachers—Training of.   I. Title.
    LB1025.2.0762   1990
    371.1′02—dc20
                                                                89-48348
                                                                    CIP

90 91 92 93 9 8 7 6 5 4 3

Dedication

All of us have had teachers whom we remember with fond memories and who were apparently good teachers. I remember six:

Mrs. Katz, P.S. 42 Queens: a warm, friendly, and understanding teacher who was concerned more with social development than with cognitive development.

Mrs. Schwartz, P.S. 42 Queens: a tough school marm who drilled the facts and enforced the rules.

Mr. Tietz, Far Rockaway High School: a good natured, quick-witted teacher with a booming voice.

Dr. Kohn, City College of New York: the scholar type, who through dialogue and questioning made me think.

Dr. Greene, Brooklyn College: humanistic and philosophical, she emphasized the personal, emotional, and moral aspects of education.

Dr. Clift, New York University: both friend and teacher, he balanced the talents and tempers of his students, and animated the best plans for their good.

Contents

Tips for Teachers

Professional Viewpoints

To the Instructor

This book is written for all who are interested in learning how to teach or improve their teaching, as well as teaching students how to learn. It will help prepare novice teachers for their new roles, and provide seasoned teachers with new insights into what they are doing.

The text focuses on the theory and practice of teaching. It attempts to blend theory with practice by reporting and analyzing important research, then presenting practical procedures and adaptive strategies for teachers to use. For example, what do successful teachers do to start a lesson? How do they monitor classroom activities? How do they deal with disruptive students? How do they proceed with a student who doesn't know the answer? These are problems that teachers must deal with on a daily basis. The answers to these questions depend on how we apply the theory we have learned in our course work to the classroom setting.

Prospective teachers and beginning teachers need to master theoretical concepts and principles and then *integrate* these concepts and principles into practice by developing specific methods and strategies that work on the job. The integration process, or the leap from theory to practice, is not easy. However, this book helps by interweaving practical strategies and methods with research. Many theories and practices are presented with the understanding that the reader can pick and choose those methods and strategies that coincide with his or her personality and philosophy. In each chapter look for "Tips for Teachers," "Guidelines for Implementing . . ." the research, and a section entitled "Theory into Practice" at the end of each chapter. These sections of the text are designed to help the reader apply the theory to practice.

The book adopts a cognitive science approach, blending cognitive-developmental research with informational-processing research. Consequently, a good deal of the subject matter is rooted in educational psychology, linguistics, and subject-related methods—and there is little that deals with philosophy, history, or sociology of teaching.

Cognitive science focuses on how teachers teach and how learners learn; it has reached a point that it can be used to derive strategies that guide effective teaching and learning. The book presents research on how students process information or what we call "learning strategies": how to skim data, summarize information, take notes, do homework, read text material, take tests, and so forth. Existing research can be used to teach students to think critically: to classify, infer, interpret, extrapolate, evaluate, and predict.

Research also exists to help identify effective teaching strategies. This is one of the first books that use recent cognitive science research to discuss how to teach by explaining, questioning, monitoring, and reviewing; how to diagnose, assess, and place students into groups for instruction; how to teach basic skills, concepts, and problem solving; how to manage the surface behavior of students on an individual and group basis; how to plan for instruction; and how to use textbooks and improve instructional materials.

The new emphasis in cognitive science, and in this text, is no longer concerned with the students' answers, but rather with how they derived the answers and what strategies the teachers used to help the student learn. The book informs teachers about recent research on how students process information and how teachers can modify their instruction to help students learn more effectively.

The book is organized into three parts with twelve chapters. Part I is comprised of four chapters and deals with students. It assumes that before one teaches one has to understand students. Part II, which contains six chapters, concerns instruction. It assumes that planning precedes instruction and that one should employ multiple instructional methods, materials, and activities. Part III, about teachers and teaching, has two chapters and provides additional help on what is good teaching and how teachers can grow professionally.

There are many distinctive features to the text, including the following:

- Focusing questions at the beginning of each chapter help orient the reader, set the stage for what is to follow, and highlight the main ideas in the chapter.

- Short, easy-to-read headings and subheadings facilitate understanding and illustrate relationships among ideas.

- Short descriptors and categories serve as anchors to help classify and conceptualize information.

- Tables and charts organized as overviews make learning more meaningful.

- Current research findings are applied to classroom teaching.

- "Professional Viewpoints," original statements by experts in the field, written specifically for the text, highlight a major concept or principle and/or give advice for both the beginning and the experienced teacher.

· Lists of practical tips for teachers give insights into teaching.

· Summaries at the end of each chapter contain a short list of main ideas, coinciding with the sequence in the narrative.

· "Things to Do," "Questions to Consider," "Key Terms," and Suggestions for "Further Readings" at the end of each chapter aid in reading comprehension and application.

ACKNOWLEDGMENTS

I wish to thank the following reviewers who read the manuscript and provided important insights and comments:

Nancy Bacharach, Syracuse University

James Bell, Arizona State University

Burton Boxerman, University of Missouri-St. Louis

Gwendolyn Henderson, University of North Carolina-Asheville

Anne Lally, University of Missouri-St. Louis

Frank Olson, Pacific Lutheran University

Dennis Showers, SUNY-Geneseo

Edward Smith, Longwood College

Evelyn Swartz, University of Kansas

Darlean Sydnor, Pacific Lutheran University

Philip Wishon, University of Northern Colorado

In addition, there are some 40 people who wrote "professional viewpoints." They were kind enough to take time from their busy schedules to jot down some valuable advice or personal views about teachers and teaching. Their thoughts add a timely and unusual dimension to the text while providing useful information in an appealing manner. I appreciate their cooperation.

Special thanks also go to Judy Kahn, who did a very capable job in editing the manuscript, and Alan McClare, the sponsoring editor for the project, who worked with me on it from start to finish and gave me wise counsel.

Allan C. Ornstein

To the Student

This book has five major purposes. The first is to help beginning teachers develop an understanding of what goes on in the classroom, and what the job of teaching involves. Despite your familiarity with education from a student's point of view, you probably have limited experience with teaching from a teacher's point of view. And even if you are experienced, you can always integrate your own experiences about teaching with new information to achieve professional improvement and development.

A second purpose is to provide classroom teachers with concrete and realistic suggestions about ways of teaching—and how they can improve the teaching-learning process. Often teachers are unaware of their behavior, or the effects they have on students; others can sharpen their expertise in what methods and strategies work with different students.

Another purpose is to apply theoretical and research-based data to teaching practices. Social scientists and educators have discovered many things about human behavior, and they have established many principles that can be translated into practices. In still other cases, existing practices of the teacher can be clarified and refined through understanding of research. The idea is to convert "knowledge of" teaching into "knowlege of how" to teach.

A fourth purpose is to show how teachers can make a difference, and how they can have a positive influence on students. The data in the text indirectly suggest that teachers affect students, and that some teachers because of their practices have better results than others.

Finally, the text deals with how teachers can teach students how to learn—that is, learning strategies that will increase students' chances for achievement and reduce the loss of human potential so pervasive in our society today. Coming to know is the goal of the learner; helping students learn how to learn is the goal of the teacher. The extent students come to know and learn how to learn is influenced by how well the teacher can teach.

Allan C. Ornstein

Teaching and Learning

FOCUSING QUESTIONS

1. What reasons do people give for teaching? How do these reasons compare with your own reasons?

2. To what extent do teachers make a difference in student achievement?

3. What measures would you take to improve teaching?

4. What are the major distractions from academic time? How can academic time be improved in the classroom?

5. What are the differences between moral knowledge, moral character, and moral development? How does value clarification foster moral thinking?

6. How can students learn how to learn? Which cognitive processes contribute to learning?

7. What is critical thinking? Can teachers teach critical thinking? How?

8. How would you describe creativity? How can creativity in the classroom be enhanced?

*T*his chapter first briefly addresses issues related to teaching: reasons for teaching, views of teaching, determining whether teachers make a difference in student outcomes, improving the quality of teaching, and characteristics of effective teaching. Next, classroom activities and academic tasks are discussed in terms of instructional variables and time spent in school. We also consider the school's responsibility in transmitting moral knowledge and values. Finally, we look at different kinds of cognitive processes that students can learn—learning to learn, critical thinking, and creative thinking.

ISSUES RELATED TO TEACHING

There are many ways to start a chapter on teaching and learning. To paint a balanced picture of what teaching is, we start with some general comments about teachers, then more precise discussions about teaching. The object of the chapter and text is to develop teachers, not only teaching strategies. We begin with motives for choosing a career in teaching. Those who are entering the teaching profession, or even those who are already teaching, should ask why they wish to teach.

Reasons for Teaching

There are many reasons why people choose teaching as a career. One strong motivation for many teachers is their identification with adult models—parents and especially teachers—during their childhood. Research indicates that women are influenced by their parents slightly more than by their teachers in their decisions to become teachers. Men are influenced by their teachers more than twice as often as by their parents.[1]

The data suggest, further, that parents encourage their daughters to become teachers more than their sons. Perhaps this is due to the wider range of professional choices that have been available for men in the past and the traditional view that teaching is a respected occupation for women but does not hold similar status for men.[2] Although job opportunities for women have increased recently, females still made up 68 percent of the public school teaching force in 1988. More than 80 percent of the elementary teachers and 45 percent of

---

[1] Philip Hosford, ed., *Using What We Know About Teachers* (Alexandria, Va.: Association for Supervision and Curriculum Development, 1984); Ann Lieberman and Lynne Miller, *Teachers, Their World, and Their Work* (Alexandria, Va.: Association for Supervision and Curriculum Development, 1984).

[2] Robert B. Howsam et al., *Educating a Profession* (Washington, D.C.: American Association of Colleges for Teacher Education, 1976); Allan C. Ornstein, "Toward Teacher Professionalism," *High School Journal*, December–January 1986.

the secondary teachers were females. Moreover, these percentages have not changed much since the mid-1960s.[3]

The view that the choice of teaching as a career is based on early psychological factors has been explored by many researchers. For example, Wright and Tuska contend that teaching is rooted in the expression of early yearnings and fantasies.[4] Dan Lortie holds that early teaching models are internalized during childhood and triggered in adulthood.[5] Although these two investigations have different theoretical bases, both hold that to a considerable extent the decision to teach is based on experiences that predate formal teacher training and go back to childhood. You might ask how accurate this is in your own case.

Views of Teaching

The kind of teacher you become is to a large extent influenced by how you view teaching and the teaching profession. The questions below are designed to explore your views. The questions are open-ended and subjective; there are no right answers.

What are your reasons for teaching? Which are positive and which are negative?

Is teaching a profession or a semiprofession? Is it an art or a science?

What degree of autonomy or input should teachers have in making decisions about curriculum? About text purchases?

What professional knowledge or content is most important in preparing teachers? What pedagogy or teaching strategies should be part of the teacher's training? Are there general principles of teaching that are applicable to most students? What grade level? Subject?

Should teachers focus on the whole child or should they focus on academic skills? How much time should content teachers spend on teaching reading skills?

Can we define good teaching? Who should define it? Students? Parents? Teachers? Administrators? Taxpayers? What is the difference between *good* teaching and *effective* teaching? Should teachers be held accountable? For what? To whom? How should teachers be evaluated? On merit or objective criteria (such as experience and education)?

---

[3]*Digest of Education Statistics 1988* (Washington, D.C.: U.S. Government Printing Office, 1988), Table 54, p. 70; *Estimates of School Statistics, 1988-89* (Washington, D.C. National Education Association, 1989), Table 6, p. 35.

[4]Benjamin D. Wright and Shirley A. Tuska, "From a Dream to Life in the Psychology of Becoming a Teacher," *School Review*, September 1968, pp. 259–393.

[5]Dan C. Lortie, "Observations on Teaching as Work," in R. M. Travers, ed., *Second Handbook of Research on Teaching* (Chicago: Rand McNally, 1973), pp. 474–497.

Who should prepare teachers? Hire them? Evaluate them?

What philosophy of teaching is best for teaching students?

What theories of learning are most conducive to students' learning?

How do teachers maintain their mental health from year to year?

What teaching organizations should teachers join? How can the working conditions of teachers be improved?

What changes would you make in schools if you were asked to make them? Why?

These questions should not be skimmed over and then forgotten. They get to the heart of what teaching is all about. They deserve answers in teacher preparation programs, and they must be continually reexamined by teachers on the job. The answers are personal and subjective; they change with time as different social, political, and personal events affect us, the schools, and society. The answers involve what and who we are as teachers and people. By analyzing our own views and comparing the views of others, we can clarify what type of teachers we are or wish to be.

Teachers Make a Difference

A good deal of well-publicized research has promoted the idea that teachers and schools contribute little to student achievement; that IQ, family life, peer groups, and social class are the most important variables; and that all other variables are secondary or irrelevant.[6] Although we cannot precisely define or measure the effects teachers have, research over the last 15 years does indicate that teachers and schools *do* make a difference.

The teacher effectiveness research, exemplified by the works of David Berliner, Jere Brophy, Walter Doyle, Carolyn Evertson, N. L. Gage, Thomas Good, Barak Rosenshine, and Herb Walberg, has shown, mainly through correlational studies, that teacher behaviors and teaching methods consistently relate to student achievement.[7] (Most of this research will be discussed in Chapter 11.)

The problem is, however, that many teacher behaviors and teaching methods that seem to have an effect in one situation may be ineffective and inappropriate in another.[8] Different teacher behaviors and methods have different

---

[6] Allan C. Ornstein, "How Good Are Teachers in Effecting Student Outcomes?" *National Association of Secondary School Principals*, December 1982, pp. 61–70; Ornstein, "A Difference Teachers Make," *Educational Forum*, Fall 1984, pp. 109–118.

[7] Thomas L. Good, Bruce J. Biddle, and Jere E. Brophy, *Teachers Make a Difference* (New York: Holt, Rinehart and Winston, 1975); Good and Brophy, *Looking in Classrooms*, 4th ed. (New York: Longman, 1988).

[8] Gary D. Fenstermacher and Jonas F. Soltis, *Approaches to Teaching* (New York: Teachers College Press, Columbia University, 1985); Karen K. Zumwalt, ed., *Improving Teaching*, 1986 ASCD Yearbook (Alexandria, Va.: Association for Supervision and Curriculum Development, 1986).

Figure 1.1 Student drawings can reveal a great deal about their feelings toward their teacher. (Photo © David Strickler/Monkmeyer)

effects on different students, grades, subjects, and classroom groups and school settings. Compounding the problem is the fact that variables such as socioeconomic status, personality traits, and human behaviors mean different things to different researchers.[9] Also, it is often difficult to isolate teacher effects from the effects of other agents (parents, peer groups, and other teachers), and we are unable to assess accurately changes in learning in short-term intervals.[10]

Despite these and other measurement problems the findings clearly show that teachers can make a difference (positive or negative). Teachers and schools influence achievement. And if they did not make a difference, then there would be (1) minimal need for teacher preparation, since there would be of little value in well-prepared teachers; (2) minimal need for concern about teacher competence, since it would not matter much; and (3) little justification for holding teachers accountable for student performance.

---

[9]Allan C. Ornstein, "Research on Teaching: Issues and Trends," *Journal of Teacher Education*, November–December 1985, pp. 27–31; Ornstein, "How Good Are Teachers in Effecting Student Outcomes?"

[10]Samuel Messick, "Meaning and Values in Test Validation," *Educational Researcher*, March 1989, pp. 5–11; Ornstein, "Research on Teaching: Issues and Trends."

Improving the Quality of Teaching

Demands for improving teacher quality and for holding teachers accountable for student achievement have increased over recent years. Some educators and policy makers claim that we need to identify indicators of effectiveness and to evaluate schools and teachers on the basis of these indicators. A growing number of educators and policy makers believe we need to raise school standards for teacher certification and performance.[11] In general, many parents' expectations for their children's education have not been met. The taxpayers, who want to keep the lid on school spending and want to know where their money is being spent, want to hold educators responsible for outcomes of instruction. Moreover, if teachers do make a difference, as the recent literature claims, then they should be accountable for the outcomes of instruction, whether the outcomes are positive or negative.

According to a recent NEA nationwide survey involving more than 2,132 parents and 2,107 teachers (Table 1.1), the strategies for improving the quality of teaching most favored by the *public* are: (1) requiring students in teacher training programs to meet specific graduation requirements (82 percent), (2) requiring teachers to pass rigorous exams assessing their knowledge of the subject they wish to teach (77 percent), and (3) requiring teachers to complete an internship (76 percent). *Teachers* show strong support for two of these strategies. As many as 85 percent of teachers favor an internship program and 78 percent favor specific graduation requirements. Their third highest ranking strategy (72 percent) is requiring candidates for teaching programs to meet specific admission requirements. Among the general public the attitude is stronger than among the teachers that the six measures listed in the table would help improve the quality of teaching.

A number of educators maintain that undergraduate teacher preparation is the gatekeeping process for the teaching profession. Prospective teachers must be able to demonstrate a specified level of competence by the end of the preservice stage in order to be allowed entry into the profession.[12] Other educators advocate delaying judgment until the end of a two- or three-year internship under the tutelage of experienced teachers. They would permit beginning teachers to learn on the job, but would require a demonstration of competency at an early stage in their career.[13]

---

[11] Thomas E. Eissenberg and Lawrence M. Rudner, "State Testing of Teachers: A Summary," *Journal of Teacher Education*, July–August 1988, pp. 21–22; Allan C. Ornstein, "Teacher Accountability: Trends and Policies," *Education and Urban Society*, February 1986, pp. 221–229; and Ornstein, "The Evolving Accountability Movement," *Peabody Journal of Education* (in print 1990).

[12] Judith E. Lanier and Joseph Featherstone, "A New Commitment to Teacher Education," *Educational Leadership*, November 1988, pp. 18–22; Andrew C. Porter, "Understanding Teachers: A Model for Assessment," *Journal of Teacher Education*, July–August 1988, pp. 2–7.

[13] Frederick J. McDonald and Patricia Elias, "The Transition into Teaching: The Problems of Beginning Teachers and Programs to Solve Them." Paper prepared for the Educational Testing Service, Berkeley, Calif., 1983; Lawrence J. O'Shea, Nora L. Hoover, and Robert G. Carroll, "Effective Intern Conferencing," *Journal of Teacher Education*, March–April 1988, pp. 17–21; and Lee S. Schulman, "Assessment for Teaching: An Initiative for the Profession," *Phi Delta Kappan*, September 1987, pp. 38–44.

Table 1.1   MEASURES TO IMPROVE TEACHER COMPETENCE

Measures	Ratings (percent)		Rankings	
	Teachers	General public	Teachers	General public
Requiring teachers to complete an internship under an experienced teacher before being certified	85	76	1	3
Requiring students graduating from teacher training programs to meet specific graduation standards	78	82	2	1
Requiring students entering teacher training programs to meet specific admission requirements	72	72	3	4.5
Requiring teachers to earn a four-year college degree in the academic subject they will teach and take a fifth year of teacher training	60	72	4	4.5
Requiring teachers to pass exams evaluating their knowledge of the subject they will teach before being certified	41	77	5	2
Requiring teachers to pass rigorous exams evaluating their knowledge of teaching theory before being certified	25	66	6	6

Source: Public and K-12 Teacher Members (Washington, D.C.: National Education Association, 1988), Table 21, p. 31.

Identifying Effective Teaching

To describe what **effective teachers** do in the classroom, Levine and Ornstein have reviewed 10 years of research and hundreds of research studies. The research reviewed deals primarily with low-achieving students in inner-city schools, but it applies to many other student types and many grade levels and subjects.

1. *Classroom management*. Effective teachers develop good managerial techniques. They make sure students know what they expect; they make certain that students know what to do if they need help; they follow through with reminders and rewards to enforce rules; and they do not respond to discipline problems emotionally.

2. *Direct instruction*. Effective teachers have a clear, systematic method of teaching, called *direct instruction* or *explicit teaching*. They proceed in small steps, provide ample review and explanation before proceeding to the next step, ask questions and check for understanding, and provide systematic feedback and correction.

3. *Time on task.* Effective teachers provide students with relevant academic activities and see to it that students spend an adequate amount of time actually engaged in these learning activities.

4. *Questioning.* Effective teachers ask appropriate questions in a manner that ensures participation and facilitates mastery of academic content. Questioning focuses on both facts and abstract thinking.

5. *Comprehension instruction.* Effective teachers emphasize independent learning and learning to learn. They teach students to apply concepts, solve problems, and monitor their own comprehension.

6. *Level of cognitive instruction.* Most instruction for low-achieving students emphasizes mechanical rote learning. Effective teachers try to move toward high-order thinking skills and independent learning by motivating students to learn and by using appropriate materials and activities.

7. *Grouping.* Effective teachers are able to group students for individualized and small-group instruction. They are able to work with more than one student or group at a time.[14]

In general, there is a relationship between effective teachers and effective schools. Teachers, to be effective, need a supportive and positive atmosphere. This includes (1) a manageable class size, (2) available and suitable instructional materials, (3) high staff expectations for student achievement, (4) an orderly school climate, (5) systems for monitoring student progress, (6) a strong and supportive principal, and (7) a school spirit or identity that is felt in the classroom.[15]

CLASSROOMS: WHAT WORKS

Classrooms are where the action is, where all the participants involved in teaching and learning interact. They are where the lesson is usually taught, where instructional methods and materials are introduced by the teacher, where students deal with learning tasks and skills and respond to subject matter, and where students are evaluated by the teacher. Classrooms can be organized or disorganized, the climate can be positive or negative, and students can experience success and pleasure or frustration and tension in dealing with the teaching and learning processes.

[14]Daniel U. Levine and Allan C. Ornstein, "Characteristics of Effective Classrooms and Schools," *Urban Review* (in print 1990), Allan C. Ornstein and Daniel U. Levine, "Social Class, Race, and School Achievement," *Journal of Teacher Education*, September–October 1989, pp. 17–23.

[15]Ronald R. Edmonds, "Characteristics of Effective Schools," in U. Neiser, ed., *The School Achievement of Minority Children* (Hillsdale, N.J.: Erlbaum, 1986), pp. 93–104; Daniel U. Levine and Eugene E. Eubanks, "Organizational Arrangements at Effective Secondary Schools," in J. J. Lane and H. J. Walberg, eds., *Organizing for Learning* (Reston, Va.: National Association of Secondary School Principals, 1989), pp. 41–49; and Robert E. Slavin and Nancy A. Madden, "What Works for Students at Risk: A Research Synthesis," *Educational Leadership*, February 1989, pp. 4–13.

Professional Viewpoint

Teaching and Learning Theories

The shift in emphasis in the last few years from a psychology of learning, which might hopefully be applied in the classroom, to a psychology of instruction has had promising consequences, encouraged both by the development of cognitive psychology and by a greater awareness of the contexts in which instruction is effective. A distinction between the mastery model, in which instruction is engineered to reach goals set by the teacher, is being contrasted with the acquiring of self-regulatory skills in which knowledge is structured for problem solving in various contexts.

If the teacher understands the difference between such strategies, steps can be taken to improve the interaction with the student as learner.

Ernest R. Hilgard
Emeritus Professor of Psychology
and Education
Stanford University

Classroom Tasks

Instructional tasks are the core of the classroom setting. Most teachers maintain control over instructional tasks by making the decisions about what is to be taught, what materials and methods are to be used, and how much students are to be allowed to interact. There are teachers, however, who do permit student input in planning content and activities. Secondary school classrooms tend to be more controlled settings than elementary school classrooms.[16] The key variable, of course, is the teacher and not the grade level. When the teacher has complete control over instruction, it is likely that most students, if not all, will be engaged in a single classroom task and work toward the same goal with the same content. When students have input, it is likely that they will work on different classroom tasks.[17]

Teacher control over tasks affects the social setting and nature of evaluation. Under single-task conditions with high teacher control, students usually

---

[16] John I. Goodlad, *A Place Called School* (New York: McGraw-Hill, 1984); Sara Lawrence Lightfoot, *The Good High School* (New York: Basic Books, 1983).

[17] Ronald W. Marx and John Walsh, "Learning from Academic Tasks," *Elementary School Journal*, January 1988, pp. 207–219; Mary J. Partridge, Roger Gehlbach, and Ronald W. Marx, "Social Contingencies, Physical Environment, and Prosocial Behavior in Children's Play," *Journal of Research and Development in Education*, Summer 1987, pp. 25–29; and Penelope L. Peterson et al., "Students' Cognition and Time on Task During Mathematics Instruction," *American Educational Research Journal*, Fall 1984, pp. 487–516.

work alone, and evaluation of academic abilities and achievement is based on comparison to others in the class or to standardized achievement levels. Under multiple-task conditions with low teacher control, there is more social interaction and cooperative learning; evaluation is conducted more on the basis of individual progress than by comparison to others.[18]

Most classroom tasks are initiated by the teacher; students usually act in response to the teacher's expectations. Most tasks are structured by the teacher and concentrate on the acquisition and comprehension of knowledge, as well as practice. Basically, classroom tasks that are initiated by the teacher fall into four categories: (1) *incremental tasks*, which focus on new skills or ideas and require recognition; (2) *restructuring tasks*, which involve the discovery of an idea or pattern and require some reorganization of data; (3) *enrichment tasks*, which involve application of familiar skills and ideas to new problems; and (4) *practice tasks*, which are aimed at making new skills and ideas automatic so they can be used in other task situations and cognitive processes.[19]

In order to facilitate learning, the teacher must learn to match appropriate tasks with the students' abilities and background knowledge. Matching becomes more difficult as students get older and have the potential to learn more. It is also more difficult in heterogeneously grouped classrooms because of the range in students' abilities and interests. The teacher must consider which tasks contribute most to students' learning, and when it is appropriate to introduce these tasks so students gain new insights and skills.

Success in matching can be judged by student performance. The more errors that students make in working on the tasks, the greater the mismatch. Fewer errors mean that students are capable of working on the tasks, but not necessarily that a good match has been made, because the tasks may be too easy to contribute to learning.

In observing 17 second- and third-grade classes in math and language activities, Bennett and Desforges found that approximately 40 percent of all instructional tasks were matched, 28 percent were too difficult, and 26 percent were too easy (remaining tasks were not characterized). Children with different abilities had different experiences. High achievers were underestimated on 41 percent of the tasks assigned to them, and low achievers were overestimated on 44 percent of the tasks.[20]

This pattern of over- and underestimation of tasks was found in another study of 21 third- to sixth-grade classes in math, language arts, and social studies. In this study 500 academic tasks were analyzed, and the extent of mismatching was greater for both high- and low-achieving students.[21]

[18]Susan J. Rosenholtz and Carl Simpson, "The Formation of Ability Conceptions: Developmental Trend or Social Construction," *Review of Educational Research*, Spring 1984, pp. 31–63.

[19]Neville Bennett and Charles Desforges, "Matching Classroom Tasks to Students' Attainments," *Elementary School Journal*, January 1988, pp. 221–234.

[20]Ibid.

[21]Neville Bennett et al., "Task Processes in Mixed and Single Age Classes," *Education*, Fall 1987, pp. 43–50.

In both studies teachers were more concerned with overestimating than underestimating tasks. In fact, no teacher saw any task as too easy. Actually, both types of mismatching lead to failure to meet the needs of the students. When tasks are underestimated, too many students are not learning up to potential, and they also may become bored. When tasks are overestimated, too many students fail to learn because they don't understand what they are being asked to do and they are likely to become discouraged. Furthermore, the research cited studied grades 2 to 6. If the assumption that matching becomes more difficult in the upper grades is correct, then mismatching may help explain why so many students drop out of school at adolescence.

Altering Instructional Variables

Researchers are focusing on elements of the classroom that teachers and schools can change, or what some call **alterable environments** for purposes of measuring the effect they have on student achievement. According to Robert Slavin, there are four components of instruction: (1) *quality* of instruction, (2) *appropriate* level of instruction, (3) *incentives* to work on instructional tasks, and (4) *time* needed to learn tasks.[22] He concludes that all four components must be adequate for instruction to be effective. For example, if the quality of instruction is low, it matters little how much students are motivated or how much time they have to learn. Each of the components "is like a link in a chain, and the chain is only as strong as its weakest link."[23]

Benjamin Bloom lists 19 teaching and instructional variables based on a summary of several hundred studies conducted during the past half century. His research synthesizes the magnitude of effect these variables have on student achievement. The five most effective ones in rank order are: (1) tutorial instruction (1:1 ratio), (2) instructional reinforcement, (3) feedback and correction, (4) cues and explanations, and (5) student class participation. The next most effective variables for student achievement are (6) improved reading and study skills, (7) cooperative learning, (8) graded homework, (9) classroom morale, and (10) initial cognitive prerequisites.[24]

Bloom concludes that the *quality* and *quantity* of instruction (teacher performance and time devoted to instruction) are the most important factors related to teaching and learning. Moreover, most of the instructional variables that are effective tend to be emphasized in individualized and small-group instruction (see Chapter 9). Bloom assumes that two or three variables "used together contribute more learning than any one of them alone, especially those in the first five rankings."[25]

[22] Robert E. Slavin, "A Theory of School and Classroom Organization," *Educational Psychologist*, Spring 1987, pp. 89–128.

[23] Ibid., p. 92.

[24] Benjamin S. Bloom, "The 2 Sigma Problem: The Search for Methods of Group Instruction as Effective as One-to-One Tutoring," *Educational Researcher*, June–July 1984, pp. 4–16.

[25] Ibid, p. 6. Also see Benjamin S. Bloom, "Helping All Children Learn," *Principal*, March 1988, pp. 12–17.

According to Herb Walberg's review of hundreds of studies, nine general factors influence student achievement: (1) ability, (2) stage of development, (3) motivation, (4) instructional quality, (5) instructional quantity, (6) home environment, (7) classroom social group, (8) peer group, and (9) use of out-of-school time[26] (Table 1.2). Walberg (with Waxman) lists 23 variables under instructional quality. The variables are similar to Bloom's. For Walberg, teacher reinforcement (reward for correct performance) has the largest overall effect on student achievement, slightly more than one standard deviation; it ranked second with Bloom. Reading training (programs designed to help students improve reading) was ranked third by Walberg and sixth by Bloom. The variable labeled "cues, participation, and feedback" was ranked fourth by Walberg; it was split in two and ranked third and fourth by Bloom. Graded homework and cooperative learning ranked fifth and sixth for Walberg and ninth and tenth for Bloom. The only major differences within the top rankings are tutorial instruction, which ranked first with Bloom and tenth with Walberg; and instructional acceleration, which Bloom did not rank and was second with Walberg.

The general conclusion is that the classroom environment, that is, both the quality and quantity of instruction, can be modified for the students' benefit. The instructional variables discussed by Bloom and Walberg provide excellent guidelines for improving instruction. They seem to be effective across school districts, ethnicity and gender, grade level, classroom size, and subject area. They deal mainly with improving the process, not increasing inputs or spending.

Time in Classrooms and Schools

Time in school can be divided into four categories relating to academic work. (1) *Mandated time* is the number of days and hours in the school calendar specified by state and school district laws. (2) *Allocated time* is the portion of time in school allocated to different subjects and other activities in academic and nonacademic areas. Allocation is often suggested in state guidelines and is influenced by attitudes and interests of the local community and school superintendent. (3) *Academic instructional time* is the time the teacher actually spends in class giving instruction by various means in particular subjects and skills. It is influenced by class size, student abilities and interests, program tracking, and instructional level. (4) *Academic engaged time* is the time the students spend in performing academic work. It is influenced by routine practices, classroom management, student motivation, and instructional quality.[27]

---

[26] Herbert J. Walberg, "Improving the Productivity of America's Schools," *Educational Leadership,* May 1984, pp. 19–27; Walberg, "Synthesis of Research on Teaching," in M. C. Wittrock, ed., *Handbook of Research on Teaching,* 3rd ed. (New York: Macmillan, 1986), pp. 214–229.

[27] Nancy Karweit, "Time on Task: The Second Time Around," *National Association of Secondary School Principals,* February 1988, pp. 31–39; Allan C. Ornstein, "Private and Public School Comparisons: Size, Organization, and Effectiveness," *Education and Urban Society,* February 1989, pp. 192–206.

Table 1.2   INSTRUCTIONAL FACTORS RELATED TO LEARNING

Factor	Mean correlation or effect
Ability (IQ)	.71
Development (Piagetian stage)	.47
Motivation	
Motivation	.34
Self-concept	.18
Instructional Quality	
Reinforcement	1.17
Acceleration	1.00
Reading training	.97
Cues, participation, and feedback	.97
Graded homework	.79
Cooperative learning	.76
Reading experiments	.60
Personalized instruction	.57
Adaptive instruction	.45
Tutoring	.40
Higher-order questions	.34
Diagnostic prescriptive methods	.33
Individualized instruction	.32
Teacher expectations	.28
Computer-assisted instruction	.24
Sequenced lessons	.24
Advanced organizers	.23
Direct instruction	.23
Homogeneous groups	.10
Class size	.10
Praise	.08
Programmed instruction	− .03
Mainstreaming	− .12
Quantity of instruction	
Instructional time	.38
Assigned homework	.28
Home environment	.37
Home interventions	.50
Home environment	
Socioeconomic status	.25
Classroom social group (class morale)	.60
Peer group	.24
Use of out-of-school time (leisure-time television)	− .05

Source: Hersholt C. Waxman and Herbert J. Walberg, ''Teaching and Productivity,'' *Education and Urban Society*, February 1986, p. 214.

Mandated Time   **Mandated time** averages about 178 days per year and about 5 hours and 8 minutes per day. The longer school term and days of Japan (220 days and more than 6 hours per day), the Soviet Union, and western European nations (200–215 days) lead some educators to conclude that one reason for poor performance of U.S. students is the shorter time in school. But research indicates that increasing time in school by itself, without changing other aspects of instruction, does not result in increased achievement.[28] Nonetheless, common sense suggests that if instructional quality is kept constant, then extra instructional quantity should have positive effects. Students who have more time to study specific knowledge, skills, or tasks, should learn more than students who have less time. Increasing school time in U.S. public schools about 40 minutes per day would add 119 hours in one school year, about 290 school days over 12 years, and 1⅔ extra years of schooling.[29] This is an important point that has future consequences in terms of American human capital, productivity, and in turn, our standard of living for all age groups.

Allocated Time   **Allocated time** is the portion of the school day (or school year) the school assigns to academic and nonacademic instruction. About 60 to 80 percent of the school day is allocated to academic content.[30] Secondary schools are subject-oriented and allocate more time to academic content than do elementary schools. The younger students have need for more time for socialization and personal growth.

More than half of the states make recommendations, and some have requirements for allocating time in curriculum content at the elementary grade levels. School districts can and usually do modify the recommendations or requirements upward, especially in math and English (perhaps because of the recent publicity given to the results of statewide programs to test performance in math and reading). Modifications of allocated time at the school level also reflect the philosophy of the local community, district superintendent, and school principal: For example, a "progressive" educator might allocate more time for socialization than an "essentialist," who might put more emphasis on the three R's and subtract time from a sports or music/art program.

Although state policies vary, as illustrated in Table 1.3, English (reading) receives the most allocated time in the early grades, after which the time decreases. Math receives the second most attention and remains relatively constant throughout the grades. Note, however, that the difference in recommendations among the states for allocated time in English is 102 minutes per day in the third grade and 75 minutes in the sixth grade. In math the difference is as much as 45 minutes. The time allocated to science and social

---

[28] Gene V. Glass, "What Works: Politics and Research," *Educational Researcher*, April 1987, pp. 5–11; Nancy Karweit, "Should We Lengthen the School Term?" *Educational Researcher*, June 1985, pp. 9–15.

[29] Allan C. Ornstein, "Academic Time Considerations for Curriculum Leaders," *National Association for Secondary School Principals*, September 1989, pp. 103–110.

[30] Karweit, "Time on Task: The Second Time Around."

Table 1.3   ALLOCATED TIME BY SUBJECT AND GRADE LEVEL

Subject	Grade	Illinois (Minimum recommendations)	Michigan (Minimum recommendations)	Texas (Minimum requirements)
Math	3	50	15	60
	6	49	15	60
	8	47	15	45
Science	3	26	9	20
	6	39	9	45
	8	44	15	45
English	3	142	40	120
	6	107	32	90
	8	87	15	45
Social Studies	3	45	4	20
	6	42	9	45
	8	44	15	45

Source: Based on telephone conversations with curriculum specialists from the respective State Departments of Education, January 27, 1989.

studies increases from the early grades to grade 8, when it is equal to the time for other subjects (except in Illinois). If standardized testing in grades 3 to 6 included science and social studies, then there would most likely be more allocated time for them in those grades. The states that do not establish time allocations (such as California, Florida, and New York) focus on instructional objectives and test for performance in subject areas.

At the secondary level allocated time is better defined and is influenced by the nature of the students' program (academic, technical, vocational). In response to national demands for upgrading academic requirements and increasing academic productivity, the curriculum was changed in the 1980s to put more emphasis on such core subjects as English, social studies, math, and science—and academic course requirements for graduation were also increased.

Table 1.4 shows that there has been a marked increase in required course work for public high school graduation in all major academic subjects, especially in math and science, between 1981 and 1988. Graduation requirements in English and social studies for public schools are now only slightly below the recommendations of the National Commission on Excellence in Education; they are still substantially below the recommended levels in math, science, and, especially, foreign languages. Moreover, the proportion of high school seniors who completed more than three years of course work in English was 26 percent in 1980 and 87 percent in 1987; in mathematics, 8.5 percent in

Table 1.4 AVERAGE YEARS OF COURSE WORK REQUIRED FOR PUBLIC HIGH SCHOOL
GRADUATION

School year	Subject area				
	Mathematics	Science	English	Foreign languages	Social studies
1981–1982	1.6	1.5	3.6	a	2.6
1984–1985	1.9	1.8	3.8	.1	2.8
1987–1988[b]	2.3	2.0	3.9	.2	2.9
Recommendations of National Commission on Excellence in Education[c]	3.0	3.0	4.0	2.0[d]	3.0

[a]Less than 0.05 year.

[b]Expectations as of fall 1985 about requirements for seniors graduating in 1988.

[c]Another half year of coursework was recommended in computer science. Almost no school districts had requirements in this area in 1981–82. That situation changed by 1984–85, when the average for all school districts was 0.1 year of coursework required for graduation in computer science; the expected average for 1987–88 was 0.2 year.

[d]The Commission's recommendations about foreign languages applied only to the college-bound, not to all students. The figures for actual requirements represent requirements for all graduates.

Source: The Condition of Education 1987 (Washington, D.C.: U.S. Government Printing Office, 1987), Table 1.37B, p. 84.

1980 and 36 percent in 1987; in science, 6 percent in 1980 and 23 percent in 1987; in social studies, 10 percent in 1980 and 12 percent in 1987.[31]

Considering that we live in a highly technological society, and in a world in which the push of a button can have enormous impact on our lives, the small enrollments in science and mathematics have serious implications for our future. A similar concern was voiced nearly thirty years ago, when our standard of living was increasing more rapidly, when we were more influential as a superpower, and when we were jolted by the Soviet Union's rapid advances in space. Then, James Conant stressed that our educational programs needed more emphasis on science, mathematics, and foreign languages.[32] Our failure to heed Conant's warning may be viewed as one reason for our decline as the

[31]*The Condition of Education 1983* (Washington, D.C.: U.S. Government Printing Office, 1984), Table 1.11, p. 34; "High School Transcript Study of Percentage of Graduates Earning Various Number of Credits, Carnegie Units," Preliminary Data for Educational Research and Improvement (Washington, D.C.: U.S. Department of Education, 1988), Table 2, p. 42; and Ornstein, "Private and Public School Comparisons: Size, Organization, and Effectiveness," Table 7, p. 203.

[32]James B. Conant, *The American High School Today* (New York: McGraw-Hill, 1959).

political and economic giant of the world, the general decline of our manufacturing capability and standard of living, and today's urgency of the problem.

Consider that Japanese students are required to take 23 percent of their total junior high school curriculum in science and mathematics. In high school they are required to take 1.25 science courses per year and 1.5 math courses per year (including calculus and statistics). As a point of comparison, American graduating high school seniors average a total of 2.3 years in math and 2.0 years in science. Because 94 percent of the Japanese attend high school, their requirement produces a more scientifically literate public than ours.[33] In addition, Japanese students have continuously outperformed United States students in science and mathematics on the International Association for the Evaluation of Educational Achievement (IEA) study since comparisons were started in the mid-1970s. In fact, according to recent comparisons of student achievement in math and science, Americans score slightly below the mean among 14 industrial nations and more than 15 percent below Japanese scores in both subject areas.[34]

Academic Instructional Time   Whereas allocated time is the maximum possible time (or opportunity time) that might be spent in subject areas, **academic instructional time**, sometimes referred to as "academic learning time" or "content covered," is the actual amount of time the teacher spends on specific content.

Goodlad and Klein observe that teachers devote most academic learning time to reading activities at all elementary grade levels (except kindergarten). This includes related activities in phonics instruction, listening to stories, and discussion of library books and elements of language. In terms of time allocation, this curriculum area is followed by "independent activities" such as filling in workbooks, looking up words in the dictionary, writing in journals, spelling words, and attending to class projects (almost all of which deal with language and have a reading component). Mathematics was the third most popular activity.[35]

According to David Berliner, the academic instructional time in reading per day over a school year at the second-grade level ranges from 47 to 118 minutes and at the fifth-grade level, from 68 to 137 minutes (Table 1.5). There are similar ranges in mathematics: 16 to 51 minutes per day in the second grade and 20 to 73 minutes in the fifth grade. Thus one teacher may spend two to three times more academic learning time on reading and math than

---

[33] Allan C. Ornstein, "Sources of Change and the Curriculum," *High School Journal*, April–May 1988, pp. 192–199; Kay M. Troost, "What Accounts for Japan's Success in Science Education?" *Educational Leadership*, December–January 1984, pp. 26–29.

[34] *Digest of Education Statistics 1988* (Washington, D.C.: U.S. Government Printing Office, 1988), Tables 289–290, pp. 342–343.

[35] John I. Goodlad and Francis Klein, *Behind the Classroom Door* (Worthington, Ohio: Jones Publishers, 1970). Also see Goodlad, *A Place Called School*.

Table 1.5   ACADEMIC INSTRUCTIONAL TIME FOR READING AND MATHEMATICS IN SELECTED GRADES 2 AND 5

| Grade 2 | | | | Grade 5 | | | |
| Reading | | Mathematics | | Reading | | Mathematics | |
Class	Allocated minutes per day	Class	Allocated minutes per day	Class	Allocated minutes per day	Class	Allocated minutes per Day
4	47	16	16	6	68	3	20
16	66	6	24	27	88	9	36
23	85	10	35	1	102	6	58
14	103	3	42	23	121	25	64
11	118	4	51	12	137	24	73

Source: David C. Berliner, "Recognizing Instructional Variables," in D. E. Orlosky, ed., *Introduction to Education* (Columbus, Ohio: Merrill, 1980), p. 203. Originally adapted from Marilyn Dishawi, *Descriptions Allocated Time to Content Areas for the A-B Period, Technical Notes IV-11a and IV-11b of the Beginning Teacher Evaluation Study* (San Francisco: Far West Laboratory for Educational Research and Development, 1977).

another teacher. Over a school year this difference in instructional time affects achievement.[36]

Even in junior and senior high schools, where departmentalization forces time allocation for each subject, teachers must still make decisions on actual time for lesson units or topics. How much time should be spent on subjects such as creative writing that achievement tests don't usually test? Berliner found that one fifth-grade teacher spent 56 minutes all year on creative writing, while another spent 573 minutes. One teacher spent 400 minutes on fractions, while another teacher spent no time. Obviously, the students who had no instruction in fractions are at a disadvantage compared with students at the same grade level who received instruction. Of course, one must also ask what content was taught in lieu of fractions (perhaps more practice in word problems)—and/or whether this time was overkill, wasteful (disciplinary problems were attended to), or put to good use.

Two cautionary observations should be noted. First, Berliner and others do not conclude that "more is always better." Quality is crucial, and there is a point at which "more" becomes boring. On the other hand, teachers must allocate sufficient time for their students to learn the required material.

Second, teachers vary in how efficiently they use time. A good portion of classroom time that seems to be devoted to instruction is often wasted on clerical and housekeeping activities and managerial problems. According to

---

[36]David C. Berliner, "Tempus Educare," in P. L. Peterson and H. J. Walberg, eds., *Research on Teaching: Concepts, Findings, and Implications* (Berkeley, Calif.: McCutchan, 1979), pp. 120–135; Berliner, "Recognizing Instructional Variables," in D. E. Orlosky, ed., *Introduction to Education* (Columbus, Ohio: Merrill, 1980), pp. 198–225.

researchers, no more than 50 to 60 percent of an elementary school day and 30 to 45 percent of a high school day is devoted to academic instruction.[37] The rest of the time is spent on nonacademic subjects, recess, lunch, and/or study time, transitions between classes, announcements, and procedural and maintenance tasks.

Also, there is a problem of absenteeism, and in many inner-city schools the absenteeism among students is high. When a student is absent or late, it does not matter how much time the teacher devotes to instruction. A student who is not present receives no instruction.

To increase academic learning time, teachers should have a system of rules and procedures that facilitate noninstructional tasks and reduce disruptions and disciplinary problems. Similarly, the schools need to implement policies that decrease absenteeism and lateness. See Tips for Teachers 1.1.

Academic Engaged Time   **Academic engaged time** is the time a student spends attending to academic tasks or content. For some educators, it also means that students must perform the tasks or be engaged in the content with a high success rate (80 percent or more).[38] Although actual classroom instructional time is a more important variable than engaged time in the sense that it shows a higher correlation with improved performance, there is more data on engaged time because it is easier to measure. Moreover, different teachers use different materials and methods to cover the same content, and they focus on different aspects of content. Since researchers have not developed a way to code content in such situations, they often turn to academic engaged time as a proxy for instructional time, or content covered.[39]

Barak Rosenshine's review of instruction in reading and mathematics in 50 classrooms, grades 2 and 5, shows the importance of how time is spent in the classroom. About 58 percent of the school day is allocated to academic activities, about 23 percent to nonacademic activities (music, art, physical education), and about 19 percent to noninstructional activities (transitions between activities and class business). On the average, students are engaged about 73 percent of the time allocated to academic activities in reading and math. Students in the lower grades (grade 2) spent 1 hour and 30 minutes on

---

[37] Walter Doyle, "Academic Work," *Review of Educational Research*, Summer 1983, pp. 159–199; Allan C. Ornstein, "Emphasis on Student Outcomes Focuses Attention on Quality of Instruction," *National Association of Secondary School Principals*, January 1987, pp. 88–95; Ornstein, "Private and Public School Comparisons: Size, Organization, and Effectiveness"; and Richard A. Rossmiller, "Time on Task: A Look at What Erodes Time for Instruction," *National Association of Secondary School Principals*, October 1983, pp. 45–49.

[38] James H. Block, Helen E. Efthim, and Robert B. Burns, *Building Effective Mastery Learning Schools* (New York: Longman, 1989); Benjamin S. Bloom, *Human Characteristics and School Learning* (New York: McGraw-Hill, 1976).

[39] Ornstein, "Emphasis on Student Outcomes Focuses Attention on Quality of Instruction"; Barak Rosenshine, "Content, Time, and Direct Instruction," in P. L. Peterson and H. J. Walberg, eds., *Research on Teaching: Concepts, Findings, and Implications* (Berkeley, Calif.: McCutchan, 1979), pp. 28–56.

Tips for Teachers 1.1

Increasing Academic Time

Too much instructional time is wasted in today's classrooms. Two educators contend that as much as 50–60 days or nearly one-third of the school year may be wasted but can be regained without increasing the school day or school year simply by improving or changing some procedures. Here are some major time wasters to resolve.

1. *Working on homework during the school day.* It is not uncommon to find teachers allocating 20 to 30 minutes in class for students to work on homework assignments. This is equivalent to about 10 school days if only one teacher per day is guilty of this practice. *Action to be taken:* Time used for homework in class should be converted to instructional time. Teachers should still explain the homework assignment and review common problems, but not permit work on homework in class.

2. *Excessive viewing of films.* Too many teachers use too many films, especially on Fridays. Viewing films for one hour per week uses up 36 hours or 7 days. *Action to be taken:* Use of instructional tools should be justified in terms of student results. A cumulative record of film time used by teachers should perhaps be kept.

3. *Changing and beginning classes.* In most middle and secondary schools, students move from room to room. It is not unusual for teachers to use 5 or 10 minutes per class to take attendance and make announcements. If only 5 minutes were used, 75 hours or 15 days would be saved. *Action to be taken:* Teachers need to devise systems, such as assigned seats, printed lists, or diagrams, to show quickly who is absent from class.

4. *Teacher absences.* Learning suffers when teachers are absent (The average teacher is absent three to five times a year.), since most substitute teachers are unable to reach desired academic objectives. *Action to be taken:* Excellent substitute teachers need to be identified by the school principal. Also, the regular teacher needs to make available the lesson plan for the day, along with related materials, when he or she expects to be absent.

5. *Registration and testing.* About 3 days a year are lost on registration and another 3 on schoolwide testing. In both cases students are often free for portions of the day. *Action to be taken:* Registration should be scheduled prior to the school year. Schoolwide and standardized testing should be incorporated into the regular class time, not treated as a separate testing day.

continued

6. *Extracurricular activities.* Although it is impossible to state the exact number of days lost by students who are dismissed early for athletic events, school tournaments, community and state activities, music and dance workshops, band, and other activities, a good estimate is 5 to 10 days. *Action to be taken:* Students must be encouraged to make up their academic work. Special events should be scheduled on activity days, not regular academic days, or during after school hours (in the afternoon, evenings, or on weekends), not during class time.

Source: Adapted from Robert Lowe and Robert Gervais, "Increasing Instructional Time in Today's Classroom," *National Association of Secondary School Principals,* February 1988, pp. 19–22.

these two activities, and older students (grade 5) spent 30 minutes longer on an average. (This somewhat contradicts Table 1.3.)

During time allocated for academics, students are not engaged about 16 minutes an hour, during which they are passing out and collecting papers, waiting for help, or completely off task. Overall, students spend about two-thirds of the allocated time in seatwork (or self-paced activities), mainly practice and drill, and about one-third engaged with an adult. Student engagement is higher in teacher-directed settings (about 84 percent) than in other seatwork settings (about 70 percent).[40] Thus, if a teacher divides a class into three groups and engages one group at a time while the other two groups work alone, student academic engaged time substantially falls off. Many educators object to emphasis on teacher-directed activities and would prefer more independent activities for students—just what seems to create academic waste of time.

Both the quality and quantity of academic engaged time (as well as instructional time) are considered to be important in improving the outcomes of student learning, although quantity is easier to agree upon and measure. All things being equal, students of teachers who provide more academic engaged time and instructional time learn more than students of teachers who provide relatively less.

MORAL EDUCATION

How a person develops morally is partially, if not predominantly, based on the way he or she interacts with family, schools, and society—more precisely, on

---

[40]Barak Rosenshine, "How Time Is Spent in Elementary Classrooms," in C. Denham and A. Lieberman, eds., *Time to Learn* (Washington, D.C.: National Institute of Education, 1960), pp. 107–126.

the roles and responsibilities he or she learns and deems important based on contact with people who are considered important.

Schools have traditionally been concerned with moral education of children. In the nineteenth century moral education became linked to obedience and conformity to rules and regulations. Standards of moral behavior were enforced by rewards and punishments and were translated into grades in what at different times was called morals and manners, citizenship, conduct, or social behavior.[41]

Until the middle of the nineteenth century public schools typically exhibited a strong, nonsectarian Protestant tone, which was reflected in activities such as Bible readings, prayers, and the content of instructional materials such as the McGuffey readers. By the turn of the century the schools shifted the notion of moral education to purely secular activities such as student cooperation in class, extracurricular activities, student councils, flag salutes, assembly rituals, and school service. In short, schools have never ignored moral education, but teachers have often avoided the teaching of morality because of its subjective nature and its potential overlap with religious indoctrination.

Moral Knowledge

It is possible to give instruction in moral knowledge and ethics. We can discuss philosophers such as Socrates, Immanuel Kant, and Jean-Paul Sartre, religious leaders such as Moses, Jesus, and Confucius, and political leaders such as Abraham Lincoln, Mohandas Gandhi, and Martin Luther King. Through the study of the writings and principles of these moral people, students can learn about moral knowledge. For young readers there are "Aesop's Fables" and "Jack and the Beanstalk." For older children, there are *Sadako, Up from Slavery*, and the *Diary of Anne Frank*. And for teenagers, there are *Of Mice and Men, A Man for all Seasons*, and *Death of a Salesman*. All these books deal with moral and value-laden issues. Whose morality? Whose values? Well, there are agreed-upon virtues such as honesty, integrity, civility, caring and so forth, that represent an American consensus. It is out there, if we have sufficient moral conviction to find it.

According to Philip Phenix, the most important sources of moral knowledge are the laws and customs of society, and they can be taught in courses dealing with law, ethics, and sociology. However, moral conduct cannot be taught; rather it is learned by "participating in everyday life of society according to recognized standards of society."[42] Although laws and customs and obedience to them are not always morally right, accepted standards do provide guidance for conduct and behavior.

---

[41] See Ellwood P. Cubberley, *The History of Education* (Boston: Houghton Mifflin, 1920); Allan C. Ornstein and Francis P. Hunkins, *Curriculum: Foundations, Principles, and Issues* (Englewood Cliffs, N.J.: Prentice-Hall, 1988).

[42] Philip Phenix, *Realms of Meaning* (New York: McGraw-Hill, 1964), pp. 220–221.

Professional Viewpoint

On Right and Wrong

I raise a problem: How does one reconcile, as a teacher, openness toward various points of view, with the need—the necessity—of taking an absolute position on certain issues: drug trafficking, drug use, stealing from fellow students, teachers or the school, and the like? This is the problem confronted by various kinds of values education, which, perhaps reflecting their origins in the late 1960s and early 1970s, emphasize openness, arguments on both sides of most issues, autonomous decision making by the pupil on the basis of information, etc. I do not know how widespread this orientation is among teachers; perhaps most of them, reflecting their backgrounds, take an absolutist view on moral issues (if they do, it would raise the question of why these views seem to have so modest an influence on student behavior). Reflecting on my own behavior as a teacher, admittedly with college students, I know I find it very difficult to firmly take the position on moral issues that this is right and that is wrong. With younger students, I think it is essential that teachers be able to take that position, and defend it. That is no simple task: One cannot take the position that something is wrong simply because there is a rule or law against it; or simply because it will make your parents feel bad; or simply because it is bad for your health; or because it's against your religion. All these are evasions of the core of moral prescription. But how do we teach to teachers, and how do they teach to students, the essence of that core, the basis of morality and civil society?

Nathan Glazer
Professor of Education
and Sociology
Harvard University

The content of moral knowledge, according to Phenix, covers five main areas: (1) human rights, involving conditions of life that ought to prevail, (2) ethics concerning family relations and sex, (3) social relationships, dealing with class, racial, ethnic, and religious groups, (4) economic life, and (5) political life, involving justice, equity, and power.[43] The way we translate moral content into moral conduct defines the kind of people we are. It is not our moral knowledge that counts; rather it is our moral behavior in everyday affairs with people that is important.

---

[43] Ibid.

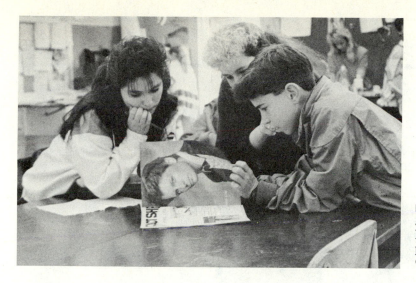

Figure 1.2 Peer group interaction influences moral behavior as well as student performance in school. (Photo © Elizabeth Crews)

Moral Character

A person can have moral knowledge and obey secular and religious laws, but still lack moral character. **Moral character** is difficult to teach because it involves patterns of attitudes and behavior that result from stages of growth, distinctive qualities of personality, and experiences. It involves a coherent philosophy and the will to act in a way consistent with that philosophy.

To have moral character also means to help people, to accept their weaknesses without exploiting them, to see the best in people and to build on their strengths, to act civilly and courteously in relations with classmates, friends, or colleagues, to express humility, and to act as an individual even if it means being different from others. Perhaps the real test of moral character is to cope with a crisis or setback, to deal with adversity, and to be willing to take risks (that is, possible loss of job, even life itself) because of one's convictions. Courage, conviction, and compassion are the ingredients for character. What kind of person do we want to emerge as a result of our efforts as teachers? We can engage in moral education and teach moral knowledge, but can we teach moral character? See Tips for Teachers 1.2. The world is full of people who understand the notion of morality, but take the expedient way out or follow the crowd. Who among us (including our colleagues) possess moral character? Who among our students will develop into morally mature individuals? To be sure, moral character cannot be taught by one teacher, rather it takes a concerted effort by the entire school and involves the nurturing of children and youth over many years.

Tips for Teachers 1.2

The Morally Mature Person

The Association for Supervision and Curriculum Development has tried to write a description of the morally mature person. The characteristics it lists offer teachers a framework for classroom discussion and classroom interaction with their students.

I. *Respects human dignity*, which includes
   1. Showing regard for the worth and rights of all persons
   2. Avoiding deception and dishonesty
   3. Promoting human equality
   4. Respecting freedom of conscience
   5. Working with people of different views
   6. Refraining from prejudiced actions
II. *Cares about the welfare of others*, which includes
   1. Recognizing interdependence among people
   2. Caring for one's country
   3. Seeking social justice
   4. Taking pleasure in helping others
   5. Working to help others reach moral maturity
III. *Integrates individual interests and social responsibilities*, which includes
   1. Becoming involved in community life
   2. Doing a fair share of community work
   3. Displaying self-regarding and other-regarding moral virtues— self-control, diligence, fairness, kindness, honesty, civility—in everyday life
   4. Fulfilling commitments
   5. Developing self-esteem through relationships with others
IV. *Demonstrates integrity*, which includes
   1. Practicing diligence
   2. Taking stands for moral principles
   3. Displaying moral courage
   4. Knowing when to compromise and when to confront
   5. Accepting responsibility for one's choices
V. *Reflects on moral choices*, which includes
   1. Recognizing the moral issues involved in a situation
   2. Applying moral principles (such as the golden rule) when making moral judgments
   3. Thinking about the consequences of decisions
   4. Seeking to be informed about important moral issues in society and the world

continued

VI. *Seeks peaceful resolution of conflict*, which includes
1. Striving for the fair resolution of personal and social conflicts
2. Avoiding physical and verbal aggression
3. Listening carefully to others
4. Encouraging others to communicate
5. Working for peace

In general, then, the morally mature person understands moral principles and accepts responsibility for applying them.

Source: ASCD Panel on Moral Education, "Moral Education and the Life of the School," *Educational Leadership*, May 1988, p. 5.

Moral Values

Good moral character requires a clear set of values. The values a person holds depend on many factors, including environment, education, and personality. Teachers and schools are always transmitting values to students, both consciously and unconsciously. Sometimes the transmission occurs through what educators call the "hidden curriculum," the unstated meanings conveyed by teacher attitudes and behavior, class routines, school policies, and the curriculum in general.[44] **Values clarification** (sometimes called *values building*) is now considered part of the teaching-learning process. Advocates of values clarification have a high regard for creativity, freedom, and self-realization. They prefer that learners explore their own preferences and make their own choices.

Confusion over values can result in apathy, uncertainty, inconsistency, extreme conformity, or extreme dissension. Values clarification is designed to help persons overcome values confusion and become more positive, purposeful, and productive, as well as to have better interpersonal relationships. There are many ways of teaching values clarification. *Inculcation* is teaching accepted values with the support of common law. *Moral development* is highlighting moral and ethical principles and applications. *Analysis of issues* is the examination of situations involving values. *Action learning* is trying and testing values in real-life situations. *Valuing* is a method of choosing, prizing, and acting among alternatives.[45]

Louis Raths and his colleagues have outlined the major components in a

[44] Allan C. Ornstein, "The Irrelevant Curriculum: A Review from Four Perspectives," *National Association of Secondary School Principals*, September 1988, pp. 26–32; Clark Power and Lawrence Kohlberg, "Moral Development: Transforming the Hidden Curriculum," *Curriculum Review*, September–October 1986, pp. 14–17.

[45] Ronald C. Doll, *Curriculum Improvement: Decision Making and Process*, 7th ed. (Boston: Allyn and Bacon, 1989).

process of values clarification (see Chapter 6). They developed various strategies, employing dialogue, writing, questioning, and other activities—for teaching
the process of valuing. The value activities are not intended to impart specific
values to students, but to probe their thoughts and feelings so that they make
choices.[46]

How might the teacher engage students in the clarification of values that
have moral overtones (that is, that deal with right and wrong)? Merrill Harmin
makes five general recommendations.

1. *Speaking up for morality*. Teachers sometimes do not express moral
   indignation, claiming that they should maintain value neutrality. On
   important issues teachers should voice their concerns or take a stance
   in front of the class.
2. *Stating personal positions*. Students should be encouraged to express
   their position or viewpoint on controversial issues. They should not
   feel that it is best to avoid stating a personal viewpoint.
3. *Explaining rules.* Sometimes teachers merely state classroom or school
   rules without explanation. Giving the reasons for required behavior
   may help teachers gain respect, trust, and cooperation among students.
4. *Speaking forthrightly*. There is no reason why teachers cannot be honest with students; indeed, such honesty has positive influence on student behavior. When teachers speak forthrightly for their values, without
   condemning others who have different values, they advance understanding of their values and respect for free speech and a free press,
   which our society demands.
5. *Increasing moral experience*. Sometimes a gap exists between words
   and deeds. If teachers want people to speak truthfully, be tolerant of
   others, and keep an open mind, then they must monitor their own
   behavior to see if they exemplify these characteristics.[47]

Moral Development: Piaget and Kohlberg

Developmental theories address the change that occurs as a consequence of
learning (or failing to learn) appropriate tasks during critical stages of life. The
theories emphasize the study of learning and behavior as a totality and thus
tend to look at the whole child as he or she grows and develops. They describe
various aspects of growth and development, including the biological, psychological, social, cognitive, and moral.

While some self-control of behavior may be seen in the preschool years,
researchers agree that not until the child is about 4 years old do moral standards

---

[46] Louis E. Raths, Merrill Harmin, and Sidney B. Simon, *Values and Teaching*, 2nd ed. (Columbus,
Ohio: Merrill, 1978).

[47] Merrill Harmin, "Value Clarity, Higher Morality: Let's Go for Both," *Educational Leadership*,
May 1988, pp. 24–30.

begin to develop at a rapid rate. During the period when the child begins to abandon behavior governed by whatever he or she wants to do at a particular moment, conscience tends to be erratic, largely confined to prohibitions against specific behaviors, and based on external sanctions. Before age 5, morality does not exist for children because they have little or no conception of rules. From about 5 to 6 years, conscience becomes less confined to specific behaviors and begins to incorporate more generalized standards; it becomes determined less by external rewards or punishments and more by internal sanctions.[48]

Piaget's Theory of Moral Development   Piaget's theory was based on techniques of investigation that included conversing with children and asking them questions about moral dilemmas and events in stories. For example, he might ask a child, "Why shouldn't you cheat in a game?" Piaget's observations suggest that from age 5 to 12, children's concept of justice passes from a rigid and inflexible notion of right and wrong, learned from parents, to a sense of equity in moral judgments. Eventually, it takes into account specific situations or circumstances.

As children grow older, they become more flexible and realize that there are exceptions to rules. As they become members of a larger, more varied peer group, rules and moral judgments become less absolute and rigid and more dependent on the needs and desires of the people involved. Wrote Piaget, "For very young children, a rule is a sacred reality because it is traditional; for the older ones it depends upon a mutual agreement."[49]

On the basis of numerous studies, Piaget concluded:

> . . . There are three great periods of development of the sense of justice in the child. One period, starting at age 5 and lasting up to age 7–8, during which justice is subordinated to adult authority; a period contained approximately between 8–11, and which is that of progressive equalitarianism; and finally a period that sets in toward 11–12, and during which purely equalitarian justice is tempered by consideration of equity.[50]

Kohlberg's Theory of Moral Reasoning   More recently, Lawrence Kohlberg studied the development of children's moral standards and concluded that the way people think about moral issues reflects their culture and their stage of growth. He outlined six developmental stages of moral judgment grouped into three moral levels that correspond roughly to Piaget's three stages of cognitive development.

I. *Preconventional level.* Children have not yet developed a sense of right or wrong. The level comprises two stages: (1) children do as

---

[48] Paul H. Mussen, John J. Conger, and Jerome Kagan, *Child Development and Personality* (New York: Harper & Row, 1969).

[49] Jean Piaget, *The Moral Development of the Child* (New York: Free Press, 1965), p. 192.

[50] Ibid., p. 314.

they are told because they fear punishment, and (2) children realize that certain actions bring rewards.

II. *Conventional level*. Children are concerned about what other people think of them, and their behavior is largely other-directed. The two stages in this level are (3) children seek their parents' approval by being "nice," and (4) children begin thinking in terms of laws and rules.

III. *Postconventional level*. Morality is based not only on other people's values, but also on internalized precepts of ethical principles and authority. This level also includes two stages: (5) children view morality in terms of contractual obligations and democratically accepted laws, and (6) children view morality in terms of individual principles of conscience,[51] as well as a higher being.

Unless a reasonable degree of moral development takes place during childhood and adolescence, that is, unless standards of right and wrong are established, the child, and later the adult, is likely to engage in asocial behavior, and/or aggressive behavior. On the other hand, if the acceptance of others' standards or the internalization of standards and prohibitions is unduly strong, guilt may develop in association with a wide variety of actions and thoughts. Ideally, individuals work out an adequate sense of morality and at the same time avoid self-condemnation in the context of the culture in which they live.

Kohlberg's theory has been widely criticized on the grounds that moral reasoning does not necessarily conform to development and involves many complex social and psychological factors; that particular moral behaviors are not always associated with the same reasoning (and vice versa); and that his prescriptions are culture-bound and sexist. However, he has made researchers and practitioners aware of moral reasoning and provides a theory, along with Piaget's, to guide teaching.

Guidelines for Moral Education

The process of moral education is cumulative and involves the student's total environment (home, peer group, media, community, schools). However, teachers can play a role in promoting various aspects of moral education.

There are some general principles that apply to teachers and students and can be integrated into the classroom setting. First, many teachers who loudly

---

[51] Lawrence A. Kohlberg, "The Development of Children's Orientations Toward a Moral Order, I: Sequence in the Development of Moral Thought," *Vita Humana* (vol. 6, 1963), pp. 11–33; Kohlberg, "Development of Moral Character and Moral Ideology," in M. L. Hoffman and L. W. Hoffman, eds., *Review of Child Development*, vol. 1 (New York: Russell Sage Foundation, 1964), pp. 383–431.

proclaim the need for moral education in the schools often want students to adopt their moral and ethical beliefs.[52] Teachers must allow students to explore moral issues in the curriculum. They must encourage students to reflect, not to accept dogma; to think and question, not merely to accept "facts" from someone else's interpretation of the world; and to develop rational and appropriate standards of behavior, not to follow standards because they are convenient or socially approved.

Second, there are universal values, which are held across cultures, and particular values, which are specific to certain groups or individuals. Universal values of love, honesty, integrity, trust, justice, kindness, and fairmindedness are easy to agree on. It is the particular values of an ethnic, political, or social group or organization that may cause problems. They evoke considerable emotion. They are often used to identify some people as "different."[53] They are used to rationalize behavior. They may be subtle and thought almost unconsciously. The work of the teacher is to help students recognize their particular values, to consider the consequences of these values, and to become aware of how they conflict with universal values. In general, the more students move toward universal values, the more they improve their moral attitudes and behaviors.

Third, almost all subjects have moral implications. There is a need for students to grasp the moral significance of what they study in English literature, science, and social science. Almost everyone interprets reality and the meaning of events to serve their own values. Values affect our perceptions of our nation, community, ethnic or religious group, and self. We can justify slavery as our founding fathers did; we can justify nuclear arms as a military necessity; and we can fight wars in the name of destiny, religion, or truth. Students must examine the actions of their nation, community, ethnic or religious group in terms of universal moral values. Moral and ethical judgment is a selective process that is conceptualized from some point of view, and students must be made to understand that this perspective is the key to their own beliefs and behaviors.

Fourth, teachers can influence their students' moral thought and judgment in class by discussing admirable character traits and role models, permitting group discussions of value-laden issues, and insisting that students obey legitimate authority and rules of behavior such as getting to class on time, paying attention and applying themselves in class, doing homework, and so forth.[54]

[52] Phyllis Berger, "Reforging the Historic Intellectual-Moral Connection," *Educational Horizons* Spring 1989, pp. 59–61; Richard W. Paul, "Ethics Without Doctrination," *Educational Leadership*, May 1988, pp. 10–19.

[53] Ann N. Dapice et al., "Teaching and Learning Values," *Educational Horizons*, Spring 1988, pp. 107–110; Thomas Lickona, "Educating the Moral Child," *Principal*, November 1988, pp. 6–10.

[54] Robert Coles, "The Moral Life of Children," *Educational Leadership*, December–January, 1986, pp. 19–25; Ron Miller, "Two Hundred Years of Holistic Education," *Holistic Education*, Spring 1988, pp. 5–12; and Edward A. Wynne and Herbert J. Walberg, "The Complimentary Goals of Character Development and Academic Excellence," *Educational Leadership*, December–January 1986, pp. 15–18.

Students must understand that they alone are responsible for their own thoughts and actions and as they get older are held increasingly responsible for their behavior. In a classroom and school environment where students are permitted to express their inner feelings, make choices, and develop creative and critical skills of thinking, moral dimensions of learning can exist.

What practical strategies can teachers use to promote moral education? The strategies listed below fall into three categories: teacher actions that set the stage for learning; general cognitive strategies; and specific cognitive strategies. The cognitive strategies or latter two categories combine critical thinking skills and moral reasoning skills.

I. Teacher Actions
   1. Trying to establish a clear understanding of what morality is.
   2. Focusing on the group (the school, classroom) in initial discussions before proceeding to individual students.
   3. Involving all students in making rules and enforcing them.
   4. Speaking up as an advocate of justice, reason, and enlightenment in the classroom and in school meetings.
   5. Assuring that advocacy does not become a form of indoctrination of self-assertiveness.[55]

II. General Cognitive Strategies
   6. Avoiding oversimplification of moral issues.
   7. Developing one's moral perspective.
   8. Clarifying moral issues and claims.
   9. Clarifying moral ideas.
   10. Developing criteria for moral evaluation.
   11. Evaluating moral authorities.
   12. Raising and pursuing root moral questions.
   13. Evaluating moral arguments.
   14. Generating and assessing solutions to moral problems.
   15. Identifying and clarifying moral points of view.
   16. Engaging in Socratic discussion on moral issues.
   17. Practicing dialogical thinking on moral issues.
   18. Practicing dialectical thinking on moral issues.

III. Specific Cognitive Strategies
   19. Distinguishing facts from moral principles, values, and ideals.
   20. Using critical vocabulary in discussing moral issues.
   21. Distinguishing moral principles or ideas.
   22. Examining moral assumptions.
   23. Distinguishing morally relevant from morally irrelevant facts.
   24. Making plausible moral inferences.
   25. Supplying evidence for a moral conclusion.
   26. Recognizing moral contradictions.

---

[55]Clark Power and Lawrence A. Kohlberg, "Moral Development: Transforming the Hidden Curriculum," *Curriculum Review*, September–October 1986, pp. 14-17.

27. Exploring moral implications and consequences.
28. Refining moral generalizations.[56]

COGNITIVE LEARNING AND THINKING

It is important for teachers to understand the ways students learn and the components of critical and creative thinking. Learning is a reflective process, whereby the learner either develops new insights and understanding or changes and restructures his or her mental process. So constructed, learning combines both inductive thought (general to specific) and deductive thought (specific to general). Whereas learning connotes a general process, critical thinking and creativity connote specific aspects of learning.

Principles of Learning

There have been three major schools of learning theories in the last 100 years. (1) Behavioral theories see learning in terms of changing what we do. They emphasize behavioral modification through conditioning by means of reinforcement. (2) Field and gestalt theories consider how the individual perceives the learning environment or situation. They emphasize observational learning, imitation, and modeling. (3) Cognitive theories consider how the learner thinks, reasons, and transfers information to new learning situations.

In the last 15 years or so the cognitive theories have had the greatest impact on educational thought, but at the same time some ideas from the three schools have been fused. This new development in theories about how learners process information is called "cognitive psychology" or "cognitive science." The following list of principles of learning is derived from contemporary cognitive psychology and has implications for teachers today.

1. *Learning by doing is good advice.* But teachers should also understand that students learn by direct and indirect means, by observing others (peers and teachers), by obtaining corrective feedback, and through encouragement to try again or to go to the next task or skill level.
2. *One learns to do what one does.* If students are unwilling to read or to play tennis, they will not learn how to read or to play tennis. Students who do not study are not going to learn as much as students who do. What students already know influences what and how they learn.
3. *The amount of reinforcement necessary for learning is relative to the students' needs and abilities.* An important part of teaching is to know who needs additional instruction and who is ready to learn new tasks.
4. *The principle of **readiness** is related to the learners' stage of development and their previous learning.* The teacher must consider the

---

[56] Paul, "Ethics Without Indoctrination," p. 12.

Figure 1.3 Ideally students are taught not by being told but by being encouraged to problem solve, explore, and discover. (Photo © Bruce Roberts/Photo Researchers)

students' age in presenting certain content and in expecting certain cognitive processes. (A third grader can deal with concrete operations, but cannot make inferences.) The teacher should also periodically assess the current skills of students and adjust instructional objectives, subject matter, and cognitive expectations accordingly.

5. *The students' self-concept and beliefs about their abilities are extremely important.* Teachers sometimes forget that these personal factors affect learning and that teachers' attitudes toward students influence the students' perceptions of themselves.

6. *Teachers should provide opportunities for meaningful and appropriate practice (rehearsal).* Practice tasks should be varied to engage students more fully and to take advantage of different ways of learning the same thing.

7. *Transfer of learning to new situations can be horizontal (across subject matter) or vertical (increased complexity of the same subject).*

8. *Learning should be goal-directed and focused.* Teachers must assist students to become task-oriented, purposive, and efficient in their use of time for learning and studying. Teachers should discourage students from memorizing facts and encourage them to focus on "big" ideas or concepts. New information is made more meaningful to students through relating it in a meaningful way to knowledge they already know.

9. *Positive feedback, realistic praise, and encouragement are motivating in the teaching-learning process.* Teachers must also consider situational factors (home and classroom environment), basic human needs (a hungry child or one who lacks love is concerned with things other than learning), and personal factors (student self-concept).

10. *Metacognition is an advanced cognitive process whereby students acquire specific learning strategies and also sense when they are not learning or having trouble learning.* Teachers need to help students learn how to organize their thoughts, how to assess their own thinking, and how to study.[57]

   Teachers also need to assist students in making meaningful connections between prior knowledge or experiences and new information, as opposed to teaching facts or drilling the "basics" in an isolated manner or routine. These processes are more important than the immediate acquisition of particular content or teaching basic facts or tasks. To apply these new principles may require teachers who are test- and results-oriented to rethink their approach and methods. Right-answer oriented teachers should learn to become more process oriented.

Learning How to Learn

The concept of learning in this text differs from the notion that the learner merely remains passive, reacts to stimuli, and waits for some reward. Here the learner is regarded as active and able to monitor and control cognitive activities. He or she processes new information through assimilation and integration with old information. Without this integration, new information is lost to memory and task performance dependent on the information is unsuccessful.[58] Learning new information results in modification of long-term memory. The responsibility for engaging in learning, including control, direction, and focus, belongs to the individual. The teacher can facilitate the process through explicit or direct instruction and by linking new information with existing relevant and related information.[59]

---

[57] Stephen F. Foster, "Ten Principles of Learning Revised in Accordance with Cognitive Psychology," *Educational Psychologist*, Summer 1986, pp. 235–243; Velam I. Hythecker, Donald F. Dansereau, and Thomas R. Rockline, "An Analysis of the Processes Influencing the Structured Dyadic Learning Environment," *Educational Psychologist*, Winter 1988, pp. 23–38.

[58] David P. Ausubel, Joseph D. Novak, and Helen Hanesian, *Educational Psychology: A Cognitive Perspective*, 2nd ed. (New York: Holt, Rinehart, 1978); John Flavell, *Cognitive Development*, 2nd ed. (Englewood Cliffs, N.J.: Prentice-Hall, 1985).

[59] Penelope L. Peterson, "Making Learning Meaningful: Lessons from Research on Cognition and Instruction," *Educational Psychologist*, Fall 1988, pp. 365–374; Lauren B. Resnick and Leopold E. Klopfer, "Toward the Thinking Curriculum," in L. B. Resnick and L. E. Klopfer, eds., *Toward the Thinking Curriculum: Current Cognitive Research*, 1989 ASCD Yearbook (Alexandria, Va.: Association for Supervision and Curriculum Development, 1989), pp. 1–18.

Cognitive structures are searched when students want to identify, categorize, and process new information. If the cognitive structures are disorganized, unclear, or not fully developed (for the person's age), then new information will not be clearly identified, categorized, and assimilated. To be sure, new learning based on previous learning should be meaningful to students—in context with prior knowledge and real-life experiences, regardless of whether the students are low or high achieving.[60] The difference is that low-achieving students have more limited knowledge and cognitive base than high-achieving students.

From a review of the literature, Charles Letteri has compiled a list of seven comprehension or thinking skills that students can develop to enhance the way they process and integrate information. They are skills that teachers should understand and help students acquire.

1. *Analysis* (sometimes called field dependence-independence), the ability to break down complex information into component parts for the purpose of identification and categorization.
2. *Focusing* (scanning), the ability to select relevant or important information without being distracted or confused by the irrelevant or secondary information.
3. *Comparative analysis* (reflective-impulsivity), the ability to select a correct item from among several alternatives and to compare information and make proper choices.
4. *Narrowing* (breadth of categorization), the ability to identify and place new information into categories through its attributes (physical characteristics, principles, or functions).
5. *Complex cognitive* (complexity-simplicity), the ability to integrate complex information into existing cognitive structures (long-term memory).
6. *Sharpening* (sharpening-leveling), the ability to maintain distinctions between cognitive structures (including old and new information) and to avoid confusion or overlap.
7. *Tolerance* (tolerant-intolerant), the ability to monitor and modify thinking; the ability to deal with ambiguous or unclear information without getting frustrated.[61]

A cognitive framework proposed by Weinstein and Mayer consists of eight comprehension or thinking strategies.

1. *Basic rehearsal strategies*, the ability to remember names or words and the order of things.
2. *Complex rehearsal strategies*, making appropriate choices or selec-

---

[60]Flavell, *Cognitive Development.*

[61]Charles A. Letteri, "Teaching Students How to Learn," *Theory into Practice*, Spring 1985, pp. 112–122.

tions (such as knowing what to copy when the teacher explains something or what to underline or outline while reading).

3. *Basic elaboration strategies*, relating two or more items (such as nouns and verbs).
4. *Complex elaboration strategies*, analyzing or synthesizing new information with old information.
5. *Basic organizational strategies*, categorizing, grouping, or ordering new information.
6. *Complex organizational strategies*, putting information in hierarchical arrangements (such as in outlining notes or homework).
7. *Comprehension monitoring*, checking progress, recognizing when one is on the right track or confused, right or wrong.
8. *Affective strategies*, being relaxed yet alert and attentive during a test situation and when studying.[62]

All of these learning skills combined represent knowledge about and control over cognitive processes, what some educators refer to as metacognition. The specific strategies deal with the identification, categorization, and integration of information.

Of all the specific strategies discussed, **comprehension monitoring** is often considered the most important. This skill permits the student to monitor, modify, and direct his or her cognitive activities. The student remains focused on the task, is aware of whether he or she is getting closer to or farther away from an answer, and knows when to choose alternative methods to arrive at the answer.[63] A student with good comprehension monitoring has developed self-correcting cognition processes, including how to determine what part of a problem needs further clarification, how to relate parts of a problem to one another, and how to search out information to solve the problem. In short, the student is able to identify what has to be done, focus attention, cope with errors, and make modifications in steps to work out a solution—all without losing control, getting frustrated, or giving up.

Learning to learn skills are basic thinking skills that are used in all content areas. Although some of these learning skills are generic and can be taught solely as general strategies, without reference to content, it is impossible to avoid a certain amount of subject matter,[64] especially in the upper (secondary) grades. Many average and high-achieving students develop learning skills on their own, yet the skills can be taught to all students. Most of these learning skills can be incorporated into regular classroom activities or taught as a special

[62] Claire E. Weinstein and Richard E. Mayer, "The Teaching of Learning Strategies," in M. C. Wittrock, ed., *Handbook of Research on Teaching*, 3rd ed. (New York: Macmillan, 1986), pp. 315–327.

[63] Weinstein and Mayer, "The Teaching of Learning Strategies"; Jan Sheinker and Alan Sheinker, *Metacognitive Approach to Study Strategies* (Rockville, Md.: Aspen, 1989).

[64] Ron Brandt, "On Learning Research: A Conversation with Lauren Resnick," *Educational Leadership*, December–January 1989, pp. 12–16.

course that incorporates content from several subjects and focuses on cognitive processes that cut across subjects. The classroom activities or special course should be designed to make all students independent learners in all subjects. The training should begin early in the elementary grades, say around the third or fourth grade. It should continue thereafter with additional time devoted to these skills, perhaps twice the time by the sixth or seventh grade, when students must gather and organize increasing amounts of subject-related information. It cannot be postponed until high school, when the job of learning how to learn has become more difficult because of increasing academic deficiencies.

Guidelines for Teaching Learning Skills

How do teachers help students learn different learning skills? The teacher's role is essentially fivefold: (1) Teachers do not merely mention a particular learning skill; they direct and explain what a particular skill is and how to use it. (2) Teachers provide progressively more difficult items for students to practice on until students can complete the tasks on their own. (3) Teachers determine whether students can perform the task and use related skills and then give the students opportunities to apply the skills to new and different learning situations.[65] (4) Teachers identify the processes or thinking operations students use to perform tasks or solve problems by asking appropriate questions and listening to students' responses. (5) Teachers learn to use diagnostic and assessment tools to make appropriate connections between learning skills and concepts or problems being taught in the particular subject.

All too often teachers are more interested in whether students know the facts or can complete tasks than in whether they understand the skill for performing the task; they are more concerned with test scores than with the development of cognitive process. Teachers have to redirect their efforts to focus on teaching students how and when to employ different learning skills. This type of teaching has immense potential for students in all subjects and grade levels.

One instructional framework for enhancing students' learning strategies is based on a form of direct instruction and consists of six components.

1. *Modeling* (sometimes called *introduction*). The teacher identifies the skill required and shows how it is used. In effect, the teacher "shares a cognitive secret" of how to execute a strategy.

---

[65] Richard E. Mayer, "Aids to Text Comprehension," *Educational Psychologist,* Winter 1984, pp. 30–42; Peterson, "Making Learning Meaningful: Lessons from Research on Cognition and Instruction"; and Weinstein and Mayer, "The Teaching of Learning Strategies."

2. *Guided practice.* Teachers and students work together on a skill or task and figure out how to apply the strategy. The teacher stays in the background, but guides students by asking such questions as why they have rejected or accepted some information or some specific strategy.

3. *Consolidation* (sometimes called *extension*). The teacher helps students to consider a skill in relation to several examples and to determine when the skill should or should not be used. The teacher corrects imperfect examples of the skill. He or she may also test the students' skills by the technique of providing misinformation or irrelevant information to see how students cope.

4. *Independent practice.* The students complete assignments by themselves, first in class with the teacher present to provide aid if necessary and then at home or on their own without the assistance of the teacher. The teacher checks the students' work and then gives the students an opportunity to consolidate and modify the skill to prevent patterns of failure, if they exist.

5. *Application.* The teacher asks students to apply the skill in a new problem.

6. *Review.* The teacher periodically reviews the when, why, and how of the skill. It is incorporated into classroom and homework assignments over an extended period. It is discussed and integrated into new tasks until students have mastered it and integrated it into the learning of new skills. Test results are used for assessing the amount of review needed.[66]

According to Barry Beyer, instruction in each learning skill should occur 10 to 15 times a year in the subject in which it was introduced. When previously learned skills are being reinforced and applied in new contexts, the number of practice or application lessons can be reduced. A curriculum guide should provide the teacher with content and activities for integrating skills into the subject.[67] Either the curriculum by itself or the instructional leader should see to it that the same skills or strategies are taught horizontally across subjects or by more than one teacher at the same grade level as well as vertically in each subject, to ensure review of old strategies and integration with new ones. (See Tips for Teachers 1.3.)

Critical Thinking

One of the most important things a teacher can do in the classroom, regardless of subject or grade level, is to make students aware of their own thinking processes—to examine what they are thinking about, to make distinctions

---

[66] Barry K. Beyer, "Teaching Thinking Skills," *National Association of Secondary School Principals*, January 1985, pp. 70–81; P. David Pearson and Janice A. Dole, "Explicit Comprehension Instruction: A Review of Research," *Elementary School Journal*, November 1987, pp. 151–165.

[67] Barry K. Beyer, *Practical Strategies for the Teaching of Thinking* (Boston: Allyn and Bacon, 1987).

Tips for Teachers 1.3

Enhancing Learning Skills

Here is a teaching inventory for enhancing learning skills among students. The first part is what the school can do; the second part is what the teacher can do.

I. The school district or school should have:
1. A list of major learning skills to be taught throughout the system
2. Agreement among all subject areas that these skills should be taught throughout the system
3. A K–12 curriculum document that clearly specifies which learning skills are to be taught at each grade level in each subject area
4. A K–12 curriculum document that presents skills to be taught in a developmental sequence based on the cognitive development of learners
5. A learning skills curriculum that provides for continuing instruction in key thinking skills across many grade levels and subjects
6. Detailed descriptions of the operating procedures, rules, and distinguishing criteria of each major skill to be taught
7. Appropriate learning skill descriptions available to every teacher and administrator
8. Provisions for instruction in each skill with a variety of media, in a variety of settings, and for a variety of goals

II. The teacher should:
1. Use a common terminology and instructional language to describe the learning skills they are required to teach
2. Provide instruction in learning skills when these skills are needed to accomplish subject matter learning goals
3. Understand the major components of the skills they are teaching
4. Provide continuing instruction in each skill through stages of introduction, guided practice, extension, practice, and application
5. Introduce learning skills as explicitly as possible by explaining and modeling each skill and having students apply the skill with their guidance
6. Provide frequent guided practice in each skill with appropriate instructive feedback
7. Require students to reflect on and discuss how they make each skill operational
8. Use instructional materials appropriate to learning the skills

continued

9. Test on their own unit tests the learning skills or strategies they are responsible for teaching

Source: Barry F. Beyer, "Teaching Thinking Skills," *National Association of Secondary School Principals,* January 1985, pp. 82–83.

and comparisons, to see errors in what they are thinking about and how they are thinking about it, and to make self-corrections.

It is now believed that **critical thinking** is a form of intelligence that can be taught. The leading proponents of this school are Matthew Lipman, Robert Sternberg, and Robert Ennis.

Lipman's program was originally designed for elementary school grades but is applicable to all grades. He seeks to develop the ability to use (1) concepts, (2) generalizations, (3) cause-effect relationships, (4) logical inferences, (5) consistencies and contradictions, (6) analogies, (7) part-whole and whole-part connections, (8) problem formulations, (9) reversibility of logical statements, and (10) applications of principles to real-life situations.[68]

In Lipman's program for teaching critical thinking, children spend a considerable portion of their time thinking about thinking and about ways in which effective thinking differs from ineffective thinking. After reading a series of stories, children engage in classroom discussions and exercises that encourage them to adopt the thinking process depicted in the stories.[69] Lipman's assumptions are that children are by nature interested in such philosophical issues as truth, fairness, and personal identity, and that children can and should learn to explore alternatives to their own viewpoints, to consider evidence, to make distinctions, and to draw conclusions.

Lipman distinguishes between *ordinary thinking* and *critical thinking.* Ordinary thinking is simple and lacks standards; critical thinking is more complex and is based on standards of objectivity, utility, or consistency. He wants teachers to help students change (1) from guessing to estimating, (2) from preferring to evaluating, (3) from grouping to classifying, (4) from believing to assuming, (5) from inferring to inferring logically, (6) from associating concepts to grasping principles, (7) from noting relationships to noting relationships among relationships, (8) from supposing to hypothesizing, (9) from offering opinions without reasons to offering opinions with reasons, and (10) from making judgments without criteria to making judgments with criteria.[70]

---

[68] Matthew Lipman, "The Culturation of Reasoning through Philosophy," *Educational Leadership,* September 1984, pp. 51–56.

[69] Matthew Lipman et al., *Philosophy for Children,* 2nd ed. (Philadelphia: Temple University Press, 1980).

[70] Matthew Lipman, "Critical Thinking—What Can It Be?" *Educational Leadership,* September 1988, pp. 38–43.

Table 1.6   CRITICAL THINKING SKILLS UNDERLYING INTELLIGENT BEHAVIOR

1. Recognizing and defining the nature of a problem
2. Deciding upon the processes needed to solve the problem
3. Sequencing the processes into an optimal strategy
4. Deciding upon how to represent problem information
5. Allocating mental and physical resources to the problem
6. Monitoring and evaluating one's solution processing
7. Responding adequately to external feedback
8. Encoding stimulus elements effectively
9. Inferring relations between stimulus elements
10. Mapping relations between relations
11. Applying old relations to new situations
12. Comparing stimulus elements
13. Responding effectively to novel kinds of tasks and situations
14. Effectively automatizing information processing
15. Adapting effectively to the environment in which one resides
16. Selecting environments as needed to achieve a better fit of one's abilities and interests to the environment
17. Shaping environments so as to increase one's effective utilization of one's abilities and interests

Source: Robert J. Sternberg, "How Can We Teach Intelligence?" *Educational Leadership,* September 1984, p. 40.

Sternberg seeks to foster many of the same skills (listed in Table 1.6), but in a different way. He points to three categories of components of critical thinking: (1) *meta-components,* high-order mental processes used to plan, monitor, and evaluate what the individual is doing; *(2) performance components,* the actual steps the individual takes; and (3) *knowledge-acquisition components,* processes used to relate old material to new material and to apply new material.[71] Sternberg does not specify how to teach these skills; rather he gives general guidelines for developing or selecting a program.

Robert Ennis identifies 13 attributes of critical thinkers. They tend to (1) be open minded, (2) take a position (or change a position) when the evidence calls for it, (3) take into account the entire situation, (4) seek information, (5) seek precision in information, (6) deal in an orderly manner with parts of a complex whole, (7) look for options, (8) search for reasons, (9) seek a clear statement of the issue, (10) keep the original problem in mind, (11) use credible sources, (12) remain relevant to the point, and (13) be sensitive to the feelings and knowledge level of others.[72]

[71] Robert J. Sternberg, "How Can We Teach Intelligence?" *Educational Leadership,* September 1984, pp. 38–48; Robert J. Sternberg and Joan B. Baron, "A Statewide Approach to Measuring Critical Thinking Skills," *Educational Leadership,* October 1985, pp. 40–43.

[72] Robert H. Ennis, "Logical Basis for Measuring Critical Thinking Skills," *Educational Leadership,* October 1985, pp. 44–48; Ennis, "A Taxonomy of Critical Thinking Skills," in J. B. Barron and R. J. Sternberg, eds., *Critical Thinking* (New York: Freeman, 1987), pp. 19–26.

Professional Viewpoint

Critical Thinking in the Everyday World

Every teacher believes she teaches children to think. If she didn't, she would probably have tried a different occupation. But the way we teach children to think in schools often has little to do with the everyday world, and, indeed, what works in school thinking may not work outside. For example, in the everyday world, we need to recognize problems when faced with them; in school, teachers hand problems to students. In the everyday world, we have to figure out the exact nature of the problem confronting us at a given time; in school, teachers define problems for us. In the everyday world, problems are highly contextualized: There is a great deal of background information that enters into our solutions to problems and the decisions we make. For example, the information needed to decide whether to buy a car, and, if so, what kind to buy, can't be stated in a couple of sentences.

School problems, in contrast, are often decontextualized, with the result that children come to think that problems can be stated much more simply than is true outside academia. School problems, too, are well-structured: There is usually a clear path to solution. In contrast, everyday problems tend to be ill-structured, with no clear path leading to an answer. Indeed, in everyday life, usually there is no one right answer, so unlike the multiple-choice and fill-in-the-blanks tests we give. Schools also ill-prepare us for working in groups, despite the fact that in the everyday world, there are few problems that are solved totally on one's own, without the need to talk to others about possible solutions. The bottom line is that to teach children to think, we need to teach them in a way that prepares them for life outside of school, not just life in the classroom, which may bear little resemblance to what goes on outside it.

Robert J. Sternberg
IBM Professor of Psychology and Education
Yale University

Some educators contend that teaching a person to think is like teaching someone to swing a golf club; it requires a holistic approach, not a piecemeal effort, as implied by Lipman, Sternberg, and Ennis. "Trying to break thinking skills into discrete units may be helpful for diagnostic proposals," say Sadler and Whimbey, "but it does not seem to be the right way to move in the teaching of such skills." Critical thinking is too complex to be divided into small processes; teaching must involve "a student's total intellectual functioning, not . . . a set of narrowly defined skills."[73]

Perhaps the major criticism of thinking skills programs has been raised by Sternberg. He cautions that the kinds of critical thinking skills stressed in school and the way they are taught "inadequately prepares students for the kinds of problems they will face in everyday life."[74]

Further caution is needed. Thinking skills programs often stress "right" answers and "objectively scorable" test items; therefore, they are removed from real-world relevance. Most problems and decisions in real life have social, economic, and psychological implications. They involve interpersonal relationships and judgments about people, personal stress and crisis, and dilemmas involving responsibility and choice. How a person deals with illness, aging, or death or with less momentous events such as starting a new job or meeting new people has little to do with the way a person thinks in class or on critical thinking tests. But such life situations are important matters. In stressing cognitive skills, educators tend to ignore the realities of life. Being an A student in school guarantees little after school and in real life. There are many other factors associated with the outcomes of life—and many of them have little to do with thinking. Thus, we need to keep in mind social, psychological and moral components of learning, as well as "luck" or what some of us might call the unaccounted for variables in the outcomes of life.

Guidelines for Teaching Critical Thinking

Teachers must understand the cognitive processes that constitute critical thinking, be familiar with the tasks, skills, and situations to which these processes are applied, and employ several classroom activities that develop these processes. Ennis provides a framework for such instruction. He divides critical thinking into four components, each consisting of several specific skills that can be taught to students.

   I. Defining and clarifying
      1. Identifying conclusions.
      2. Identifying stated reasons.
      3. Identifying unstated reasons.
      4. Seeing similarities and differences.

---

[73]William A. Sadler and Arthur Whimbey, "A Holistic Approach to Improving Thinking Skills," *Phi Delta Kappan*, November 1985, p. 200.

[74]Robert J. Sternberg, "Teaching Critical Thinking: Possible Solutions," *Phi Delta Kappan*, December 1985, p. 277.

    5. Identifying and handling irrelevance.

    6. Summarizing.

II. Asking appropriate questions to clarify or challenge

    1. Why?

    2. What is the main point?

    3. What does this mean?

    4. What is an example?

    5. What is not an example?

    6. How does this apply to the case?

    7. What difference does it make?

    8. What are the facts?

    9. Is this what is being said?

   10. What more is to be said?

III. Judging the credibility of a source

    1. Expertise.

    2. Lack of conflict of interest.

    3. Agreement among sources.

    4. Reputation.

    5. Use of established procedures.

    6. Known risk to reputation.

    7. Ability to give reasons.

    8. Careful habits.

IV. Solving problems and drawing conclusions

    1. Deducing and judging validity.

    2. Inducing and judging conclusions.

    3. Predicting probable consequences.[75]

In general, teachers must ask students a great many questions; require students to analyze, apply, and evaluate information; take opposing sides to tease and test students; and require them to support their answers or conclusions. Supplementary materials, beyond the workbook and textbook, will be needed; it is recommended that teachers work together to develop such materials. David and Roger Johnson point out that students must learn to respect and value one another, so they can learn from each other. Students must feel secure enough to challenge each other's ideas and reasoning, and they must be encouraged to engage in controversial discussions, debates, problem-solving activities, and decision-making activities.[76] By varying instructional activities, ensuring that groups are heterogeneous in skills, distributing relevant materials, and giving instruction in constructing logical arguments, teachers can help students learn to think critically in a variety of academic situations.

---

[75] Ennis, "A Logical Basis for Measuring Critical Thinking Skills."

[76] David W. Johnson and Roger T. Johnson, "Critical Thinking Through Structured Controversy," *Educational Leadership*, May 1988, pp. 58–64.

No one teacher can do the job alone. It is a process that takes years to develop. It behooves the school administration to establish the tone and instill in its teachers of all subjects and grades the need for cooperation to make students aware of what it means to be a critical thinker.

Creative Thinking

Standardized tests do not always measure creativity accurately; in fact, we have difficulty agreeing on what creativity is and who is creative. All children who are normal are potentially creative, yet many parents and teachers impose so many restrictions on their natural behaviors that the children learn that creativity gets them into trouble and earns them disapproval. Parents often react negatively to children's inquisitiveness and "messing around." Teachers and parents impose rules of order, conformity, and "normalcy" to suit themselves, not the children.

There are many types of **creativity**—artistic, dramatic, scientific, athletic, manual—yet we tend to talk about creativity as an all-encompassing term and usually limit the term to cognitive or intellectual endeavors. Educators tend to assess people as smart or dumb based on their performance in one or two areas of intelligence, say, linguistic or mathematical ability. Because of this narrow view of human abilities and this insensitivity to how individuals differ, schools often prevent the development of a positive self-concept in young children who have creative abilities other than in the cognitive domain. The potential talents of many creative children are lost because of our fixation on specific and limited kinds of knowledge.

Creative students are often puzzling to teachers. They are difficult to characterize, their novel answers are threatening, and their behavior often deviates from what is considered normal or proper. Curriculum specialists tend to ignore them in their plans, and teachers usually ignore them in their program and classroom assignments. Little money is earmarked to support special programs and personnel for them. Even if creativity is recognized, educators often lump "gifted" children together without distinguishing between intellectual and creative talents or between different types of creativity.

In a classic cross-cultural study, E. P. Torrance investigated elementary and secondary teachers' concepts of the "ideal" creative personality.[77] He sampled from 95 to 375 teachers in each of five countries: the United States, Germany, Greece, India, and the Philippines. Cultural values were reflected in definitions of creativity. For example, teachers in the United States and Germany (technologically developed countries) gave high ratings to independent thinking, industriousness, curiosity, and independent judgment; these traits were not regarded as important by teachers in the less-developed countries. Greek and Philippine teachers valued remembering, but many American

---

[77] E. P. Torrance, *Rewarding Creative Behavior: Experiments in Classroom Creativity* (Englewood, N.J.: Prentice-Hall, 1965).

teachers considered this type of thinking to be anticreative. Teachers in the three less-developed countries linked creativity with obedience, courtesy or sincerity, being well liked, and having self-confidence, but many of these traits were associated with conformity by American teachers.

Robert Steinberg identified six attributes associated with creativity from a list of 131 mentioned by laypeople and professors in the arts, science, and business: (1) lack of conventionality, (2) intellectuality, (3) esthetic taste and imagination, (4) decision-making skills and flexibility, (5) perspicacity (in questioning social norms), and (6) drive for accomplishment and recognition.[78] He also makes important distinctions among creativity, intelligence, and wisdom. Although they are mutually exclusive categories, they are interrelated constructs. **Wisdom** is more clearly associated with intelligence than is creativity, but differs in emphasis upon mature judgment and use of experience with difficult situations. Creativity overlaps more with intelligence than it does with wisdom, but there is more emphasis on imagination and unconventional methods with creativity, as opposed to intelligence, which deals with logical and analytical absolutes.

According to Carl Rogers, the essence of creativity is novelty, and, hence, we have no standard by which to judge it. In fact, the more original the product, the more likely it is to be judged by contemporaries as foolish or evil.[79] The individual creates primarily because creating is self-satisfying and because the behavior or product is self-actualizing. (This is the humanistic side of creativity, even though the process and intellect involved in creating are cognitive in nature.)

Erich Fromm defines the creative attitude as the willingness to be puzzled (to orient oneself to something without frustration), the ability to concentrate, the ability to experience oneself as a true originator of one's acts, and the willingness to accept the conflict and tension caused by the lack of tolerance for creative ideas.[80]

The above studies show that there is little agreement on a definition of creativity except that it represents a quality of mind and is associated with intelligence. For teachers, the definition of creativity comes down to how new ideas have their origin. We are dealing with processes that are both conscious and unconscious and both observable and unrecognizable. Because unconscious and unrecognizable processes are difficult to deal with in the classroom, there is often misunderstanding between teachers and creative students.

---

[78]Robert J. Steinberg, "Intelligence, Wisdom, and Creativity: Three Is Better Than One," *Educational Psychologist*, Summer 1986, pp. 175–190.

[79]Carl Rogers, "Toward a Theory of Creativity," in M. Barkan and R. L. Mooney, eds., *Conference on Creativity: A Report to the Rockefeller Foundation* (Columbus, Ohio: Ohio State University Press, 1953), pp. 73–82.

[80]Erich Fromm, "The Creative Attitude," in H. H. Anderson, ed., *Creativity and Its Cultivation* (New York: Harper & Row, 1959), pp. 44–54.

Guidelines for Teaching Creativity

Teachers generally require "reactive" thinking from their students; that is, they expect them to react to questions, exercises, or test items and give a preferred answer. They tend to discourage "proactive" thinking, that is, generating novel questions and answers. This is the way most teachers were taught, and they feel uneasy about not having "right" answers. Some teachers do try to develop critical thinking in their students, but they need to go beyond reactive thinking and even beyond critical thinking and encourage learners to generate ideas. Society needs generative thinkers to plan, to make decisions, to deal with social and technological problems. Teachers need to let students know that having the right answer is not always important, that depth of understanding is important, that different activities require different abilities. Teachers need to understand that nearly all students have the potential for creative thinking.

In order to stimulate creative thinking, teachers should encourage students to make inferences, encourage them to think intuitively, and use inquiry-discovery teaching techniques. Three types of inferences have creative potential: (1) elaboration of characteristics, categories, or concepts (For example, a student is told some of the objects in a category are "right," some "wrong." The problem is to infer from this information the definition of the category.); (2) elaboration of causality (What were the causes of World War I? Why did the compound turn into gas?); and (3) elaboration of background information (making inferences about possible effects of events or facts from past events or facts in order to make decisions and solve problems).[81]

Intuitive thinking is a cognitive process that has been discouraged because traditional teaching relies on facts and rote. A good thinker, according to Jerome Bruner, is creative and has an intuitive grasp of subject matter. Intuition is part of the process of discovery; investigating hunches and playing with ideas can lead to discoveries and additions to the storehouse of knowledge. The steps involved in intuitive thinking often cannot be differentiated or defined; intuition involves cognitive maneuvers "based on implicit perception of the total problem. The thinker arrives at an answer, which may be right or wrong, with little, if any, awareness of the process by which he reached it."[82]

Teachers must encourage students to make educated guesses, to follow hunches, and to make leaps in thinking. Having a clear account of how we

---

[81] Robert Marzano, *A Unitary Model of Cognition and Instruction in Higher Order Thinking Skills* (Denver: Midcontinent Regional Laboratory, 1985); David N. Perkins, *Knowledge as Design* (Hillsdale, N.J.: Erlbaum, 1986). Also see Robert J. Marzano and Daisy E. Arredondo, "Restructuring Schools Through the Teaching of Critical Skills," *Educational Leadership*, May 1986, pp. 20–26.

[82] Jerome S. Bruner, *The Process of Education* (Cambridge, Mass.: Harvard University Press, 1959), p. 57.

obtain an answer is sometimes secondary; understanding cognitive nuances and larger concepts is more important.

In inquiry-discovery techniques of teaching, students are not presented with subject matter in its final form; questions, answers, solutions, and information are devised and derived by the students. The techniques can be adapted to students of all ages.

Most people would agree that it is tremendously important to society that the creative abilities of our children and youth be identified and developed—important for the welfare of our civilization. Torrance, who is probably the best known expert on the subject, points out that students can be taught in such ways that their creative thinking abilities are nourished. Teachers need to recognize that highly creative children learn in different ways than do children who have high IQ's but are not highly creative, and there are social pressures in school and outside of school that interfere with the development of their creative abilities.[83]

The teacher must provide for, and give credit for, self-initiated learning. Creative kids are sometimes mislabeled as lazy or as daydreamers because they spend some of their time sitting and thinking—not visibly busy; sometimes their thoughts are interrupted, their questions rejected, their daydreams ridiculed; their ideas go unexpressed and their judgments are unsought. Even worse, because they don't always fit the conventional mold in the classroom, they are increasingly labeled as disabled learners and funneled into an educational wasteland. Teachers must wake up to the unused talents of these students, and how we sometimes mislabel them. Torrance recommends 20 principles for developing creativity in class and for enhancing students' creative processes—ten of which are listed below:

1. Make students more sensitive to their environment.
2. Encourage manipulation of objects and ideas.
3. Develop tolerance toward new ideas.
4. Resist one acceptable answer or a set pattern.
5. Teach skills for avoiding peer sanctions.
6. Encourage individualized learning.
7. Make available different resources for working out ideas.
8. Encourage the habit of working out the full implication of ideas.
9. Integrate knowledge in a variety of fields.
10. Develop adventure and spirit in the classroom.[84]

According to Torrance, the teacher needs to recognize that students can learn in both active and quiet environments. Important ideas occur to some people in the heat of activity as well as in quiet periods of relaxation. As for

---

[83]J. Pansy Torrance, ed., *Over the Years: Research Insights of E. Paul Torrance* (Athens, Ga.: University of Georgia, Department of Educational Psychology, 1984).

[84]Ibid.

the teacher, he or she must have the courage and maturity to accept the original answers of these students,[85] and be willing to accept some degree of nonconforming behavior—not an easy concept for some teachers to accept. To be sure, teachers are better able to free and develop the creative capacities of their students so long as their own behavior and values support creativeness.

In the final analysis, teachers are going to have to learn to accept an inquiring and divergent mind—one that questions and challenges common thinking and is willing to avoid the ordinary and think of the unusual. The information age is upon us, and those who can digest, assimilate, and question data, and see different perspectives and opportunities when they are confronted with problems, will be better able to cope with the future. Managers and executives of business and industry, even the government and military, are going to have to learn to deal with creative people—who can creatively deal with complex information—in order to stay ahead. The quicker teachers come to realize that a narrow classroom mold, one that breeds conformity, complacence, and rote learning, is old fashion and out of tune with the future, the better off will be our students, schools, and society.

THEORY INTO PRACTICE

One overriding factor in all the elements of this chapter is that teachers must face themselves and be honest about themselves and what they are trying to achieve in the classroom. To teach moral values, learning skills, critical thinking, or creativity calls for a teacher who has these skills and has a healthy self-concept. Teachers must be willing to ask tough questions that deal with feelings, attitudes, and behaviors. More than 35 years ago Arthur Jersild, a well-known psychologist, asked teachers to deal with crucial issues of personal and professional life—such issues as striving, conflicts, anxiety, loneliness, self-doubt, alienation, hostility, guilt, anger, and despair. He asked teachers to search for meaning, to go beyond surface facts and behaviors and analyze motives.[86]

To gain knowledge of oneself as a teacher and person, and to face the looking glass to see how others view oneself, requires courage and humility. All of us should be able to analyze our strengths and weaknesses as teachers and our anxieties and aspirations as people. We cannot run from our feelings or mask them for long. They effect our relations with others, especially our students. A teacher who is not timid and not fearful, who has a realistic and positive self-concept, can help others understand themselves, which is at the core of teaching.

Similarly, our students have personal problems of growing up, problems

---

[85] Ibid.

[86] Arthur T. Jersild, *When Teachers Face Themselves* (New York: Teachers College Press, Columbia University, 1955).

with parents and peers, that eventually affect their school work and behavior. Most teachers ignore these problems, for many of us are afraid to deal with the emotions of our students. We prefer dealing with subject matter, not the realities of life. But to teach children to be moral or to think critically calls for a psychologically healthy learning environment and learner. Teachers must help students search for meaning and face themselves, because the cognitive processes (involving content, discovery, critical thinking, and creativity) and the affective processes (feelings and emotions) are interlinked and depend on one another for full development.

SUMMARY

1. The kind of teacher you choose to be is based in part on your reasons for teaching, professional knowledge, and pedagogical skills.

2. Teachers do make a difference in student achievement. However, the differences vary with classroom and school conditions and are not easy to discern.

3. Effective teachers are good classroom managers, provide direct instruction, keep students on task, ask appropriate questions, emphasize comprehension monitoring and learning-to-learn skills, and provide small group and individualized instruction.

4. Variables that affect student achievement are instructional feedback, reinforcement and correction, cues and explanations, reading and study skills, graded homework, and cooperative learning.

5. Quality and quantity of academic instructional and engaged time affect student performance.

6. Moral knowledge can be acquired through academic content, but moral character takes many years to develop and reflects the whole person.

7. Students can be taught learning-to-learn skills, critical thinking skills, and creative thinking skills.

QUESTIONS TO CONSIDER

1. Why is it important for teachers to be willing to face themselves? How can this be accomplished at the preservice level? In-service level?

2. To what extent do teachers make a difference in student achievement? Which of your teachers made the most difference to you? Why?

3. How would you improve academic instructional time and academic engaged time as a teacher?

4. What teaching methods and approaches can be used to improve students' thinking skills?

5. What are the attributes of critical thinking and of creative thinking? Which type of thinking is more important for students to develop in school?

THINGS TO DO

1. Observe two or three teachers at work in the classroom and try to describe the classroom interactions taking place. Why do things happen in the classroom?

2. Observe the same teachers again. Make a list of the dominant instructional patterns that you observe. Compare them with the descriptions in this chapter.

3. Speak to a local school principal or teacher to find out the school's allocated time by subject and grade level. Compare this with Table 1.3. Try to explain the reasons for whatever differences may exist.

4. Some observers argue that Piaget and Kohlberg ignored women in developing their moral theories. What books would you include in the curriculum to ensure the voice of women in moral education?

5. School success is partially based on the students' ability to think critically. Identify the cognitive processes, or the things teachers can do, to foster critical thinking among students.

RECOMMENDED READINGS

Beyer, Barry. *Developing Thinking Skills Program.* Boston: Allyn and Bacon, 1988. Explains the thinking process, including critical thinking, information processing, problem solving, and decision making, and gives guidelines for improving thinking skills programs.

Flavell, John. *Cognitive Development,* 2nd ed. Englewood Cliffs, N.J.: Prentice-Hall, 1985. A discussion of cognitive development with an analysis of problem solving and metacognition.

Hunter, Madeline. *Mastery Learning.* El Segundo, Calif.: Tip Publishers, 1982. A step-by-step approach to improve teaching and instructional effectiveness in elementary and secondary schools.

Kohlberg, Lawrence. *Psychology of Moral Development.* New York: Harper & Row, 1984. A theory of moral reasoning in relation to cognitive abilities and age of children.

Piaget, Jean. *The Equilibration of Cognitive Structures,* trans. and rev. ed. Chicago: University of Chicago Press, 1985. Theory of cognitive development, intelligence, and cognitive processes involved in thinking.

Raths, Louis E., Merrill Harmin, and Sidney Simon. *Values and Teaching,* 2nd ed. Columbus, Ohio: Merrill, 1978. An important text on how teachers can help students clarify values and thinking, with instructional strategies discussed in detail.

Rogers, Carl. *Freedom to Learn,* 2nd ed. Columbus, Ohio: Merrill, 1983. Methods of building freedom and choice in classrooms and developing person-centered (humanistic) teachers.

KEY TERMS

Effective teachers

Alterable environments

Mandated time

Allocated time

Academic instructional time

Academic engaged time

Moral character

Values clarification

Developmental theories

Readiness

Metacognition

Comprehension monitoring

Learning to learn skills

Critical thinking

Creativity

Wisdom

Intuitive thinking

Chapter 2

Classroom Management and Discipline

FOCUSING QUESTIONS

1. Why is classroom management an integral part of teaching?

2. What are some approaches to classroom management? Which ones best fit your personality and philosophy?

3. What is the best way to decide on which approach best fits your classroom management goals?

4. What are some characteristics of successful classroom managers? How many of these characteristics coincide with your management behaviors?

5. How can preventive disciplinary measures improve classroom management? Which ones best fit your personality and philosophy?

6. How can you analyze your strengths and weaknesses as a classroom manager? What means or techniques would you use to evaluate your management abilities?

*I*n order to teach, you must be able to manage your students. No matter how much potential you have as a teacher, if you are unable to control the students in your classroom, little learning will take place. Classroom management is an integral part of teaching, and techniques of managing students both can and must be acquired by the teacher.

Inadequate classroom management and discipline are widely considered by the public to be the major educational problem, even though the media have centered on school busing, school financing, declining test scores, and student drugs. In annual Gallup polls in education, taken among parents since 1970, student discipline, or the lack of it, is listed as the number one or number two school problem each year for the last 20 years.[1]

According to a recent NEA teacher opinion poll, 90 percent of the teachers maintain that student misbehavior interferes with their teaching, and nearly 25 percent claim that it greatly interferes. The same poll revealed that approximately 100,000 teachers suffer personal attack from students annually, most often in front of other students in the classroom.[2]

The problem of discipline is persistent, especially in inner-city schools, because (1) many students lack inner control and are unwilling to defer to teacher authority, (2) many teachers lack systematic methods for dealing with discipline problems, and (3) many school administrators do not provide adequate support for teachers. According to the same NEA poll, the four major reasons the public gives for disciplinary problems in schools nationwide are: parents' failure to discipline youth in the home (84 percent), increased use of drugs and alcohol (83 percent), breakup of traditional family values (72 percent), and schools' lack of authority to deal with the problem (67 percent).

APPROACHES TO CLASSROOM MANAGEMENT

Your personality, philosophy, and teaching style will directly affect your managerial and disciplinary approach. There are many approaches, but the one you adopt must be comfortable for you and coincide with your personal characteristics.

The seven of these approaches, or models, that are considered below are grounded in research and are applicable to classrooms. Although they are presented as distinct approaches, they do share common features. All are based on a mixture of psychology, classroom experience, and common sense. All blend elements of prevention with techniques for intervention. They recom-

---

[1] The annual poll is published in the September or October issue of *Phi Delta Kappan*. The twenty-first survey was published in *Phi Delta Kappan*, September 1989, pp. 41–58.

[2] *Public and K–12 Teacher Members* (Washington, D.C.: National Education Association, 1988).

mend somewhat similar measures. They differ as to the relative importance of prevention and intervention, the degree of control and supervision exercised by the teacher, and the relative emphasis on tasks and personalities. They form a continuum from firm, direct, and structured to flexible, indirect, and democratic.

Assertive Approach

The **assertive approach** to classroom management expects teachers to specify rules of behavior and consequences for disobeying them and to communicate these rules and consequences clearly. The classroom is managed in such a way that students are not allowed to forget who is in charge of the classroom. According to Duke and Meckel, "Students come to realize that the teacher expects them to behave in a certain way in class." Teachers hold students accountable for their actions. Students who disobey rules receive "one warning and then are subjected to a series of increasingly more serious sanctions."[3] The idea is for the teacher to respond to a student's misbehavior quickly and appropriately; mild misbehavior is matched by mild sanctions, but if the misbehavior continues, the sanctions toughen. The approach assumes that misbehavior is contagious and will snowball unless checked early. If misbehavior is ignored or not stopped at an early stage, it will eventually become uncontrollable and more and more students will become disruptive.[4]

The assertive approach is based on Lee and Marlene Canter's model of discipline in which teachers insist on responsible behavior by their students. The teacher takes charge of the classroom immediately, sets the ground rules, and interacts with students in a calm yet forceful way.[5] The teacher is expected to combine clear expectations, active response to misbehavior, and consistent follow-through with warmth and support for all students. The technique assumes that students expect this insistence on responsible behavior, that parents want it, and that the educational process comes to a halt without it.

The technique also assumes that firm classroom management liberates students because it allows them to develop their best traits, skills, and abilities, and provides them with psychological security in the classroom, and an effective learning environment. It also assumes that good teachers can handle discipline problems on their own and that teaching failure is directly related to the inability to maintain adequate classroom discipline. Success, if not predicated on, at least correlates with, good discipline. The approach probably is most effective at the secondary level and in inner-city classrooms where it is now recognized that chronic student behavior problems often exist.

---

[3] Daniel L. Duke and Adrienne M. Meckel, *Teacher's Guide to Classroom Management* (New York: Random House, 1984), p. 23.

[4] Allan C. Ornstein, "Techniques and Fundamentals for Teaching the Disadvantaged," *Journal of Negro Education*, Spring 1967, pp. 136–145.

[5] Lee Canter and Marlene Canter, *Assertive Discipline* (Los Angeles: Canter Associates, 1979).

This type of approach was criticized in the 1960s as "authoritarian," "repressive," "militaristic," and "prejudicial" toward minority students. Its acceptance today is due in part to the student disruptions of the 1970s and the general public demand in the 1980s for firmer discipline and higher academic standards for all students.

The Canters make the following suggestions for teachers applying assertive discipline.

1. Clearly identify expectations.
2. Take positions. (Say, "I like that" or "I don't like that.")
3. Use a firm tone of voice.
4. Use eye contact, gestures, and touches to supplement verbal messages.
5. Say no without guilt feelings.
6. Give and receive compliments genuinely.
7. Place demands on students and enforce them.
8. Set limits on students and enforce them.
9. Indicate consequences of behavior and why specific action is necessary.
10. Be calm and consistent; avoid emotion or threats.
11. Follow through regularly.
12. Persist; enforce minimum rules; don't give up.
13. Establish positive expectations for student behavior; eliminate negative expectations about students.
14. Gain confidence and skills in working with chronic behavior problems in the classroom.[6]

The last point relates to the impact that assertive discipline has on the teacher. Teachers who are able to apply assertive discipline techniques not only have more confidence in their own abilities as teachers, but also get along better with students. The assumption is that a nonassertive approach is typical of teachers who have given in to students or feel it is wrong to place demands and limitations on students. Nonassertive teachers are basically powerless to control students and often passively accept what students do or react with sarcasm, hostility, or idle threats.

The assertive model holds that teachers must establish firm management at the beginning of the year by (1) clarifying appropriate expectations of responsible behavior, (2) identifying existing or potential discipline problems, (3) deciding on negative and positive consequences of behavior that fit the students and situation, and (4) learning how to follow through and implement these consequences. The plan is best achieved through mental rehearsal (having a good idea of what to do before something occurs) and practice (learning from mistakes).

---

[6]Ibid.

Business-Academic Approach

Well-run classrooms free from disruptions, where students behave in an orderly manner and are highly involved in learning, are not accidental. They exist where teachers have a clear idea of the type of classroom conditions (arrangement, materials), student behaviors (rules, procedures), and instructional activities (assignments, tasks) they wish to produce. The **business-academic approach,** developed by Evertson and Emmer, emphasizes the organization and management of students as they engage in academic work.[7] Task orientation, that is, focusing on the businesslike and orderly accomplishment of academic work, leads to a clear set of procedures for students and teachers to follow.

Evertson and Emmer divide organizing and managing student work into three major categories: establishment and communication of work assignments, standards, and procedures; monitoring of student work; and feedback to students.

I. *Clear communication of assignments and work requirements.* The teacher must establish and explain clearly to students work assignments, features of the work, standards to be met, and procedures.
   1. *Instruction for assignments.* Explanations should be made in both oral and written forms. In addition to telling the students about assignments, teachers should post assignments on the chalkboard or distribute duplicated copies. Students should be required to copy assignments posted on the chalkboard into their notebooks.
   2. *Standards for form, neatness, and due dates.* Before students start, they should be given general rules for all assignments: type of paper and writing material to use (pencil, pen, typewriter), page numbering system, form for headings, due dates, and so forth. Students will then know what is expected of them without having to be told each time.
   3. *Procedures for absent students.* Routines should be established for makeup work for absent students. These must include meeting briefly with students at a set time before or after school, assigning class helpers who will be available at particular times of the day (usually during seatwork activities) to help the students, and having a designated place where students can pick up and turn in makeup work.
II. *Monitoring student work.* Monitoring student work helps the teacher to detect students who are having difficulty and to encourage students to keep working.
   1. *Monitoring group work.* Before helping any individual student with work, the teacher must be sure that all students start work and

---

[7]Carolyn M. Evertson et al., *Classroom Management for Elementary Teachers*, 2nd ed. (Englewood Cliffs, N.J.: Prentice-Hall, 1989); Edmund T. Emmer et al., *Classroom Management for Secondary Teachers*, 2nd ed. (Englewood Cliffs, N.J.: Prentice-Hall, 1989).

Figure 2.1 The classroom setting is a place where a structured and organized teacher is often successful. (Photo © Richard S. Orton)

    are able to do the assignment; otherwise, some students will not even start the assignment and others may start incorrectly.

2. *Monitoring individual work.* Work can be monitored several ways, including circulating around the room and giving feedback where needed, having students bring their work to the teacher one at a time at some designated point during an activity, and establishing due dates that correspond with stages in an assignment.

3. *Monitoring completion of work.* Procedures for turning in work must be established and enforced. When all students are turning in work at the same time, the best procedure is to have the work passed in a given direction with no talking until all the work is collected.

4. *Maintaining records of student work.* It is important for teachers to keep a record of the students' work and to incorporate it as part of the grade. The record should be divided into several headings, such as workbook assignments, major assignments or projects, daily homework, and quizzes and tests.

III. *Feedback to students.* Frequent, immediate, and specific feedback is important for enhancing academic monitoring and managerial procedures. Work in progress, homework, completed assignments, tests, and other work should be checked promptly.

1. *Attention to problems.* It is important for teachers to pay careful attention at the beginning of the year to completion of classroom and homework assignments. The first time a student fails to turn in an assignment without a good reason is the time to talk to the student. If the student needs help, the teacher should provide it, but should insist at the same time that the student do the work. If the student has persistent problems completing work, then parental communication may be needed. The teacher should not wait until the grading period is over to note the problems that exist.
2. *Attention to good work.* Part of giving feedback is to acknowledge good work. This may be done by displaying the work, giving oral recognition, or providing written comments.[8]

According to Evertson and Emmer, an effective manager incorporates 11 managerial methods, all of which have been shown to correlate with improved student achievement and behavior. These methods are listed in Table 2.1.

The general approach and methods used by Evertson and Emmer are appropriate for both elementary and secondary teachers. The approach coincides with various instructional techniques, especially Rosenshine's direct instruction (see Chapter 6), Bloom's mastery learning (Chapter 9), Ryan's pattern Y teacher (Chapter 11), and Good and Brophy's methods of effective teaching (Chapter 11).

The business-academic approach involves a high degree of "time on task" and "academic engaged time" for students. The idea is that when students are working on their tasks, there is little opportunity for discipline problems to arise. The teacher organizes students' work, keeps them on task, monitors their work, gives them feedback, and holds them accountable by providing rewards and penalties.[9] It is a no-play, no-frills approach, corresponding to old-fashioned "three Rs" and now packaged as part of the "academic productivity" movement in education.

Behavioral Modification Approach

Behavioral modification is rooted in the classic work of James Watson and the more recent work of B. F. Skinner. It involves a variety of techniques and methods, ranging from simple rewards to elaborate reinforcement training. Behaviorists assume that behavior is shaped by environment and pay little attention to the causes of problems.

Teachers using the **behavior modification approach** spend little time on the personal history of students or on searching for the reasons for a particular problem. They strive to increase the occurrence of appropriate behavior through a system of rewards and reduce the likelihood of inappropriate behavior through

---

[8]Ibid.

[9]Allan C. Ornstein, "Emphasis on Student Outcomes Focuses Attention on Quality of Instruction," *National Association of Secondary School Principals*, January 1987, pp. 88–95.

Table 2.1   METHODS OF EFFECTIVE CLASSROOM MANAGERS

1. *Readying the classroom.* Classroom space, materials, and equipment are ready at the beginning of the year. Effective managers have better arranged their rooms, and they have coped more effectively with existing constraints.
2. *Planning rules and procedures.* Teachers make sure students understand and follow rules and procedures; they spend more time in the beginning of the year explaining and reminding students of rules.
3. *Teaching rules and procedures.* Rules and procedures are systematically taught (i.e., lining up, turning work in, etc.) and reinforced. Most of these teachers have taught their students to respond to certain cues or signals, such as a bell or the teacher's call for attention.
4. *Consequences.* Consequences for not following rules and procedures are clearly established by the teachers; there is consistent follow through.
5. *Beginning of school activities.* The first few days are spent getting students ready as a coherent and cooperative group. Once established, these teachers sustain a whole-group focus.
6. *Strategies for potential problems.* Strategies for dealing with potential problems are planned in advance. With these strategies teachers can deal with misbehavior more quickly than can less effective managers.
7. *Monitoring.* Student behavior is closely monitored; the teacher does not lose audience contact; student academic work is also monitored.
8. *Stopping inappropriate behavior.* Inappropriate or disruptive behavior is handled promptly and consistently—before it worsens or spreads.
9. *Organizing instruction.* Teachers organize instructional activities at suitable levels for all students in the class. There is a high degree of student success and content related to student interests.
10. *Student accountability.* Procedures have been developed for keeping students for their work and behavior.
11. *Instructional clarity.* Teachers provide clear instructions; these help keep students on task and allow them to learn faster, while reducing discipline problems. Directions are clear, thus confusion is minimized.

Source: Edmund T. Emmer and Carolyn M. Evertson, "Synthesis of Research on Classroom Management," *Educational Leadership,* January 1981, pp. 342–347; Emmer et al., "Effective Classroom Management at the Beginning of the School Year," *Elementary School Journal,* May 1980, pp. 219–231; and Evertson et al., "Improving Classroom Management: An Experiment in Elementary School Classrooms," *Elementary School Journal,* November 1983, pp. 173–188.

punishments. According to Albert Bandura, teachers would ask the following questions: (1) What is the specific behavior that requires modification (increase, reduction, elimination)? (2) When does the behavior occur? (3) What are the consequences of the behavior? Or, what happens in the classroom when the behavior is exhibited? (4) How do these consequences reinforce inappropriate behavior? How can the consequences be altered? (5) How can appropriate behavior be reinforced?[10]

---

[10] Albert Bandura, *Principles of Behavioral Modification* (New York: Holt, Rinehart and Winston, 1969); Bandura, *Social Foundations of Thought and Action: A Social-Cognitive Theory* (Englewood Cliffs, N.J.: Prentice-Hall, 1986).

Professional Viewpoints

Effective Classroom Management

The foremost concern of new teachers is managing the classroom effectively, but, too often, managing effectively is seen as simply dealing with misbehavior. To view good classroom management as a set of strategies for disciplining students is to misunderstand the basis on which good management rests. Effective classroom managers are distinguished by their success in preventing problems from arising in the first place, rather than by special skills in dealing with problems once they occur. Good management practice begins on the first day of school with carefully organized, systematic plans for accomplishing classroom tasks and activities. Good managers also make clear their expectations for students' work and behavior, rules and procedures, routines for checking and monitoring student academic work, procedures for grading and giving feedback to students, incentives and deterrents, methods for grouping students, and a whole variety of seemingly minor but essential procedures. Proactive planning helps avert behavior problems by providing students with ways to be successful.

Carolyn M. Evertson
Professor of Education Psychology
Vanderbilt University

The basic principles of the behavioral modification approach are as follows:

1. Behavior is shaped by its *consequences*, not by the causes of problems in the history of the individual or by group conditions.
2. Behavior is strengthened by immediate reinforcers. *Positive reinforcers* are praise or rewards. *Negative reinforcers* take away or stop something that the student doesn't like.[11] For example, the student is reprimanded by the teacher; the student agrees to behave according to classroom rules, and the teacher stops reprimanding. In a negative reinforcing situation the student behaves in such a way as to remove aversive stimuli (such as nagging, scolding, and threats) from the environment.
3. Behavior is strengthened by *systematic reinforcement* (positive or negative). Behavior is weakened if not followed by reinforcement.[12]

[11]B. F. Skinner, "The Evolution of Behavior," *Journal of Experimental Analysis of Behavior,* March 1984, pp. 217–222; Skinner, "Cognitive Science and Behaviorism," *British Journal of Psychology,* August 1985, pp. 291–301.

[12]Gordon H. Bower and Ernest Hilgard, *Theories of Learning,* 5th ed. (Englewood Cliffs, N.J.: Prentice-Hall, 1981).

4. Students respond better to positive reinforcers than they do to punishment (aversive stimuli). Punishment can be used to reduce inappropriate behavior, but sparingly.

5. When a student is not rewarded for appropriate or adaptive behavior, inappropriate or maladaptive behavior may become increasingly dominant and will be utilized to obtain reinforcement.

6. *Constant reinforcement*—the reinforcement of a behavior every time it occurs—produces the best results, especially in new learning or conditioning situations.

7. Once the behavior has been learned, it is best maintained through *intermittent reinforcement*—the reinforcement of a behavior only occasionally.

8. Intermittent reinforcement schedules include (a) *variable ratio*, supplying reinforcement at unpredictable intervals, (b) *fixed ratio*, supplying reinforcement after a preselected number of responses, and (c) *fixed interval*, supplying reinforcement at preselected intervals.[13]

9. There are several types of reinforcers, each of which may be positive or aversive. Examples of positive reinforcers are: (a) *social reinforcers*, such as verbal comments ("Right", "Correct," "That's good"), facial expressions, and gestures, (b) *graphic reinforcers*, such as written words of encouragement, gold stars, and checks, (c) *tangible reinforcers*, such as cookies and badges for young students and certificates and notes to parents for older students, and (d) *activity reinforcers*, such as being a monitor or sitting near the teacher for young students and working with a friend or on a special project for older students.[14]

10. *Rules* are established and enforced. Students who follow rules are praised and rewarded in various ways. Students who break rules are either ignored, reminded about appropriate behavior, or punished immediately. The response to rule-breaking differs somewhat in different variations of the behavioral modification approach.[15]

Each teacher has an undetermined value as a potential reinforcing agent for each student. This value is assigned initially by students on the basis of past experiences, and it changes as a result of the teacher's actions. The teacher must realize that this evaluation process is going on in the student and that a positive relationship with the student will enhance his or her potential for influencing their behavior in class. Moreover, the teacher is one of many adults who serve as reinforcing agents in the student's life. In order to facilitate the classroom management process the teacher may have to enlist the support of others.

[13] Robert F. Biehler and Jack Snowman, *Psychology Applied to Teaching*, 6th ed. (Boston: Houghton Mifflin, 1990).

[14] C. M. Charles, *Building Classroom Discipline*, 3rd ed. (New York: Longman, 1989).

[15] Ellen P. Reese, "Learning about Teaching from Teaching about Learning," in V. P. Makosky ed., *The G. Stanley Hall Lecture Series*, vol. 6 (Washington, D.C.: American Psychological Association, 1986), pp. 65–128.

There are a number of systems or variations of behavioral modification that are applicable to classroom management. They basically build limits and consequences into behavior and employ various rules, rewards, and punishments. A well-known system utilized in various social learning situations is termed **modeling.**

Models are effective in modifying behavior to the degree that they capture attention, hold attention, and are imitated. Effective models may be parents, relatives, teachers, other adults (community residents), public figures (sports people, movie stars), and peers. The best models are those that individuals can identify with on the basis of one or more of the following traits: (1) sex, (2) age, (3) ethnicity, (4) physical attractiveness, (5) personality attractiveness, (6) competence, (7) power, and (8) ability to reward imitators. Teachers who want to use modeling in classroom management should recognize that the first five are personal characteristics that are hard to change, but the last three are institutional and role characteristics that are easier to manipulate to increase their effectiveness as models.

Building good discipline through modeling includes the following.

1. *Demonstration.* Students know exactly what is expected. In addition to having expected behavior explained to them, they see and hear it.
2. *Attention.* Students focus their attention on what is being depicted or explained. The degree of attention correlates with the characteristics of the model (teacher) and characteristics of the students.
3. *Practice.* Students are given opportunity to practice the appropriate behavior.
4. *Corrective feedback.* Students receive frequent, specific, and immediate feedback. Appropriate behavior is reinforced; inappropriate behavior is suppressed and corrected.
5. *Application.* Students are able to apply their learning in classroom activities (role playing, modeling activities) and other real-life situations.[16]

The teacher's role in modeling is summarized in Table 2.2. Data suggest that teachers who do not know much about how students learn from models produce less learning in their students and have more discipline problems than teachers who are successful at using modeling.

Group Managerial Approach

The **group managerial approach** to discipline is based on Jacob Kounin's research. He emphasizes the importance of responding immediately to group

---

[16] Albert Bandura et al., "Representing Personal Determinants in Causal Structures," *Journal of Personality and Social Psychology*, June 1985, pp. 406–414; Shelby R. Cohen, "Models Inside and Outside the Classroom: A Force from Desirable Learning," *Contemporary Education*, Summer 1980, pp. 186–188; and B. F. Skinner, "The Evaluation of Verbal Behavior," *Journal of Experimental Analysis of Behavior*, January 1986, pp. 115–122.

Table 2.2   THE TEACHER'S ROLE IN MODELING

1. Selects behavior to be learned.
2. Selects most appropriate models.
3. Sees that the behavior is modeled clearly, accurately, and succinctly.
4. Assists in helping observers focus attention on what is being modeled.
5. Assists observers in remembering what they saw.
6. Provides for suitable practice in reenacting the observed behavior.
7. Provides corrective feedback during student reenactment.
8. Provides reinforcement following desired behaviors.

Source: C. M. Charles, *Building Classroom Discipline*, 2nd ed. (New York: Longman, 1985), p. 161.

student behavior that might be inappropriate or undesirable in order to prevent problems rather than having to deal with them after they emerge. He describes what he calls the "ripple effect."[17] If a student misbehaves, but the teacher stops the misbehavior immediately, it remains an isolated incident and does not develop into a problem. If the misbehavior is not noticed, is ignored, or is allowed to continue for too long, it often spreads throughout the group and becomes more serious and chronic.

Kounin analyzes classroom activities for purposes of management by dividing them into categories of pupil behavior and teacher management behavior (see Table 2.3). Major categories of pupil behavior are work involvement and deviancy. Major categories of teacher behavior are desist techniques, movement management, and group focus.

Work involvement is the amount of time students spend engaged in assigned academic work. (It closely resembles what other researchers call "time on task" or "academic engaged time.") Students who are involved in work (writing in a workbook, reciting, reading, watching a demonstration) exhibit fewer disciplinary problems than students who are not involved in any assigned task. If the teacher keeps students involved in work, there is less chance that boredom and discipline problems will arise.

Deviancy ranges from no misbehavior to serious misbehavior. *No misbehavior* means the student is not purposefully but nevertheless upsetting another student or teacher or is slightly off task. *Mild misbehavior* includes such actions as whispering, making faces, teasing, reading a comic, passing notes. *Serious misbehavior* is aggressive or harmful behavior that interferes with others or violates school or social codes. The point is not to permit mild misbehavior to degenerate into serious misbehavior by dealing with the mild misbehavior as soon as it occurs.

Desist techniques are teacher actions taken to stop misbehavior. Kounin feels that they depend on two abilities. *With-it-ness* is the ability to react on

[17]Jacob S. Kounin, *Discipline and Group Management in Classrooms* (New York: Holt, Rinehart and Winston, 1970); Kounin, *Discipline and Classroom Management* (New York: Holt, Rinehart and Winston, 1977).

Table 2.3   KOUNIN'S BEHAVIORS AND CATEGORIES FOR OBSERVING CLASSROOM MANAGEMENT

Categories of pupil behavior

I. Work Involvement	II. Deviancy
A. Definitely in	A. No misbehavior
B. Probably in	B. Mild misbehavior
C. Definitely out	C. Serious misbehavior

Categories of teacher management behavior

I. Desist Techniques	III. Group Focus
A. "With-it-ness"	A. Alerting
1. Target	1. Create suspense
2. Timing	2. Pick reciter randomly
B. Overlapping	3. Mass unison response
1. None	4. Alert nonperformers to possibility of being called on
2. Some	5. Present new or novel material
	6. Ignore group in favor of reciter
II. Movement Management	7. Prepick reciter before asking question
A. Smoothness-Jerkiness	8. Predetermine sequence of reciters
1. Stimulus-bounded	B. Accountability
2. Thrust	1. Ask students to hold up props
3. Dangle	2. Actively attend to mass unison response
4. Truncation	3. Call on others to help student
5. Flip-flop	4. Ask for raised hands and require performance
B. Momentum	5. Circulate and check products of nonreciters
1. Overdwelling	6. Require student to demonstrate and check performance
2. Fragmentation	

Source: Adapted from Jacob Kounin, *Discipline and Group Management in Classrooms* (New York: Holt, Rinehart and Winston, 1970), chaps. 3–6.

target (react to the proper student) and in a timely fashion. It also involves communicating to students that one knows what is happening, or, as Kounin puts it, that one "has eyes in the back of one's head." *Overlapping* behavior refers to the teacher's ability to handle more than one matter at a time. He or she can attend to more than one student at the same time—say, a student who is reciting and another student who is interrupting with a question or comment.

Movement management is the organization of behavior in transitions from task to task within and between lessons. Movement may be characterized as smooth or jerky. *Smoothness* is an even and calm flow of activities. It involves uninterrupted work periods and short, fluid transitions that are made automatically and without disruption. In particular, the teacher (1) avoids unnecessary announcements and interruptions when students are busy doing work,

(2) finishes one activity before starting on the next, and (3) doesn't abruptly end or start an activity. *Jerkiness* is a disorderly flow of activities. It may result if the teacher tries to do too many things at once or does not make clear to students procedures for ending one task and changing to a new one. The teacher may have to shout during transitions, disorder may arise as students have to ask questions about what to do, and unengaged students may create disruptions. In order to prevent jerkiness, five subcategories of behavior should be avoided.

1. *Stimulus-bounded.* The teacher is so immersed in a small group of students or activity that he or she ignores other students or misses an event that is potentially disruptive.
2. *Thrust.* The teacher bursts into activities without assessing student readiness and gives orders, statements, or questions that only confuse the students.
3. *Dangle.* The teacher ends an activity or drops a topic before it is completed.
4. *Truncation.* The teacher ends an activity abruptly.
5. *Flip-flop.* The teacher terminates one activity, goes to another, and then returns to the previously terminated activity. The teacher lacks clear direction and sequence of activities.

Movement management also involves *momentum*, that is, keeping activities at an appropriate "pace." Momentum is slowed or impeded if the teacher engages in overdwelling or fragmentation. *Overdwelling* may take the form of giving explanations beyond what is necessary for most students' understanding, or lecturing, preaching, nagging, overemphasizing, or giving too many directions. *Fragmentation* takes the form of giving too much detail, breaking things down into too many steps, or duplicating or repeating activities. For example, a teacher who calls students to the desk to read, one by one, when one student can read aloud while the others listen, is engaging in fragmentation.

Group focus is keeping the students focused on the group activity or task. It can be achieved by what Kounin calls *alerting*. Alerting activities include creating suspense, presenting new material, choosing reciters randomly, and selecting reciters (see Table 2.3 for other methods Kounin lists). Group focus can also be achieved by using *accountability*. This involves such methods as asking students to hold up props, circulating to check the products of nonreciters, and requiring students to perform and checking their performance (see Table 2.3).

Kounin believes that work involvement, smoothness and momentum are enhanced by instructional techniques that facilitate learning. See Tips for Teachers 2.1. Student *satiation* (boredom) can be avoided in three ways: by providing a feeling of *progress*, providing *challenges*, and adding *variety* to the lessons.

In summary, Kounin believes that student engagement in lessons and activities is the key to successful classroom management. Students are expected to work and behave. The successful teacher monitors student work in a sys-

---

Tips for Teachers 2.1

Enhancing Smooth Transitions and Maintaining Momentum

A variety of related instructional techniques help students make smooth transitions from one activity to another and facilitate momentum in the classroom.

1. Use structured curricula rather than discovery learning.
2. Emphasize small, briskly paced instructional components.
3. Provide detailed and repetitious instructions and explanations.
4. Provide numerous examples.
5. Include frequent questions and opportunities to practice activity.
6. Include frequent and immediate feedback and correction, especially in the early phases of instruction.
7. Design instruction for high rates of success.
8. Limit the duration of seatwork.
9. Arrange for overlearning to occur through frequent drill and practice.

Source: Elizabeth M. Reis, "Effective Teacher Techniques: Implications for Better Discipline," *Clearing House*, April 1988, p. 357.

---

tematic fashion, clearly defines acceptable and unacceptable behavior, and exhibits with-it-ness and overlapping abilities. The successful teacher has a clear sense of direction and sequence for tasks. Smooth transitions are made from one activity to another, so that student attention is turned easily from one activity to another. Similarly, lessons are well paced.

Almost all the major theorists of classroom management—Brophy, Doyle, Emmer, Evertson, and Good—have been influenced by Kounin and sometimes give him some credit when they discuss their own managerial views. The point is, however, that most of what they have to say was said by Kounin twenty years ago.

Group Guidance Approach

The **group guidance approach** is based on manipulating (a better word is "changing") the surface behavior of the students on a group basis. Since teachers have few opportunities to work with students on an individual basis, they must learn to work with groups of students and to maintain group focus on the content and tasks of the group. Discipline and classroom control are produced through the group atmosphere and enhanced through group rapport.

The work of Fritz Redl and his colleagues with delinquent and disruptive youth is the basis for much of the group guidance approach. He holds that disciplinary problems have three causes.

1. *Individual case history.* The problem is related to the psychological disturbance of one child; disruptive behavior in class is part of the child's larger emotional problem. The surface problems are repetitive since they arise from the individual case history.
2. *Group conditions.* The problem reflects unfavorable conditions in the group. It is easier to resolve than a problem produced by a case history.
3. *Mixture of individual and group causes.* The problem centers around an individual, but is triggered by something in the group. A remedy must consider both elements.[18]

According to Redl's research, 10 percent of all cases of school discipline are simple cases of individual disturbances, about 30 percent involve group conditions or inadequacies, and 60 percent seem to include both individual and group factors. This means 90 percent of all discipline cases indicate a need for group remediation, or what he refers to as "group psychological engineering."[19]

In analyzing a disciplinary situation, Redl contends that teachers must ask themselves to what extent problems reflect elements of the group, the teachers' own behavior, and the behavior of the students. To maintain good discipline, the teacher must understand the group—its needs and interests—and be able to manipulate the surface behavior of the group. Group elements to be considered include the following.

1. *Dissatisfaction with classroom work.* The work is too easy or too difficult. The work load is too light or too heavy. Assignments are poorly planned or poorly explained. Assignments are considered unfair by students because they have not been prepared for them. Learning experiences emphasize verbalization, omitting motor skills and manipulative activities. Work is badly scheduled, badly sequenced, or confusing.
2. *Poor interpersonal relations.* Problems are caused by friendships or tensions among individuals, cliques, or subgroups; by badly filled group roles (for example, teacher assistant, tutor-tutoree); and by student-teacher friction.
3. *Disturbances in group climate.* The climate is punitive, tinged with partiality (certain children can do no wrong, others are accused for almost anything), too competitive (leading to hostile or defeatist attitudes), too exclusive (the group rejects individuals who don't fit).
4. *Poor group organization.* The group is characterized by too much autocratic pressure or too little supervision and security. Standards for group behavior are too high or too low. The group is too highly organized (too many rules) or too unstructured. The group organization

---

[18] Fritz Redl and David Wineman, *Children Who Hate* (New York: Free Press, 1951); George V. Scheviakov and Fritz Redl, *Discipline for Today's Children and Youth* (Washington, D.C.: National Education Association, 1957).

[19] Scheviakov and Redl, *Discipline for Today's Children and Youth.*

is out of focus with the age, developmental maturity, social back-ground, needs, or abilities of the group members.

5. *Sudden changes and group emotions.* The group is experiencing a high level of anxiety (for example, just before exam period). Contemporary events lead to unusual depression, fear, or excitement. Students are bored (there is lack of interest or emotion).[20]

According to Redl and his colleagues, boredom is one of the major causes of disciplinary problems, and it leads to withdrawal, frustration and irritability, or aggressive rejection of the entire group on the part of students.[21] Another key factor is the organization of the group. Whenever something is wrong with the organizational composition (for example, in relation to student needs, abilities, or age), discipline problems are inevitable.

Perhaps one of the most difficult managerial tasks for the teacher is dealing with a hostile or aggressive group. Such a classroom group subtly and overtly defies the teacher and disrupts instructional activities. Among the symptoms that reveal this condition are:

1. Continual talking, lack of attention when instructional tasks are pre-sented.
2. Constant disruptions that interfere with teaching.
3. Overall nonconformity to classroom rules or school practices.
4. Overt challenges and refusal to obey.
5. Group solidarity in resisting the teacher's efforts.[22]

A class group with these symptoms usually continues to be aggressive and resistant long after the cause of the behavior is removed. When group members act together to defy and resist the teacher's efforts, the teacher may react by trying to match force with force. In some cases the teacher's behavior is the source of the problem—being inconsistent in enforcing rules, yelling or making idle threats, displaying frequent outbursts of emotion, giving assignments that lack challenge, variety, or interest. In such situations teachers often mistakenly identify the ringleaders or the entire group as causes of the problem rather than looking to their own behavior.

In other cases the problem can be traced to the students' attitudes toward authority, and has little to do with the teacher. Here the teacher must be able to change the students' feelings of hostility to trust and confidence. According to educators, this difficult task of developing a positive working relationship with the students on an individual and group basis involves reacting with sensitivity to the needs and feelings of students, making an effort to understand

---

[20] Fritz Redl and David Wineman, *Controls from Within* (New York: Free Press, 1952); Scheviakov and Redl, *Discipline for Today's Children and Youth.*

[21] Ibid.

[22] James S. Cangelosi, *Classroom Management Strategies* (New York: Longman, 1988); Johanna K. Lemlech, *Classroom Management: Methods and Techniques for Elementary and Secondary Teachers* (New York: Longman, 1988).

Professional Viewpoint

On Humanistic Approaches

The humane school recognizes that all children (indeed, all human beings) need to be valued and respected as people—that they need to have some measure of control over their lives and activities, in school and out, and that they need, above all, to experience a reasonable amount of success in order to develop feelings of competence and self-worth. Rules are needed, but whatever rules govern the school are fair and primarily serve the needs of the students, not the needs of teachers.

The humane school places great faith in the importance of the classroom teacher as the key to its success or failure. The teacher is the link between the child and the curriculum; the "humaneness" of that curriculum will be directly related to the teacher's perceptiveness, sensitivity, and responsiveness. Wordsworth could have had the teacher in mind when he wrote of the poet as "a man endued with more lively sensibility, more enthusiasm and tenderness, who has a greater knowledge of human nature and a more comprehensive soul."

This is, of course, asking a great deal of teachers; yet I see no other way if schools are to become the sort of place where children learn not only to read and to write, but also to understand and to care.

It matters, then, how time is spent, for the quality of children's lives in school probably has the most direct relationship to the quality of the lives they will live later as adults.

Vincent Rogers
Professor of Education
University of Connecticut, Storrs

---

students' individual problems, showing trust and respect for them, listening to and observing them, diagnosing what has to be done to manipulate their surface behavior in a group, providing meaningful work, and encouraging on-task behavior.[23]

Of course, if teachers do not diagnose management problems correctly, especially group managerial problems, the problems will persist and increase.

---

[23] Arlene Breckenridge, "Performance Improvement Program Helps Administrators Assess Counselor Performance," *National Association of Secondary School Principals*, February 1987, pp. 23–28; Jere E. Brophy, "Educating Teachers About Managing Classrooms and Students," *Teaching and Teacher Education* (vol. 4, 1988), pp. 1–18; and Penelope L. Peterson, "Making Learning Meaningful: Lessons from Cognition and Instruction," *Educational Psychologist*, Fall 1988, pp. 365–374.

When such problems exist, having group discussions with students can be helpful for exploring differences and identifying causes of conflict. But the teacher needs human relation skills in working with groups. A safer and more conservative strategy is for the teacher, alone or with colleagues, to analyze how his or her own behavior affects the group, how individual student case histories create difficulties, and how group factors are reflected in the problem.

Acceptance Approach

The **acceptance approach** to discipline is rooted in humanistic psychology and maintains that every person has a prime need for acceptance. Students, like everyone else, strive for acceptance. They want to belong and to be liked by others who are important to them more than they want to learn. Similarly, they would rather behave than misbehave. The acceptance approach is also based on the democratic model of teaching in which the teacher provides leadership by establishing rules and consequences, but at the same time allows students to participate in decisions and to make choices.

Rudolph Dreikurs is noted for a disciplinary approach based on the need for acceptance.[24] He maintains that acceptance by peers and teachers is the prerequisite for appropriate behavior and achievement in school. People try all kinds of behavior to get status and recognition. If they are not successful in receiving recognition through socially acceptable methods, then they will turn to mistaken goals that result in antisocial behavior. Dreikurs identifies four mistaken goals:

1. *Attention getting.* When students are not getting the recognition they desire, they often resort to attention-getting misbehavior. They want other students or the teacher to pay attention to them. They may act as the "class clown," ask special favors, continually seek help with assignments, or refuse to work unless the teacher hovers over them. They function as long as they obtain their peers' or teacher's attention.
2. *Power seeking.* Students may also express their desire for recognition by defying adults to achieve what they perceive as power. Their defiance is expressed in arguing, contradicting, teasing, temper tantrums, and low-level hostile behavior. If the students get the teacher to argue or fight with them, they win, because they succeed in getting the teacher involved in a power struggle.
3. *Revenge seeking.* Students who fail to gain recognition through power may seek revenge. Their mistaken goal is to hurt others to make up for being hurt or feeling rejected and unloved. Students who seek revenge don't care about being punished. They are cruel, hostile, or violent toward others. Simple logic doesn't always work with them.

---

[24]Rudolph Dreikurs, *Psychology in the Classroom*, 2nd ed. (New York: Harper & Row, 1968); Rudolph Dreikurs and Pearl Cassel, *Discipline Without Tears*, rev. ed. (New York: Dutton, 1988).

Figure 2.2 Teachers must learn to control minor infractions that disrupt learning. (Photo © Elizabeth Crews)

Being punished gives them renewed cause for action. The more trouble they cause for themselves, the more justified they feel.

4. *Withdrawal.* If students feel helpless and rejected, the goal of their behavior may become withdrawal from the social situation, rather than confrontation. They guard whatever little self-esteem they have by removing themselves from situations that test their abilities. Such withdrawal displays their feelings of inadequacy. If not helped, they eventually become isolated.[25]

The first thing teachers need to do is to identify students' mistaken goals. The type of misbehavior indicates the type of expectations students have or their mistaken goal.

1. If students stop the behavior and then repeat it, their goal is *getting attention.*
2. If students refuse to stop or increase their misbehavior, their goal is *power seeking.*
3. If students become hostile or violent, their goal is *getting revenge.*
4. If students refuse to cooperate or participate, their goal is *withdrawal.*

After teachers identify the mistaken goals, they need to confront the students with an explanation of what they are doing. Dreikurs maintains that by

---

[25] Rudolph Dreikurs, Bernice B. Grunwald, and Floyd C. Pepper, *Maintaining Sanity in the Classroom,* 2nd ed. (New York: Harper & Row, 1982); Rudolph Dreikurs and Loren Grey, *Logical Consequences: A New Approach to Discipline* (New York: Dutton, 1988).

doing this in a friendly, nonthreatening way, teachers can get students to examine—even change—their behavior. The teachers should then encourage students in their efforts to recognize their mistaken goals and to change their behavior. Dreikurs sees an important distinction between encouraging and praising. *Encouragement* consists of words or actions that convey respect and belief in students' abilities. It tells students they are accepted; it recognizes efforts, not achievements. *Praise,* on the other hand, is given when a task is achieved. It promotes the idea that an action is worthless unless it receives praise. (This concept contradicts Good and Brophy, who believe in moderate praise; see Chapter 6.)

Finally, the teacher needs to be sure the students are aware of and understand the consequences of inappropriate behavior. The consequences must be as closely related to the misbehavior as possible, and the teacher must apply them consistently, immediately, and in a calm manner, displaying no anger or triumph. For example, failing to complete a homework assignment means staying after school and finishing it. Disturbing others in class results in isolation from the group for a short period. Students gradually learn that poor choices result in unpleasant consequences, which are nobody's fault but their own. Eventually, students learn to control their actions and to make better decisions, and thus they reach a point where their behavior is controlled by self-discipline.

Dreikurs suggests several strategies for working with students who exhibit mistaken goals to encourage them and to enforce consequences. These points are listed in Table 2.4.

Success Approach

The **success approach,** like the acceptance approach, is rooted in humanistic psychology and the democratic model of teaching. However, instead of dealing with inappropriate behavior and the consequences of such behavior, it deals with general psychological and social conditions. William Glasser, most noted for this approach, which he calls *reality therapy*, insists that although teachers should not excuse bad behavior on the part of the student, they need to change whatever negative classroom conditions exist and improve conditions so they lead to student success.[26]

Glasser's view about discipline is simple but powerful. Behavior is a matter of choice. Good behavior results from good choices; bad behavior results from bad choices. A teacher's job is to help students make good choices. Students make choices according to whether they see the results of those choices as desirable. If bad behavior gets them what they want, they will make bad choices.

Students who have feelings of positive self-worth and experience success

---

[26]William W. Glasser, *Reality Therapy: A New Approach to Psychiatry* (New York: Harper & Row, 1965).

Table 2.4   STRATEGIES FOR CARRYING OUT THE ACCEPTANCE APPROACH

To encourage students	To enforce consequences
1. Be positive; avoid negative statements.	1. Give clear directions.
2. Encourage students to improve, not be perfect.	2. Establish a relationship with each student based on mutual trust and respect.
3. Encourage effort; results are secondary if students try.	3. Consequences must be logical; a direct relationship between misbehavior and consequences must be understood by students.
4. Emphasize strengths; minimize weaknesses.	4. Perceive behavior in its proper perspective; avoid making issues out of trivial incidents.
5. Teach students to learn from mistakes.	5. Permit students to assume responsibility for their own behavior.
6. Stimulate motivation; do not exert undue pressure.	6. Treat students as social equals.
7. Encourage student independence.	7. Combine friendliness with firmness; students must see the teacher as a friend, but limitations must be established.
8. Exhibit faith in student's abilities.	8. Distinguish between the deed and doer; react to the behavior, not the person.
9. Offer to help overcome student's obstacles.	9. Set limits at the beginning, but work toward a sense of responsibility on the part of the student.
10. Encourage cooperative or team effort among students.	10. Keep demands or rules simple.
11. Send positive notes home; note improvement.	11. Mean what you say; carry out your rules.
12. Show pride in student's work; display it.	12. Close an incident quickly; revive good spirits; mistakes are corrected, then forgotten.
13. Be optimistic, enthusiastic, supporting.	
14. Set up situations that lead to success for all.	
15. Use encouraging remarks: "I know you can"; "Keep trying"; "That a boy."	

Source: Adapted from Rudolf Dreikurs, *Maintaining Sanity in the Classroom,* 2nd ed. (New York: Harper & Row, 1982).

will make good choices most of the time. The road to positive self-worth and to success begins with a good relationship with people who care. For some students school may be the only place where they meet people who genuinely care for them. Yet, some students resist entering into positive relationships with adults, especially teachers. Teachers, therefore, must show that they care and are positive and be persistent about both. The emphasis is on helping—exactly what the teaching profession is about—and therefore the approach is attractive to many educators.

Glasser makes the following suggestions.

1. *Stress students' responsibility for their own behavior continually.* Since good behavior comes from good choices, their responsibility for their choices and behavior must be explored and clarified on a regular basis.
2. *Establish rules.* Rules are essential, but they should be established and agreed upon early in the term by the teacher and students. Rules should

facilitate group achievement and group morale. Rules can be evaluated and changed, but as long as they are retained, they must be enforced.

3. *Accept no excuses.* The teacher should not accept excuses for inappropriate behavior as long as the student is able to distinguish right from wrong. This is especially true if the student has made a commitment to a rule.

4. *Utilize value judgments.* When students exhibit inappropriate behavior, the teacher should call on them to make value judgments about their behavior. This enhances the students' responsibility to make better choices.

5. *Suggest suitable alternatives.* Alternatives to inappropriate behavior should be suggested by the teacher. The students should make the choice, one which reinforces their responsibility.

6. *Enforce reasonable consequences.* Reasonable consequences must follow whatever behavior the students choose. The consequences of inappropriate behavior should not be erratic, emotional, sarcastic, or physically punishing. The consequences of good behavior should be satisfying to students. The teacher should never manipulate events or make excuses, so that reasonable consequences do not occur after a behavior is exhibited.

7. *Be persistent.* The teacher must repeatedly and constantly make sure that students are committed to desirable behavior. The teacher must always help students make choices and have them make value judgments about bad choices.

8. *Continually review.* Topics and issues relevant to these procedures should be discussed and developed during a classroom meeting separate from academic activities. This is the time for students and teacher to seek plausible solutions to problems. Students should never be allowed to find fault with or place blame on others, to shout or threaten. If attention is directed to real matters of concern, a bonding or caring attitude between teacher and students may have a chance to take form.[27]

In a recent summary of his views Glasser makes the point that teachers must be supportive and meet with students who are beginning to exhibit difficulties, and they must get students involved in making rules, making commitments to the rules, and enforcing them. School must be a friendly, warm place, especially for students who have previously experienced failure in school. Student misbehavior is often intertwined with academic problems. The failing student, frustrated by an inability to function in the classroom, frequently expresses uneasiness by acting out. To correct an academic problem, the student, teacher, and school must make a specific commitment to overcome the problem. But too often the student is unaware of how to deal with

[27] William R. Glasser, *School Without Failure* (New York: Harper & Row, 1969).

the problem, the teacher is too burdened with other problems, and the school lacks the resources for helping the student and teacher.[28]

For Glasser, school reform is not linked to stimulating teachers and students to work harder. People, including students, will not be more productive unless what is being asked of them is psychologically satisfying. We have to change school not by changing the length of the school day or year or the amount of homework, but by making it more satisfying to students and more consistent with their interests, so that they gain a sense of power, fulfillment, and importance in the classroom. Solutions to the problems of discipline and achievement are related and based primarily on making students feel that someone listens to them, thinks about them, cares for them, and feels they are important.[29]

Although Glasser is somewhat vague on just what teachers can do in dealing with academic or behavior problems, most of his ideas involve time set aside for therapeutic sessions, encounter groups, or other forms of group discussion. For this reason, more elementary and junior high school teachers use this approach than high school teachers. The high school teachers are not expected to deal with social or psychological problems of students on a regular basis, and they tend to be more concerned with subject matter. His approach also involves a certain amount of warmth, genuineness, and concern for the whole child, his or her social, psychological, and cognitive needs. For this reason, progressive educators tend to adapt many of Glasser's ideas without even knowing that they are his, since many of his ideas also coincide with classic progressive thinkers from Pestalozzi and Froebel to Parker and Washburne.

Guidelines for Implementing Alternative Approaches to Classroom Management

---

All seven approaches have elements of prevention and intervention, and all, regardless of how firm or flexible they appear to be, deal with a set of rules, limitations, and consequences of behavior. In all the approaches students must complete academic work and they are held accountable for their behavior and work.

Whereas all the approaches advocate having clear and well-communicated *rules*, the firmer approaches expect the teacher to assert more power and authority with students. The more flexible approaches rely more on mutual trust

---

[28] William R. Glasser, *Control Theory in the Classroom* (New York: Harper & Row, 1986).

[29] Pauline B. Gough, "The Key to Improving Schools: An Interview with William Glasser," *Phi Delta Kappan*, May 1987, pp. 656—662.

and respect between teacher and students. The more assertive approaches look to the teacher to take control of the classroom and quickly establish rules. The more humanistic approaches emphasize positive expectations of students; they have more faith in the students' ability to exhibit self-control and to work out the rules with their peers and the teacher.

Although all the approaches establish *limitations*, the flexible approaches permit greater latitude in enforcing rules and allow the students to share power with the teacher. In the firmer approaches the teacher asserts authority, takes charge, and tends to intervene immediately and automatically in all cases of misbehavior, even mild ones (on the theory that this will prevent more serious problems).

All the approaches rely on *consequences*. The difference is that the firm approaches advocate stricter imposition of generally more severe sanctions as a consequence of disobedience. Punishment for inappropriate behavior is permissible as long as it is logical and related to the severity of the disturbance. The flexible approaches impose sanctions, but emphasize making students aware that their behavior influences others, helping them to examine their behavior, and helping them to identify the consequences of their misbehavior.

All the approaches hold students *accountable* for academic work. The firmer approaches limit students' socializing and group activities, determine academic tasks, and demand that they complete assignments. Students are told what is expected of them and little time is spent in any activities other than academic work. The classroom is organized so that students' engagement in academic work is continuous. In the more flexible approaches students are still accountable for academic work, but they participate in planning the curriculum, and socializing is tolerated. Engagement in academic tasks is less intense and work is often performed on a cooperative or group basis.

In choosing an approach, teachers must be objective about their personality and philosophy and what they are trying to accomplish. It is important that they be honest about themselves—their strengths and weaknesses. To help determine the approach that is best, Duke and Meckel have constructed a series of questions that try to identify teacher goals and values and also consider specific student and school criteria, such as the age of students and established school policies (see Table 2.5).

Still another point to consider is that some educators are quick to package programs that are discussed in the professional literature or advertised as "reform" or a "quick fix." It is wrong to assume that a process as complicated and multidimensional as managing students, can be understood by reading a list of do's and don'ts or attending a two-day workshop.[30]

Certain rules are central to all the models, but they are conceptual and must be modified according to the classroom situation and personalities in-

---

[30] Richard L. Curwin and Allen N. Mendter, "Packaged Discipline Programs: Let the Buyer Beware," *Educational Leadership*, October 1988, pp. 68–71; Gary F. Render et al., "What Research Really Shows About Assertive Discipline," *Educational Leadership*, March 1989, pp. 72–75.

Table 2.5   QUESTIONS TO HELP DETERMINE WHAT CLASSROOM MANAGEMENT
APPROACHES TO ADOPT

Teacher criteria: consider your goals and values

1. What are my primary goals in classroom management?
2. Which classroom management approaches address these goals?
3. What are my values or beliefs concerning classroom management?
4. Which classroom management approaches consider these values and beliefs?
5. Which classroom approaches are consistent with my goals and values?

Student criteria: consider their needs and problems

1. What are the age and maturity of my students?
2. Which classroom management approaches are best suited to my students' age and maturity?
3. What is the past disciplinary record of my students?
4. Which classroom management approaches are best suited to my students' past disciplinary record?
5. What are the backgrounds of my students?
6. Which classroom management approaches are most suited to my students' backgrounds?
7. What are the abilities and interests of my students?
8. Which classroom management approaches are most suited to my students' abilities and interests?
9. How much support can I expect from my students' parents?
10. Which classroom management approaches are best suited to the expected level of parental support?

School criteria: consider its policies and procedures

1. How much support can I expect from the school administration?
2. Which classroom management approaches coincide with the administrative philosophy or policy?
3. What aspects of each approach coincide with school district or school guidelines?
4. What aspects of each approach conflict with school district or school guidelines?
5. Which classroom management approaches coincide most and conflict least with school district or school guidelines?

Source: Adapted from Daniel L. Duke and Adrienne M. Meckel, *Teacher's Guide to Classroom Management* (New York: Random House, 1984), pp. 123–125, 127.

volved. The models should not be construed as set in stone; for example, "Always raise your hand when you wish to speak." There are many gray areas involved in managing students that involve common sense and maturity by the teacher. The models, if taken literally, limit teacher discretion and judgment, and in some cases only offer one preferred reaction or option for teachers when a rule is violated.

The point is, teachers need to be flexible and examine the models in relationship to their own classroom situation and personality. But, according to experts, the models are supported by research and they provide an effective strategy for teachers to use, as well as a way to respond to real discipline problems.[31] They are the best we have now, and teachers do need a strategy now to apply in the classroom.

In considering what is best for you, you must consider your teaching style, your students' needs and abilities, and your school's policies. As you narrow your choices, remember that approaches overlap and are not mutually exclusive. Also remember that more than one approach may work for you. You may borrow ideas from various approaches and construct your own hybrid. The approach you finally arrive at should make sense to you on an intuitive basis. Don't let someone impose his or her teaching style or disciplinary approach on you. Remember, what works for one person (in the same school, even with the same students) may not work for another person.

STUDENT AND TEACHER DISCIPLINE TYPES

Students and teachers interact with each other in the classroom situation, and eventually they make assessments of each other. This sizing up goes on all the time, whether or not teachers recognize it. Most of the assessment takes place in the beginning of the school year, but judgments are modified throughout the year as students perceive teachers' strengths and weaknesses as disciplinarians and as teachers gain insight into students' mental health and personal adjustment.

There is evidence that these assessments and perceptions influence how teachers and students respond to each other when behavior problems occur, and to a lesser extent how students perceive their own academic abilities.[32] For example, if students see the teacher as a weak disciplinarian they tend to engage in more disruptive behavior than if they perceive the teacher as a strong disciplinarian. Teachers' perceptions of students can serve as a basis for understanding and coping with particular problem situations. However, according to researchers, attributional judgments can be harmful if the teacher uses them to create self-fulfilling prophecies and to categorize students. This way of interacting with the students can contribute to misbehavior.[33] Teachers need to make attributional judgments about their students to guide their managerial

---

[31] Lee Canter, "Let the Educator Beware," *Educational Leadership*, October 1988, pp. 71–73; Sammie McCormack, "Response to Render, Padilla, and Krank: But Practitioners Say it Works," *Educational Leadership*, March 1989, pp. 77–79.

[32] Alexis L. Mitman and Andrea A. Lash, "Students' Perceptions of their Academic Standing and Classroom Behavior," *Elementary School Journal*, September 1988, pp. 55-68.

[33] Harris M. Cooper, "Pygmalion Grows Up: A Model for Teacher Expectation Communication and Performance Influence," *Review of Educational Research*, Summer 1979, pp. 389–410; Thomas L. Good, "Two Decades of Research on Teacher Expectations," *Journal of Teacher Education*, July–August 1987, pp. 32–47.

techniques; however, they need to balance their perceptions of their students with an analysis of their own behavior. As long as teacher judgments and classifications of students are open to modification, they can be useful as a framework for dealing with students who engage in misbehavior. Table 2.6 lists some student problem types based on teacher descriptions.

Parents (and teachers) have identified problem children who exhibit 1 of 31 disorderly behaviors (Table 2.7). The behaviors can be classified into four general attributes or dimensions: (1) *hyperactivity*, defined as high level of activity, nonaggressive conduct, (2) *inattentiveness*, inability to complete work and activities, high level of distractibility; (3) *conduct disorder*, inability to accept correction, tendency to tease others, high level of defiance, and (4) *impulsivity*, constant demand for attention, present orientation, unpredictability.

Table 2.7 indicates those behavior items that correlate with (have a factor loading of more than .40) one of the four attributes. Two items (1, 7) correlate with more than one attribute. Follow-up data reveal that parent and teacher ratings correspond closely. They also reveal that the characterizations of the children show no differences by age, meaning that the items and attributes are representative of problem children in kindergarten through twelfth grade.

Just as there are categories for students who exhibit managerial problems and disorderly behaviors, there are ways of classifying teachers who are successful managers of such students. Recent research in this area deals with general characteristics or descriptors. For example, Brophy and Putnam describe successful classroom managers using mental health terms such as emotional maturity, sincerity, and personal adjustment. Successful managers have "ego strength"—that is, they are confident and comfortable with themselves and with their students, and they have realistic perceptions of themselves, the students, and the classroom situation. They remain calm in a crisis. These teachers act and react without becoming defensive or authoritarian. They can cope with student "games" or "one-upmanship" contests; they know how to "win" without creating resentment on the part of the students. They can integrate clear rules and procedures into a workable system and apply the system with patience and persistence. All of these characteristics connote what we refer to as maturity and confidence in a person.[34]

A few problem students in a class can create great anxiety, battle fatigue, and even fear for some teachers. But the student who may be the teacher's "biggest problem," if handled correctly, can become the teacher's "best friend." The knowing teacher devotes extra time to the student to get to the root of the student's problem before it comes to a head in class. He or she seeks out information and advice from parents, former teachers, guidance counselors, and supervisors. The idea is to get to know the student and the cause of the

---

[34]Jere E. Brophy and Joyce Putnam, "Classroom Management in the Elementary Grades", in D. Duke, ed., *Classroom Management*, Seventy-eighth Yearbook of the National Society for the Study of Education, Part II (Chicago: University of Chicago Press, 1979), pp. 182–216.

Table 2.6 STUDENT PROBLEM TYPES BASED ON TEACHER DESCRIPTIONS

1. *Failure syndrome*. These children are convinced that they cannot do the work. They often avoid starting up or give up easily. They expect to fail, even after succeeding. Signs: easily frustrated, gives up easily, says "I can't do it."

2. *Pefectionist*. These children are unduly anxious about making mistakes. Their self-imposed standards are unrealistically high, so that they are never satisfied with their work (when they should be). Signs: often anxious, fearful, or frustrated about quality of work; holds back from class participation unless sure of self.

3. *Underachiever*. These do the minimum to "get by." They do not value schoolwork. Signs: indifferent to schoolwork, minimum work output, not challenged by schoolwork, poorly motivated.

4. *Low achiever*. These children have difficulty, even though they may be willing to work. Their problem is low potential or lack of readiness rather than poor motivation. Signs: difficulty following directions, difficulty completing work, poor retention, progresses slowly.

5. *Hostile aggressive*. These children express hostility through direct, intense behaviors. They are not easily controlled. Signs: intimidates and threatens, hits and pushes, damages property, antagonizes, hostile, easily angered.

6. *Passive aggressive*. These children express opposition and resistance to the teacher, but indirectly. It often is hard to tell whether they are resisting deliberately or not. Signs: subtly oppositional and stubborn, tries to control, borderline compliance with rules, mars property rather than damages, disrupts surreptitiously, drags feet.

7. *Defiant*. These children resist authority and carry on a power struggle with the teacher. They want to have their way and not be told what to do. Signs: resists verbally with statements such as "You can't make me . . ."; and derogatory statements about teacher and others; resists nonverbally with frowns and grimaces, arms folded and hands on hips, foot stomping, looking away when being spoken to; laughs at inappropriate times; mimics posture of teacher, may be physically violent toward teacher; deliberately does what the teacher says not to do.

8. *Hyperactive*. These children show excessive and almost constant movement, even when sitting. Often their movements appear to be without purpose. Signs: squirms, wiggles, jiggles, scratches; excitable; blurts out answers and comments; often out of seat; bothers other children with noises, movements; energetic but poorly directed; excessively touches objects or people.

9. *Distractible*. These children have short attention spans. They seem unable to sustain attention and concentration and are highly distractible. Signs: has difficulty adjusting to changes, rarely completes tasks, easily distracted by sights, sounds, or speech.

10. *Immature*. These children have poorly developed emotional stability, self-control, self-care abilities, social skills, or responsibility. Signs: often exhibits behavior normal for younger children; may cry easily; loses belongings; frequently appears helpless, incompetent, or dependent.

11. *Rejected by peers*. These children seek peer interaction but are rejected, ignored, or excluded. Signs: forced to work and play alone; lacks social skills; often picked on or teased.

12. *Withdrawn*. These children avoid personal interaction, are unobtrusive, and do not respond well to others. Signs: quiet and sober, does not initiate or volunteer, does not call attention to self.

Source: Adapted from Mary M. Rohrkemper and Jere E. Brophy, "Teachers' Thinking About Problem Students," in J. M. Levine and M. C. Wang, eds., *Teacher and Student Perceptions* (Hillsdale, N.J.: Erlbaum, 1983), pp. 77–78.

Table 2.7 DISORDERLY BEHAVIOR OF CHILDREN RATED BY PARENTS

	Attributes			
	1	2	3	4
1. Unable to sit still, fidgets	.44	.44		
2. Talks too much	.67			
3. Quickly wears out toys, furniture				.54
4. Gets into things				.51
5. Has lots of accidents				.49
6. Reckless, acts carelessly				.70
7. Doesn't stay with games or activities		.52	.47	
8. Cannot wait for pleasant things to happen	.46			
9. Doesn't complete hobbies or projects		.44		
10. Adapts slowly				
11. Inattentive, distractible		.77		
12. Unpredictably affectionate				
13. Constant demand for attention	.50			
14. Cannot accept correction			.65	
15. Teases others			.45	
16. Discipline doesn't change behavior for long			.58	
17. Defiant, talks back			.60	
18. Doesn't follow directions		.44		
19. Lies				
20. Unpopular with others his or her age				
21. Unusually aggressive in behavior with others				
22. Must be continually supervised during leisure time activities				
23. Withdraws from new people, is shy		.48		
24. Sits fiddling with small objects		.46		
25. Hums and makes other odd noises	.43			
26. Excitable	.66			
27. Overly anxious to please	.60			
28. Awkward, poor general coordination	.60			
29. Moody			.46	
30. Fights			.46	
31. Difficulty in handling frustration			.43	

Source: Adapted from Nadine M. Lambert and Caroyln S. Hartsough, "The Measurement of Attention Deficit Disorder with Behavior Ratings of Parents," *American Journal of Orthopsychiatry* (July 1987), p. 366.

Note: 1 = Hyperactivity; 2 = Inattentiveness; 3 = Conduct Disorder; 4 = Impulsivity.

student's poor work and behavior quickly. Serious incidents do not just happen; anxieties collect and build up. The teacher who has common sense, emotional maturity, and good professional training can translate the student's inappropriate behavior into better efforts before his or her behavior becomes threatening or uncontrollable and before direct action is needed. See Tips for Teachers 2.2.

Tips for Teachers 2.2

Strategies for Managing Problem Students

Below are general strategies for dealing with problem students, sometimes called "difficult" students, based on the experience of teachers. Although originally developed for junior high school inner-city students, the strategies apply to most school settings and grade levels.

1. *Accept the students as they are,* but build on and accentuate their positive qualities.
2. *Be yourself,* since these students can recognize phoniness and take offense at such deceit.
3. *Be confident;* take charge of the situation, and don't give up in front of the students.
4. *Provide structure,* since many of these students lack inner control and are restless and impulsive.
5. *Explain your rules and routines* so students understand them. Be sure your explanations are brief; otherwise you lose your effectiveness and you appear to be defensive or preaching.
6. *Communicate positive expectations* that you expect the students to learn and you require academic work.
7. *Rely on motivation,* and not on your prowess to maintain order; an interesting lesson can keep the students on task.
8. *Be a firm friend,* but maintain a psychological and physical distance so your students know you are still the teacher.
9. *Keep calm,* and keep your students calm, especially when conditions become tense or upsetting. It may be necessary to delay action until after class, when emotions have been reduced.
10. *Size up the situation,* and be aware of undercurrents of behavior, since these students are sizing you up and are knowing manipulators of their environment.
11. *Anticipate behavior;* being able to judge what will happen if you or a student decide on a course of action may allow you to curtail many problems.
12. *Expect, but don't accept, misbehavior.* Learn to cope with misbehavior, but don't get upset or feel inadequate about it.

Source: Adapted from Allan C. Ornstein, "Teaching the Disadvantaged," *Educational Forum,* January 1967, pp. 215–223; Ornstein, "The Education of the Disadvantaged, *Educational Researcher,* June 1982, pp. 197–221.

PUNISHMENT

Educators disagree as to the extent to which misbehavior should be ignored. Although it seems contrary to the teacher's normal tendency, some researchers have found repeatedly that the best procedure is to ignore undesirable behavior while paying attention to and reinforcing desirable behavior.[35] If this is the case, then teachers have been undermining their own managerial purposes by scolding, shaming, threatening, or punishing students for misbehavior.

Brophy and Evertson are skeptical about avoiding or ignoring inappropriate behavior.[36] They contend that certain misbehaviors are too disruptive or dangerous to be ignored. Ignoring such behavior leaves students with the impression that the teacher is unaware of what is going on or is unable to cope with it. Another observer takes the middle stance that undesirable behavior can be ignored by the teacher when it is momentary, not serious, unlikely to be disruptive, and attributable to a student who is usually well behaved.[37]

Robert Slavin makes still another distinction. Many forms of misbehavior are motivated by the desire for peer attention and approval. Students who disobey the teacher are usually (consciously or unconsciously) weighing the effect of their defiance on their standing among classmates; this is especially true as students enter adolescence. Slavin concludes that ignoring misbehavior is ineffective if it is reinforced or encouraged by peers. Such behavior cannot be ignored, for it will worsen and attract more peer support.[38]

Ornstein makes still another distinction among misbehaving students. He asserts that emotionally disturbed children and children who lack healthy ego development pose a special challenge. Their inability to get along with normal children makes them isolated and rejected. Often, they are unaware of their responsibility for or contribution to events. They have almost no feelings of guilt and are not responsive to others' feelings. When they realize they are wrong, they tend to withdraw. He claims that "by threatening or punishing, the teacher makes the mistake of appearing hostile; in turn, these children feel they have a right to hate the teacher and be 'bad.'" It is advisable, Ornstein asserts, for the teacher "to be sympathetic," not overly assertive, and even "make special allowances." The other children know these disturbed children are different and will accept the fact that concessions are made "or rules are modified to accommodate their special needs."[39]

---

[35] K. Daniel O'Leary and Susan G. O'Leary, *Classroom Management: The Successful Use of Behavior Modification,* 2nd ed. (New York: Pergamon, 1977).

[36] Jere E. Brophy, "Classroom Organization and Management," *Elementary School Journal,* March 1983, pp. 265–286; Carolyn Evertson et al., "Effective Classroom Management," Final Report for the National Institute of Education, *Improving Classroom Management,* June 1985. Also see Brophy and Evertson, *Student Characteristics and Teaching* (New York: Longman, 1981).

[37] Laurel N. Tanner, *Classroom Discipline for Effective Teaching and Learning* (New York: Holt, Rinehart and Winston, 1978).

[38] Robert E. Slavin, *Cooperative Learning* (New York: Longman, 1983); Slavin, *Educational Psychology: Theory into Practice,* 2nd ed. (Englewood Cliffs, N.J.: Prentice-Hall, 1988).

[39] Allan C. Ornstein, "Teaching the Disadvantaged," *Educational Forum,* January 1967, p. 221.

For situations in which it is decided that punishment is appropriate and will be effective, the teacher must decide on its form and severity. The teacher should establish criteria for using it. Punishment is construed by behaviorists as an unpleasant stimulus that an individual will try to avoid. Common punishments, according to Gage and Berliner, are soft reprimands (heard only by the student concerned), reprimands coupled with praise, social isolation (detention, missed recess), point loss in academics, and being reported to someone outside the classroom (disciplinarian, principal, parent).[40]

Corporal punishment should not be used; the negative side effects outweigh the temporary advantages of squashing inappropriate behavior. It tends to demoralize the class. Although it may keep young and physically immature students in check, it creates anger and resentment in them. If it is to have any effect, the teacher will at some point have to use it with physically stronger students, and the teacher who backs down loses face and authority. Moreover, it is outlawed in many states.

One researcher, who refers to punishment as "management strategies," has assessed 24 common strategies employed by junior high school teachers.[41] The sample consisted of 281 students and 80 teachers who were asked to rate the severity of each strategy. As shown in Table 2.8, those with a mean rating of 5 or 4 were classified as "very severe," those with a rating of 3 were classified as "moderately severe," and those with a rating of 2 or 1 were classified as "relatively unsevere."

The data reveal that teachers tend to employ as many relatively unsevere strategies as moderately severe and very severe strategies combined. Relatively unsevere strategies involve task assignments or removal of privileges. Moderately severe strategies impose constraints on students' freedom or time. Very severe strategies involve removal or transfer of the student or conferring with another authority about the problem.

Although there were significant differences between student and teacher mean ratings for about half the items, their rank orderings of the strategies were similar (correlation of .84), implying comparable perceptions of the severity of punishment.

Table 2.9 lists principles for using punishment. The first column, based on the work of O'Leary and O'Leary lists seven principles that coincide with behavioral modification theory; punishment is combined with reinforcement of desired behavior. The second column is based on the work of Good and Brophy. These measures are stop-gap measures to suppress overt misbehavior, but they do not change underlying desires to misbehave or causes of misbehavior. There are similarities between the columns; both lists represent firm approaches to discipline.

---

[40]N. L. Gage and David C. Berliner, *Educational Psychology*, 4th ed. (Boston: Houghton Mifflin, 1988).

[41]Moshe Zeidner, "The Relative Severity of Common Classroom Management Strategies: The Student's Perspective," *British Journal of Educational Psychology*, February 1988, pp. 69–77.

Table 2.8 MEAN RATINGS OF COMMON CLASSROOM MANAGEMENT STRATEGIES

Strategies	Students (N = 281) M	Teachers (N = 80) M
1. Permanent suspension from school	4·78	4·60
2. Shaming or personally insulting student	4·32	3·14
3. Permanent removal from class	4·30	4·18
4. Parent-principal conference	4·21	3·14
5. Temporary demotion to lower grade	4·03	3·91
6. Withdrawal or denial of special privileges	4·00	3·74
7. Communicating problem to parents	3·46	3·34
8. Lowering school mark	3·46	4·03
9. Throwing student out of class	3·40	3·65
10. Learning material by heart	3·22	2·90
11. Summons of student to principal's office	3·17	2·80
12. Surprise quiz	3·09	3·06
13. Busy work	2·93	2·63
14. Detention after class	2·90	3·00
15. Teacher-student conference	2·70	3·08
16. Additional monitor duty	2·70	2·66
17. Cleaning up school grounds	2·60	2·59
18. Shortening recess	2·59	2·41
19. Reporting early to school	2·52	2·55
20. Teacher's aversive nonverbal communication	2·49	2·93
21. Verbal reprimand	2·47	2·88
22. Additional homework	2·22	2·22
23. Being placed in corner	1·90	2·70
24. Special classroom seating	1·73	2·16

Source: Moshe Zeidner, "The Relative Severity of Common Classroom Management Strategies: The Student's Perspective," *British Journal of Educational Psychology,* February 1988, p. 73.

Guidelines for Using Punishment

The 12 guidelines listed below supplement the principles listed in Table 2.9 and can be used for all disciplinary approaches. Underlying the guidelines is the idea that punishment should be flexible and tailored to the specific student and situation.

Table 2.9   PRINCIPLES FOR PUNISHING STUDENTS

O'Leary & O'Leary (1977)	Good and Brophy (1984, 1985)
1. Use punishment sparingly.	1. Threat of punishment is usually more effective than punishment itself especially when phrased in such a way that there are unknown consequences.
2. Make it clear why the student is being punished.	2. Punishment should be threatened or warned before implemented. This is done in a way that the teacher hopes it will not be used and the students are responsible if it has to be used.
3. Provide the student with alternative means of obtaining some positive reinforcement.	3. The punishment should be accompanied with positive statements of expectations and rules, focusing on what the students should be doing.
4. Reinforce student behaviors which are incompatible with those you wish to weaken or eliminate. For example, if you punish for being off task, reward for being on task.	4. Punishment should be combined with negative reinforcement, so that student must improve to escape punishment. For example, the student will lose a privilege until behavior improves.
5. Avoid punishing while you are angry or emotional.	5. Punishment should be systematic and deliberate; avoid emotional reaction or provocation to reaction when punishing.
6. Punish when inappropriate behavior starts rather than when it ends.	6. Do not punish an entire class or group because of the misbehavior of an individual.
7. Avoid corporal punishment.	7. Avoid excessive punishment, since this may unite the students in sullen defense against the teacher.

Source: Adapted from K. Daniel O'Leary and Susan O'Leary, *Classroom Management: The Successful Use of Behavior Modification*, 2nd ed. (New York: Pergamon, 1977); Thomas L. Good and Jere E. Brophy, *Looking into Classrooms*, 3rd ed. (New York: Harper & Row, 1984); and Good and Brophy, *Educational Psychology: A Realistic Approach*, 3rd ed. (New York: Longham, 1985).

1. *Learn what type of punishment school authorities allow.* Different schools have different guidelines for punishment and punish students for infringement of different rules.
2. *Don't threaten the impossible.* Make sure the punishment can be carried out. Telling a student to stay after class at 3:00 P.M. when you have a 3:30 appointment with the dentist illustrates that you reacted hastily and cannot follow through.
3. *Don't punish when you are at a loss for what else to do or in an emotional state.* Sometimes it is best to immediately react, that is,

to tell the student to see you after class. The delay gives you time to think and be more rational. All things being equal, the quiet, cool approach is more effective than the angry, emotional approach.

4. *Don't assign extra homework as punishment.* This creates dislike for homework as well as the subject.

5. *Be sure the punishment follows the offense as soon as possible.* Don't impose punishment two days after the student misbehaves.

6. *Be sure the punishment fits the misbehavior.* Don't overreact to mild misbehavior or underplay or ignore serious misbehavior.

7. *Be consistent with punishment.* If you punish one student for something, don't ignore it when another student does the same thing. However, students and circumstance differ, and there should be room for modification.

8. *Don't use double standards when punishing.* You should treat both sexes the same way, and low-achieving and high-achieving students the same way. (Perhaps the only allowance or difference can be with emotionally disturbed children.) Avoid having teacher "pets."

9. *Give the student the benefit of doubt.* Before accusing or punishing someone, make sure you have the facts right.

10. *Don't hold grudges.* Once you punish the student, put the incident behind you and try to start with a clean slate.

11. *Don't personalize the situation.* React to misbehavior, not the student. Do not react to the student's anger or personal remarks. He usually doesn't mean them and is reacting out of emotion. Stay focused on the deed, remind the student he doesn't mean what he is saying and that things will worsen unless he calms down. When the student is out of control, the main thing is to get him to calm down. Punishment comes later, if it is required, after the student is calm.

12. *Document all serious incidents.* This is especially important if the misbehavior involves sending the student out of the room or possible suspension.[42]

PREVENTIVE DISCIPLINE

Preventive discipline refers to establishing control systems in the classroom and avoiding the breakdown of controls. It involves a series of strategies to modify the surface behavior of the students so they are engaged in appropriate classroom tasks. It also involves preventing students from getting out of control by reacting to small, manageable incidents before they become big and unmanageable. Preventive discipline permits the teacher to cope with student adjustment problems in class while helping students cope with their feelings.

---

[42] Allan C. Ornstein, "Techniques and Fundamentals for Teaching the Disadvantaged"; *Journal of Negro Education*, Spring 1967, pp. 136–145; Ornstein, "Teaching the Disadvantaged"; and Ornstein, "A Difference Teachers Make: How Much?" *Educational Forum*, Fall 1984, pp. 109–117.

The task is to establish ways of dealing with behavior that do not disrupt the group but still may be helpful to the students. It involves making judgments as to when to *tolerate* certain student behaviors (without approving them), when to *modify* behaviors, and when to *interfere* with behaviors in order to allow learning to take place. Indeed, a certain amount of common sense and emotional maturity on the part of the teacher is important in managing and modifying behavior.

Professional Viewpoint

Learning from Your Mistakes

When I stepped before my first class as a teacher, I was totally unprepared. I had little training in education and no practice teaching. The high school in which I taught was in my hometown, an area of heavy industry and oil refineries—all belching smoke and fumes. The students I taught were young men and women who eventually went to work in these factories, along with a few who would make their way to college. As an English major fresh out of college, I came with a mission to teach lyric poetry and writing to these students. I quickly found out that I could not maintain discipline in my classroom.

The students were noisy continually. I could not keep control. I found myself shouting at them, resorting to desperate attempts at discipline. When one of the tough boys would not sit down, I confronted him face to face, chest to chest. After a tense moment he finally backed down without violence. A week later, after attending a school function at night, I found the canvas top of my new MGA roadster slashed. I still remember the long walk to the principal's office to report what had happened.

The help I received from my fellow teachers that first year was not much. The algebra teacher next door complained about the noise: "Can't you keep those kids quiet?!" No, I could not. My first year of teaching was pure misery. I hated to see Monday roll around. During the summer I decided this was no way to live. It was either them or me.

That fall I entered the classroom as a disciplinary ogre. Nothing moved unless I said so. Nobody talked unless I gave permission. I doubt that anyone learned anything that year, but it was quiet. But at least I didn't dread going to school every morning.

By my third year I became confident enough to relax my totalitarian grip so that spontaneous learning could occur. By my fourth year I might even have been a good teacher. But what a struggle.

Looking back, I discovered that discipline in the classroom depends on what the teacher does in the first few weeks of school. The students watch

continued

to see what the teacher will allow, then behave accordingly. If the teacher establishes and enforces simple rules, the students will behave properly. The key is consistency. I learned that the teacher must be consistent in the disciplinary pattern, especially the first few weeks. Also I found that the pattern for the entire year is usually determined the first weeks of school. It is possible to relax discipline later in the year but it is difficult to tighten it once it is gone. The idea is to be a manager of students, not a disciplinarian.

Ernest R. House
Professor and Director of
Laboratory for Policy Studies
University of Colorado-Boulder

General Preventive Measures: For All Teachers

Redl and Wineman established 21 specific influence techniques that were workable with aggressive boys in treatment centers. They later developed 12 of these for managing students in regular classrooms. They are classic techniques, based on clinical psychology and diagnostic insight into student behavior. They seek to enhance psychological protection of students on an individual and group basis. They attempt to avoid conflict, to enhance the comfort of the individual with himself, and to enhance cooperation with group members. Most important, the 12 influence techniques seem to apply to all disciplinary approaches.

1. *Planned ignoring.* Much inappropriate behavior has limited influence and will exhaust itself, especially if it is low level or mild. If it appears that the behavior will not spread to others, it is sometimes best to ignore it and not feed the student's secondary need for attention.
2. *Signal interference.* A variety of signals can be used to communicate disapproval to the student. Signals such as eye contact, hand gestures, snapping fingers, clearing one's throat, facial expressions, and body gestures are effective in handling the beginning stages of inappropriate behavior.
3. *Proximity control.* In some cases teacher proximity acts as a deterrent against misbehavior, and in other cases it can operate as a source of protection, strength, and identification. Some students need to have a teacher stand close by before they are able to control their impulses. (However, caution is recommended; in some cases proximity can spark a child to lose control or to get further out of control.)
4. *Interest boosting.* When a student shows signs of restlessness or boredom, it is often helpful for the teacher to show genuine interest in the student's work or incorporate his or her personal interests (for example, in athletics or music) into the discussion.

Figure 2.3 Warm, friendly encounters with students enhance rapport and teacher-student relations. (Photo © Elizabeth Crews)

5. *Humor.* Almost everyone is aware that humor can defuse a tense situation and that it can make students relax. It is also an excellent way of showing that the teacher is secure during a stressful incident. (However, the teacher must be careful to distinguish between humor and sarcasm. Sarcasm should not be viewed as a technique, since it means that there is a winner and a loser.)

6. *Hurdle lessons.* Sometimes students misbehave because of frustration with a particular assignment. Students who do not understand the work may translate their frustration into disruptive behavior. The teacher should try to provide academic assistance before students get to the stage of not paying attention or disturbing others.

7. *Restructuring the program.* The classroom schedule may have to be modified because of some circumstances or problems. Tension levels may have to be reduced before the class can involve itself in the regular assignment. If students do not understand parts of the lesson, they may have to be retaught, or parts may have to be skipped because retracking would only increase student frustration.

8. *Routine.* Some degree of routine and structure makes most students feel comfortable and secure. Those who lack inner control need more routine and structure. Daily schedules of activities provide the kind

of routine that eliminates aimless behavior while students wait for teachers to announce the next activity.

9. *Direct appeal.* Overreacting or intervening severely in order to demonstrate authority can backfire. An alternative technique is to appeal to values that the students have internalized regarding their image ("Gentlemen don't engage in that kind of behavior. You know better"), the teacher-student relationship ("Have I been unfair to you?"), group codes or peer reaction ("You are spoiling it for the rest of your classmates"), authority ("You know I can't allow this behavior to go unnoticed"). The trick is to learn what appeal works with what students.

10. *Removing seductive objects.* Certain objects elicit a particular type of behavior that leads to problems. For example, a water gun, flashlight, or ball may set off impulsive or mischievous behavior that disrupts the class. The objects to be eliminated in the classroom are determined by the age, maturity, and inner controls of the students.

11. *Antiseptic bouncing.* If a student's behavior reaches a point where he or she cannot be controlled, it is best to have the student removed from the room—either for a few minutes (for example, getting a drink or delivering a message) or for a full period (waiting in the guidance counselor's office). The intent of antiseptic bouncing is to protect and help the student and the group get over their immediate feelings of anger, disappointment, emotion, or silliness. It is not meant as punishment, which would defeat the original purpose of prevention.

12. *Physical restraint.* A student who loses control or threatens others must be restrained. The student should be held firmly, but not roughly. Once again, the intent is protection, not punishment. The teacher substitutes a control system until the student's controls are operating again. (Punishing a student who lost complete control is not a solution; it adds to the student's anguish and can make him or her more enraged.) If the teacher is unable to restrain the student, one of the other students should be sent out to get help from a colleague or administrator.[43]

Moderate Preventive Measures: Enhancing Routine and Academic Work

From a review of the literature on classroom order and management, Walter Doyle has compiled a series of "management functions" for successful teachers.[44] These functions, which coincide with our term *preventive measures*, tend to stress cooperation, social participation, and social harmony, as well as academic accountability. Taken as a whole, they correspond with middle-of-

[43]Fritz Redl and David Wineman, *The Aggressive Child* (New York: Free Press, 1957); Redl and Wineman, *Children Who Hate.*

[44]Walter Doyle, "Classroom Order and Management," in M. C. Wittrock, ed., *Handbook of Research on Teaching*, 3rd ed. (New York: Macmillan, 1986), pp. 392–431.

the-road disciplinary approaches such as the group managerial and group guidance approaches, and to lesser extent the firmer business-academic approach. The functions are rooted in the work of Kounin and also the work of Brophy, Emmer, Evertson, and Good (who were influenced by Kounin).

For Doyle, preventive discipline is a matter of understanding events in the classroom—how processes evolve and how people interact. He claims that classroom order is fragile, a condition that can be easily disrupted by mistakes, intrusions, and unpredictable events. Order is not something that is achieved once and for all so that teaching can take place; rather, there is permanent pressure on the classroom life, and a teacher must be vigilant in preventing disorder. The managerial functions are important for enhancing the inherent delicacy of classroom order. Such functions correlate, according to Doyle, with being an effective manager at both the elementary and secondary levels.

1. *Establishing classroom activities.* The early class sessions of a school year are critical. During this period order is defined and procedures for sustaining order are put into place.
2. *Rules and procedures.* Life in classrooms must be governed by rules and procedures, with specific formats for opening, closing, and conducting lessons. Rules should be focused on behavior that is likely to disrupt activities, such as lateness, talking during lessons, gum chewing, being unprepared, or fighting.
3. *Academic work and activities.* Students are told what to do, beginning the first day in class, so that little time is lost finding seats, getting organized, or waiting between activities. Warm-up activities have a simple, whole-class instructional structure, and the work is familiar and easy to accomplish. Effective teachers establish a procedure for maintaining whole-group focus on academic work and protect it from intrusion and disruption.
4. *Routines.* Routinization makes classroom activities less susceptible to breakdowns and interruptions because students know the normal sequence of events and what is expected of them. The more familiar the "lesson contexts," that is, classroom processes, schedules, and structures, the more stable and predictable is student behavior. Establishing routines is also somewhat prerequisite for performing academic work.
5. *Enacting processes.* Rule systems are complex and vary with lesson contexts or distinctive phases of a class session. For example, quiet talk is often permitted among peers during entry and seatwork, but not during teacher presentations or question-answer recitation. Students know the difference, with little explanation needed, in well-controlled classes. With older children, rules often do not have to be explicitly articulated, but are part of commonsense knowledge and past experience.
6. *Hidden curriculum.* Emphasis on authority, responsibility, orderliness, and task orientation is common in well-run classrooms. There

is a heavy emphasis on following directions, accepting responsibility, and working quietly and diligently. Students are socialized to the world of work, that is, to modern bureaucracy, in classrooms; institutional constraints prevail over student preferences.

7. *Monitoring.* Monitoring consists of three levels. First, effective managers watch *groups*: they attend to what is happening in the entire room, while they attend to individual students. Second, they watch *conduct or behavior*, that is, they are quick to react to misbehavior before it spreads. Third, they monitor the *pace, rhythm, and duration* of classroom events (avoiding what Gump calls "hesitations" and "lags" and emphasizing what Kounin calls "smoothness" and "momentum").[45]

8. *Maintaining group lessons.* Instructional strategies, such as grouping and questioning, ensure that all students in the class stay involved in the lesson, even when one or two students are performing. Materials and activities provide a group focus. In many classrooms the teacher sets specific limits on the type and amount of student participation. For example, the teacher sets the topics, formulates narrow rather than open-ended questions, and calls on students to secure a "right answer" to keep a planned discussion going.

9. *Seatwork.* Seatwork is well organized and monitored by the teacher. The teacher is available to work with students and circulates around the room to see how students are doing. The extent of whole-class supervision decreases when the teacher focuses attention on a small group, but the rest of the class works independently.

10. *Transitions.* Transitions are made with minimal loss of momentum or time. The teacher monitors them closely to see that students move from one task to another, and provides considerable direction.

11. *Engaged time.* Opening routines are established, and enough work is assigned to fill the scheduled time. The opening routines—for example, copying down the assignments or writing in a journal—engage students immediately in work. Well-planned assignments mean that students do not run out of work, so they remain engaged throughout the period.

12. *Cueing.* Teachers and students adjust to the unfolding processes of the classroom. Order is held in place, even during disruptions by unforeseen events, by means of cues and messages (verbal and nonverbal) that teachers use to tell students what is happening or to announce a transition. (This is similar to Kounin's "signal systems.")

13. *Maintaining academic work.* Academic work can be used to achieve order by selecting tasks that are easy for students. The more demanding the academic work, the greater the risk that classroom rou-

[45] Paul Gump, *The Classroom Behavior Setting* (Washington, D.C.: U.S. Government Printing Office, 1967); Gump, *Ecological Psychology and Children* (Chicago: University of Chicago Press, 1975); and Kounin, *Discipline and Group Management in Classrooms.*

tines will be slowed down or disrupted. Thus some teachers may simplify task demands and lower the risk for mistakes. When academic work is demanding, teachers often break down the work into small, sequenced tasks and heavily prompted increments.

14. *Cooperative learning teams.* Small groups in which students work together on assignments have positive effects on achievement, so long as instruction is carefully structured, individuals are accountable for performance, and a well-defined reward system is used. The effect on discipline is unclear, although it is assumed that cooperation among students enhances group morale and group rapport, which in turn has a positive effect on the organization and management of the classroom.

15. *Subject matter as procedure.* For purposes of control, subject matter is sometimes presented with an emphasis on practice and drill. Academic work in this case is reduced by the teacher to completing one assignment or exercise and then going on to the next exercise. Neither teacher nor students talk much about the meaning or purpose of the work or the processes involved in doing the work. Although there is an appearance of engaged time, the work may be faked or performed without real understanding. So long as there is some feedback or evaluation, students are willing to spend time on these activities.

16. *Teacher expectations.* Some teachers appear to solve the problem of order in large group instruction by excluding low-ability students from participation in classroom activities. From a management perspective, such action is reasonable because it avoids conditions that lead to breakdown in momentum, pacing, and rhythm; it also avoids confusion and slowing down (hesitations, lags) of content flow and activities. From a teaching perspective, however, such actions restrict the opportunities of low-ability students.[46]

Humanistic Preventive Measures: Feedback, Trust, and Communication

David Johnson has written several books that deal with interpersonal relations, cooperation, and self-actualization. His methods of enhancing self-awareness, mutual trust, and communication among people serve as excellent preventive strategies. Johnson's methods correspond with flexible and democratic approaches to discipline such as the acceptance and success approaches. They might be used by anyone who wishes to build a humanistic classroom based on student rapport and understanding. The specific methods can be applied on a one-to-one basis or on a group basis in which teachers emphasize interpersonal relations and cooperative processes.

Building Self-Awareness Through Feedback   Feedback tells students what effect their actions are having on others. It is important for the teacher to provide

---

[46] Doyle, "Classroom Order and Management."

feedback in a way that does not threaten the student. The more threatened and defensive the student becomes, the more likely it is that he or she will not understand the feedback correctly. Increasing a student's self-awareness through feedback gives the students a basis for making informed choices in future behavior.

1. *Focus feedback on behavior, not on personality.* Refer to what the person does, not to what you believe her traits to be. The former is a response to what you see or hear, and the latter is an inference or interpretation about character.

2. *Focus feedback on descriptions, not on judgments.* Refer to what occurs, not to your judgments of right or wrong, good or bad. ("You are not spelling the word correctly" or "We cannot hear you," rather than "You are a terrible speller" or "You don't know how to speak up in public.")

3. *Focus feedback on a specific situation, not on abstract behavior.* Feedback tied to a specific situation leads to self-awareness. Feedback that is abstract is open to interpretation and is often misunderstood.

4. *Focus feedback on the present, not on the past.* The more immediate the feedback, the more effective it is. ("You are becoming angry now as I talk to you," rather than "Sometimes you become angry.")

5. *Focus feedback on sharing feelings, not giving advice.* Sharing feelings gives people the opportunity to make a choice in light of their own needs and perceptions. Giving advice or telling people what to do limits their freedom and responsibilities.

6. *Do not force feedback on a person.* Feedback must be presented as an offer, not as something being forced on the receiver.

7. *Do not give more feedback than can be understood at one time.* Don't overload receivers with feedback; it reduces the chances they will understand or use it. When you give feedback that cannot be understood or used, you are satisfying your own needs and not the needs of others.

8. *Focus feedback on action that can change the person.* It does little good to tell a person that you don't like the color of his eyes. This is something that cannot be changed.

Developing and Maintaining Trust To build a healthy relationship among students and between students and teacher, a climate of mutual trust must grow and develop. Fears of rejection or betrayal must be reduced, and acceptance, support, and respect must be promoted. Trust, like order, is not something that can be built once and forgotten about; it constantly changes and constantly needs nourishment.

1. *Building trust.* Trust begins as people take the risk of disclosing more and more of their thoughts and feelings to each other. If they do not receive acceptance or support, they back off from the relationship. If

they receive acceptance or support, they will continue to risk self-disclosure, and the relationship continues to grow.

2. *Being trusting.* The level of trust that develops between two people is related to both individuals' willingness and ability to be trusting. Each must be willing to risk the consequences of revealing oneself to and depend on the other person. Each must be openly accepting and supporting of the other to ensure that the other experiences beneficial consequences from the risk taken.

3. *Trusting appropriately.* A person must be able to size up a situation and make a wise judgment about when, whom, and how much to trust. Trust is appropriate when a person is reasonably confident that the other person will not react in a way that will be harmful.

4. *Trusting as a self-fulfilling prophecy.* Assumptions made about another person or a situation affect an individual's behavior. That behavior often elicits the expected reactions from the other person. The assumptions become a self-fulfilling prophecy. If you make other people feel they can trust you, they will often do so.

Communicating Effectively   All behavior conveys messages. A person sends messages to evoke a response from the receiver. The messages and responses are verbal and nonverbal. Effective communication takes place when the receiver interprets the sender's messages in the way that was intended; effective communication enhances understanding and cooperation among individuals. Ineffective communication arises when there is a discrepancy between what the sender meant and what the receiver thought the sender meant. This reduces understanding and cooperation. Mutual trust enhances the possibility of effective communication; distrust is a primary cause of miscommunication. Skill in sending messages can increase communication between teachers and students.

1. *Use the first person singular.* Take responsibility for your own ideas or feelings. People doubt messages that use terms like "most people," "some of your classmates."

2. *Make messages complete and specific.* People often make incorrect assumptions about what their listeners know, leave out steps in describing their thinking, and do not mention specific items or ideas that are necessary if their intentions are to be conveyed to their listeners.

3. *Make verbal and nonverbal messages congruent.* Communication problems arise when a person's verbal and nonverbal messages are contradictory.

4. *Be redundant.* Use more than one means of communication, such as verbal and nonverbal cues, to reinforce your message.

5. *Ask for feedback.* The only way to learn how a person is actually receiving and interpreting your message is to seek feedback from the receiver.

6. *Consider the listener's frame of reference.* The same information might be interpreted differently by a child and by an adult. It may be necessary to use different words or different nonverbal cues depending on the listener's age, maturity level, educational level, and cultural background.
7. *Make messages concrete.* It is important to be descriptive, to use verbs (I like *working*), adverbs (Your homework is due *tomorrow*), and adjectives (Johnnie is an *excellent* student) to communicate your feelings clearly.
8. *Describe behavior without evaluating it.* Describe the student's behavior ("You are interrupting Johnnie") rather than evaluating it ("You are self-centered and won't listen to anyone else's ideas").[47]

Guidelines for Implementing Preventive Measures

The preventive disciplinary measures discussed above range widely—from firm to flexible. No teacher will use all these measures. It is up to each to pick and choose according to what coincides with teaching style, personality, philosophy, and teaching situation.

In trying to establish your own preventive measures, it is worthwhile to note the **coping strategies** developed by Gerald Caplan. (For our purposes, coping strategies mean understanding the demands of a situation and adjusting to them, knowing what resources are available to help deal with problems, and possessing a self-awareness that allows intelligent reactions.)

1. Active exploration of reality issues and search for information.
2. Free expression of both positive and negative feelings and a tolerance of frustration.
3. Active invoking of help of others.
4. Breaking down problems into manageable bits and working them through one at a time.
5. Awareness of fatigue and tendencies toward disorganization.
6. Active mastery of feelings . . . flexibility and willingness to change.
7. Basic trust in oneself and others and basic optimism about outcomes.[48]

In developing your approach to preventive strategies as one aspect of classroom management, you must know yourself, be capable of learning from your

[47]David W. Johnson, *Reaching Out: Interpersonal Effectiveness and Self-Actualization,* 3rd ed. (Englewood Cliffs, N.J.: Prentice-Hall, 1986).

[48]Gerald Caplan, "Human Competence and Coping: An Overview," in R. H. Moss, ed., *Human Adaptation: Coping with Life Crisis* (Lexington, Mass.: Heath, 1976), p. 14.

own mistakes, and know where to go for assistance. One way to improve your classroom management skills is to analyze sample cases presented on videotapes of actual and role-play teacher situations. You can work on your own by reading on the subject, or enroll in an appropriate in-service or staff development course to benefit from group discussion and analysis. Other suggestions are given in Tips for Teachers 2.3.

Most important, don't be afraid to admit to disciplinary problems, to seek advice, or to think about transferring to another school if your disciplinary problems persist. Remember, if you wish to teach, if you expect to be an effective teacher, and if you want your students to learn, you will have to be an effective manager. For most of us, this should come with experience. For those of us who are unable to teach difficult students, a transfer is perhaps the most practical remedy. If this is the case, do it early in your career. Don't hang on in a school where you are unable to control the students or where you feel intense pressure, sense serious inabilities in yourself, or are afraid.

THEORY INTO PRACTICE

To move from the theory to the practice of good management and discipline, you must grasp the answers to some common and important questions and be able to translate those answers into action.

I. How do I encourage students to behave and work with me in the class?
   1. Act as if you *expect students to be orderly* from the first day on.
   2. *Expect everyone's attention* before you start teaching. Stop when there is noise. Don't teach over individual or group chatter.
   3. *Don't talk too much.* After a while, you lose the students' attention. Involve the students in activities, ask questions, pose problems, etc.
   4. *Hold students accountable* for abiding by rules.
   5. *Be businesslike but friendly.* It is important to establish reasonable limits and enforce them. It is also important to smile, to have a sense of humor, and to be warm and supportive.
   6. *Maintain your dignity.* Students should know there are limitations in a teacher-student relationship. You may wish to establish an imaginary line or keep a psychological distance from your students.
   7. *Treat minor disturbances calmly.* Small incidents can be ignored verbally; a stern look or gesture will suffice. Know when to pass over a situation quickly without making a fuss.
II. How do I handle group infractions or misbehavior?
   1. *Don't wait until a class is out of control.* When students are restless, change the activity. When students are beginning to engage in disturbances, take measures to stop the behavior in the initial stages.

Tips for Teachers 2.3

Suggestions for Analyzing Preventive Measures

Some of the causes of misbehavior are beyond your control. Knowing what measures to take to avoid common discipline problems and to handle problem student behaviors will increase your time for teaching and general teacher effectiveness. Below are suggestions for analyzing your measures.

1. Obtain private counseling to better understand your own emotional reactions to student behavior.
2. Organize rap sessions with students to better understand their concerns and emotional needs.
3. Meet privately with other teachers to discuss problems and successful strategies.
4. Identify and analyze the strengths of colleagues in dealing with discipline problems.
5. Determine which supervisors and administrators will provide support when necessary.
6. Ask another teacher, supervisor, or administrator to visit your classroom on a regular basis to analyze your classroom management.
7. Communicate with parents on a regular basis to learn about their management philosophies for purposes of support and follow-up in the class.
8. Keep informed on current legal issues concerning discipline. Read education journals, state law digests; talk to union representatives.
9. Document carefully all serious student behavior problems.
10. Evaluate your expectations about your disciplinary measures and what you ought to accomplish.

Source: Adapted from Daniel L. Duke and Adrienne M. Meckel, *Teacher's Guide to Classroom Management* (New York: Random House, 1984).

2. *Focus on the individual* rather than the class. Try to divert individuals by asking questions, assigning tasks, or reminding them they are wasting class time or spoiling it for the entire group.
3. *Don't punish the group* when you are unable to deal with the individual or to find which individual is causing a disturbance.
4. *Maintain your temper and poise.* Students will test their teacher to see how far they can go; they are not being personal. Don't overreact; maintain your poise.

5. *Avoid threats*, but if you make one, carry it out. Don't threaten the impossible. Think before you threaten. Follow through on a threat.

6. *Analyze your own behavior for possible causes of misbehavior*, especially if the difficulty continues. Look at your mannerisms, speech, attitudes. Analyze your rules and routines. Is your teaching interesting? Organized? Suitable to the level of the students? Be objective in your analysis.

7. *Seek help from others.* Check with another teacher, guidance counselor, disciplinarian, or supervisor. All of them have different roles with regard to the students and will give different views. Don't wait until a situation is beyond control.

III. How do I deal with individual offenders in the classroom?

1. When a student is involved in a minor infraction (whispering, annoying a neighbor, calling out), use nonverbal signals such as facial expressions or gestures while you continue to teach. If the infraction stops, don't reprimand the student.

2. If these signals fail, *move closer* to the student while you continue to teach. If this stops the student, don't reprimand any further.

3. If proximity fails, quietly *talk to the student* while the rest of the class continues to work.

4. *Avoid physical contact*, especially in a tense situation.

IV. How do I deal with discipline problems that cannot be resolved in class?

1. *Talk to the offender in private*, before or after class. Try to determine causes of the problem. Try to reach an understanding or agreement with the student.

2. If you have to punish, *make the punishment fit the misbehavior.* The first offense, unless it is quite serious, need not be punished.

3. Leave the misbehaving student with the feeling that he is *ruining things for himself and the group.*

4. Ignore a student's claims that she "doesn't care." This is usually a defensive reaction. *Remind the student that she really does care.*

5. Give the student a *chance to redeem himself.*

6. *Use the resources at your disposal.* For example, use student records, suggestions from other teachers and the guidance counselor, advice and authority of the dean of discipline or a supervisor.

7. *Communicate with the parents* (via telephone or letter). Most parents will support the teacher in matters of discipline involving their children.

8. *Analyze your methods.* What are you doing wrong, or how are you contributing to the problem?

9. If you have to *refer the student* to a counselor, disciplinarian, or supervisor, be specific. Avoid subjective remarks. Stick to the facts.

10. Don't rely too much on others to *solve your classroom problems*. Eventually this diminishes your authority. Save only the major discipline problems, the ones you really have trouble handling, for others to resolve.[49]

V. How do I develop and maintain a positive approach to classroom management (whatever discipline approach I wish to adopt)?

1. *Be positive.* Stress what should be done, not what shouldn't be done.

2. *Use praise.* Give praise according to merit. Show that you appreciate hard work and good behavior.

3. *Trust.* Trust students, but don't be an easy mark. Make students feel you believe in them as long as they are honest with you and don't take advantage of you.

4. *Express interest.* Talk to individual students about what interests them, what they did over the weekend, how school work is progressing in other areas or subjects. Be sensitive and respectful about social trends and styles and school events that affect the behavior of the group. Be aware that peer group pressure affects individual behavior.

5. *Be fair and consistent.* Don't have "pets" or "goats." Don't condemn an infraction one time and ignore it another time.

6. *Show respect; avoid sarcasm.* Be respectful and considerate toward students. Understand their needs and interests. Don't be arrogant or condescending or rely on oneupmanship to make a point.

7. *Establish classroom rules.* Make rules clear and concise and enforce them. Your rules should eventually be construed as their rules.

8. *Discuss consequences.* Students should understand the consequences for acceptable and unacceptable behavior. Invoke logical consequences, that is, appropriate rewards and punishment. Don't punish too often; it loses its effect after a while.

9. *Establish routines.* Students should know what to do and under what conditions. Routine procedures provide an orderly and secure classroom environment.

10. *Confront misbehavior.* Don't ignore violations of rules or disruptions of routines. Deal with misbehavior in a way that does not interfere with your teaching. Don't accept or excuse serious or contagious misbehavior, even if you have to stop your teaching. If you ignore it, it will worsen.

11. *Guide.* There is a difference between guidance, whereby you help students deal with problems, and discipline, whereby you main-

---

[49] *Getting Started in the Elementary School*, rev. ed. (New York: Board of Education of the City of New York, 1986); *Getting Started in the Secondary School*, rev. ed. (New York: Board of Education of the City of New York, 1986).

tain order and control by reacting to student surface behavior. Your main goal should be guidance rather than discipline. Good guidance will serve as a preventive measure, whereby you can establish order and control without having to assert authority.

12. *Avoid overcontrolling.* Assert your authority only when you need to and without overdoing it. Be confident without being condescending or egotistical. The need is to show you are in control of the classroom without overcontrolling students.

13. *Reduce failure, promote success.* Academic failure should be kept to a minimum since it is a cause of frustration, withdrawal, and hostility. When students see themselves as failures, they will act as failures. When students see themselves as winners and receive recognition for success, they become more civil, calm, and confident; they are easier to work with and teach.

14. *Set a good example.* Model what you preach and expect. For example, speak the way you want students to speak; keep an orderly room if you expect students to be orderly; check homework if you expect students to do the homework.

15. *Be willing to make adjustments.* Analyze your disciplinary approach and preventive strategies by yourself and with the help of experienced colleagues. Be objective about your abilities. Learn to compensate for your weaknesses by making adjustments in your disciplinary approach and preventive measures. Be sure your managerial techniques fit your disciplinary approach.

SUMMARY

1. Seven approaches to establishing and maintaining good discipline are presented. All establish clear rules and expectations, all include recommendations for preventive measures, and all are positive and practical. They differ as to the degree of control exercised by the teacher and the emphasis on tasks.

2. The approaches are the *assertive approach*, based on firm rules and forceful intervention and control by the teacher; the *business-academic approach*, based on classroom work requirements and assignments and organized instructional activities to enhance discipline; the *behavioral modification approach*, based on the systematic reinforcement of good behavior and punishment of inappropriate behavior; the *group managerial approach*, based on the teacher's maintaining group focus and group participation and holding all members of the group accountable; the *group guidance approach*, based on manipulating the surface behavior of students as individuals and groups; the *acceptance approach*, based on the assumption that when students are given such acceptance by the teacher and peers, behavior and achievement improve; and the *success approach*, based on the teacher's helping students make proper choices by experiencing success.

3. Which approach or combination of approaches a teacher adopts largely

depends on the teacher's philosophy, personality, teaching style, and teaching situation.

4. Educators have identified student and teacher types in reference to classroom management. Students can be classified in terms of discipline problem types, and teachers can be classified in terms of various strategies for maintaining good discipline.

5. Punishment is sometimes necessary to enforce rules and regulations. Punishment should fit the situation and take into consideration the developmental stage of the student. It should also be in line with school policy.

6. Preventive measures for maintaining and enhancing discipline are based on the need to curtail classroom problems before they become disruptive and affect teaching.

QUESTIONS TO CONSIDER

1. What goals do you expect classroom management to achieve?
2. What approaches to classroom management do you prefer? Why?
3. How do a teacher's personality characteristics affect his or her disciplinary strategies?
4. Which student problem types discussed in the chapter do you feel you may have the fewest problems with? The most problems with?
5. Which preventive measures discussed in the chapter seem to coincide best with your personality and philosophy?

THINGS TO DO

1. Arrange a conference with a teacher who is known as a "good" disciplinarian. Which of the approaches described in the chapter does the teacher's approach resemble? What are the constructive or positive factors in the teacher's methods and strategies?
2. Arrange to visit a nearby school to observe a teacher. Does that teacher have any special "tricks of the trade" for preventing disorder or confusion? What methods do you like? Dislike? Why?
3. Invite a guidance counselor, dean of discipline, or supervisor to the classroom. Discuss the procedures used at his or her school for handling discipline cases.
4. Prepare a list of preventive disciplinary techniques and common errors of discipline. Discuss the preventive techniques and common errors in class. Which common errors could have been prevented with which preventive techniques?
5. Discuss in class how you would respond as a teacher to the following classroom situations: (a) student constantly calls out; (b) student refuses to do work; (c) student uses improper language as an affront against a classmate; (d) student begins to argue with another student.

RECOMMENDED READINGS

Canter, Lee, and Marlene Canter. *Assertive Discipline: A Take Charge Approach for Today's Educator.* Los Angeles: Canter & Associates, 1976. A tough-minded approach to dealing with discipline.

Charles, C. M. *Building Classroom Discipline*, 3rd ed. New York: Longman, 1989. Outline of various disciplinary models and practices.

Duke, Daniel L., and Adrienne M. Meckel. *Classroom Management: A Teacher's Guide.* New York: Random House, 1984. An analysis of several discipline problems and how to deal with them as a teacher.

Emmer, Edmond T., et al. *Classroom Management for Secondary Teachers*, 2nd ed. Englewood Cliffs, N.J.: Prentice-Hall, 1989. A business-academic approach to organizing and controlling students, including several practical techniques for secondary teachers.

Evertson, Carol M., et al. *Classroom Management for Elementary Teachers*, 2nd ed. Englewood Cliffs, N.J.: Prentice-Hall, 1989. The companion book to the one above, mainly for elementary teachers.

Glasser, William. *Schools Without Failure.* New York: Harper & Row, 1969. A classic book on discipline that emphasizes humanitarian and democratic strategies and a positive approach to discipline.

Kounin, Jacob S. *Discipline and Group Management in Classrooms.* New York: Holt, Rinehart and Winston, 1970. A classic piece of research, emphasizing group discipline problems.

KEY TERMS

Assertive approach	Group guidance approach
Business-academic approach	Acceptance approach
Behavioral modification approach	Success approach
Modeling	Preventive discipline
Group managerial approach	Coping strategies

Chapter
3

Testing Students

FOCUSING QUESTIONS

1. What does it mean when we say a test is reliable? Valid?

2. What are the most common methods for testing reliability? Validity?

3. What are the differences between norm-reference measurements and criterion-reference measurements?

4. How can criterion-reference tests be improved?

5. How can classroom tests be improved?

6. What short-answer test questions generate the most controversy? Why?

7. How can the teacher improve the writing and scoring of essay test questions?

8. What test-taking skills can be taught to students? When was the last time you taught these skills to your students?

*E*valuation is a process in which we put a value on or assign worth to something. The essential characteristic of evaluation is judgment. Measurement is quantitative. It describes something in terms of specific numbers or percentages. In evaluation a judgment is made in attaching a value or a qualitative description to a measurement derived from a test.

For example, a student scores 65 on a test. This score is a measurement. However, the number does not indicate if the score should be judged good or poor, high or low. If most students score over 65, we may decide that the score is low and indicates poor performance. If most students score in the 60s, we may decide that the score is not so low. Measurement provides us with test data (numbers, percentages); judgment interprets the numbers and turns them into evaluations.

Evaluation is a two-step process. The first step is measurement, in which the data are obtained by the use of one or a series of tests. Once the measurement has been made, judgments are made about the adequacy of the performance, usually in the context of instructional objectives.

Problems in test content, sampling (norming), and procedures can result in errors in measurement, and all evaluations are subject to error, since human judgment is involved. The best we can hope for is to reduce the chance for and margin of error by careful measurement and evaluation procedures. In this chapter we will focus on testing and in the next, on evaluation.

CRITERIA FOR SELECTING TESTS

Two major criteria for selecting tests are reliability and validity. No matter what type of test you use, it should be reliable and valid. By **reliability** we mean that the test yields similar results when it is repeated over a short period of time or when a different form is used. A reliable test can be viewed as consistent, dependable, and stable. By **validity** we mean that the test does measure what it is represented as measuring. An invalid test does not measure what it should. For example, a pen-and-pencil test is not suitable for measuring athletic abilities.

Reliability

Test reliability can be expressed numerically. A coefficient of .80 or higher indicates high reliability, .40 to .79 fair reliability, and less than .40 low reliability. Many standardized tests are comprised of several subtests or scales and thus have coefficients to correspond to each of the subtests, as well as the entire test. For example, reliability for a reading test might be reported as .86 for comprehension, .77 for vocabulary, .91 for analogies, and .85 for the test as a whole.

There are three basic methods for determining test reliability. In the method called *test-retest* a test is administered twice, usually with 10 to 30 days between tests.[1] The rank ordering of individual test scores on the two tests is compared. If the rank ordering of scores is exactly the same, then the correlation coefficient is 1.00, or perfect reliability. A correlation of .86 indicates that the test is highly consistent over time.

A number of objections have been raised to the test-retest method. If the same items are used on both tests, the respondents' answers on the second test may be influenced by their memory of the first test and by discussions about the items with classmates or teachers between tests. If the interval between tests is too short, memorization is a factor. If the interval is too long, scores may change as a result of learning. The two test conditions might also differ. Lack of interest on the student's part during one of the test situations, a change in a student's health or diet, a change in the mood of the student or the test administrator may affect the scores.

To overcome the problems introduced by repeated test items in the test-retest method, the *parallel forms* method may be used. Two different but equivalent forms of the test are produced, and students are given both forms of the test. The correlation between scores on the two tests provides a good estimate of reliability. One drawback to this method is that parallel forms are not always available, especially with teacher-made tests, but even with many standardized tests. The two forms are not always equivalent and may differ in difficulty.[2] Also, the parallel forms method does not address the problem of differing test conditions.

The difficulties associated with the test-retest and parallel forms methods have led to the development of the *split-half* reliability method. A single test is split into reasonably equivalent halves, and these two subtests are used as if they were two separate tests to determine reliability coefficients. One common method of splitting a test is to score the even-numbered and odd-numbered items separately. Of course, splitting a test in half means that the reliability scores are determined by half the number of items. Too few items in calculations can lead to greater distortions and more chance effects.

Test reliability can be improved by the following factors.

1. *Increased number of test items.* Reliability is higher when the number of items is increased, because the test involves a larger sample of the material covered.
2. *Heterogeneity of the student group.* Reliability is higher when test scores are spread over a range of abilities. Measurement errors are smaller than from a group that is more homogeneous in ability.

---

[1] Anne Anastasi, *Psychological Testing,* 6th ed. (New York: Macmillan, 1988); Lee J. Cronbach, *Essentials of Psychological Testing,* 4th ed. (New York: Harper & Row, 1984).

[2] Jum C. Nunnally, "Reliability of Measurement," in M. C. Wittrock, ed., *Encyclopedia of Educational Research,* 5th ed. (New York: Macmillan, 1982), pp. 1589–1601.

3. *Moderate item difficulty.* Reliability is increased when the test items are of moderate difficulty because this spreads the scores over a greater range than a test composed mainly of difficult or easy items.

4. *Objective scoring.* Reliability is greater when tests can be scored objectively. With subjective scoring, the same responses can be scored differently on different occasions, even if the scorer is the same person. A machine-scored test is more reliable than a hand-scored test because it is less subject to human error.

5. *Limited time.* A test in which speed is a factor is more reliable than a test that all students can complete in the time available.[3]

Validity

Several different types of validity exist. Basically, we try to determine whether we are measuring what we think we are measuring. Depending on a person's knowledge of research and reason for administering the test, an individual can choose from several different types of validity.

Content Validity   When constructing a test for a particular subject, we must ask whether the items adequately reflect the specific content of that subject. If test items can be answered on the basis of basic intelligence, general knowledge or test wiseness, the content of a course or knowledge of a subject is not being tested adequately. The test lacks content validity.

Of all the forms of validity, content validity is perhaps the most important one. An eighth-grade science test should measure scientific knowledge and skills taught in eighth grade, not reading comprehension, not mathematics, and not tenth-grade science.

Curricular Validity   A standardized test that covers a good sample of a subject, but not the subject or course as taught in a particular school, would have content validity, but not curricular validity. A test that reflects the knowledge and skills presented in a particular school's curriculum has curricular validity. In such a test the items adequately sample the content of the curriculum the students have been studying.[4]

The problem of curricular validity arises more often with standardized (or norm-reference) tests than with teacher-made (or criterion-reference) tests. Many standardized tests have excellent content validity on a nationwide or statewide basis, but the items are not matched on a local school basis.

---

[3] Cronbach, *Essentials of Psychological Testing*; Tim Kubiszym and Gary D. Borich, *Educational Testing and Measurement*, 2nd ed. (Glenview, Ill.: Scott, Foresman, 1987); and William A. Mehrens and Irwin J. Lehmann, *Measurement and Evaluation in Education and Psychology*, 3rd ed. (New York: Holt, Rinehart, and Winston, 1984).

[4] Samuel Messick, "Validity," in R. L. Linn, ed., *Educational Measurement*, 3rd ed. (New York: Macmillan, 1989), pp. 13–103; Richard M. Wolf, "Validity of Tests," in M. C. Wittrock, ed., *Encyclopedia of Educational Research*, 5th ed. (New York: Macmillan, 1982), pp. 1991–1998.

Construct Validity   Construct validity is the extent to which the test measures the attributes or "constructs" it is supposed to measure. If we are using an aptitude test, we ask if we are really measuring the construct of aptitude. If it is measuring something else—general intelligence, reading comprehension, or creativity—then it is not measuring what it claims to measure.

A construct—for example, scientific aptitude, mechanical ability, or IQ— can be defined as a measurable quality that exists and explains some behavior or performance. When we interpret test scores in terms of a construct, say, mechanical ability, we make the assumption that there is an attribute or quality that we can properly call mechanical ability and that it can be measured by some objective means.

Criterion Validity   Criterion validity is the extent to which a particular test correlates with some other acceptable and valid test or measure of performance. Suppose, for example, a test for creativity is given to students. Scores of the test are compared with scores on another test or measure of creativity that is accepted as valid.[5] If there is a high correlation between the high and low scores of the new and established tests, then the new test is considered to have criterion validity. In effect, the test scores are related to a criterion that is independent of the test but is established as measuring what it purports to measure.

Predictive Validity   Predictive validity is concerned with the relation of test scores to performance at some future time. For example, valid aptitude tests, administered in the twelfth grade or first year of college, can predict success in college. This is what the Scholastic Aptitude Tests (SATs) that students take in high school are supposed to do. Information on how a student is likely to perform in an area of study or work can be helpful in counseling students and in selecting students for different programs. (It is important to consider other factors as well, including previous grades and letters of recommendation.)

Usability

A third criterion for selecting a test is **usability.** A test should be easy for students to understand, easy to administer and score, within budget limitations if it has to be purchased, suitable to the test conditions (for example, time available), and appropriate in degree of difficulty.[6]

---

[5] Anne Anastasi, "Coaching, Test Sophistication, and Developed Abilities," *American Psychologist,* October 1981, pp. 1086–1093; Samuel Messick, "Test Validity and the Ethics of Assessment," *American Psychologist,* November 1980, pp. 1012–1028. and Robert L. Linn, *Intelligence: Measurement Theory and Public Policy* (Urbana, Ill.; University of Illinois Press, 1988).

[6] Norman E. Gronlund, *Measurement and Evaluation in Teaching,* 5th ed. (New York: Macmillan, 1985); William A. Mehrens and Irwin J. Lehmann, *Using Standardized Tests in Education,* 4th ed. (New York: Longman, 1986).

A test may be valid in content, but the questions may be so ambiguous or the directions so difficult to follow that a student who understands the material may give the wrong answer. Or the questions may be phrased in such a way that a student who does not understand the material may give the right answer. For example, students expect a true-false or multiple-choice item containing the word "always" or "never" to be false or an inappropriate choice. They sometimes answer such an item correctly when they are ignorant of the facts. By the same token, the vocabulary of the test should not be too difficult for students taking the test.

Table 3.1 lists nine factors that affect usability and in turn influence reliability and validity.

Table 3.1 FACTORS AFFECTING USABILITY

1. *Unclear directions.* Directions that do not clearly indicate to the pupil how to respond to the items, whether it is permissible to guess, and how to record the answers will tend to reduce validity.

2. *Reading vocabulary and sentence structure too difficult.* Vocabulary and sentence structure that are too complicated for the pupils taking the test will result in the test's measuring reading comprehension and aspects of intelligence rather than the aspects of pupil performance it intended to measure.

3. *Inappropriate level of difficulty of the test items.* In norm-referenced tests, items that are too easy or too difficult will not provide reliable discriminations among pupils and will therefore lower validity. In criterion-referenced tests, failure to match the difficulty specified by the learning outcome will lower validity.

4. *Poorly constructed test items.* Test items that unintentionally provide clues to the answer will tend to measure the pupils' alertness in detecting clues as well as the aspects of pupil performance that the test is intended to measure.

5. *Ambiguity.* Ambiguous statements in test items contribute to misinterpretations and confusion. Ambiguity sometimes confuses the better pupils more than the poorer pupils, causing the items to discriminate in a negative direction.

6. *Test items inappropriate for the outcomes being measured.* Attempting to measure understandings, thinking skills, and other complex types of achievement with test forms that are appropriate only for measuring factual knowledge will invalidate the results.

7. *Test too short.* A test is only a sample of the many questions that might be asked. If a test is too short to provide a representative sample of the performance we are interested in, validity will suffer accordingly.

8. *Improper arrangement of items.* Test items are typically arranged in order of difficulty with the easiest items first. Placing difficult items early in the test may cause pupils to spend too much time on these and prevent them from reaching items they could easily answer. Improper arrangement may also influence validity by having a detrimental effect on pupil motivation.

9. *Identifiable pattern of answers.* A systematic pattern of correct answers (e.g., T, T, F, F or A, B, C, D, A, B, C, D) will enable pupils to guess answers, and this will lower validity.

Source: Norman E. Gronlund, *Measurement and Evaluation in Teaching,* 5th ed. (New York: Macmillan, 1985), pp. 79–80.

Figure 3.1 The standardized testing process has developed on a large scale over the years. (Photo Arthur Grace/Stock, Boston)

STANDARDIZED AND NONSTANDARDIZED TESTS

A **standardized test** is an instrument that contains a set of items that are administered and measured according to uniform scoring standards. The test has been pilot tested and administered to representative populations of similar individuals to obtain normative data. Most standardized tests are published and distributed by testing companies (such as Educational Testing Service and Psychological Corporation), publishing companies (such as Houghton Mifflin and Macmillan), which usually publish reading and math tests to accompany their textbooks, and universities (such as Iowa University and Stanford University), which have developed and validated specific achievement and IQ tests.

Standardized tests are widely used in schools, and you most certainly have taken a number of them throughout your academic career. Standardized tests usually have high reliability coefficients and good validity, since they have been tested on representative sample populations. The unreliable or invalid test items have been eliminated through this pilot testing over the years. Normative data are useful in interpreting individual test scores and in ranking individual scores within a comparative population. However, normative data are less useful in special school or class situations in which the students have abilities, aptitudes, needs, or learning problems that are quite different from the normative population. The content of standardized tests does not always coincide with the content in a particular school or classroom—that is, the tests may lack curricular validity for that school or classroom.

Nonstandardized tests, usually referred to as **teacher-made tests** or classroom tests, have not been tested on several sample populations and therefore are not accompanied by normative data. These test scores cannot indicate an individual's position with reference to a standard or larger sample. Standardized tests are usually administered only once or twice a year; teacher-made tests provide more frequent evaluations. Teacher-made tests are more closely related to the school's and/or teacher's objectives and content of the course. Who knows better than the teacher what content was covered and emphasized and hence should be tested? Who knows better than the teacher what are the needs, interests, and strengths of the students, when to test, and when, based on test outcomes, to proceed to the next instructional unit?[7]

The relative advantages and disadvantages of standardized and nonstandardized tests are listed in Table 3.2. These advantages and limitations are analyzed in terms of our previous discussion of reliability, validity, and usability.

Norm-Reference Tests (NRT)

Standardized tests are **norm-referenced**—that is, the performance of sample populations has been established and serves as a "basis for interpreting a [student's] relative test performance. A norm-reference measure allows us to compare one individual with other individuals."[8] The idea of norms, especially if the norms are based on a larger population, say, nationwide or statewide, is to compare the score of a student on a test with students from other schools. Suppose, for example, on a statewide achievement test Jack's score places him in the 98th percentile in his school, but in the 58th percentile in the state. Although Jack's score is extremely high when compared with scores of students in his school, it is barely above average compared to scores of a large pool of students. Students who attend inner-city schools may exhibit excellent performance when compared with classmates or peer groups, but poor performance on a national or statewide basis. If their scores are compared only with other inner-city schools or even with the city norms rather than statewide or national norms, their percentile scores are likely to be higher since the norm group is different.

Norm-reference tests tend to have high estimates of reliability and validity because the norms are based on large populations. The test manual usually

---

[7]W. Bruce Walsh, *Tests and Measurements*, 4th ed. (Englewood Cliffs, N.J.: Prentice-Hall, 1989); Mehrens and Lehmann, *Measurement and Evaluation in Education and Psychology*.

[8]N. L. Gage and David C. Berliner, *Educational Psychology*, 4th ed. (Boston: Houghton Mifflin, 1988), p. 572.

Table 3.2   ADVANTAGES AND DISADVANTAGES OF STANDARDIZED AND
NONSTANDARDIZED TESTS WITH RESPECT TO RELIABILITY, VALIDITY,
AND USABILITY

Standardized	Advantages	Limitations
1. Reliability	For best tests, fairly high—often .85 or more for comparable form.	High reliability is no guarantee of validity. Also, reliability depends upon range of ability in group tested.
2. Validity a. Curricular	Careful selection by competent persons. Fits typical situations.	Inflexible. Too general in scope to meet local requirements fully, especially in unusual situations.
b. Statistical	With best tests, high.	Criteria often inappropriate or unreliable. Size of coefficients dependent upon range of ability in group tested.
3. Usability a. Ease of Administration	Definite procedure, time limits, etc. Economy of time.	Manuals require careful study and are sometimes inadequate.
b. Ease of Scoring	Definite rules, keys, etc. Largely routine.	Scoring by hand may take considerable time and be monotonous. Machine scoring preferable.
c. Ease of Interpretation	Better tests have adequate norms. Useful basis of comparison. Equivalent forms.	Norms often confused with standards. Some norms defective. Norms for various types of schools and levels of ability are often lacking.
Summary	Convenience, comparability, objectivity. Equivalent forms may be available.	Inflexible. May be only slightly applicable to a particular situation.

Nonstandardized (essays)	Advantages	Limitations
1. Reliability		Reliability usually quite low.
2. Validity a. Curricular	Useful for English, advanced classes; affords language training. May encourage sound study habits.	Limited sampling. Bluffing is possible. Mixes language factor in all scores.
b. Statistical		Usually not known.
3. Usability a. Ease of Administration	Easy to prepare; easy to give.	Lack of uniformity.
b. Ease of Scoring		Slow, uncertain, and subjective.
c. Ease of Intepretation		No norms. Meaning doubtful.
Summary	Useful for part of many tests and in a few special fields.	Limited sampling. Subjective scoring. Time-consuming.

Table 3.2   Continued

Nonstandardized (objective)	Advantages	Limitations
1. Reliability	Sometimes approaches that of standardized tests.	No guarantee of validity.
2. Validity		
a. Curricular	Extensive sampling of subject matter. Flexible in use. Discourages bluffing.	Narrow sampling of tested functions. Negative learning possible.
	Compares favorably with standard tests.	May encourage piecemeal study.
b. Statistical		Adequate criteria usually lacking.
3. Usability		
a. Ease of Administration	Directions rather uniform. Economy of time.	Time, effort, and skill required to prepare well.
b. Ease of Scoring	Definite rules, keys, etc. Largely routine. Can be done by clerks or machine.	Monotonous.
c. Ease of Interpretation	Local norms can be derived.	No norms available at beginning.
Summary	Extensive sampling. Objective scoring. Flexibility.	Preparation requires skill and time.

Source: Julian C. Stanley, *Measurement in Today's Schools*, 4th ed. (Englewood Cliffs, N.J.: Prentice-Hall, 1964), pp. 304–305.

reports reliability and validity data obtained for various sample populations. A test manual should provide a comprehensive description of procedures in establishing normative data. Although norms can be reported for almost any characteristic (sex, ethnicity, geographical setting, and so forth), such data are usually not shown or are incomplete for students who have special characteristics or backgrounds.

Criterion-Reference Tests (CRT)

Sometimes an educator is not concerned with how well a student performs compared to other students, but whether the student exhibits progress in learning. The educator establishes a set of objectives with corresponding proficiency or achievement levels and then determines whether the student can achieve an acceptable proficiency or achievement level.[9] Rather than compare the

---

[9]Norman E. Gronlund, *How To Construct Achievement Tests*, 4th ed. (Englewood Cliffs, N.J.: Prentice-Hall, 1988); W. James Popham, *Criterion-Referenced Measurement* (Englewood Cliffs, N.J.: Prentice-Hall, 1978).

student to other students, the teacher assesses the student only on the basis of a predetermined standard. Scores can demonstrate progress (or minimal progress) in learning over time.

Criterion-reference tests measure individuals' ability in regard to a criterion, that is, a specific body of knowledge or skill. The tests are used to determine what students know or can do in a specific domain of learning rather than how their performance compares with other students.

Criterion-reference tests are usually locally developed and sometimes teacher-made. Norm-reference tests usually have better overall reliability and validity, since they have been constructed by test experts and tested on larger sample populations.[10] However, the criterion-reference tests allow the teacher to judge students' proficiency in specific content areas, and therefore they usually have better curricular validity than norm-reference tests.

Criterion-reference measurements may be practical in areas of achievement that focus on the acquisition of specific knowledge (for example, the Civil War in history or gas laws in physics) and in special programs such as individually prescribed instruction, mastery learning, and adaptive instruction.[11] It is important to note that it is difficult to develop reliable or valid criterion measurements, since most instructional units and special programs deal with specific curriculum and instruction of information. See Tips for Teachers 3.1.

Differences Between Norm-Reference and Criterion-Reference Tests

The norm-reference test measures a student's level of achievement at a given period of time compared to other students elsewhere. Scores from a criterion-reference test do not indicate a relative level of achievement or produce standards because no comparisons are made. The test indicates how proficient a student is in terms of a specific body of learning. It can measure changes in learning over time, but it cannot produce meaningful comparisons or standards.

According to researchers, the norm-reference test is valuable for measuring higher and abstract levels of the cognitive domain, whereas the criterion-reference test is valuable for measuring lower and concrete levels of learning. The norm reference is valuable for heterogeneous groups in which the range of abilities is wide and a test is intended to measure a wide range of performance. The criterion-reference test is more useful in homogeneous groups in

---

[10]William A. Mehrens and Robert L. Ebel, "Some Comments on Criterion-Referenced and Norm-Referenced Tests," *Measurement in Education*, August 1979, pp. 43–53; W. James Popham, "Can High-Stakes Tests Be Developed at the Local Level?" *National Association of Secondary School Principals*, February 1987, pp. 77–84.

[11]Edward Haertel, "Construct Validity and Criterion-Reference Testings," *Review of Educational Research*, Spring 1985, pp. 47–86; W. James Popham, "Measurement Driven Instruction: It's on the Road," *Phi Delta Kappan*, May 1985, pp. 628–634; and Herbert C. Rudman, "Classroom Instruction and Tests," *National Association of Secondary School Principals*, February 1987, pp. 3–22.

Tips for Teachers 3.1

Constructing Criterion-Reference Tests

In criterion-reference tests (1) performance is related to a set of behavioral objectives or referents, (2) the test items represent samples of actual performance or behavior, and (3) performance can be interpreted in terms of predetermined cutoff scores or achievement levels (such as low, average, high). If, for example, the test is on grammar, we must have some basis for saying that a student knows his or her grammar, and what kind of questions can be answered (dealing with nouns, verbs, adjectives, and so forth).

To construct a criterion-reference test, the following steps are recommended.

1. Prepare a content outline of the knowledge or skills that the test will measure. This should coincide with the course or unit outline.

   Example: Classifying singular nouns
   Classifying possessive nouns
   Classifying adjectives
   Classifying verbs
   Identifying pronouns
   Identifying adverbs
   Placing commas
   Placing semicolons
   Placing colons

2. Restate the knowledge or skills in behavioral terms—that is, identify the required performances. Include an *action* word and performance *criteria*.

   Example: Action: Write commas in appropriate places.
   Criteria: Use a comma to separate parts of a compound sentence, after an adverbial clause, before a conjunction, and connecting the last two elements in a series of three or more.

3. To increase the content validity of the test, write test items to cover particular domains or areas, with at least two items per objective.

   Example: Domain: Compound sentences
   Objective: Given a short paragraph containing compound sentences, place all necessary commas properly.
   Test Item: In the paragraph below insert five missing commas in the appropriate places.
   Test item: The paragraph below contains several sentences. Change two simple sentences to compound sen-

   continued

tences, placing commas in the appropriate places in the sentences.

Test item: Write a paragraph of four or five sentences. Include two compound sentences. Place the commas in the appropriate places.

4. Validate the fact that the knowledge and skills measured by the test are prerequisite for moving to the next objective. This is based on judgment. To validate your assumption, give the test items to a group of experts or colleagues or obtain actual data by giving the test to a group of students who have overall proficiency to see which test items are more difficult than others.

5. Decide upon scores to indicate proficiency levels (below average, average, above average).

Source: Adapted from Bruce W. Tuckman, *Testing for Teachers*, 2nd ed. (San Diego: Harcourt Brace Jovanovich, 1988), pp. 44–46, 197. All examples and test items are this author's; the steps are based on Tuckman.

which the range of abilities is narrow and a test is intended to measure a limited or predetermined range of objectives and outcomes. With norm-reference tests external standards can be used to make judgments about a student's performance, whereas criterion-reference tests lack uniform standards, and the interpretation of the scores is only as good as the process used to set the proficiency levels.[12]

Norman Gronlund points out five differences: (1) Whereas the norm-reference test covers a *large or general domain* of learning tasks, with only a few items measuring each task, the criterion-reference test covers a *limited or specific domain*, with a relatively large number of items measuring each task. (2) The norm reference emphasizes *discrimination* among students in terms of relative levels of learning or achievement, whereas the criterion reference focuses on *description* of what learning tasks students can or cannot perform. (3) The norm-reference test favors *average difficulty* and omits easy or difficult items; the criterion-reference test *matches* item *difficulty* to the difficulty of learning tasks and does not omit easy or difficult items. (4) The norm-reference test is used for *survey or general testing*, while the criterion-reference test is used for *mastery or specific test situations*. (5) Interpretation

[12]Ronald K. Hambleton et al., "Criterion-Referenced Testing and Measurement: A Review of Technical Issues and Developments," *Review of Educational Research*, Winter 1978, pp. 1–47; Robert L. Linn, "Educational Testing and Assessment," *American Psychologist*, October 1986, pp. 1153–1160; and Craig G. Schoon et al., "An Alternative Criterion-Reference Passing Point Method," paper presented at the annual meeting of the American Educational Research Association, New Orleans, April 1988.

of a norm-reference score is based on a *defined group*, and the student is evaluated by his or her standing relative to that group. Interpretation of a criterion-reference score is based on a *defined learning domain*, and the student is evaluated by the items answered correctly.[13]

Criterion-reference tests are usually teacher-made and are used by teachers to tailor tests to their objectives, to develop more efficient and appropriate teaching strategies, and to fit the needs of the classroom population. Because norm-reference tests are prepared for many different school districts, with different curricular and instructional emphases, they are unable to do these individualized things. Criterion-reference tests better coincide with the actual teaching-learning situation of a particular class or school. The problem is that local school officials and teachers often lack the expertise in test construction needed to develop criterion-reference tests. Thus, it is recommended that teachers develop these tests in a group, where they can exchange information with colleagues and perhaps with a test consultant. Table 3.3 provides a guide for constructing such tests that meet the five criteria of appropriateness, validity, reliability, interpretability, and usability.

Types of Standardized Tests

There are basically four types of standardized tests. The scores from these tests will appear in the student record, often called the *cumulative record*.

Intelligence Tests **Intelligence tests** have come under attack in recent years, and most school systems use them only for special testing or placement of students. The two most commonly used intelligence tests are the Stanford-Binet (SB) and the Wechsler Intelligence Scale for Children (WISC). The first is a group intelligence test; the second is administered on an individual basis.

Achievement Tests The use of **achievement tests** has increased in recent years, replacing intelligence testing as the prime source of information for educators about students and how they perform in comparison to each other and to students elsewhere. Every elementary student is exposed to a series of reading, language, and mathematics standardized tests to evaluate performance at various grade levels. There are several types of achievement tests, as stated below.

1. The most common *survey* or *general achievement tests* are the Stanford Achievement Tests (grades 2 through 9) and the Iowa Test of Basic Skills. The National Assessment of Educational Progress (NAEP) exams are designed to measure the knowledge and skills of American students in 10 subject areas (with emphases in the arts, science, math, and career development) at ages 9, 13, and 17.
2. Many elementary and junior high school students are required to take *diagnostic tests*, usually in the basic skills and in study skills, to reveal

---

[13]Gronlund, *Measurement and Evaluation in Teaching.*

Table 3.3   CHECKLIST FOR CRITERION-REFERENCED TESTS

I. *Is My Test APPROPRIATE?*
  1. Does It Fit My Objectives?
    a. Are there two items or more for each and every objective and zero items that fit no objectives?
    b. Do the number of items per objective accurately reflect the relative importance of each objective?
  2. Does It Reflect the Action Verbs:
    a. Does each item for a given objective measure the action called for by the verb in that objective?
    b. Have I used the item format most appropriate for each action?
  3. Does It Utilize the Conditions:
    a. Does each item for a given objective employ the statement of givens or conditions set forth in that objective?
  4. Does It Employ the Criteria:
    a. Is the scoring of each item for a given objective based on the criteria stated in that objective?

II. *Is My Test VALID?*
  1. Does It Discriminate between Performance Levels:
    a. Do students who are independently judged to perform better in the test area perform better on the test?
    b. Do different students with different degrees of experience perform differently on the various items?
  2. Does It Fit Any External Standard:
    a. Does success on the test predict subsequent success in areas for which the test topic is claimed to be a prerequisite?
    b. Do students who receive appropriate teaching perform better on the test than untaught students (or does a student perform better on the test after teaching than before)?
  3. How Do My Colleagues View the Coverage:
    a. Do my colleagues in the topic area or at the grade level agree that all necessary objectives and no unnecessary ones have been included?
    b. Do they agree that the items are valid for measuring the objectives?
  4. Does It Measure Something Other than Reading Level or Life Styles:
    a. Are the demands it makes on reading skills within the capabilities of the students?
    b. Is performance independent of group membership or any other socioethnic variable?

III. *Is My Test RELIABLE?*
  1. Are There Paired Items That Agree:
    a. Do students who get one item of a pair (per objective) right also get the other right and those who get one wrong get the other wrong?
    b. Have nonparallel items been rewritten?
  2. Is Item Performance Consistent with Test Performance:
    a. Is each item consistently passed by students who do well on the total test?
    b. Have inconsistent items been removed?
  3. Are All Items Clear and Understandable:
    a. Have the student responses been used as a basis for evaluating item clarity?
    b. Have ambiguous items been removed or rewritten?
  4. Have Scoring Procedures Proved to Be Systematic and Unbiased:
    a. Have multiple scorings yielded consistent results?
    b. Are scoring criteria and procedures as detailed and as suitable as they can be?

Table 3.3 Continued

IV. *Is My Test INTERPRETABLE?*
  1. Do I Know How the Scores Relate to Relevant Performance:
     a. Is my test referenced in terms of some criterion (e.g., my objectives)?
     b. Can I tell what a high score and a low score mean? Or, can I report the specific objectives on which proficiency has been demonstrated?
     c. Can the results for an individual student be used as a specific indication of level or degree of proficiency?
  2. Do I Know What Defines Acceptable Performance:
     a. Have I preestablished cutoff scores (e.g., passing grade) and if so, on what basis?
     b. Do I have some concrete and verifiable way to say whether a particular performance suffices in terms of objective specifications of acceptability?
  3. Does the Test Provide Diagnostic and Evaluative Information:
     a. Does it tell me the areas in which a student needs help?
     b. Does it tell me the areas in which the class needs help?
     c. Does it tell me the areas in which instruction needs improvement?
  4. Does It Provide Useful Relative Information:
     a. Does it provide the kind of data that I can compare meaningfully with results of past and future testings?
     b. Can the results be interpreted on a norm-referenced basis if that is desired?

V. *Is My Test USABLE?*
  1. Is it Short Enough to Avoid Being Tedious:
     a. Does it stop short of creating fatigue? stress? boredom?
     b. Have I tried to make it as short as possible within the limits of reliability?
  2. Is It Practical for Classroom Use:
     a. Can it be used conveniently in a classroom?
     b. Is it within the limit of available teacher time?
     c. Can it be used to test all students?
     d. Is it realistic about the kinds of equipment and physical set-up it requires?
  3. Are There Standard Procedures for Administration:
     a. Are there clear, written instructions?
     b. Can it be administered by someone other than me?
     c. Can it be given in a nonthreatening, nondiscriminatory way?
  4. Can Students Comprehend It and Relate to It:
     a. Is it written at a level students can understand?
     b. Is it interesting, clever, or provocative?
     c. Is it written to engage students?

Source: Bruce W. Tuckman, *Measuring Educational Outcomes: Fundamentals of Testing* (New York: Harcourt, Brace, 1975), pp. 304–306.

strengths and weaknesses for purposes of placement and formulating an appropriate instructional program.

3. An increasing number of students in many school systems must pass *competency tests* to prove they are competent in reading, language, and math. Students who fail are usually provided some type of re-

Figure 3.2 At higher age levels in I.Q. tests, verbal and abstract items replace physical and concrete items. (Photo © Judith D. Sedwick/Picture Cube)

mediation. In some cases the tests are used as "break points" or "gate guards" between elementary, junior high, and high school, and as a requirement for graduation from high school. Students in some states are denied promotion or a diploma until they pass the examinations.[14]

4. *Subject exit tests* are used in a few school systems at the high school level. Students must pass tests to graduate, to receive a particular diploma, or to enroll in certain programs. For example, New York State uses the Regents examination in basic academic subject areas (English, history, science, mathematics, foreign language) as a screen for eligibility to matriculate full time in a state college or university; the student must also pass these examinations to receive an academic diploma. Actually, these exams may be considered competency tests.

Aptitude Tests   The difference between aptitude and achievement tests is mainly one of purpose. Achievement tests provide information about present achievement or past learning on a cumulative basis. **Aptitude tests** predict achievement. Whereas achievement tests deal with content that the schools teach (or

---

[14]Allan C. Ornstein, "Accountability Report from the USA," *Journal of Curriculum Studies*, December 1985, pp. 437–439; Ornstein, "Teacher Accountability: Trends and Policies," *Education and Urban Society*, February 1986, pp. 221–229.

should be teaching), aptitude tests may stress what is not taught in schools. The most common aptitude tests are briefly discussed below.

1. Most students who wish to go on to college have to take a number of *general aptitude tests* to provide information to college admissions officers. You probably took the Scholastic Aptitude Tests (SAT) or the American College Testing Program (ACT) exam. Students applying to graduate school may take the Miller Analogies Test (MAT) or the Graduate Record Examination (GRE). The MAT is a general aptitude test in logic and language skills. The GRE is a general aptitude test, but the advanced parts are considered a *professional aptitude test.*

2. *Special* or *talent aptitude tests* are frequently administered as screening devices for students who wish to enroll in a special school (such as music, art, or science) or for students who wish to enroll in a special course (such as an honors course or a college course with credit) or a special program (such as creative writing or computers).

Personality Tests   **Personality tests** are generally used for special placement of students with learning problems or adjustment problems. Most students in school are not tested for personality. The most commonly used personality tests are the California Test of Personality, the Pinter Personality Test, and the Thematic Apperception Test, all intended for use in primary grades to college and designed to measure various social and personal adjustment areas.

1. A number of general *attitudinal scales*, which estimate attitudes in diverse economic, political, social, and religious areas, are available; among the more common ones are the Allport Submission Reaction Study and the Allport-Vernon-Lindsey Study of Values.

2. Among *occupational attitudinal tests,* the Occupational Interest Inventory is suitable for students with at least a sixth-grade reading level, and the Kuder Preference Record is designed for high school and college students.

3. The most popular *projective test* is the Rorschach Inkblot Test. The test has some reliability and validity problems, especially in prediction from trait scores to behavioral situations, but it is still widely used in many schools.

Trends in Standardized Testing

It is important to recognize that a student's placement and progress in school, from grades 1 to 12, is largely determined by his or her scores on achievement tests in reading and math and, later on, aptitude tests of general knowledge or literacy. On a practical basis most standardized tests, at all grade levels (with the exception of personality tests), focus on declarative or simple content, and not on important or high-level cognitive processes, which cut across subject matter and are useful for critical thinking in several subjects.

As many as 22 cognitive processes have been identified by thinking skills theorists. However, in a review of 6,942 test items on standardized tests,

Marzano and Costa found that only nine cognitive processes were involved in answering the items. Two were involved in some way in answering every item: retrieving information from long-term memory, and comparing different pieces of information. The seven other processes, with corresponding percentage of use, were: referencing, or identifying explicit or implicit information (17 percent); visual matching, or relating a picture or symbol to a linguistic term (8.5 percent); inferring, or deducing unstated information (6.5 percent); ordering, or ranking or sequencing data (5.5 percent); representing, or devising a graphic or pictorial representation of information (5 percent); transposing, or translating information from one source to another (5 percent); and summarizing, or combining information (3 percent). The remaining 13 high-order thinking skills were considered absent on standardized tests.[15]

Until standardized tests are revised to reflect important cognitive processes such as extrapolating, synthesizing, verifying, and predicting, teachers will continue to stress these nine cognitive processes during teaching and instructional practices to prepare students for the tests they must take. To be sure, curriculum and instruction are test driven. It behooves test developers to improve their tests if they wish teachers to upgrade and incorporate critical thinking or problem solving in the content or subject matter.

So long as school authorities focus their attention on test results and not on how students think, standardized tests will continue to emphasize low-level cognitive operations. Some states, for example, Illinois and Michigan, are beginning to develop standardized tests in reading that attempt to determine how well readers process information.[16] To assess readers' processes, that is, the way they think, is a step toward providing information about how students read. This information is much more important than reading results if we are going to help students become better readers. The same is true in math, science, and other subject areas.

Questions to Consider in Selecting Tests

Hundreds of standardized tests exist, and selecting an appropriate one is difficult. Individual classroom teachers usually do not have to make this choice, but you may be called upon to make selections if you serve as a member of a test or evaluation committee for your school district. Below are 12 questions to assist you in selecting an appropriate standardized test. They are based on criteria formulated by W. James Popham.

    1. *Is the achievement test in harmony with course instructional objectives?* An achievement test should correspond with the objectives of the course, and it should assess the important knowledge, concepts, and skills of the course.

---

[15]Robert J. Marzano and Arthur L. Costa, "Question: Do Standardized Tests Measure General Cognitive Skills? Answer: No," *Educational Leadership*, May 1988, pp. 66–71.

[16]Roger Farr, "New Trends in Reading Assessment: Better Tests, Better Uses," *Curriculum Review*, September–October 1987, pp. 21–23. Sheila W. Valencia et al., "Theory and Practice in Statewide Reading Assessment," *Educational Leadership*, April 1989, pp 57-63.

Professional Viewpoint

Learning About Students' Thinking

Teachers need to know how students do certain tasks, not just how well they perform those tasks. For example, in helping a student develop reading comprehension, the teacher needs to know if the student has the background knowledge to read various social studies or science texts or whether the student has had experiences to read specific stories with understanding. The problem may be lack of vocabulary knowledge or the student may not have established thinking strategies such as prediction and visualization that will help him to comprehend a story.

Test scores provide information about how well a student has performed, but the score doesn't tell the teacher how the student arrived at the answers. It is important to know how well students perform, but the most important information for the teacher concerns the things a student does, or doesn't do, to comprehend.

A useful procedure to learn about how a student performs is to administer a formal test informally. This can be done with standardized tests, chapter and unit tests included in textbooks, and teacher-made tests. The procedure is actually quite simple. After the test has been administered in the usual fashion, and the results as to how well students can perform have been recorded, the tests are returned to the students and the teacher and students discuss the answers. This strategy is more effective if it is done with small groups of students—or even on an individual basis when possible.

In discussing the answers, the teacher is not just pointing out to students their errors and telling them the correct answers. Rather, the teacher should focus on asking students why they chose the answer they did—regardless of whether the answer is correct or incorrect. Discussion of so-called wrong answers should also take place. The alert teacher will learn a great deal about each student's background knowledge, comprehension strategies, and vocabulary strengths and weaknesses. The teacher will learn what needs to be taught to help students comprehend.

The key to success in using this technique is getting students to discuss answers—and to probe beyond merely checking answer choices. Important questions are: "Why do you think that?" "What made you answer that way?" "Could another answer be correct?" or "If we changed this part of the question could another answer be correct?" It is also important for the teacher to be open and accepting of all rationales for answer choices. The goal for the teacher is to help students to reflect about their thinking.

Roger Farr
Professor of Education
Indiana University

2. *Do the test items measure a representative sample of the learning tasks?* The test items cannot measure the entire course or subject matter, but they should cover the major objectives and content.

3. *Are the test items appropriate for measuring the desired outcomes of learning?* The test items should correspond to behaviors or performance levels consistent with the course level.

4. *Does the test fit the particular uses that will be made of the results?* For example, a diagnostic achievement test should be used for analyzing student difficulties, but an aptitude test should be used for predicting future performance in a given subject or program.

5. *Is the achievement test reliable?* The test should report reliability coefficients for different types of students, and they should be high for the student group you are testing.

6. *Does the test have retest potential?* Equivalent forms of the test should be available so that students can be retested if necessary. There should also be evidence that the alternative forms are equivalent.

7. *Is the test valid?* Standardized tests usually have poor curricular validity, but the test should have good construct validity and good criterion validity.

8. *Is the test free of obvious bias?* It is difficult to find a test that is totally free of bias toward all student groups, but teachers should look for tests that are considered culturally fair or at least sensitive toward minority groups and that provide normative data (reliability and validity data) for minority groups.

9. *Is the test appropriate for students?* The test must be suitable for the persons being tested in terms of reading level, clarity of instructions, visual layout, and so forth. It must be at the appropriate level of difficulty for students of a given age, grade level, and cultural background.

10. *Does the test improve learning?* Achievement tests should be seen as part of the teaching and learning process. This means a test should provide feedback to teachers and students and be used to guide and improve the teacher's instruction and the student's learning.

11. *Is the test easy to administer?* Tests that can be administered to large groups are more usable than tests that can only be given to small groups or individuals. Tests that require less time and are still reliable are more usable than lengthy tests.

12. *Is the cost of the test acceptable?* The total cost of the test, including the time involved in administering and scoring it, should be commensurate with the benefits to be derived. If similar information can be obtained by some other method that is just as reliable and valid, and less costly, then that method should be considered.[17]

---

[17] W. James Popham, *Modern Educational Measurement*, 2nd ed. (Englewood Cliffs, N.J.: Prentice-Hall, 1990).

CLASSROOM TESTS

Teachers are expected to write their own classroom tests. Most of these tests will be subject-related, will focus on a specific domain of learning, and will assess whether a subject has been mastered and when it is time to move on to a new area. In this context classroom tests are criterion-reference measurements.

Two researchers report that the majority of teachers develop more than half the tests used in class. About a third of the teachers surveyed estimate they spend between 11 and 20 percent of their professional time on developing and correcting teacher-made tests, and slightly more than a third estimate they spend more than 20 percent of their time on such tests.[18] William Mehrens estimates that a student may take as many as 400 to 1,000 teacher-constructed tests prior to high school graduation.[19]

It may be said that teachers and schools are in the business of testing and that they are highly influenced (sometimes hypnotized) by test scores. However, according to researchers, the bulk of the testing is done with teacher-made tests that have unknown or low reliability, and most teachers do not know how to check for reliability or how to ensure appropriate weighting of content (which impacts on validity).[20] Analysis of teacher-made tests reveals that about 80 percent of test questions emphasize knowledge or specific content, that tests frequently do not give adequate directions or explain scoring, and that about 15 to 20 percent contain grammatical, spelling, and punctuation errors.[21]

In spite of these limitations, classroom tests still serve important and useful purposes. They provide information related to (1) formulating and refining objectives for each student, (2) deciding on curriculum content, (3) evaluating and refining instructional techniques, and (4) evaluating the degree to which learning outcomes have been achieved.[22] One study states that classroom tests are used by teachers (1) to group or place students initially, (2) to decide on what to teach and how to teach it to students of different abilities or achievement levels, (3) to monitor student progress, (4) to change student

---

[18]Deena C. Newman and William M. Stallings, "Teacher Competency in Classroom Testing, Measurement Preparation, and Classroom Testing Practices," paper presented at the annual meeting of the National Council on Measurement in Education, March 1982.

[19]William A. Mehrens, "Educational Tests: Blessing or Curse?" unpublished, 1987.

[20]William A. Mehrens and Irwin J. Lehmann, "Using Teacher-Made Measurement Devices," *National Association of Secondary School Principals*, February 1987, pp. 36–44; Popham, "Can High-Stakes Tests Be Developed at the Local Level?"

[21]Margaret Fleming and Barbara Chambers, "Teacher-Made Tests: Windows in the Classroom," in W. E. Hathaway, ed., *Testing in Schools* (San Francisco: Jossey-Bass, 1983), pp. 29–38.

[22]Mehrens and Lehmann, "Using Teacher-Made Measurement Devices"; Richard J. Stiggens and Nancy J. Bridgeford, "The Ecology of Classroom Assessment," *Journal of Educational Measurement*, Winter 1985, pp. 271–286.

Tips for Teachers 3.2

Preparing Classroom Tests

Teacher-made tests are frequently the major basis for evaluating students' progress in school. Although the specific purposes of the tests and intended use of the outcomes vary among schools and teachers, tests play an important part in the life of the students and teachers.

Detailed planning goes into the development of standardized tests, and the same must be true for teacher-made tests. Good tests do not just happen! They require appropriate planning so that instructional objectives, curriculum content, and instructional materials are related in some meaningful fashion. Below is a checklist to consider when preparing classroom tests.

1. What is the purpose of the test? Why am I giving it?
2. What skills, knowledge, attitudes, and so on, do I want to measure?
3. Have I clearly defined my instructional objectives in terms of student behavior?
4. Have I prepared a table of specifications?
5. Do the test items match the objectives?
6. What kind of test (item format) do I want to use? Why?
7. How long should the test be?
8. How difficult should the test be?
9. What should be the discrimination level of my test items?
10. How will I arrange the various item formats?
11. How will I arrange the items within each item format?
12. What do I need to do to prepare students for taking the test?
13. How are the pupils to record their answers to objective items? On separate answer sheets? On the test booklet?
14. How is the objective portion to be scored? Hand or machine?
15. How is the essay portion to be graded?
16. For objective items, should guessing instructions be given? Should a correction for guessing be applied?
17. How are the test scores to be tabulated?
18. How are scores (grades, or level of competency) to be assigned?
19. How are the test results to be reported?

Source: William A. Mehrens and Irwin J. Lehmann, *Measurement and Evaluation in Education and Psychology*, 3rd ed. (New York: Holt, Rinehart and Winston, 1984), p. 64.

grouping and placement, (5) to guide changes in their teaching approach, and (6) to evaluate students on their performance.[23]

Differences Between Short-Answer and Essay Tests

Most classroom tests fall into two categories: *short-answer tests* (multiple choice, matching, completion, and true-false), sometimes called *objective tests*, and *essay* (or *discussion*) *tests*, sometimes called *free-response tests*. **Short-answer tests** require the student to supply a specific and brief answer, usually one or two words; essay tests require the student to organize and express an answer in his or her own words and do not restrict the student to a list of responses.

An **essay test** usually consists of a few questions, each requiring a lengthy answer. A short-answer test consists of many questions, each taking little time to answer. Content sampling and reliability are likely to be superior in short-answer tests. Essay tests provide an opportunity for high-level thinking, including analysis, synthesis, and evaluation. Most short-answer items emphasize low-level thinking or memorization, not advanced cognitive operations. See Tips for Teachers 3.2.

The quality (reliability, validity, usability) of an objective test depends primarily on the skill of the test constructor, whereas the quality of the essay test depends mainly on the skill of the person grading the test. Short-answer tests take longer to prepare, but are easier to grade. Essay tests may be easier to prepare, but are difficult to grade. Short-answer items tend to be explicit, with only one correct answer. Essays permit the student to be individualistic and subjective; the answer is open to interpretation, and there is more than one right answer. Short-answer tests are susceptible to guessing and cheating; essay tests are susceptible to bluffing (writing "around" the answer).[24] Table 3.4 provides an overview of some reasons for selecting short-answer and essay tests. The relative advantages of the two types of tests are suggested by the characteristics noted in the table.

According to Mehrens and Lehmann, there are six factors to consider in choosing between short-answer and essay tests.

1. *Purpose of the test.* If you want to measure written expression or critical thinking, then use an essay. If you want to measure broad knowledge of the subject or results of learning, then use short-answer items.
2. *Time.* The time saved in preparing an essay test is often used up in grading the responses. If you are rushed before the test and have suf-

---

[23]D. W. Dorr-Bremme, "Assessing Students: Teacher's Routine Practice and Reasoning," paper presented at the annual meeting of the American Educational Research Association, New York, March 1982.

[24]Ebel, *Essentials of Educational Measurement*; R. L. Linn, ed., *Educational Measurement*, 3rd ed. (New York: Macmillan, 1989); and Anthony Nitko, *Educational Tests and Measurements* (San Diego, Calif.: Harcourt Brace Jovanovich, 1983).

Table 3.4   ADVANTAGES OF AND REASONS FOR SELECTING SHORT-ANSWER
AND ESSAY TESTS

	Relative advantage of test	
	Short answer: multiple choice, matching, completion, true-false	Essay (or discussion)
1. Provides good item pool	+	
2. Adequately samples objectives and broad content	+	
3. Independent of writing ability (quality of handwriting, spelling) and verbal fluency	+	
4. Discourages bluffing by writing or talking "around the topic"	+	
5. Easy and quick to score	+	
6. Reliable for scoring and grading	+	
7. Calls for higher levels of cognitive thinking		+
8. Measures student's ability to select and organize ideas		+
9. Easy and quick to prepare		+
10. Useful to test writing ability		+
11. Eliminates guessing or answering by process of elimination		+
12. Useful for measuring problem-thinking skills and originality		+

Source: Adapted from Robert L. Thorndike and Elizabeth Hagen, *Measurement and Evaluation in Psychology and Education,* 3rd ed. (New York: Wiley, 1969), p. 71. (Additional items added by author.)

ficient time after it, you might choose an essay examination. If you must process the results in two or three days, you should use short-answer items—provided you have sufficient time to write good questions.

3. *Numbers tested.* If there are only a few students, the essay test is practical. If the class is large or if you have several different classes, short-answer tests are recommended.

4. *Facilities.* If typing and reproduction facilities are limited, the teacher may be forced to rely on essay tests. Completion and true-false questions can be administered by reading the question aloud, but it is best that all short-answer tests be typed, reproduced, and put in front of students to respond to at their own pace.

5. *Age of students.* Not until about the fifth or sixth grade should students be required to answer essay questions. Older students (sixth grade and above) can deal with a variety of types of short-answer items, but younger students are confused by changing item formats and accompanying directions.

6. *Teacher's skill.* Some types of items (true-false) are easier to write than others, and teachers tend to prefer one type over another. However, different types should be included. Test writing is a skill that can be improved with practice.[25] See Tips for Teachers 3.2.

SHORT-ANSWER TESTS

Short-answer items include multiple-choice, matching, and completion, and true-false. Regardless of the type of objective test, the writing of the test questions or items by the teacher generally involves finding the most appropriate manner in which to pose problems to students. The test questions or items often involve the recall of information, exemplified by knowledge of facts, terms, names, or rules, but they can also involve higher-order cognitive abilities. (Multiple choice items are easier to devise for testing advanced cognitive abilities; the other short-answer types are more difficult.) A number of suggestions should be considered when preparing and writing short-answer tests.

1. The test items should measure all the important objectives and outcomes of instruction.
2. The test items should reflect the approximate emphasis given the various objectives and content of the subject or course. They should not focus on esoteric or unimportant content and should not overemphasize one aspect of instruction.
3. The test items should be clearly phrased so that a knowledgeable person will not be confused or respond to a wrong choice. The test items should not contain clues that might enable an uninformed person to answer correctly.
4. Trick or trivia test items should be avoided since they may penalize students who know the material and benefit students who rely on guessing or chance.
5. Every test item should separate students who know the material from those who do not.
6. Test items should not be included just to add length to the test or be used if most students will answer them correctly (too easy) or incorrectly (too difficult).
7. Test items should not be interrelated. Knowing the answer to one item should not furnish the answer to another.
8. Test items should be grammatically correct.
9. Test items should be appropriate to the students' age level, reading level, and cognitive and developmental levels.
10. Test items should not be racially, ethnically, or sexually biased.

---

[25] Mehrens and Lehmann, *Measurement and Evaluation in Education and Psychology.* (The fifth point is mainly based on the author's ideas about testing students at various ages.)

11. Test items should have a definitely correct answer, that is, an answer that all experts (other teachers) can agree on.
12. The number of test items should be appropriate to the abilities of the student group as well as to the time available for testing; low-achieving students should have fewer test items or more time to answer than high-achieving students.
13. The test should consider the physical conditions under which the test is administered—heat, ventilation, lighting, noise, and other physical conditions.
14. Tests should not be the only basis for evaluating the students' classroom performance or for deriving a grade for a subject.

In order to write an appropriate test the teacher must obviously know the course content (specific knowledge, skills, concepts, common misconceptions, difficult areas, etc.). But knowledge of content is not enough. The teacher must be able to translate the objectives of the course into test items that will distinguish between students who know the material and who do not, and that will measure qualitative differences (preferably in higher-order thinking) related to the course as well as knowledge.

Multiple-Choice Questions

These are the most popular objective test items, especially at the secondary level, and some students think they are fun to answer because they see the task almost as a puzzle, putting pieces together: doing easy pieces first and saving the hard pieces for last. The basic form of the **multiple-choice** item is a *stem* or *lead*, which defines the problem, to be completed by one of a number of alternatives or choices. There should be only one correct response, and the other alternatives should be plausible but incorrect. For this reason the incorrect alternatives are sometimes referred to as "distractors." In most cases four or five alternatives are given.

The idea in writing the question is to have the knowledgeable student choose the correct answer and not be distracted by the other alternatives; the other alternatives serve to distract the less knowledgeable student. The effect of guessing is reduced, but not totally eliminated, by increasing the number of alternatives. In a 25-item four-alternative multiple-choice test, the probability of obtaining a score of at least 70 percent by chance alone is 1 in 1,000. To achieve a similar freedom from the effect of guessing in a true-false test requires 200 items.[26]

The use of plausible distractors helps the teacher to control the difficulty of the test. They should not be tricky or trivial. The major limitation of the multiple-choice format is that the distractors are often difficult to construct, particularly as the number of choices increases to five.[27] Unless the teacher

[26] Allen E. Edwards, *Experimental Design in Psychological Research*, 5th ed. (New York: Harper & Row, 1985); David A. Payne, *The Assessment of Learning* (Lexington, Mass.: D.C. Heath, 1974).

[27] Gronlund, *Construction of Achievement Tests*; Linn, *Educational Measurement*.

knows the content of the course well, he or she is usually limited in the number of good multiple-choice test items that can be constructed.

Following are three examples of multiple-choice questions. The first tests simple knowledge, the second the application of a formula, and the third the application of a concept.

1. Henry Kissinger is a well-known (a) corporate lawyer, (b) avante-garde playwright, (c) surrealistic artist, (d) international statesman, (e) pop musician.

2. What temperature, in degrees Fahrenheit, is equivalent to 10° Centigrade? (a) 0°F (b) 32°F (c) 50°F (d) 72°F (e) 100°F

3. Based on the map provided, which product is most likely to be exported from Bango (a fictitious country for which longitude, latitude, and topography are shown)? (a) fish (b) oranges (c) pine lumber (d) corn.

Guidelines for Writing Multiple-Choice Questions

Below are some suggestions for writing multiple-choice questions.

1. The central issue or problem should be stated in the stem. It should be a singular statement, topic, or problem.
2. In the stem a direct question is preferable to an incomplete statement. A direct question will result in less vagueness and ambiguity, especially among inexperienced test writers.
3. Include in the stem any words that might otherwise be repeated in the alternative responses. This reduces wordiness in the alternatives and increases clarity in the stem.
4. Negative statements in the stem and alternatives should be avoided, since they lead to confusion.
5. Use numbers to label stems and letters to label alternatives.
6. Avoid absolute terms ("always," "never," "none"), especially in the alternatives; a test-wise person usually avoids answers that include them.
7. Avoid using items directly from the text or workbook, since this practice encourages memorization.
8. Arrange alternatives in some logical order—for example, alphabetically or chronologically.
9. Alternatives should be parallel in content, form, length, and grammar. Avoid making the correct alternative different from wrong alternatives: longer or shorter, more precisely stated, having a part of speech others lack.
10. Correct responses should be in random order. Do not use one particular letter more often than others or create a pattern for the placement of correct responses.

11. Alternatives should be mutually exclusive. Overlapping or similar responses permit the student to eliminate two or more alternatives in one choice or result in poor discrimination of the correct alternative.

12. Alternative responses should be plausible to less knowledgeable students.

13. The answers should be objectively correct; that is, other teachers who might grade the test should agree on the correct answers.

14. The alternatives "All of the above" and "None of the above" should be used sparingly, since the test writer may fail to take into consideration all the nuances in the choices or the test taker may see other nuances.

Matching Questions

In a **matching test** there are usually two columns of items. For each item in one column, the student is required to select a correct (or matching) item in the other. The items may be names, terms, places, phrases, quotations, statements, or events. The basis for choosing must be carefully explained in the directions.

Matching questions have the advantages of covering a large amount and variety of content, being interesting to students (almost like a game), and being easy to score. Matching questions may be considered a modification of multiple-choice questions in which alternatives are listed in another column instead of in a series following a stem. The questions are easier to construct than multiple-choice questions, however, since only one response item has to be constructed for each stem. One problem with matching tests, according to test experts, is finding homogeneous test and response items that are significant in terms of objectives and learning outcomes. A test writer may start with a few good items in both columns, but may find it necessary to add insignificant or secondary information to maintain homogeneity.[28]

Another problem is that matching questions often require recall rather than comprehension and more sophisticated levels of thinking. Higher levels of cognition may be called for in matching questions that involve analogies, cause and effect, complex relationships, and theories, but such items are hard to construct.[29]

---

[28] Gronlund, *Measurement and Evaluation in Teaching;* Mehrens and Lehmann, *Measurement and Evaluation in Education and Psychology.*

[29] Benjamin S. Bloom, J. Thomas Hastings, and George F. Madaus, *Evaluation to Improve Learning* (New York: McGraw-Hill, 1981); Walter R. Borg, *Applying Educational Research: A Practical Guide for Teachers,* 2nd ed. (New York: Longman, 1987).

Below is an example of a matching exercise.

Famous American presidents are listed in column A, and descriptive phrases relating to their administration are listed in column B. Place the letter of the phrase that describes each president in the space provided. Each match is worth 1 point.

Column A: Presidents
1. George Washington
2. Thomas Jefferson
3. Abraham Lincoln
4. Woodrow Wilson
5. Franklin Roosevelt

Column B: Descriptions or Events
a. Civil War president
b. "New Deal"
c. First American president
d. Purchased Louisiana Territory
e. "New Frontier"
f. World War I president

Guidelines for Writing Matching Questions

The following suggestions may improve the construction of matching questions.

1. The directions should briefly and clearly indicate the basis for matching items in column A with items in column B.
2. An entire matching question should appear on a single page. Running the question on two pages is confusing and distracting for students.
3. Wording of items in column A should be shorter than those in column B. This permits students to scan the test question quickly once or twice.
4. Column A should contain no more than 10 test items; 5 or 6 items is probably ideal. Longer lists confuse students.
5. There should be more alternatives in column B than there are items in column A to prevent answering the last one or two items by simple elimination. Column B should contain 6 or 7 items if column A contains 5. A list of 10 items in column A should be accompanied by about 12 items in column B.
6. Column A items should be numbered, as they will be graded as individual questions, and column B items should be lettered.
7. Column B items should be presented in a logical order, say alphabetically or chronologically (but not one that gives away the answer), so the student can scan them quickly in search for correct answers.
8. Items in both columns should be similar in terms of content, form, grammar, and length. Dissimilar alternatives in column B result in irrelevant clues that can be used to eliminate items or guess answers by the test-wise student.
9. Negative statements (in either column) should be avoided, since they confuse students.
10. Many multiple-choice questions can be converted to a matching test; therefore, many of the suggestions are applicable to both.

Completion Questions

In the **completion test**, sentences are presented from which certain words have been omitted. The student is to fill in the blank to complete the meaning. This type of short-answer question, sometimes called a *fill-in* or *fill-in-the-blank* question, is suitable for measuring a wide variety of content. Although it usually tests recall of information, it can also demand thought and ability to understand relationships and make inferences. Little opportunity for guessing and for obtaining clues is provided, as with other short-answer questions. The major problem of this type of test question is that the answers are not always entirely objective, so the scoring for the teacher is time-consuming and the grading may vary subjectively with the grader. Combining multiple-choice and completion is an effective method for reducing ambiguity in test items and making scoring more objective. However, this combination does restore the opportunity for guessing.

The examples below illustrate how guessing is reduced. To answer the completion item (question 1), the student must know the capital of Illinois. To arrive at an answer to the multiple-choice question (question 2), the student may eliminate alternatives through knowledge about them or simply choose one of them as a guess.

1. The capital of Illinois is _____.
2. The capital of Illinois is (a) Utica, (b) Columbus, (c) Springfield, (d) Cedar Rapids.

Guidelines for Writing Completion Questions

General suggestions for writing completion items are listed below.

1. The direction "Fill in the blanks" is usually sufficient, but the student should be informed about how detailed the answer should be.
2. Do not use questions or statements that are copied from the textbook or workbook, since this encourages memorization.
3. Fill-in items should be clearly worded to avoid unexpected responses.
4. The completion part should be near the end of the item.
5. It is simpler and clearer to write the completion item as a question than as a statement.
6. There should only be one possible correct answer, even though students are expected to make their own response rather than choose among given responses.
7. If more than one answer is correct, equal credit should be given to each one.
8. The fill-in should be plausible to the knowledgeable student; it should not be based on trivia or trick data.

9. The correct response should not be part of a particular grammatical form, common expression, or well-known saying. An item such as "Give me liberty or give me _____" is a famous American revolutionary slogan which should be avoided.

10. Use one blank, or certainly no more than two, in any item, since more than two blanks leads to confusion and ambiguity.

11. The required completion should be a specific term (person, place, object, concept), since an item requiring a more general phrase may elicit more subjective responses and be harder to score.

12. When combining multiple-choice and completion formats, the alternative responses should be homogeneous in form, length, and grammar to avoid clues.

True-False Questions

Of all types of short-answer questions used in education, the **true-false** question is the most controversial. Advocates contend that the basis of "logical reasoning is to test the truth or falsity of propositions" and that "a student's command of a particular area of knowledge is indicated by his [or her] success in judging the truth or falsity of propositions related to it."[30] The main advantages of true-false items are their ease of construction and ease of scoring. A teacher can cover a large content area, and a large number of items can be presented in a prescribed time period. This allows the teacher to obtain a good estimate of the student's knowledge. If the items are carefully constructed, they can also be used to test understanding of principles.

Critics assert that true-false items have almost no value, since they encourage, and even reward, guessing, and measure memorization rather than understanding. Others note that true-false questions tend to elicit the response set of acquiescence, that is, the response of people who say yes (or "true") when in doubt.[31] The disadvantages of true-false questions may outweigh their advantages unless the items are well written. Precise language that is appropriate for the students taking the test is essential so that ambiguity and reading ability do not distort test results.

Here are a few examples of ambiguous true-false questions. True or false:

1. Australia, the island continent, was discovered by Captain Cook.
2. Early in his career, Will Rogers said, "I never met a man I didn't like."[32]
3. A body immersed in a fluid is buoyed up by a force equal to half the weight of the fluid displaced.[33]

---

[30]Ebel, *Essentials of Educational Measurement*, pp. 164–165.

[31]Gage and Berliner, *Educational Psychology*.

[32]Bruce W. Tuckman, *Measuring Educational Outcomes*, 2nd ed. (San Diego: Harcourt, Brace, Jovanovich, 1985).

[33]Ebel, *Essentials of Educational Measurement*.

In question 1 two statements are made, and it is unclear whether the student is to respond to both or only one; moreover, the meaning of *island* and *continent* is also being tested. In question 2 is the student being asked whether Rogers made the statement early or late in his career or whether this is the exact statement? A test-wise person might say false, because there are two ways of being wrong in this question, but the person would be wrong in this case. Question 3 tests knowledge of Archimedes' principle, not understanding of the principle. The principle states that the force is not half, but equal to, the weight. A test-wise student should know the correct answer is false.

Guessing is the biggest disadvantage to true-false tests. When students guess, they have a fifty-fifty chance of being right. Clues in the items and being test-wise improve these odds. The purpose of the test is to measure what students know, not how lucky or clever they are. This disadvantage can be compensated for to some extent by increasing the number of test items and by penalizing (deducting a quarter- or one-third point) for an incorrect answer. True-false items should be used sparingly for older students, who are more test-wise and able to sense clues in questions. They are more appropriate for younger students, who respond more to the content than to the format of questions.

Guidelines for Writing True-False Questions

Here are some suggestions for writing true-false items.

1. Each true-false item should test an important concept or piece of information, not just a specific date or name. The knowledge being tested should be significant.
2. True-false statements should be completely true or false, without exception.
3. The intended correct answer should be clear only to a knowledgeable person. The true-false item should not test general knowledge or experience, and its answer should not be given away by unintentional clues.
4. Avoid specific determiners and absolute statements ("never," "only," "none," "always"), since they are unintentional clues. Most important, do not use them in statements you want to be considered true.
5. Avoid qualifying statements and words that involve judgment and interpretation ("few," "most," "usually"). Most important, do not use them in statements you want to be considered false.
6. Avoid negative statements and double negatives, since they confuse students and may cause knowledgeable students to give the wrong answer.

7. Avoid verbatim textbook and workbook statements, since use of such statements promotes memorization.
8. Use the same form and length for true and false statements. For example, do not make true statements consistently longer than false statements; test-wise students will recognize a pattern.
9. Present a similar number of true and false items.
10. Use simple grammatical structure. Avoid dependent clauses and compound sentences, since they may distract the student from the central idea. There is also a tendency for the knowledgable student to see a more complex item as a trick question or to read more into the meaning than is intended.
11. Be clear and concise. Avoid unfamiliar language and wordiness since they confuse the student and test reading comprehension rather than knowledge.
12. Place the idea being tested at the end of the statement. Most students focus more attention on the last portion of the item; thus the teacher's intent and student's attention will coincide.

Overview of Short-Answer Questions

The different types of short-answer tests all have advantages and disadvantages, and some teachers will eventually prefer certain types and avoid others. Although each has features that make it useful for specific testing situations, the different types can be used together to add variety for the test taker and to test different types and levels of knowledge.

Multiple-choice questions are the most difficult and time-consuming items to construct. However, they can be used more readily to test higher levels of learning than other short-test items. Matching questions are also difficult and time-consuming to write, but they are interesting for students and can be used for variety. Completion questions are open to subjective interpretation and scoring, but they can be used also to test higher levels of learning. True-false questions tend to focus on trivia, but they are easy to construct and score. See Tips for Teachers 3.3.

ESSAY QUESTIONS

Short-answer questions, no matter how well formulated, cannot measure divergent thinking, subjective or imaginative thought. To learn how a student thinks, attacks a problem, writes, and utilizes cognitive resources, something beyond the short-answer test is needed. Essay questions, especially where there is no specific right answer, produce evaluation data of considerable value.

Authorities disagree on how structured and specific essay questions should be. For example, some authorities advocate using words such as "why," "how," and "what consequences." They claim questions worded in this way (which we call type 1 essay questions) call for a command of essential knowledge and

Tips for Teachers 3.3

When To Use Short-Answer and Essay Tests

The tips below provide the reader with a brief overview of when to use what type of test—short answer or essay. It is best, perhaps, to maintain a balance between both types of tests, since some students do better on one type than the other.

Use short-answer tests in the measurement of educational achievement when:

1. The group to be tested is large, or the test may be reused.
2. Highly reliable test scores must be obtained as efficiently as possible.
3. Impartiality of evaluation, absolute fairness, and freedom from halo effects are essential.
4. The teacher is more confident of his or her ability to express objective test items clearly than of his or her ability to judge essay test answers correctly.
5. There is more pressure for speedy reporting of scores than for speedy test preparation.

Use essay tests in the measurement of educational achievement when:

1. The group to be tested is small, and the test should not be reused.
2. The teacher wishes to do all possible to encourage and reward the development of student skill in written expression.
3. The teacher is more interested in exploring the student's attitudes than in measuring his or her achievements.
4. The teacher is more confident of his or her proficiency as a critical reader than as an imaginative writer of good objective test items.
5. Time available for test preparation is shorter than the time available for test grading.

Use either short-answer or essay tests to:

1. Measure almost any important educational achievement a written test can measure.
2. Test understanding and ability to apply principles.
3. Test ability to think critically.
4. Test ability to solve novel problems.
5. Test ability to select relevant facts and principles, to integrate them toward the solution of complex problems.
6. Encourage students to study for command of knowledge.

Source: Robert L. Ebel, *Essentials of Educational Measurement,* 2nd ed. (Englewood Cliffs, N.J.: Prentice-Hall, 1972), p. 144.

concepts and require students to integrate the subject matter, analyze data, make inferences, and show cause-effect relations.[34] Other test specialists urge words such as "discuss," "examine," and "explain," claiming that this wording (type 2 essay questions) gives the student less latitude in responding, but provides an opportunity to learn how the student thinks.[35] Although more restricted than the first type, this type of question may still lead to tangential responses by some students. It is useful when the object is to see how well the student can select, reject, and organize data from several sources. Other test specialists advocate more structure or precision through the use of words such as "identify," "compare," and "contrast."[36] We call these type 3 questions. They feel that in addition to giving more direction to the student, such wording demands that the student select and organize specific data. Thought processes elicited by different essay questions are listed in Table 3.5.

In effect, we are talking about the degree of freedom permitted the student in organizing a response to a question. All types have their disadvantages. The first two types of essay questions allow an "extended response"; they can lead to disjointed, irrelevant, superficial, or unexpected discussions by students who have difficulty organizing their thoughts on paper. The third type of essay question suggests a "focused response"; it can lead to simple recall of information and a mass of details.

Essay questions can be used effectively for determining how well a student can analyze, synthesize, evaluate, think logically, solve problems, and hypothesize. They can also show how well he or she can organize thoughts, support a point of view, and create ideas, methods, and solutions. The complexity of the questions, and the complexity of thinking expected of the student, can be adjusted to correspond to students' age, abilities, and experience. Another advantage is the ease and short time involved in constructing an essay question. The major disadvantages of essay questions are the considerable time to read and evaluate answers and the subjectivity of scoring. (The length and complexity of the answer, as well as the standards for responding, can lead to reliability problems in scoring.)

Some studies report that independent grading of the same essay by several teachers results in appraisals ranging from excellent to failing. This variation illustrates a wide range in criteria for evaluation among teachers. Even worse,

---

[34]Phyllis C. Blumenfeld and Judith L. Meece, "Task Factors, Teacher Behavior, and Students' Involvement and Use of Learning Strategies in Science," *Elementary School Journal*, January 1988, pp. 235–250; Thomas P. Carpenter and Penelope L. Peterson, "Learning Through Instruction," *Educational Psychologist*, Spring 1988, pp. 79–86; and Allan C. Ornstein, "Questioning: The Essence of Good Teaching," *National Association of Secondary School Principals*, February 1988, pp. 72–80.

[35]Gage and Berliner, *Educational Psychology*; John R. Hayes and Linda S. Flower, "Writing Research and the Writer," *American Psychologist*, October 1986, pp. 1106–1113; and Bruce W. Tuckman, *Testing for Teachers*, 2nd ed. (San Diego: Harcourt Brace Jovanovich, 1988).

[36]Gronlund, *Measurement and Evaluation in Teaching*; Tuckman, *Measuring Educational Outcomes*; and Walsh, *Tests and Measurements*.

Table 3.5   SAMPLE THOUGHT QUESTIONS AND COGNITIVE LEVELS OF THINKING

1. Comparing
   Describe the similarities and differences between . . .
   Compare the following two methods for . . .
2. Relating cause and effect
   What are the major causes of . . . ?
   What would be the most likely effects of . . .
3. Justifying
   Which of the following alternatives would you favor, and why?
   Explain why you agree or disagree with the following statement.
4. Summarizing
   State the main points included in . . .
   Briefly summarize the contents of . . .
5. Generalizing
   Formulate several valid generalizations from the following data.
   State a set of principles that can explain the following events.
6. Inferring
   In light of the facts presented, what is most likely to happen when . . . ?
   How would (Senator X) be likely to react to the following issue?
7. Classifying
   Group the following items according to . . .
   What do the following items have in common?
8. Creating
   List as many ways as you can think of for . . .
   Make up a story describing what would happen if . . .
9. Applying
   Using the principle of . . . as a guide, describe how you would solve the following problem situation.
   Describe a situation that illustrates the principle of . . .
10. Analyzing
    Describe the reasoning errors in the following paragraph.
    List and describe the main characteristics of . . .
11. Synthesizing
    Describe a plan for proving that . . .
    Write a well-organized report that shows . . .
12. Evaluating
    Describe the strengths and weaknesses of the following . . .
    Using the criteria developed in class, write an evaluation of . . .

Source: Norman E. Gronlund, *Measurement and Evaluation in Teaching*, 5th ed. (New York: Macmillan, 1985), p. 220.

one study showed that the same teacher grading the same essay at different times gave the essay significantly different grades.[37] It has also been demonstrated that teachers are influenced by such factors as penmanship, quality of

[37] Albert E. Meyers, Carolyn McConville, and William E. Coffman, "Simplex Structure in the Grading of Essay Tests," *Educational and Psychological Measurement*, Spring 1966, pp. 41–54; Ernest W. Tiegs, *Educational Diagnosis* (New York: McGraw-Hill, 1952).

composition, and spelling, even when they are supposed to grade on content alone.[38]

One way to increase the reliability of an essay test is to increase the number of questions and restrict the length of the answers. The more specific and restricted the question, the less ambiguous it is to the teacher and the less affected by interpretation or subjectivity in scoring.[39]

An entire test composed of essay questions can cover only limited content because only a few questions can be answered in a given time period. However, this limitation is balanced by the fact that in studying for an essay test high-achieving students are likely to look at the subject or course as a whole, and at the relationships of ideas, concepts, and principles.

The essay answer is affected by the student's ability to organize written responses. Many students can comprehend and deal with abstract data, but have problems writing or showing that they understand the material in an essay examination. Students may freeze and write only short responses, write in a disjointed fashion, or express only low-level knowledge. One way of helping to alleviate this problem is to discuss in detail how to write an essay question. Sadly, few teachers take the time to teach students how to write essay examinations. They often expect English teachers to perform this task, and English teachers are often so busy teaching grammar, spelling, and punctuation that they cannot approach the mechanics of essay writing.

On the other hand, there are students who write well, but haven't learned the course content. Their writing ability may conceal their lack of specific knowledge. It is important for the teacher to be able to distinguish irrelevant facts and ideas from relevant information. Even though essay questions appear to be easy to write, careful construction is necessary to test students' cognitive abilities, that is, to write valid questions. Many essay questions can be turned around by the student so that he or she merely lists facts without applying or integrating information to specific situations and without showing an understanding of concepts. "What were the causes of World War II?" can be answered by listing specific causes without integrating them. A better question would be "Assume that Winston Churchill, Franklin Roosevelt, and Adolph Hitler were invited to speak to an audience on the causes of World War II. What might each of them say? What might each select as the most important causal factors? On what points would they agree? Disagree?"

Factors to be considered in deciding whether to use essay questions are the difficulty and time involved in grading essays, the low reliability of grading, the limited sampling of content, and the validity of the essay itself versus the ease in formulating questions, the testing of advanced levels of cognition, and

---

[38] Ray Bull and Julia Stevens, "The Effects of Attractiveness of Writer and Penmanship on Essay Grades," *Journal of Occupational Psychology*, April 1979, pp. 53–59; Jon C. Marshall and Jerry M. Powers, "Writing Neatness, Composition Errors, and Essay Grades," *Journal of Educational Measurement*, Summer 1969, pp. 97–101.

[39] Howard Wainer and Henry Braun, *Test Validity* (Hillsdale, N.J.: Erlbaum, 1988); Payne, *The Assessment of Learning*.

the fostering of the integration of the subject as a whole. Many teachers take advantage of what both short-answer questions and essay questions have to offer by writing tests consisting of both, perhaps 40 to 60 percent short-answer and the remainder, essay. This balance to some extent is determined by grade level. In the upper grades there is a tendency to require students to answer more essay questions since it is believed they should have the ability to formulate acceptable answers. According to Piagetian developmental stages, students should begin to be able to handle essays (actually, short essays) at the formal operation stage, beginning at age 11.

Guidelines for Writing Essay Questions

Here are suggestions for preparing and scoring essay tests.

1. Make directions specific, indicating just what the student is to write about. Write several sentences of directions if necessary.
2. Word each question as simply and clearly as possible. Use a vocabulary consistent with the student's level. Avoid excess verbiage since it may confuse the student.
3. Prepare enough questions to cover the material of the unit or course broadly. Write questions that are germane to the course and cover its major objectives.
4. Allow sufficient time for students to answer the questions. A good rule of thumb is for the teacher to estimate how long he or she would take to answer the questions, and then multiply this time by two or three depending on the students' age and abilities. Suggest a time allotment for each question so students can pace themselves.
5. Ask questions that require considerable thought. Use essay questions to focus on organizing data, analysis, interpretation, formulating theories, rather than on reporting facts.
6. Give students a choice of questions, say, two out of three, so as not to penalize students who may know the subject as a whole, but happen to be limited in the particular area asked about.[40]
7. Determine in advance how much weight will be given to each question or part of a question. Give this information on the test, and score accordingly.

---

[40] Most authorities (for example, Ebel, Gronlund, and Payne) recommend that students answer all questions and that no choice be provided because a common set of questions tends to increase reliability in scoring while options tend to distort results. However, weighed against this advantage is the fact that being able to select an area they know well increases student morale, reduces test anxiety, and gives students a greater chance to show they can organize and interpret the subject matter.

8. Ask questions that have an answer that is generally accepted by other teachers as better than other answers.
9. Ask more than one essay question. Increasing the number of questions increases the content coverage of the test and increases the reliability of the test score. Asking only one essay question puts too much pressure on students and penalizes many who may know the material but not the answer to the specific question.
10. Provide sample questions (which will not be on the test) to students before the test so they have an idea of what to expect and how to respond.
11. Explain your scoring technique to students before the test. It should be clear to them what weight will be given to knowledge, development and organization of ideas, grammar, punctuation, spelling, penmanship, and any other factor to be considered in evaluation.
12. Be consistent in your scoring technique for all students. Try to conceal the name of the student whose answer you are grading to reduce biases that have little to do with the quality of the student's response and more to do with the "halo effect" (the tendency to grade students according to impressions of their capabilities, attitudes, or behavior).
13. Grade one question at a time, rather than one test paper at a time, to increase reliability in scoring. This technique makes it easier to compare and evaluate responses to each specific question.
14. Write comments on the test paper for the student, noting good points and explaining how answers could be improved. Do not compare a student to others when making comments.

Discussion Questions

The **discussion question,** or short essay question, is an essay question that requires a short response. The response can either be oral or written. In a test situation it is usually written and requires an answer that may range from one or two sentences to one or two paragraphs (or a page at most).

The discussion question is excellent for examining the causes of an event, for describing the advantages or disadvantages of a technique, for making comparisons, for briefly explaining concepts, and for evaluating data. Of crucial importance are the directions you give that specify the approximate detail and the approximate length expected in the response. Because of the brevity of the response, the quality of the answers depends heavily on the ability to phrase ideas, on writing skills, and on the ability to select the most relevant data.[41]

The discussion questions should coincide with the objectives of the course, and focus on the most important content. It is common for teachers, especially at the secondary level, to use a number of short discussion questions to cover

---

[41] Robert E. Slavin, *Educational Psychology: Theory into Practice*, 2nd ed. (Englewood Cliffs, N.J.: Prentice-Hall, 1988).

several important objectives and areas of content. Less important content can be covered by short-answer questions.

The advantages and disadvantages of discussion questions are similar to those of essay questions, but there are a few differences. Essays emphasize the integrative, subjective, and imaginative thought processes of students rather than their presentation of objective information. Discussion questions are more specifically focused on knowledge and short generalizations relating to a particular topic. Compared to essay questions, the discussion question takes less time to answer and to evaluate, and therefore more can be included in a test. Following are some examples of discussion questions.

1. Briefly list the reasons why the United States entered World War I.
2. Evaluate the poem below in 200 words or less.
3. Identify two ways in which the Democratic party and the Republican party differ in their attitude toward social spending.
4. Explain three ways in which you can improve breakfast eating habits.

Guidelines for Writing Discussion Questions

Here are some suggestions for writing discussion questions. Most of the suggestions for writing essay questions also apply.

1. Give clear and concise directions, indicating the length of response and amount of detail expected. "List at least three factors," "Describe the reasons," "Briefly evaluate" are more specific terms than "Discuss," "Tell about," and "Examine."
2. Ask questions that focus on important instructional objectives and course content.
3. Allow sufficient time for students to answer the questions. Estimate about three to four times longer than it takes the teacher to answer, depending on the age and abilities of the students.
4. Match questions and expected responses with the age and abilities of the students.
5. Use the same techniques and criteria for evaluating all the students' responses.

Every test, regardless of type, should be checked for errors before it is duplicated and distributed. Directions and time allotments should be clearly stated. Any errors, vagueness, or omissions should be corrected. Most important, the teachers should be clear on the reasons for using short answers, essays, or a combination. See Tips for Teacher 3.3.

With older students or high-achieving students, there should be an increasing emphasis on essay examinations because they elicit critical thinking. This does not mean, however, that short-answer tests are suitable only for

Figure 3.3 Teachers need to be clear about test instructions. (Photo © Peter Vandermark, Stock, Boston)

testing knowledge and recall. Given an appropriate command of the subject, the teacher should be able to develop short-answer questions that extend beyond knowledge and rote learning. The worth of a classroom test is based on how all the items relate to each other, integrate, and measure what has been taught by the teacher and, one hopes, learned by the students.

ADMINISTERING AND RETURNING TESTS

As early as possible in the term, it should be decided when and how often tests will be given. Teachers who consider testing important often give several short tests at short intervals of time. Those for whom testing is not so vital may give fewer tests. Teachers who prefer a mastery or competency approach to instruction generally give several criterion-reference tests for purposes of diagnosing, checking on learning progress, and individualizing instruction, as well as for grading. Those who prefer a broad, cognitive approach may rely more on standardized tests or fewer classroom tests that integrate the subject matter. Whatever their approach to testing, it is recommended that teachers announce tests well in advance. Discuss what will be covered, how it will be evaluated, and how much it will count toward a final grade.[42] Be considerate in scheduling tests. It is unwise to schedule a test on the same day as or the day before a big game, dance, or student activity, on Friday afternoon, or before a major holiday such as the Easter or Christmas vacation.

Test Routines

Both short-answer and essay tests must be administered carefully to avoid confusion. A routine should be established by the teacher for handing out the test questions and answer sheets, papers, or booklets. The answer sheets, paper, or booklets should be passed out first, for example, with the exact number for each row given to the first student in each row and then passed back along the row for distribution. Students should be instructed to fill out information required on the answer papers, such as their names and class. To avoid confusion the test should not be handed out until the answer papers have been distributed. In some cases, the answer paper can be inserted into the test so as to hand out the necessary papers in one step.

Before the test begins, be sure that students understand the directions and questions, that the test papers are clear, complete, and in proper order, and that students have any necessary supplies, such as pencil or pen, ruler, calculator, or dictionary. It is important for the teacher to have on hand extra copies of the test and extra supplies.

Establish a procedure for clarifying directions and test items during test time. Once the test begins, a student with a question should raise his or her hand without talking out loud or disturbing classmates. With young students, the teacher should go to the student's desk and both should whisper. Older students may be permitted to come to the teacher. If several students have the same question or a problem with the same item, the teacher should interrupt the students briefly to clarify it for all. This should be done sparingly to limit distractions.

To further reduce distractions or interruptions, the door to the hallway should be closed and a sign, "Testing—Do Not Disturb," should be posted on the door.

Late students will disturb the others no matter how quiet they are in picking up the test papers and getting seated. Unless they have a proper pass or excuse for being late, the teacher should not give them extra time to complete the examination. If students enter the room late for a standardized examination, they should not be permitted to take the exam since the norms are based partially on time allotments.

Pressure on students for good grades causes some to cheat. Short-answer tests are particularly vulnerable to cheating, because a student can easily see

---

[42] Robert F. Biehler and Jack Snowman, *Psychology Applied to Teaching*, 6th ed. (Boston: Houghton Mifflin, 1990).

someone else's answer by glancing at his or her paper.[43] To reduce cheating, some teachers have students sit in alternate seats if sufficient seats are available, or have students sit at a distance from each other if seats can be moved. Using two versions of the same test or dividing the test into two parts and having students in alternate rows start on different parts also helps reduce cheating. One of the best deterrents to cheating is the teacher's presence. To what extent the teacher needs to police students during the test depends on how common cheating is. Even if there is no cheating problem, a teacher should stay alert and not bury his or her head in a book while the test is being administered.

Routines should be established for collecting tests at the end of the period. Students who finish early should be reminded to review their answers. When the test period ends, the papers should be collected in an orderly fashion, for example, with papers being passed forward to the first student in each row and then collected by the teacher.

Table 3.6 indicates some things a teacher can do to improve test conditions and help students. Most of these strategies are geared to limiting confusion and interruptions before and during the test, ensuring that students know what to do, curtailing their anxieties and nervousness, and motivating them to do their best.

In this connection, a review of 562 studies, involving more than 20,000 students, shows that test anxiety strongly correlates with feelings of academic inadequacy, helplessness, and anticipation of failure. After grade 4, students who exhibit high **test anxiety** (that is, emotions and worry) wish to leave the test situation early and consistently score low on tests, thus reinforcing the original view of themselves. Performance on tests also strongly varies with students' perception of the test's difficulty, affecting average-achieving students more than other student groups.[44]

The high test anxiety/low test performance cycle is difficult to reverse. Incentives, praise, rewards, and prompt feedback all have minimal benefits, as do frequent tests, detailed test instructions, and test reviews. What works best, according to the research, is to teach students study skills and test-taking skills.[45] However, it needs to be reaffirmed that good study skills and test skills are already associated with high achievement, although one might now argue these measures are possibly modified by test anxiety.

---

[43] Jean D. Grambs and John C. Carr, *Modern Methods in Secondary Education*, 4th ed. (New York: Holt, Rinehart and Winston, 1979); Milbrey W. McLaughlin and R. Scott Pfeifer, *Teacher Evaluation: Improvement, Accountability, and Effective Learning* (New York: Teachers College Press, Columbia University, 1988)

[44] Ray Hembree, "Correlates, Causes, Effects, and Treatments of Test Anxiety," *Review of Educational Research*, Spring 1988, pp. 47–77.

[45] Ibid.

Table 3.6   TEST GIVER'S LIST OF THINGS TO DO

1. Before giving a standardized test:
   a. Order and check test materials in advance of the testing date.
   b. Be sure there are sufficient tests and answer sheets.
   c. Securely store all test materials until the testing date.
   d. Follow the testing instructions, including how to administer the test.

2. Before giving a teacher-made test:
   a. Check the questions for errors and clarity.
   b. Be sure there are sufficient tests and answer sheets.
   c. Be sure the test pages are sequenced properly.
   d. Securely store all test materials until the testing date.
   e. Announce testing date; avoid days that are before holidays or coincide with major events.

3. Be sure classroom conditions are adequate:
   a. Is there adequate workspace, desks, chairs?
   b. Is there sufficient light, heat, and ventilation?
   c. Is it a quiet location?
   d. Is there a wall clock that is visual to the students? If not, you will need your own watch to post the time or announce it at intervals.
   e. See that desks are cleared.

4. Study the test materials before the test:
   a. Are the directions clear?
   b. Are the time limits clear?
   c. Are the methods for indicating answers clear?

5. Minimize distractions and interruptions during the testing period:
   a. Decide the order in which materials are to be distributed and collected.
   b. Be sure that students have pencils or pens, and other needed supplies. Have extra pencils or pens handy for students who are unprepared.
   c. Close the hallway door.
   d. Poster a sign "Testing in Progress: Do Not Disturb."
   e. Decide what students who finish early are to do.

6. Motivate students to do their best:
   a. Explain the purpose of the test.
   b. Ask students to do their best: "I will be pleased if you try your best," for example.
   c. Reduce test anxiety: "Take it easy." "Take a deep breath." "Shake your fingers and wrist." "Relax, it's only a test."

7. Reassure students; provide positive expectations and strategies:
   a. "Some test questions are difficult. Don't worry if you can't answer all of them."
   b. "It is all right to guess. Choose the answer you think is best. Don't blindly guess."
   c. "If you don't finish, don't worry about it. Just try your best."
   d. "Don't work too fast, whereby you start making careless mistakes."
   e. "Don't work too slow, whereby you start falling behind. Work at a moderate pace."
   f. "Don't dwell on a difficult question; return to it when you finish and if there is time to do so."
   g. "Pay close attention to your work and to the time."
   h. "Good luck."

8. Follow directions and monitor time:
   a. Distribute materials according to predetermined time allotment.
   b. Read test directions, if permitted.

Table 3.6 Continued

   c. Give signal to start.

   d. Do not help students during the test, except for mechanics (i.e., providing an extra pencil or answer sheet).

   e. Stick to the time schedule, especially if you are administering a standardized test.

   f. Periodically post or announce time; provide 5- to 10-minute time announcements during last 15 or 20 minutes of test.

9. Observe significant events:

   a. Pay attention to students; monitor the test situation.

   b. Make sure students are following directions and answering in the correct place.

   c. Replace pens or pencils if needed; provide extra test booklets, sheets, or papers if needed.

   d. Note if any student displays behavior that might affect his or her test results; curtail cheating

   e. Note any major distractions or interruptions that could affect the test results. If administering a standardized test, report these problems to the administration.

10. Collect test materials:

   a. Attend to students who finish early; remind them to check answers before handing in test.

   b. Collect materials promptly and without confusion.

   c. If administering a teacher-made test, perhaps provide a few minutes extra for slow students or students who walked in late. Use good judgment.

   d. Count and check to see that all materials have been turned in.

Source: Adapted from Norman E. Gronlund, *Measurement and Evaluation of Teaching*, 5th ed. (New York: Macmillan, 1985), p. 331; Charles Hopkins and Richard Antes, *Classroom Testing* (Itasca, Ill.: Peacock, 1979), pp. 8–17; and David A. Payne, *The Assessment of Learning* (Lexington, Mass.: D. C. Heath, 1974), pp. 84–86.

Returning Tests and Feedback

Tests should be returned to students as quickly as possible. As the papers are returned the teacher should make some general comments to the class about awareness of the group effort, level of achievement, and general problems or specific areas of the test that gave students trouble.

Each question on the test should be discussed in class; questions that many students missed should be gone over in detail. If the missed test items are fundamental for mastery, then the teacher should take extra time to explain the material and provide similar but different exercises for students to review.[46] Some teachers call on volunteers to redo and explain parts of the test that were missed, although this method may not always be the most profitable use of time.

For students who have achieved a good grade, especially an unexpectedly good grade, the teacher should provide approval. Students who have performed poorly should be given special help in the form of extra reading, selective

---

[46] Neville Bennett and Charles Desforges, "Matching Classroom Tasks to Students' Attainments," *Elementary School Journal*, January 1988, pp. 207–220; Grambs and Carr, *Modern Methods in Secondary Education*.

Professional Viewpoint

Rules of Thumb for Taking a Test

Once upon a time, when I was a student, I was a good test taker. While all my friends were busy being overcome by test anxiety and forgetting everything they had crammed into their heads the night before, I was being focused and super "cool" and looking for any advantage I could get. I figured that all was fair in love, war, and taking a test. I had studied hard, outlined all my notes and all the chapters that would be covered, and tried to figure out what the teacher thought was important enough to ask about on the test. But I also had some ideas about what kinds of *clues* to look for on the test itself. Back then I was working on intuition, but today, as a person who teaches teachers how to build tests, I have tried to specify what all those clues I used to use were so that the teachers I taught wouldn't inadvertently provide them for their students.

Since we don't want to reward test-taking skills as a substitute for acquiring knowledge through hard work such as coming to class and studying, these are the clues that students should *not* be given in the tests that you build.

1. Do not include any obviously wrong answer choices. If you do, students can just cross them out and thereby reduce their odds of guessing the correct answer.
2. Do not write one item that actually contains the answer to another item on the same test. If you do, clever students will skim over the whole test, find the items that overlap, and then use one to answer the other.
3. Do not make the right answer choice longer, more complex, or in any way visibly different from the wrong answer choices or else the wise test taker, when in doubt, will always choose the "meatier" choice and invariably be right.
4. Do not follow a pattern in choosing what choice, a, b, c, d, or e, will be the correct choice. Pick letters out of a hat or use some other truly random procedure. Otherwise, when in doubt, the wily fox will choose the letter choice that has not been right for the longest time.
5. Make all the answer choices grammatically consistent with the question. Any choices that are not will be automatically disregarded by the sharp-eyed student.

Beyond these five rules of thumb, in scoring the test include a penalty for guessing (for example, test score equals number right minus ¼ number wrong) if you do not want students to benefit unduly from guessing. In

continued

addition, while giving the test be wary of students who ask a lot of questions about the items that require you to give them explanations. You may be giving away the right answer without knowing it.

If you want to try to help your students, tell them to skip items they cannot answer and come back to them, to guess at answers they do not know (if there is no penalty for guessing), and to try to answer each question before they look at the answer choices. And wish them EFFORT rather than luck.

> Bruce W. Tuckman
> Professor of Educational Research
> Florida State University

homework, or tutoring. In some cases, teachers will retest them after they have restudied the material. The teacher should meet with students who have questions about their grades after class privately, or possibly in a small group if several students have the same question. Regardless of the type of test, the teacher should make some comments about the individual student's answers and progress, with more personal comments directed at younger children. Personal comments, so long as they are objective and positive, help motivate students and make them aware that they need to improve in specific areas.

THEORY INTO PRACTICE

Conditions other than students' knowledge can affect their performance on tests. One such factor is their general test-taking ability, completely apart from the subject matter of particular tests. Test-taking skills are important for all students. Almost any student who has taken a few tests and who has common sense can learn certain skills that will improve his or her scores. Developing good test strategies should not be construed as amoral or dishonest. Rather it is a way of reducing anxiety in test situations. A number of test authorities contend that all students should be given training in test-wiseness.[47]

Table 3.7 lists important test skills that can be taught to students. When students are given practice in diagnosing test questions and in strategies involved in taking tests, their test scores usually improve (although researchers differ as to the size of the effect).[48]

---

[47]Ebel, *Essentials of Educational Measurement;* Randolph E. Sarnacki, "An Examination of Test-Wiseness in the Cognitive Test Domain," *Review of Educational Research,* Spring 1979, pp. 252–279.

[48]Henry S. Dyer, "The Effects of Coaching for Scholastic Aptitude," *National Association of Secondary School Principals,* February 1987, pp. 46–53; Samuel Messick, "Issue and Equity in the Coaching Controversy: Implications for Educational Testing and Practice," *Educational Psychologist,* Summer 1982, pp. 67–91.

Table 3.7   TEST-WISE STRATEGIES

1. Determine the basis of how the responses will be scored. Will points be subtracted for wrong answers, punctuations, spelling, etc.?
2. Read each test item carefully.
3. Be aware that both human scores and machine scores place a premium on neatness and legibility.
4. Establish a pace that will permit sufficient time to finish; check the time periodically to see if the pace is being maintained.
5. Bypass difficult test questions or problems; return to them at the end of the test.
6. If credit is given only for the number of right answers, or if correction for guessing is less severe than a wrong response (i.e., $-\frac{1}{2}$ for a wrong response and $+1$ for a correct response), it is appropriate to guess.
7. Eliminate items known to be incorrect on matching or multiple choice questions before guessing.
8. Make use of relevant content information on other test items and options.
9. Consider the intent of the test constructor; answer the item as the test constructor intended; consider the level of sophistication of the test and audience for which the test is intended.
10. Recognize idiosyncracies of the test constructor that distinguish correct and incorrect options; for example, correct (or incorrect options; (a) are longer or shorter, (b) are more general or specific, (c) are placed in certain logical positions within each set of options, (d) include or exclude one pair of diametrically opposed statements, and (e) are grammatically inconsistent or consistent with the stem.
11. Check to be sure the item number and answer number match, especially when using an answer sheet.
12. Reflect on and outline an essay before starting to write; decide how much time you can afford to write given the available time. In all cases, attempt an answer, no matter how poor, to gain some points.
13. Write short paragraphs for an essay; develop one idea or concept around each paragraph to make it easier for the reader (teacher) to discern. Include several short paragraphs as opposed to a few long paragraphs that tend to blend or fuse distinct ideas.
14. If time permits, return to omitted items, if any; then check answers and correct careless mistakes.

Source: Adapted from Robert L. Ebel, *Essentials of Educational Measurement*, 2nd ed. (Englewood Cliffs, N.J.: Prentice-Hall, 1972), pp. 234–235; Norman E. Gronlund, *Measurement and Evaluation in Teaching*, 5th ed. (New York: Macmillan, 1985), p. 291; and Jason Millman and Walter Pauk, *How to Take Tests* (New York: McGraw-Hill, 1969), p. 176. Additional items included by author.

In addition to the strategies listed in the table, it is important to tell students that consistent studying or review over the course is more effective than cramming. Advise them to get a good night's sleep before the test. There is nothing wrong in telling students to chew gum or to nibble on candy (as long as they don't wrinkle papers or make a mess) if it will reduce their anxiety. Remind them to wear a watch if there is no clock in the room to help pace themselves and to come prepared with more than one pen or pencil.

Professional Viewpoint

Testing What We Intend To Teach

Too often, testing never gets beyond seeing what a student can remember from reading, discussions, and/or class activities. And yet, the course goals and lesson objectives seldom begin with the verbs "remember" or "recall." It is reasonable, then, to expect skills and competencies in quizzes and examinations that coincide with the verb forms in the statement of goals and objectives.

Some who are intimately involved with competency-based and/or behavioral learning strategies are guilty of defining the competencies or behaviors for mastery as lists that can be transferred to test items that require recognition of definitions in multiple-choice items, a matching of terms with definitions, or a short answer item requiring a straightforward definition or elaboration. Such recall does not assure learning and often negates the value of identifying goals and objectives for the classroom.

Effective teachers use their goals to select a curriculum that is a vehicle for meeting those goals, instructional strategies to drive the vehicle, and skills in testing that match the actions used in the goal statements. Too many of us espouse general goals, proceed with telling students information that we know, and evaluate student retention of this information. Such is a common temptation for many beginning teachers. However, as we mature and have time to ponder what our testing actions do, we are humbled as we note the mismatch between what we purport to be our goals and the measures we select or create to assess student success.

Robert E. Yager
Professor of Science Education
University of Iowa

In addition to these items, the attitude of the test administrator is important. Consider these questions raised by Jerome Sattler:

1. Did you prepare the students for the test?
2. Were you friendly, sympathetic, and interested during the test?
3. Did you avoid any distracting mannerisms and speech?
4. Was your appearance appropriate?
5. Were you fair or nonbiased?
6. Were you at ease?
7. Did you put your students at ease?[49]

---

[49]Jerome M. Sattler, *Assessment of Children's Intelligence and Special Abilities,* 2nd ed. (Boston: Allyn and Bacon, 1982).

Your answer should be "yes" for each question. Whenever your answer is "no" or "unsure," you should work to improve your behavior in test situations.

SUMMARY

1. A good test is reliable and valid. Methods for establishing reliability are test-retest, parallel test forms, and split-half reliability. Forms of validity are content, curricular, construct, criterion, and predictive.

2. There are two major types of tests: norm-reference and criterion-reference. Norm-reference tests measure how a student performs relative to other students. Criterion-reference tests measure a student's progress and appraise his or her ability relative to a specific criterion.

3. For general appraisal of an individual's performance or behavior, the standardized (norm-reference) test is an excellent instrument. There are four basic types of standardized tests: intelligence, achievement, aptitude, and personality.

4. Teacher-made tests may be short-answer tests or essay tests. Short-answer questions include multiple-choice, matching, completion, and true-false. Essay, or free-response, questions also include discussion questions.

5. Proper test administration reduces confusion, curtails students' anxieties, and motivates and helps them to do as well as possible.

6. Important test-taking skills can be taught to students.

QUESTIONS TO CONSIDER

1. What are the most important factors to consider in choosing a test?
2. What are the advantages and disadvantages of a norm-reference test?
3. What are the advantages and disadvantages of a criterion-reference test?
4. What are the advantages of teacher-made tests over standardized tests? What are the advantages of standardized tests over teacher-made tests?
5. What strategies or principles should be considered in administering a test?

THINGS TO DO

1. Explain the differences between reliability, validity, and usability.
2. Visit a school and talk to a few teachers, the school counselor, or one of the administrators about the standardized tests the school uses. Try to find out which ones are used, and why. What are the advantages and disadvantages of the tests? Report back to the class.
3. Discuss in class five guidelines for constructing multiple-choice questions and five guidelines for constructing matching questions.
4. Develop five essay questions (in the subject you plan to teach or are

teaching) that test critical thinking. Indicate in class what type of thinking these questions test.

5. Invite a test specialist to class to discuss strategies that students can learn to increase their test-wiseness.

RECOMMENDED READINGS

Gronlund, Norman E. *Measurement and Evaluation in Teaching*, 5th ed. New York: Macmillan, 1985. Several suggestions for constructing various types of tests, including short-answer and essay tests.

Lehman, Irwin J. *Standards for Educational and Psychological Testing*, 2nd ed. Washington, D.C.: American Psychological Association, 1985. Testing standards and procedures adopted by the number-one psychological association.

Linn, Robert L., ed. *Educational Measurement*, 3rd ed. New York: Macmillan, 1989. An up-to-date treatment of measurement theory with emphasis on test reliability and validity.

Mehrens, William A., and Irwin J. Lehmann. *Measurement and Evaluation in Education and Psychology*, 3rd ed. New York: Holt, Rinehart and Winston, 1984. A major text dealing with the basic principles involved in constructing, selecting, administering, and interpreting tests.

Popham, W. James. *Modern Educational Measurement*, 2nd ed. Englewood Cliffs, N.J.: Prentice-Hall, 1990. Describes the differences between norm-reference and criterion-reference tests and their application.

Tuckman, Bruce W. *Testing for Teachers*, 2nd ed. San Diego: Harcourt Brace Jovanovich, 1988. A brief text on testing, written for the practitioner, that puts measurement and evaluation in perspective.

Worthington, Blaine R., Walter R. Borg, and Karl R. White. *Measurement and Evaluation in the Schools*. New York: Longman, 1988. Describes the difference between measurement and evaluation, and how they should be used by teachers and school administrators. Important concepts and issues dealing with testing and evaluation of students and teachers.

KEY TERMS

Reliability	Aptitude test
Validity	Personality test
Usability	Short-answer test
Standardized test	Essay test
Nonstandardized test	Multiple-choice test
Teacher-made test	Matching test
Norm-reference test	Completion test
Criterion-reference test	True-false test
Intelligence test	Discussion test
Achievement test	Test anxiety

Chapter
4

Evaluating
Students

FOCUSING QUESTIONS

1. Why should students be evaluated?

2. What is the difference between placement evaluation and diagnostic evaluation? Formative and summative evaluation?

3. What methods other than tests are available for evaluating students?

4. What are the advantages and disadvantages of absolute grade standards and relative grade standards?

5. When is it appropriate to grade students on the basis of contracts, mastery learning, and effort?

6. Why is it important to communicate with parents about their children's work and progress? How might communication with parents be improved?

7. How might the grading system in schools be changed to reduce student anxiety and student competition?

*T*esting of students is more objective than evaluation, since it is based on quantifiable data. Evaluation is more subjective, since it involves human judgment. We make evaluations of people and their performance not only in school, but also on the job and at home. Similarly, we make evaluations of consumer goods (food, clothing, cameras, televisions) and services (auto repair, insurance, medical treatment, legal advice). We use various kinds of information, including test data and other objective measurements. We weigh our information against various criteria and make an evaluation about people or products. As teachers, we strive to reduce the chance for misjudgment in the evaluation of students by carefully designing evaluation procedures.

REASONS FOR EVALUATION

According to Robert Slavin, there are basically five purposes for evaluating students.

1. *Motivation of students.* Evaluations, if properly conducted and presented to students, can motivate them. For example, high grades, gold stars, certificates of achievement, and prizes that are used as rewards for good work can stimulate further good work.
2. *Feedback to students.* Students need to know the results of their efforts. Regular evaluation can reveal strengths and weaknesses, and the teacher should relay this information to the students with recommendations for improvement. Explanations of grades and examination of performance are more helpful for students' learning than grades without explanations.
3. *Feedback to teachers.* Evaluation provides information to teachers on the effectiveness of their instruction, how well the students have learned the material, and to what extent they are improving. Evaluation data (student records and teacher evaluations) also provide information to other teachers who instruct the students in other classes or later grades.
4. *Information to parents.* School evaluations of many kinds—test papers, certificates, prizes, letters, report cards—provide information to parents. Evaluations should be sent to parents regularly, and parents should be instructed in home-based reinforcement and follow-up procedures.
5. *Information for selection.* Evaluations can be used to select and sort students for different types of instruction, such as homogeneous or heterogeneous grouping in classrooms and special courses or programs.[1]

---

[1] Robert E. Slavin, *Educational Psychology: Theory into Practice*, 2nd ed. (Englewood Cliffs, N.J.: Prentice-Hall, 1988).

To be of any use to students, teachers, or parents, evaluation of students must be *fair*. Students must feel that the evaluation of their performance is objective and the same for all students. If students feel that some students are evaluated more leniently or more strictly than others, the effectiveness of the evaluation will be reduced.[2]

Students must feel that their academic efforts will lead to success. The evaluation process should *motivate* them; it should encourage them to set progressively higher goals for personal achievement. If students feel the evaluation process will lead to failure, or if they feel the process is unfair, then they will be discouraged by it.

The evaluation process should also be *realistic*. Students should be able to assess their own performance in relation to classmates and normative standards. In a class where most students cannot read well, a student who is an average reader may get an inflated impression about his or her real abilities. Evaluations are more effective when students are provided with valid norms of what constitutes success.

Every student, during his or her school career, will experience the pain of failure and the joy of success as a result of the evaluation process. The student must learn, according to Philip Jackson, "to adapt to the continued and pervasive spirit of evaluation that will dominate his school year." Although school is not the only place "where the student is made aware of his strengths and weakness," school evaluation happens most frequently and has the most lasting impact.[3]

The impact of school evaluation is profound because students are forming their identities during their school years, because they are going through their most critical stages of development, and because they lack defensive mechanisms to ward off extreme or continuous negative evaluations. Whether evaluation focuses on academic work, behavior, or personal qualities, it affects the student's reputation among his or her peers, confidence in his or her abilities, and motivation in work. The student's popularity, confidence, personal adjustment, career goals, even physical and mental health are related to the judgments that others communicate to him or her throughout school. We are what we see ourselves to be, and like it or not, we see ourselves as others perceive and evaluate us. The self is a social product that emerges as the child grows and interacts with others.

TYPES OF EVALUATION

There are four basic evaluation techniques that are appropriate for and commonly used in the classroom. (1) Placement evaluation helps to determine

---

[2]Gary Natriello and Stanford M. Dombusch, *Teacher Evaluative Standards and Student Effort* (New York: Longman, 1984); Blaine R. Worthen, Walter R. Borg, and Karl R. White, *Measurement and Evaluation in the Schools* (New York: Longman, 1989).

[3]Philip W. Jackson, *Life in Classrooms* (New York: Holt, Rinehart and Winston, 1968), p. 19.

Professional Viewpoint

Reasons for Evaluation

The most important reasons to evaluate are:

1. To assure that one is doing all one can to help each student to learn.
2. To find ways to conduct group instruction as efficiently and effectively as possible.
3. To provide students and their parents with progress reports they can use to guide the learning process.
4. To certify levels of achievement.
5. To provide records and reports that will help other professionals work with individual students.

It is noteworthy that four of the five purposes denote the need for individualized evaluation and continuous assessment and feedback. While evaluation is also needed to assist the search for efficient teaching methods that work well with groups, it is crucial that the teacher become skilled in those kinds of evaluation that can lead to individual diagnoses, reinforcement, and direction for growth. Unfortunately, many of the evaluation devices for sale, especially standardized tests, and many of the evaluation designs in the literature, especially pre-test/post-test designs, have little utility to teachers for doing the types of evaluation that are most important to them and to the individual students and families they serve. Hence, teachers should not fall into a pattern of using whatever standardized measures are available but instead should become proficient in designing evaluations that produce useful information about their students, and in devising homespun instruments that will respond well to the pertinent data requirements.

Daniel L. Stufflebeam
Professor and Director, The Evaluation Center
Western Michigan University

---

student placement or categorization before instruction begins. (2) Diagnostic evaluation is a means of discovering and monitoring learning difficulties. (3) Formative evaluation monitors progress. (4) Summative evaluation measures the products of instruction at the end of instruction.

Placement Evaluation

Placement evaluation, sometimes called *preassessment*, takes place before instruction. The teacher wants to find out what knowledge and skills the students have mastered to establish a starting point of instruction. Sufficient mastery might suggest that some instructional units may be skipped or treated briefly. Insufficient mastery suggests that certain basic knowledge or skills should be emphasized. Students who are required to begin at a level that is too difficult or beyond their understanding will encounter frustration and will most likely be unable to gain new knowledge and skills. Students who are required to review old material they already know are wasting instructional time and may eventually become bored.

It is also important to find out how much a student knows and what his or her interests and work habits are in order to decide on the best type of instruction (group or independent, inductive or deductive), methods, and materials for that student.

A third reason for placement evaluation is to place students in specific learning groups. Although this procedure may lead to tracking, which is criticized by many researchers, teachers find that grouping students by knowledge and skills facilitates teaching and learning. Placement evaluation is based on readiness tests, aptitude tests, pretests on course objectives, and observational techniques.

Diagnostic Evaluation

Diagnostic evaluation attempts to discover the causes of students' learning problems. If a student continues to fail a particular subject or is unable to learn basic skills in elementary school or basic content in secondary school, diagnosis of the cause of the failure may point to ways to remedy it. According to Bruce Tuckman, "where proficiency has not been demonstrated, remedial instruction aimed directly at those [deficiencies] can be instituted." Evaluation can "provide the kind of information that will make it possible to overcome failure."[4]

In many cases diagnostic and formative evaluation (discussed below) overlap. Formative evaluation is mainly concerned with progress, but the lack of progress may indicate a problem, which should then be investigated with more specific diagnostic evaluation. According to Gronlund, formative evaluation serves as a guide to general, everyday treatment, but diagnostic evaluation is necessary for detailed, remedial treatment.[5] Diagnostic evaluation is based on teacher-made and published tests and observational techniques.

Formative Evaluation

Formative evaluation and summative evaluation are terms coined by Michael Scriven in his analysis of program and curriculum evaluation.[6] **Formative eval-**

---

[4]Bruce W. Tuckman, *Measuring Educational Outcomes*, 2nd ed. (San Diego: Harcourt Brace Jovanovich, 1985), p. 300.

[5]Norman E. Gronlund, *Measurement and Evaluation in Teaching*, 5th ed. (New York: Macmillan, 1985).

[6]Michael Scriven, "The Methodology of Evaluation," in R. W. Tyler, R. Gagné, and M. Scriven, eds., *Perspectives on Curriculum Evaluation* (Chicago: Rand McNally, 1967), pp. 39–83.

uation monitors progress during the learning process, while summative evaluation measures the final results at the end of an instructional unit or term. Benjamin Bloom and his associates describe formative evaluation as a major tool of instruction: "Too often in the past evaluation has been entirely summative in nature, taking place only at the end of the unit, chapter, course, or semester, when it is too late, at least for that particular group of students, to modify either . . . the teaching [or] learning . . . process."[7]

If evaluation is to help the teacher and student, it should take place not only at the end point of instruction, but also at various points during the teaching-learning process while modifications can be made. Instruction can be modified, based on the feedback that formative evaluation yields, to correct learning problems or to move ahead more rapidly.

Formative evaluation focuses on small, comparatively independent units of instruction and a narrow range of objectives. It is based on teacher-made and published tests administered throughout the term, homework and classroom performance of students, informal teacher observations of students, student-teacher conferences, and parent-teacher conferences.

Summative Evaluation

As the phrase implies, **summative evaluation** is an evaluation that takes place at the end of an instructional unit or course. It is designed to determine the extent to which the instructional objectives have been achieved by the students and is used primarily to certify or grade students.[8] It can also be used to judge the effectiveness of a teacher or a particular curriculum or program. Whereas formative evaluation provides a tentative judgment of teaching and learning, summative evaluation, coming when teaching and learning are over, is a final judgment.

Summative evaluation focuses on a wide range of objectives and relies on an accumulation of student work and performance. Although teacher-made tests can be used for this purpose, it is often based on formal observation scales or ratings and standardized tests.

Table 4.1 provides a summary of the four evaluation categories, which the teacher can use during the instructional process.

EVALUATION METHODS AND APPROACHES

Everyone is evaluated and makes evaluations on a daily and informal basis. Students and teachers are continuously evaluating each other in class on an informal basis. When teachers observe students at work or answer students'

---

[7]Benjamin S. Bloom, J. Thomas Hastings, and George F. Madaus, *Handbook on Formative and Summative Evaluation of Student Learning* (New York: McGraw-Hill, 1971), p. 20.

[8]Norman E. Gronlund, *How To Construct Achievements Tests*, 4th ed. (Englewood Cliffs, N.J.: Prentice-Hall, 1988); Robert F. Mager, *Making Instruction Work* (Belmont, Calif.: Fearon, 1988),

Table 4.1   TYPES OF EVALUATION

Type	Function	Illustrative instruments used
Placement	Determines skills, degree of mastery before instruction to determine appropriate level and mode of teaching	Readiness tests, aptitude tests, pre-tests, observations, interviews, personality profiles, self-reports, videotapes, anecdotal reports
Diagnostic	Determines causes (cognitive, physical, emotional, social) or serious learning problems to indicate remedial techniques	Published diagnostic tests, teacher-made diagnostic tests, observations, interviews, anecdotal reports
Formative	Determines learning progress, provides feedback to facilitate learning and to correct teaching errors	Teacher-made tests, tests from test publishers, observations, checklists
Summative	Determines end-of-course achievement for grading or certification	Teacher-made tests, rating scales, standardized tests

Source: Adapted from Peter W. Airasian and George F. Madaus, "Functional Types of Student Evaluation," *Measurement and Evaluation in Guidance*, January 1972, pp. 221–233; Norman E. Gronlund, *Measurement and Evaluation in Teaching*, 5th ed. (New York: Macmillan, 1985), p. 17.

questions, they are engaging in **informal evaluation**. When they make a decision to assign one of two alternative books for students to read, they are also engaging in informal evaluation. Evaluation, when it is thorough and precise, is usually formal. When it is impressionistic or based on hunches, it is informal.

Informal Evaluation

Testing is the most obvious method by which students are evaluated, but it is not the only one. In fact, evaluation without tests occurs on a daily basis and is considered by Philip Jackson to be more powerful and influential than tests. He asserts that students quickly come to realize "when things are right or wrong, good or bad, largely as a result of what the teacher tells them." The *teacher* "continuously makes judgments of students' work and behavior [and communicates] that judgment to the students in question and to others."[9]

A second source of daily evaluation is the judgment of *peers.* "Sometimes the class as a whole is invited to participate in the evaluation of a student's work, as when the teacher asks, 'Who can correct Billy?' or "How many believe that Shirley read the poem with a lot of expression?' " At times an obvious error evokes "laughter" or destructive criticism, while outstanding performance wins "spontaneous applause."[10] Little urging on the part of the teacher

[9]Jackson, *Life in Classrooms,* p.19.

[10]Ibid., p. 20.

is needed, although the teacher may consciously or unconsciously egg the students on.

A third source of daily evaluation is student *self-judgment*. Students appraise their own performance without the "intervention of an outside judge." This type of evaluation is more difficult to discern and describe, but it occurs throughout instruction, for example, when the student works on the chalkboard and knows that the work is correct or incorrect, although the teacher may not bother to indicate one way or another.[11]

There are many other types of evaluation, according to Jackson, which are both *private*, such as IQ and personality test scores (that always follow the student and lead to labels) or certain communications to parents or other teachers about students and *public*, such as the display of work for others to see or a teacher review for the class of someone's mistake. Evaluations in class and school never cease.

Although critics make many negative comments about the evaluation process, evaluation is still necessary. Although it can be argued that tests are not always necessary for grading, classifying, or judging students, evaluation is. Teachers need to evaluate students' performance and progress; otherwise, they are surrendering an important role in teaching. On the other hand, the evaluation process should consider the students' feelings and self-concept; it should avoid labels that lead to traps, embarrassment, and despair among students whose performance is less than average.

Evaluation Other Than Testing

Student performance and progress can be measured through a variety of formal methods other than tests, although testing is the most common source of data and should be included as part of the total evaluation. The various other methods and approaches can be used to supplement formal test data.

Observation of Student Work   The teacher has the opportunity to watch students perform various tasks on a daily basis, under various conditions, alone and with different students. The teacher sees students more or less continually simply by virtue of being in the classroom, but he or she needs to know what to look for and to have some objective system for collecting and assessing data.

Although the teacher should observe all students, individuals who exhibit atypical behavior or learning outcomes are often singled out for special study. The keys to good observation are objectivity and documentation. Teachers cannot depend on memory or vague statements, such as "Johnny misbehaves in class." They must keep accurate, specific written records.

If observations are free from bias and tempered with common sense, this

---

[11] See Mary C. Ellwein, Gene V. Glass, and Mary L. Smith, "Standards of Competence Propositions on the Nature of Testing Reforms," *Educational Researcher*, November 1988, pp. 4–9; Ray Hembree, "Correlates, Causes, Effects, and Treatment of Test Anxiety," *Review of Educational Research*, Spring 1988, pp. 47–78.

informal, nonstandardized evaluation method can provide more insightful information about a student than would test scores alone.

Group Evaluation Activities   Teachers can set aside a time to allow students to participate in establishing instructional objectives, to evaluate their strengths and limitations, and to evaluate their own progress in learning. Students can evaluate themselves or their classmates on study habits and homework, class participation, quizzes, workbook or textbook activities, and other activities. They can keep anecdotal reports or logs about their own work in which successes and difficulties are recorded and then discussed in class. They can check off assignments they complete and evaluate their work in group discussions.

Evaluation techniques such as these "make it possible for teachers . . . to diagnose [student] errors and to measure student progress. Teachers can also use these [activities] to show students how well they are getting on and what their faults and strengths are."[12]

Class Discussions and Recitations   Many teachers consider a student's participation in class discussion an essential source of data for evaluation. Teachers are impressed by students who volunteer, develop thoughts logically, and discuss relevant facts and relationships. Answering the teacher's questions frequently and carrying out assignments in class are considered to be evidence of progress. The inability to answer questions and the inability to perform assignments in class are taken to be indications of learning problems or lack of motivation.

Homework   The teacher can learn much about students' achievements and attitudes by checking homework carefully. A good rule is not to assign homework unless it is going to be checked in some way, preferably by the teacher and in some cases by another student or by the student herself. The idea is to provide prompt feedback to the student, preferably emphasizing the positive aspects of work while making one or two major recommendations for improvement. As Herbert Walberg points out, student achievement increases significantly when teachers assign homework on a regular basis, students conscientiously do it, and comments and feedback are provided when the work is completed.[13]

Notebooks and Note Taking   Notebooks should be used as an assessment tool for evaluating the writing and understanding of subject matter for students in elementary school and, to a lesser extent, in the middle grades and junior high school.

Note taking is more important for secondary school students, especially

---

[12] Leonard H. Clark and Irving S. Starr, *Secondary and Middle School Teachers' Methods*, 5th ed. (New York: Macmillan, 1986), p. 355.

[13] Herbert J. Walberg, "Homework's Powerful Effects on Learning," *Educational Leadership*, April 1985, pp. 76–79.

at the high school level. At this level students should begin to be able to take notes on some of the unwritten ideas that emerge from the classroom discussions. According to William Rohwer, good note taking consists of arranging information in a systematic form, focusing on major points of discussion, condensing material, and integrating new with old information.[14] Verbatim note taking or simple paraphrasing or listing of information are not as effective.[15]

Reports, Themes, and Research Papers   Written work serves as an excellent way to assess students' ability to organize thoughts, to research topics, to develop new ideas. In evaluating projects, the teacher should look to see how well students have developed their thoughts in terms of explanations, logic, and relationship of ideas; whether ideas are expressed clearly; whether facts are documented or distinguished from opinion; and what conclusions or recommendations are evidenced. Spelling and grammar should not be the key to evaluating students; rather, emphasis should be on the thinking process of the students, the use of reference materials, and the ability to keep to the topic and develop it logically.

Discussions and Debates   Evaluating oral work is less reliable than evaluating written samples, but oral work may reveal creative and critical thinking that cannot be measured with other methods. Louis Raths and others point out that when students freely discuss topics that are of interest to them, their thinking is based on many skills, insights, and experiences not evidenced in a one-hour written test.[16]

Free discussion in groups brings values out in the open and forces students to think about other people's values. Analysis of problems and attempts to find solutions to problems through debates, panel discussions, or buzz sessions are valuable tools for teachers to use to understand how their students think and feel.

During discussions students can be rated not only on their mastery of and ability to analyze material, but also on several social and cognitive characteristics. According to Peter Martorella, such characteristics would include the way in which the student "(1) accepts ideas of others, (2) initiates ideas, (3) gives opinions, (4) is task oriented, (5) helps others, (6) seeks information, (7) encourages others to contribute, (8) works well with all members, (9) raises provocative questions, (10) listens to others, (11) disagrees in a constructive fashion, and (12) makes an overall positive contribution to the group."[17]

---

[14] William Rohwer, "An Invitation to an Educational Psychology of Studying," *Educational Psychologist*, Winter 1984, pp. 1–14.

[15] Kenneth A. Kiewra, "Providing the Instructor's Notes: An Effective Addition to Student Note-Taking," *Educational Psychologist*, Winter 1985, 33–39.

[16] Louis E. Raths et al., *Teaching for Thinking: Theory, Strategies, and Activities for the Classroom* (New York: Teachers College Press, Columbia University, 1985). Also see Lauren B. Resnick, *Education and Learning To Think* (Washington, D.C: National Academy Press, 1987).

[17] Peter M. Martorella, *Elementary Social Studies* (Boston: Little, Brown, 1985), p. 247.

Figure 4.1 Learning how to study for exams is essential for academic achievement. (Photo © Richard S. Orton)

Quizzes

Quizzes are brief informal exams. They provide an excellent basis for checking homework and for evaluating the progress of students. Some teachers give unannounced quizzes at irregular intervals, especially quizzes related to specific assignments. Others give regular, scheduled quizzes to assess learning over a short period of time, say a week or two. Quizzes encourage students to keep up with the assignments and show them their strengths and weaknesses in learning.

Frequent and systematic monitoring of students' work and progress through short quizzes helps teachers improve instruction and learning. Errors serve as early warning signals of learning problems that then can be corrected before they worsen. According to researchers, student effort and achievement improves when teachers provide frequent evaluation and prompt feedback on quizzes.[18] Quizzes are easy to develop, administer, and grade, thus providing an avenue for multiple and prompt evaluation.

---

[18]Benjamin S. Bloom, George F. Madaus, and J. Thomas Hastings, *Evaluation to Improve Learning* (New York: McGraw-Hill, 1981); Robert Mager, *Developing Attitudes Toward Learning*, 2nd ed. (Belmont, Calif.: Fearon, 1984); *What Works: Research About Teaching and Learning* (Washington, D.C.: U.S. Government Printing Office, 1986); and Blaine R. Worthen and James R. Sanders, *Educational Evaluation: Alternative Approaches and Practical Guidelines*, 2nd ed. (New York: Longman, 1987).

GRADING

The purpose of grading is somewhat different for teachers at different grade levels. Some studies indicate that elementary school teachers tend to say they give grades because the school district requires it, not because the function of grades as a yardstick is important to them. In contrast, secondary school teachers feel grades are necessary for informing students, other teachers, and colleges about performance.[19] The same studies showed that elementary school teachers rely more on their observations of student participation in class, motivation, and attitudes than on tests. Secondary school teachers assign grades mainly on the basis of test results. On average, no more than 15 percent of the grade is based on professional judgment.

Teachers need to recognize, also, that young students (grade 4 or lower) have little understanding of the meaning of grades and that understanding of grading concepts increases with age. It is not until grade 9 that most students understand complex schemes such as a grading curve, grade point average, and weighted grading. Students below grade 6 attach less importance to grades and consider external and uncontrollable factors to be important influences on grading; older students attach more importance to grades, see them as linked to internal and controllable factors, and are aware of the reasons for grading. However, older students are more likely to be critical of grading practices and less accepting of low grades received than are younger students.[20] Such findings indicate that teachers might consider postponing formal grading until grades 5 or 6, if school policy permits, and that teachers should expect concern and even criticism among older students, especially since they increasingly see grades as important for their future.

Researchers tend to list general purposes for grading: (1) certification, or assurance that a student has mastered specific content or achieved a certain level of accomplishment; (2) selection, or identifying or grouping students for certain educational paths or programs; (3) direction, or providing information for diagnosis and planning; and (4) motivation, or emphasizing specific material or skills to be learned and helping students to understand and improve their performance.[21]

Grades often result in the same group of students being "winners" or "losers" from grade to grade. Robert Slavin puts it this way: "In the usual, competitive reward structure, the probability of one student's receiving a re-

[19] Fred Burton, *A Study of the Better Grade System and Its Effects on the Curriculum*, ERIC No. 238143, March 1983; Gary Natriello and James McPartland, *Adjustments in High School Teachers' Grading Criteria* (Baltimore: John Hopkins University Press, 1988). Also see Thomas L. Good and Jere E. Brophy, *Educational Psychology: A Realistic Approach*, 3rd ed. (New York: Longman, 1986).

[20] Ellis D. Evans and Ruth A. Engleberg, "Student Perceptions of School Grading," *Journal of Research and Development in Education*, Winter 1988, pp. 45–54.

[21] Robert L. Linn, "Testing and Instruction: Links and Distinction," *Journal of Education Measurement*, Summer 1983, 179–189; Gary Natriello, "The Impact of Evaluation Processes on Students," *Educational Psychologist*, Spring 1987, 155–175.

Professional Viewpoint

Evaluation: Where to Begin?

The great challenge for teachers is to challenge themselves and their students to extend their own thinking, to learn independently, and to take responsibility for the quality of their own work. To do this, teachers must create environments in which students are actively involved in their learning in a context that is meaningful to them. In that way, students learn to integrate the information under study; they discover meaning and relevance within the information. Given opportunities to practice learning with one another, students learn the importance of flexibility and collaboration in life.

To evaluate this learning requires more than standardized tests. It requires that teachers resist pressures to let standardized tests drive instruction in their classrooms. It requires that students create responses, rather than simply select responses. It requires that teachers create problems and contexts that require students to demonstrate the learning that has occurred. Such evaluation need not always occur within the classroom, within a class period, or within the confines of a paper and pencil format. Such evaluation should reflect the broader context within which students will live their lives and demonstrate their competence.

Evaluation begins with self-evaluation for both teachers and students. Narrow teacher appraisal instruments, just as standardized tests, are inadequate demonstrations of competence. When teachers model reflection by thinking aloud and monitoring the effectiveness of their own problem-solving strategies, students learn to do this as well. Students start to evaluate their own learning, both during and after the process. This enables them to monitor their progress and determine where and when they may need assistance. It also enables them to look objectively at their products and compare them to standards set within the class. Evaluation must focus on these key goals—thinking, independent learning, and quality of work—to prepare students for success.

Joan M. Raymond
General Superintendent
Houston Independent School District

Figure 4.2 Record keeping is an essential role of teachers, yet rarely discussed in teacher training programs. (Photo © Miriam Reinhart/ Photo Researchers)

ward (good grade) is negatively related to the probability of another student's receiving a reward."[22]

A demonstrable relationship exists between formal instruction and student performance at all grade levels, but constructing tests and grading accurately to reflect classroom tasks and intended learning are difficult for most teachers.[23] Although teachers report that they feel they are able to interpret test results and transfer test scores into grades or grade equivalents, when teachers are tested on these abilities, the majority misinterpret concepts presented to them.[24]

Assigning grades to students' school work is inherently subjective, regardless of the method used. Not only is a high degree of expertise required for being accurate in grading, there is the false assumption that teacher-made tests reflect precisely what is being taught. Teachers are required to make judgments, and few, if any, are purely objective or accurate.[25] What test items should be included and how the items should be weighted are matters of judgment. Should points be deducted for wrong answers? How many As or Bs or Fs should be awarded? Will grading be on a curve or absolute? And what about all those special cases ("I lost my notebook") and problems ("I was sick last week")? Are students to be allowed to retake an exam because the results deviate from past performance? Should extra credit assignments be used to modify grades and to what extent? If test modification, additional tests, or extra credit as-

[22]Robert E. Slavin, "Classroom Reward Structure: An Analytical and Practical Review," *Review of Educational Research*, Fall 1977, pp. 633–650. Slavin, "Cooperative Learning and Student Achievement," *Educational Leadership*, October 1988, pp. 31–34.

[23]Neville Bennett and Charles Desforges, "Matching Classroom Tasks to Students' Attainments," *Elementary School Journal*, January 1988, pp. 221–234.

[24]Herbert C. Rudman, "Classroom Instruction and Tests: What Do We Really Know about the Link?" *National Association of Secondary School Principals*, February 1987, pp. 3–22.

[25]Marv Nottingham, "Grading Practices—Watching Out for Land Mines," *National Association of Secondary School Principals*, April 1988, pp. 24–28.

signments are permitted, then teachers are forced into a more subjective role.[26] But, if a teacher fails to consider extraneous circumstances, possibly modifying the scoring results, then it can be argued that grades are being used as a weapon, certainly as a cold symbol of learning. It can also be argued that students are entitled to extra coaching and practice, but retaking exams or extra credit is unfair because it affects the grades of some, but not all, students.

Homework is another consideration. Who should grade the homework, students or teacher? Prompt scoring by students enables the teacher to decide promptly what material needs further analysis. When the teacher grades the homework, however, it increases his or her paper load, and feedback to students is delayed. But grading the homework adds to the teacher's information about the specific thinking skills and problems of the students. Moreover, researchers point out that when the teacher takes time out to write encouraging and constructive comments on the homework (or other student papers), it has positive measurable effects on achievement.[27]

Homework may be important in the learning process, but there is a question about whether it should be counted in the grading system. Some educators say no. There are similar questions about lowering grades for minor discipline problems (for example, chewing gum), not typing a paper, not doing an assignment on time, and coming to class late. A student whose behavior is unacceptable must be held accountable, but most educators are against reducing grades as a deterrent.[28] Many teachers, however, take another view, especially when classroom discipline is at stake.

There is also considerable disagreement about the value of using routine class activities, class participation, recitations, oral reading, chalkboard work, oral presentations, and even reports as part of the grade system. Although such practices broaden the base of information on student performance and also give students a chance to be evaluated on grounds other than tests, there are serious questions about the quality of information they provide.[29] For example, some students "talk a good game" and know little, while others are introverted or shy but know the material. Other educators maintain that grades should be divided into primary measures of performance (unit tests, term papers) and secondary measures (homework, quizzes). The secondary measures are con-

[26] Nottingham, "Grading Practices—Watching Out for Land Mines"; James S. Terwilliger, "Classroom Standard Setting and Grading Practices," paper presented at the annual meeting of the American Educational Research Association, New Orleans, April 1988.

[27] Gary Natriello and Edward L. McDill, "Performance Standards, Student Effort on Homework and Academic Achievement," *Sociology of Education,* January 1986, pp. 18–31; Linda G. Stewart and Mary A. White, "Teacher Comments, Letter Grades and Student Performance," *Journal of Educational Psychology,* August 1976, pp. 488–500.

[28] Natriello, "The Impact of Evaluation Processes on Students"; Nottingham, "Grading Practices —Watching Out for Land Mines."

[29] Joan Herman and Don W. Dorr-Bremme, *Testing and Assessment in American Public Schools* (Los Angeles: University of California at Los Angeles, Center for the Study of Education, 1984); Gary Natriello and Sanford M. Dornbusch, *Teacher Evaluative Standards and Student Effort* (New York: Longman, 1984).

sidered less important and are given less weight, since their purpose is to prepare students to achieve the primary learning outcomes.[30]

Combining and Weighting Data

Some researchers recommend that grades at all levels be based on exams, 50 percent; class work, 30 percent; assigned papers, 10 percent; and homework, 10 percent.[31] Another group of experienced teachers maintain that grades should be based on tests and quizzes, 60 percent; class participation, 15 percent; written and oral projects, 15 percent; and notebook and homework, 10 percent.[32] Although researchers generally agree that grading should be based on several indicators that are directly related to the instructional program, there is less agreement on what should be included, and how the indicators should be weighted, and whether indicators not directly related to instruction, such as participation, effort, neatness, and conduct, are appropriate at all.[33]

Grades based on little information, say one or two tests, are unfair to students and probably invalid. Assigning too much importance to term papers or homework is also invalid and unwise because these indicators say little about whether the students have really learned the material. Relying more heavily on test data is preferred, especially at the secondary school level, as long as there are several quizzes or examinations and the tests are weighted properly.

There are a number of problems related to combining several test scores into a single measure (or grade) for each student, including the fact that test scores may have different significance. For example, a teacher who wishes to combine scores on two separate tests might consider that each contributes 50 percent to the composite score. However, this rarely is the case, especially if one test was more difficult than the other; the composite score is a function not only of the mean but also of the standard deviation.[34]

Another question is whether scores from different sources, representing different learning outcomes and levels of difficulty, can be combined into a composite score. Although there are arguments for and against this procedure, it is acceptable as long as the composite score is based on several sources that are independent of each other. (See Tips for Teachers 4.1.)

---

[30] Robert F. Madgic, "The Point System of Grading: A Critical Appraisal," *National Association of Secondary School Principals,* April 1988, pp. 29–34.

[31] Good and Brophy, *Educational Psychology: A Realistic Approach.*

[32] Association of Teachers of Social Studies in the City of New York, *A Handbook for the Teaching of Social Studies,* 2nd ed. (Boston: Allyn and Bacon, 1985).

[33] Natriello, "The Impact of Evaluation Processes on Students"; Rudman, "Classroom Instruction and Tests: What Do We Really Know about the Link?" and Robert E. Slavin, "Separating Incentives, Feedback, and Evaluation," *Education Psychologist,* Spring 1978, 97–100.

[34] Walter R. Borg, *Applying Educational Research: A Practical Guide for Teachers,* 2nd ed. (New York: Longman, 1987); David A. Payne, *The Assessment of Learning* (Lexington, Mass.: Heath, 1974).

Tips for Teachers 4.1

Advantages and Disadvantages of Point System of Grading

Most teachers, especially from the middle grades onwards, rely on a point system of grading whereby the teacher identifies points or percentages for various tests and class activities. Some teachers even post summaries at regular intervals so students can see their point totals as the term progresses. The point system has advantages and disadvantages. Special caution is recommended with the problems associated with this system.

ADVANTAGES

1. Is fair and objective. The teacher is not apt to be swayed by subjective factors, and the need for interpretation is minimized.
2. Is quantifiable, explicit, and precise. Students and teachers know exactly what the numbers are and what they represent.
3. Minimizes conflict over what grade a student should receive.
4. Facilitates the weighting of tests and class activities. For example, teacher may choose 5 points for each quiz, 25 points for a special project, 25 points each for the midterm and final.
5. Is cumulative. The final grade can be determined by a single computation at the end of the grading period.
6. Facilitates grading by establishing clear distinctions. Once categories are weighted and points totaled, assigning the grade for each student is a straightforward task.

DISADVANTAGES

1. Emphasizes objectivity of scoring, not learning. Conveys the message that learning is equivalent to the accumulation of points, not the acquisition of skills and knowledge.
2. Presents an illusion of objectivity. Every test and assignment results from a series of subjective decisions by the teacher—what areas to cover, how to weight particular answers or aspects of performance, and so forth.
3. Reduces teacher's judgment. A point system minimizes the teacher's professional judgment and results in a somewhat inflexible grading system.
4. Hides importance of patterns. Average or total scores at any point, rather than improvement or decline, are emphasized.
5. Gives undue weight to fine distinctions. A single point difference, which may represent only a small difference in learning, may be the difference between a B− and a C+.

continued

6. Leads to cumulative errors. A particular test score or classroom activity may not truly reflect the student's abilities or learning. The final total represents the sum of all such errors.
7. Is subject to misinterpretation. Without norms it is false to assume that a certain range (90 to 100) or number (93) represents a valid indicator (e.g., an A) of performance or that categories (breakpoints) can be decided in advance.

Source: Adapted from Robert F. Madgic, "The Point System of Grading: A Critical Appraisal," *National Association of Secondary School Principals,* April 1988, pp. 29–34.

Form of Grades

The most popular form in which grades are presented is the *letter grade.* According to David Payne, the letter grade "represents a translation from a number base, resulting from a combination of test scores, ratings, and the like . . . [and has a] common meaning for most people, and for this reason should probably be retained."[35]

A disadvantage is that the conversion from numbers to letters to some extent distorts meaning and masks individual differences. Since a letter represents a range of numbers, different students may receive the same letter grade from the same teacher for different levels of performance. However, although the number system is more precise, the difference between two or three points for a final grade is often not that meaningful.

Most schools convert letters to an even more general statement of evaluation as follows:

A = superior, excellent, outstanding

B = good, above average

C = fair, competent, average

D = minimum passing, weakness or problems

F = failure, serious weakness or problems

The standards upon which grades are based vary considerably among school districts, so that a C student in one school may be an A student in another school. Hence schools and school districts eventually get reputations about how low or high standards are.

---

[35] Payne, *The Assessment of Learning,* p. 425.

Table 4.2   EXAMPLES OF ABSOLUTE AND RELATIVE
STANDARDS OF GRADING

Absolute standard		Relative standard	
		Percent of students*	Number of students (total = 32)
A = 90% or above	A =	7%	2–3
B = 80–89%	B =	24%	7–8
C = 70–79%	C =	38%	12–13
D = 60–69%	D =	24%	7–8
F = Below 60%	F =	7%	2–3

*Based on a normal curve.

Source: Adapted from Robert E. Slavin, *Educational Psychology: Theory into Practice* (Englewood Cliffs, N.J.: Prentice-Hall, 1986), pp. 556–557.

Absolute Grade Standards

Grades may be given according to fixed or **absolute standards**, as illustrated in Table 4.2. One disadvantage of this approach, is that the standards may be subject to the *error of leniency*; that is, if students have an easy grader, many As and Bs will be assigned, or if they have a tough grader, many Cs and Ds will be assigned.[36] Also, student scores depend on the difficulty of the tests given. In some tests a score of 65 percent may be above average, but with an absolute or fixed standard, as indicated on the table, this score would be a D. Hence, many students would be given a minimum passing grade under an absolute grading approach.

Despite these limitations, most teachers use this method of grading. It makes a great deal of sense as long as teachers have a firm idea of what students should be able to do and as long as standards are realistic and fair. The main advantage, according to Good and Brophy, is that "it puts control of grades in students' hands." If the standards are fair, students should work hard to earn good grades. "However, if standards are too high, students will give up."[37]

Relative Grade Standards

Grades may be given according to how a student performs in relation to others. If a student scores 80 on an examination, but most others score above 90, the student has done less than average work. Instead of receiving a B under the relative, or norm-reference, method of grading, the student might receive a C.

[36] Allan C. Ornstein, "How Good Are Teachers in Effecting Student Outcomes?," *National Association of Secondary School Principals*, December 1982, pp. 61–70; Ornstein, "Research in Teaching: Measurements and Methods," *Education and Urban Society*, February 1986, pp. 176–181.

[37] Good and Brophy, *Educational Psychology: A Realistic Approach*, p. 793.

If a student scores 65, but most others score below 60, he or she has done well and might receive a B instead of a D.

Relative grading can be based on a curve, either a normal bell-shaped curve or a curve derived from a simple ranking system. In a normal curve few students receive As or Fs, the majority receive Cs (midpoint of the curve), and many receive Bs and Ds. This is also shown in Table 4.2, which uses a 7-24-38-24-7 percent grade distribution. In a ranking system, which is more common, the teacher determines in advance percentage equivalents for each letter grade: for example, the top 25 percent will receive A, the next 30 percent B, the next 25 percent C, and the next 20 percent D or F. The grading on this curve is not always as precise as with the normal curve, and it tends to be a little easier for students to score higher grades.

Grading on a curve and other relative grading practices assure that grades will be distributed on the basis of scores in relation to one another, whatever the difficulty of the test. However, according to research, this can create competition among students, inhibit them from helping each other, and affect social relations.[38]

Contracting for Grades

A few schools permit teachers and students considerable flexibility in formulating grading standards. Teachers and students come to an agreement early in the term concerning grades for specific levels of performance or achievement on various tasks. Maximum, average, and minimum standards or performance levels are usually established for those who wish to receive passing and progressively higher grades. In effect, the teacher promises to award a specific grade for specified performance; a **contract** grade is established. With this approach students know exactly what they have to do to receive a certain grade; depending on the amount of work they wish to do, they can receive a particular grade.

The plan seems suited to criterion-reference learning and to teaching and learning by a set of objectives. The approach is not recommended for elementary school students because of their lack of maturity and their inability to engage in independent work for a sustained period of time and to follow through on individual activities.[39] The contract can be implemented at the upper elementary level (grade 5 or higher) if great care is taken to match student maturity and abilities with performance requirements. Different standards will be needed with different students.

---

[38] Carole Ames, Russell Ames, and Donald W. Felker, "Effects of Competitive Reward Structure and Valence of Outcome on Children's Achievement Attributions," *Journal of Educational Psychology*, February 1977, pp. 1–8; David W. Johnson, *Reaching Out: Interpersonal Effectiveness and Self-Actualization* 3rd ed. (Englewood Cliffs, N.J.: Prentice-Hall, 1986); and Robert E. Slavin and Nancy A. Madden, eds., *Effective Programs for Students at Risk* (Boston: Allyn and Bacon, 1989).

[39] Ronald A. Berk, "Setting Passing Scores on Competency Tests," *National Association of Secondary School Principals*, February 1987, pp. 69–76.

Revised contracts can be designed for students whose work is not satisfactory or who expected a higher grade than they received. This grading system provides more latitude for teachers in responding to unsatisfactory work and gives students a chance to improve their work and their grade.

Mastery and Continuous Progress Grading

Many elementary schools and a few middle grade and junior high schools now stress **mastery grading** and **continuous progress grading.** Both approaches require that teachers maintain specific records for each student and report on the student's progress. Schools using these approaches usually do not use grades, but rather evaluate the student in terms of expected and mastered skills and behaviors.[40] Reports for the student and parents describe how the student is performing and progressing without any indication of how the student is doing in relation to others. Although a judgment is made about the student, the absence of a standard for comparison reduces some pressure related to grades. In mastery learning situations and continuous progress reporting, grades are usually based on criterion-reference measurements. In more traditional situations grades are also based on normative data.[41]

Grading for Effort or Improvement

To what extent should teachers consider effort or improvement as part of the grade? This question surfaces with most teachers when they grade their students. Problems with considering effort are that bright students may show the least improvement and effort and that by raising the grade or average of low-achieving students to reflect effort rather than achievement, you are to some extent lowering the value of the grade given to high-achieving students.[42] Also low-achieving students have more opportunity to improve by simple regression toward the mean.

Most teachers, especially in the elementary and middle grade schools, leave some room for judgment in grading. The more effort and improvement are considered in deciding on final grades, the more subjective the grades will be and the more biased they are likely to be. The teacher must examine his or her perceptions for accuracy. If the teacher feels strongly about a judgment,

---

[40]Benjamin Bloom, "The 2 Sigma Problem: The Search for Methods of Instruction as Effective as One-to-One Tutoring," *Educational Researcher*, June/July 1984, pp. 4–16; Robert E. Slavin, "Grouping for Instruction in the Elementary School," *Educational Psychologist*, Spring 1987, pp. 109–128; and Slavin, *Educational Psychology: Theory into Practice*.

[41]William A. Mehrens and Irving J. Lehmann, *Measurement and Evaluation in Education and Psychology*, 3rd ed. (New York: Holt, Rinehart and Winston, 1984); Mehrens and Lehmann, "Using Teacher-Made Measurement Devices," *National Association of Secondary School Principals*, February 1987, pp. 36–45.

[42]Thomas L. Good and Rhona S. Weinstein, "Schools Make a Difference: Evidence, Criticisms, and New Directions," *American Psychologist*, October 1986, pp. 1090–1097; Allan C. Ornstein, "Evaluation of Students: A Practitioner's Perspective," *National Association of Secondary School Principals* (in print 1990).

Professional Viewpoint

Great Expectations

Some call it the knowledge explosion. It is better often to think of it as an ignorance explosion.

Not to belittle people but to realize that when any one person discovers something, billions of people become ignorant of one more thing.

Each of us learners is a mouse gnawing at an exploding castle.

Grading someone down for not mastering a "body of knowledge" is like faulting the mouse for not gnawing the entire castle.

> Robert E. Stake
> Professor and Director
> Center for Instructional Research
> University of Illinois

---

then the movement in a grade from a B+ to a B or an A or A− is acceptable. A major change in a grade, say from a C to an A, cannot be justified on the basis of the student's effort or teacher's hunches about the student.

RECORDS AND REPORTS OF PERFORMANCE

There is usually a difference in the way student performance is recorded and reported in elementary and secondary school. Elementary teachers are usually more sensitive about the student's feelings, attitudes, and effort, and are willing to consider these factors in reporting performance. Elementary school report cards often contain a narrative or a combination of grades and narrative about the child's progress. The parents may be asked to write a reply, instead of merely signing the report card, or to schedule a conference perhaps two or three times a year during which the parent and teacher discuss the child's work.

Fewer middle grade and junior high schools have such elaborate reporting systems, and at the high school level this human (or social) dimension of reporting is almost nonexistent, partly because teachers have more students (perhaps 150 or more) and thus cannot easily write narratives and hold conferences for the parents of each student.

Report Cards

The teacher's judgments and scores on tests are communicated to students and parents by means of a report card. The reports should not come as a surprise to students. Both students and parents should know how marks or grades are to be computed and to what extent tests, class participation, homework, and other activities contribute to their overall grade. Many students and parents become anxious if they do not know the basis for the marks or grades on the report card.

At the lower elementary grade level (below grade 4), and to a lesser extent at the upper elementary and junior high school levels, the school may use a **mastery** or **progress report card** on which a list of descriptors or categories is given and the teacher indicates what the student can do by checking off terms such as "yes" or "no" or "outstanding," "satisfactory," or "unsatisfactory." Below is a list of common reading descriptors for which "yes" or "no" are indicated.

	Yes	No
1. Reads orally at appropriate level	___	___
2. Reads with comprehension	___	___
3. Identifies main ideas in stories	___	___
4. Recognizes main characters in stories	___	___
5. Finds details in stories	___	___
6. Draws conclusions from reading stories	___	___
7. Demonstrates appropriate vocabulary	___	___
8. Reads with appropriate speed	___	___
9. Finishes reading assignments on time	___	___
10. Persists even if understanding does not come immediately	___	___

Teachers can make up their own lists for any basic skill or subject. A mastery report might also involve descriptions of progress or problems rather than yes/no evaluations. At some levels and for some types of course content the list of descriptors or categories can be precise, with a date for achievement or mastery to be shown.

	Date Mastered
Simple Addition	
1. Performs simple counting 1 to 100	___
2. Adds one-digit numbers up to 10 (e.g., 4 + 3 = 7)	___
3. Adds one-digit numbers up to 19 (e.g., 9 + 4 = 13)	___
4. Adds two-digit numbers without carrying (e.g., 22 + 30 = 52)	___
5. Adds two-digit numbers with carrying (e.g., 22 + 79 = 101)	___

Concepts in Addition
1. Understands cumulative property of addition (e.g., 4 apples + 7 apples = 11 apples) ____
2. Understands place value (e.g., 3 tens + 7 ones = 37) ____
3. Supplies missing number (e.g., 4 + ? = 10)[43]

This approach fits in with a criterion-reference system of evaluation and is useful for schools that wish to eliminate grades and put more emphasis on progress or mastery.

The same approach can be used for all subjects and grade levels. For example, the list below illustrates a science progress report for junior high school students.[44] The descriptors are checked if the student shows strength in a specific area (absence of a check suggests need for improvement). A three- or five-point scale could also be used to give a more precise report.

Areas of strengths are checked below

	First Quarter	Second Quarter	Third Quarter	Fourth Quarter
Obeys school and classroom rules	____	____	____	____
Completes homework	____	____	____	____
Follows directions	____	____	____	____
Brings materials to class	____	____	____	____
Completes work neatly and carefully	____	____	____	____
Works independently	____	____	____	____
Cleans up lab	____	____	____	____
Uses equipment carefully	____	____	____	____
Participates in class discussions	____	____	____	____
Makes good use of class time	____	____	____	____
Seeks help when needed	____	____	____	____
Gets to class on time	____	____	____	____
Puts forth satisfactory effort	____	____	____	____
Listens attentively	____	____	____	____

A typical report card for grades 1 to 8 might look like the one in Figure 4.1. The grades are designated by letters, with explanations for each letter.

---

[43] Allan C. Ornstein, "The Nature of Grading," *Clearing House*, April 1989, pp. 365–369.

[44] Adapted from Science Report Card, Miner Junior High School Progress Report, Aptakisic-Tripp Community Consolidated School District 102, Illinois, no date.

CPS CHICAGO PUBLIC SCHOOLS

REPORT OF STUDENT ACHIEVEMENT AND EFFORT GRADES 1-8

19___ TO 19 ___ SCHOOL YEAR

School_____

School Address _____

Principal_____

Teacher_____

REPORTING PERIODS	1	2	3	4
Enrolled in Bilingual Program				
Bilingual Program Category				

Dear Parents or Guardian:

This report card gives you information about your child's achievement and progress in school. The marks are given by the teacher, based upon the expectations for your child and your child's performance. You will receive the report card four times a year.

You can make a real difference in how well your child does in school. You can encourage your child to do all homework and can even help with assignments. You can visit the school and talk with the teachers and the principal. You can take an active part in school affairs. We need and want you to help us give your child the best possible education.

Yours truly,

Manford Byrd Jr.

Manford Byrd, Jr.
General Superintendent of Schools

EL 131 · Rev. 10-86
Com. No. 216

Figure 4.1 Typical report card for grades 1–8.

GROWTH IN KNOWLEDGE, SKILLS, AND UNDERSTANDINGS

The following marking codes will be used to report your child's achievement:

A - Excellent **D** - Needs Improvement

B - Good **F** - Unsatisfactory

C - Satisfactory **(/)** - Indicates an area not to be marked at this time

Each mark represents your child's achievement for one 10-week reporting period. An average mark of the four marks is recorded at the end of the school year in the column headed FINAL.

The instructional level in reading is the grade level at which your child is performing and being taught in the basal reader. The instructional level may differ from the assigned grade.

	ACHIEVEMENT				
	1	2	3	4	FINAL
READING IN THE ENGLISH LANGUAGE					
Instructional Level					
Your child's reading level is below grade level, at grade level, or above grade level.	below	below	below	below	below
	at	at	at	at	at
	above	above	above	above	above
READING IN THE NATIVE LANGUAGE					
Instructional Level					
Your child's reading level is below grade level, at grade level, or above grade level.	below	below	below	below	below
	at	at	at	at	at
	above	above	above	above	above
ENGLISH AS A SECOND LANGUAGE (ESL)					
Reading					
Writing					
Listening					
Speaking					
LANGUAGE ARTS or NATIVE LANGUAGE ARTS					
Oral Expression					
Written Expression					
Spelling					
Handwriting					
MATHEMATICS					
SCIENCE					
SOCIAL STUDIES					
ART					
MUSIC					
HEALTH and SAFETY EDUCATION					
PHYSICAL EDUCATION					
LIBRARY SCIENCE					

Figure 4.1 (*continued*)

Name _____

ID Number _____   Grade _____ Room _____

GROWTH IN HABITS AND ATTITUDES

A student must show progress in social, work, and health and safety habits to gain the greatest benefit from the school program. (✓) means that your child needs to improve.

SOCIAL HABITS	REPORTING PERIODS			
	1	2	3	4
Exercises self-control				
Accepts responsibility				
Obeys school rules and regulations				
Plays well alone and in a group				
Respects rights and property of others				
WORK HABITS				
Comes prepared to work				
Listens well				
Follows directions				
Works independently and in a group				
Takes part in class activities				
Cares for materials				
Completes assigned classroom work				
Does homework assignments				
Puts forth effort				
HEALTH AND SAFETY HABITS				
Practices good health habits				
Obeys safety rules				

ATTENDANCE

Regular attendance and promptness are necessary for successful progress in school. A note dated and signed by the parent or guardian is required each time a student is absent or is tardy.

REPORTING PERIODS	1	2	3	4	TOTAL
Days Absent					
Times Tardy					

Figure 4.1 (*continued*)

TEACHER COMMENTS AND
REQUEST FOR CONFERENCE

A check in the box indicates that the teacher desires a conference with you.

COMMENTS

Period 1

☐ Conference
Requested

Period 2

☐ Conference
Requested

Period 3

☐ Conference
Requested

Period 4

PARENT OR GUARDIAN COMMENTS AND
REQUEST FOR CONFERENCE

Please sign below to show that you have read this report. If you wish to confer with the teacher, place a check in the box.

COMMENTS

Period 1

Signature of
Parent or Guardian _____   ☐ Conference
Requested

Period 2

Signature of
Parent or Guardian _____   ☐ Conference
Requested

Period 3

Signature of
Parent or Guardian _____   ☐ Conference
Requested

Conference held on

Period 1 _____

Period 2 _____

Period 3 _____

Next Assignment	
Grade	
Room	

It is the policy of the Board of Education of the City of Chicago not to discriminate on the basis of race, color, creed, national origin, religion, age, handicap unrelated to ability, or sex in its educational program or employment policies or practices

Inquiries concerning the application of Title IX of the Education Amendments of 1972 and the regulations promulgated thereunder concerning sex discrimination should be referred to the Title IX Coordinator, Board of Education of the City of Chicago, 1819 West Pershing Road, Chicago, Illinois 60609

CHICAGO PUBLIC SCHOOLS   **BOARD OF EDUCATION**   **CITY OF CHICAGO**

Figure 4.1 (*continued*)

Note the emphasis on reading and language skills. Because the school district in this case has a large number of bilingual students, there is a place for reporting native language achievement. Grades for citizenship or conduct (called "social habits" in this card) and work habits, separated from academic grades, are given. The term is divided into four periods, with the periods averaged for the fourth and final grade. Absenteeism and lateness (called "tardiness" in this figure) should be shown on all report cards, regardless of grade level. Places for a parent's signature, teacher comments, and parent or teacher requests for a conference to discuss the report are usually provided. (See Tips for Teachers 4.2.)

Electronic Recordkeeping

The need for careful record keeping is an important part of the teacher's job and has financial and legal implications for the school. Research shows that the average teacher, with the assistance of a calculator, takes 87 minutes to record grades for 30 students in a traditional record book. This time does not include actual grading, rather (1) alphabetizing and entering names, (2) entering grades, (3) averaging grades for five categories, (4) performing statistical analysis such as means or frequency distributions, and (5) providing progress reports. The same teacher with a computerized recordkeeper takes 15 minutes to do the same work—a saving of 62 minutes for one class during a single grading period.[45]

Elementary school teachers usually have four grading periods per year for one class (a savings of four hours), but secondary school teachers usually have three or four grading periods and four or five classes per semester or half year (a savings of up to 40 hours for the year or about one week's work). The savings in time for all teachers is further increased, considering that teachers are required to generate reports that include grades to school administrators on a weekly and monthly basis and reports to parents about their children's progress. The **computerized recordkeeper** can generate school reports and parental reports, as well as customized letters and printout lists concerning student grades by numerous categories, in 10 to 20 seconds per report, compared to an average of 20 minutes per report with traditional methods. Figuring on a minimum of one school report per week for 40 weeks and two customized letters or progress reports per year for 30 parents the savings is another 33 hours.

Two researchers have listed 22 tasks that computerized recordkeeping can accomplish more effectively than a traditional recordkeeping book. Ten are listed below.

1. Permitting the teacher to make easy and quick modifications of recorded scores, to correct clerical errors, or to accommodate retest scores or new test scores.

---

[45] Edward L. Vockell and Donald Kopenec, "Record Keeping Without Tears," *Clearing House*, April 1989, pp. 355—359.

2. Computing grade averages and applying weighted formulas to grade students on various categories: 40 percent for exams, 30 percent for weekly quizzes, 15 percent for homework, and 15 percent for class participation.
3. Converting numerical grades to letter grades according to specific standards.
4. Providing records of student performance by ranking, percentages, frequency distributions, etc., for subgroups or the entire class.
5. Making comparisons of one student or subgroups on any recorded category for purpose of placement, diagnostic, formative, or summative evaluation.
6. Providing printouts of student performance on specific tests or subtests for purposes of instruction.
7. Designating or flagging students according to specific levels of performance on specific tests (students who failed, or who received 80 percent or higher).
8. Generating reports that include standardized comments for one student or groups of students.
9. Generating personal letters for individual students, including specific comments about grades.
10. Reusing names for different reports, labels, printouts, or another grading period; creating class lists for attendance, lateness, extra credit, phone numbers, addresses, etc.[46]

We must keep in mind that we are in the age of electronics, and the pen-and-pencil method of recording data is quickly becoming dated. It behooves teachers to efficiently manage information, and use various data bases and spreadsheets for grading, evaluating, and reporting student performance. These methods provide many alternatives to help busy teachers take advantage of the tools of the twenty-first century.

Cumulative Record

Each student has a permanent record in which important data are filed during his or her entire school career. It contains information about subject grades, standardized test scores, family background, personal history, health, school service, parent and pupil interviews, special aptitudes, special learning, behavioral, or physical problems, number of absences, and tardiness. Samples of cumulative records are reproduced in Figures 4.2 and 4.3—one for elementary schools and the other for secondary schools.

The **cumulative record** is usually stored in the main office or guidance office. Teachers are permitted access to the cumulative records of the students in their classes to obtain information about them. They are also required to

---

[46]Ibid.

Tips for Teachers 4.2

Innovative Practices for Reporting Student Performance

In lieu of traditional report cards, teachers might experiment with new reporting procedures for providing information on student performance and progress. A number of innovative ideas are listed below. Some are in practice in a few schools. Just how innovative you can be will depend to a large extent on your school's policy and philosophy about grading.

1. Consider more than a single grade or mark. Develop a progress report for each activity detailing specific instructional tasks and student performance.
2. List more than cognitive development and specific subjects. Include social, psychological, and psychomotor behaviors and creative, esthetic, and artistic learning as well as scientific and technical abilities.
3. Develop forms of report cards specifically suited to particular grade levels rather than using one form for the entire school.
4. Grade students on the basis of both an absolute standard and a relative standard (especially in lower grades).
5. Report each student's progress (especially in lower grades).
6. Replace or use in addition to standard letter grades or categories (such as "excellent," "good," and "fair") new categories or written individual statements such as "needs more time to develop," "advanced understanding for the child's age."
7. Stress strengths of the student. Point out only two or three weaknesses or problem areas, and specify ways for improving weak or problem areas.
8. Replace or supplement the standard card with a larger more detailed folder, one that contains explanations for students and parents and perhaps pictures or cartoons at the younger grade levels.
9. Provide space for comments by both teachers and parents, not just for their signatures.
10. Provide space for requests by both parents and teachers for parent-teacher conferences.
11. Organize committees of students, teachers, and parents to meet periodically (every three or four years) to improve the school district's standard report card.
12. Supplement report cards with frequent informal letters to parents, parent-teacher conferences, and student-teacher conferences.

Source: Adapted from Allan C. Ornstein, "The Nature of Grading," *Clearing House*, April 1989, pp. 65–69; and David A. Payne, *The Assessment of Learning* (Lexington, Mass.: D.C. Heath, 1974), p. 417.

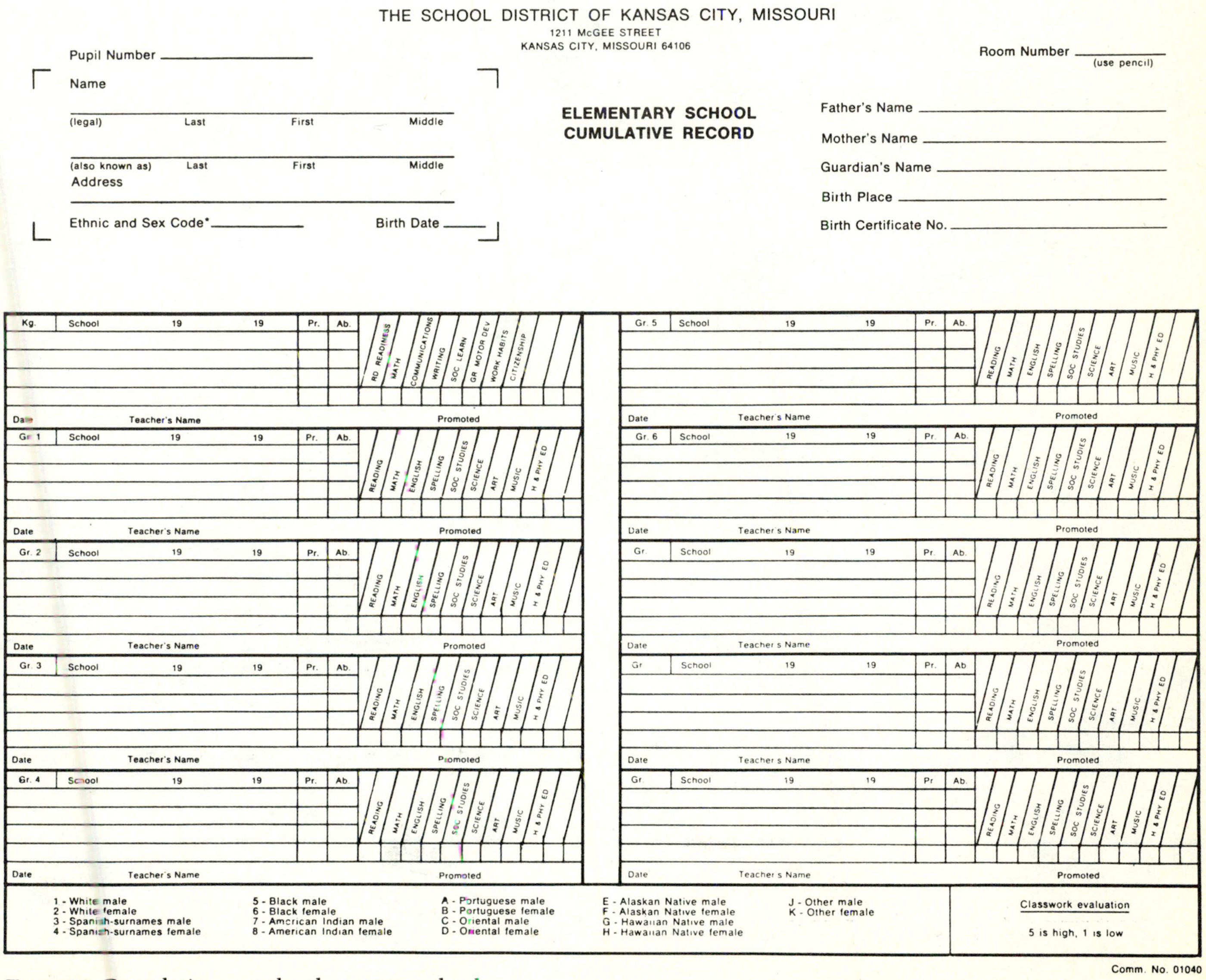

THE SCHOOL DISTRICT OF KANSAS CITY, MISSOURI

1211 McGEE STREET
KANSAS CITY, MISSOURI 64106

**ELEMENTARY SCHOOL
CUMULATIVE RECORD**

Room Number _____ (use pencil)

Pupil Number _____

Name _____

| (legal) | Last | First | Middle |

Father's Name _____

Mother's Name _____

Guardian's Name _____

| (also known as) | Last | First | Middle |

Address _____

Birth Place _____

Ethnic and Sex Code* _____   Birth Date _____

Birth Certificate No. _____

Kg.   School   19   19   Pr.   Ab.   READING   MATH   ENGLISH   SPELLING   SOC STUDIES   SCIENCE   ART   MUSIC   H & PHY ED

Date   Teacher's Name   Promoted

Gr. 1   School   19   19   Pr.   Ab.   RD READINESS   MATH   COMMUNICATIONS   WRITING   SOC LEARN   GR MOTOR DEV   WORK HABITS   CITIZENSHIP   ART   MUSIC   H & PHY ED

Date   Teacher's Name   Promoted

Gr. 2   School   19   19   Pr.   Ab.   READING   MATH   ENGLISH   SPELLING   SOC STUDIES   SCIENCE   ART   MUSIC   H & PHY ED

Date   Teacher's Name   Promoted

Gr. 3   School   19   19   Pr.   Ab.

Date   Teacher's Name   Promoted

Gr. 4   School   19   19   Pr.   Ab.

Date   Teacher's Name   Promoted

Gr. 5   School   19   19   19   Pr.   Ab.   READING   MATH   ENGLISH   SPELLING   SOC STUDIES   SCIENCE   ART   MUSIC   H & PHY ED

Date   Teacher's Name   Promoted

Gr. 6   School   19   19   Pr.   Ab.

Date   Teacher's Name   Promoted

Gr.   School   19   19   Pr.   Ab.

Date   Teacher's Name   Promoted

Gr.   School   19   19   Pr.   Ab.

Date   Teacher's Name   Promoted

Gr.   School   19   19   Pr.   Ab.

Date   Promoted

1 - White male
2 - White female
3 - Spanish-surnames male
4 - Spanish-surnames female

5 - Black male
6 - Black female
7 - American Indian male
8 - American Indian female

A - Portuguese male
B - Portuguese female
C - Oriental male
D - Oriental female

E - Alaskan Native male
F - Alaskan Native female
G - Hawaiian Native male
H - Hawaiian Native female

J - Other male
K - Other female

Classwork evaluation

5 is high, 1 is low

Comm. No. 01040

Figure 4.2 Cumulative record—elementary school.

195

Directions For Recording Test Scores

Interpretation Of Test Statistics

STANINES	LEVELS	PERCENTILES
7-9	ABOVE AVERAGE	75-100
4-6	AVERAGE	26-74
1-3	BELOW AVERAGE	1-25

Enter District Test Results In Chronological Order (A-I)

Printed Labels Attach Label In Appropriate Box

Hand Recording Complete ALL Blanks In Appropriate Box Enter Test Results In Corresponding Box

Name _____

Room Number _____ (use pencil)

Enter large labels for tests from outside the District here

School _____
Test _____
Grade _____
Test Date _____

A

School _____
Test _____
Grade _____
Test Date _____

D

School _____
Test _____
Grade _____
Test Date _____

G

School _____
Test _____
Grade _____
Test Date _____

B

School _____
Test _____
Grade _____
Test Date _____

E

School _____
Test _____
Grade _____
Test Date _____

H

School _____
Test _____
Grade _____
Test Date _____

C

School _____
Test _____
Grade _____
Test Date _____

F

School _____
Test _____
Grade _____
Test Date _____

I

Special Evaluations

Immunization Record

DPT/DT 1___ 2___ 3___ 4___ 5___
Polio 1___ 2___ 3___ 4___
Measles 1___ Mumps 1___ Rubella 1___

Basic Competency and/or IEP Conferences

Date	Teacher	Date	Teacher	Date	Teacher	Date	Teacher

NOTE: Altered scores will invalidate the test results. Questionable results should be verified by the Educational Testing Office.

Figure 4.2 (continued)

HIGH SCHOOL PERMANENT RECORD

	COURSE	TEACHER	GRADE	CREDITS	COMMENTS
9					
10					
11					
12					

NAME		BIRTH DATE	DATE GRADUATED

JEFFERSON COUNTY
PUBLIC HIGH SCHOOL RECORD
P.O. Box 34020, Louisville, Ky. 40232

LOCAL SCHOOL NAME & ADDRESS

Accredited by the Ky. Dept. of Education
and the Southern Assn. of Colleges & Schools

OFFICIAL SIGNATURE

KEY TO HIGH SCHOOL RECORD

Program
* Advance—Last digit of course number = 9
  Honors—Designated By H
  Special Education—Course number
                    Prefix W or Q
  Regular—All other course numbers
* Advance Program students are identified
  by specific criteria which indicate the students
  are selected from the top 3% of the population.

GRADES	Quality Points
A—93-100	4
B—86-92	3
C—79-85	2
D—70-78	1
F—69-0	0
WP—Withdrawn Passing	
WF—Withdrawn Failing	

	TRANSCRIPT RECORD	
Rank 9 thru 11	COLLEGE	DATE
TOTAL QUAL. PTS.		
TOTAL CREDITS Attempted ___ Earned ___		
GRADE POINT AVERAGE		
RANK IN CLASS		
NO. IN CLASS		

Completed Advance Program _____
Completed Honors Program _____
Beta Club _____   NHS _____

TOTAL CREDITS	G.P.A.	RANK

Figure 4.3 Cumulative record—secondary school.

HIGH SCHOOL PERMANENT RECORD

Last Name	First	Middle	Sex	Race	Birthplace			Birth Date: Mo. Day Year		
Parents			School		Entry Date and Code	WD Date and Code	School		Entry Date and Code	WD Date and Code
Address		Telephone								
Change of Address		Telephone								
Change of Address		Telephone								
Change of Address		Telephone								

Date

IMMUN. CERT. EXPIRES _____ _____ _____   PUPIL NUMBER: _____

T.B. CERT. _____ _____ _____

HIGH SCHOOL STANDARDIZED TEST SCORES

Proficiency Test

P.S.A.T.

S.A.T.

A.C.T.

Figure 4.3 (*continued*)

add to the information at the end of the term to keep the records complete and up to date.

Although the information found in the cumulative records is extremely helpful, a major criticism of using these records is that the teacher may make prejudgments about students before even meeting them in class. For this reason, some educators argue that a teacher should not look at cumulative records until a month or more after the school year begins.

Since federal legislation (Records Law 93-830) permits the records of a child to be open to inspection and review by the child's parents, most educators are reluctant to write statements or reports that may be considered controversial or negative, unless supported with specific data. Sometimes important information is omitted. When parents review information in cumulative records (they also have the right to challenge the information), a qualified employee of the school (principal's secretary or guidance counselor) should be present to give assistance.

HIGH SCHOOL PERMANENT RECORD

Achievement Test Record

NAME _____

9

10

11

12

E
X
T
R
A

F-435-1 Rev. 7/10/86

Figure 4.3 *(continued)*

Guidelines for Grading Students

Here are some suggestions for deriving grades.

1. *Explain your grading system to the students.* For young students, explain your grading system orally and with concrete examples. Older students can read handouts that describe assignments, tests, test schedules, and grading criteria.

2. *Base grades on a predetermined set of standards.* For example, a student who is able to perform at a significantly higher performance standard than another student should receive a higher grade.

3. *Base grades on the student's degree of progress.* The student who comes to a class with poor skills and improves greatly might get a higher grade than a student who was slightly less than average when he came to class and showed no marked improvement.

4. *Base grades on the student's attitude, as well as achievement, especially at the elementary or junior high school level.* Some educators argue this is unfair, and the citizenship or conduct grade, not the academic grade, should reflect attitude. Others argue that penalizing a disruptive child in the subject grade is a legitimate method for shaping behavior.

5. *Base grades on the student's relative standing compared to class-mates.* The teacher needs to consider the student's work in relation to others in class, not only for grading but also for grouping purposes.

6. *Base grades on a variety of sources.* The more sources of information used and weighted properly, the more valid is the grade. Although most of the grade should be based on objective sources, some subjective sources should also be considered. For example, a student who frequently participates in class may be given a slightly higher grade than her test average.

7. *As a rule, do not change grades.* Grades should be arrived at after serious consideration, and only in rare circumstances should they be changed. Of course, an obvious mistake or error should be corrected, but if students think you will change grades, they will start negotiating or pleading with you for changes.

8. *Become familiar with the grading policy of your school and with your colleagues' standards.* Each school has its own standards for grading and procedures for reporting grades. Your standards and practices should not conflict with those of the school and should not differ greatly from those of your colleagues.

9. *When failing a student, closely follow school procedures.* Each school has its own procedures to follow for failing a student. You may be required to have a warning conference, to send a pending failure notice to parents, and so forth.

10. *Record grades on report cards and cumulative records.* Report cards usually are mailed to parents or given to students to give to parents every six to eight weeks. Cumulative records are usually completed at the end of the school year.[47]

Remember to use the evaluation procedure as a teaching and learning device, to be fair in your evaluation of students, to interpret evaluative data properly, and to give students the benefit of the doubt.

COMMUNICATION WITH PARENTS

The importance of parent involvement is well documented. How the teacher can help the parents to improve the child's academic work and behavior is often the major concern among parents and teachers alike. According to Joyce Epstein, more than 85 percent of parents spend 15 minutes or more helping their child at home when asked to do so by the teacher. Parents claim they can spend more time, 40 minutes on the average, if they are told specifically how to help, but fewer than 25 percent receive systematic requests and directions from teachers to assist their children with specific skills and subjects.[48] Epstein further notes that parents become involved most often with reading activities at the lower grades: reading to the child or listening to the child read, taking the child to the library, and helping with teaching materials brought home from school for practice at home.[49] Parents of older students (grade 4 and above) become more involved with specific homework and subject-related activities. Research shows that children have an advantage in school when their parents support, participate, and communicate on a regular basis with school officials.[50] Schools typically communicate with parents in three ways: reports cards (already discussed), conferences, and letters. Parents expect feedback from the teacher and school, and usually welcome the opportunity to meet with the teacher and to stay in touch through phone calls and letters.

Parent Conferences

Scheduling parent-teacher conferences is becoming increasingly difficult because an increasing number of children have only one adult living at home,

---

[47] Ornstein, "The Nature of Grading."

[48] Joyce L. Epstein, "Parents' Reactions to Teacher Practices of Parent Involvement," *Elementary School Journal*, 1986, pp. 277–294; Epstein, "Parent Involvement: What Research Says to Administrators," *Education and Urban Society*, February 1987, pp. 119–136.

[49] Joyce L. Epstein, "How Do We Improve Programs for Parent Involvement?" *Educational Horizons*, Winter 1988, pp. 58–59; Epstein, "Parent Involvement: What Research Says to Administrators."

[50] Anne T. Henderson, "An Ecologically Balanced Approach to Academic Improvement," *Educational Horizons*, Winter 1988, pp. 60–62; Beth Sattes, "Parental Involvement in Student Learning," *Education Digest*, January 1989, pp. 37–39.

Figure 4.3 Parent-teacher conferences can greatly affect student learning. (Photo Vivienne della Grotta 1983/Photo Researchers)

or have two parents in the work force, or have parents with more than one job. Few parents are able to attend school activities or conferences during normal school hours, and many have trouble scheduling meetings at all. Today's teacher must adjust to these new circumstances with greater efforts through letters and telephone calls to set up meetings and greater flexibility to accommodate the needs of the parents.

Usually both teachers and parents are a little apprehensive before a conference, want to impress each other favorably, and don't know exactly what to expect. Teachers can reduce their anxiety by preparing for the conference, assembling in advance all the information pertinent to the student and the subject to be discussed with parents. This might include information regarding the student's academic achievement, other testing results, general health, attendance and lateness, social and emotional relations, work habits, special aptitudes, or other noteworthy characteristics or activities. If the conference is about subject grades, the teacher should assemble the student's tests, reports, and homework assignments. If it is about discipline, he or she might have on hand written and detailed accounts of behavior.

The conference should not be a time for lecturing parents. If the teacher asked for the conference, the teacher will set the agenda, but should remain sensitive to the needs of the parents. The atmosphere should be unrushed and quiet. The information presented should be based on as many sources as pos-

---

Professional Viewpoint

Evaluating Students in Schools

I learned two lessons while teaching second grade in the stone age. The first was from Arthur, who should have been in a special class but we liked each other and I never sent him to the school psychologist to be tested. Arthur had trouble learning anything and if he did, he had trouble remembering it the next hour. In order to "encourage" him (but also to be fair to the others) I gave him C's on his first report card. The next day he came in with a black eye and some facial cuts. His sister explained that their parents had beaten him because he hadn't come home with all A's. After meeting the parents I learned that they were religious zealots who believed that God told them to beat Arthur to shape him up; indeed, it was their duty. I saw to it that Arthur got all A's on his subsequent report cards and included some specific information on the permanent record of just what Arthur's achievements were in the various subjects.

My second lesson also came from parents. Martha was a "sweet" little second grader who played with a doll all day, every day. When I met with her father, I was surprised to see a Danish sailor who was at least 6'6". He picked Martha up and perched her on his shoulder while I gave him one-half hour of jargon about how he might interpret norm-referenced test scores related to Martha's achievement. When I finished using every bit of jargon that I knew, he said, "Ah, that Martha, she's got a head like a chicken!" I noticed he was holding her just like she held her doll and the only thing I thought to say was that it was a real pleasure to have Martha in class.

I never did learn how to communicate honestly with abusive parents but with doting ones I learned to enjoy how much they loved their kids. I'll bet some people might not think this has anything to do with "evaluation."

Martin Haberman
Professor of Curriculum and Instruction
University of Wisconsin-Milwaukee

---

sible. It is advisable to begin and end on a positive note, even if a problem has to be discussed. The idea is to encourage parents. The teacher should not monopolize the discussion, should be truthful, yet tactful and constructive, and should remain poised. The teacher should be cautious about giving too much advice, especially with regard to the child's home life.[51] The average

---

[51]J. Karen Chapman, "Advice for Parents," *PTA Today*, October 1988, pp. 9–10; Allan C. Ornstein, "The Parent-Teacher Conference," *PTA Today*, October 1988, pp. 8–9.

Tips for Teachers 4.3

Guide to Discussion During a Parent-Teacher Conference

During a conference the teacher can expect parents to ask about certain things. And if parents don't ask about them, the teacher should be prepared to introduce the topics into the discussion. Below is a list of questions (that may be introduced by the parent or teacher) that can guide your discussion.

1. How does the student behave in class? In school?
2. How does the student get along with classmates?
3. Is the student working up to full potential?
4. How does the student's progress compare with that of classmates?
5. What are the potential strengths of the student? In what skill area or subject?
6. What problems does the student have, if any? In what skill area or subject?
7. What interests or special abilities does the student demonstrate in class?
8. In what way has the student performed well?
9. How can the parent help the student?
10. How can the parent help the teacher?

Source: Adapted from Leonard H. Clark and Irving S. Starr, *Secondary and Middle School. Teaching Methods*, 5th ed. (New York: Macmillan: 1986), p. 393; Jeffrey I. Gelfer and Peggy G. Perkins, "Effective Communication with Parents," *Childhood Education*, October 1987, pp. 19–22.

---

conference, unless there is an important problem, lasts 20 to 30 minutes (See Tips for Teachers 3.3).

The parent-teacher conference is helpful for both parties. The conference helps teachers (1) understand and clarify parents' impressions and expectations of the school program or particular classes, (2) obtain additional information about the child, (3) report on the child's developmental progress and suggest things the parents can do to stimulate development, (4) develop a working relationship with parents, and (5) encourage parents' support of the school. The conference helps parents (1) gain a better understanding of the child's school program, (2) learn about school activities that can enhance the child's growth and development, (3) learn about the child's performance and progress, (4) learn about the school's faculty and support staff, (5) communicate concerns and ask questions about the child, and (6) both provide and receive information that can benefit the child's development in school and at home.[52]

Letters to Parents

Letters to parents fall into three categories. First, letters are sent to make parents aware of or invite them to participate in certain classroom or school activities or functions. Second, letters may be sent out regularly, perhaps weekly or bimonthly, to keep parents up to date about their children's academic work and behavior. Parents are entitled to and appreciate this communication. Informing parents and seeking their input and support may help to stop minor problems before they become serious. Of course, letters can be about commendable behavior. Third, letters are written to address specific problems. In such letters problems are described, parents are asked for their cooperation in one or more ways, and a conference may be requested.

Guidelines for Communicating with Parents

Over the years many suggestions have been offered for teachers in conducting a parent conference and communicating to them. The guidelines below emphasize the need for (1) establishing a friendly atmosphere, (2) discussing the child's potential and limitations in an objective manner, (3) avoiding arguments and remaining calm, and (4) observing professional ethics.

Mechanics with the Parent

1. Make an appointment for the conference well in advance.
2. Provide two or more options for the parent's visit.
3. Greet the parent courteously using his or her proper name. Stand up to greet the person.
4. Take the parent's wraps and show him to a comfortable chair.
5. If the parent is upset or emotional, let him express his feelings without interruptions. Do not become defensive; remain calm.
6. Be objective in analyzing the child's progress; also, show interest in the child's development, growth, and welfare.
7. Never get trapped into criticizing another teacher or the principal.
8. Explain how you and the parent can work together to help the student.
9. Set up a date for a follow-up conference, if needed.
10. Walk the parent to the door. If possible, end on a positive note.

---

[52]Jeffrey L. Gelfer and Peggy B. Perkins, "Effective Communication with Parents," *Childhood Education*, October 1987, pp. 19–22.

Discussion About the Child

1. Begin on a postive note.
2. Be truthful and honest.
3. Accept the parent's feelings.
4. Emphasize the child's strengths.
5. Be specific about the student's learning difficulties.
6. Have ready samples of the student's class work and homework as well as a record of his or her test scores, attendance, etc.
7. Be receptive to the parent's suggestions.
8. Let the parent have the opportunity to talk about his or her concerns.
9. Avoid arguments; avoid pedantic language.
10. Provide constructive suggestions.
11. Be willing to explain activities or changes in the school curriculum that meet the needs of the child.
12. Close on a positive note, with a plan of action.[53]

THEORY INTO PRACTICE

Your evaluation of students and your grading of them can be useful in making decisions about where to place students in class or in programs. Errors in evaluation need to be reduced, and both students and teachers must see marks and grades as representative of actual achievement (or behavior) but also amendable. Most important, grades should not be dropped from your teaching or from school practice because of criticism. We live in groups, and regardless of how competitive or uncompetitive we want others to be, we will always be evaluating people. What we need to do is to seek ways to improve our evaluation system. According to Gage and Berliner, we need to temper our judgments with "sensibility" and "humaneness." We need to give students the benefit when in doubt, and we need to reduce the anxiety, stress, and unnecessary competition that often accompanies testing, grading, and evaluation.[54]

Seven research-based generalizations about grading students have practical application.

1. Grades should be derived from multiple sources (tests, quizzes, homework, papers, projects, class participation, and so forth), but the sources should be weighted differently.
2. Grades should reflect the most significant instructional objectives and learning outcomes.
3. Students should understand the grading system. The more sophisticated the system, the older the students should be.

---

[53] Allan C. Ornstein, "Parent Conferencing: Recommendations and Guidelines," *Kappa Delta Pi Record* (Winter 1990), in print.

[54] Gage and Berliner, *Educational Psychology.*

4. Students should know in advance how grades are to be determined.

5. Higher standards generally lead to greater student effort on school tasks, but too demanding a system or the absence of sufficient reward is likely to hamper students' achievement and students' self-concept.

6. Grading should be fair and objective, not subject to arbitrariness or undue subjectivity.

7. The teacher should accept the responsibility that grading involves professional judgment and not use an artificial or biased set of numbers to discourage effort or growth in personal achievement.[55]

Below are some practical questions to consider in evaluating and improving your grading and reporting system.

1. Does your evaluation system coincide with your instructional objectives?

2. Is your evaluation system understood by your students and their parents?

3. Does your evaluation system motivate student learning?

4. Is your evaluation system detailed enough to be diagnostic, yet broad enough to be operational for all students?

5. Do you make use of evaluation information for purposes of beginning instruction?

6. Do you use both summative and formative evaluation techniques?

7. Does your evaluation system promote two-way communication between home and school?

8. Does your evaluation system promote good public relations?

9. Is your evaluation system economical in terms of teacher time?

10. Does the evaluation system coincide with school policy or school guidelines[56]

Your evaluation system may not meet all of these criteria, but it should come close. It is expected, too, that your evaluation procedures accommodate the grade level and maturity of your students and consider the students' self-concept and well-being. Finally, we would expect your evaluation system to be fair.

SUMMARY

1. The reasons for evaluating students include motivating students, providing feedback to students and teachers, informing parents, and making selection decisions.

---

[55] Tamar Gendler, "The Testing Paradox," *Education Digest*, January 1989, pp. 27–29; Madgic, "The Point System of Grading"; and Natriello, "The Impact of Evaluation Processes of Students."

[56] Mehrens and Lehmann, *Measurement and Evaluation in Education and Psychology*; Ornstein, "Evaluation of Students."

2. Four types of evaluation are placement, diagnostic, formative, and summative.

3. Sources of information for evaluation in addition to formal tests include classroom discussion and activity, homework, notebooks, providing reports, and quizzes.

4. Grades are based on absolute or relative scales. Alternative grading practices include contracts, mastery grading, and grades for effort and progress.

5. The conventional report card emphasizes basic subject areas and uses letters to designate grades; more contemporary methods of reporting include mastery and progress reports and statements about process.

6. The cumulative record is a legal document that includes important data about the student's performance and behavior in school; it follows the students thoughout their school career.

7. Communication with parents takes place in the form of report cards, conferences, and letters.

DISCUSSION QUESTIONS TO CONSIDER

1. Can a teacher be objective in evaluating student performance? Explain.

2. How would you distinguish between placement, diagnostic, formative, and summative evaluation?

3. How might you improve your own grading practice compared to that of teachers you had in school?

4. What are the differences between absolute and relative standards in grading? Which do you prefer? Why?

5. Why is it desirable to use several sources of data when arriving at a grade for a student?

THINGS TO DO

1. From your past school experiences, list some examples of inappropriate evaluation techniques.

2. List and discuss criteria for good grading.

3. Outline a grading procedure you expect to follow as a teacher.

4. Visit local schools, obtain sample report cards, and discuss their major characteristics in class. Analyze how various report cards differ.

5. Pretend you are about to have a general conference with a parent for the first time. Discuss with your classmates what topics might be important to include in a conference.

RECOMMENDED READINGS

Bloom, Benjamin S., J. Thomas Hastings, and George F. Madaus. *Handbook of Formative and Summative Evaluation of Student Learning.* New York: McGraw-Hill, 1971. A mammoth-size text that can serve as an excellent source for technical questions about evaluation.

Gronlund, Norman E. *Measurement and Evaluation in Teaching,* 5th ed. New York: Macmillan, 1985. An appreciation of the advantages and disadvantages of various tests and evaluation procedures.

House, Ernest R. *Evaluating With Validity.* Berkeley, Calif.: Sage, 1980. Comparison of various methods of evaluating school programs.

Mehrens, William A., and Irving J. Lehmann. *Measurement and Evaluation in Education and Psychology,* 4th ed. New York: Holt, Rinehart and Winston, 1984. An important reference on testing and evaluation that is both theoretical and practical, comprehensive but easy to read.

Popham, W. James. *Modern Educational Measurement,* 2nd ed. Englewood Cliffs, N.J.: Prentice-Hall, 1990. Various models and strategies for evaluating student outcomes.

Walsh, W. Bruce. *Tests and Measurements,* 4th ed. Englewood Cliffs, N.J.: Prentice-Hall, 1989. Practical advice on how to plan, conduct, and use evaluation techniques.

Worthen, Blaine R., Walter R. Borg, and Karl R. White. *Measurement and Evaluation in Schools.* New York: Longman, 1989. Helps the reader assess the quality and function of evaluation tools and how to interpret them; how to set up schoolwide evaluation programs.

KEY TERMS

Placement evaluation

Diagnostic evaluation

Formative evaluation

Summative evaluation

Informal evaluation

Absolute grades

Relative grades

Contract grading

Mastery grading

Continuous progress grading

Mastery report card

Computerized recordkeeper

Cumulative record

Chapter 5

Instructional Objectives

FOCUSING QUESTIONS

1. What should the schools teach?

2. How are aims, goals, and objectives formulated?

3. How do aims, goals, and objectives differ?

4. How would you characterize the approaches to writing objectives by the following: Tyler, Bloom, Gronlund, Mager, and Gagné?

5. How does each approach differ? In what way should teachers use enabling objectives?

6. How specific should course objectives be? Classroom objectives?

*T*o understand why and how to use instructional objectives results in more effective teaching and testing. The use of instructional objectives helps the teacher focus on what students should know at the end of the lessons plan or unit plant (a series of lessons related to a specific topic), likewise, helps students know what is expected of them. Instructional objectives help the teacher plan for teaching and organize instruction; they identify what to teach and when to teach it, and thus serve as a "map" or guide for both teachers and students. Instructional objectives are stated in observable and measurable terms, and clarify whether what we intended was achieved or to what extent it was (or was not) achieved.

Aims, *goals*, and *objectives* are terms that can be defined in many ways. We use the term **aims** to refer to broad statements about the intent of education. They are value-laden statements, written by panels, commissions, or policy-making groups, that express a philosophy of education and concepts of the social role of schools and the needs of children and youth. In short, they are broad guides for translating the needs of society into educational policy. Aims, sometimes called *purposes*, are written on a societal (or national) level. They are descriptive and vaguely written statements. For example, what does the phrase "Preparing students for Democratic citizenship" mean? What do we have in mind when we stress "Citizenship preparation"?

Educators need to translate aims into statements that will describe what schools are expected to accomplish (which is more focused than stating the purpose of education). These translations are called **goals.** Goals make it possible to organize learning experiences in terms of what the state, school district, or school plans to stress on a systemwide basis. In effect, goals are statements that cut across subjects and grade levels and represent the entire school program. Goals are more definite than aims, but they are still nonbehavioral and therefore nonobservable and nonmeasurable. Goals provide direction for educators, but they do not specify achievement levels or proficiency levels. Examples of goals are "Development of reading skills," "Appreciation of art," and "Understanding of mathematical concepts." Goals are written by professional associations and state and local educational agencies to be published as school and curriculum guidelines for what all students should accomplish over their entire school career.

Objectives are descriptions of what is to eventually take place at the classroom level. They specify content and sometimes the proficiency level to be attained. Objectives are stated in behavioral terms. They state specific skills, tasks, content, and attitudes to be taught and learned, and give teachers and students a standard by which to judge if they are achieving the objectives. According to Hilda Taba, "The chief function of . . . objectives is to guide the making of . . . decisions on what to cover, what to emphasize, and what content to select, and what learning experiences to stress."[1] Because the possibilities

---

[1]Hilda Taba, *Curriculum Development: Theory and Research* (New York: Harcourt Brace Jovanovich, 1962), p. 197.

of content, learning, and teaching are endless, teachers face the problem of selection: What content is most important? What learning activities are most appropriate? What unit plan is most effective? Objectives supply criteria for these decisions, according to Taba. No matter what its nature, the statement of objectives in terms of desired outcomes "sets the scope and limits for what is to be taught and learned."[2]

Naturally, objectives should be consistent with the overriding goals of the school system and state and the general educational aims of society. Each teacher, when planning for instruction, may contribute to these goals and aims in a different way. Recalling our three examples of goals, we can now give examples of objectives to be attained in their pursuit: (1) goal: Development of reading skills; objective: To gain knowledge in word recognition; (2) goal: Appreciation of art; objective: To recognize the paintings of major artists; (3) goal: Understanding of mathematical concepts; objective: To understand mathematical proofs.

AIMS

Aims are important statements that guide our schools and give educators direction. However, we will discuss them only briefly because they are not written by teachers. Perhaps the most widely accepted list of educational aims in the twentieth century was compiled by the Commission on the Reorganization of Secondary Education in 1918. Its influential bulletin was entitled *Cardinal Principles of Secondary Education.* The seven principles, or aims, designated by the commission are listed below.

1. *Health.* The secondary school should . . . provide health instruction, inculcate health habits, organize an effective program of physical activities, regard health needs in planning work and play, and cooperate with home and community in safeguarding and promoting health interests.
2. *Command of fundamental processes.* The facility that a child of twelve or fourteen years may acquire . . . is not sufficient for the needs of modern life. [Further instruction in the fundamentals is urged.]
3. *Worthy home membership.* Worthy home membership as an objective calls for the development of those qualities that make the individual a worthy member of a family, both contributing to and deriving benefit from that membership.
4. *Vocation.* Vocational education should equip the individual to secure a livelihood for himself and those dependent on him, to serve society well through his vocation, to maintain the right relationships toward his fellow workers and society, and, as far as possible, to find in that vocation his own best development.

---

[2]Ibid.

5. *Civic education.* Civic education should develop in the individual those qualities whereby he will act well his part as a member of neighborhood, town or city, state, and nation, and give him a basis for understanding international problems.

6. *Worthy use of leisure.* Education should equip the individual to secure from his leisure the recreation of body, mind, and spirit, and the enrichment and enlargement of his personality.

7. *Ethical character.* In a democratic society ethical character becomes paramount among the objectives of the secondary school. Among the means for developing ethical character may be mentioned the wide selection of content and methods of instruction in all subjects of study and the social contacts of pupils with one another and with their teachers.[3]

The Commission's work was the first statement of educational aims to address the need to assimilate immigrant children and to educate an industrial work force, reflecting events in the country at that period. The most important aspect of the document is that it emphasized the need to educate all students for "complete living," not to educate only students headed for college and not to develop only cognitive abilities. It endorsed the concept of the whole child, meeting the various needs of students, while it provided a common ground for teaching and enhancing American ideals and educating all citizens to function in a democratic society. These aims are still relevant for all levels of education and are still found today in one form or another in statements of educational aims.

GOALS

Goals tend to reflect the developmental needs of children and youth. According to Peter Oliva, goals "are timeless, in the sense that no time is specified by which the goals must be reached" and at the same time they "are not permanent," in the sense that they "may be modified wherever necessary or desirable." Goals usually cut across subjects and grades and apply throughout the school. They do not delineate specific items of content or corresponding activities. Goals should be stated broadly enough "to be accepted at any level of the educational enterprise," but specifically enough to lead to desired outcomes.[4]

Increasingly, the schools are being burdened by the rest of society with roles and responsibilities that other agencies and institutions no longer do well

---

[3]Commission on the Reorganization of Secondary Education, *Cardinal Principles of Secondary Education* (Washington, D.C.: U.S. Government Printing Office, 1918), pp. 11–15.

[4]Peter F. Oliva, *Developing the Curriculum,* 2nd ed. (Glenview, Ill.: Scott, Foresman, 1988), p. 265.

Figure 5.1 All teachers can benefit from collegial discussion of aims and goals. (Photo © Richard S. Orton).

or want to do.[5] The schools are seen as ideal agents to solve the problems of the nation, community, and home. Many people and groups refuse to admit to their own responsibilities in helping children develop their capabilities and adjust to society. More and more, the schools are being told that they must educate and socialize all children, regardless of the initial input and support from home. The schools may now be attempting to accomplish too many things and therefore not performing many of them effectively.

In preparing his classic *Study of Schooling*, John Goodlad surveyed the school goals that had been published by state and local boards of education across the country. From approximately 100 different statements of goals, he constructed 12 that represent the spirit of the total list (Table 5.1). He further defined each with subgoals and a rationale statement. The goals summarize what educators are expected to attend to and what they might be held accountable for.

Goal statements are often written by professional associations for educators at the state and local level to modify and adopt. One of the more influential list of goals was published by the Association for Supervision and Curriculum Development (Table 5.2). Many of the goals are interrelated, and the achievement of some facilitates the achievement of others. The acquisition of basic

---

[5] Mario D. Fantini, "Adapting to Diversity—Future Trends in Curriculum," *National Association of Secondary School Principals*, May 1985, pp. 15–22; Allan C. Ornstein, "How Do Educators Meet the Needs of Society?" *National Association of Secondary School Principals*, May 1985, pp. 36–47; and Ornstein, "The Evolving Accountability Movement," *Peabody Journal of Education* (in print 1990).

skills, for example, is prerequisite to all other goals. Anything that prevents the achievement of one goal may thereby restrict the attainments of other goals.

When we formulate our goals, we might ask the following questions:

To what extent should our schools emphasize the needs of society and the needs of the individual? Should schools emphasize excellence or equality? Should we put equal emphasis on academic, vocational, and general education?

Table 5.1   MAJOR GOALS OF AMERICAN SCHOOLS

---

1. *Mastery of basic skills or fundamental processes.* In our technological civilization, an individual's ability to participate in the activities of society depends on mastery of these fundamental processes.
2. *Career or vocational education.* An individual's personal satisfaction in life is significantly related to satisfaction with her or his job. Intelligent career decisions require knowledge of personal aptitudes and interests in relation to career possibilities.
3. *Intellectual development.* As civilization has become more complex, people have had to rely more heavily on their rational abilities. Full intellectual development of each member of society is necessary.
4. *Enculturation.* Studies that illuminate our relationship with the past yield insights into our society and its values; furthermore, these strengthen an individual's sense of belonging, identity, and direction for his or her own life.
5. *Interpersonal relations.* Schools should help every child understand, appreciate, and value persons belonging to social, cultural, and ethnic groups different from the child's own and to increase affiliation with and decrease alienation toward them.
6. *Autonomy.* Unless schools produce self-directed citizens, they have failed both society and the individual. As society becomes more complex, demands on individuals multiply. Schools help prepare children for a world of rapid change by developing in them the capacity to assume responsibility for their own needs.
7. *Citizenship.* To counteract the present human ability to destroy humanity and the environment requires citizen involvement in the political and social life of this country. A democracy can survive only with the participation of its members.
8. *Creativity and aesthetic perception.* Abilities for creating new and meaningful things and appreciating the creations of other human beings are essential both for personal self-realization and for the benefit of society.
9. *Self-concept.* The self-concept of an individual serves as a reference point and feedback mechanism for personal goals and aspirations. Factors for a healthy self-concept can be provided by the school environment.
10. *Emotional and physical well-being.* Emotional stability and physical fitness are perceived as necessary conditions for attaining the other goals, but they are also worthy ends in themselves.
11. *Moral and ethical character.* Development of the judgment needed to evaluate events and phenomena as right or wrong and a commitment to truth, moral integrity, moral conduct, and a desire to strengthen the moral fabric of society are the values manifested by this goal.
12. *Self-realization.* Efforts to develop a better self contribute to the development of a better society.

Source: John I. Goodlad, *What Schools Are For* (Bloomington, Ind.: Phi Delta Kappa, 1979), pp. 44–52. Also see Goodlad, *A Place Called School* (New York: McGraw-Hill, 1984).

Table 5.2   EDUCATIONAL GOALS OF THE ASSOCIATION OF SUPERVISION AND
CURRICULUM DEVELOPMENT

1. *Basic skills:* Acquires information and meaning through observing, listening, and reading, as well as through reflective thinking.

2. *Self-conceptualization:* Recognizes that self-concept is acquired in interaction with other people, and distinguishes between significant and nonsignificant others.

3. *Understanding others:* Bases actions and decisions on the knowledge that individuals differ and are similar in many ways, and that values and behaviors are learned and differ from one social group to another; acts on belief that each individual has value as a human being and should be respected as a worthwhile person in his or her own right.

4. *Using accumulated knowledge to interpret the world:* Applies basic principles and concepts of the sciences, arts, and humanities to interpret personal experiences; analyzes and acts upon public issues: understands natural phenomena, evaluates technological progress, and appreciates aesthetic events.

5. *Continuous Learning:* Bases actions and decisions on the knowledge that it is necessary to continue to learn throughout life because of the inevitability of change.

6. *Mental and physical well-being:* Consumes a nutritionally balanced, wholesome diet, exercises sufficiently to maintain personal health; avoids, to the extent possible, consuming materials harmful to health, particularly addictive ones; behaves rationally based upon reasonable perceptions of self and society; and perceives self positively with a generally competent sense of well-being.

7. *Participation in the economic world of production and consumption:* Selects and pursues career opportunities consonant with social and personal needs and capabilities; makes informed consumer decisions based on appropriate knowledge of products, needs, and resources.

8. *Responsible societal membership:* Acts consonant with an understanding of the basic interdependence of the biological and physical resources of the enviroment; acts in accordance with a basic ethical framework incorporating those values contributing to group living, such as honesty, fairness, compassion, and integrity; assumes responsibility for own acts, works in groups to achieve mutual goals; and invokes law and authority to protect the rights of all persons.

9. *Creativity:* Generates a range of imaginative alternatives to stimuli; entertains and values the imaginative alternatives of others.

10. *Coping with change:* Works for goals on realistic personal performance standards; decides when a risk is worth taking; works now for goals to be realized in the future.

Source: Adapted from ASCD Committee on Research and Theory, *Measuring and Attaining the Goals of Education* (Aldexandira, Va.: Association for Supervision and Curriculum Development, 1980), pp. 9–12.

Should we put more emphasis on cognitive learning or humanistic learning? Which is more important—national commitment or a higher morality? Should we educate students to their own ability level (and for some, that might only mean an eighth-grade education) or should we push students beyond their aptitude and achievement level? How should we apportion money to be spent on talented and gifted students, average students, and handicapped students? How do we compare the payoff to society and the obligations of society in educating different student populations?

These questions are tough and complicated that not only do educators disagree about them, but wars have been fought over them. Indeed, the way we answer these questions both reflects and determines the kind of people we are. Most people in this country readily say they believe in democracy, but how they answer these questions determines what democracy means and how it affects and controls our lives. Trying to resolve these questions, at least in this country, ideally involves a balancing act and particularly, the question as to whether our moral and legal restraints overrule our political and economic considerations and whether needs of the group can be placed in perspective with the rights of the individual.

LEVELS OF OBJECTIVES

Instructional objectives help the teacher focus on what students should know at the end of a lesson, unit, or course, and also help students know what is expected of them. They help the teacher plan and organize instruction by identifying what is to be taught and when it is to be taught. Instructional objectives are stated in observable and measurable terms (outcomes, proficiencies, or competencies). Their specificity enables the teacher to determine whether what was intended was achieved, and to what extent.

When we move from goals to instructional objectives, the role and responsibility of the teacher become evident. Objectives are behavioral in nature and are observable and measurable in some way. They are formulated on three levels with increasing specificity: program, course, and classroom. Objectives at the classroom level can be further divided into unit plan and lesson plan objectives.

Program Objectives

Program objectives stem from the goals of the school and are written at the subject and grade level. Although they do not usually state specific content or competencies, they do focus on general content and behaviors. Like goals, they refer to the accomplishments of all students, rather than to those of individual students.[6]

Nearly every state and school district has an overview or set of program

---

[6]Ivor K. Davies, *Objectives in Curriculum Design* (New York: McGraw-Hill, 1976); Oliva, *Developing the Curriculum.*

objectives at the subject and grade level to facilitate what teachers should be teaching. In most cases these instructional objectives are formulated by curriculum committees made up of administrative, teacher, and community (or parent) groups. Table 5.3 provides a detailed list of the instructional objectives for grades 1 through 8 in four subject areas for the Chicago Public Schools. (The original list included eight other subject areas—language arts, art, music, physical education, health and safety, library science, homemaking, and industrial arts—not shown on the table.) The table helps the reader envision program objectives on a vertical and horizontal basis, to see relationships that exist by subjects and grade levels.

Course Objectives

Course objectives are derived from program objectives: They categorize and organize content and sometimes concepts, problems, or behaviors, but do not specify the exact content to be examined or exact instructional methods and materials to be used. Course objectives are stated in the form of topics, concepts, or general behaviors.

Objectives stated as *topics* for an American history course might be "The Colonial Period," "The Revolutionary Period," "The Framing of the Constitution," "Manifest Destiny," "The Civil War Period," "The Reconstruction Period," "Industrialization and Colonialization," "Immigration and Nationalism," "World War I." Objectives stated as *concepts* for a science course might be "Science and Knowledge," "Science and Method," "Science and Humanity," "Science and Environment," "Science, Products, and Technology," "Science and Space." Examples of objectives stated as general *behaviors* (which are not easy to measure or observe) might be phrased "To develop critical thinking in . . .," "To increase understanding of . . .," "To have experience for. . . ."

Course objectives (as well as program objectives) help the teacher organize the content in terms of *scope* (topics, concepts, behaviors to be covered), *continuity* (recurring and continuing opportunity to teach important content and practice certain skills and tasks), *sequence* (cumulative development or successive treatment of topics, concepts, or behaviors that build upon preceding ones), and *integration* (relationships of content in one course to content in another course).[7]

Classroom Objectives

Classroom objectives are usually formulated by the teacher. Classroom objectives divide course objectives into several units. Unit plan objectives usually encompass one to three weeks of instruction, organized in a sequence and

---

[7]David G. Armstrong, *Developing and Documenting the Curriculum* (Needham Heights, Mass.: Allyn and Bacon, 1989); Allan C. Ornstein and Francis P. Hunkins, *Curriculum: Foundations, Principles and Issues* (Englewood Cliffs, N.J.: Prentice-Hall, 1988); and Taba, *Curriculum Development: Theory and Practice.*

Table 5.3 OVERVIEW OF THE INSTRUCTIONAL PROGRAM OF THE CHICAGO PUBLIC SCHOOLS—K TO 8

Kindergarten

Reading	Mathematics	Science	Social Studies
Follows simple oral directions.	Compares sets of 0 to 9 objects.	Develops an awareness of the senses and proper care of the body.	Tells about self, including name, address and city.
Understands left-to-right orientation.	Names the number in a set of 0 through 9 objects.	Describes the purpose of the family and the roles of family members.	Describes interests, such as pets, games, and toys.
Recognizes differences in shapes.	Identifies the first, second, and third object in a sequence.	Identifies some animals.	Identifies new friends at school.
Identifies beginning, middle, and end objects.	Joins and separates sets, and names the new groups.	Describes the interrelation of the sun, moon, and earth.	Describes the many ways of being a friend.
Supplies missing elements in pictures.	Orders sets of 1 through 9 objects.	Develops an awareness of matter and energy.	Describes the physical appearance and characteristics of the schoolroom.
Identifies numerals.	Identifies and names congruent parts of whole as one-half or one-third.	Identifies characteristics of plants.	Tells what the schoolroom rules and regulations are.
Infers story outcome from picture sequences.	Names one-half of a group of up to four objects.		Explains the purpose of a family and the roles of family members.
Understands the five senses.	Tells time to the hour.		Describes some interests and activities of family life.
Distinguishes fact from fantasy.	Compares lengths of objects to one another and to a meter.		Explains what is involved in caring for a home.
Completes simple abstract patterns.	Identifies models of circles, triangles, rectangles, and squares.		Explains how leisure time is used.
Interprets nursery rhymes.			Recognizes the importance of responsibility at home and in school.
Pantomimes character parts.			Participates in room and school activities in accordance with rules and regulations.
			Tells what is happening in a picture portraying an urban area.
			Uses the globe to learn the shape of the earth.

	Grade 1		
Reading	**Mathematics**	**Science**	**Social Studies**
Identifies details in pictures.	Names, reads, writes, compares, and renames numbers to 99.	Recognizes characteristics of animals.	Identifies rules and reasons for proper behavior at school.
Places pictures in sequence.	Identifies the fourth through the ninth object in a sequence.	Describes how mammals grow inside the mother's body and resemble their parents at birth.	Develops a respect for individuals of ethnic and racial groups.
Differentiates among the five senses.	Recalls basic addition and subtraction facts with sums through 10.	Identifies basic concepts about air.	Tells ways of becoming a good friend.
Chooses titles for pictures.	Divides a unit or a group whole into sixths, eighths, and tenths, and names each part.	Recognizes winter preparation of plants and animals.	Identifies school workers.
Answers "how" and "why" questions.	Demonstrates that 2/2, 3/3, 4/4, 6/6, 8/8, and 10/10 equal one whole.	Identifies some physical properties of matter.	Recognizes the need for love, cooperation, and understanding in a family.
Uses word clues to identify the correct picture.	Tells time to the half-hour.	Recognizes spring changes in plants and animals.	Identifies neighborhood areas of homes, businesses, and recreation.
Uses words in context to identify a word with a similar meaning or an opposite meaning.	Tells the month, day, and year shown on calendar.	Identifies the uses of simple machines.	Recognizes examples of cooperation in the neighborhood.
Understands words that describe.	Makes change for money up to a quarter.		Identifies different ways of travel.
Understands and compares the seasons.	Estimates and measures length using nonstandard units.		Compares an urban community with a farm community.
Identifies initial, final, and medial consonants.	Compares the mass of two objects by estimating and by weighing.		Identifies animals that are seen at the zoo.
Knows first grade sight words.	Classifies three-dimensional objects.		Compares people in the neighborhood with people in neighborhoods in other urban areas.
Identifies compound words.			Distinguishes between a map and a globe.
Knows consonant digraphs *ch, sh, th,* and *wh.*			Recognizes land and water areas on a map and on a globe.
Knows two-letter consonant blends.			Identifies *north* and *south* on maps and on a globe.
Knows plural forms *-s* and *-es.*			Identifies pictorial symbols on maps.
Knows short vowels.			
Knows alphabetical order.			
Reacts to humor in poetry.			
Recognizes rhyming patterns.			

Reading	Mathematics	Science	Social Studies
		Grade 2	

Reading	Mathematics	Science	Social Studies
Matches pictures with phrases. Arranges sentences in sequence. Draws details outlined in a short story. Understands simple cause-effect relationships. Uses letter clues to determine word meaning in sentences. Applies categorizing to word lists. Uses questions to understand the literal meaning of sentences. Chooses titles for short, written stories. Identifies topic sentences in short stories. Understands inferences and predicts outcomes. Knows pronunciation of vowels controlled by *l, w,* and *r.* Identifies diphthongs *ew, oi, ou, ow,* and *oy.* Knows hard and soft sounds of *c, g,* and *s.* Alphabetizes to the second letter. Applies long vowel generalizations. Knows consonant blends and digraphs. Identifies symbols on picture maps. Understands plural forms of nouns ending in *-y, -e,* and *-fe.* Knows verb endings *ed, ing,* and *-s.* Identifies rhyming patterns. Recognizes alliteration in poetry.	Names, reads, writes, compares, and renames numbers to 9,999. Recalls basic addition and subtraction facts with sums through 18. Adds and subtracts up to three-digit numbers with regrouping. Recalls multiplication and division facts 0, 1, 2, 5, and 10. Writes numerals for halves, thirds, fourths, sixths, eighths, or tenths of a unit whole or group. Tells time to the quarter-hour. Marks a given date on the calendar. Counts money up to $1.00. Estimates and measures lengths in centimeters and decimeters. Tells the number of objects in a dozen and in a half-dozen. Distinguishes between a line and a line segment.	Recognizes characteristics of living things. Describes the dependence of the earth upon the sun. States basic concepts of matter and energy. Explains the importance of water to living things. Lists the parts of plants and their functions. Explains the relationship of man to domestic animals. Distinguishes between animals which are hatched from eggs and those which are born alive.	Describes the people and customs of the community. Explains available community public services. Names types of foods, clothing, and homes that are available in the community. Identifies community workers. Explains the importance of respecting school property. Describes places and types of recreation in the community. Explains how weather and climate affect the community. Explains the benefits of modern transportation. Identifies various kinds of communication. Describes the differences between two communities within the same state. Describes the differences between a local community and an overseas community. Reads information on charts. Uses picture maps. Locates information on a globe. Computes distance in blocks from home to parks and playgrounds. Locates the equator on a globe and maps.

Grade 3

Reading	Mathematics	Science	Social Studies
Applies categorizing to paragraphs.	Names, reads, writes, compares, and renames numbers to 999,999.	Explains man's dependence upon green plants.	Lists factors that make Chicago a great city.
Analyzes response choices for best answer.	Adds three or more four-digit numbers.	Explains basic principles about the earth.	Explains how Chicago functions as the "heart" of the metropolitan area.
Understands concepts of past, present, and future in passages.	Finds the difference between two numbers of up to five digits, with regrouping.	Explains basic principles of air.	Explains why Chicago is a famous city.
Understands complex cause-effect relationships.	Recalls multiplication and division facts with products to 81.	Explains basic principles about matter and energy.	Identifies symbols on the flag of Chicago.
Discriminates between simple facts and opinions.	Multiplies and divides two-digit numbers by one-digit numbers.	Identifies basic characteristics of birds.	Recognizes famous names in Chicago history.
Uses basic phonics skills to recognize and reproduce sounds of consonants, long and short vowels, and three-letter combinations of consonants and vowels.	Compares, names, and writes equivalent fractions for halves, thirds, fourths, sixths, eighths, and tenths.	Identifies basic characteristics of cold-blooded animals.	Identifies three important events in the early history of Chicago.
Knows silent letter combinations.	Tells time to the minute.	Identifies the parts of the body.	Explains some of the duties of a citizen of Chicago.
Alphabetizes to the third letter.	Makes change for money up to $5.00.	Categorizes animals in terms of how they care for their young.	Compares Chicago with another metropolitan area in the United States.
Recognizes meanings of words in context.	Estimates and measures to find mass in kilograms, capacity in liters, and lengths in customary and metric units.		Compares Chicago with an overseas metropolitan area.
Understands synonyms, antonyms, and homonyms.	Estimates and reads temperature.		Obtains information from simple line and bar graphs.
Locates places on a street map.	Measures perimeters of polygons.		Locates Chicago on a map and globe in relation to Illinois and other states in the region.
Identifies the correct meaning for words with two meanings.	Identifies a right angle.		Locates main streets of Chicago on city map.
Understands the purpose of a pronunciation key, guide words, and a glossary.	Identifies the radius and diameter of a circle.		Locates home and school on a map of Chicago.
Understands lyric poetry and narrative.			Identifies major bodies of water and land on maps and on a globe.
Understands onomatopoeia.			
Reads fables.			

Reading	Mathematics	Science	Social Studies
		Grade 4	

Reading	Mathematics	Science	Social Studies
Answers questions about simple charts, diagrams, graphs, and globes.	Names, reads, writes, renames, and compares numbers up to 9,999,999.	Recognizes the importance of insects and spiders.	Describes the physical features of the regions of the United States.
Understands time sequences.	Names the value of each digit in a decimal up to two digits.	Identifies the relationships among living things and their environment.	Explains how natural resources have contributed to the growth and development of the state.
Locates topic sentences in short paragraphs.	Multiplies mentally using 10, 100, and 1,000 as factors.	Describes the characteristics of cells as the basic unit of life.	Explains how natural resources have contributed to the growth and development of the various regions of the United States.
Uses specific questions to make inferences.	Names the product of two 2-digit factors.	Recognizes the relationship of the earth to the solar system.	Explains how the people in the various regions of the United States meet their basic needs.
Identifies author's purpose as revealed through characterization and plot.	Divides a three-digit dividend by a one- or two-digit divisor.	Describes the composition of matter and its relationship to energy transfer.	Compares and contrasts regions of the United States with similar regions in other parts of the world.
Uses clues and definitions to discriminate between fact and opinion.	Writes the family of equations related to a given multiplication equation.	Recognizes characteristics of tree growth and the dependence of man upon trees.	Identifies on maps such surface features as mountains, plains, lands, and water.
Understands root words and affixes.	Finds the average of a set of numbers.		Locates land and water boundaries of the continental United States.
Uses questions and structural analysis to infer word meanings.	Names sets of equivalent fractions.		Groups states within the United States according to regional locations.
Knows comparative adjectives.	Names fractional parts of numbers.		
Understands negative contractions.	Compares and orders two rational numbers.		Recognizes natural and political boundaries on maps.
Uses five syllabication rules to syllabicate two-syllable words.	Renames common fractions as decimal fractions and decimal fractions as common fractions.		Uses map symbols to find the capitals and the population of cities.
Understands the relationship of north, south, east, and west in map reading.	Tells time to the nearest second.		
Uses a scale of miles to estimate distances.	Computes equivalence of measures.		
Identifies alliteration in poetry.	Constructs and interprets picture graphs and scale drawings.		
Identifies the setting of stories and dramas.	Classifies models of curves.		
Distinguishes between fiction and nonfiction.	Names models as triangles, quadrilaterals, rectangles, squares, hexagons, or pentagons.		
	Constructs triangles.		

Grade 5

Reading	Mathematics	Science	Social Studies
Makes simple inferences about who, where, when, what, and why.	Reads and writes Roman numerals.	Identifies the properties of air and its relationship to weather.	Identifies the routes used by the people who discovered the New World.
Identifies main topics and subtopics in lists and identifies topic sentences in three different types of paragraphs.	Names, reads, writes, and renames numbers up to 99,999,999.	Recognizes the basic principles of aviation and space flight.	Lists reasons why people came to the New World.
Infers mood from short paragraphs of fiction.	Names the value of each digit in a decimal fraction through thousandths.	Recognizes the behavior of heat energy and its relationship to light energy.	Describes some of the problems encountered in building the new nation.
Summarizes descriptive, explanatory, and sequential paragraphs.	Multiplies two 3-digit numbers.	Classifies animals.	Explains some of the causes of the westward movement.
Analyzes information for true/false statements and time comparisons.	Divides a five-digit dividend by a two-digit divisor.	Identifies characteristics of human reproduction and pubertal development.	Compares and contrasts the government of Canada with that of the United States.
Recognizes metaphors and sensory images.	Renames fractions in higher or lower terms.	Recognizes the characteristics and importance of birds.	Explains the current relationship between Mexico and the United States.
Recognizes elements of plot in lengthy, complex stories.	Adds and subtracts fractions and decimals.	Describes the life processes and uses of plants.	Describes the ways of life in Central and South America.
Identifies origin of words and differentiates the meanings of words that have four or more meanings.	Orders any two rational numbers.		Explains the relationship of Puerto Rico to the United States.
Identifies three propaganda techniques.	Uses longitude and latitude.		Exhibits a knowledge of the geography of Latin America.
Uses an index to obtain information.	Makes and interprets charts, bar graphs, and line graphs.		Uses a scale of miles in computing distances.
Constructs new words using roots and affixes.	Estimates and measures length to the nearest millimeter.		Uses parallels of latitude and meridians of longitude to locate places on a map and a globe.
Relates word patterns and rules.	Computes the areas of rectangles, squares, and triangles.		Compares flat maps with a global representation of the world.
Uses latitude and longitude to locate places.	Determines congruency of angles.		Uses maps to relate natural factors to the economic development of a region.
Applies eight syllabication rules to divide multi-syllabic words.	Classifies rectangles as quadrilaterals with opposite sides conguent and four right angles.		
Critiques author's point of view.	Defines and identifies relationship between the radius and diameter of the same circle.		
Relates conflict to plot.	Performs operations with denominate numbers.		
	Measures angles to the nearest degree.		

Reading	Mathematics	Science	Social Studies

Reading	Mathematics	Science	Social Studies
Makes complex inferences about who, when, where, and what in lengthy passages.	Uses exponents to rename numbers that are products of like factors.	Recognizes that animals adapt to their environment and are influenced by man.	Explains how the land and climate influence cultural patterns in the Eastern Hemisphere.
Contrasts authors' opinions.	Renames percents as decimals and common fractions.	Identifies the atomic structure of matter.	Describes how the historical development of countries in the Eastern Hemisphere has influenced present conditions.
Shows how character traits are revealed.	Rounds three-place decimals to the nearest tenth and nearest hundredth.	Describes the universe.	Compares and contrasts the people and their ways of living in countries of the Eastern Hemisphere.
Completes three-level outlines based on long, concrete, familiar passages.	Adds and subtracts decimal fractions.	Describes the structure of the earth's crust and its role in helping to reveal the earth's history.	Compares and contrasts the political systems of the Union of Soviet Socialist Republics and the United States.
Makes inferences from facts in short texts.	Multiplies and divides decimal fractions.	Recognizes basic characteristics of seed-bearing plants.	Describes present conditions in countries of the Eastern Hemisphere.
Analyzes character differences and motivation.	Multiplies two mixed numbers.	Explains the role of heredity in human growth and development.	Recognizes the interdependence of the United States and the regions of the Eastern Hemisphere.
Identifies and defines descriptive phrases.	Divides fractions.	Identifies how simple machines help man.	Uses the globe and maps to locate areas of the world discussed in current events.
Answers identification and comparison questions from tables in textbooks.	Finds the missing term of a proportion.		Develops the ability to use a map scale for measuring distance.
Analyzes word patterns and style (propaganda techniques).	Solves problems involving percents.		Locates time zones and the International Date Line on a map and on a globe.
Uses guide words, syllabication, pronunciation key, and definitions.	Orders decimal fractions.		
Uses information in complex diagrams.	Estimates and computes the areas of circles, parallelograms, and other figures.		
Provides base words and their definitions for words that have affixes.	Renames metric measures.		
Completes analogies.	Computes the circumference of a circle.		
Compares information obtained from interpreting picture graphs.	Computes the volume of a rectangular prism.		
Identifies figures of speech in imagery.	Identifies and names models of triangular and rectangular prisms, cones, spheres, cylinders, and tetrahedrons.		
Recognizes characteristics of a ballad.	Identifies and tells the number of faces, vertices, and edges of a model of a space region.		
Identifies three elements to differentiate an autobiography from a biography.			
Analyzes rhymed and unrhymed poetry.			

Grade 7

Reading	Mathematics	Science	Social Studies
Distinguishes fact from opinion in lengthy, complex passages.	Identifies a set as finite or infinite and lists its members.	Compares the relationship of heat energy to the earth's atmosphere.	Describes life in primitive times.
Uses classification, association, and response choices to infer word meanings.	Describes the union and intersection of two or more sets.	Recognizes the basic principles of heat energy.	Lists contributions of early civilizations.
Interprets implied comparisons.	Expresses numbers in scientific notation.	States basic principles of solids, liquids, and gases.	Compares and contrasts Greek and Roman civilizations.
Analyzes paragraphs.	Solves for the missing term of an open sentence.	Interprets view regarding matter and energy.	Identifies the contributions of African cultures.
Infers mood and setting from complex passages.	Applies the identity elements in the solution of addition and multiplication problems.	States various types of chemical and physical changes.	Describes changes in the ways of living during the Middle Ages.
Identifies connotative words that create mood.	Names the least common multiple and greatest common factor of two numbers.	Recognizes the interrelation of the systems in the human body.	Describes the problems the English colonists encountered when settling the new nation.
Uses parts of a textbook to obtain reference information.	Renames common fractions as terminating or repeating decimals.	Relates the causes and prevention of diseases in humans to sexually transmitted diseases.	Compares and contrasts the viewpoints of the Loyalists and Tories.
Summarizes and uses information from charts and from line, bar, and circle graphs.	Solves problems involving ratios.	Compares the similarities and differences between the life processes of plants and animals.	Lists some of the problems encountered by the political leaders when trying to unite the nation.
Uses titles, subtitles, and illustrations to preview content-area texts.	Uses properties to solve equations.		Explains how the acquisition and development of western lands strengthened the nation.
Takes notes and summarizes passages from content-area texts.	Computes the areas of trapezoids, rhombuses, and other closed regions.		Explains the conflicting interests that resulted in the Civil War.
Distinguishes major from minor ideas.	Identifies adjacent angles.		Relates how the physical features of a region influence its history.
Constructs three-level outlines from notes and from complex paragraphs.	Compares measures of angles.		
Identifies techniques of characterization.			
Identifies characteristics of legends.			
Distinguishes lyric from narrative poetry.			
Recognizes irony and point of view.			
Uses letters of the alphabet to denote rhyme schemes.			

Reading	Mathematics	Grade 8 Science	Social Studies
Differentiates among figures of speech.	Pictures unions and intersections of sets.	Identifies the characteristics of the geology of Chicago.	Lists the characteristics of a modern industrial nation.
Infers word meaning from context to generate new sentences.	Graphs ordered pairs and solution sets.	Recognizes the basic principles of sound energy.	Lists several reasons that explain the emergence of the United States as a world power.
Infers mood, setting, and plot in complex stories and plays.	Solves problems involving buying, saving, borrowing, budgeting, investing, insurance, and taxes.	Recognizes the uses of electrical energy.	Identifies the major conflicts in which the United States has been involved since the 1930s.
Judges true/false inferences in lengthy narrative texts.	Performs basic operations with integers.	Recognizes the basic principles of radiant energy.	Explains the role of the United States in an interdependent world.
Completes a story involving a conflict of goals.	Performs basic operations with positive and negative rational numbers.	Explains the mechanics of simple machines.	Reads and interprets historical documents.
Understands symbolism.	Identifies greatest possible error and number of significant digits.	Interprets basic facts about atomic energy.	Demonstrates knowledge of the national and state governments by fulfilling requirements of Public Law 195.
Uses all parts of a road map to obtain information.	Calculates surface areas and volumes of prisms, pyramids, cylinders, and spheres.	Explains concepts about space.	Compares and contrasts the functions of state and local governments.
Constructs a three-level outline based on lengthy, content-area passages.	Solves problems using the Pythagorean theorem.	Summarizes the role of the life sciences in contributing knowledge of the physical, emotional, and social growth and development of human beings.	Identifies the future needs of the city of Chicago and the state of Illinois.
Selects and uses appropriate reference aids to do research.	Uses a table to find square roots.		Develops effective skills in the interpretation of current events.
Summarizes compare-and-contrast paragraphs and paragraphs revealing a principle.	Constructs congruent line segments and angles.		Uses maps to discover patterns of land use.
Identifies facts that support generalizations.	Bisects line segments and angles.		Uses the globe to demonstrate the importance of geographic positions in the world.
Comprehends instructions on forms.	Identifies congruent triangles.		
Identifies elements of style.	Finds the sum of the measures of the angles in a triangle.		
Identifies and reacts to imagery in poetry.	Defines the set of real numbers.		
Identifies characterization in plays.	Applies the formula to compute probability.		
	Gathers, organizes, and analyzes statistical data.		
	Identifies mean, median, and mode of a set of data.		

Source: Copyright © 1981 Board of Education of the City of Chicago, Chicago, Illinois.

229

Professional Viewpoint

Thinking About Teaching

Trial and error is a magnificent approach to learning. However, its efficacy as an heuristic process depends on knowing when an error has been made. One problem with teaching as a field of study is that there is no consensus as yet as to what counts as an "error." Put another way, there is very little agreement about what comprises "effective" teaching. One approach to this problem is arbitrarily to define narrow, measurable, short-term goals, and argue that the effective teacher is the one who can reach those goals. That is tantamount to defining effective medical practice in terms of putting Band-Aids on scratches. Another is to think of teaching in lofty, ethereal terms which have no observable indicators. Under this approach, almost any practice can be justified. Teachers must learn to live with the ambiguity of the profession, without taking on dogmatic views, but by working with colleagues who are nearby, across the hall, in the building, in the district to build some sort of consensus of what education might be while at the same time positing some indicators that might suggest the consensus is credible.

James Raths
Dean of Education
College of Education and Social Services
University of Vermont

---

corresponding to expectations for the entire class, not for particular individuals or groups. Unit plan objectives are then further divided to create lesson plan objectives, organized ideally around one day of instruction on a particular subject.

Unit Plan Objectives **Unit plan objectives** are usually categorized into topics or concepts. Recall the history course objective, "The Framing of the Constitution." This *topic* might be divided into the following units: "To understand the system of American government," "To comprehend the rights of American citizens," "To identify characteristics of a democratic society," "To apply the principles of American government to classroom and school activities."

The science objective, written as a *concept*, "Science and Method," might be broken down into the following unit plan objectives: "To organize inductive, deductive, and intuitive methods in answering questions about the (a) biological world, (b) chemical world, and (c) physical world"; "To organize scientific

Table 5.4   CHARACTERISTICS OF INSTRUCTIONAL OBJECTIVES AT THE CLASSROOM
LEVEL

1. A statement of objectives should describe both the kind of behaviors expected and the content or the context to which that behavior applies.
2. Complex objectives need to be stated analytically and specifically enough so that there is no doubt as to the kind of behavior expected, or what the behavior applies to.
3. Objectives should also be formulated so that clear distinctions are required among learners to attain different behaviors.
4. Objectives are developmental, representing roads to travel rather than terminal points.
5. Objectives should be realistic and should include only what can be translated into . . . classroom experience.
6. The scope of objectives should be broad enough to encompass all types of outcomes for which the school [or teacher] is responsible.

Source: Hilda Taba, *Curriculum Development: Theory and Practice* (New York: Harcourt Brace Jovanovich, 1962), pp. 200–205.

information according to (a) logic, (b) explanations, (c) causal relations, (d) hypotheses, and (e) projections"; "To gain understanding in the methods of (a) inquiry, (b) experimentation, and (c) problem-solving"; "To show interest in scientific hobbies or projects."

Unit plan objectives are sometimes called *general instructional objectives.* They should be specific enough to provide direction for instruction, but not so specific that they restrict the teacher's selection of instructional methods, materials, and activities. Almost any appropriate instructional technique—lectures, discussions, demonstrations, laboratory work, textbook assignments, additional readings—might be used to achieve the unit plan objectives.[8]

Lesson Plan Objectives   **Lesson plan objectives**, sometimes called *specific instructional objectives*, further define the unit objectives by providing clear direction for teaching and testing. Instructional objectives at the lesson plan level state (1) *expected behaviors*, in terms of specific skills, tasks, or attitudes, and (2) *content*. They may also state (3) *outcomes*, sometimes called *standards*, in terms of level of achievement, proficiency, or competency, and (4) *conditions* of mastery. There is currently debate on how detailed these objectives should be and whether too much specificity leads to concern with the trivial.

Lesson plan objectives are more specific than unit plan objectives. Whereas lesson plan objectives may include outcomes and conditions for a specific instructional sequence, unit plan objectives do not. Whereas lesson plan objectives usually include specific methods, materials, or activities, unit plan objectives may or may not, and if they do they are more general. However, the two levels of objectives do have several characteristics in common. Such characteristics as described by Taba are listed in Table 5.4.

---

[8]Norman E. Gronlund, *Measurement and Evaluation in Teaching,* 5th ed. (New York: Macmillan, 1985); Robert E. Mager, *Measuring Instructional Results* (Belmont, Calif.: Fearon, 1984).

To illustrate the kind of specificity involved in the two levels of classroom objectives, consider the unit plan objective, stated as a concept, "To gain understanding of graphs." Lesson plan objectives for this unit might read:

1. To identify different types of graphs when using different types of data.
2. To identify important terms of a graph.
3. To discover practical application of graphs.

Some educators would feel that these lesson objectives are not specific enough, since they lack outcomes and mastery level.[9] They might rewrite the above instructional objectives in the following way.

1. All students will be required to identify which sets of data are best represented by a bar graph, line graph, and circle graph. Seventy-five percent of the class are expected to earn 75 percent or higher.

2. High-achieving students will be required to demonstrate understanding of five terms associated with graphs by (a) defining them and (b) supplying appropriate illustrations of each term. No more than one error will be permitted for moving to the next sequence of material.

3. All students will be required to read an annual corporate report and translate the narrative into at least three graphs to state the financial condition of the company: (a) income, (b) operating cost, and (c) assets and liabilities. A panel of three students must unanimously agree that the graphs are accurate.

FORMULATING GOALS AND OBJECTIVES

In our discussion so far, we have been using several words—*aims, goals, objectives, standards, conditions, outcomes*—that have subtle differences in meaning related to different levels of education (national to classroom) and different levels of abstractness. At one end of the continuum are the value-laden abstract aims of society; at the other end are concrete objectives describing a specific behavior. Most teachers tend to favor the middle of the continuum, where goals and objectives are observable, but not necessarily clearly measurable, or if they are measurable, they are stated without proficiency levels. They may use such terms as "list," "describe," and "identify" in writing their classroom objectives, but unless they are behaviorists or sensitive to preparing tests, they may not always incorporate precise outcomes and conditions of mastery.

Goals and Objectives: The Tyler Model

Ralph Tyler uses the term *purposes* when discussing what we call the goals of the school.[10] He indicates that educators need to identify purposes (goals)

---

[9]James H. Block, Helen E. Efthim, and Robert B. Burns, *Building Effective Mastery Learning Schools* (New York: Longman, 1989); Robert E. Slavin, *Educational Psychology: Theory into Practice*, 2nd ed. (Englewood Cliffs, N.J.: Prentice-Hall, 1988).

[10]Ralph Tyler, *Basic Principles of Curriculum and Instruction* (Chicago: University of Chicago Press, 1949).

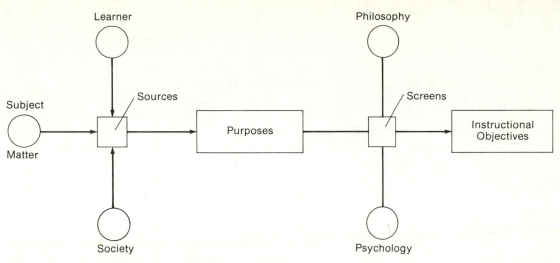

Figure 5.1 Tyler's method for formulating objectives.

by gathering data from three *sources:* learners, society, and subject specialists. Educators then filter their identified purposes (or goals) through two *screens:* philosophy and psychology. What results from the screening are more specific and agreed-upon objectives, or what he calls *instructional objectives* (Figure 5.1).

Even though Tyler uses the term *instructional objectives,* he is not advocating narrow behavioral objectives. For Tyler, objectives cannot be deduced from tiny bits of data or only from objective data. The formulation of objectives involves intelligence, insight, values, and attitudes of people involved in making decisions. Wise choices cannot be made without the most complete data available, but judgments must still prevail. We now turn to Tyler's three sources from which to select goals and two screens for refining goals into objectives.

1. *Studies of the learners.* The responsibility of the school is to help students meet their needs and develop to their fullest potential. Studies that focus on educational needs of students, that distinguish between what the schools do and what other social institutions do, that distinguish between what is done and what should be done, that identify or differentiate gaps between students of the particular school (or school district) and students elsewhere, provide a basis for the selection of goals for the school program. It is possible to identify needs that are common to most students on a national, state, and local basis, as well as other needs that are common to all students in a school or to a certain group of students within a school or school district.

2. *Studies of contemporary life outside of school.* Educators must be aware of the tremendous impact of the increasingly rapid rate of change, the explosion of knowledge, and the increasing complexity of technology on our lives today and tomorrow. The trouble is that preparation for the future involves skills

and knowledge that we may not fully understand today. As we analyze contemporary life, we might break it into manageable categories that are likely to result in implications for school goals.

Tyler emphasizes the need to study life at the community level in terms of needs, resources, and trends, but societal studies might also be extended to state, national, and international levels. For example, in preparing students for the world of work, it is necessary to look at local conditions, but some students will move to other states or regions. Further, we live in a "global village," one that is strongly interconnected: state, national and international conditions eventually affect conditions at the community level.

3. *Suggestions from subject specialists.* Every subject area has its professional associations that list goals and important knowledge in its field. What the subject specialists propose, however, is often too technical, too specialized, or inappropriate for goal setting that cuts across subject matter and is concerned with all students. The inadequacy of many of these lists for schools grows out of their misplaced emphasis. What schools need to ask is not what a specialist in a particular field needs to learn, but, according to Tyler, what the subject can contribute to the general education of young people who are not going to be specialists in the field.[11]

As an example, in science as a goal for all students in all schools, we would not be as concerned with preparing scientists as with producing a scientifically literate citizenry that can understand and use science and technology. In the field of English literature, the idea is not to produce literary scholars, but rather to emphasize how reading and learning from literature can expand the ideas and experiences of young people, regardless of educational level, and to develop reading interests and habits that are satisfying and significant to students in general.

4. *The use of philosophy.* Once purposes have been identified from studies of the learner, society, and subject areas, the educator must review and refine them in light of philosophy and psychology, or as Tyler says, filter them through two screens. The first screen is *philosophy*. As a school tries to outline its educational program, "the educational and social philosophy of the school can serve as the first screen. The original list of [goals] can be culled by identifying those that stand high in terms of values stated or implied in the school's philosophy."[12]

For Tyler, goals should concern important values, be consistent with one another, and be clearly stated. We need not focus on unimportant goals or goals that create confusion or contradictory behavior. We should be aware of the values and way of life we are trying to preserve and what aspect of society we wish to improve. Goals should be consistent with the democratic values and ideals of our society, in all aspects of living, and not just politics. Education

---

[11] Ibid.

[12] Ibid., p. 34.

is for democracy, and this overriding philosophy must be reflected in our school goals.

5. *The use of psychology*. Goals must be in conformity with the psychology of learning, that is, the theories, concepts, and specific findings we accept. "A psychology of learning includes a unified formulation of the processes involved, such as how learning takes place, under what conditions, and what mechanisms and variables operate."[13] Again moving beyond Tyler, in formulating goals, teachers need to consider how appropriate they are in terms of what is known about learning—whether they can be achieved, how they can be achieved, and what the cost and time will be. Goals that conflict with an acceptable psychological viewpoint about learning should be rejected. Of course, there is more than one psychological viewpoint, and many theories, concepts, and even data are contradictory. However, even opposing theories of learning can agree on many of the same goals.

Taxonomy of Educational Objectives

Another way of formulating instructional objectives is to categorize the desired behaviors and outcomes into a system analogous to classification of books in a library, chemical elements in a periodic table, or divisions of the animal kingdom. Through this system, known as a *taxonomy*, standards for classifying objectives have been established, and educators are able to be more precise in their language. The taxonomy is rooted in Tyler's ideas that all words in a scientific system should be defined in terms of observable events and that educational objectives should be defined operationally in terms of performances or outcomes. This method of formulating objectives can be used for writing objectives at the program and course level. By adding specific content, the objectives can be used at the classroom level, including the lesson plan level.

The educational taxonomy calls for the classification of learning into three domains: **cognitive**, **affective**, and **psychomotor.** The *Taxonomy of Educational Objectives, Handbook I: Cognitive Domain* was developed by a committee of 36 researchers from various universities headed by Benjamin Bloom.[14] The cognitive domain includes objectives that are related to recall or recognition of knowledge and the development of higher intellectual skills and abilities. The *Taxonomy of Educational Objectives, Handbook II: Affective Domain* by David Krathwohl and associates is concerned with aims and objectives related to interests, attitudes, and feelings.[15] The description of the psychomotor domain, dealing with manipulative and motor skills, was never com-

---

[13]Ibid., p. 41.

[14]Benjamin S. Bloom et al., ed., *Taxonomy of Educational Objectives, Handbook I: Cognitive Domain* (New York: Longman-McKay, 1956).

[15]David R. Krathwohl, Benjamin S. Bloom, and Bertram Masia, ed., *Taxonomy of Educational Objectives, Handbook II: Affective Domain* (New York: Longman-McKay, 1964).

pleted by the original group of researchers. A classification of psychomotor objectives by Anita Harlow closely resembles the intent of the original group.[16] The fact that it was published by the same company that published the original two taxonomies adds to the validity of this version of the psychomotor domain. Below is a brief listing of the types of objectives of the three domains of learning.

Cognitive Domain

1. *Knowledge.* This level includes objectives related to (a) knowledge of specifics, such as terminology and facts; (b) knowledge of ways and means of dealing with specifics, such as conventions, trends and sequences, classifications and categories, criteria, and methodologies; and (c) knowledge of universals and abstractions, such as principles, generations, theories, and structures. *Example:* To identify the capital of France.

2. *Comprehension.* Objectives at this level relate to (a) translation, (b) interpretation, and (c) extrapolation of materials. *Example:* To interpret a table showing the population density of the world.

3. *Application.* Objectives at this level relate to the use of abstractions in particular situations. *Example:* To predict the probable effect of a change in temperature on a chemical.

4. *Analysis.* Objectives relate to breaking a whole into parts and distinguishing (a) elements, (b) relationships, and (c) organizational principles. *Example:* To deduce facts from a hypothesis.

5. *Synthesis.* Objectives relate to putting parts together in a new form such as (a) a unique communication, (b) a plan of operation, and (c) a set of abstract relations. *Example:* To produce an original piece of art.

6. *Evaluation.* This is the highest level of complexity and includes objectives related to judging in terms of (a) internal evidence or logical consistency and (b) external evidence or consistency with facts developed elsewhere. *Example:* To recognize fallacies in an argument.

Affective Domain

1. *Receiving.* These objectives are indicative of the learner's sensitivity to the existence of stimuli and include (a) awareness, (b) willingness to receive, and (c) selective attention. *Example:* To identify musical instruments by their sound.

2. *Responding.* This includes active attention to stimuli such as (a) acquiescence, (b) willing responses, and (c) feelings of satisfaction. *Example:* To contribute to group discussions by asking questions.

3. *Valuing.* This includes objectives regarding beliefs and evaluations in the form of (a) acceptance, (b) preference, and (c) commitment. *Example:* To argue over an issue involving health care.

4. *Organization.* This level involves (a) conceptualization of values and

---

[16]Anita J. Harlow, *Taxonomy of the Psychomotor Domain: A Guide for Developing Behavioral Objectives* (New York: McKay, 1972).

(b) organization of a value system. *Example:* To organize a meeting concerning a neighborhood's housing integration plan.

5. *Characterization.* This is the level of greatest complexity and includes behavior related to (a) a generalized set of values and (b) a characterization or philosophy of life. *Example:* To demonstrate in front of a government building in behalf of a cause or idea.

Psychomotor Domain

1. *Reflex movements.* Objectives relate to (a) segmental reflexes (involving one spinal segment) and (b) intersegmental reflexes (involving more than one spinal segment). *Example:* To contract a muscle.

2. *Fundamental movements.* Objectives relate to (a) walking, (b) running, (c) jumping, (d) pushing, (e) pulling, and (f) manipulating. *Example:* To run a 100-yard dash.

3. *Perceptual abilities.* Objectives relate to (a) kinesthetic, (b) visual, (c) auditory, (d) tactile, and (e) coordination abilities. *Example:* To distinguish distant and close sounds.

4. *Physical abilities.* Objectives relate to (a) endurance, (b) strength, (c) flexibility, (d) agility, (e) reaction-response time, and (f) dexterity. *Example:* To do five sit-ups.

5. *Skilled movements.* Objectives relate to (a) games, (b) sports, (c) dances, and (d) the arts. *Example:* To dance the basic steps of the waltz.

6. *Nondiscursive communication.* Objectives relate to expressive movement through (a) posture, (b) gestures, (c) facial expressions, and (d) creative movements. *Example:* To act a part in a play.

One point needs to be made about the cognitive domain. While Bloom acknowledges that the teaching of knowledge is essential, he asserts that "many teachers . . . prize knowledge . . . because of the simplicity with which it can be taught or learned."[17] Quite frequently we stop at the knowledge category, because it is easy to teach and test. Thus we ask our students: "What are three products of Brazil? What is the chemical formula for water?" Also, we tend to equate knowledge with intelligence. This is illustrated by our misconception that when someone can recall trivia information on a television quiz show, we often consider the person to be intelligent. It is not how much knowledge an individual possesses, but what the individual can do with the knowledge that characterizes intelligence.

Once we study the taxonomy, it becomes apparent that most teaching and testing we have been exposed to as students stressed knowledge—knowledge of facts, terms, conventions, classifications, categories, methods, and principles. As a teacher, you should not make the same mistake; rather you should advance into other cognitive dimensions that use knowledge for advanced teaching and learning.

---

[17] Bloom, *Taxonomy of Educational Objectives, Handbook I,* p. 34.

Professional Viewpoint

Appreciating the Taxonomy

One of my earliest contacts with the taxonomy came as a University of Chicago graduate student attending a campus seminar on programmed learning (PL). It was the heyday of the "teaching machine," and its proponents (from commercial enterprises) told the audience how their PL materials would elevate achievement in all subjects to stratospheric levels. One stated that he had obtained information on the great success of PL directly "from the horse's mouth," represented by a leading behaviorist researcher. Professor Bloom, who was one of my instructors, and his colleagues did not think much of the suggestion that the low-level, knowledge-oriented programmed materials of the 1960s could help students advance very far on the taxonomy. Professor Herbert Thelen, another one of my instructors, summed up their reaction in stating that the information presented must have come from the "other end of the horse."

Since that time my contact and experience with the taxonomy has been alternately sad and exciting: Sad in the case of the many school administrators I have observed who treated it as a public-relations tool by distributing it to teachers and then pretending their faculties were addressing its higher domains, but exciting in instances where teachers were given substantial training, technical assistance, materials, time, and other resources so that they really could move their instruction beyond drill and regurgitation of knowledge. Unfortunately, the public-relations approach seems to be much more common than are systematic efforts to help teachers use the taxonomy in an effective manner, but this pattern is no different, I suppose, from what usually happens with respect to many promising prosposals for improving instruction in our schools.

Teachers who want to draw on the taxonomy to improve their instruction should keep their initial efforts simple. Do not begin with a grandiose scheme for using and assessing objectives at all taxonomic levels in every unit. As usual when a new approach or technique is introduced, teachers should have a chance to see what happens when they analyze objectives and materials with a view to increasing emphasis on "application" or "analysis" or other higher-level objectives, and opportunities should be provided to discuss what happened with other teachers who also have agreed to make this effort.

Daniel Levine
Professor and Director of Education
Center for Studies of Metropolitan
Problems in Education
University of Missouri-Kansas City

Guidelines for Applying the Taxonomy of Educational Objectives

The categories of the three taxonomies describe levels of complexity from simple to more advanced. Each level is built upon and assumes acquisition of skills of the previous level. One must have knowledge of facts, for example, before one can comprehend material. The taxonomy as a whole is a useful source for developing educational objectives and for categorizing and grouping existing sets of objectives. Perhaps the greatest difficulty is deciding between adjacent categories, particularly if the objectives have not been clearly stated. To avoid becoming frustrated while categorizing objectives into appropriate categories, classroom teachers are advised to work in groups and share opinions. By studying and using the taxonomy, they may eventually appreciate it as a valuable tool for implementing objectives and formulating test items.

After you have decided you want to use the taxonomy and after you have determined what you want your students to learn, you might systematically review the major classifications of the various domains to make sure you are familiar with each classification. You might then ask the following questions when formulating objectives in the cognitive domain.

1. *Knowledge.* What specific facts do you want the students to learn? What trends and sequences should they know? What classifications, categories, and methods are important for them to learn? What general principles and theories should they learn?
2. *Comprehension.* What types of translation will students need to perform? What types of interpretation? What types of extrapolation?
3. *Application.* What will students be required to perform or do to show they can use the information in practical situations?
4. *Analysis.* What kinds of elements should students be able to analyze? What relationships? What organizational principles?
5. *Synthesis.* What kinds of communication should students be able to synthesize? What kinds of operation? What kinds of abstraction?
6. *Evaluation.* What kinds of evaluation should students be able to perform? Can they use internal evidence? Can they use external evidence?

When asking these questions and when formulating instructional objectives according to the taxonomy, the teacher should keep in mind that the classifications represent a hierarchy. Before students can deal with analysis, they must be able to function at the three previous levels, that is, knowledge, comprehension, and application. The same kinds of questions should be asked when writing objectives in the affective and psychomotor domains. The teacher needs to look at each level within the domain and ask what students are to be expected to achieve.

As an aid in writing and categorizing objectives, a list of key infinitives and direct objects for the cognitive, affective, and psychomotor domains are shown in Tips for Teachers 5.1, 5.2, 5.3. In all of these examples, no specific content is described so as to keep them applicable to all subjects.

General Objectives and Specific Learning Outcomes: The Gronlund Method

Norman Gronlund has developed a flexible way of formulating instructional objectives, whereby the teacher moves from a general objective to a series of specific learning outcomes, each related to the general objective. Gronlund's **general objectives** coincide with program (subject and grade) and course level objectives, and his **specific learning outcomes** coincide with unit plan and lesson plan objectives. He recommends that teachers start with general objectives because learning is too complex to be described in terms of specific behaviors or specific outcomes and because higher levels of thinking cannot be achieved by one specific behavior or outcome. To illustrate the difference between general objectives and specific learning outcomes, Gronlund has prepared a list of general objectives that can be used for almost any grade, subject, or course.

1. Knows basic terminology
2. Understands concepts and principles
3. Applies principles to new situations
4. Interprets charts and graphs

Figure 5.2 A teacher's willingness to help students pays big dividends in achieving the desired outcomes of the lesson. (Photo © Hugh Rogers/Monkmeyer)

Tips for Teachers 5.1

Key Words for the Taxonomy of Educational Objectives:
Cognitive Domain

Taxonomy classification	Examples of infinitives	Examples of direct objects
1.0 Knowledge		
1.1 Knowledge of specifics	to define, to distinguish, to acquire, to identify, to recall, to recognize	vocabulary terms, terminology, meaning(s), definitions, referents, elements, facts, factual information, (sources), (names), (dates), (events), (persons), (places), (time periods), properties, examples, phenomena
1.2 Knowledge of ways and means of dealing with specifics	to acquire, identify, to recall, to recognize	forms, conventions, uses, usage, rules, ways, devices, symbols, representations, styles, formats, actions, processes, movements, continuity, developments, trends, sequences, causes, relationships, forces, influences, areas, types, features, classes, sets, divisions, arrangements, classifications, categories, criteria, basics, elements, methods, techniques, approaches, uses, procedures, treatments
1.3 Knowledge of universals and abstractions in a field	to acquire, to identify, to recall, to recognize	principles, generalizations, propositions, fundamentals, laws, principal elements, implications, theories, bases, interrelations, structures, organizations, formulations
2.0 Comprehension		

continued

2.1 Translation	to translate, to transform, to give in own words, to illustrate, to prepare, to read, to represent, to change, to rephrase, to restate	meanings, samples, definitions, abstractions, representations, words, phrases
2.2 Interpretation	to interpret, to reorder, to rearrange, to differentiate, to distinguish, to make, to draw, to explain, to demonstrate	relevancies, relationships, essentials, aspects, new views, qualifications, conclusions, methods, theories, abstractions
2.3 Extrapolation	to estimate, to infer, to conclude, to predict, to differentiate, to determine, to extend, to interpolate	consequences, implications, conclusions, factors, ramifications, meanings, corollaries, effects, probabilities
3.0 Application	to apply, to generalize, to relate, to choose, to develop, to organize, to use, to employ, to transfer, to restructure, to classify	principals, laws, conclusions, effects, methods, theories, abstractions, situations, generalizations, processes, phenomena, procedures
4.0 Analysis		
4.1 Analysis of elements	to distinguish, to detect, to identify, to classify, to discriminate, to recognize, to categorize	elements, hypotheses, conclusions, assumptions, statements of fact, statements of intents, arguments, particulars
4.2 Analysis of relationships	to analyze, to contrast, to compare, to distinguish, to deduce	relationships, interrelations, relevance, relevancies, themes, evidence, fallacies, arguments, cause-effects, consistency, consistencies, parts, ideas, assumptions
4.3 Analysis of organizational principles	to analyze, to distinguish, to detect, to deduce	forms, patterns, purposes, points of view, techniques, biases, structures, themes, arrangements, organizations

continued

5.0 Synthesis		
5.1 Production of a unique communication	to write, to tell, to relate, to produce, to constitute, to transmit, to originate, to modify, to document	structures, patterns, products, performances, designs, works, communications, efforts, specifics, compositions
5.2 Production of a plan or proposed set of operations	to propose, to plan, to produce, to design, to modify, to specify	plans, objectives, specifications, schematics, operations, ways, solutions, means
5.3 Derivation of a set of abstract relations	to produce, to derive, to develop, to combine, to organize, to synthesize, to classify, to deduce, to develop, to formulate, to modify	phenomena, taxonomies, concepts, schemes, theories, relationships, abstractions, generalizations, hypotheses, perceptions, ways, discoveries
6.0 Evaluation		
6.1 Judgments in terms of internal evidence	to judge, to argue, to validate, to assess, to decide	accuracies, consistencies, fallacies, reliability, flaws, errors, precision, exactness
6.20 Judgments in terms of external criteria	to judge, to argue, to consider, to compare, to contrast, to standardize, to appraise	ends, means, efficiency, economies, utility, alternatives, courses of action, standards, theories, generalizations

Source: Newton S. Metfessel, William B. Michael, and Donald A. Kirsner, ''Instrumentation of Bloom's and Krathwohl's Taxonomies for the Writing of Educational Objectives,'' *Psychology in the Schools,* July 1969, pp. 227–231.

5. Demonstrates skill in critical thinking
6. Writes a well-organized theme
7. Appreciates poetry, art, literature, dance, etc.
8. Demonstrates scientific attitude
9. Evaluates the adequacy of an experiment.[18]

Note that the behavior (verb) in each statement is general enough to permit a host of specific learning outcomes. Such outcomes provide useful guides for teachers and students. There may be six or seven related specific outcomes

---

[18]Gronlund, *Measurement and Evaluation in Teaching,* pp. 41–42.

Tips for Teachers 5.2

Key Words for the Taxonomy of Educational Objectives: Affective Domain

Taxonomy classification	Examples of infinitives	Examples of direct objects
1.0 Receiving		
1.1 Awareness	to differentiate, to separate, to set apart, to share	sights, sounds, events, designs, arrangements
1.2 Willingness to receive	to accumulate, to select, to combine, to accept	models, examples, shapes, sizes, meters, cadences
1.3 Controlled or selected attention	to select, to posturally respond to, to listen (for), to control	alternatives, answers, rhythms, nuances
2.0 Responding		
2.1 Acquiescence in responding	to comply (with), to follow, to commend, to approve	directions, instructions, laws, policies, demonstrations
2.2 Willingness to respond	to volunteer, to discuss, to practice, to play	instruments, games, dramatic works, charades, burlesques
2.3 Satisfaction in responding	to applaud, to acclaim, to spend leisure time in, to augment	speeches, plays, presentations, writings
3.0 Valuing		
3.1 Acceptance of a value	to increase measured proficiency in, to increase numbers of, to relinquish, to specify	group memberships, artistic productions, musical productions, personal friendships
3.2 Preference for a value	to assist, to subsidize, to help, to support	artists, projects, viewpoints, arguments
3.3 Commitment	to deny, to protest, to debate, to argue	deceptions, irrelevancies, abdications, irrationalities
4.0 Organization		
4.1 Conceptualization of a value	to discuss, to theorize (on), to abstract, to compare	parameters, codes, standards, goals

continued

4.2 Organization of a value system	to balance, to organize, to define, to formulate	systems, approaches, criteria, limits
5.0 Characterization by value or value concept		
5.1 Generalized set	to revise, to change, to complete, to require	plans, behaviors, methods, efforts
5.2 Characterization	to be rated high by peers in, to be rated high by superiors in, and to be rated high by subordinates in and	humanitarianism, ethics, integrity, maturity
	to avoid, to manage, to resolve, to resist	extravagance(s), excesses, conflicts, exorbitancy/ exorbitancies

Source: Newton S. Metfessel, William B. Michael, and Donald A. Kirsner, "Instrumentation of Bloom's and Krathwohl's Taxonomies for the Writing of Educational Objectives, *Psychology in the Schools*, July 1969, pp. 227–231.

for each general objective to clarify what students will do to demonstrate achievement of the general objective.

Guidelines for Applying Gronlund's Objectives

The two examples below illustrate how we move from general objectives to a series of related, intended learning outcomes.

I. Understands the meaning of terms
1. Defines the terms in own words
2. Identifies the meaning of a term in context
3. Differentiates between proper and improper usage of a term
4. Distinguishes between two similar terms on the basis of meaning
5. Writes an original sentence using the term
II. Demonstrates skill in critical thinking
1. Distinguishes between fact and opinion
2. Distinguishes between relevant and irrelevant information
3. Identifies fallacious reasoning in written material
4. Identifies the limitations of given data

Tips for Teachers 5.3

Key Words of the Taxonomy of Educational Objectives: Psychomotor Domain

Taxonomy classification	Examples of infinitives	Examples of direct objects
1.0 Reflex movements	to flex, to stretch, to straighten, to extend, to inhibit, to lengthen, to shorten, to tense, to stiffen, to relax	reflexes
2.0 Fundamental movements	to crawl, to creep, to slide, to walk, to run, to jump, to grasp, to reach, to tighten, to support, to handle	changes location, moves in space while remaining in one place, moves extremities in coordinated fashion
3.0 Perceptual abilities	to catch, to bounce, to eat, to write, to balance, to bend, to bounce, to draw from memory, to distinguish by touching, to explore	discriminates visually, discriminates auditory, discriminates kinesthetically, discriminates tactually, coordinates two or more perceptual abilities
4.0 Physical abilities	to endure, to improve, to increase, to stop, to start, to move precisely, to touch, to bend	exerts tension, moves quickly, stops immediately, endures fatigue
5.0 Skilled movements	to waltz, to type, to play the piano, to plane, to file, to skate, to juggle, to paint, to dive, to fence, to golf, to change	changes or modifies basic body movement patterns, uses a tool or implement in adaptive or skilled manner
6.0 Nondiscursive communication	to gesture, to stand, to sit, to express facially, to dance skillfully, to perform skillfully, to paint skillfully, to play skillfully	moves expressively, moves interpretatively, communicates emotions, communicates esthetically, expresses joy

Source: Adapted from Anita J. Harlow, *A Taxonomy of the Psychomotor Domain* (New York: McKay, 1972).

5. Formulates valid conclusions from given data
6. Identifies the assumptions underlying conclusions.[19]

The learning outcomes listed above are good examples of content-free objectives that can fit many different grade levels, subjects and courses. Because Gronlund feels it is important to keep specific learning outcomes content-free, they are not really applicable to the lesson plan level, which should be content-oriented.

The teacher can add content to objectives. For example, an objective might be to identify three causes of World War I or to differentiate between a triangle and a rectangle. Gronlund maintains that once a teacher identifies content, there is a risk of writing too many objectives for each general objective or topic. But instead of identifying the causes of World War I, as most teachers would do, Gronlund would say the objective is to identify important historical causes and events. Instead of differentiating between a triangle and a rectangle, the objective, for Gronlund, is to differentiate between geometric shapes. Gronlund's content-free specific outcomes can be used up to the unit plan level that focuses on concepts; only by including content can they be used at the lesson plan level.

Table 5.5 highlights Gronlund's steps for stating instructional objectives and can serve as a guide if you wish to adopt his method.

Specific Objectives: The Mager Method

Robert Mager is more precise in his approach to formulating instructional objectives. His objectives have three components.

1. *Behavior*, or performance, which describes what the learner is expected to do. *Example:* to know, to use, to identify.
2. *Condition*, which describes under what circumstances or condition the performance is to occur. *Example:* Given five sentences with adjectives . . ., Based on the statement. . . .
3. *Proficiency level*, or criterion, which states an acceptable standard, competency, or achievement level. *Example:* 80 percent, 9 out of 10, judged correctly by the teacher.[20]

Mager is controversial in his approach to writing instructional objectives, and therefore it might be worthwhile to state some of the arguments for and against his approach. Some educators (including Tyler and Gronlund) claim that Mager's method produces an unmanageable number of objectives, leads to trivia, and wastes time. They also contend that the approach leads to teaching that focuses on low levels of cognitive and psychomotor objectives, em-

---

[19]Ibid., p. 43.

[20]Robert F. Mager, *Preparing Instructional Objectives*, rev. ed. (Belmont, Calif.: Fearon, 1984). The examples of each component are derived from the author.

Table 5.5 STEPS FOR STATING GENERAL OBJECTIVES AND SPECIFIC LEARNING
OUTCOMES

Stating general instructional objectives

1. State each general objective as an intended learning outcome (i.e., pupils' terminal performance).
2. Begin each general objective with a verb (e.g., knows, applies, interprets). Omit "The pupil should be able to . . ."
3. State each general objective to include only one general learning outcome (e.g., not "Knows and understands").
4. State each general objective at the proper level of generality (e.g., it should encompass a readily definable domain of responses). Eight to twelve general objectives will usually suffice.
5. Keep each general objective sufficiently free of course content so that it can be used with various units of study.
6. State each general objective so that there is minimum overlap with other objectives.

Stating specific learning outcomes

1. List beneath each general instructional objective a representative sample of specific learning outcomes that describes the terminal performance pupils are expected to demonstrate.
2. Begin each specific learning outcome with an action verb that specifies observable performance (e.g., identifies, describes). Check that each specific learning outcome is relevant to the general objective it describes.
4. Include a sufficient number of specific learning outcomes to describe adequately the performance of pupils who have attained the objective.
5. Keep the specific learning outcomes sufficiently free of course content so that the list can be used with various units of study.
6. Consult reference materials for the specific components of those complex outcomes that are difficult to define (e.g., critical thinking, scientific attitude, creativity).
7. Add a third level of specificity to the list of outcomes, if needed.

Source: Norman E. Gronlund, *Measurement and Evaluation in Teaching*, 5th ed. (New York: Macmillan, 1985), p. 46.

phasizes learning of specific bits of information, and does not foster comprehension and whole learning.[21]

Mager and other educators argue that the approach clarifies what teachers intend, what students are expected to do, and what to test to show evidence of learning.[22] It provides a structured method for arranging sequences of skills, tasks, or content, provides a guide for determining instructional methods and materials, and adds precision for constructing tests. Most teachers prefer a less specific approach, corresponding more to the methods of Bloom or Gronlund.

---

[21] Ornstein and Hunkins, *Curriculum: Foundations, Principles, and Issues*; Robert M. W. Travers, *Essentials of Learning*, 5th ed. (New York: Macmillan, 1982); and Bruce W. Tuckman, *Conducting Educational Research*, 3rd ed. (San Diego: Harcourt Brace Jovanovich, 1987).

[22] Robert J. Kibler, Larry L. Baker, and David T. Miles, *Behavioral Objectives and Instruction*, 2nd ed. (Boston: Allyn and Bacon, 1981); W. James Popham, *Criterion-Referenced Measurement* (Englewood Cliffs, N.J.: Prentice-Hall, 1978); and Paul D. Plowman, *Behavioral Objectives* (Chicago: Science Research Associates, 1971).

Guidelines for Applying Mager's Objectives

Using Mager's approach, a teacher could write hundreds of objectives for each unit, certainly for each course. If we decide on his approach, we would first ask ourselves to identify or describe what the learner will be *doing*. Next we would identify or describe the *conditions* under which the behavior is to occur. Finally, we would state the *performance* criteria or achievement level we expect the learner to meet.

Here are some examples. The behavior, condition, and proficiency level are identified.

1. *Given six primary colors, students will be able to identify five.* The behavior is to identify, the condition is given six primary colors, and the proficiency level is five out of six.
2. *Based on the reading passage in Chapter 7, students will compare the writing styles of Ernest Hemingway and John Steinbeck. Performance will be judged pass-fail by the teacher.* The behavior is to compare writing styles, the condition is after reading the passage in Chapter 7, and the proficiency level is to pass, a subjective judgment by the teacher.
3. *From the required list of 10 words, students will correctly spell 9 of them.* The behavior is to spell, the condition is the required list of words, and the proficiency level is 90 percent (9 out of 10).
4. *From the foul line, students will make 6 out of 10 baskets.* The behavior is to throw a basketball, the condition is from the foul line, and the proficiency level is 60 percent (6 out of 10).
5. *The student will be able to complete a 100-item multiple-choice examination on the topic of pollution, with 80 items answered correctly within 60 minutes.* The behavior is to complete an exam, the condition is 60 minutes, and the proficiency level is 80 percent (80 out of 100).

Mager lists eight words or phrases that he considers "fuzzy" and to be avoided in formulating objectives: to know, to understand, to appreciate, to grasp the significance of, to enjoy, to believe, to have faith in, and to internalize. He lists nine words or phrases that are open to fewer interpretations and are more appropriate to use: to write, to recite, to identify, to sort, to solve, to construct, to build, to compare, and to contrast.[23]

Performance Objectives: The Gagné Method

Robert Gagné is just as precise as Mager in his formulation of objectives. He contends that there are five basic types of **learned capabilities** that can be observed and measured in terms of exhibited performances.[24] The five capa-

---

[23] Mager, *Preparing Instructional Objectives.*

[24] Robert M. Gagné, *The Conditions of Learning,* 4th ed. (New York: Holt, Rinehart and Winston, 1985).

bilities overlap the three domains of the taxonomy of educational objectives. (The first three capabilities mainly fall within the cognitive domain.)

1. *Intellectual skills.* The capability first to use symbols for learning how to read, write, and use numbers and later to distinguish, combine, tabulate, classify, analyze, and quantify objects, events, and other symbols. Intellectual skill is divided into five subcategories: (1) discrimination, (2) concrete concept, (3) defined concept, (4) rule, and (5) higher-order rule (problem-solving).

2. *Cognitive strategies.* This involves tasks related to problem-solving and independent learning. It involves searching for applicable information and values to arrive at solutions to problems and to understand how a solution applies to other instances. The learner has internalized various techniques to remember the main points of a lecture or text —search for relationships, analyze problems, and determine approaches to solving problems.

3. *Information.* The capability to state a fact or a set of events by using oral speech, written language, or pictorial or symbolic representation. The learner is able to retrieve, restate, and recount ideas and events.

4. *Motor skills.* The capability to execute simple to complex motor acts and movements. Complex acts, such as playing golf or driving an automobile, involve organized and comprehensive movements.

5. *Attitudes.* What influences the learner's response to situations and choice of actions. It is a mental state that affects performance rather than a specific performance, unlike the other learned capabilities.

The mental "operation" involved in each of the five capabilities is different. Writes Gagné, "Learning intellectual skills requires a different design of instructional events from those required for learning verbal information or from those required for learning motor skills, and so on."[25] The five categories underlie different types of performance and outcomes and are assessed differently. Gagné, Briggs, and Wager summarize the five major areas for sequencing information within a lesson plan. Each category represents a central focus for teaching and learning, and each category is based on prerequisite relationships among the objectives of the lesson plan.[26]

For Gagné, the ultimate aim of school is to equip learners with learning capabilities whereby they can apply what they learn in class to situations outside of class. In other words, learners learn how to learn on their own and to apply what they learn to everyday problems. There is an implication that intellectual skills and cognitive strategies are more important learned capabilities than the others, although Gagné never states there is a hierarchy.

[25]Ibid., p. 245.

[26]Robert M. Gagné, Leslie J. Briggs, and Walter W. Wager, *Principles of Instructional Design*, 3rd ed. (New York: Holt, Rinehart and Winston, 1988).

Figure 5.3 High-achieving students can independently perform the appropriate tasks involved in learning. (Photo © Rafael Macia 1987/ Photo Researchers)

Task Analysis and Enabling Objectives

As part of his system of formulating objectives, Gagné introduces the concept of **task analysis,** which is a common procedure used in business, industry, and the military. A task is broken down into the logical sequence of steps necessary to achieve an intended outcome. By analyzing a learning task into skills required, a teacher can pinpoint problem areas, make appropriate corrections, and make sure students have the necessary skills and subskills to complete the task. For example, an assignment to report on information found in the library involves the following separate skills:

1. Knowing how to look up words alphabetically
2. Using the card catalog system
3. Using tables of contents and indexes
4. Understanding the concepts of the topic
5. Reading and comprehending material
6. Getting the main idea from material
7. Distinguishing facts and opinions

8. Drawing conclusions or summarizing
9. Organizing or outlining a report
10. Knowing and applying basic rules of spelling, punctuation, and usage[27]

Of course, all tasks can be broken down into subtasks all the way back to letter recognition. The point is that the teacher must be aware of the tasks involved in learning a new skill or concept and must be certain that students know what they need to know to succeed. This may mean reviewing certain tasks or even teaching something new that students should have learned years earlier. The process of task analysis recognizes the importance of what the learner brings to a learning situation, or what Glaser calls the "entering behavior" of the learner.[28] And Gagné says, "Previously learned capabilities provide necessary support for new learning, regardless of what is being learned. For example, cognitive strategies of one kind or another must be brought to bear upon [various] phases of the learning process."[29] Intellectual skills learned many years ago can support new learning situations, and previously learned motor skills become refined and part of new advanced skills, which may lead in turn to a set of still more advanced motor skills.

Gagné calls the prerequisites for learning **enabling objectives.** Some prerequisites make sense as separate tasks, each of which the learner might perform by itself. Other prerequisites function only to facilitate the objective. For example, in learning to add double-digit numbers, one of the enabling objectives is to add single-digit numbers. This is by itself a useful task to be learned. In contrast, the enabling objective of carrying numbers to the second column is useful only for the operation of adding double- (or triple-, etc.) digit numbers and is not useful for other purposes.

Guidelines for Applying Gagnés Objectives

According to Gagné, to enhance learning, an objective must be analyzed in terms of enabling objectives. These tasks may have been learned a few minutes ago or long ago; nevertheless, at the time the new learning takes place, they must be retrieved by the learner.

Following are some examples of task analysis.

    I. To solve subtraction problems
       1. To arrange sets of numbers to be subtracted

---

[27]See Anita E. Woolfolk and Lorraine McCune-Nicolich, *Educational Psychology for Teachers,* 3rd ed. (Englewood Cliffs, N.J.: Prentice-Hall, 1988).

[28]Robert Glaser, "Trends and Research Questions in Psychological Research on Learning and Schooling," *Educational Researcher,* November 1979, pp. 6–13.

[29]Gagné, *The Conditions of Learning,* p. 268.

Professional Viewpoint

"The Function of Prior Knowledge"

In teaching new knowledges and skills, nothing is more important for a teacher to know than the answer to the question "What do my students already know?" This information is helpful to the act of teaching in a number of ways.

First, knowledge of prior experience helps the teacher formulate an introduction to the lesson that relates to students' backgrounds and interests. Introductory communication of this sort helps to arouse and maintain motivation. There is also a more specific function of prior knowledge for learning. When new skills are being learned, students will acquire them more easily if their subordinate skills are recalled and readily available. The recall of previously acquired knowledge also makes possible the formation of cognitive models that guide the use of newly learned knowledge in situations requiring application.

Teachers can discover the nature and extent of students' prior knowledge in a number of ways. Published curricula objectives usually give the basic information. Student exercises may be conducted to reveal the scope of knowledge and skills already learned. Armed with such information, the teacher can devise instruction that maintains student interest, achieves a memorable organization, and aids the transfer of learning to new and unfamiliar situations that require knowledge application.

Robert M. Gagné
Professor Emeritus of Education Research
Florida State University

---

2. To add numbers
3. To identify plus and minus signs
4. To recognize the meaning of numbers
5. To write numbers
II. To evaluate statements made by government officials concerning the economy
   1. To know economic principles and relationships
   2. To know national and international events
   3. To distinguish between evidence and opinion
   4. To identify limitations of evidence
   5. To draw conclusions from evidence
   6. To know how to read with comprehension

III. To identify musical instruments
   1. To identify an instrument by its appearance
   2. To differentiate between instruments of an orchestra and band when pictures of each are displayed
   3. To identify an instrument by its sound
   4. To differentiate between instruments of an orchestra and band when each is played on a recording
   5. To state the differences between the instruments of an orchestra and of a band
IV. To shoot a bow with accuracy
   1. To estimate the balance point of a bow
   2. To gauge string pressure
   3. To place the arrow in the bow correctly
   4. To hold the arrow and the bow correctly
   5. To achieve balance when arching the bow
   6. To aim, estimating distance and required angle of arrow flight

Figure 5.2 provides a more detailed look at a task analysis. The objective, or task, is map reading. It can be achieved if enabling objectives have been achieved. The enabling objectives of discrimination, then defining, then identifying serve as the prerequisite or foundation before the learner understands the rules and concepts of longitude and latitude.

Task analysis is appropriate for many behavioral learning theories. It appears in the step-by-step frames of programed instruction and computer-assisted instruction and in various mastery learning and adaptive learning programs that present subskills or tasks leading to the acquisition of more complex skills or tasks. For many experienced teachers it is second nature, and they do it as part of the teaching process without using the terms "task analysis" and "enabling objectives."

THEORY INTO PRACTICE

The task of writing goals and objectives for a school district, school, program, or course usually falls to a school committee. Individual classroom teachers are usually responsible for developing unit plans or lesson plans. If you are a member of a district or school committee, it is advisable to consult the following sources to be sure that your list corresponds to prescribed educational goals and objectives.

1. Federal and state mandates and legislation.
2. National and state commission reports that identify aims and goals.
3. Professional association reports that identify goals and objectives.
4. Community concerns voiced by state and local business organizations and pressure groups.
5. Parental concerns expressed in parental advisory committees, parent-teacher associations, and individual letters from parents.
6. Professional literature on theories of learning and child development.

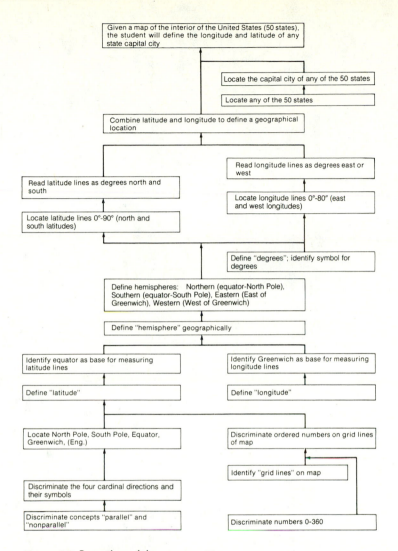

Figure 5.2 Locating cities on a map.

7. Professional literature on student needs, assessments, and career choices.
8. Books and reports on college and employee requirements.
9. Teacher reports and comments.
10. Subject specialist reports and comments.
11. Evaluation reports about school programs and curriculum.
12. Reports and studies about trends in society.[30]

[30]Lynn L. Morris and Carol T. Fitz-Gibbon, *How to Deal with Goals and Objectives* (Beverly Hills, Calif.: Sage, 1978); Allan C. Ornstein, "The National Reports on Education: Implications for Directions and Aims," *Kappa Delta Pi Record*, Winter 1985, pp. 58–64.

Table 5.6 ASSIGNING PRIORITIES TO OBJECTIVES

Method	Summary	Advantages	Disadvantages	Recommendations
Sampling objectives	Objectives randomly selected from the total set	Can be done by evaluator alone (without cooperation from others) Quickest, simplest method Treats all program objectives (on the test or not) as instructionally important	Risk of missing important objectives or items thus reducing the credibility of the evaluation	Highly recommended when all objectives are of about equal importance
Sampling important objectives	Pool of most important objectives chosen by two or three raters Objectives randomly chosen from pool, or all objectives rated as important used	Fairly fast Gives raters a say in the evaluation Unlikely that important objectives will be missed	Focuses evaluation on a small number of objectives Depends on cooperation of raters Raters' choices perhaps not representative of other concerned persons	Highly recommended when credible raters are available, objectives are not all of equal importance, and there are many objectives
Matrix sampling	All objectives assigned to parts of a test, and each part given to a randomly selected group of students	Can be done by evaluator alone (without cooperation from others) All objectives tested, albeit with samples of students rather than all students	Somewhat involved procedure Data not entirely appropriate for use with some statistical tests	Only method by which all objectives are assessed Due to procedure's complexity, however, best to use only when testing all objectives or items cannot be avoided
Ratings of objectives (retrospective needs assessment)	All objectives rated by about 15 raters on a 5-point scale, with priorities determined by mean ratings	Yields accurate assessment of priorities of interest groups represented by the raters Involves raters in evaluation and is therefore likely to increase credibility	Focuses evaluation on a small number of objectives Depends on cooperation of raters Time-consuming for evaluators and raters	Recommended if time is available and enough raters will cooperate Especially recommended when acceptance of evaluation by various education or lay groups is a major concern
Objectives hierarchies	Objectives grouped into content areas, then charted from simple to complex, with most complex or "terminal" ones receiving highest priority	Can be done by evaluator alone (without cooperation from others) Assigns priority to most complex objectives, avoiding attention to simple ones	Relatively time-consuming, depending on the number of objectives May not be desirable to test only terminal, difficult objectives	Best if used only when evaluator must narrow down number of objectives without assistance and when the subject matter lends itself to logical hierarchies

Source: Lynn L. Morris and Carol T. Fitz-Gibbons, *How to Deal with Goals and Objectives* (Beverly Hills, Calif.: Sage, 1978), pp. 50–51.

It is also advisable to consult already published lists of goals and objectives. Most published lists deal with the cognitive domain; only a few concern the affective and psychomotor domains. Lists of goals and objectives that have been published can be obtained from government agencies (state departments of education and regional educational agencies), professional agencies (Association of Supervision and Curriculum Development, Phi Delta Kappa), publishing companies and businesses, universities, and school districts. Objectives published by the government and schools can be obtained free of charge; professional agencies may charge a nominal fee.

Several techniques are available for assigning priorities to goals and objectives. These techniques can assist both committee members formulating school goals or program and course objectives and teachers formulating unit plan and lesson plan objectives. A summary of these methods, with advantages, disadvantages, and recommendations, is given in Table 5.6. It should be noted that the first three methods involve sampling from a pool of objectives, while the remaining two use ratings based on people's opinions. Rating techniques have many advantages, but they are more complex and difficult to develop. However, if teachers and other school people want to establish priorities of goals or objectives, then ratings techniques should be used for purposes of objectivity.

In formulating classroom-level objectives, either unit or lesson plans, eight concerns or general rules should be kept in mind.

1. They should be related to the developmental needs and tasks of the learners, which in turn are related to the age and experiences of the students.
2. They should be an outgrowth of diagnostic data (achievement, aptitude, personality, behavioral tests) and student records.
3. They should be consistent with professional and subject specialist opinions.
4. They should be consistent with teaching and learning theories and procedures.
5. They should build on student interests and strengths, not on adult interests and student weaknesses.
6. They should relate to the whole child, and several domains of learning, not only one aspect of learning or the cognitive domain.
7. They should foster higher-order thinking skills, rather than focus mainly on knowledge or busy work.
8. They should be based on subject and grade level objectives.
9. They should be flexible enough to keep pace with changing educational and social situations.

Theoretically sound and practical recommendations concerning the content, form, and specificity of objectives are given in Tables 5.7 and 5.8 and Tips for Teachers 5.4.

Finally, no matter how carefully you plan your objectives, there are likely to be some unintended outcomes of instruction. These outcomes may be de-

Table 5.7   RECOMMENDATIONS FOR STATING OBJECTIVES: INSTRUCTIONAL CONTENT AND FORM

Content	Form
1. Objectives should be appropriate in terms of the level of difficulty and prior learning experience (of students).	1. Objectives should be stated in the form of expected pupil changes.
2. Objectives should be "real" in the sense that they describe behaviors the teacher actually intends to act on in the classroom situation.	2. Objectives should be stated in behavioral or performance terms.
3. A useful objective will describe both the content and the mental process or behavior required for an appropriate response.	3. Objectives should be stated singly.
4. The content of the objectives should be responsive to the needs of the individual and society.	4. Objectives should be parsimonious [and] trimmed of excessive verbiage.
5. A variety of behaviors should be stated, since most courses attempt to develop skills other than "recall" [or simple motor or affective skills].	5. Objectives should be grouped logically, so they make sense in determining units of instruction and evaluation.
	6. The conditions under which the expected pupil behavior will be observed should be specified.
	7. If possible, the objective should contain criteria for acceptable performance. Criteria might involve time limits or a minimum number of correct responses.

Source: Adapted from Allan C. Ornstein and Francis P. Hunkins, *Curriculum: Foundations, Principles and Issues* (Englewood Cliffs, N.J.: Prentice-Hall, 1988), pp. 153–155; David A. Payne, *The Assessment of Learning: Cognitive and Affective* (Lexington, Mass.: D.C. Heath, 1974), pp. 43–45.

sirable or undesirable, and most are likely to fall into the affective domain of attitudes, feelings, and motivation about learning. For example, as a result of a language arts lesson on a Tolstoy novel, some students may become more interested in reading novels on their own or be motivated to read more books by Tolstoy. Other students may become bored with language arts or uninterested in reading novels. According to educators, teachers may fail to notice or may ignore such side effects, because they result more from the method than from the content of instruction, more from the teacher's behavior than from students' attitudes.[31]

---

[31] Walter Dick and Robert A. Reiser, *Planning Effective Instruction* (Englewood Cliffs, N.J.: Prentice-Hall, 1989); Norman E. Gronlund, *Stating Objectives for Classroom Instruction*, 3rd ed. (New York: Macmillan, 1985).

Table 5.8 RECOMMENDATIONS FOR WRITING GENERAL OBJECTIVES AND PRECISE
OBJECTIVES

General objectives	Precise objectives
1. Determine the major objectives you wish to stress. (You may wish to arrange them in order of importance.)	1. Make a clear and precise determination of *what* you want the learner to accomplish.
2. Be sure the objectives are related to the goals of the school.	2. Decide on *who* is to perform the desired behavior (e.g., the student).
3. Be sure the objectives are related to sound principles of learning.	3. Detail through an action word the actual *behavior* to be employed in demonstrating mastery of the objective (e.g., to write, to describe).
4. Be sure the objectives are realistic in terms of the students' abilities and the time and facilities available.	4. Establish the limiting and/or facilitating *conditions* under which the learner is to do what is asked (e.g. in one hour, with the textbook open).
5. Be sure the objectives are related to important learning outcomes.	5. Describe the *product* or *performance* of the behavior to be evaluated to determine whether the objective is achieved (e.g., an essay, a report, a speech).
6. Arrange the objectives according to domains of learning or high-order/low-order cognitive, social, or psychological categories.	6. Decide on a *standard* or achievement level that will be used to evaluate the success of the product or performance (e.g., 80 percent correct).
7. Arrange the content and activities of the subject, course, etc., so they correspond with the objectives.	
8. Be sure the objectives satisfy or at least do not conflict with the views of the parents and community.	

SUMMARY

1. Aims are broad statements about the intent of education as a whole. Goals are general statements about what schools are expected to accomplish. Objectives specify content and behavior, and sometimes a proficiency level to be achieved at some level of instruction.

2. Objectives are written at several levels, including program, grade, subject, course, classroom, unit plan, and lesson plan, and at several degrees of specificity, from broad to precise.

3. The most popular approaches to formulating objectives are based on the work of Tyler, Bloom, Gronlund, Mager, and Gagné. Tyler identifies purposes

and then interprets them in the light of philosophical and psychological concerns to arrive at instructional objectives. Bloom's work (taxonomy of educational objectives) entails three domains of learning: cognitive, affective, and psychomotor. Gronlund distinguishes between general objectives and specific learning outcomes. Mager relies on three major characteristics for writing objectives: behavior, condition, and proficiency level. Gagné defines types of learned capabilities and stresses the importance and the identification of enabling objectives.

4. A number of recommendations for writing objectives are provided to facilitate teacher planning and instruction.

QUESTIONS TO CONSIDER

1. In terms of aims and goals, why is the question "What is the purpose of school?" so complex?

2. Why is it important for aims and goals to change as society changes?

3. What sources of information does Tyler recommend in formulating his objectives? Which source is most important? Why?

4. How does Gronlund distinguish between general objectives and specific learning outcomes?

5. What are the three components of Mager's objectives?

THINGS TO DO

1. Find a list of school goals in a textbook or curriculum guide and revise them to conform to the guidelines in writing objectives at a particular subject and grade level.

2. Arrange the six categories of the cognitive domain into a hierarchy from simple to complex. Give an example of an instructional objective for each category.

3. Arrange the five categories of the affective domain into a hierarchy from simple to complex. Give an example of an instructional objective for each category.

4. Formulate ten unit plan objectives in your area of specialization. Use either Gronlund's or Bloom's method to write these objectives. Give an example of an instructional objective for each category.

5. Write six objectives for the subject you wish to teach at the lesson plan level. Use the methods of Bloom, Mager, or Gagné to write these objectives.

RECOMMENDED READINGS

Benjamin S. Bloom et al. *Taxonomy of Educational Objectives: Handbook I, Cognitive Domain.* New York: Longman-McKay, 1956. Describes six categories of the cognitive domain and objectives and test items related to knowledge and problem-solving skills.

Dick, Walter, and Robert A. Reiser. *Planning Effective Instruction*. Englewood Cliffs, N.J.: Prentice-Hall, 1989. How to plan for instruction with emphasis on setting goals, establishing objectives, and developing tests to determine if the objectives have been achieved.

Gagné, Robert M. *The Conditions of Learning*, 4th ed. New York: Holt, Rinehart and Winston, 1985. How to plan and write objectives based on learned capabilities and task analysis.

Gronlund, Norman E. *Stating Objectives for Classroom Instruction*, 3rd ed. New York: Macmillan, 1985. Step-by-step procedures for writing and using objectives for instruction and testing.

Harlow, Anita J. *Taxonomy of the Psychomotor Domain*. New York: McKay, 1972. Examines six categories of the psychomotor domain and presents sample objectives and test items in the domain.

Krathwohl, David R., Benjamin S. Bloom, and Bertram Maisa. *Taxonomy of Educational Objectives, Handbook II: Affective Domain*. New York: Longman-McKay, 1964. Describes five categories of the affective domain and objectives and test items related to feelings, attitudes, and values.

Mager, Robert F. *Preparing Instructional Objectives*, rev. ed. Belmont, Calif.: Fearon, 1984. Describes objectives that specify behavior, condition, and proficiency.

KEY TERMS

Aims
Goals
Objectives
Program objectives
Course objectives
Classroom objectives
Unit plan objectives
Lesson plan objectives
Taxonomy of educational
   objectives

Cognitive domain
Affective domain
Psychomotor domain
General objectives
Specific learning outcomes
Learned capabilities
Task analysis
Enabling objectives

Chapter 6

Instructional Methods

FOCUSING QUESTIONS

1. When is the method of practice and drill useful?

2. How can practice and drill be made most effective?

3. Why is the method of questioning crucial to good instruction?

4. What are the characteristics of well-formulated questions?

5. What factors should be considered in preparing a lecture?

6. Why should lecture and explanation times be limited?

7. What are good strategies for the problem-solving method?

*T*o appreciate instruction, we need to make a distinction between teaching and instruction. *Teaching* is the behavior of the teacher that evolves during the instructional process. *Instruction* is the specific methods and activities by which the teacher influences learning. In this chapter we will explore four basic and traditional instructional methods: (1) practice and drill, (2) questioning, (3) lecturing and explaining, and (4) problem solving. These methods are supported by many years of research and practice.

PRACTICE AND DRILL

The mention of practice and drill summons up images of the old-fashioned schoolmaster, the drillmaster who made learning a repetitive response whereby students either memorized their lessons or experienced his wrath. However, it is an instructional method that does serve certain purposes well and can be used to advantage in classrooms today.

Applications of Practice and Drill

Practice and drill is a common method used by elementary teachers to teach the fundamentals to students, especially young children. The method is also employed by secondary teachers who teach students who still lack basic skills or knowledge of academic subject matter before asking them to move on to other tasks or transfer their learning to a new situation. Some teachers (K–12) believe it is essential to provide lots of practice on related problems in order to learn a basic skill or task, to the extent that they repeatedly drill their students. Most teachers are less drill-oriented and more open to other instructional approaches.

PROBLEM / DISADVANTAGE

Busywork   A major problem with the practice and drill method is that although it is supposed to enhance student knowledge, it can turn into busywork, especially if the tasks are either too easy or too difficult for the majority of students, or if it supplants other methods. This is true whether the teachers use published practice and drill material or design the material themselves.[1]

Teachers who emphasize routine and structure or who feel the need for a quiet and ordered environment sometimes disregard the classroom nuances or activities that produce those conditions and substitute busywork for meaningful practice and drill. According to one review of the research, about 25 to

---

[1]Jean Osborn, "Do Workbooks Reflect the Rest of the Work?," paper presented at the annual meeting of the American Educational Research Association, San Francisco, April 1986; Barak V. Rosenshine, "Teaching Functions in Instructional Programs," *Elementary School Journal*, March 1983, pp. 335–351.

30 percent of elementary teachers[2] (especially new teachers who need a safe environment) fall into this category.

<u>Seatwork Activities</u>   Elementary school students spend about 70 to 85 percent of their time engaged in seatwork activities, and practice and drill take up about two-thirds of this time for students involved in learning the basic skills of reading, writing, and arithmetic.[3] High school students spend more time in seatwork activities, but the activities are more varied and challenging and involve less practice and drill;[4] this is the case regardless of whether the high school teachers are experienced or beginning teachers.

<u>Back-to-Basics Approach</u>   Because of the dramatic decline in SAT scores over the past 20 years, and because many high schools have permitted functional illiterates to graduate, there has been a popular cry to return to the basics—the so-called three Rs at the elementary school level, and "essential" academic subjects (math, science, English, history, foreign language) at the high school level.

The proponents of back-to-basics argue that students should be drilled until they acquire basic knowledge in the three Rs and academic subjects; then they can become involved in inquiry-discovery learning. The real question is not whether they like reading or math, but whether they can read or compute.[5]

<u>Behaviorist Approaches</u>   Thorndike's **law of exercise,** which states that the more often a stimulus-response connection is made, the stronger it becomes, and Skinner's finding that reinforcement of a response increases the likelihood of its occurrence both provide some basis for the old maxim that practice makes perfect.[6]

Practice and drill can be provided by instructional techniques, such as teaching machines and computerized instruction, that rely on a schedule of

---

[2] Louis M. Heil, "Personality Variables, an Important Determinant in Effective Elementary School Instruction," *Theory into Practice,* February 1964, pp. 12–15.

[3] John I. Goodlad and Frances M. Klein, *Behind the Classroom Door* (Worthington, Ohio: Jones, 1970); Barak V. Rosenshine, "How Time Is Spent in Elementary Classrooms," in C. Denham and A. Lieberman, eds., *Time to Learn* (Washington, D.C.: National Institute of Education, 1980), pp. 107–126.

[4] Eric J. Cooper, "Toward a New Mainstream of Instruction in American Schools," *Journal of Negro Education,* Winter 1989, pp. 102–116; John I. Good, *A Place Called School* (New York: McGraw-Hill, 1984); Jane A. Stallings, "Using Time Effectively: A Self-Analytic Approach," in K. K. Zumwabt, ed., *Improving Teaching,* 1986 ASCD Yearbook (Alexandria, Va.: Association for Supervision and Curriculum Development, 1986), pp. 15–28.

[5] Allan C. Ornstein, "Curriculum Contrasts: A Historical Overview," *Phi Delta Kappan,* February 1982, 404–408; Claire E. Weinstein et al., "Helping Students Develop Strategies for Effective Learning," *Educational Leadership,* December–January 1989, pp. 17–19.

[6] See Ernest R. Hilgard and Gordon H. Bower, *Theories of Learning,* 5th ed. (Englewood Cliffs, N.J.: Prentice-Hall, 1981).

Figure 6.1 Workbooks have a double edge quality: they are an excellent tool for practice and drill yet over use can lead to busywork and student boredom. (Photo © Elizabeth Crews)

reinforcement. Instructional materials are arranged in logical order and broken down into units, called *frames*, that lead students through the program in small steps from the simplest to the most complex material. A program may have hundreds or thousands of frames. Repetition is used to maximize correct responses and to prevent misconceptions. Continuous reinforcement is supplied by getting answers right, and the program presents material in a way designed to enable students to have a high rate of success. From time to time, frames review previous material or present the same material in different contexts. Practice is essential when the learner makes a mistake and before advancing to another level of difficulty.[7]

Mastery Learning Methods Instruction that is arranged in a logical, progressive order and that matches materials and activities to individual needs and abilities

---

[7]Albert Bandura, *Social Learning Theory* (Englewood Cliffs, N.J.: Prentice-Hall, 1977); B. F. Skinner, *The Technology of Teaching* (New York: Appleton-Century-Crofts, 1968), and Skinner.

is most effective in fostering achievement. The basis of mastery learning, and similar forms of teaching such as adaptive instruction and individualized instructions, is to make certain that adequate learning and mastery of certain concepts and skills have taken place, usually through practice and drill, "before progressing to more complex concepts and skills."[8] Mastery instruction, especially when it is individualized as opposed to group-based instruction, accommodates varying rates of learning among students. A student who has difficulty in attaining a specific level of performance or mastery can improve by working on the necessary prerequisites through practice and drill.[9]

Where learning tasks are arranged in sequential order, mastery of the first task is a prerequisite of the second task, and all subsequent tasks build on preceding tasks. Uncorrected difficulties in a task are likely to create and to be compounded by further difficulties on following tasks. According to Bloom, the early tasks in the sequence are the most critical, since if these are not adequately learned, "the student is likely to have difficulty with all the later tasks." The most important techniques for teaching simple or prior learning tasks involve practice and drill.[10]

Remedial Instruction   Low-achieving (and at-risk) students need more practice and drill than high-achieving students before they can move on to subsequent tasks. The teacher may have to reduce the breadth of the work for more depth and reduce the pace and difficulty of the material.[11] The teacher will need to monitor the practice and drill closely, providing corrective feedback to help students grasp the material and avoid confusion or frustration.

Much of teaching for low-achieving students will be remedial in nature. Students who have learning problems often need extra practice and drill and a variety of learning experiences that relate new learning with prior learning; they cannot easily keep up with more advanced students and should not be allowed to become embarrassed or defensive. In heterogeneous classes, teachers must challenge high-achieving students and let them move on to other content. Practice and drill, and other direct forms of instruction, have limited value for these students.[12] But at the same time teachers must be sure that slower

---

[8]Robert Glazer, *Adaptive Education: Individual Diversity and Learning* (New York: Holt, Rinehart and Winston, 1977), p. 77.

[9]John H. Block, Helen E. Efthim, and Robert Burns, *Building Effective Mastery Learning Schools* (New York: Longman, 1984); Benjamin S. Bloom, *Human Characteristics and School Learning* (New York: McGraw-Hill, 1976).

[10]Bloom, *Human Characteristics and School Learning*, p. 35.

[11]Larry Cuban, "The 'At-Risk' Label and the Problem of Urban School Reform," *Phi Delta Kappan*, June 1989, pp. 780–784; Allan C. Ornstein and Daniel U. Levine, "Social Class, Race, and School Achievement," *Journal of Teacher Education*, September–October 1989, in print.

[12]Beau F. Jones and Lawrence B. Friedman, "Active Instruction for Students at Risk," *Educational Psychologist*, Summer 1988, pp. 299–308; Weinstein et al., "Helping Students Develop Strategies for Effective Learning."

Professional Viewpoint

The Persistence of Practice and Drill

The decade of the 1890s was one in which a spirit of reform in education permeated the atmosphere. A young pediatrician, Joseph Mayer Rice, was caught up in this desire to remake American education and embarked on a tour of thirty-six American cities to observe what was going on in American schools. In one New York City school, Rice observed how children learned tiny bits of information by memorizing facts and reciting loudly and rapidly. Rice was properly outraged and dedicated himself to eradicating as far as possible such puerile forms of teaching.

Now, about a century later, such extreme forms of drill are virtually unknown, but all contemporary evidence indicates that the recitation remains the predominant form of classroom discourse. This is despite the fact that many astute and sensitive educational reformers have called for a much greater measure of teaching procedures that involve, say, critical thinking or discovery activities. But, even if teachers are not quite as rigid as in Rice's day, they continue to rely on ditto sheets and workbooks to an unconscionable extent.

Why, we may ask, have classsroom practices changed so little from Rice's day to the present? To my way of thinking, the most plausible answer lies in a conflict between two seemingly compatible tasks that teachers are asked to perform: control and teaching. Hardly anyone will argue against the need for a measure of control in classroom situations in order to carry forward the task of teaching. In practice, however, the emphasis on control has so predominated that we can be counted as good teachers so long as our classrooms are orderly. It almost does not matter whether we really teach or not. Practice and drill of the sort that Rice observed persist not because they have specific pedagogical sanction but because they are proven instruments of control. It is only when teachers are able to see their primary role as teaching, not as enforcing a precarious order, that routine practice and drill will be relegated to their appropriately subordinate role in the classroom.

Herbert M. Klieband
Professor of Curriculum
University of Wisconsin-Madison

students learn some material thoroughly, in some cases only a limited amount, instead of racing through a large amount of material, with little comprehension and retention.

Functions of Practice and Drill

The main goal of practice and drill is to make sure that students understand the prerequisite skills for the day's lesson. Practice and drill activities include: (1) reviewing the previous day's work and homework, (2) presenting skills and concepts necessary for new content, (3) providing student practice and checks to evaluate student responses, (4) receiving feedback from student work and questions and reteaching common problems, (5) providing students with methods for independent practice, and (6) conducting weekly or monthly reviews in test or nontest forms. These activities are presented in greater detail in Table 6.1.

In elementary and secondary grades the technique of beginning a lesson by checking or reviewing the previous day's assignment is common in many mastery learning and direct instructional approaches. In a 45-minute period in mathematics, for example, Thomas Good recommends that daily practice and drill be used to start the lesson, that it consist of approximately 8 minutes, and that it be related to homework assignments and computation exercises. He also recommends practice as part of seatwork activity, when students are engaged in learning new concepts and skills.[13] Practice and drill varies by subject and grade level; the data suggest that it occurs in 50 to 60 percent of the classes, less at the high school than elementary level and more in mathematics and English than in social studies or science.[14]

<hr>

Guidelines for Implementing Practice and Drill

In order to acquire many basic skills, especially in arithmetic, grammar, and foreign languages, certain things need to be learned to the point of automatic response, such as simple rules of grammar and speech, word recognition, and mathematical calculations (adding, subtracting, multiplying). These things are needed for more advanced learning and are best learned through practice and drill.

---

[13] Thomas L. Good, Douglas A. Grouws, and Howard Ebermeier, *Active Mathematics Teaching* (New York: Longman, 1983).

[14] Carolyn M. Evertson et al., "Relationship Between Classroom Behaviors and Student Outcomes in Junior High School Mathematics and English," *American Educational Research Journal*, Spring 1980, pp. 43–60; Thomas L. Good and Douglas A. Grouws, "The Missouri Mathematics Effectiveness Project," *Journal of Educational Psychology*, June 1979, pp. 355–362; and Rosenshine, "Teaching Functions in Instructional Programs."

Table 6.1   PRACTICE AND DRILL ACTIVITIES

1. *Daily review, checking previous day's work, and reteaching (if necessary):*
   Checking homework
   Reteaching areas where there were student errors
2. *Presenting new content/skills:*
   Provide overview
   Proceed in small steps (if necessary), but at a rapid pace
   Give detailed and redundant instructions and explanations, if necessary
   Phase in new skills while old skills being mastered
3. *Initial student practice:*
   High frequency of questions and overt student practice (from teacher and materials)
   Prompts provided during initial learning (when appropriate)
   All students have a chance to respond and receive feedback
   Teacher checks for understanding by evaluating student responses
   Continue practice until students are firm
   Success rate of 80% or higher during initial learning
4. *Feedback and correctives (and recycling of instruction, if necessary):*
   Feedback to students, particularly when they are correct but hesitant
   Feedback of student errors to teacher, that corrections and/or reteaching is necessary
   Corrections by simplifying question, giving clues, explaining or reviewing steps, or reteaching
     last steps
   When necessary, reteaching using smaller steps
5. *Independent practice so that students are firm and automatic:*
   Seatwork
   Unitization and automaticity (practice to overlearning)
   Need for procedure to ensure student engagement during seatwork (i.e., teacher or aide moni-
     toring)
   95% correct or higher
6. *Weekly and monthly reviews:*
   Reteaching, if necessary

Source: Barak V. Rosenshine, "Teaching Functions in Instructional Programs," *Elementary School Journal* (March 1983), p. 338.

Although practice and drill is accepted in theory, realistic guidelines need to be applied for the classroom setting. Below is a recommended list, based on practice and research.

   1. *Practice must follow understanding and can enhance understanding.* Students will learn more easily and remember longer if they practice what they understand or have learned through prior classroom experiences.[15] At the same time understanding can be further increased through practice and drill of what is to be learned.

---

[15] Neville Bennett, "The Search for a Theory of Pedogogy," *Teaching and Teacher Education* (no. 1, 1988), pp. 19–30; David E. Somerville and David J. Leach, "Direct or Indirect Instruction," *Educational Research*, February 1988, pp. 46–53.

2. *Practice is more effective if students have a desire to learn what is being practiced.* Students will practice what they believe has value and if they are motivated. For these reasons, it is important for the teacher to provide situational variety (repetition can become boring), interesting aspects of a particular skill as well as interesting drill items, situations in which students can use the skill or knowledge in other phases of learning, drill items related to students' experiences and interests, and explanations of the relationship between the skill or knowledge being learned and more advanced learning.

3. *Practice should be individualized.* Exercises should be organized so that each student can work independently at his or her own level of ability and rate of learning. In this way low-achieving or slow students can devote more time to items that are difficult for them, and high-achieving or bright students can advance without waiting for the others.

4. *Practice should be specific and systematic.* A drill exercise should be related to a specific objective or skill, and students should know in advance what is being practiced. Drill on specific skills in which students need practice will produce better results than indiscriminate drill. Digressions should be avoided.[16] A systematic, step-by-step procedure fits well with all learners, especially low-achieving students.

5. *Practice should be intermixed with different materials and parts of the lesson.* Drill items can constitute part of chalkboard exercises, mimeographed materials, workbook and textbook exercises, homework, and reviews for tests.[17] Drill may also be used in conjunction with independent seatwork, small learning groups, or student learning teams.

6. *There should be much practice on a few skills rather than a little practice on many skills.* It is best to focus on one or two of skills at one time and emphasize more practice on those few skills.

7. *Practice should be organized so that students experience high rates of achievement.* Effective drill is characterized by high rates of correct response. Correct responses serve as reinforcement. When students discover that their answers are correct, they are encouraged to go to the next question or item. This is especially important for slow learners. Research suggests that most students need at least a 90 percent rate of correct response while doing practice and drill activities (also for completing homework) in material that has supposedly been

---

[16]Block, Efthim, and Burns, *Building Effective Mastery Learning Schools*; Robert M. Gagné, Leslie J. Briggs, and Walter W. Wager, *Principles of Instructional Design*, 3rd ed. (New York: Holt, Rinehart and Winston, 1988).

[17]Gaea Leinhardt and William Bickel, "Instruction's the Thing Wherein to Catch the Mind that Falls Behind," *Educational Psychologist*, Spring 1987, pp. 177–207; Barak V. Rosenshine, "Explicit Teaching and Teacher Training," *Journal of Teacher Education*, May–June 1987, pp. 34–38.

learned.[18] Success rate can be as low as 70 percent with students who will not become overly confused or frustrated, as long as the teacher is available to correct their work immediately.[19]

8. *Practice should be organized so that students and teacher have immediate feedback.* Either drill should be self-scoring, or teacher-scored, with correct answers provided—and should be done as soon as possible. The teacher needs to know scores or results in order to know if he or she can proceed to the next point or skill.[20] The student, especially the low-achieving student, needs to know the correct responses here and now, not next week or when the teacher has had time to mark the papers. Based on a review of 53 students, for best results tests should be returned within one or two days, and for specific lists (or items) to be learned the feedback time should be 4 to 10 seconds.[21] However, as well as classroom practice, should be graded each day, with teacher suggestions given for what to do for wrong answers.

9. *Practice material should be used for diagnostic purposes.* Drill items should be constructed to reveal individual problem areas. Much of practice material can be used for diagnostic purposes as long as the teacher knows what skills each student is working on and what skills each student has mastered.[22] Studying and keeping a record of students' performance can help the teacher recognize and treat problems before they become habits, seriously affect later work, or cause students to be branded as "remedial" or having a "learning disability."

10. *Practice material should provide progressive continuity between learning tasks.* Too often a skill is taught and left without testing. To foster continuous mastery and systematic recall, there should be a whole sequence of practice for a specific unit or course, making certain that there is intermittent drill at desirable intervals. Practice should be given frequently; it should cover tasks in order of difficulty,

[18]Bloom, *Human Characteristics and School Learning;* Rosenshine, "Teaching Functions in Instructional Programs."

[19]Thomas L. Good and Jere E. Brophy, *Looking into Classrooms,* 4th ed. (New York: Harper & Row, 1988). Richard S. Marliave and Nikola N. Filby, "Success Rate: A Measure of Task Appropriateness," in C. W. Fisher and D. C. Berliner, eds., *Perspectives on Instructional Time* (New York: Longman, 1985), pp. 217–236.

[20]Linda M. Anderson, Carolyn M. Evertson, and Jere E. Brophy, "An Experimental Study of Effective Teaching in First-Grade Reading Groups," *Elementary School Journal,* March 1979, pp. 193–223; Velma I. Hythecker, Donald F. Dansereau, and Thomas R. Rocklin, "An Analysis of the Processes Influencing the Structured Dyadic Learning Environment," *Educational Psychologist,* Winter 1988, pp. 23–37.

[21]James A. Kulik and Chen-Lin C. Kulik, "Timing and Feedback and Verbal Learning," *Review of Educational Research,* Spring 1988, pp. 79–97.

[22]Stephen F. Foster, "Ten Principles of Learning Revised in Accordance with Cognitive Psychology," *Educational Psychologist,* Summer 1986, pp. 235–243; Somerville and Leach, "Direct or Indirect Instruction."

Tips for Teachers 6.1

Improving Practice and Drill

Research has identified several recommendations for improving practice and drill and other seatwork activities to enhance academic learning.

1. *Have a clear system of rules and procedures for general behavior.* This allows students to deal with personal needs (for example, permission to use the bathroom pass) and procedural routines (sharpening or borrowing a pencil) without disturbing classmates seated and engaged in academic work.

2. *Move around the room to monitor students' seatwork.* Students should feel that the teacher is aware of their behavior and alert to difficulties they may encounter. The extent of monitoring is correlated with the students' academic ability and the related demands they make for the teacher's attention.

3. *Provide comments, explanations, and feedback.* The more recognition or attention students receive, the more they are willing to pursue seatwork activities. Watching for signs of confusion by students and briefly dealing with it increases students' willingness to persist and helps teachers to know how students are doing and to plan the next instructional task. Common problems should be explained immediately by interrupting the practice exercise if the problems are serious, or after the practice if they can wait.

4. *Spend more time teaching and reteaching the basic skills.* Elementary and low-achieving youngsters should be exposed to heavy doses of skills learning, which requires practice and drill. When students have difficulty with basic skills, it is important to instruct in small steps to the point of overlearning.

5. *Use practice during and after learning.* Practice and drill should be used sparingly for initiating new learning, rather in conjunction with and after the learning. Practice activities can be mixed with other activities such as demonstrations, explanations, and questions, depending on the students' age and abilities. However, games and simulations for young children and field trips and buzz sessions for older students are not as effective (in terms of use of time) as practice and drill and other paper-and-pencil activities (for review or reteaching).

6. *Provide variety and challenge in practice and drill.* Practice can easily drift into busywork and frustrate or bore students if it is too easy, too difficult, or too monotonous. The teacher should motivate

continued

the students to work at optimum levels of their ability, gradually shifting into different activities to interest and challenge them.

7. *Keep students alert and focused on the task.* Teachers need to keep students on task—occasionally questioning them, calling on both volunteers and nonvolunteers, elaborating on incorrect answers (preferably by asking other students to do so).

8. *Maintain a brisk pace.* There should be little confusion about what to do during practice and drill, and activities should not be interrupted by minor disturbances or environmental conditions. A snap of the finger, eye contact, or other "signal" procedures should help in dealing with inattentive or disruptive students without stopping the lesson.

and the range of items should be wide enough to connect prerequisite learning tasks with new learning tasks.[23] See Tips for Teachers 6.1.

QUESTIONING

Good teaching involves good questioning, especially when large groups of students are being taught. Skillful questioning can arouse the students' curiosity, stimulate their imagination, and motivate them to search out new knowledge. It can challenge the students, make them think, and help clarify concepts and problems related to the lesson. The type and sequence of the questions and how students respond to them influence the quality of classroom discussion and the effectiveness of instruction. Good teachers usually have skill in striking a balance between factual and thought-provoking questions and in selecting questions to emphasize major points and to stimulate lively discussion.

Types of Questions

Questions can be categorized in many ways: (1) according to thinking process involved, from low level to high level or (according to the cognitive taxonomy) from knowledge to evaluation, (2) according to type of answer required, convergent or divergent, and (3) according to the degree of personal exploration, or valuing. Some authorities have also developed descriptive categories of questions that deal with academic tasks and activities.

---

[23] The ten recommendations for practice and drill are based on Allan C. Ornstein, "Practice and Drill: How to Improve Learning," *National Association of Secondary School Principals* (in print 1990).

Figure 6.2 Waiting and delayed gratification are part of the instructional process that students must learn to cope with. (Photo © Steve Payne)

Low-Level and High-Level Questions   **Low-level questions** emphasize memory and recall of information. When was the Declaration of Independence signed? Who won the Civil War? Where is the Statue of Liberty? These questions focus on facts and do not test understanding or problem-solving skills. They correspond to lower cognitive processes—what J. P. Guilford calls *information*, Jerome Bruner calls *concrete operations*, and Arthur Jensen calls *level-one thinking.*

High-level questions go beyond memory and factual information and deal with complex and abstract thinking. Low-level questions have a place in the sequence of questioning. They are used to assess readiness for complex and abstract thinking, to see whether students can deal with higher cognitive processes and high-level questions that deal with analysis, synthesis, and problem solving. The ideal is to reach a balance between the two types of questions. The trouble is that many teachers do not progress beyond the knowledge-oriented questions. In fact, according to researchers, it is not uncommon to find that 70 to 90 percent of the questions teachers ask are low level.[24]

---

[24] Michael J. Dunkin and Bruce J. Biddle, *The Study of Teaching* (New York: Holt, Rinehart and Winston, 1974); David A. Payne, *The Assessment of Learning* (Boston: Heath, 1974); Meredith Gall, "Synthesis of Research on Teachers' Questioning," *Educational Leadership*, January 1984, pp. 40–47; and William W. Wilen, "Implications of Research on Questioning for the Teacher Education," *Journal of Research and Development in Education*, Winter 1984, pp. 31–35.

Criticism of the use of low-level questions is complicated by recent research that indicates that low-level and narrowly defined questions characterize an effective instructional program for inner-city and low-achieving learners.[25] Teachers who ask high-level questions and encourage student-initiated comments are least effective with these types of students,[26] the reason being that these students lack a knowledge base and need more low-level questions and feedback from teachers before they can move to problem-solving skills and high-level questions. The problem is that teachers often become set in their use of low-level questions and thus keep these students permanently in a cognitively second-rate instructional program.

Low-level questions can foster learning, especially with students who lack prerequisite knowledge and who are developing a knowledge base and need to experience simple questions to build their confidence in learning. According to researchers, low-order questioning is effective for such students when it is taught in relation to instructional activities involving basic reading and math. The new low-order information must be related in a meaningful way to knowledge and information level the learner already has.[27] But we would expect teachers to progress to asking as many high-level questions as possible. If we return to the subjects of our three examples of low-level questions, we can ask a series of high-level questions. What were the reasons for signing the Declaration of Independence? What other alternative courses of action were available to the revolutionists? How would these other actions have affected history? What economic, political, and social events led to the Civil War? Why did the North win the Civil War? How did the results of the war affect black-white relations for the remainder of the nineteenth century? or this century? What does the Statue of Liberty mean to you? To an immigrant arriving in America by ship in 1920? To a Vietnamese political refugee today? To a Hispanic worker today crossing the Rio Grande in search of a job?

These questions are obviously more advanced, more stimulating, and more challenging, and in many cases there are no right or wrong answers. As the questions become more advanced, they involve more abstractions and points of view. Asking high-level questions demands patience and clear thinking on

---

[25] Carl Bereiter and Siegfried Englemann, *Teaching Disadvantaged Children in the Preschool* (Englewood Cliffs, N.J.: Prentice-Hall, 1966); Barak V. Rosenshine, "Content, Time, and Direct Instruction," in P. L. Peterson and H. J. Walberg, eds., *Research on Teaching: Concepts, Findings, and Implications* (Berkekey, Calif.: McCutchan, 1979), pp. 28–56.

[26] Walter Doyle, "Effective Teaching and the Concept of the Master Teacher," *Elementary School Journal*, September 1985, pp. 27–34; Donald S. Medley, "The Effectiveness of Teachers," in Peterson and Walberg, eds., *Research on Teaching*, pp. 11–27; and Jane Stallings and David H. Kaskowitz, *Follow Through Classroom Observation Evaluation* (Menlo Park, Calif.: Stanford Research Institute, 1974).

[27] Penelope L. Peterson, "Making Learning Meaningful: Lessons from Research on Cognition and Instruction," *Educational Psychologist*, Fall 1988, pp. 365–373. Patricia A. Herman, "Incidental Requisition of Word Meaning from Expositions with Varied Text Features," *Reading Research Quarterly*, Summer 1987, pp. 263–284.

the part of the teacher; creating appropriate timing, sequencing, and phrasing is no easy task for even the experienced teacher.

Benjamin Bloom's cognitive taxonomy can be related to the categories of low-level and high-level questions just described. Low-level questioning and knowledge correspond to the knowledge category of the taxonomy, what Bloom calls the "simplest" form of learning and the "most common educational objective."[28] High-level questioning and problem-solving skills correspond to the next five categories of the taxonomy—comprehension, application, analysis, synthesis, and evaluation. This is shown in Table 6.2. As we saw in Chapter 5, the six categories of the cognitive taxonomy form a hierarchy of levels of complexity from simple to more advanced, with each level dependent upon the acquisition of skills at the lower levels. The sample questions in the table correspond to the cognitive categories of the taxonomy.

Convergent and Divergent Questions   **Convergent questions** tend to have one correct or best answer. For this reason they are often mistakenly identified as low-level and knowledge questions, but they can also be formulated to demand the selecting of relevant concepts and the working out of problems dealing with steps and structure. Convergent questions can deal with logic and complex data, abstract ideas, analogies and multiple relationships. According to research, convergent questions can be used when students work on and attempt to solve difficult exercises in math and science, especially dealing with analysis of equations and word problems.[29]

Divergent questions are often open ended and usually have many appropriate, different answers. Stating a "right" answer is not always most important; rather it is how the student arrives at his or her answer. Students should be encouraged by the teacher to state their reasoning and to provide supporting examples and evidence. Divergent questions are associated with high-level thinking processes and can encourage creative thinking and discovery learning. Often convergent questions must be asked first to clarify what students know before advancing to divergent questions. But the ideal is to ask fewer convergent questions, especially low-level ones, and more divergent questions. The mix of convergent to divergent questions will reflect the students' abilities, the teacher's ability to phrase such questions, and the teacher's comfort in handling varied responses.

Convergent questions usually start with what, who, when, or where; divergent questions usually start with how or why. What or who questions, followed by why, are really divergent questions that are introduced by what to get to the why aspect of the question. (For example, "Who won the Civil War?" leads to the ultimate question: "Why?") The differences are highlighted

[28]Benjamin S. Bloom, ed., *Taxonomy of Educational Objectives, Handbook I: Cognitive Domain* (New York: Longman-McKay, 1956), p. 28.

[29]Lauren B. Resnick and Leopold E. Klopfer, eds., *Toward the Thinking Curriculum: Current Cognitive Research*, 1989 ASCD Yearbook. (Alexandria, Va.: Association for Super and Curriculum Development, 1989).

Table 6.2 QUESTIONS RELATED TO THE COGNITIVE TAXONOMY

Category	Sample question
1.0 Knowledge	
1.1 Knowledge of specifics	Who discovered the Mississippi River?
1.2 Knowledge of ways and means of dealing with specifics	What word does an adjective modify?
1.3 Knowledge of universals and abstractions in a field	What is the best method for calculating the circumference of a circle?
2.0 Comprehension	
2.1 Translation	What do the words *hasta la vista* mean?
2.2 Interpretation	How do Democrats and Republicans differ in their views of spending?
2.3 Extrapolation	Given the present birth rate, what will be the world population by the year 2000?
3.0 Application	
	How has the *Miranda* decision affected civil liberties?
	Given a pie-shaped lot 120 ft. × 110 ft. × 100 ft., and village set-back conditions of 15 ft. in all directions, what is the largest size one-story home you can build on this lot?
4.0 Analysis	
4.1 Analysis of elements	Who can distinguish between fact and opinion in the article we read?
4.2 Analysis of relationships	How does Picasso organize colors, shapes, and sizes to produce images?
4.3 Analysis of organizational principles	How does John Steinbeck use his characters to discuss the notion of friendship in *Of Mice and Men*?
5.0 Synthesis	
5.1 Production of a unique communication	Who can write a simple melodic line?
5.2 Production of a plan or proposed set of operations	How would you go about determining the chemical weight of an unknown substance?
5.3 Derivation of a set of abstract relations	What are the common causes for cell breakdown in the case of mutations, cancer, and aging?
6.0 Evaluation	
6.1 Judgment in terms of internal evidence	Who can show the fallacies of Hitler's *Mein Kampf*?
6.2. Judgment in terms of external evidence	Who can judge what is wrong with the architect's design of the plumbing and electricity?

Source: Allan C. Ornstein, "Questioning: The Essence of Good Teaching," *National Association of Secondary School Principals,* May 1987, pp. 73–74.

by the sample questions in Table 6.3. Most teachers ask far more *what, who, when*, and *where* questions than *how* or *why* questions; the ratio is about 3 or 4 to one.[30] This is because the convergent questions are simple to phrase and to grade; they help keep students focused on specific data; and they give many students a chance to participate. Convergent questions thus make good questions for practice and review. Divergent questions require more flexibility on the part of the teacher. For the student they require the ability to cope with not being sure about being right and not always getting approval from the teacher. In general, the pace of questioning is slower. There is more opportunity for students to exchange ideas and differing opinions. There is also more chance for disagreement among students and between students and teacher—which is often discouraged or viewed as tangential by teachers.

Right Answers Count   In the majority of classrooms, teachers ask convergent questions, which entail a "right" answer, and students are expected to give the answer—often resulting in teacher approval. These questions and answers, coupled with the stidents' need for approval (especially at the elementary grade level) permit teachers to dominate classroom interaction and students learn to give the answer expected of them. According to Jule Henry, students "learn the signal response system called docility and thus obtain approval from the teacher."[31] Indeed, right answers count in school, not necessarily how you arrived at the answer, because teachers are keyed to and approve right answers.

For low-achieving students, and for students who need teacher approval, the magic words from the teacher is often "yes" or "right." The teacher determines what is right in the classroom, and the easiest way to test students is to ask convergent questions. Divergent questions, on the other hand, lead to novel responses, responses that the teacher does not always expect, and responses that take up class time (or time out from the formal curriculum). This may be difficult to deal with by students who have come through the educational system being right answer-oriented, or for teachers who have been trained to provide and then look for correct answers.

John Holt points out that as students become right answer-oriented, they become *producers*, producing what teachers want, not *thinkers*. It is only the rare student who is willing to play with ideas, not caring whether the teacher confirms an answer is right. But the average child must be right. "She cannot bear to be wrong. When she is wrong . . . the only thing to do is to forget it as quickly as possible."[32] Under these circumstances, divergent questions, which may not have right answers, only prolong the child's agony in the classroom.

---

[30]J. T. Dillon, "Research on Questioning and Discussion," *Educational Leadership*, November 1984, pp. 50–56; Gall, "Synthesis of Research on Teachers' Questioning." Also see J. T. Dillon, *Questioning and Teaching* (New York: Teachers College Press, Columbia University, 1988).

[31]Jules Henry, "Docility, or Giving Teacher What She Wants," in J. H. Chilcott, N. C. Greenberg, and H. B. Wilson, eds., *Readings in the Socio-Cultural Foundations of Education* (Belmont, Calif.: Wadsworth, 1969), p. 249.

[32]John Holt, *How Children Fail* (New York: Pitman, 1964), p. 12.

Table 6.3 SAMPLE CONVERGENT AND DIVERGENT QUESTIONS

Subject and grade level	Convergent questions	Divergent questions
Social Studies, 5th–7th	Where did the Boston Tea Party take place?	Why did the Boston Tea Party take place?
	Where did it take place?	Why did it take place in Boston, not New York or Philadelphia?
Social Studies, 7th–9th	What are the three products from Argentina?	How does wheat production in Argentina affect wheat export in our country?
English, 5th–7th	What is the verb in the sentence, "The girl told the boy what to do."?	How do we rewrite the present and future tense of the verb in the sentence, "The girl told the boy what to do."?
English, 10th–11th	Who wrote *Farewell to Arms*?	How does Hemingway's experience as a news reporter affect the story *Farewell to Arms*?
Science, 2nd–5th	Which planet is closest to the sun?	How would you compare living conditions on Mercury with those on Earth?
	Who was the first American astronaut to travel in space?	What planet, other than Earth, would you prefer to visit, if you were an astronaut? Why?
Science, 9th–11th	What are two elements of water?	How is water purified?
Math, 4th–5th	What is the definition of a triangle?	How have triangles influenced architecture?
Math, 6th–8th	What is the shortest distance between two points?	What is the best air route to take from New York City to Moscow? Why?

Asking questions to which there is only one right answer fosters a highly convergent mind, even an authoritarian mind—one that looks for simple "right" answers and simple solutions to complex problems, one that relies on authority rather than on rational judgment to find the "right" answer. It also breeds a rigid and narrow mind that fails to recognize or is unwilling to admit that facts and figures are screened through a filtering process of personal and social experience and interpretation.[33]

Valuing Questions A number of educators and psychologists have advocated different ways of enhancing the creative and human potential of students. All

---

[33] Allan C. Ornstein, "Questioning: The Essence of Good Teaching: Part I," *National Association of Secondary School Principals*, May 1987, pp. 71–79.

these procedures and techniques stress **valuing**—a process in which students explore their feelings and attitudes, analyze their experiences, and express their ideas. The emphasis is on the personal development of the learner through clarifying attitudes and aspirations and making choices.

A teacher can stimulate valuing through probing questions. Keep in mind, however, that a 6-year-old cannot be confronted or probed in terms of feelings or attitudes in the same way as a 16-year-old. The teacher must also consider how far to get students to express themselves (or to reveal their inner thoughts) in the classroom, especially in front of their peers, to avoid unexpected, unintended, or extreme emotional reactions.

Louis Raths and his colleagues have developed a model for clarifying the values of learners. For him, valuing consists of seven components in three levels: *choosing*—(1) choosing freely, (2) choosing from alternatives, (3) choosing after considering the consequences of each alternative; (4) *prizing*—cherishing the choice, (5) affirming the choice to others; (6) *acting*—doing something with the choice, and (7) repeating the action.[34] Raths has also developed several general questions that can be used in any classroom to encourage students to clarify their values along his model. A sample of these questions is shown in Table 6.4.

Descriptive Categories of Questions   Several authorities have formulated their own categories and models of questions that correspond to the basic types we have just described. James Gallagher sorts questions into four categories.

1. *Cognitive-memory* questions require students to reproduce facts or remember content through processes such as rote memory or selective recall. For example, "What is the capital of France?"
2. *Convergent* questions require students to recall information that leads to a correct or conventional answer. Given or known information is usually the expected response; novel information is usually considered incorrect. For example, "Summarize the author's major points."
3. *Divergent* questions require students to generate their own data or a new perspective on a given topic. Divergent questions have no right answer; they suggest novel or creative responses. For example, "What might the history of the United States have been if the Nazis had won World War II?"
4. *Evaluative* questions require students to make value judgments about the quality, correctness, or adequacy of information, based on some criterion usually set by the student or by some objective standard. For example, "How would you judge the art of Picasso?"

Gallagher found that in classrooms with gifted students, cognitive-memory questions comprised more than 50 percent of the total questions asked. It is

---

[34]Louis E. Raths, Merrill Harmin, and Sidney B. Simon, *Values and Teaching*, 2nd ed. (Columbus, Ohio: Merrill, 1978).

Table 6.4   QUESTIONING STRATEGIES FOR THE VALUING PROCESS

1. *Choosing freely*
   a. Where do you suppose you first got that idea?
   b. How long have you felt that way?
   c. What would people say if you weren't to do what you say you must do?

2. *Choosing from alternatives*
   a. What else did you consider before you picked this?
   b. How long did you look around before you decided?
   c. Was it a hard decision? What went into the final decision? Who helped? Do you need any further help?

3. *Choosing thoughtfully and reflectively*
   a. What would be the consequences of each alternative available?
   b. Have you thought about this very much? How did your thinking go?
   c. This is what I understand you to say . . . [interpret statement].

4. *Prizing and cherishing*
   a. Are you glad you feel that way?
   b. How long have you wanted it?
   c. What good is it? What purpose does it serve? Why is it important to you?

5. *Affirming*
   a. Would you tell the class the way you feel?
   b. Would you be willing to sign a petition supporting that idea?
   c. Are you saying that you believe . . . [repeat the idea]?

6. *Acting upon choices*
   a. I hear what you are for; now, is there anything you can do about it? Can I help?
   b. What are your first steps, second steps, etc.?
   c. Are you willing to put some of your money behind this idea?

7. *Repeating*
   a. Have you felt this way for some time?
   b. Have you done anything already? Do you do this often?
   c. What are your plans for doing more of it?

Source: Louis E. Raths, Merrill Harmin, and Sidney B. Simon, *Values and Teaching*, 2nd ed. (Columbus, Ohio: Merrill, 1978), pp. 64–66.

assumed that teachers ask even more cognitive-memory questions with average or low-achieving students. Convergent questions were the second most frequently used category. Few divergent and evaluative questions were asked. Gallagher surmises that teacher-student discussions can operate normally if only the first two categories of questions are used.[35]

Hilda Taba categorizes questions according to cognitive operations pertaining to high-level thinking or what some have termed *reflective thinking*.

---

[35]James J. Gallagher, "Expressive Thought by Gifted Children in the Classroom," in *Language and the Higher Thought Processes* (Champaign, Ill.: National Council of Teachers of English, 1965), pp. 56–65; James J. Gallagher and Mary J. Aschner, "A Preliminary Report on Analyses of Classroom Interaction," *Merrill Palmer Quarterly*, July 1963, pp. 183–194.

The questions are designed to engage the learner in levels of cognitive tasks: (1) concept formation, (2) generalizing and inferring, and (3) application of principles.[36]

The cognitive tasks are defined in terms of overt activities (see Table 6.5). These cognitive tasks, overt activities, and eliciting questions form a hierarchy in which each is prerequisite to the next. As students proceed through the steps in each cognitive task, qualitative transformations occur in the thought process.

According to Taba's model, the teacher formulates appropriate questions for the cognitive activities within each cognitive task. The questions elicit from students different levels of complexity and abstraction. Taba relies heavily on divergent questions. The nature of the activities dictates the type of question to be used.

Dillon classifies research questions, or what we might also refer to as high-level questions, into four types.

1. *Theoretical:* Examples: How are the principles (or methods) consistent with the underlying rationale? What are the rationale and principles of the scheme?
2. *Reliability:* Examples: How precisely has each of the categories been defined? What is the definition of the thing whose kinds are being classified? How consistent is the performance?
3. *Logical:* Examples: What characteristics do these categories exhibit? What principle has been identified? What relationship exists among the catergories exhibited?
4. *Utility:* Examples: For what use has the plan been designed? How well does it satisfy these uses? What kinds of action does the scheme permit?[37]

Unquestionably, these are tough questions that deal with abstractions and academic research. They are the kinds of questions that are appropriate only for high-achieving students who can deal with reflective questions and who are not concerned with right answers.

Formulating Questions

Through appropriate strategies in formulating and asking questions the teacher can help students understand and utilize content and formulate ideas, concepts, relationships, and principles. Several different approaches to formulation have been suggested.

---

[36] Hilda Taba, *Teaching Strategies and Cognitive Functioning in Elementary School Children,* Cooperative Research Project No. 2404 (San Francisco: San Francisco State College, 1966); Hilda Taba and Freeman F. Elzey, "Teaching Strategies and Thought Processes," *Teachers College Record,* March 1964, pp. 524–534.

[37] J. T. Dillon, "The Classification of Research Questions," *Review of Educational Research,* Fall 1984, pp. 327–361.

Table 6.5   COGNITIVE OPERATIONS AND LEVELS OF QUESTIONS

Overt activity	Eliciting questions
Cognitive task 1: concept formation	
1. Enumeration and listing	What did you see? Hear? Note?
2. Grouping together	What belongs together? On what criterion?
3. Labeling, categorizing	What would you call these groups? What belongs under what?
Cognitive task 2: generalizing and inferring	
1. Identifying points	What did you note? See? Find?
2. Explaining identified items of information	Why did so-and-so happen? Why is so-and-so true?
3. Making inferences or generalizations	What does this mean? What would you conclude? What generalizations can you make?
Cognitive task 3: application of principles	
1. Predicting consequences, explaining unfamiliar phenomena, hypotheses	What would happen if . . . ?
2. Explaining and supporting predictions and hypotheses	Why do you think this would happen?
3. Verifying predictions and hypotheses	What would it take for so-and-so to be true? Would it be true in all cases? At what times?

Source: Hilda Taba, *Teaching Strategies and Cognitive Functions in Elementary School Children,* Cooperative Research Project No. 2404 (San Francisco: San Francisco State College, 1966), pp. 39–40, 42.

A teacher can formulate basic questions as he or she prepares each lesson. At this stage the teacher can reduce the number of questions to four or five, sometimes called **pivotal questions,** that relate to the major objectives or parts of the lesson. These questions can be used to introduce and clarify major ideas and to motivate students. The questions are written in advance, as part of the lesson plan, because they evolve naturally from the lesson plan so that the teacher will have them available to use at appropriate places during the classroom discussion.

As the lesson proceeds and teacher-student interaction occurs, it is necessary for the teacher to formulate other questions, called **emerging questions.** These questions cannot be prepared in advance, since it is impossible to know exactly what discussion will lead to, but they are crucial for keeping the flow of ideas and the interaction alive.

Some researchers suggest examining questions in terms of five major characteristics.

1. *Conciseness.* Questions should be simple and easily understood by all students. Good questions center on one specific point related to an objective topic or concept. Vague questions and multiple questions can lead to student confusion and frustration.

2. *Challenge.* Good questions promote inquiry-discovery learning. Questions that repeat subject material or facts in the text are not thought-provoking. Challenging questions are conceptual, analytical, evaluative, divergent, and valuing. They lead to student participation, student problem formulation, and student explanation of problems. They encourage students to support their responses, express opinions, and use their own experiences.

3. *Group orientation.* Classroom questions are addressed to an entire class or group of students, not an individual. (Students should not receive any indication as to who will be called upon to respond; this helps keep students alert.) Using the words *we* and *us* rather than *I* and *me* enhances group spirit and unites the class in working toward common goals: "Can *we* identify the reasons for . . . ?" rather than "Can anyone tell *me* the reasons for . . . ?"

4. *Appropriateness to age and ability of students.* Questions should push students to think and imagine, but they must be within their comprehension. Easier questions allow low-ability students to participate, and difficult questions can challenge high-achieving students. While it is important not to embarrass or frustrate students by asking them questions in class that they cannot handle, it is just as important not to track low-achieving students by asking them only the easy questions. (After a while the students will sense you are dividing the class into low and high achievers by the way you direct questions.) Slower students need more background information, more time to respond, and more convergent questions, but they should also be challenged and expected to stretch their thinking and imagination.

5. *Variety.* Depending on the objectives of the lesson and the age and ability of the students, questions should be mixed in terms of type (what, who, how, and why), difficulty, (low and high level), direction (convergent and divergent), and subjectivity (objective and valuing). The effective teacher utilizes several different kinds of questions and knows when and how to use which kind to achieve instructional objectives and increase student participation.[38]

Two researchers prescribe six steps in questioning: (1) Prepare questions in advance; (2) adapt questions to various student skill levels; (3) word questions so as to involve all students or as many as possible; (4) encourage students to take time to answer; (5) question students in a way that causes them (not

---

[38] Allan C. Ornstein, "Questioning: The Essence of Good Teaching: Part II," *National Association of Secondary School Principals*, February 1988, pp. 72–80.

the teacher) to answer; and (6) use questions to get feedback on students' learning and how they think.[39]

Still another point to consider is that most questioning sequences have two major purposes, instruction and diagnosis. **Instructional questioning** is generally convergent and tends to be used in new learning and practice situations. **Diagnostic questioning** is generally divergent and is designed to elicit information from students about their understanding of the topic. It usually results in a natural dialogue between teacher and students.[40] There are often right or preferred responses to instructional questions; diagnostic responses are not labeled as right or wrong, but are viewed as information for the teacher. Both types of questions can give the teacher information about students' knowledge and level of cognitive development, but diagnostic questions permit more exploration of students' thought processes.

Guidelines in Asking Questions

Good questioning is both a methodology and an art; there are certain rules to follow that have been found to apply in most cases, but good judgment is also needed. See Tips for Teachers 6.2 and 6.3 for some review of formulating questions and for some recommendations for procedures in asking questions.

In preparing and asking questions in class, a number of instructional strategies have been shown to be effective with a large number of different teachers and students. Most of these instructional strategies come from educational psychology and the teacher effectiveness movement, not from the curriculum, instruction, or teaching method schools, which one might think would contribute to this field of knowledge.[41]

Wait-Time   The interval between asking a question and the student response is referred to as **wait-time.** One study by Mary Rowe indicated that the average amount of time teachers wait is 1 second. Increasing the wait-time to 3 to 4 seconds has several beneficial effects on student responses: (1) length of response increases, (2) unsolicited but appropriate responses increase, (3) failure to respond decreases, (4) confidence (as reflected in an affirmative, rather than

---

[39]Dorothy McCullough and Edye Findley, "How to Ask Effective Questions," *Arithmetic Teacher*, March 1983, pp. 8–9.

[40]Donald M. Fairbairn, "The Art of Questioning Your Students," *Clearing House*, September 1987, pp. 19–22.

[41]Allan C. Ornstein and Francis P. Hunkins, *Curriculum: Foundations, Principles, and Issues* (Englewood Cliffs, N.J.: Prentice-Hall, 1988). Also see Francis P. Hunkins, *Effective Questions, Effective Thinking* (Needham, Mass.: Gordon, 1989).

Tips for Teachers 6.2

Don'ts in Asking Questions

Good questioning techniques have to be developed slowly and over the years. They must become second nature, a habit. Just as you can form good or bad habits in driving a car or swinging a golf club, you can develop good and bad habits in questioning. Try to eliminate the *don'ts* in asking questions before they become ingrained as habits and to practice the *do's*. Below is a list of things a teacher should *not* do.

1. *Ask yes or no questions or questions that allow a 50–50 chance of getting the right answer.* Example: "Did Orwell write *Animal Farm?*" "Who won the Civil War?" These kinds of questions encourage guessing, impulsive thinking, and right-answer orientation, not conceptual thinking or problem solving. If the teacher accidentally asks this kind of question, he or she should follow up immediately with a why or how question.

2. *Ask indefinite or vague questions.* Example: "What are the important cities of the United States?" "How would you describe the sentence?" Such questions are confusing and often must be repeated or refined. Questions should be clearly worded and coincide with the intent of the teacher.

3. *Ask guessing questions.* Guessing questions can also be "yes" or "no" questions, indefinite or vague questions. Ask students to explain ideas and show relationships, rather than searching for detailed or trivial information.

4. *Ask double or multiple questions.* Example: "What is the chemical formula for salt?" "What is its chemical weight?" Before students can respond to the first question, the second is asked. As a result, they don't know which question the teacher wants them to answer and they respond to the question they feel more knowledgeable about.

5. *Ask suggestive or leading questions.* Example: "Why was Andrew Jackson a great president?" The question really calls for an opinion, but a position or judgment is already stated.

6. *Ask fill-in questions.* Example: "The New Frontier occurred during whose presidency?" The question is embedded in the statement rather than being clearly expressed. "Which president implemented the New Frontier?" is a better wording of the question.

7. *Ask overload questions.* Example: "In connection with pollution factors and the sun's rays, what conclusions can we make about the future water level?" "How did Manifest Destiny lead to im-

continued

perialism and colonialism, while enhancing the industrialization of the country?" These questions are indefinite, multiple, and wordy. Trim excess verbiage, use simple rather than overly formal or obscure vocabulary, and ask clear, simple questions to avoid concealing the meaning of your question and confusing the student.

8. *Ask tugging questions.* Example: "What else? Who else?" These tug at the student and do not really encourage thought.

9. *Cross-examination questions.* You may be able to assist a student by asking a series of questions to draw out information. However, this should be distinguished from asking many or rapid questions of the same student. Also, the rest of the class tends to be neglected.

10. *Call the name of a student before asking a question.* As soon as students know that someone else is responsible for the answer, their attention lessens. First ask a question, pause to allow comprehension, and then call on someone to answer it.

11. *Answer a question asked by a student if students should know the answer.* Turn the question back to the class and ask "Who can answer that question?"

12. *Repeat questions or repeat answers given by students.* Reiteration fosters poor work habits and inattentiveness. A good practice is to say "Who can repeat that question or that answer?"

13. *Exploit bright students or volunteers.* The rest of the class becomes inattentive and loses contact with discussion.

14. *Allow choral responses or handwaving.* Both are conducive to undesirable behavior.

15. *Allow improper speech or incomplete answers to go unnoticed.* Youngsters are quick to cultivate wrong habits. Supply the correction without stopping the recitation.

Source: Adapted from Allan C. Ornstein, "Questioning: The Essence of Good Teaching: Part II," *National Association of Secondary School Principals,* February 1988, p. 77.

a questioning, tone of voice) increases, (5) speculative responses increase, (6) student-to-student responses increase, (7) evidence-inference statements increase, (8) student questions increase, and (9) responses from students rated by teachers as relatively slow increase.[42]

No negative side effects of increasing wait-time have been observed, and

---

[42]Mary B. Rowe, "Wait-Time and Reward as Instructional Variables," *Journal of Research in Science Teaching,* February 1974, pp. 81–97. Also see David C. Berliner, "Laboratory Settings and the Study of Teacher Education," *Journal of Teacher Education,* November–December 1985, pp. 2–9.

Tips for Teachers 6.3

Do's in Asking Questions

Now that you know what not to do, here is a list of things to do in questioning. Practice them so they become second nature in your instructional process.

1. *Ask questions that are stimulating* and not merely memory testing or dull. A good teacher arouses students and makes them reflect with thought-provoking questions. Questions that ask for information recall will not sustain the attention of a class and that's when discipline and management problems begin.

2. *Ask questions that are commensurate with students' abilities.* Questions that are dramatically below or above the abilities of students will bore or confuse them. Target questions, even on difficult subjects, within the ability level of the majority of the class.

3. *Ask questions that are relevant to students.* Questions that draw on their life experiences will be relevant.

4. *Ask questions that are sequential.* Questions and answers should be used as stepping stones to the next question. This contributes to continuous learning.

5. *Vary the length and difficulty of questions.* Questions should be diversified so that both high- and low-achieving students will be motivated to participate. Observe individual differences and phrase questions so that all students take part in the discussion.

6. *Ask questions that are clear and simple.* Questions should be easily understood and trimmed of excess verbiage.

7. *Encourage students to ask questions of each other and to make comments.* This results in students' becoming active learners and cooperating on a cognitive and social level, which are essential for reflective thinking and social development. Good questions stimulate further questions, even questions by students. The idea is to encourage student comments and interaction among themselves, and to refer student questions and comments to other students to promote discussion, even when they are directed at the teacher.

8. *Allow sufficient time for deliberation.* Pausing for a few seconds until several hands go up gives everyone, particularly the slow learners, a chance to consider the question. As a result, everyone profits from the discussion, and learning takes place for all.

9. *Follow up incorrect answers.* Take advantage of wrong or marginal answers. Probe the student's mind. Encourage the student to think

continued

about the question. Perhaps the student's thinking is partially correct, even novel.

10. *Follow up correct answers.* Use a correct answer as a lead to another question. A correct answer sometimes needs elaboration or can be used to stimulate student discussion.

11. *Call on nonvolunteers and volunteers.* Some students are shy and need coaxing from the teacher. Other students tend to daydream and need assistance from the teacher to keep attentive. Distribute questions among the entire class so that everyone can participate.

12. *Call on disruptive students.* This stops troublesome students without having to interrupt the lesson.

13. *Prepare five or six pivotal questions.* Such questions test students' understanding of the lesson as well as give the lesson unity and coherence.

14. *Write the objective and summary of the lesson as a question, preferably as a problem.* Questions encourage the class to think. The students are made to consider the new work by presenting it as a question or problem.

15. *Change your position and move around the room* Teacher energy and vitality induce class activity, rapport, and socialization. They also foster an active audience and prevent daydreaming and disciplinary problems.

Source: Adapted from Allan C. Ornstein, "Questioning: The Essence of Good Teaching: Part II," *National Association of Secondary School Principals*, February 1988, p.78.

the positive effects are numerous. Yet, many teachers do not employ this instructional strategy. Other data suggest that asking one to four questions per minute is reasonable and that beginning teachers ask too many questions, averaging only 1½ seconds wait-time.[43] Also, although all students need time to process information, low-achieving students need more time, and the data indicate that teachers tend to wait less for an answer from the students they perceive as slow.[44]

Directing   As mentioned earlier, the recommended strategy in directing questions to students is to ask the question and then call a student's name, because

---

[43] Paulette P. Harris and Kevin J. Swick, "Improving Teacher Communications: Focus on Clarity and Questioning Skills," *Clearing House*, September 1985, pp. 13–15.

[44] Rowe, "Wait-Time and Reward as Instructional Variables"; J. Nathan Swift and C. Thomas Gooding, "Interaction of Wait-Time Feedback and Questioning in Middle School Science Teaching," *Journal of Research in Science Teaching*, August 1983, pp. 721–730; and Good and Brophy, *Looking in Classrooms.*

more students will think about the question. Research on classroom management also confirms that it is better to be unpredictable in calling on students to answer questions than to follow a predictable order.[45] On the other hand, a predictable order seems to be more effective when calling on students to read in the lower grades.[46] The reason is perhaps that predictability reduces anxiety, which is important for young children who are reading in front of the class.

The research also indicates that calling on nonvolunteers can be effective as long as students who are called on can answer the question most of the time. It is a good idea to call on nonvolunteers when it is believed that students can respond correctly, but it is not wise to embarrass them with their inability to answer the questions.[47] This is probably true at all grade levels and subjects. It is acceptable, however, to call on nonvolunteers with the understanding that they may not be able to answer the question correctly, in order to curtail disruptive or inattentive behavior—then to link their inability to answer to their behavior.

Although the research indicates that teachers should call on nonvolunteers no more than 15 percent of the time,[48] practice indicates this figure may be too low. By emphasizing volunteers, there is a tendency to call on high-achieving students more often than low-achieving students. Calling on more nonvolunteers increases the likelihood that low-achieving students will be included in the discussion. It is generally a good idea to call on low achievers who usually do not volunteer, and they should periodically be called on as nonvolunteers as long as they are likely to be able to answer the question correctly.

Redirecting and Probing   If a student response to a question is incorrect or inadequate, an effective strategy for the teacher is not to provide the answer, but to redirect the question to another student or to probe for a better answer from the same student. Redirecting the question is better for high-achieving students, but probing is better for low-achieving students. High-achieving stu-

[45] Jere E. Brophy, "Classroom Organization and Management," *Elementary School Journal*, March 1983, pp. 265–286; Carolyn M. Evertson et al., "Effective Classroom Management: An Exploration of Models," Final Report for the National Institute of Education, Washington, D.C., 1985; and Jacob Kounin, *Discipline and Group Management in Classrooms* (New York: Holt, Rinehart and Winston, 1970).

[46] Linda M. Anderson, Carolyn M. Evertson, and Jere E. Brophy, "An Experimental Study of Effective Teaching in First Grade Reading Groups," *Elementary School Journal*, March 1979, pp. 193–223; Anderson, Evertson, and Brophy, "Principles of Small Group Instruction in Elementary Reading," paper prepared for the Institute for Research on Teaching, Michigan State University, 1982.

[47] Thomas L. Good and Jere E. Brophy, "Changing Teacher and Student Behavior: An Empirical Investigation," *Journal of Educational Psychology*, June 1974, pp. 390–405; Mary Rohrkemper and Lyn Corno, "Success and Failure in Classroom Tasks: Adaptive Learning and Classroom Teaching," *Elementary School Journal*, January 1988, pp. 297–312.

[48] Alexis L. Mitman and Andrea Lash, "Students' Perceptions of the Academic Learning and Classroom Behavior," *Elementary School Journal*, September 1988, pp. 55–68; Jones and Friedman, "Active Instruction for Students at Risk."

dents seem to be able to cope better with minor academic failure in front of their peers and thus are better able to accept redirection. Teacher persistence in seeking improved responses from low-achieving or at-risk students is also related to positive teacher expectations, which is important in trying to reach and teach such students.

In **probing** the teacher stays with the same student, asking for clarification, rephrasing the question or asking related questions, and restating the student's ideas.[49] It is important not to overdo it, lest the probing becomes cross-examination. On the other hand, if the teacher feels that the student was not paying attention, it is best not to probe and give the student a second chance; unwittingly, the teacher would be condoning the student's lack of attention. During the probing process the teacher may ask a series of easier questions that lead toward the answer to the original question. If the student answers correctly (either initially or in response to a rephrased question), the teacher may want to follow with a related question to pursue the implications of the answer and to ensure student understanding.

Probing is acceptable for all students. With high-achieving students it tends to foster high-level responses and discussion. With low-achieving students it tends to reduce the frequency of "no responses" or "incorrect responses." In both cases probing is positively correlated with increased student achievement.[50]

Commenting and Praising   While research on the use of praise is mixed, it is generally agreed that honest praise increases achievement and motivation. Positive reactions can simply mean a smile, nod of approval, or brief comment ("Good," "Correct," "That's true") indicating approval or acceptance. Phoney praise or too much praise can have detrimental effects. See Table 6.6.

Most teachers do not use sufficient or genuine praise, however, while questioning or with other methods of instruction. A summary of 10 studies, for example, shows that teachers on the average use it no more than 6 percent of the total time in regular classrooms.[51] In another study it was observed that praise of good answers to questions or good work in general was used less than

[49] Jere E. Brophy and Carolyn M. Evertson, *Learning from Teaching: A Developmental Perspective* (Boston: Allyn & Bacon, 1976); N. L. Gage, *The Scientific Basis of the Art of Teaching* (New York: Teachers College Press, Columbia University, 1978); and Sherri Gibson and Myron H. Dembo, "Teacher Efficacy: A Construct Validation," *Journal of Educational Psychology*, August 1984, pp. 569–582.

[50] Anderson, Evertson, and Brophy, "An Experimental Study of Effective Teaching"; Jere E. Brophy and Carolyn M. Evertson, "Process-Product Correlations in the Texas Teacher Effectiveness Study," Final Report for the Research and Development Center for Teacher Education, University of Texas, 1974; and Robert S. Soar, "An Interactive Approach to Classroom Learning," report published for the School of Education, Temple University, 1965.

[51] Dunkin and Biddle, *The Study of Teaching*.

Table 6.6   GUIDELINES FOR GIVING PRAISE

Effective praise	Ineffective praise
1. Is delivered contingently	1. Is delivered randomly or unsystematically
2. Specifies the particulars of the accomplishment	2. Is restricted to global positive reactions
3. Shows spontaneity, variety, and other signs of credibility; suggests attention to the students' accomplishment	3. Shows a bland uniformity that suggests a conditioned response made with minimal attention
4. Rewards attainment of specified performance criteria (which can include effort criteria, however)	4. Rewards mere participation, without consideration of performance processes or outcomes
5. Provides information to students about their competence and the value of their accomplishments	5. Provides no information at all or gives students no information about their status
6. Orients students toward better appreciation of their own task-related behavior and thinking about problem solving	6. Orients students toward comparing themselves with others and thinking about competing
7. Uses own prior accomplishments as the context for describing present accomplishments	7. Uses the accomplishments of peers as the context for describing students' present accomplishments
8. Is given in recognition of noteworthy effort or success at difficult tasks (for *this* student)	8. Is given without regard to the effort expended or the meaning of the accomplishment
9. Attributes success to effort and ability, implying that similar successes can be expected in the future	9. Attributes success to ability alone or to external factors such as luck or task difficulty
10. Fosters endogenous attributions (students believe that they expend effort on the task because they enjoy the task and/or want to develop task-relevant skills)	10. Fosters exogenous attributions—students believe that they expend effort on the task for external reasons like pleasing the teacher or winning a competition or reward
11. Focuses students' attention on their own task-relevant behavior	11. Focuses students' attention on the teacher as an external authority figure who is manipulating them
12. Fosters appreciation of and desirable attributions about task-relevant behavior after the process is completed	12. Intrudes into the ongoing process, distracting attention from task-relevant behavior

Source: Jere E. Brophy, "Teacher Praise: A Functional Analysis," *Review of Educational Research*, Spring 1981, p. 26.

five times per hour at the elementary school level and considerably less at the secondary school level.[52]

The research is also mixed about negative comments. While the research

---

[52]Jere E. Brophy, "Teacher Praise: A Functional Analysis," *Review of Educational Research*, Spring 1981, pp. 5–32; Brophy, "On Praising Effectively," *Elementary School Journal*, May 1981, pp. 269–280.

suggests that teachers use criticism and disapproval sparingly, even less than praise, criticism can have a detrimental effect on student achievement. Similarly, if used by a teacher in response to a student question or comment, it can curtail students' asking questions or responding to the teacher's questions.[53] While low achievers receive more criticism than high achievers, it is possible that low achievement causes teachers to use more criticism. While boys receive more criticism from teachers than girls, we also know that boys achieve less than girls in the elementary school grades.[54] In other words, a correlation exists between criticism and achievement, but the cause and effect is unclear.

Finally, comments can be categorized as negative but be used in a supporting way or be followed by positive suggestions or peer group recognition, as illustrated by the underlined statements. (1) "You don't understand. *Let's see who can help you*"; (2) "Your response is wrong. *Try it again, you can answer it*"; (3) "That's not really right. *But it was a difficult question. Let's see how we can improve the answer*"; (4) "Johnny, please be quiet. *You are spoiling it for the entire class. Besides, you know better.*" The criticism, moreover, is justified when the answer is wrong or the behavior is interfering with the rules or procedures of the classroom. The point is that it is not only what you say that counts, but how you say it, why you say it, and how you follow up.

LECTURES AND EXPLANATIONS

Lectures are divided into three types for our discussion.

1. *Formal lectures* last for most of or the entire class session; student questions and comments are discouraged. Formal lectures should be used only at the advanced high school and college levels, where students are mature enough to sit for long periods of time and take notes on their own.
2. *Informal lectures* last about 5 to 10 minutes; student responses and questions are permitted but not encouraged.
3. *Brief lectures* last no more than 5 minutes; student responses are encouraged.

Formal and informal lectures generally require extensive preparation; brief lectures involve less preplanning, perhaps only a one- or two-sentence reminder in the lesson plan.

Explanations take only a few moments of teacher talk and are focused on

---

[53] J. T. Dillon, "A Norm Against Student Questioning," *Clearing House*, November 1981, pp. 136–139.

[54] Dunkin and Biddle, *The Study of Teaching*; Thomas L. Good, Bruce J. Biddle, and Jere E. Brophy, *Teachers Make a Difference* (New York: Holt, Rinehart and Winston, 1975).

a specific problem, task, or activity. Explanations are spontaneous, not pre-planned or outlined in advance.

Discussions can be an outgrowth of lectures or explanations. They are oral exchanges between the teacher and students or among the students. Discussions permit students to respond to teacher statements, to ask questions, and to clarify ideas. The more involved students are in discussion, the more effective the exchange of ideas is likely to be, since students' thoughts tend to wander as teacher talk increases. Younger and low-achieving students become inattentive more readily than older and high-achieving students. The implication is clear: Teachers should make an effort to maintain student attention by limiting lecture and explanation times and increasing discussion time.

Problems of Lecturing and Explaining

During lectures and explanations delivered by a teacher, there is little give and take between the teacher and students and among students. Lecturing is often described as "unnecessary," "dull," and a "waste of time." One observer has pointed out that it increases student passivity and reduces the student's role to note taking instead of luring students into more active learning.[55] Another critic has noted that if a student misses a point or is lost, he or she cannot interrupt for a personal explanation or stop and review as with a book, computer program, or tape.[56]

For levels below senior high school (grades 10–12) these criticisms are valid for formal lectures, especially when teachers do not allow for student response and when the lectures are not adequately prepared and are repetitive or digressive. According to many researchers, attention span is correlated with age and ability, and with young and low-achieving students attention span is limited.[57] For such students it is essential that teacher talk in any form (especially lecturing and explaining) be limited to a few minutes' duration at any one time and be intermixed with other instructional activities (audio, visual, and physical). There should be more concrete activities than verbal and abstract presentations.

Benefits of Lecturing and Explaining

Based on a review of several studies of the lecture method, Gage and Berliner feel that it is appropriate when (1) the basic purpose is to disseminate infor-

---

[55] John McLeish, *The Lecture Method* (Cambridge, England: Cambridge Institute of Education, 1968).

[56] William J. Seiler et al., *Communication in Business and Professional Organizations* (Reading, Mass.: Addison-Wesley, 1982).

[57] Robert F. Biehler and Lynne M. Hudson, *Developmental Psychology*, 4th ed. (Boston: Houghton Mifflin, 1990); Robert E. Slavin, *Educational Psychology: Theory and Practice*, 2nd ed. (Englewood Cliffs, N.J.: Prentice-Hall, 1988).

Teach Them to Write

The most important lessons presented by a teacher are those embodied in his being. I try to convey to students my knowledge and my ignorance, my passion for the subject, the ways in which I approach problems, how I launch, carry out (and sometimes abandon) projects, how I think and write. I then try to work with the students on these same issues, helping them to think about their own areas of knowledge and ignorance, projects of meaning to them, their own working styles, and their own short- and long-term aspirations.

Because I am particularly interested in writing, I work intensively with students on their papers. In a typical course, a student will communicate with me several times about his paper: at the time of inception, when it is in outline form, when it is in first draft, and when it is in final draft form. The student must submit each "installment" on time and I provide rapid feedback. This entails lots of work for both of us but I think the process works reasonably well. My procedure is based on an empirical observation that has been much supported: One rarely learns from a single experience (i.e., writing a single draft and getting a single grade) but one can learn much from accumulated efforts over time.

Howard Gardner
Professor of Education
Harvard University

---

mation, (2) the information is not available elsewhere, (3) the information needs to be presented in a particular way or adapted to a particular group, (4) interest in a subject needs to be aroused, (5) the information needs to be remembered for a short time, and (6) the purpose is to introduce or explain other learning tasks. They further state that the lecture method is inappropriate when (1) objectives other than acquisition of information are sought, (2) long-term learning is desired, (3) the information is complex, abstract, or detailed, (4) learner participation is important for achieving the objectives, (5) higher cognitive learning, such as analysis and synthesis, is sought, and (6) students are below average in ability.[58]

There are administrative and practical reasons for using informal and brief lectures, as well as explanations. These methods are well suited to large groups,

---

[58]N. L. Gage and David C. Berliner, *Educational Psychology*, 4th ed. (Boston: Houghton Mifflin, 1988).

and few materials and equipment are needed, giving the methods the additional benefit of being economical. The methods are flexible and can be used in regular classrooms, small groups, and large settings. Teachers who travel or change classrooms need only to carry with them their lesson plans or notes. Although good lectures need considerable preparation, their delivery does not require elaborate advance planning to have materials ordered or equipment scheduled and moved about. The fact that teachers are not dependent on others to carry out the lecture, explanation (or discussion) makes it easy and comfortable for them.

Procedures for Presenting Lectures and Explanations

When preparing and presenting informal or brief lectures and providing explanations, you might consider the following steps and suggestions.

1. *Establishing rapport with students.* At the beginning of a talk you should take measures to establish rapport with students. (Periodically telling a story or joke helps maintain their interest in the subject and rapport with you.) Always keep in mind the need to maintain the interest of students and the fact that students will react to you first on a personal basis, then on a cognitive basis.

2. *Preparing lectures and explanations.* The major concepts or ideas should be outlined in advance. Corresponding activities and materials might be indicated—say, in the lesson plan—to introduce at a certain point. Except for short passages or quotations to make a point, you should not read from notes. You must know the material well enough to speak clearly and with animation and to speak extemporaneously as you sense the need of the moment and the interests of the students.

3. *Length of lectures and explanations.* Although there are exceptions, the less you talk and the more your students talk, the more effective you are as a teacher. The greatest danger is that by talking too much you will create a passive audience and lose their interest. Brief lectures and explanations of 3 to 5 minutes at most are suitable for elementary school students. Short, informal lectures or explanations of 5 to 10 minutes are acceptable at the middle grade and junior high school levels. High school students can tolerate up to 10 to 15 minutes of interesting teacher talk. Always try to limit your lecturing and explaining and use questions, discussions, various student activities, and media as supplementary tools of instruction.

4. *Motivating students to pay attention.* Relevant lectures motivate students. To achieve relevance, you should consider the students' age, ability, educational experiences, environment, interests, needs, perceived goals, and career aspirations. You can make the lesson more understandable and interesting by combining other methods, materials, and media with your talk. When

students perceive the relevance of, understand, and are interested in the topic, they become *success-oriented* and acquire *intrinsic motivation*—that is, they pursue "the goal of achievement for the sake of achievement."[59]

5. *Structure and sequence.* A disorganized talk confuses and bores its audience. Present major concepts and difficult ideas in a linear and logical fashion, with examples and questions to test students' understanding. Facts and concepts should be developed systematically and sequentially from statement to statement. The overall topic should be related to the topic of the previous lesson. Sentence structure and vocabulary must be appropriate for the students' level of development. Although this sounds obvious, many beginning teachers speak over the vocabulary level and content level of their students.

Criteria of a structured lecture, according to one researcher, are (1) *continuity*, a sequenced arrangement of ideas expressed in intelligible and grammatically correct sentences, (2) *simplicity*, the absence of complex sentences and the use of language within the students' vocabulary range, and (3) *explicitness*, the identification and explanation of major concepts and relationships.[60]

Explanatory talk that is considered effective tends to correspond with what we often mean by *coaching*. The explanations can be *physical* through demonstrations; *visual* through pictures or models; or *verbal* through oral discussion or tapes. It is this kind of teacher talk by elementary teachers of low-achieving students that was found to be effective. The more effective teachers engaged in highly structured explanations and were: (1) more responsiveness to student questions, (2) more adequate for presenting content, (3) more complete in providing specific information, and (4) better in giving students feedback to help them learn.[61]

6. *Providing appropriate organizers.* Teachers can provide for students what David Ausubel terms "advanced organizers." They can provide means for the students to organize the ideas to be presented by telling them in advance what the lecture or explanation will focus on and how it will be structured. Gage and Berliner use the terms *hooks* and *anchors* to mean major topics or concepts around which teachers structure information.[62] Another technique is to outline the major topics or parts of the lesson, either orally or in writing (on the chalkboard), as they unfold (not in advance) during the discussion. This is especially helpful when students are listening to the teacher and must select, process, and assimilate information with which they are working.

7. *Avoiding vagueness.* Lectures and explanations that are free of vague language are easier to follow and to understand. Researchers have labeled nine

---

[59] Robert M. W. Travers, *Essentials of Learning*, 5th ed. (New York: Macmillan, 1982), p. 436.

[60] Elizabeth Perrott, *Effective Teaching: A Practical Guide to Improving Your Teaching* (New York: Longman, 1982).

[61] Gerald G. Duffy, "Conceptualizing Instructional Explanation," *Teaching and Teacher Education*, 2, 1986, pp. 197–214.

[62] David P. Ausubel, "In Defense of Advanced Organizers: A Reply to the Critics," *Review of Educational Research*, Spring 1978, pp. 251–259; Gage and Berliner, *Educational Psychology*.

kinds of vague terms: (1) *ambiguous designation*—"somewhere, somehow," (2) *approximation*—"about, almost, nearly, sort of," (3) *bluffing*—"anyway, as you know, so forth, to make a long story short," (4) *error admission*—"I'm not sure, I guess, perhaps," (5) *indeterminate amount*—"a couple, few, some, many," (6) *negated intensifiers*—"not many, not very much," (7) *multiplicity* —"aspects, kind of, type," (8) *possibility*—"chances are, perhaps, it seems, could be," and (9) *probability*—"frequently, generally, usually, often."[63]

Smith and Land point out that vague terms include what they call *mazes*—false starts, incomplete words and sentences, redundant words, and tangled words. The mazes are italicized in the following paragraph.

> This mathematics lesson *will enab* ... will get you to understand *number, uh,* number patterns. Before we get to the *main idea of the,* main idea of the lesson, you need to review *four conc* ... four prerequisite concepts. The first *idea, I mean, uh,* concept you need to review is positive integers. A positive *number* ... *uh* integer is any whole *integer, uh,* number greater than zero.[64]

Another factor that leads to vagueness is discontinuous and irrelevant content. The content may be important at another time, but when introduced at an inappropriate time, it becomes distracting from the main ideas. In a clear lecture, the sequence of the flow of ideas from sentence to sentence is clear, and the language is free of ill-defined and redundant words.

8. *Combining instructional materials.* The use of audiovisual aids and special materials and activities can liven a talk and reinforce its content. Varied stimuli are important for all learners, but younger students especially benefit from less verbalization and more illustrations and activities.

9. *Summarizing Content.* The classroom discussion should always end with a **final summary** or conclusion, what some educators call *postorganizers.*[65] The lesson may also have **internal summaries,** what some educators call *medial summaries* or *chunking strategies.*[66] Medial summaries, with accompanying summary activities and transitions, subdivide a lesson into clear parts. It is more important to incorporate medial summaries for low-achieving and young students than high-achieving or older students.

The best type of summary (medial or final) briefly reviews the presentation and gives students a chance to see whether they understand the material by

[63]Jack Hiller, Gerald A. Fischer, and Walter Kaess, "A Computer Investigation of Verbal Characteristics of Effective Classroom Lecturing," *American Educational Research Journal,* November 1969, pp. 661–675.

[64]Louis Smith and Michael L. Land, "Low Inference Verbal Behaviors Related to Teacher Clarity," *Journal of Classroom Interaction,* April 1981, p. 38.

[65]Robert B. Burns and Lorin W. Anderson, "The Activity Structure of Lesson Segments," *Curriculum Inquiry,* Spring 1987, pp. 31–53; Robert E. Mayer, "Elaboration Techniques that Increase the Meaningfulness of Technical Text," *Journal of Educational Psychology,* December 1980, pp. 770–784.

[66]Good and Brophy, *Educational Psychology: A Realistic Approach;* Ornstein, "Questioning: The Essence of Good Teaching."

asking them to explain ideas, provide examples, evaluate data, and do some exercises. It lets them know what they have learned and helps identify major ideas of the lesson.[67]

After the final summary, the teacher should explain related homework and prepare students for any problems they may encounter in it. Also, the teacher might establish a connection between the just completed lesson and the next lesson.

If time is running short, it is best for the teacher to stop at some logical point (not in the middle of a thought or while a student is speaking), leaving enough time to give a quick summary. Each lesson should be concluded by the teacher, not by the bell or by the students' closing their books or walking out. Don't try to keep talking at this point, and be sure you dismiss them to maintain good discipline.

10. *Style of presentation.* Appropriate gestures, movements, and voice quality can improve a talk and make it more interesting and understandable. Without being overly theatrical, it is effective to match nonverbal communication (facial expressions, body movements, eye contact) with the objectives of the talk. Similarly, teacher enthusiasm and expectations during the talk are likely to affect student attitudes and achievement. It should be clear from the presentation that the teacher finds the content interesting and expects students to learn. However, unusual gestures or speech inflections, extreme nervousness, inappropriate dress, and other idiosyncratic characteristics are things that students notice, remember, and are distracted by.

Thorough preparation is essential. Check your lesson to be sure that you have followed these guidelines: (1) State the objectives at the beginning, (2) define new terms and concepts, (3) use relevant examples, (4) explicitly relate new ideas to familiar ones, (5) use alternative explanations when necessary, (6) go more slowly through more difficult material, (7) provide occasional summaries and restatements of important ideas, (8) include questions to clarify information being presented, and (9) provide a final summary.[68] A teacher must study his or her own style, become aware of strengths and weaknesses in delivery, and try to eliminate or reduce the weaknesses. Someone who is uncomfortable in talking or standing in front of an audience is unable to communicate as effectively as someone who is relaxed. The less a teacher is able to overcome nervousness and distracting mannerisms, the more he or she should use methods other than lectures, involve the students in talking, and engage them in other instructional activities. The kind of image the teacher projects will influence the teaching-learning process.

---

[67] Mary Rohrkemper and Lyn Corno, "Success and Failure on Classroom Tasks: Adaptive Learning and Classroom Teaching," *Elementary School Journal,* January 1988, 397–312; Rosenshine, "Explicit Teaching and Teacher Training."

[68] Larry A. Braskamp, Dale C. Brandenburg, and John C. Ory, *Evaluating Teaching Effectiveness* (Berkeley, Calif: Sage, 1984).

PROBLEM SOLVING

A great deal of literature since the beginning of the twentieth century has focused on problem solving and related thinking skills. Educators and psychologists have identified various methods to teach students how to problem-solve since Charles Judd (at the University of Chicago) and Edward Thorndike (at Columbia University) showed that learning could be explained in terms of general principles of thinking and methods of attacking problems transferred to different situations.

John Dewey's process of **reflective thinking** was considered the classic model for problem solving from 1910 until the 1950s, when Piaget's work and other models employing various cognitive and information-processing strategies were introduced. Although Dewey's model is viewed as an oversimplification by cognition theorists, it is still considered practical, especially by science and math teachers. Since one of the chief functions of school, for Dewey, was to improve the reasoning process, he recommended adopting the problem-solving method for all subjects and grade levels. Reflective thinking involves five steps: (1) Become aware of difficulty, (2) identify the problem, (3) assemble and classify data and formulate hypotheses, (4) accept or reject tentative hypotheses, and (5) formulate and evaluate conclusions.[69]

Dewey's model is based on a mixture of theory and practice, and many problem-solving models today are also based on the same ingredients. For example, Bransford and Stein outline the IDEAL method for problem-solving: (1) *I*dentify the problem, (2) *D*efine it, (3) *E*xplore possible strategies, (4) *A*ct on the strategies, and (5) *L*ook at the effects of your efforts.[70]

A number of educators describe successful problem solving as relying on a **heuristic** approach, that is, engaging in exploratory processes that have value only in that they may lead to the solution of a problem. Physicians often diagnose problems in this manner, for example, doing tests to eliminate what is not the problem in order to narrow the possibilities down to a few probable diagnoses of what is the problem.[71] According to Newell and Simon's method for dealing with a problem, the person first constructs a representation of the problem, called the "problem space," and then works out a solution that involves a search through the problem space. The problem solver may break the problem into components, activate old information from memory, or seek new information. If an exploratory solution proves to be successful, the task ends.[72] If it fails, the person backtracks, sidetracks, or redefines the problem or method

---

[69] John Dewey, *How We Think* (Lexington, Mass.: Heath, 1910).

[70] John Bransford and Barry Stein, *The IDEAL Problem Solver* (San Francisco: Freeman, 1985).

[71] Good and Brophy, *Educational Psychology: A Realistic Approach*; Richard E. Mayer, *Thinking, Problem Solving, and Cognition* (San Francisco: Freeman, 1983).

[72] Allen Newell and Herbert Simon, *Human Problem Solving* (Englewood Cliffs, N.J.: Prentice-Hall, 1972).

Figure 6.3 Large amounts of experimental and discovery activities is correlated with student problem solving. (Photo © Paul Conklin/ Monkmeyer)

used to solve it. This type of problem solving is not linear; the problem solver may jump around, skip, or combine steps.

Richard Cyert also suggests a heuristic model. It includes 10 steps: (1) Keep the basic problem in mind without being distracted by details, (2) avoid early commitment to a particular hypothesis when several hypotheses are possible, (3) simplify the problem by using phrases, symbols, or formulas, (4) change an approach that is not working, (5) ask questions and attempt to answer them, (6) be willing to question assumptions, (7) work backwards if necessary to work out solutions, (8) keep in mind partial solutions that later may be combined, (9) use metaphors and analogies, and (10) talk about the problem.[73]

Successful and Unsuccessful Problem Solvers

An individual is confronted with a problem when he encounters a situation to which he must respond but does not know immediately what the response should be. Regardless of the method, the student needs relevant information to assess the situation and to arrive at a response, that is, to solve the problem. What strategies are used is related to the student's age and the specific problem. According to researchers, not all successful students will use the same strategy to solve the same problem, and often more than one strategy can be used.[74]

---

[73] Richard M. Cyert, "Problem-Solving and Education Policy," in D. Tuma and F. Reif, eds., *Problem Solving and Education: Issues in Teaching and Research* (Hillsdale, N.J.: Erlbaum, 1980), pp. 3–8.

[74] Michael Pressley, "The Relevance of the Good Strategy User Model to the Teaching of Mathematics," *Educational Psychologist*, Spring 1986, pp. 139–161; David N. Perkins and Gavriel Saloman, "Teaching for Transfer," *Educational Leadership*, September 1988, pp. 22–32.

Even with simple addition or subtraction, students use different strategies in solving problems and therefore have a different framework about the relative difficulty of the problems. For example, John has 6 marbles and Sally has 8. How many marbles do they have together? In a *join strategy*, elements are added (6 + 6 = 12, 2 more is 14). With a *separate strategy*, elements are removed (8 + 8 = 16, 2 less is 14). A *part-part-whole strategy* involves undertaking two, or more elements ("I tabulated both numbers by adding 1 and 6 and subtracting 1 from 8. That makes 7 + 7, which is 14.") All three students are using correct strategies.[75]

Although teachers often stress one specific strategy to solve specific problems, students often use a variety of strategies, especially with more complex problems. In fact as the problems become more abstract so do their strategies. The teacher who insists on one strategy and penalizes students who use another appropriate strategy is discouraging their problem-solving potential. Teachers need to become aware of how students process information and what strategies they use to solve problems, in order to teach problem solving according to the way *students* think. They can do this by asking them questions, listening to their responses, and inspecting their work.

Some basic problem-solving strategies do seem to emerge, however. In a classic study Benjamin Bloom pointed out several differences between successful and unsuccessful students engaged in problem-solving activities. Although the subjects were college age, the findings apply to students of various ages so long as they have reached the developmental stage (between age 11 and 15) of logical thinking or what Piaget called "formal mental operations."

1. *Comprehending the problem.* Successful problem solvers reacted to selected cues and immediately began to work out a solution. Unsuccessful students missed cues and often misinterpreted the problem.
2. *Employing previous knowledge.* The successful group utilized previous knowledge to solve the problem. The unsuccessful students possessed the accessory information, but did not utilize it. They often did not know where or how to start.
3. *Style of problem-solving behavior.* Successful students were more active and could verbalize what they were doing. They simplified the problem, whenever possible, or broke it down into parts, if they could not deal with the whole. The unsuccessful students rarely were able to clarify or state concisely what they were doing. They often did not attempt to analyze the various parts.
4. *Attitude toward problem solving.* The successful students had confidence and viewed the problem as a challenge. The unsuccessful students lacked confidence, became frustrated, and gave up.[76]

[75]Penelope L. Peterson, Elizabeth Fennema, and Thomas Carpenter, "Using Knowledge of How Students Think About Mathematics," *Educational Leadership*, December-January 1989, pp. 42–46.

[76]Benjamin S. Bloom and Lois J. Broder, "Problem-Solving Process of College Students," in *Supplementary Educational Monograph*, no. 73 (Chicago: University of Chicago Press, 1950).

Professional Viewpoint

Methods for Teaching

There is much rote learning in schools throughout the world. However, in a small number of countries—for example, Japan, South Korea, Israel, and Thailand—I find great emphasis on such higher mental processes as problem solving, application of principles, analytical skills, and creativity. These countries have very active central curriculum centers charged with responsibility constantly to improve textbooks and other learning materials, and to provide inservice training for teachers, especially as it relates to the curriculum and teaching methods.

In these countries, subjects are taught as methods of inquiry into the nature of science, mathematics, the arts, and the social studies. Subjects are taught as much for the ways of thinking they represent as for their traditional content. Much of this learning makes use of observations, reflections on observations, experimentation with phenomena, and the use of firsthand data and daily experiences, as well as primary printed sources.

In sharp contrast to these teaching methods, teachers in the United States use textbooks that rarely pose real problems. The textbooks I observe emphasize specific content to be remembered and give students little opportunity to discover underlying concepts and principles—and even less opportunity to attack real problems in their environments. I estimate that over 90 percent of the test questions that American students are expected to answer deal with little more than remembered information. Our instructional materials, classroom teaching methods, and testing methods rarely rise above *knowledge*.

Benjamin S. Bloom
Emeritus Professor
University of Chicago and
Northwestern University

There is a consensus today that metacognitive skills (or processes) are transferable competencies that play a significant role in problem solving and high-order thinking. Metacognitive skills represent knowledge of how to do something (usually involving a plan, set of steps, or procedures) as well as the ability to evaluate and modify performance. Based on a review of the research, some metacognitive skills that have been found to distinguish successful problem solvers and that can translate into instructal methods are:

1. *Comprehension monitoring.* Knowing when one understands or does not understand something; evaluating one's performance.
2. *Understanding decisions.* Understanding what one is doing and the reasons why.
3. *Planning.* Taking time to develop a strategy; considering options; proceeding without impulse.
4. *Estimating task difficulty.* Estimating difficulty and allocating sufficient time for difficult problems.
5. *Task presentation.* Staying with the task; being able to ignore internal and external distractions; maintaining direction in one's thinking.
6. *Coping strategies.* Staying calm; being able to cope when things are not going easily; not giving up or becoming anxious or frustrated.
7. *Internal cues.* Searching for context clues when confronted with difficult or novel problems.
8. *Retracking.* Looking up definitions, rereading previous information; knowing when to backtrack.
9. *Noting and correcting.* Using logical approaches; double-checking; recognizing inconsistencies, contradictions, or gaps in performance.
10. *Flexible approaches.* Willingness to use alternative approaches; knowing when to search for another strategy; trying random approaches that are sensible and plausible, when one's original approach has been unsuccessful.[77]

It should be noted that low-achieving and younger students have fewer metacognitive skills compared to high-achieving and older students.[78] The implication for teaching is that an increase in knowledge of subject matter does not necessarily produce changes in metacognitive skills. These skills in general reflect high-order thinking processes that cannot be learned or developed overnight or in one subject. Developmental age is crucial in limiting potential metacognitive skills among students. An 8-year-old student is capable of just so much and cannot be pushed beyond her cognitive stage. According to Piaget, not until age 11 is a child capable of employing many of these metacognitive skills (corresponding to formal mental operations), and not until

---

[77]Jere E. Brophy, "Research Linking Teacher Behavior to Student Achievement," *Educational Psychologist,* Summer 1988, pp. 235–286; David F. Lohman, "Predicting Mathemathanic Effects in the Teaching of High-Order Thinking Skills," *Educational Psychologist,* Summer 1986, pp. 191–208; and Richard K. Wagner and Robert J. Sternberg, "Alternative Conceptions of Intelligence and Their Implications for Education," *Review of Educational Research,* Summer 1984, pp. 179–224.

[78]Brophy, "Research Linking Teacher Behavior to Student Achievement"; Lyn Corno and Richard E. Snow, "Adapting Teaching to Individual Differences Among Learners," in Wittrock, ed., *Handbook of Research in Teaching,* pp. 605–629; and Lohman, "Predicting Mathemathanic Effects in the Teaching of High-Order Thinking Skills."

age 15 is the child capable of fully employing all metacognitive skills in an efficient manner.[79]

Guidelines for Teaching Problem Solving

While most teachers acknowledge that problem solving is important, many have not learned how to incorporate it into their lessons. Others view problem solving as interfering with or taking time away from curriculum coverage, since many skills and processes are required. More important, problem solving does not express itself in easily observed behaviors and outcomes that can be simply listed in lesson plans, taught to students, and evaluated. Some teachers do not see problem solving as part of their instructional function. Rather they see it as a chore, not as a commitment, and in competition with, not complimentary to, the teaching-learning process.

Good and Grouws have identified five problem-solving processes for mathematics, but they can be applied to the teaching-learning process in all subjects.

1. *Attending to prerequisites.* Solving new problems is based largely on understanding previously learned skills and concepts of the subject. The teacher should use the skills and concepts mastered by the students as a basis for solving problems.
2. *Attending to relationships.* Subjects comprise a large body of logical and closely related ideas; the teacher should emphasize meaning and interpretation of ideas.
3. *Attending to representation.* The more the student is able to represent a problem in context with concrete or real-world phenomena, the better able the student is to solve the problem.
4. *Generalizability of concepts.* Teachers need to explain the general applicability of the idea to students; skills and processes that apply to many settings should be practiced.
5. *Attending to language.* Teachers should use precise terminology of their subject, and students must learn basic terms and concepts of the subject.[80]

Matthew Lipman adds five other processes that cut across situational contexts and subject matter. Problem-solving teaching should take into account:

---

[79]Jean Piaget, *The Origins of Intelligence in Children* (New York: International Universities Press, 1952); Jean Piaget and Barbel Inhelder, *The Early Growth of Logic in the Child* (London: Routledge & Kegan Paul, 1964).

[80]Thomas L. Good and Douglas A. Grouws, ''Increasing Teachers' Understanding of Mathematical Ideas Through In Service Training,'' *Phi Delta Kappan,* June 1987, pp. 778–783.

1. *Exceptional or irregular circumstances.* Certain things may be permissible under certain conditions and not under others.
2. *Special limitations or constraints.* Almost all theories, principles, and concepts have certain limitations or contingencies under which they don't apply or are not valid.
3. *Overall configurations.* A concept or fact may be wrong or objectionable when taken out of context, but valid or proper in context.
4. *Atypical evidence.* Overgeneralizing from a small sample or one experiment is somewhat risky.
5. *Context-specific meanings.* There are terms and concepts for which there are no precise equivalents in other languages or subjects and whose meanings are therefore context-specific.[81]

In general, the improvement of students' thinking depends upon students' ability to identify good criteria for their opinions or solutions. The criteria should be based on one or more of the above processes, which can be taught. Students can also learn that for an opinion or solution to be good, it must be "relevant," "reliable," "coherent," and "consistent" with acceptable standards.[82] In this connection, the most characteristic feature of problem solving is that it discovers its own weakness and rectifies what is at fault in its procedures; thus, it is *self-correcting.* See Tips for Teachers 6.4.

THEORY INTO PRACTICE

Regardless of students' socioeconomic status, grade level, and subject, the four instructional methods—practice and drill, questioning, lecturing and explaining, and problem solving—characterize the teaching-learning process in classrooms. Adams and Biddle found that teacher talk—in the form of these instructional methods—characterizes most of instructional time in a sample of first-, sixth-, and eleventh-grade classrooms.[83] Elementary school teachers are more diverse in their instructional activities and encourage more student interaction and feedback, but even at this grade level teacher talk dominates the classroom activities. "In fact, it seems as if teachers and pupils have tacitly agreed that the teacher is the expert and that she ought to be doing the telling."[84]

Elementary teachers tend to rely on practice and drill more than other

---

[81] Matthew Lipman, "Critical Thinking—What Can It Be?," *Educational Leadership,* September 1988, pp. 38–43.

[82] Robert H. Ennis, "A Taxonomy of Critical Thinking Dispositions and Abilities," in J. B. Baron and R. J. Sternberg, eds., *Teaching Thinking Skills* (New York: Freeman, 1987), pp. 9–26; Lipman, "Critical Thinking—What Can It Be?"

[83] Raymond S. Adams and Bruce J. Biddle, *Realities of Teaching* (New York: Holt, Rinehart and Winston, 1970).

[84] Ibid., 45.

Tips for Teachers 6.4

Problem-Solving Strategies

Teachers need to provide students with good problem-solving strategies and practice in using such strategies. An extensive catalog of strategies is discussed below, all grounded in current research.

1. The problem-solving process in most cases is either *schema-driven*, with little search for solution procedures because appropriate procedures are activated by recognizing the particular problem type, or based on *search strategies*, in which the problem solver looks for or decides on a particular strategy before solution procedures are implemented.

2. Experts and subject specialists possess schemata relevant to problems in their area of expertise or subject. Consequently, they rarely engage in search strategies as novices or students often do.

3. In the absence of appropriate schemata, problem solvers proceed to a search strategy. Search strategies include, among others, means-ends analysis, analogies, matching, sequencing, and examining problems already worked out.

   a. *Means-ends* analysis is goal-based for a specific problem and requires that the problem solver eliminate differences between the current state and goal condition; this strategy usually leads to memory overload, and does not result in learning moves that can be used in different problems.

   b. *Analogies* are important for making the unfamiliar problem more familiar. Novice problem solvers are likely to engage in superficial analogies, as opposed to analogies based on solution procedures.

   c. *Matching* involves selecting a plan of action and carrying it out accordingly; the process of matching plans and actions continues until the problem is solved.

   d. *Sequencing* strategies (step by step) is an integral part of training and can be used for solving straightforward problems.

   e. *Examining problems* already worked out results in general strategies for a similar set of problems. It does not prepare the problem solver for an atypical problem or a new set of problems.

4. The use of different problem-solving strategies is influenced by the age and knowledge base of the problem solver and the problem itself.

continued

5. As students gain more knowledge in a subject area, they are better able to deal with problems without engaging in search strategies.

6. In analyzing a problem, students should be taught how to obtain a solution: Where to begin, how to move forward, how to backtrack, how to combine parts of problems, and how to know when they have a satisfactory answer or solution.

7. Knowledge of when, where, and how to apply certain specific strategies is also crucial. The problem solver learns that errors are often the result of applying the incorrect strategies to problems, rather than lack of ability or effort.

8. Although some problem strategies cut across several subjects, others are supported by a knowledge base. Without an adequate base in a given subject, it is nearly impossible to solve many complex problems.

9. An extensive knowledge base permits both skipping and intermixing of strategies to solve problems.

10. Perhaps the most fundamental problem-solving skill is monitoring progress—knowing when little is being achieved, when mistakes are being made, and when to modify strategies.

11. In working at solutions to problems, students should be taught by the teacher to compare, relate parts to the whole, decompose whole to parts, control variables, understand causal relationships, recognize inconsistencies in statements or findings, distinguish between bias and objective data, generalize from experience, generalize from findings, move from concrete to abstract, and then abstract to abstract. In all cases, there is need to stress objectivity of judgment and calm emotions in light of existing conditions.

12. Students should be taught to identify what they know and don't know, when new or extra information is needed, what new information will effect the unknown, and how to deal with incomplete information.

13. Students can learn to use specific strategies through consistent practice in a variety of settings so that eventually their strategies develop into broad schemata. Diverse opportunities to use strategies increase abstraction and strategy knowledge; abstraction of the above strategies broadens one's ability to cope with different problems.

14. Abstraction of strategies is less likely with low-achieving and younger students. More explicit teaching is necessary for these students.

15. Students need to learn that time and effort are important for problem solving. Time and effort should be matched with task situations; students should be cognizant of wasting time because of distractions or nonfocused behavior.

continued

Source: Adapted from Allan C. Ornstein, "Problem Solving: What Is It? How Can We Teach It?," *National Association of Secondary School Principals* (in print 1990). Note: For points 1–3, see Mary L. Glick, "Problem-Solving Strategies," *Educational Psychologist,* Winter/Spring 1986, pp. 99–120; Michael Pressley, "The Relevance of the Good Strategy User Model to the Teaching of Mathematics," *Educational Psychologist,* Winter/Spring 1986, pp. 139–161.

instructional methods and focus on four content areas: reading silently, reading aloud, completing worksheets, and writing assignments.[85] This is not to say they don't use other instructional methods, but problem-solving activities are used the least at all grade levels, and it is not until the third or fourth grade that such activities are introduced as part of the instructional process.[86]

At the high school level, informal and brief lectures, explanations, and questions dominate the teaching-learning process. In observing 525 high school classrooms, John Goodlad and his research team found that in a typical class the teacher lectured and explained to the whole class, asked questions, and watched students work. Generally the teacher initiated discussions and students listened and responded to the teacher's questions.[87] In another nationwide review of 5,000 high school teachers of mathematics, science, and social studies, nearly 80 percent of actual academic engaged time in each period was used for (1) explaining, lecturing, and discussing, (2) questioning, (3) working on assignments, and (4) taking tests.[88]

Teachers and students across grade levels spend about 80 to 90 percent of their classroom time on practice and drill, questioning, explaining, and problem solving. According to educators, the remaining time is spent on other instructional methods: role playing, small group discussions, scientific inquiry, independent learning, and class projects.[89]

---

[85] Jerome Freiberg and Hersholt C. Waxman, "Alternative Feedback Approaches for Improving Student Teachers' Classroom Instruction," *Journal of Teacher Education,* July–August 1988, pp. 8–14; Goodlad and Klein, *Behind the Classroom Door;* and Ronald W. Marx and John Walsh, "Learning from Academic Tasks," *Elementary School Journal,* January 1988, pp. 207–220.

[86] David C. Berliner, "Recognizing Instructional Variables," in D. E. Orlosky, ed., *Introduction to Education* (Columbus, Ohio: Merrill, 1980), pp. 198–225; Phyllis C. Blumenfeld and Judith L. Meece, "Task Factors, Teacher, Behavior, and Students' Involvement and Use of Learning Strategies During Science," *Elementary School Journal,* January 1988, pp. 235–250.

[87] Goodlad, *A Place Called School.*

[88] *Report of the 1977 National Survey of Science, Mathematics, and Social Studies Education* (Washington, D.C.: National Science Foundation, 1977).

[89] Walter Doyle, "Content Representation in Teachers' Definitions of Academic Work," *Journal of Curriculum Studies,* October 1986, pp. 365–379; Goodlad and Klein, *Behind the Classroom Door;* and Jack Martin, *Mastering Instruction* (Boston: Allyn and Bacon, 1983).

Some recommendations can be made for implementing the four instructional methods. Thirteen techniques are listed below to use in conjunction with practice and drill, questioning, lecturing and explaining, and problem solving:

1. Lessons are planned in advance by the teacher; student choices are limited within the boundaries established by the teacher.
2. Directions are clear, and students know what to expect and when to change activities. The pace of the lesson is brisk.
3. Materials and media are prepared in advance and incorporated without disturbing the momentum of the lesson.
4. The teacher is responsible for teaching the content of the lesson. The teacher explains, illustrates, and demonstrates what is to be learned.
5. The lesson proceeds in sequenced steps. Each academic task or skill builds on the preceding one. Students are helped to see relationships between previous and present learning.
6. In lecturing and explaining, the teacher matches style and content to students' abilities and interests, prepares and organizes content well, uses materials and media to clarify ideas, and asks questions to maintain student attention and to gauge student understanding and progress. Problem-solving activities are also introduced as part of lectures and explained, when possible.
7. In asking questions, the teacher makes sure that students have the opportunity to respond by using a variety of types of questions (low level and high level, convergent and divergent, valuing), allowing sufficient wait-time, calling on nonvolunteers as frequently as or more than volunteers, and calling on low achievers as frequently as or more than high achievers.
8. The teacher aims at a high success rate in student responses to questions. With low achievers, easier questions and factual questions may be emphasized to ensure high success rates and to build a knowledge base before proceeding to more difficult questions.
9. The teacher redirects incorrectly answered questions to other students or rephrases and probes for a better answer from the same student. Prompt comments and feedback are provided by the teacher, including moderate praise. Correct answers are noted. Students who respond with no answer or a wrong answer are encouraged to try again to improve.
10. The teacher uses practice and drill before and after new learning to ensure that students master required academic tasks. The drill may be incorporated into several parts of the lesson, including preliminary reviews and summaries.
11. Elementary school students and low-achieving students are provided with more practice and drill and less problem solving than older and high-achieving students. Practice exercises are checked and corrected promptly.

12. Problem-solving activities are introduced in detail and at a much slower pace than practice and drill.

13. Homework is given frequently and returned promptly with corrective feedback. By the third or fourth grade, problem solving is introduced into boardwork and homework activities and it increasingly replaces practice and drill in higher grades.

All these instructional techniques must be modified to suit the classroom situation—age and academic abilities of the students, subject matter, teacher style, and student learning style. To be sure, the methods discussed in this chapter have broad application for most teachers, students, and classrooms.

SUMMARY

1. Most instructional activities can be categorized as one of four instructional methods: practice and drill, questioning, lecturing and explaining, and problem solving.

2. The method of practice and drill has applications for seatwork activities, back-to-basics approaches, behaviorist learning, individualized instruction, and remedial instruction.

3. Questioning is perhaps the most important instructional method used today in whole-group instruction. Types of questions include low-level and high-level, convergent and divergent questions, and valuing.

4. Lecturing and explaining is the oldest instructional method. Different types of teacher talks (formal, informal, and brief lectures and explanations) can be effective with different students, but in general the length, complexity, and frequency of teacher talks should be reduced for younger and slower students.

5. Problem-solving models and strategies were discussed. There is real need to increase problem solving in our instructional approach; likewise, teachers need to teach their students how to problem solve.

QUESTIONS TO CONSIDER

1. Why is practice and drill used more often in elementary grades than secondary grades?

2. What is the difference between convergent and divergent questions? Why do most teachers rely on convergent questions?

3. Why is the wait-time important in questioning?

4. When should different types of lecturing and explaining be used?

5. What are the advantages and disadvantages of problem solving as an instructional method?

THINGS TO DO

1. List five recommendations for conducting practice and drill. Indicate any that you feel particularly comfortable or uncomfortable with as a teacher. Based on these preferences, what conclusions can you make about how you will use practice and drill?

2. Outline ten do's and don'ts in asking questions. Discuss each one with your classmates.

3. Teach a short lesson to your class by asking questions. Refer to Tips for Teachers 6.2 and 6.3 as guides to see how well you performed.

4. Develop a checklist for improving the lecture method. In doing so, review the procedures for preparing a lecture and recommendations for lecturing.

5. Identify five characteristics of successful problem solvers. What characteristics coincide with your own problem-solving strategies? How can these strategies be used to enhance your problem-solving instruction?

RECOMMENDED READINGS

Baron, Joan, and Robert J. Sternberg, eds. *Teaching Thinking Skills: Theory and Practice.* New York: Freeman, 1987. A discussion of strategies for critical thinking, problem solving, and strategic learning.

Dillon, J. T. *Questioning and Teaching.* New York: Teachers College Press, Columbia University, 1988. A concise guide to questioning, when and how to ask questions.

Gage, N. L., and David C. Berliner. *Educational Psychology*, 4th ed. Boston: Houghton Mifflin, 1988. Examination of the research pertaining to practice and drill, lecturing, and problem solving—among other subjects.

Good, Thomas L., and Jere E. Brophy. *Educational Psychology: A Realistic Approach*, 3rd ed. New York: Longman, 1986. Examination of the research pertaining to practice and drill, questioning, and problem solving.

Hunkins, Francis P. *Effective Questions, Effective Thinking.* Needham, Mass.: Gordon, 1989. A practical approach to the technique of questioning.

McLeish, John. *The Lecture Method.* Cambridge, England: Cambridge Institute of Education, 1968. Perhaps the most comprehensive text on how and when to lecture, including advantages and disadvantages of lecturing.

Raths, Louis E., Merril Harmin, and Sidney B. Simon. *Values and Teaching*, 2nd ed. Columbus, Ohio: Merrill, 1978. An important book on how to use valuing and strategies for lecturing and questioning, among other instructional approaches.

KEY TERMS

Law of exercise
Low-level questions
High-level questions
Convergent questions
Divergent questions
Valuing questions
Pivotal questions
Emerging questions
Instructional questions

Diagnostic questions
Wait-time
Probing
Lectures
Explanations
Final summaries
Internal summaries
Reflective thinking
Heuristic thinking

Chapter 7

Instructional Materials

FOCUSING QUESTIONS

1. How can instructional materials enhance learning?

2. What are the best methods for incorporating instructional materials into lessons?

3. How can the value and appropriateness of commercially produced or teacher-made instructional materials be estimated?

4. What are the characteristics of a good textbook?

5. How is the reading level of textbooks determined?

6. Why are workbooks often criticized? How can they be improved?

7. What problems might the teacher encounter in providing journals, magazines, or newspapers in the class?

8. What are the best methods for incorporating simulations and games into lessons?

*R*eal-life experiences provide the most direct type of learning, but they are difficult to supply in the traditional classroom. Most experiences in the classroom occur through verbal symbolism—written and spoken words. These classroom experiences may be easier for teachers to supply, but they may be more difficult for many students to understand. Verbal symbolism depends on the ability to conceptualize and think in the abstract, while the impact of firsthand experience is immediate and concrete. Various multisensory **instructional aids**—texts, pictures, games, simulations—can substitute for firsthand experiences and enhance understanding, so they are an integral part of the learning activity.

In this chapter we survey the use of instructional aids in general and then focus on written instructional materials—with emphasis on textbooks and workbooks. In the the next chapter we examine technological tools and media equipment.

PURPOSE OF INSTRUCTIONAL AIDS

Regardless of the type of instructional aid to be used, a teacher must consider it in light of the purpose of the learning activity. The instructional aid must be suited to that objective purpose—whether it be subject matter mastery, skills improvement, or valuing. Although materials and media can stimulate and maintain student interest, they are not meant merely to entertain the students; students need to understand this fact. Unless students are properly guided, they become distracted by the attention-getting aspects of the instructional aids and lose sight of their educational significance. For example, a teacher who frequently starts the lesson with a political cartoon, picture, or film strip may, after a while, be entertaining his students, and the students may look forward to these little aids as a way of delaying or avoiding discussion and critical thinking.

High-achieving students, especially those at the secondary level, are able to cope with large doses of **verbal symbolism**. It is with slow learners and younger students that the advantages of audiovisual and tactile experiences become apparent.[1] The more senses that are involved in the learning process, the easier it is for the student to learn. Differences in learning styles must also be taken into account. Some students can learn a body of information by simply reading an assignment or listening to the teacher; others need additional stimuli and experiences involving hearing, seeing, and manipulating the subject matter. The old saying "One picture in worth a thousand words" remains true

---

[1] Robert Calfee, "Computer Literacy and Book Literacy: Parallels and Contrasts," *Educational Researcher*, May 1985, pp. 8–13; Robert E. Slavin, "A Theory of School and Classroom Organization," *Educational Psychologist*, Spring 1987, pp. 89–108.

today, but now the one picture can be a photograph, film slide, motion picture, television program, or videotape.

Instructional aids can affect students in many ways, by:

1. *Motivating students.* For example, model cars, trucks, trains, boats, and airplanes can be used to introduce a unit on transportation.
2. *Contributing to understanding.* For example, graphs can be used to clarify fluctuations of the stock market.
3. *Providing varied learning experiences.* For example, a workbook or paperback novel can supplement the assigned textbook.
4. *Reinforcing learning.* For example, when students hear the music of a composer, they can better understand a discussion of his or her style.
5. *Allowing for different interests.* For example, various sections of a newspaper can be assigned, depending on the type of lesson or the learner.
6. *Encouraging participation.* For example, role playing increases individual involvement.
7. *Providing experiences that might not otherwise be had.* For example, simulations allow students to feel and sense experiences in the classroom.
8. *Changing attitudes and feelings.* For example, a photograph can be used to illustrate and increase the emotional impact of abstract concepts such as pollution, war, and poverty.[2]

The experienced teacher will be able to use a variety of materials in a multimedia approach in any subject to vary the learning experiences. All students have different interests and abilities that determine what they attend to and learn. But what they learn also depends on the ability of the teacher to capture their attention and spark their interest through the use of appropriate instructional materials and media.

The needs of each learning situation determine the materials and media the teacher use. These are some general considerations, however, that can help in estimating their value and appropriateness.

1. *Interest* is the extent to which the learner's curiosity is aroused and sustained by the use of instructional aids.
2. *Relevance* is the degree to which the experience provided by the aids is related to the learner's personal needs or goals.
3. *Expectancy* is the degree to which the learner expects to succeed at learning and sees success as being under his or her control when using the aids.

---

[2]Allan C. Ornstein, Harriet Talmage, and Anne W. Juhasz, *The Paraprofessional's Handbook* (Belmont, Calif.: Fearon, 1975).

4. *Satisfaction* is the level of outcome and the learner's satisfaction in performing the tasks.[3]

All of these factors influence students' subsequent performance with instructional aids.

Guidelines for Using Instructional Aids

Just what instructional aids a teacher uses depends on his or her knowledge and experience, the availability of the materials, the lesson assignment, the subject and the students. However, there are some basic guidelines for their use. These are summarized below. Instructional aids are made for situations in general; it is the teacher's job to tailor them to the needs of the students.

1. *Purpose.* Ask yourself what you are trying to accomplish and why this instructional aid is important.
2. *Define objectives.* Clearly defined objectives are essential for planning the lesson and selecting and using instructional aids.
3. *Flexibility.* The same instructional aid can satisfy many different purposes.
4. *Diversity.* Use a variety of materials, media, and resources to develop and maintain student interest.
5. *Development.* Instructional aids must be related to the age, maturity, ability, and interest of students.
6. *Content.* You must know the content of the instructional aids to determine how to use them and how to make the best use of them.
7. *Guide learners.* Focus students' attention on specific things to attend while viewing, listening, or reading the materials.
8. *Evaluate results.* Check students' reactions and consider your own reactions to the instructional aids.[4]

---

[3] Walter Dick and Robert A. Reiser, *Planning Effective Instruction* (Englewood Cliffs, N.J.: Prentice-Hall, 1989); Charles M. Reigeluth *Instructional-Design Theories and Models* (Hillsdale, N.J.: Erlbaum, 1983).

[4] George W. Maxim, *Social Studies and the Elementary School* (Columbus, Ohio: Merrill, (1983); Charles F. Schuller, "Using Instructional Resources and Technology," in D. E. Orlosky ed., *Introduction to Education* (Columbus, Ohio: Merrill, 1982), pp. 400–429.

SELECTING INSTRUCTIONAL MATERIALS

Selecting appropriate commercial materials, especially textbooks, is the responsibility of teachers and administrators, sometimes acting in small professional groups (at the district, school, department, or grade level), in professional-lay groups that include parents and community members, or as individuals. The professional-lay group, according to Elliot Eisner, is subject to controversy when lay members have particular views about what students should be exposed to or when they start objecting to what teachers are teaching.[5] Although committees make decisions about purchase or adaptation of materials on a schoolwide or districtwide basis, the teacher still needs to made professional judgments about the appropriateness and worth of the materials, since he or she is closest to the students and should know their needs, interests, and abilities.

The evaluator (committee or individual) should examine as many available materials as possible. The following general questions should be considered.

1. *Do the materials fit the objectives?* Materials should fit the objectives of the course as well as unit plan and lesson plan. Given the general nature of published materials, some may fit only partially; or it may not be possible to find materials to cover all the objectives. In such cases teachers need to create all or some of their own materials. On the other hand, there may be times when the teacher expands the objectives or activities to include an outstanding set of instructional materials.

2. *Are the materials well organized?* Good instructional materials will relate facts to a few basic ideas or concepts in a logical manner.

3. *Do the materials prepare the students for the presentation?* The materials should include instructional objectives or advance organizers.

4. *Are the materials well designed?* The materials should be attractive; the size should be appropriate for the intended use; print should be readable, with adequate margins, legible typeface, and comfortable type size.

5. *Have the materials been presented in a technically appropriate manner?* The material should not be "overpresented" with too much emphasis on design, elaborate presentation for its own sake, decorative but uninformative illustrations, unnecessary type elements. Nor should it be "underpresented" so that it lacks useful guides to its organization and content. Visual presentations, side notes in margins, appropriate headings, graphics, and color should be incorporated into the material.

6. *Do the materials provide sufficient repetition through examples, illustrations, questions, and summaries to enhance understanding of content?* Young students and low-achieving students need more rep-

[5]Elliot W. Eisner, "Why the Textbook Influences Curriculum," *Curriculum Review*, January/February 1987, pp. 11–13.

etition, overviews, and internal summaries, but for all students the material should be paced properly, and they should have sufficient time to digest and reflect on it.

7. *Is the material suitable to the reading level of the students?* Many teachers can make this type of judgment intuitively by reading through the material, and others can make the judgment after students experience the materials. The most reliable method for all teachers is to use a standard readability estimate.[6]

8. *Does the difficulty of the materials match the abilities of the students?* Research indicates that highly motivated students require a minimum success rate of 65 to 70 percent when working with reading materials (or on related tasks) to maintain motivation and interest. Materials for low-achieving students, especially seatwork and drill materials, require minimum success rates of 70 to 80 percent when the teacher is nearby to provide corrective feedback and 80 to 90 percent (depending on their confidence level) when students work independently.[7]

Some questions more specifically related to content than these general considerations are listed in Table 7.1. Committees and teachers should vary the questions they ask to suit their own goals. The teacher may want to observe students using the materials for several weeks and use their reactions to them in making final judgments. See Tips for Teachers 7.1 It is also worthwhile to consult with students about the worth of textbooks, since they are the ultimate consumers of these books. They represent a fresh and a different perspective. With the proper guidance from the teacher, in terms of questions and comments, they can provide valuable insight to what texts they prefer (and why) and which texts they understand and consider more interesting.

DUPLICATED MATERIALS

The types of educational materials used most by teachers are written texts (textbooks, workbooks, pamphlets, magazines, newspapers), pictures and models, and material used in association with games. They may be **printed materials,** that is, prepared and published commercially, or **duplicated materials,** that is, prepared by the teacher or school. Duplicated materials are used when teachers produce their own materials or when they wish to copy printed material not easily available for students. Instructional aids that involve special materials and equipment, such as films, slides, computers, and videotapes will be discussed in the next chapter.

---

[6]Allan C. Ornstein, "The Development and Evaluation of Curriculum Materials," *National Association of Secondary School Principals* (in print 1990).

[7]James H. Block, Helen E. Efthim, and Robert B. Burns, *Building Effective Mastery Learning in Schools* (New York: Longman, 1989); Thomas L. Good and Jere E. Brophy, *Looking in Classrooms,* 4th ed. (New York: Harper and Row, 1988).

Table 7.1 QUESTIONS TO CONSIDER IN SELECTING INSTRUCTIONAL MATERIALS

1. Is there a need for the material?
2. Does the material further the objectives of the lesson?
3. Does the material contribute meaningful content to the unit or lesson plan?
4. Does the material build on previous learning?
5. Does the material relate to present learning in other subjects?
6. Is the material current, accurate, and defensible?
7. Is the material appropriate for the age, maturity and experience of the students?
8. Is the material suitable to the reading level of the students?
9. Is the material free from bias, stereotyping, sexism?
10. Are the ideas, concepts, and points of views well expressed?
11. Is the physical presentation of the material acceptable? Are there appropriate margins, headings, summaries, review exercises and questions?
12. Is the material presented at a pace that allows for reflection and review?
13. Is the material suited for individual and small group instruction? Can the material be used for direct instruction or mastery instruction?
14. Are the physical conditions in the room conducive to using the materials?
15. Are the materials worth the time, effort, and expense?
16. Will the materials last over a period of time so the initial cost will be worth the investment?

Source: Allan C. Ornstein, "The Development and Evaluation of Curriculum Materials," *National Association of Secondary School Principals* (in print 1990).

Developing Materials

Sometimes slight modifications or supplements to published materials will make them suitable to use. Other times totally different materials are needed. If none of the printed materials seems usable, you have to consider making your own.

Before developing new materials, you should examine your present materials carefully. There must be sufficient "no" responses to the evaluating questions in Table 7.1 to warrant producing new materials. There must be a sufficiently greater number of "yes" responses for your new material to justify the time, effort, and cost of its development.

If you decide to produce your own, take factors of time and cost into consideration. It is suggested that you take no more than 1 to 1½ hours to develop materials for each lesson; any more is not worth the time and effort, and you may eventually lose interest in producing your own materials. The materials should be of a type that can be duplicated, put on a transparency or computer disk, or used again. The overall cost per unit declines as the number of copies increases, which is related to the number of students that will use the materials. Too often teachers make their own instructional materials at a

Figure 7.1 Developing your own instructional materials is unique, and important ingredient of good teaching. (Photo © David Strickler/ Picture Cube)

high cost for themselves and their schools. There may be better uses for the teacher's time and the school's money.

A team of specialists can sometimes produce a better product than the individual teacher. The group may consist of subject specialists, learning specialists, and evaluation experts, as well as teachers who will use the package in the classroom. Estimates for the development of completely new materials for a new program run as high as 50 to 100 hours of development per hour of instruction.[8] Needs or problems must be addressed, objectives developed, methods and materials determined, tests and evaluation conducted, and parts of the program and the materials revised. The questions in Table 7.1 listed for evaluation of printed material apply as much to new material. They can be taken as guidance for your own development of materials.

Copying Materials

Many teachers supplement the required text or workbook with instructional materials obtained from various sources—library texts, magazines and journals, government reports, newspapers. They duplicate these materials without

---

[8]Elizabeth G. Cohen, *Designing Group Work for the Classroom* (New York: Teachers College Press, Columbia University, 1986); Frederick G. Knirk and Kent L. Gustafson, *Instructional Technology: A Systematic Approach to Education* (New York: Holt, Rinehart and Winston, 1986).

Tips for Teachers 7.1

Selecting and Using Instructional Materials

How do instructional materials test serve students? Well-developed materials contain well-constructed tasks and important aspects of what is being taught. Below are some guides for selecting, using, and even developing instructional materials, with emphasis on reading and subject-related tasks.

1. Materials should be relevant to the instruction that is going on in the rest of the unit or lesson.
2. A portion of the materials should provide for a systematic and cumulative review of what has already been taught.
3. Materials should reflect the most important aspects of what is being taught in the course or subject.
4. Materials should contain, in a form that is readily accessible to students and teachers, extra tasks for students who need extra practice.
5. The vocabulary and concept level of materials should relate to that of the rest of the subject.
6. The language used in the materials must be consistent with that used in the rest of the lesson and in the rest of the textbook.
7. Instructions to students should be clear, unambiguous, and easy to follow; brevity is a virtue.
8. The layout of pages should combine attractiveness with utility.
9. Materials should contain enough content so that there is a chance a student will *learn* something and not simply be *exposed* to something.
10. Tasks that require students to make discriminations must be preceded by a sufficient number of tasks that provide practice on components of the discriminations.
11. The content of materials must be accurate and precise; tasks must not present wrong information or be presented in language that contains grammatical errors and incorrectly used words.
12. At least some tasks should be fun and have an obvious payoff to them.
13. Student response modes should be consistent from task to task and should be the closest possible to reading and writing.
14. The instructional design of individual tasks and of task sequences should be carefully planned.
15. There should be a limit on the number of different materials so as not to overload or confuse students.

continued

16. Artwork in the materials must be consistent with the text of the materials.
17. Cute, nonfunctional, space- and time-consuming materials should be avoided.
18. When appropriate, materials should be accompanied by brief explanations of purpose for both teachers and students.

Source: Adapted from Jean Osborn, "The Purposes, Uses, and Contents of Workbooks and Some Guidelines for Publishers," in R. C. Anderson, J. Osborn, and R. J. Tierney, eds., *Learning to Read in American Schools* (Hillsdale, N.J.: Erlbaum, 1984), pp. 110–111.

being aware that there is a **copyright law** that controls their use. The law, enacted in 1976, permits an educator to make a single duplication for scholarly or instructional purpose of the following: (1) a chapter from a book, (2) an article from a magazine, journal, or newspaper, (3) a short story, essay, or poem, and (4) a chart, graph, drawing, or table from a book, periodical, or newspaper.[9]

Multiple copies for students, not to exceed one copy per student for a course, may be made without permission providing the following requirements are met.

1. *Brevity.* The material may be no more than 250 words from a poem; no more than 1,000 words or 10 percent, whichever is less, from a prose work; no more than 2,500 words from a complete story, article, or essay; and no more than one chart, graph, drawing or table per book or periodical issue.
2. *Spontaneity.* The materials are considered necessary for scholarly or teaching effectiveness, and the time required to obtain permission would interfere with the scholarship or teaching.
3. *Cumulative.* No more than one entire source (story, article, essay, poem) or two excerpts may be copied from the same author. No more than three sources may be copied from the same collective work, magazine, or journal during one class term.
4. *Prohibition.* The duplicated material should not create a substitute for a text or compilation of works, nor should it restrict the consumption or purchase of a published work. No charge shall be made to the student beyond the actual cost of duplication.[10]

---

[9] American Library Association, *The New Copyright Law: Questions Teachers and Librarians Ask* (Washington, D.C.: National Education Association, 1977).

[10] Knirk and Gustafson, *Instructional Technology.*

Professional Viewpoint

On Using Many Materials

Judith was a student-teacher I supervised in an MA intern program. She was a thin, quiet, almost mousy person who only received average ratings in the summer micro-teaching program because she didn't have the necessary verbal pizzazz to lead a discussion. I worried about her during that hot, dry summer.

The school year started, and as part of her intern year, Judith was assigned to teach three social studies classes in a local high school. Then, something new happened. Judith started writing extremely good worksheets which contained well-developed integrative questions and thought questions. The students prepared these before class and much of the class time focused on having students compare answers with each other and Judith elaborating upon those answers. Judith also took charts and tables from the various sources and developed extremely good factual, analytic, and skill questions based on those materials. The students were excited, they were learning new skills and developing an integrated map of the material, but they weren't doing it through the usual teacher-student discussion. Judith's means were different, but they were effective.

Judith taught me that effective teachers come in many varieties; even quiet people can be effective. We should remember that the goal of teaching is the learning, processing, and skill development that goes on in the students' heads, and there is a variety of instructional methods for achieving this: It can be done by leading discussions, by developing special materials, by finding suitable materials developed by others, by developing thoughtful assignments, by explaining with guided note taking, and/or by having students explain concepts and material to each other. Judith taught me to focus on what goes on in the students' heads, and less on whether a currently prescribed method was used.

Barak Rosenshine
Professor of Education Psychology
University of Illinois-Urbana

Teachers should be aware of the potential consequences of violating copyright laws; ignorance is no defense. When in doubt, it is best to follow the school district's policy (if it has one) or request written permission from the publisher or copyright holder to use the work.

PRESENTING MATERIALS

The teacher must incorporate instructional materials into the unit plan and lesson plan and modify them in a way that considers the students' developmental stages or age, needs and interests, aptitudes, reading levels, prior knowledge, work habits, learning styles, and motivation. The following factors should be considered when presenting materials (published or teacher-made).

Understanding   Understanding requires matching materials to the learner's abilities and prior knowledge. If students don't understand the material, frustration sets in, making learning even more difficult. The teacher must know whether the materials are appropriate for the students to begin with and whether the students are understanding the material as it is being presented. The teacher must check for student understanding; this is especially important for younger and slower students and when teaching new information.

One educator suggests that teachers ask students or try to observe if they know *when* they understand and when they don't; if they know *what* they have learned; if they know what they *need* to know; if they know *how* to detect errors and improve.[11]

Structuring   Structuring, sometimes referred to as *clarifying*, involves organizing the material so it is clear to students. This means directions, objectives, and main ideas are stated clearly. Internal and final summaries cover the content. Transitions between main ideas are smooth and well integrated. Writing is not vague. Sufficient examples are provided. New terms and concepts are defined. Adequate practice and review assignments reinforce new learning.[12] Clarity is especially important when new subject matter is introduced, and when it is being integrated into previous learning.

Sequencing   The teacher should arrange the material to provide continuous and cumulative learning and to give attention to prerequisite skills and concepts. According to two educators, there are four basic ways to sequence materials: (1) *simple to complex*—materials gradually increase in complexity and become broader and deeper in meaning; (2) *parts to whole*—parts of information are presented first to enable the student to grasp the whole; (3) *whole to parts*—whole concepts or generalizations are presented first to facilitate organizing and integrating new and isolated items, and (4) *chronological* (which

---

[11]Jill Fitzgerald, "Helping Readers Gain Self-Control over Reading Comprehension," *Reading Teacher*, December 1983, pp. 249–254.

[12]Velma I. Hythecker et al., "An Analysis of the Process Influencing the Structured Dyadix Learning Environment," *Educational Psychologist*, Winter 1988, pp. 23–38; Joseph L. McCaleb and Jacqueline A. White, "Critical Dimensions in Evaluating Teacher Clarity," *Journal of Classroom Interaction*, April 1980, pp. 27–30.

is a favorite organizer for many teachers)—topics, ideas, or events are studied in the order that they take place.[13]

Balancing   The materials need to be vertically and horizontally related or balanced. **Vertical relationships** refer to a building of content and experiences at the lesson, unit, and course levels. Ninth-grade math concepts build on eighth-grade concepts, the second unit plan builds on the first, etc. **Horizontal relationships** establish a multidisciplinary and unified view of different subjects. The content of a social studies course is related to English and science.

Explaining   This refers to the way headings, terms, illustrations, and summary exercises are integrated and elucidate the content. Do the examples illustrate major concepts? Are the major ideas identified in chapter objectives and overviews? Do the headings outline a logical development of the content? Do the materials show relationships among topics, events, or facts to present an in-depth view of major concepts? The students should be able to discover important concepts and information and relate new knowledge to prior knowledge on their own through the materials. In short, the content of the material should be explicit, related, and cumulative in nature.

Pacing   This refers to how much and how quickly material is presented. The volume or length of material should not overwhelm students, but there must be enough to have an effect. As students get older, the amount of material can increase, the presentation can be longer and more complex, and the breadth and depth can be expanded.

    The rate at which the material is presented can be more rapid when old material is being reviewed than when the content is new. High-achieving and older students can tolerate more rapid pacing than low-achieving and younger students. The teacher should always build an appropriate wait-time into his or her timing.

Elaborating   Students can better learn when they are trying to learn what they are learning in different ways. The idea is to teach students to transform information from one form to another, and to apply new information to prior knowledge—by using various techniques such as comparing and contrasting, drawing analogies, drawing inferences, paraphrasing, summarizing, and predicting. A series of elaboration strategies help students learn new materials. Students can be taught a broad list of questions (of comparing and contrasting, drawing analogies, etc.) to use while reading materials, or the teacher can raise the questions in class when discussing the materials: (1) What is the main idea of the story? (2) If I lived during that period, how would I feel? (3) What does this remind me of? (4) How can I use the information in the project I am

---

[13]Allan C. Ornstein and Francis P. Hunkins, *Curriculum: Foundations, Principles, and Issues* (Englewood Cliffs, N.J.: Prentice-Hall, 1988).

working on? (5) How do I feel about the author's opinions? (6) How can I put this material in my own words? (7) What might be an example of this? (8) How can I explain this to my father, sister? (9) If I were to interview the author, what questions would I ask? and (10) How does this apply to my own life?[14]

Transferring   Instructional materials, according to Posner and Strike, may be transferred in that they are: (1) *concept-related*, drawing heavily on structure of knowledge, the concepts, principles, or theories of the subject; (2) *inquiry-related*, derived from critical thinking skills and procedures employed by learning theorists or scholars in the field; (3) *learner-related*, related to the needs, interests, or experiences of the students; and (4) *utilization-related*, showing how people can use or proceed with them in real-life situations.[15] The first two organizers seem to work best with intrinsically motivated (self-motivated) students and that the second two work best with students who need to be extrinsically motivated. Since most students need some extrinsic motivation, learner-related and utilization-related materials will be more effective with the majority of students.

TEXTBOOKS

Traditionally, the textbook has been the most frequently used instructional material at all levels beyond the primary grades, and in some cases it is the only one used by the teacher. "The textbook and its partner, the workbook," asserts Eisner, "provide the curricular hub around which much of what is taught revolves."[16] In terms of purchasing, it receives the highest priority, with the exception of costly hardware such as computers and copying machines. Textbooks can have a strong influence or even dominate the nature and sequence of a course and thus profoundly affect the learning experiences of students.

Reliance on the textbook is consistent with the stress on written words as the main medium of education—as well as the way many teachers themselves were educated. Dependence on the textbook is also linked to the time when a majority of teachers were poorly prepared in subject matter and read

---

[14]Gaea Leinhardt and William Bickel, "Instruction's the Thing Wherein to Catch the Mind that Falls Behind," *Educational Psychologist*, Spring 1987, pp. 177–207; Claire E. Weinstein et al., "Helping Students Develop Strategies for Effective Learning," *Educational Leadership*, December-January 1989, pp. 17–19.

[15]George J. Posner and Kenneth A. Strike, "Categorization Scheme for Principles of Sequencing Content," *Review of Educational Research*, Fall 1976, pp. 401–406. Also see George J. Posner and Alan N. Rudnitsky, *A Guide to Curriculum Development for Teachers* (New York: Longman, 1986).

[16]Eisner, "Why the Textbook Influences Curriculum," p. 111.

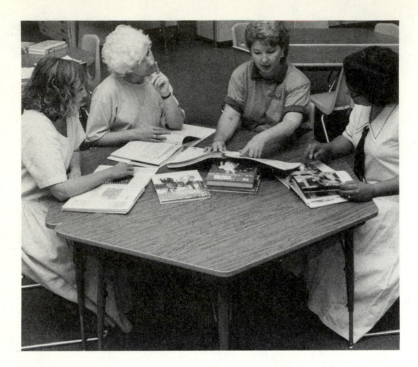

Figure 7.2 Reviewing text-books is an important re-sponsibility and brings satisfaction for those who are asked to perform this func-tion. (Photo © Richard S. Or-ton)

the text one day in advance of the students. Many of today's teachers, while better educated than their predecessors, sometimes lack time or training to prepare new materials, thus they continue to rely on the textbook and work-book.

Advantages and Disadvantages

In many classes the textbook becomes the only point of view in the course. In effect, the course is based on the theories and biases of the author of the text. Even though the author may try to maintain objectivity, what is selec-ted, what is omitted, and how the discussion is slanted reflect the author's views.

In order to have wide application, and to increase potential sales, textbooks tend to be general, noncontroversial, and bland. They are usually written for a national audience, so they do not consider local issues or community prob-lems. Because they are geared for the greatest number of "average" students, they may not meet the needs and interests of any particular group of students.

---

[17] Allan C. Ornstein, "Textbook Instruction: Processes and Strategies," *National Association of Secondary School Principals* (in print 1990).

Moreover, issues, topics, and data that might upset potential audiences or interest groups are omitted.[17]

Textbooks summarize large quantities of data and in so doing may become general and superficial and may discourage conceptual thinking, critical analysis, and evaluation. With the exception of those on mathematics, most textbooks quickly become outdated because of the rapid change of events; but because they are costly, they are often used long after they should be replaced.

Considering these criticisms, you might ask why teachers, when they have access to other instructional materials, rely so heavily on textbooks. The answer is, of course, they do have many advantages. A textbook: (1) provides an outline that the teacher can use in planning courses, units, and lessons, (2) summarizes a great deal of pertinent information, (3) enables the students to take home in convenient form most of the material they need to learn for the course, (4) provides a common resource for all students to follow, (5) provides the teacher with ideas regarding the organization of information and activities, (6) includes pictures, graphs, maps, and other illustrative material, which facilitates understanding, (7) includes other teaching aids, such as summaries and review questions, and (8) relieves the teacher of preparing material for the course, thus allowing more time to prepare the lesson.[18]

Unless a curriculum committee or teachers can develop materials that are substantially better than a text in meeting evaluative criteria (see Table 7.1), there is little reason for them to spend time, effort, and money on "homemade" materials that are sometimes put together for the sake of throwing away the textbook. Given the facts that textbooks take several years to write and revise and that publishers often spend considerable effort developing and refining them through market analysis, subject and methods consultants, writing staffs, and copy editors, it makes little sense to condemn them as a whole as being ineffective or harmful to the educational process.[19]

Good textbooks have many desirable characteristics. They are well organized, coherent, unified, relatively up-to-date, accurate, and relatively unbiased. They have been scrutinized by scholars, educators, and minority groups. Their reading level and knowledge base match the developmental level of their intended audience. They are accompanied by teacher's manuals, test items, study guides, and activity guides.[20] The textbook is an acceptable tool for instruction as long as it is selected with care and is kept in proper perspective so that it is not viewed as the only source of knowledge and it does not turn into the curriculum.

---

[18] Ibid.

[19] Ibid.

[20] Thomas H. Anderson, "Content Area Textbooks," in R. C. Anderson, J. Osborn, and R. J. Tierney, eds., *Learning to Read in American Schools* (Hillsdale, N.J.: Erlbaum, 1984), pp. 193–226; Harold L. Herber, "Subject Matter Texts—Reading to Learn," in Anderson, Osborn, and Tierney, eds., *Learning to Read in American Schools*, pp. 227–234.

Stereotyping

Basic readers and textbooks began to be criticized in the 1960s and 1970s as irrelevant to the social realities of the inner-city and minority child. According to Fantini and Weinstein, our school books depicted "happy, neat, wealthy, white people whose intact and loving families live only in clean, grassy suburbs. . . . Ethnic [and racial] groups comprising so much of our population are often omitted" or included only "as children from other lands."[21]

According to one educator, all American Indians were called "Big Horn" or "Shining Star"; people with Italian, Greek, or Polish names were likely to appear as peddlers or organ grinders, wearing red scarves and ragged clothes. Either there were no blacks or one black boy might be inserted in the background. Yellow or dark people were depicted in stories about China, India, and Africa, but they were always strangers and foreigners. Women were portrayed almost always as mothers, nurses, or teachers. Religion was rarely mentioned—except in relation to church attendance on Sunday morning. In short, the readers of these books were presented with a monocultural view of society; approximately 6.5 million nonwhite children were learning to read from books that either scarcely mentioned them, omitted them entirely, or represented them stereotypically.[22]

Today, readers, workbooks, and textbooks exclude racial, ethnic, religious, and sexual stereotyping. (Obscenity, violence, and sexual topics are still generally avoided, as are such unpleasant issues as disease and death.) Major racial, ethnic, and minority groups, including the handicapped and elderly, tend to be well represented in story characters and pictures. Women are depicted as airplane pilots, police officers, construction workers, lawyers, and doctors. Blacks, Hispanics, and other minorities have professional and managerial jobs and are not all basketball players and musicians. Girls rarely play with dolls and boys rarely play baseball, at least not without girls.[23]

Finding good literature or good texts that meet all these requirements (and many more) is difficult. To accommodate some of the new criteria, many classic works of literature have been eliminated from the curriculum, and many bland texts and instructional materials have been included. Writes Connie Muther, "The idea is to please all and offend none [and thus] many textbooks [and related materials] have no clear point of view."[24] Although many

---

[21] Mario D. Fantini and Gerald Weinstein, *The Disadvantaged: Challenge to Education* (New York: Harper & Row, 1968), p. 133.

[22] Allan C. Ornstein, "The Irrelevant Curriculum: A Review from Four Perspectives," *National Association of Secondary School Principals*, September 1988, pp. 26–32; Ornstein and Hunkins, *Curriculum: Foundations, Principles, and Issues.*

[23] Dennis Doyle, "The Unsacred Text," *American Education*, Summer 1984, pp. 3–13; Connie Muther, "What Every Textbook Evaluator Should Know," *Educational Leadership*, April 1985, pp. 4–8.

[24] Muther, "What Every Textbook Evaluator Should Know," p. 7. Also see Connie Muther, "Reviewing Research When Choosing Materials," *Educational Leadership*, February 1985, pp. 86–87.

Professional Viewpoint

Textbook Controversy

Few efforts in teaching engender more controversy than addressing the moral and/or spiritual dimension in the classroom textbooks. Yet, in our increasingly diverse society, there is a common body of values—many bearing upon moral character and development—that all would agree should be part of our American heritage that students understand, appreciate, and advance by their own conduct.

The courts properly impose boundaries that prohibit religious indoctrination in the public schools. This often is taken to mean that instructional materials in morality or religion are forbidden. And that is a mistake—probably attributable to the fact that most people view instruction in moral or religious matters as inextricably bound to the expression of belief in God.

But it does not require reference to God to teach children—either as a separate course or woven throughout the curriculum, including the text—the profound worth in life of honesty, integrity, respect for others and their differing beliefs, and various cultural values, truthfulness, civic responsibility, courage, fortitude, industry, a profound respect for our American freedoms, compassion for people poorly circumstanced, and abiding recognition of a duty to help others, and the like that, taken as a single bundle of attributes, make up the moral person.

While this approach is sometimes denigrated as "atheistic humanism," there is nothing atheistic about it. At most, it is non-theistic. But, in our religiously neutral public schools, it is the only legally viable course if the essence of our American tradition is to be imparted to our children through the public schools, as people are demanding today.

It is an abiding challenge for teachers in our free society. The way teachers face it will have significant implications for our nation in the ensuing generation.

Thomas A. Shannon
Executive Director
National School Boards Association

new books portray the populace more accurately, they remain safe and in some cases they are boring.

Readability

Concern about student reading problems has prompted educators to identify textbooks and other reading materials that are suitable for specific student populations, especially below-average readers. **Reading formulas,** first devised in the 1920s to estimate the reading difficulty of a text, have increased and are widely used by authors, publishers, teachers, reading consultants, and textbook adoption committees.

Some reading formulas count the number of syllables or the number of letters in a word, some count the number of words not on a specific word list, others measure sentence length, and still others remove words in a passage and test whether students can fill in the exact word that was removed.[25] Some formulas use graphs, regression statistics, and percentiles and range scores to calculate reading difficulty, and computer programs are now available for doing the counting and calculation chores involved in reading level determinations.[26]

The best known reading formula was developed by Edward Fry. An estimate of the approximate grade level of the reading material is obtained by plotting on a graph the average number of sentences and the average number of syllables in three 100-word passages taken at random.[27]

The Raygor Reading Estimate, developed by Alton Raygor, is a graph procedure, too, but is easier to use than the Fry method. Raygor's procedure is based on counting the number of words of six or more letters, instead of syllables. It has been validated with the Fry formula and is of equal accuracy.[28] There are many other reading formulas and methods for determining the reading level of instructional materials and textbooks.

Critics of the various reading formulas say that (1) they fail to consider students' prior knowledge, experience, and interests, all of which influence reading comprehension; (2) they assume that words with fewer syllables and shorter, simpler sentences are easier to comprehend than words with more syllables and longer sentences with subordinate clauses, which is not always

---

[25]Keith Kennedy, "Determining Readability with a Microcomputer," *Curriculum Review,* November–December 1985, pp. 40–42; Bonnie C. Konopak, "Development of a Prediction Scale for Text-Based Definitional Information," paper presented at the annual meeting of the American Educational Research Association, San Francisco, April 1986.

[26]David L. Lillie, Gary B. Stuck, and Wallace H. Hannum, *Computers and Effective Instruction* (New York: Longman, 1989); William Wresch, *A Practical Guide to Computer Uses in the English Language Arts Classroom* (Englewood Cliffs, N.J: Prentice-Hall, 1987).

[27]Edward Fry, "Fry's Readability Graph: Clarification, Validity, and Extension to Level," *Journal of Reading,* December 1977, pp. 242–252.

[28]Alton L. Raygor and George B. Schick, *Reading at Efficient Rates,* 2nd ed. (New York: McGraw-Hill, 1980).

true[29]; (3) publishers have reacted to these formulas by adjusting sentence and word length to give the appearance of certain levels of readability without necessarily providing them[30]; and (4) strict adherence to formulas robs prose of the connective words, vocabulary, and sentence structure that make it interesting and comprehensible and contribute to a style that makes the text worth reading.[31] In short, rigid following of reading formulas often results in a boring and bland text.

Whatever their faults, reading formulas do help teachers to assess reading difficulty and to select printed material that is appropriate to the students' abilities. Since most teachers work with groups of students in which there is a range of abilities, it is advisable that the difficulty of the material not be more than one year below or above the average reading grade level of the group. If there is more than a 1½- to 2-year spread in reading ability in a group, the teacher should use more than one set of instructional materials.

Some educators now urge that comprehendability, not readability, is the major quality to consider when adopting a text. Teachers and textbook committees are identifying various textbook aids such as structural overviews, introductory objectives, summaries, and review exercises as devices that contribute to comprehendability. One reading expert lists more than 40 reader aids that might be considered in selecting a text.[32] This applies not only to reading books, but to all texts.

Cognitive Task Demands

Critics have found that textbooks in nearly every subject and grade level cover too many topics, the writing is superficial, choppy, and lacking in depth and breadth (the phenomenon is called "mentioning"), and content wanders between the important and the trivial.[33] They fail to capture the imagination and interest of the students or make students think, and spurn current knowledge

---

[29]Suzanne Hidi, "The Effect of Information Salience on Text Comprehension and Recall: Lean, Salient, and Resolving Texts," paper presented at the annual meeting of the American Educational Research Association, San Francisco, April 1986; Taslina Rahman and Gay L. Bisanz, "Reading Ability and the Use of Story Schema in Recalling and Reconstructing Information," *Journal of Educational Psychology*, October 1986, pp. 323–333

[30]Alice Davidson, "Readability—Appraising Text Difficulty" in Anderson, Osborn, and Tierney, eds., *Learning to Read in American Schools*, pp. 121–139; Frank Smith, "Overselling Literacy," *Phi Delta Kappan*, January 1989, pp. 352–359.

[31]Margret T. Bernstein, "The New Politics of Textbook Adoption," *Education Digest*, December 1985, pp. 12–15; Bernstein, "The Academy's Contribution to the Impoverishment of America's Textbooks," *Phi Delta Kappan*, November 1988, pp. 193–198.

[32]Robert A. Pavlik, "Tips on Texts," *Phi Delta Kappan*, September 1985, p. 86.

[33]Bernstein, "The New Politics of Textbook Adoption"; Marcy L. Stein, "Helpfulness of Context Plus Number of Exposures," paper presented at the annual meeting of the American Educational Research Association, New Orleans, April 1988.

about cognitive information and linguistic processing.[34] The so-called best textbooks are often designed to entertain and to be decorative, but they provide only tidbits of information, lack adequate integration of subject matter, and do not stretch the student's mind. They are unintentionally geared to over-simplify and to limit thinking!

Textbook adoption committees have contributed to the problem with their demands for topic coverage and easy-to-read prose. Special interest groups, with their passions and legal challenges, have added to the problem, causing publishers to become politically sensitive to the content at the expense of linguistic and cognitive processes. Teachers have done their part, too, since most teachers emphasize answers to be found, not problems to be solved or methods to be used.

Neville Bennett and his analyzed 417 language and math tasks assigned in texts by teachers and found that 60 percent were practice tasks, or content already known to the students. New tasks accounted for 25 percent, and tasks requiring students to discover, invent, or develop a new concept or problem made up 7 percent of the tasks.[35] In another study, approximately 84 percent of teachers rely on *textually explicit* instruction, a method of using printed material in which a correct answer can be obtained by selecting verbatim information from the textbook or workbook. Rarely do teachers employ *textually implicit* instruction, in which a correct answer requires students to make an inference from the textual information supplied. Even more rarely do they use *scriptually implicit* instruction, in which a correct answer requires students to go beyond the information given and call on prior knowledge and reasoning skills.[36]

Most teachers are right-answer oriented in their teaching and testing. Hence, they are unwilling or unable to change from textbooks that are characterized by low-level cognitive demands and are divorced from how students think or reason. One might expect at least science teachers to exhibit textually implicit or scriptually implicit instruction, since they deal with scientific problems and laboratory experiments, yet the above conclusions were based on observations of seventh-grade science classes.

Teachers of mathematics, especially at the upper elementary and junior high school grades, are not much different. Some data strongly suggest that many of these "teachers don't know mathematics. They assign the basic problems but skip word problems because word problems are harder to teach."[37]

[34]Rebecca Barr, *Reading Diagnosis for Teachers* (New York: Longman, 1985); Jill Bartoli and Morton Bofel, *Reading/Learning Disability* (New York: Teachers College Press, Columbia University, 1988).

[35]Neville Bennett et al., *The Quality of Pupil Learning Experiences* (Hillsdale, N.J.: Erlbaum, 1984).

[36]John R. Mergendoller et al., "Task Demands and Accountability in Middle-Grade Science Classes," *Elementary School Journal*, January 1988, pp. 251–265.

[37]Ezra Bowen, "Flunking Grade in Math," *Time*, June 20, 1988, p. 79. Also see Lyn Corno, "The Study of Teaching for Mathematics Learning," *Educational Psychologist*, Spring 1988, pp. 181–202.

Professional Viewpoint

Beyond the Textbook

Don't be afraid to be a critic of textbooks. Sometimes they contain inaccuracies or poor writing. Sometimes they don't provide enough background information for students to understand their meaning.

The biggest drawback of textbooks is that they may bore students. Today's students are accustomed to getting information about the world from television and movies; many of them know how to get information electronically. A textbook alone may not hold the students' interest. When your students are turned off by the dull writing in their textbooks, blame the textbooks, not the kids.

Put yourself in the students' place and then ask yourself, would you read this if you didn't have to? Does it hold your attention? Would you be tempted to read more than the assigned number of pages? If the answer is "no" to all of these questions, then think about de-emphasizing the textbook in your classes.

The best way to use a textbook is to treat it like a reference work. Use it as background. The main source of learning should come from the other materials, experiences, and technology that you supply, either through hands-on activities (in or out of the classroom) or through the use of supplementary materials that are livelier, more vivid, and more motivating for students than the textbook.

Diane Ravitch
Professor of History and Education
Teachers College, Columbia University

Students may learn to deal with simple right-answer problems (Which number is closest to 27: 20, 31, 22, 35?), but they rarely learn how to think. (A better question would be: Suppose you have seven coins and have at least one quarter, dime, nickel, and penny; what is the least amount of money you could have?). Kids who cannot handle this "penny-ante" problem are in trouble, but then some teachers may have trouble handling it—and that is trouble for the nation.

TEXTBOOK AND PEDAGOGICAL AIDS

Textbook aids, sometimes called *text-based aids, instructional aids, textbook elements,* or *reader aids,* are designed to enhance understanding of the content and to facilitate learning. Aids that appear at the beginning of a chapter include overviews, instructional objectives, and focusing questions (prequestions). Aids that occur *throughout* the chapter include headings, key terms in special type, marginal notes ("trigger items"), overview tables, outlines, and discussions (point-counterpoint, pro-con), and illustrations such as graphs, charts, and pictures. Aids that come at the *end* of the chapter include summaries, discussion questions (postquestions), case studies, problems, review exercises, sample test questions, suggested activities, suggested readings, and glossaries.[38]

Pedagogical aids, sometimes called *instructional aids* or *teaching aids*, are materials designed for teacher use that are provided as supplements to the textbook. They include (1) teacher's manuals, (2) test questions, (3) skills books or exercise books, (4) transparencies or cutouts to duplicate, (5) reinforcement activities, (6) enrichment activities, (7) behavioral objectives, (8) lesson plans, (9) bulletin board displays, (10) supplementary tables, graphs, charts, maps, (11) parent involvement materials, (12) teacher resource binders, (13) computer software, and (14) audio and video cassettes.[39]

Those aids used before students start to read the chapter acquaint them with the general approach and the information and concepts to be learned. The aids used while students are reading the chapter focus on organization of the content, provide examples, supply supplementary information, and repeat objectives. Those used after the chapter reinforce learning through summaries and exercises and encourage critical thinking through problems and activities. See Tips for Teachers 7.2.

The teacher can use the aids external to the text and teach the students to use the aids internal to the text to develop the text content. Students can be taught how to note take, study and integrate information in the text by learning to utilize textbook aids; indeed, these aids are there for a reason.

Textbook aids in particular can facilitate the development of cognitive processes. Table 7.2 lists four developmental stages of cognitive processes and corresponding cognitive operations, reader activities, outcomes, and their relationship to various textbook aids. The cognitive processes, operations, activities, and outcomes, in theory, each form an untested hierarchy in which one level is prerequisite to the next. The aids are not hierarchial, but overlap in the sense that any one aid may facilitate learning at more than one level of the hierarchy.

Without good textbook aids, poor readers will learn little and capable readers will develop **default strategies**, or partially ineffective strategies for processing text information. A default strategy is likely to involve focusing on topic sentences or unusual and/or isolated information, instead of main concepts and principles.[40] A default strategy also leads to copying and memorizing

---

[38] Ornstein, "Textbook Instruction: Processes and Strategies."

[39] Sandra Conn, "Textbooks: Defining the New Criteria," *Media and Methods*, March–April 1988, pp. 30–31, 64.

[40] Richard E. Mayer, "Aids to Text Comprehension," *Educational Psychologist*, Winter 1984, pp. 30–42.

Tips for Teachers 7.2

Student Use of Textbook Aids

Textbook aids (textbook elements) have continued to grow, as publishers and authors respond to growing needs of teachers and textbook criteria for selecting texts. Below is a list of features now commonly found in textbooks, with questions to ask the students to be sure they understand how to use these tools.

Features of Text: Sample Questions for Students

Contents
1. How do you use the table of contents?
2. What is the difference between major and minor headings?
3. In what chapters would you find information about _____?

Index
1. What information do you find in an index?
2. On what pages would you find the following information _____?
3. Why is the subject on _____ cross-referenced?

Opening material (overview, objectives, focusing questions, outline)
1. What are the main points or topics of the chapter? How do we know?
2. Do the objectives correspond with the outline of the chapter?
3. In what section can we expect to find a discussion of_____?

Graphic material (charts, graphs, diagrams) and *tabular material*
1. How does the legend at the bottom of the chart explain the meaning of data?
2. Based on the lines of the graph, what will happen in the year 2000? What do the dotted lines represent?
3. Where in the narrative does the author explain the table?

Pictures
1. Are the pictures relevant? Up-to-date?
2. What is the author trying to convey in this picture?
3. How do the pictures reveal the author's biases?

Headings
1. What main ideas can you derive from the headings? Subheadings?
2. How are the subheadings related to the headings?
3. On what pages would you find a discussion of _____?

Information sources (footnotes, references)
1. Where did the author get the information for the chapter?
2. Are the footnotes important? Up-to-date?
3. What references might you use to supplement those at the end of the chapter?

continued

Key terms in text
1. Which are the important terms on this page?
2. Why are some terms in bold print? Why are other terms in italics?
3. Where can you find the meaning of these terms in the text?

Marginal notes (or trigger items)
1. Do the marginal notes catch your eye?
2. Why are these terms or phrases noted in the margin?
3. Quickly find a discussion of the following topics————

Supplementary discussion (point/counterpoint tables, lists of suggestions, lists of issues)
1. Why are the point/counterpoint discussions interesting? Which side do you take?
2. What are the important issues on this topic?
3. Which tips make sense to you? Why?

Summaries
1. If you could read only one page to find out what the chapter is about, what page would you read? Why?
2. Where can we find a summary of the main ideas of the chapter?
3. Does the summary correspond to the major headings?

End-of-chapter material (Review exercises, questions, activities, sample test items)
1. Are the exercises meaningful? Do they tie into the text?
2. Which discussion questions seem controversial? Why?
3. Why should we do the activities?
4. Take a practice test. Answer the sample test questions to see what we need to study.

long lists of information, rather than organizing, inferring, and transferring ideas of the text. A textbook may have excellent aids; however, the teacher may not know how to make good use of them. Thus there is additional need to consider Tips 7.2 and Table 7.2.

Learning to Read

All teachers, whatever the subject or grade level, are reading teachers in the sense that they should help their students read textbook material. Researchers suggest that students' comprehension of what they read is enhanced by (1) relating their knowledge and experience to the information in the text, (2) relating one part of the text to another, and (3) discussing the meaning of important new words.[41] Students need practice in inferential reasoning and

---

[41] Bonnie B. Armbuster, "Schema Theory and the Design of Content Area Textbooks," *Educational Psychologist,* Fall 1986, 253–268; Bruce K. Bromage and Richard E. Mayer, "Quantitative and Qualitative Effects of Repetition on Learning from Technical Text," *Journal of Educational Psychology,* August 1986, pp. 271–278.

Table 7.2   LEVELS OF COGNITION AND READING, WITH IMPLICATIONS FOR USING TEXTBOOK AIDS

Cognitive process	Cognitive operations	Reader activities	Outcomes	Textbook aids
Identifying	Focusing on selective information Sequencing selective information	Copying Underlining Simple notetaking or discussion	Retention of target information	Overviews Instructional objectives Prequestions Key words or terms Marginal notes Summaries Review exercises
Conceptualizing	Classifying main ideas of text Comparing main ideas of text	Logical or structured notetaking or discussion Distinguishing relevant information Relating points to each other	Retention of key concepts of text *Internal* connections (relations among ideas of text)	Headings, subheadings Marginal notes Point-counterpoint discussions Summaries Postquestions Problems Review exercises
Integrating	Analyzing main ideas of text Modifying ideas of text into variations or new ideas Deducing main ideas of text Expanding main ideas of text	Elaborate notetaking or discussion Making generalizations Hierarchical ordering of items Making inferences from text information	Understanding implications of text (explicit and implicit) External connections (relations between ideas of text and ideas outside of text)	Headings, subheadings Graphs, tables Models, paradigms Postquestions Case studies Problems Activities
Transferring	Applying main ideas of text to problems Evaluating text information Verifying text information Going beyond text information Predicting from text information	Elaborate notetaking or discussion Evaluating, problem solving, and inferring based on text information Using text information to create new information	Establishing dimensions of a problem Understanding causal relations in text information Assessing the degree of universality of text information for predicting	Graphs, tables Models, paradigms Simulations Case studies Problems Activities

Source: Allan C. Ornstein, "Textbook Instruction: Processes and Strategies," *National Association of Secondary School Principals* (in print 1990).

other comprehension processes (see Table 7.2), but this rarely occurs because they are occupied by word recognition and vocabulary demands.[42]

Relating the text to students' experience can be done through asking their opinions, having them imagine themselves part of the events described in the text, or having them think of examples from their own experience. Relating parts of the text to one another can be achieved by asking students to sum-

---

[42]Donald J. Leu, Linda J. DeGroff, and Herbert D. Simons, "Predictable Texts and Interactive-Compensatory Hypotheses," *Journal of Educational Psychology*, October 1986, pp. 347–352.

marize and analyze main points, to explain relationships and elaborate with examples, and to note main and minor headings, marginal notes, key terms, and summary statements. Defining new terms can be accomplished by discussing in class selected terms that have conceptual meaning and encouraging students to use the dictionary and glossaries on their own. Providing repetitive sentence patterns and familiar words and concepts eases word recognition and comprehension tasks for students who have trouble reading. Paying close attention to instructional objectives or focusing questions, and answering review questions, helps students determine whether they understand the text material, and what sections need to be reread or skimmed.

Other methods for improving reading comprehension, as reported by Armbuster and Anderson, include the following:

1. Explain to students why it is important to know what they are studying so they can match the text to the task.
2. Teach students how to use the textbook aids.
3. Teach students to relate what they know to the text. Have students draw on their prior knowledge and experience to think of examples that relate to what they are reading.
4. Teach students how to outline and take notes on what they read.[43]

The notion of **advance organizers,** developed by David Ausubel to enhance concept thinking, can be used in teaching students how to read.[44] The advance organizers characterize the general nature of the text, the major categories into which it can be divided, the similarities and differences among categories, and examples within different categories. The organizers state the abstraction or generality under which data can be subsumed. To be useful, the organizers should be stated in terms that are familiar to the students and prior to their reading the text material.[45] They are especially useful when the text is poorly organized or students lack prerequisite knowledge of the subject.

Although Ausubel and most other educators believe organizers should be presented before the text is read, others maintain that presenting them in the middle or after the text can also facilitate learning.[46] Other studies have shown that instructional objectives, overviews, prequestions, and specific instructions

---

[43]Bonnie B. Armbuster and Thomas H. Anderson, "Research Synthesis on Study Skills," *Educational Leadership*, November 1981, pp. 154–156.

[44]David P. Ausubel, "In Defense of Advance Organizers: A Reply to the Critics," *Review of Educational Research*, Spring 1978, pp. 251–257.

[45]Michael P. Ford and Marilyn M. Ohlhausen, "Helping Disabled Readers in the Regular Classroom." *Educational Digest*, January 1989, pp. 48–51; Ornstein, Textbook Instruction: Processes and Strategies."

[46]Livingston Alexander, Ronald G. Frankiewicz, and Robert E. Williams, "Facilitation of Learning and Retention of Oral Instruction Using Advance and Post Organizers," *Journal of Educational Psychology*, October 1979, pp. 701–707; Mayer, "Aids to Text Comprehension."

prior to chapter reading facilitate learning of reading materials.[47] These textbook aids or cues are similar to advance organizers, because they provide advance information about the nature of the material to be learned. In addition, postquestions and summary activities that apply textbook material to concepts, problems, or creative things to do also enhance learning.

Effective reading instruction is related to the needs and interests of the students. Teachers need to provide assistance and challenge, and guide each student to independent reading. Six strategies for reading instruction by the content teacher, sometimes called **scaffold instruction,** include the following: (1) *recruitment*—the teacher must obtain or focus on the students' interest; (2) *reduction in freedom*—the teacher must reduce the size and/or difficulty of the task so students can cope with task requirements; (3) *direct maintenance*—the teacher must keep the students on task; (4) *marking critical features*—the teacher must accentuate important features of the task for the students to use; (5) *frustration control*—the teacher must help reduce stress and frustration; and (6) *demonstration*—the teacher must illustrate an "ideal" completion of the task, explicating solution steps or processes needed to complete the task.[48]

Teaching Text Structure   **Text structure,** sometimes called "macro structure," refers to the main ideas of the text, how information is organized, as well as the verbal and textual cues (or pedagogical aids) that help organize and bring unity to the text. Does teaching text structure to students increase learning? The research overwhelmingly indicates that students of all ages and abilities, and using texts in various subjects, improve their ability to learn from the text when taught to identify, summarize, and integrate text structure. Students' awareness of text structure improves (1) reading comprehension, (2) retention of information, and (3) written summaries of text material.[49] Similarly, high-achieving students and skilled readers automatically abstract elaborate structures of the text.[50] They use text structure often without being taught to do so.

---

[47]John A. Ellis et al., "Effect of Generic Advance Instructions on Learning a Classification Task," *Journal of Educational Psychology,* August 1986, pp. 294–299; James Harley and Ivor K. Davies, "Preinstructional Strategies: The Role of Pretest, Behavioral Objectives, Overviews, and Advance Organizers," *Review of Educational Research,* Spring 1976, pp. 239–265.

[48]Peter Winograd and Scott G. Paris, "A Cognitive and Motivational Agenda for Reading Instruction," *Educational Leadership,* December–January 1989, pp. 30–36.

[49]Bonnie B. Arambruster, Thomas H. Anderson, and Joyce Ostertag, "Does Text Structure/Summarization Instruction Facilitate Learning from Expository Text," *Reading Research Quarterly,* Summer 1987, pp. 331–346; Lea M. McGee, "Awareness of Text Structure: Effects on Children's Recall of Expository Text," *Reading Research Quarterly,* Fall 1982, pp. 581–590: and Barbara M. Taylor and Richard W. Beach, "The Effects of Text Structure Instruction on Middle-Grade Students' Comprehension and Production of Expository Text," *Reading Research Quarterly,* Winter 1984, pp. 136–146.

[50]Ibid.

Most learning in school depends on the ability to read and understand expository text. Students, in general, have more difficulty with expository text than narrative text, because of insufficient prior knowledge, poor reading ability, lack of interest and motivation, and lack of sensitivity to how texts are organized.[51] In addition, a good many texts are poorly written, boring, and even confusing to students.[52]

The need is for teachers in all content areas to foster awareness of text structure by having students make concrete representations of the ideas within the text. Such strategies are referred to as "mapping," "networking," and "graphing," and involve a number of basic strategies: (1) *diagramming*, students develop a diagram that represents basic concepts or ideas and relationships within and among the concepts; (2) *outlining*, students use and integrate headings, subheadings, and paragraphs in the text; (3) *conventional classifications*, students use one of the following strategies: (a) compare/contrast, showing similarities and differences, (b) problem/solution, showing a problem, attempted solutions, and results, (c) cause/effect, describing stages of events and outcomes, (d) describe/enumerate, describing a major concept or theme, then listing supporting ideas for each concept, and details for each idea.[53]

In general, the strategy that is adopted will most likely provide more information about selected topics, by presenting characteristics, specifics, explanations, and details. The skilled reader becomes sensitive to the author's text structure, including pedagogical aids, and uses them if they are well structured, along with his own prior knowledge of the topic in helping to decide what information is important to emphasize and how to integrate the new information. As for the teacher, it is important that the teacher stress one strategy at a time, and have students practice it and raise questions and comments to fill in gaps in understanding.

---

[51] Armbruster, Anderson, and Ostertag, "Does Text Structure/Summarization Instruction Facilitate Learning from Expository Text"; Gerald G. Duffy et al., "Effects of Explaining the Reasoning Associated with Using Reading Strategies," *Reading Research Quarterly*, Summer 1987, pp. 347–367; and Marilyn M. Ohlhausen and Cathy M. Roller, "The Operation of Text Structure and Content Schemata," *Reading Research Quarterly*, Winter 1988, pp. 70–88.

[52] Bernstein, "The Academy's Contribution to the Improvement of America's Textbooks"; Susan M. Hubbuch, "The Trouble with Textbooks," *High School Journal*, April-May 1989, pp. 203–210.

[53] Beau F. Jones, Jean Pierce, and Barbara Hunter, "Teaching Students to Construct Graphic Representations," *Educational Leadership*, December-January 1989, pp. 20–25; Patricia A. Herman et al., "Incidental Acquisition of Word Meaning from Expositions with Varied Text Features," *Reading Research Quarterly*, Summer 1987, pp. 263—284; and Ohlhausen and Roller, "The Operation of Text Structure and Content Schema."

Guidelines for Using Textbooks

The following general guidelines should help increase the value of the text for students.

1. Do not become so hypnotized by the textbook that you follow it rigidly. Supplement the textbook with other instructional aids and printed materials (such as paperback books, for all students, and journals, magazines, and reports for junior high and high school students).
2. Before they begin to read, question students about their knowledge of what is to be read. This helps them recognize what they know about the topic, what they need to know, and what they would like to know.
3. Adapt the textbook to the needs of the students and the objectives of the lesson. Do not allow the textbook to determine either the teaching level or course content.
4. Organize guide sheets with definitions, questions, review exercises, supplementary readings, and assignments for each chapter.
5. Do not assign work in a textbook without referring to and assigning follow-up activities at the end of the chapter. Include assignments that call for understanding, evaluation, and critical thinking.
6. Teach older students how to analyze the textbook by noting when an author is editorializing, slanting the materials, or overgeneralizing.
7. Teach students how to interpret and use aids in the text, such as table of contents, headings, marginal notes, illustrations, and index.
8. With another teacher or chairperson, learn to appraise the worth of the textbook. See Tips for Teachers 7.3.

Following is a list of more specific suggestions the teacher might make to students to improve their reading.

1. Try to be aware of how you gain understanding.
2. Reread unclear or difficult passages.
3. Change speeds—slow down when the material is difficult, go faster when it is easy.
4. Rely on imagery and expression of feelings to help illustrate passages.
5. Look for main ideas, what holds the passage together.
6. Look at the total format to identify and recognize key points.
7. Search for inconsistencies; ignore irrelevant information (for older students).
8. Use the context of the passage (for older students).
9. Modify and interpret as you read.

The following sequenced steps should help the teacher realize the goal of teaching text structure to students.

1. *Introduce.* Discuss with students why and when to use a particular text structure strategy.
2. *Choose.* Select a preferred strategy; present one strategy at a time.
3. *Demonstrate.* Show how to apply the strategy; present several examples of the completed strategy; summarize major points; introduce subtle variations.
4. *Grouping.* Have students work as a whole group, then in small groups to develop their strategy the first and second time.
5. *Student participation.* Encourage students to volunteer information, to share and compare with each other; make students explain what they did—and why.
6. *Feedback.* Provide ample feedback; help students understand different parts and procedures of the strategy.
7. *Review.* Ask questions; listen to student reactions.
8. *Individualize.* Provide several opportunities for students to practice on an individual basis; provide additional feedback.
9. *Reteach.* Teach specific parts that are still considered confusing or a problem to students.
10. *Shift responsibilities.* Shift responsibilities from the whole group to small groups, to the individual; from the teacher to the students.

WORKBOOK MATERIALS

At the lower grade levels, the workbook is often used separately or independently to provide exercises for practice and drill in language arts, reading, and math; along with the textbook, it tends to dominate elementary school classrooms as the major instructional tool. In fact, in one study of 45 teachers, grades one to six, students spent as much time or more time alone on their workbooks than they did with other teacher-student activities.[54]

At the secondary grade levels, workbooks are often used in different content areas keyed to or as a supplement (rarely independently) to the textbook for purpose of practice. It sometimes exists, at the secondary grade level, in the form of a student's manual with drill exercises (sometimes problems) constituting most of the course content. Used in this context, students first engage in new learning derived from the textbook or another source. Then, the workbook is used to reinforce the new learning; ideally, the exercises or problems are concrete examples of abstract learning. For this reason, many teachers view the workbook as a pedagogical aid and check with publishers to see whether a workbook accompanies the textbook.

---

[54]Jean Osborn, "The Purposes, Uses, and Contents of Workbooks and Some Guidelines for Publishers," in Anderson, Osborn, and Tierney, eds., *Learning to Read in American Schools*, pp. 45–111.

Tips for Teachers 7.3

Appraising the Worth of a Textbook

Here are some questions to keep in mind in assessing the worth of a textbook for teacher and student. The first group of questions deals with text content, the second with mechanics, and the third with overall appraisal.

CONTENT

1. Does the text coincide with the content and objectives of the course?
2. Is it up-to-date and accurate?
3. Is it comprehensive?
4. Is it adaptable to the students' needs, interests, and abilities?
5. Does it adequately and properly portray minorities and women?
6. Does it foster methodological approaches consistent with procedures used by the teacher and school?
7. Does it reinforce the type of learning (such as critical thinking and problem solving) sought by the teacher and school?
8. Does it provide the student with a sense of accomplishment, because it can be mastered and is still challenging?

MECHANICS

1. Is the size appropriate?
2. Is the binding adequate?
3. Is the paper of adequate quality?
4. Are the objectives, headings, and summaries clear?
5. Are the contents and index well organized?
6. Is there a sufficient number of pictures, charts, maps, and so on appropriate for the students' level?
7. Does it come with instructional manuals and study guides?
8. Is it durable enough to last several years?
9. Is it reasonably priced relative to its quality? To its competitors?

OVERALL APPRAISAL

1. What are the outstanding features of the text?
2. What are the shortcomings of the text?
3. Do the outstanding features strongly override the shortcomings?

Source: Adapted from Allan C. Ornstein, ''Textbook Instruction: Processes and Strategies,'' *National Association of Secondary School Principals* (in print 1990).

Disadvantages

The value of the workbook depends on how the teacher uses it. The workbook is sometimes used as a form of "busywork," to keep students occupied, even worse, as a substitute for teaching. The workbook tends to overemphasize factual and low-level information. Students can spend hours, especially at the elementary grade level, filling in blanks, completing sentences, recognizing correct words, and working on simple mathematical computations. According to critics, workbook exercises have little to do with and often discourage critical thinking or creativity, with learning the whole, abstract thought, or hands-on activities and materials.[55]

The teacher may assign workbook exercises in order to keep students busy while he or she grades papers, performs clerical functions, or confers with an individual student or group of students. The latter, in fact, often occurs at the elementary and junior high school levels, when teachers divide students into reading or math groups. It is used, sometimes overused, in conjunction with seatwork activities—recommended by advocates of direct instruction and mastery teaching as a viable instructional approach. When workbooks are assigned either as busywork or merely to facilitate seatwork activities, and fail to link the exercises in a meaningful way to new information or to content coverage, the routine produces what critics call "management mentality" in both students and teachers, and that such dependence "deskills" teachers (they become ineffective) and curtails creative instruction.[56]

Advantages

The merit of the workbook is that it performs the practice and drill function well and is helpful with young students who need to learn a knowledge base and with low-achieving students who need extra concrete activities to understand abstract learning and repeated exercises to integrate new learning. To the extent that the workbook is used in one of these instructional contexts, and that the exercises make learning more meaningful to students, it has value.

The criteria for judging that the workbook has merit include the following: (1) exercises (or problems) are related to abstract or new learning, (2) exercises are interesting and maintain students' interest, (3) exercises exist in proper quantity—not too much or too few, (4) students understand the directions (young students and low-achieving students often don't understand written directions), (5) students can perform or answer the majority of the exercises (if they cannot, frustration will mount and most students will no longer persist),

---

[55] Richard L. Allington and Anne McGill-Franzen, "School Response to Reading Failure," *Elementary School Journal*, May 1989, pp. 529–542; Ruth Gardner and Patricia A. Alexander, "Metacognition: Answered and Unanswered Questions," *Educational Psychologist*, Spring 1989, pp. 143–158.

[56] Winograd and Paris, "A Cognitive and Motivational Agenda for Reading Instruction"; Alan Woodward, "Over-Programmed Materials: Taking the Teacher Out of Teaching," *American Educator*, Spring 1986, pp. 26–31.

(6) teacher provide needed direction and guided practice to help students learn the necessary skills and strategies for workbook comprehension or performance (the sheer ability to do something does not guarantee performance), and (7) teachers use the exercises discriminately (they supplement other instructional methods and materials).[57]

Workbooks are desirable for many students, but especially important for students for whom learning to read is difficult. It is for these children that workbooks should be geared. Workbooks have good points and bad points, and whatever bad points exist should be attended to, especially by those who write them and use them. For workbooks to be effective, Jean Osborne insists that they focus on a sequenced review of what has been taught, on the most important content, and on content that needs to be reinforced. Workbooks can provide students with (1) a means of practicing details of what has been taught, (2) extra practice for students who need it, (3) intermittent reviews of what has been taught, (4) ways for students to apply new learning with examples, (5) practice in following directions, (6) practice in a variety of formats that they will experience when they take tests, and (7) opportunity for students to work independently and at their own pace.[58]

Guidelines for Using Workbooks

In choosing, working with, or evaluating workbook materials, certain guidelines should be kept in mind. Below are a number of questions that should help make teachers aware if the workbook materials are appropriate for their specific teaching and learning situation.

1. *Objectives.* Do the workbook material meet the goals of the school? Which ones? Do the workbook materials meet the program objectives? Course objectives? Unit or lesson plan objectives?
2. *Readability.* What evidence is there that the workbook exercises coincide with the reading level of the students? Do the students understand the written directions? Wording of the exercises or problems?
3. *Utility.* What evidence is there that the workbook materials are helpful for the students? What evidence is there that students are interested in the exercises?

---

[57] Patricia M. Cunningham, "What Would Make Workbooks Worthwhile?" in Anderson, Osborn, and Tierney, eds., *Learning to Read in American Schools*, pp. 113–120; Gail M. Inlow, *Maturity in High School Teaching*, 2nd ed. (Englewood Cliffs, N.J.: Prentice-Hall, 1970); and Bonnie J. Meyer, "Text Dimensions and Cognitive Processing," in H. Mandl, N. L. Stein, and T. Trabasso, eds., *Learning and Comprehension of Text* (Hillsdale, N.J.: Erlbaum, 1984), pp. 3–52.

[58] Osborn, "The Purpose, Uses, and Contents of Workbooks."

4. *Cognition.* Do the workbook exercises supplement or reinforce abstract thinking? Are the exercises intellectually stimulating? Are sample exercises or problems worked out, step-by-step?

5. *Content coverage.* Do the exercises cover the content in depth? Do they have balance in terms of scope and sequence of the content?

6. *Audio-visuals.* Is the workbook material user friendly? Are there a variety of appropriate illustrations—charts, tables, pictures, drawings, etc.—to facilitate learning?

7. *Learning theory.* Do the workbook exercises coincide (or conflict) with current learning theory? Which theory? In what ways do the exercises stimulate learning? In what ways are individual differences provided for?

8. *Pedagogical aids.* Is the workbook used as a separate text or used in conjunction with another text? Does the workbook have a teacher edition or instructor's manual to provide assistance? Is the assistance valuable?

9. *Physical characteristics.* Is the workbook of quality material and binding? Is the workbook competitively priced? Can it be used more than once by students?

10. *Teacher training.* Are teachers trained in using the workbook (most need the training)? Does the training make any difference in how teachers use the workbook? How students integrate the material?

JOURNALS, MAGAZINES, AND NEWSPAPERS

These are primary sources and are therefore excellent materials for enhancing thinking skills and research skills of students. Journals are the publications of professional and academic associations and as such are more technical than magazines and newspapers. The most popular magazines used by teachers are *Time, Newsweek,* and *U.S. News and World Report,* although there are many others that can supplement or be the focal point of learning. (If you want to teach young students how to read, *Mad Magazine* will stimulate many of them.)[59] It is appropriate to start students with the local newspaper at the middle grade and junior high school level, but the teacher should also consider the *New York Times, Washington Post,* or *Wall Street Journal* at the high school level. These papers are written at the tenth to twelfth grade reading level; therefore, the reading abilities of the student must be seriously considered.

To enrich content, teachers in most subjects can encourage students to read journals, magazines, and newspapers. Many of these publications are in-

---

[59]Start children who are 9 or 10 years old on *Mad* and they will sharpen their reading and thinking skills—something to consider, although many educators object because they consider the views and material it contains questionable or even objectionable. Need a reason? The material is interesting to kids; content, stories, graphics, cartoons, etc., motivate and stimulate.

teresting and more informative and up-to-date than the text. Gathering suitable magazine and newspaper materials can be delegated to the class or it can be a decision made primarily by the teacher.

Journal and magazine articles have not been sanitized or toned down as textbooks have. The content expresses a point of view, and it can be used to enhance thinking and research skills. Newspapers, in theory (not always in practice), deal in reporting, not analyzing or interpreting, data. It is up to the student to draw conclusions about and evaluate what is being reported. Editorials, story columns, "op" columns, and letters to the editor are quite different, and students need to understand that the material is subjective. Although a youngster may understand that a particular point of view may be expressed in a journal, magazine, or newspaper article, he or she may be unable to identify distortions or biases and therefore accept the view as fact. In general, biases can be conveyed in eight ways: (1) through length, selection, and omission, (2) through placement, (3) by title, headline, or headings, (4) through pictures and captions, (5) through names and titles, (6) through statistics, (7) by reference source, and (8) by word selection and connotation.[60]

Although the teacher must use professional judgment in interpreting or assigning these instructional materials, students can learn to evaluate information contained in them by being trained to answer the following questions:

1. Is the account slanted?
2. Is important information treated accurately?
3. Are controversial topics discussed rationally?
4. Is there a clear distinction between fact and opinion?
5. Do the headlines, captions, and opening statements present the news accurately?
6. Are editorials and commentaries clearly designated?
7. Which groups or people usually read the publication?[61]

Guidelines for Using Journals, Magazines, and Newspapers

The following guidelines should assist teachers and students:

1. Be sure that journal, magazine, and newspaper articles are within the students' reading and comprehension range.

---

[60]Donald C. Olrich et al., *Teaching Strategies: A Guide to Better Instruction*, 2nd ed. (Lexington, Mass.: Heath, 1985); Orlich, *Staff Development: Enhancing Human Potential* (Needham Heights, Mass.: Allyn and Bacon, 1989).

[61]Association of Teachers of Social Studies in the City of New York, *A Handbook for the Teaching of Social Studies*, 4th ed. (Boston: Allyn and Bacon, 1977), p. 127.

2. Select those materials that are readily available and affordable.
3. The journal, magazine, or newspaper articles should be compatible with your teaching goals, given the fact that these materials often express a particular view.
4. Train students in reading and evaluating these materials. Children and adolescents tend to believe that whatever is printed must be true. A useful project is a comparative analysis of articles that take different views on a controversial subject.
5. Train students in the use of card catalogs, periodical catalogs, and the classification and retrieval systems of journals and magazines so they can use these materials in independent study and research.
6. Many students, especially at the secondary school and college level, clip excerpts from journals and magazines (also books) or cut out entire articles found in the library. As a teacher you must make the work of the librarian easier by discouraging this habit before students go to the library.
7. Journal, magazine, and newspaper articles are excellent sources for student reports. Encourage students to take notes, summarize main ideas, and interpret ideas in these instructional materials.
8. These instructional materials are also excellent sources for thinking about ideas, selecting and using information for assignments, and identifying and solving problems independently or in a group. High-achieving students can work independently; low-achieving students will more likely need the security of the group and the assistance of the teacher.
9. Assist students in doing research reports by providing a list of journals and magazines that are relevant to the topic and can be understood by the student.
10. Keep a file of pertinent journal, magazine, and newspaper articles to supplement the text and incorporate into the unit or lesson plan. Update the file on a frequent basis.

SIMULATIONS AND GAMES

Play is pleasurable and natural for children and adolescents, and simulations and games are formalized expressions of play. They provide a wide range of social and cognitive experiences. **Simulations** are abstractions of the real world, involving objects, processes, or situations. **Games** are activities with goals, rules, and rewards. *Simulated games* involve situations with goals, rules, and rewards.[62]

---

[62]Joel M. Levine, *Secondary Instruction: A Manual for Classroom Teaching* (Needham, Mass.: Allyn and Bacon, 1989); Elizabeth G. Cohen, *Designing Groupwork: Strategies for the Heterogeneous Classroom* (New York: Teachers College Press, Columbia University, 1986).

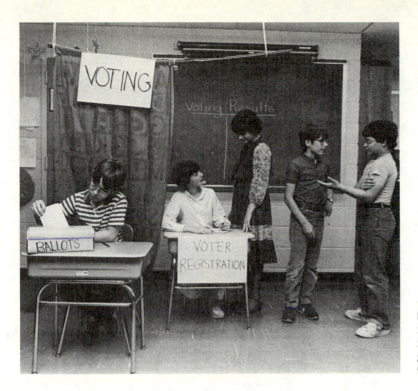

Figure 7.3 Students involved in simulations and role playing is commonplace in progressive schools. (Photo © Gale Zucker/Stock, Boston)

Simulations have become increasingly popular among educators, after much success in military, business, medical, and public administrative arenas. Many simulations are now produced commercially for teachers, especially for use in conjunction with computers and VCRs. However, teacher-made simulations (not for computer and VCR use) are more often used in the classroom, since they can be geared for specific students, subjects, or grade levels. Several "how-to-do-it" publications have been produced by teacher associations for would-be developers of simulations and games.

A simulation of a school board meeting for students permits them to explore local community issues. A simulation in health science may permit students to gain insights into the need for diagnosing medical problems or the need for empathy and care of loved ones who are ill. The dynamics of business, politics, and warfare can also be simulated. For example, in a simulation of a political situation, playing the role of president, a congressman, or a Supreme Court justice is an excellent way for students to learn about the nature of government and how the branches of government work. (If students have little or no experience in role playing, they should be briefed on the nature of role playing before the simulation starts.)

One educator reports <u>four advantages of simulations.</u>

1. A simulation is [an excellent motivating device].
2. A successful simulation demands the use of many study skills and techniques. . . . A practical relationship is forged between study and fun.
3. A full-dress simulation is a powerful way to make many . . . topics . . . come alive.
4. A successful simulation is very rewarding to the teacher. [He or she] takes a back seat to let things develop [and watches] students live, talk, and enter into [active learning].[63]

In short, simulations permit students to experience the nearest thing to reality.

Games are more informal and cover a wide range of situations, while simulations reflect a real-life situation and are more structured.[64] Games have been an important instructional tool in the kindergarten and elementary school dating back to early nineteenth-century educational pioneers such as Froebel and Pestolozzi and later, to the play wing of the Progressive movement.

Almost any teacher guide, for almost all grade levels and subjects, will list several games for enriching learning. Educational games have social and cognitive purposes and are not designed solely to amuse, but any game may contribute to learning. For example, Monopoly is a game played for amusement, yet it has some value for young children in learning to count and deal with monetary value. Checkers and chess, besides being amusing, challenge the mind; they involve math, logic, and sequencing of moves.

For younger students the value of the game may lie in the game itself, in the experience it gives them in learning to discriminate sounds or objects, to manipulate and gain facility in motor skills, or to play together and socialize.[65] For older students, the value may lie more in the post-game discussion, or what some educators call the "debriefing session." (Simulations can also incorporate post-activity discussions or debriefing sessions.) By proper questioning, the teacher brings out instances of questionable behavior, when the rules were ignored, and the reasons for such behavior. Life situations can be perceived as a series of games, where there are winners and losers, where there is cooperation and competition, and where rules are broken and enforced. In this connection, games are excellent means for teaching morality and ethics, value clarification, and affective education.

---

[63]Edmund Sutro, "Full-Dress Simulations: A Total Learning Experience," *Social Education*, October 1985, p. 634.

[64]Helen Darrow, *Independent Activities for Creative Learning*, 2nd ed. (New York: Teachers College Press, Columbia University, 1986); Cathy S. Greenblat, *Designing Games and Simulations* (Newbury Park, Calif.: Sage, 1987).

[65]David H. Russell, Elizabeth F. Russell, and Dorothy G. Hennings, *Listening Aids Through the Grades*, rev. ed. (New York: Teachers College Press, Columbia University, 1979); Lillian Stephens, *Developing Thinking Skills Through Real-Life Activities* (Boston: Allyn and Bacon, 1988).

Guidelines for Using Simulations and Games

Numerous simulations and games are commercially produced, but teachers must judge whether they are suitable for their students, whether they need or can be modified, or whether the teachers need to develop their own materials. Here are some guidelines to follow when incorporating simulations and games.

1. Every simulation and game must have an educational objective. Distinguish between amusement games and educational games, between game objectives and instructional objectives.
2. The purpose of using simulations is to enable students to understand the nature of a problem and how to solve the problem.
3. Games should be used for teaching thinking and socialization to children in the lower grades.
4. Simulations and games should be viewed as an experience for learning content. Students learn by organizing and familiarizing themselves with the content—by experiencing as much as possible the object, process, or situation.
5. Simulations and games must be related to the content (skills, concepts, values) you wish to teach; this content should correspond with reality, and the relationship between the real world and the simulation or game should be clarified to the participants.
6. Only variables, instances, or problems that are significant should be introduced as part of the simulation. Insignificant elements confuse and obscure.
7. In simulations and games, roles played by students must be clearly defined (for example, "If you were president in 1982, how would you respond to the first Iranian hostage crisis?").
8. When hindsight is being used to solve a simulated problem or to make a decision, the variables or background existing in the real-life situation should be introduced.
9. Have some students act out the simulation and other students observe. Have the students discuss the simulation.
10. Simulation and game rules must be concise and clear. Teachers must be able to answer questions from the class about hypothetical situations before a game begins.
11. Simulation and game rules should be understood with relative ease by the students (players) involved.
12. The post-game (or post-simulation) discussion is crucial for older students to clarify skills, concepts, and values to be learned.
13. The post-game (or post-simulation) discussion should incorporate case studies, draw on student experiences, apply what was observed to real-life situations, and lead to suggestions for further study.
14. The post-game (or post-simulation) discussion should not be terminated because of lack of time (rather continue the next day).

15. A class or homework writing exercise can be incorporated into the post-game (or post-simulation) discussion.

16. Employ a series of questions that require students to discuss their thoughts during the activity: What thoughts governed their behavior? What experiences resulted in certain behavior? What strategies did they use to make decisions to achieve their goals? Which strategies were most effective? Could they predict the behavior of others?

17. In most simulations and games students will interact. Participants and observers should discuss the interaction, if they are old enough, in terms of cooperation and competition, rational and emotional behavior.

18. To determine whether your objectives have been achieved by the simulations or games, use some form of evaluation, feedback, or discussion.

THEORY INTO PRACTICE

For each subject and grade level, basic instructional materials are needed to implement successful teaching and learning. Teachers, both beginning and experienced, should become familiar with the curriculum bulletins and guides for their subject and grade level. Such bulletins list necessary, recommended, and supplementary materials. They should be familiar with the materials available in their school by discussing them with experienced colleagues or supervisors. Teachers must also find out how to construct supplementary materials.

The following questions provide a guide for effective use of instructional materials.

1. What instructional materials do you plan to use?

2. What do you hope to achieve by using these materials? Do they correspond with your objectives?

3. How will you prepare students for the instructional materials?

4. How will you incorporate the instructional materials into the lesson?

5. Is the content of the materials suitable for your students? Consider sequence, scope, vocabulary, and so on.

6. Are the materials user-friendly?

7. Are there a variety of materials to coincide with various topics of the lesson?

8. How will you follow up the presentation of the materials? Are your follow-up activities appropriate?

9. Can you justify the cost and time spent in preparing and using these materials?

10. How do students react to the materials? Why do they react this way?

11. To what extent were the materials effective for this lesson? Ineffective?

12. How can you improve the use of the instructional materials for the next lesson?

SUMMARY

1. Good teachers become better teachers when they use appropriate materials in their lessons. Learning what materials to use, and how to use them, comes with experience.

2. Instructional materials may be printed (available from professional, governmental, and commercial sources) or duplicated (teacher-made or copied from printed material).

3. Materials should be selected in terms of well-defined and agreed-upon criteria, such as whether they coincide with the teacher's objectives, are well organized and designed, and are suited to the reading level of the students.

4. In presenting materials, teachers need to consider student understanding, structure, sequence, balance, explanation, pace, and elaboration strategies.

5. Types of instructional materials included textbooks and workbooks; journals, magazines, and newspapers; and simulations and games. Textbooks and workbooks tend to dominate as the major instructional material in most classrooms.

6. Important aspects of selecting textbooks deal with stereotyping, readability, textbook and pedagogical aids, and aids to student comprehension.

7. The differences between textbook aids, designed to facilitate student comprehension, and pedagogical aids, designed to facilitate the teacher's instruction, were noted. A host of examples of each type aid was discussed.

8. Several strategies for incorporating simulations and games into the daily lesson were examined.

QUESTIONS TO CONSIDER

1. What is the main purpose of using instructional materials?

2. How would you determine if a textbook presents a stereotypical picture of an ethnic or religious group, sex, labor group, or any other minority?

3. Which textbook aids are most important? Why?

4. What are important factors to consider when supplementing the textbook with the workbook?

5. Is there a danger in using too many materials in a class? Explain.

THINGS TO DO

1. Discuss in class ten questions to consider in evaluating instructional materials. Which questions or concepts are the most important? Why?

2. List five steps in developing your own materials.

3. In class prepare a checklist for evaluating textbooks.

4. Discuss which textbook aids you like in a textbook. Why?

5. Give five suggestions for using the following materials: (a) workbooks, (b) journals and magazines, and (c) simulations and games.

RECOMMENDED READINGS

Anderson, Richard C., Jean Osborn, and Robert J. Tierney, eds., *Learning to Read in American Schools*. Hillsdale, N.J.: Erlbaum, 1984. An important discussion about using textbooks and workbooks, as well as how to improve reading and learning skills of students.

Apple, Michael. *Teachers and Texts*. New York: Routledge & Kegan Paul, 1986. Analysis of the politics of textbook selection and the social and cultural implications of the content regarding class, race, and gender.

Armstrong, David C. *Developing and Documenting the Curriculum*. Needham Heights, Mass.: Allyn and Bacon, 1989. Several chapters on organizing and developing materials.

Debelak, Marianne, Judith Herr, and Martha Jacobson. *Creating Innovative Classroom Materials*. New York: Harcourt Brace Jovanovich, 1981. A collection of 150 teacher-made materials that relate to students' developmental needs.

Greenblat, Cathy S. *Designing Games and Simulations: An Illustrated Handbook*. Newbury, Calif.: Sage, 1987. A systematic guide for teachers who wish to design games and simulations.

Morlan, John E., and Leonard J. Espinoza. *Preparation of Inexpensive Teaching Materials*, 3rd ed. Belmont, Calif.: Fearon, 1988. Several ways for planning, preparing, using, and evaluating materials.

Russell, David, Etta Karp, and Anne M. Mueser. *Reading Aids Through the Grades*, rev. ed. New York: Teachers College Press, Columbia University, 1981. A classic text describing hundreds of activities and situations for teaching reading, divided into reading readiness, beginning reading, and advanced reading.

KEY TERMS

Instructional aids	Comprehendability
Verbal symbolism	Textbook aids
Printed materials	Pedogogical aids
Duplicated materials	Default strategies
Copyright law	Advance organizers
Vertical relationships	Scaffold instruction
Horizontal relationships	Text structure
Reading formulas	Simulations
	Games

Chapter
8

Instructional Technology

FOCUSING QUESTIONS

1. What technological advance do you consider most valuable in improving your instruction?

2. What problems are beginning teachers likely to have in using instructional technology?

3. For what purposes might films, filmstrips, and slides be used?

4. When is it best to use an overhead projector?

5. Why is television an important source of information? How can teachers best use television for improving instruction?

6. How do you expect to incorporate computers in the classroom?

7. What telecommunication systems might be useful in your teaching field?

8. What educational value, if any, do video games have?

*T*his chapter is an extension of the previous one and deals mainly with audiovisual aids and electronic media. Technology is conceived as instructional when, through specialized materials and equipment, it supplements the conventional process of instruction. The special materials and equipment make it possible for learners to experience stimuli that might otherwise be impossible or impractical to bring to the classroom or school. Places, objects, and events can be seen and heard in the classroom.

Just what technology you use will depend on your knowledge, the teaching assignment, the capability of the equipment, and its availability. Effective use does require some basic guidelines. Turning on a movie projector or computer is not quite as simple as opening a book, but important steps in their use are not unlike the steps recommended for all other instructional materials.

In using instructional technology, four steps are recommended:

1. *Prepare* the students for what they are going to see, hear, or do. This may entail a brief explanation.
2. *Arrange* conditions to show special materials under the best possible conditions so they do not interrupt the momentum of the lesson. This includes making necessary adjustments, such as changing a seat for a student in the rear who has trouble seeing the screen.
3. *Operate* the equipment efficiently. Either you or an assistant will probably be responsible for this task.
4. *Summarize* the experience or follow it up with a discussion.[1]

Charles Schuller lists four slightly different steps for using instructional technology in the classroom:

1. *Define your objectives.* Clearly defined objectives are essential starting points for selecting and effectively using learning resources of any kind.
2. *Know the content.* Knowledge of the content of film, software, or other material is essential in determining whether you will use it and how to use it to the best advantage.
3. *Guide learners on what to look for.* One of the "musts" in using media effectively is to focus learners' attention on specific things to attend while viewing, listening, or reacting to assigned materials.
4. *Evaluate the results.* To know whether the material and equipment have been used effectively, some kind of evaluation is necessary. Did the particular lesson accomplish your objectives? If not, why not? And what can be done to remedy the situation?[2]

---

[1] Allan C. Ornstein, Harriet Talmage, and Ann Juhaus, *The Paraprofessional's Handbook* (Belmont, Calif.: Fearon, 1975).

[2] Charles F. Schuller, "Using Instructional Resources and Technology," in D. E. Orlosky, ed., *Introduction to Education* (Columbus, Ohio: Merrill, 1982), pp. 400–429.

Professional Viewpoint

Some Quandaries in Instructional Technology

Since the transistor (1947) and the single unit microchip (1959) made their debuts they have had an enormous and rapidly increasing impact on education. On the whole, electronic gear has created a *milestone* in the history of our schools—but the era of the "information society" could become something of a *millstone* around our necks unless we use instructional technology with a measure of wisdom.

Let us review a few of the major quandaries that are besetting us as we approach a new millennium. For one thing, young learners must be protected from the habit of letting a computer *per se* rather than their minds find answers!

Another problem resides in the way teachers use electronic tools in the learning milieu. We must also avoid acquiring a "frozen curriculum" dictated by the equipment used. A particular challenge resides in utilizing suitable learning tools for pupils' varied needs in diverse schools.

Space limitations preclude the review of many other problems, but at least two more should be mentioned. One of these is the composite use of electronic gear by young people for pranks, vandalism, and fraud. This must be discouraged.

Second, there is great, and generally unrecognized, danger in the electromagnetic pulse (EMP) phenomenon. The EMP, while harmless to humans, carries an energy surge which can cause electronic damage. We must not become too dependent on microelectronic support systems when an EMP blast, caused by a nuclear explosion or fire could render much of our equipment inoperative over most of the Continental United States. Patently our schools must not be so dependent on computers and robots that an EMP blast would render them virtually impotent.

The points above are a *very* small sampling of the quandaries of which educators must be aware as we endeavor to move forward effective teaching strategies in the years before the class of 2002 is graduated!

Harold G. Shane
Emeritus Professor of Education
Indiana University-Bloomington

A wide variety of technological instructional aids are available in most schools. We will discuss the materials you are most likely to encounter and some promising new ones. You may need to seek on-the-job instruction for use of the specific equipment at your school.

CHALKBOARD AND DISPLAY BOARD

Chalkboards and display boards certainly do not represent any advanced technology, but they are definitely visual aids. The **chalkboard** is perhaps the oldest and most traditional piece of equipment found in the classroom. Next to the textbook, it is the most widely used instructional aid. According to two eduucators, the chalkboard "is so omnipresent that many of us fail to think of it as an audiovisual aid at all; yet most teachers would be hard put if they had no chalkboards available."[3]

There is usually one chalkboard at the front of the classroom and sometimes others at the sides or back. In older schools most of the chalkboards are black (hence the name blackboard), but because black tends to absorb light and make the room gloomy, it is being replaced. Light green and yellow reduce glare and eye strain, absorb less light, are cheerful, and provide a good contrast with white and colored chalk.

The chalkboard is popular because it allows for spontaneity, speed, and change. The chalkboard can fit the tempo of any lesson in any subject. It can be used for displaying pictures and important clippings; drawing sketches and diagrams to help illustrate points of a lesson; projecting films and other materials; listing suggestions or items as they are offered; writing outlines, summaries, and assignments; and working out problems and evaluating procedures and answers. The chalkboard is particularly valuable for emphasizing the major points of a lesson and working out problems for the whole class to see.

Because of the its flexibility and familiarity, the chalkboard is sometimes overused. Many secondary school teachers rely too heavily on it to the exclusion of other audiovisual aids. Instead of making elaborate drawings on the chalkboard, teachers can show them with an overhead projector. Or instead of writing long lists of problems or notes on the board for the students to copy, the teacher can duplicate them and hand them out to the students. The time saved by these procedures can be devoted to other aspects of the lesson. The daily homework assignments can be duplicated on a weekly basis and handed out to the students, thus eliminating the need for the teacher to write them on the chalkboard and the need for the students to copy them down. This method also allows absent students to keep up with their assignments at home. This does not mean that the chalkboard should not be used, but that it should not be used when other procedures that are available might work more efficiently.

---

[3]Leonard H. Clark and Irving S. Starr, *Secondary and Middle School Teaching Methods*, 5th ed. (New York: Macmillan, 1986), p. 403.

Display boards are used for displaying student projects and progress; displaying current items of interest related to a lesson or unit; posting announcements, memos, and routine assignments; and decorating the room. There are many types: bulletin board, pegboard, flannel board, magnetic board. The boards stimulate student creativity and interest, promote student participation in the learning activity, and make the room more cheerful and student-oriented. If there are no display boards in a room, a portion of the chalkboard can be reserved for this purpose. Especially in the elementary grades, the display board is important enough that this would be a good use of some chalkboard space.

Guidelines for Using the Chalkboard

1. Write legibly and large enough for all to see. If your handwriting is cursive and you have trouble making it legible on the board, then print. All words should be printed until students have switched from manuscript to cursive writing.
2. Use the chalkboard as if you were writing on paper. Proceed from left to right. If crevices divide the chalkboard, treat them as margins—that is, end lines on the right side and start new lines on the left side. Try not to go beyond the margin for the sake of inserting one or two words.
3. While writing, stand to one side of the board as much as possible so you can maintain eye contact with the students.
4. When referring to work already on the chalkboard, stand to the side so you don't block the students' view. Use a pointer (a ruler or yardstick will do).
5. Don't talk toward the chalkboard while writing on it.
6. If the chalkboard space is limited, draw a line down the middle of the board, thus creating a margin and two smaller boards. This will allow you to use the space more efficiently.
7. Organize your chalkboard work ahead of time. When possible, outline items with a letter or numbering system. There are many possible systems, but use one form for purposes of consistency.
8. Don't clutter the board. Limit your writing or drawing to major ideas of the lesson.
9. If you must abbreviate, use standard forms. Don't use unusual or personal abbreviations. Check the dictionary if you are unsure.
10. Utilize colored chalk, rulers, string, stencils, and other materials to make your illustrations more effective.
11. Don't get embarrassed or show resentment if you make a mistake and a student corrects you. Instead, thank the student for the help.

12. If you are working with young or low-achieving students, write in complete sentences. They need practice in seeing and writing correct grammar.

13. Establish routine uses for the chalkboard. Have specific spaces for homework assignments, drill problems, or the instructional objective.

14. Erase the chalkboards completely after you finish, and keep them clean. If you are busy, ask a student to erase them while you continue with another part of the lesson.

15. Don't overuse the chalkboard. You can ditto or mimeograph lengthy or complicated materials.

FILMS, FILMSTRIPS, AND FILMSLIDES

According to one educator, **film** is the most influential and seductive educational medium for transmitting ideas and persuading an audience to a point of view.[4] Because of the vivid, often larger-than-life images it presents, the motion picture has a dramatic impact on its audience. Films both interest and motivate students. Thousands of good films have been made expressly for educational purposes. They can be divided into the following categories: (1) historical, (2) dramatic, (3) special topic, (4) "slice of life," and (5) animated.[5] The movie is particularly useful for showing processes in which motion is involved or in which slow motion can be used.

The **filmstrip** is a series of pictures in a fixed sequence on a strip of 35 mm film for still projection. Filmstrips are compact, easy to store, relatively inexpensive to buy, easy to project, and somewhat flexible in use because pictures thought to be unnecessary can be skipped over. Explanatory symbols or captions are often incorporated, and filmstrips with recorded sound narrations, called *sound filmstrips*, are being produced.

Filmslides are individual pieces of film for projection, mounted on thin cardboard or plastic frames, usually 2-inch squares. They are more flexible to use than filmstrips, since unnecessary slides can be omitted. Slide sets are sometimes accompanied by audiotape narrations. Slides may be changed manually or automatically with a device that advances the slides at preset time intervals.

The speed of showing both filmstrips and filmslides is adjustable. Each frame or slide can be discussed and the time allowed for discussion can vary; thus the teacher can set and change the pace of instruction. A film, on the other hand, is presented in a fixed, continuous sequence and the speed is also fixed (unless the images are such that the projector or video equipment can

---

[4]Hart Wagner, *Teaching with Film* (Bloomington, Ind.: Phi Delta Kappa Foundation, 1977).

[5]David F. Naylor and Richard Diem, *Elementary and Middle School Social Studies* (New York: Random House, 1987).

be slowed down or the projection can be stopped). Because students are forced to think at the speed and in the sequence determined by the film, it tends to create a passive rather than an active mind set. Since filmstrips and slides can be viewed on either a small or a large screen, they are suited to individual and small-group instruction as well as whole-class instruction.[6]

Several hundred commercial companies produce films, filmstrips, and filmslides for educational purposes. Catalogs listing producers, titles, rental or purchase rates, and ordering instructions are often circulated by school districts to local schools. Most films are rented on a daily or weekly basis, and most filmstrips and slides are bought. Some school systems maintain a film library. Films are also available on free loan or for a nominal fee from university and public libraries and various political, social, and cultural groups. Enterprising students can take their own 8 mm films and 35 mm photographs for slides on field trips, in the classroom, or after school.

Guidelines for Using Films, Filmstrips, and Filmslides

1. Keep the film lists up to date.
2. When ordering from sources outside the school, be sure to order well in advance of the screening date.
3. Preview the film to make sure it is appropriate to the students' interests and maturity level and to familiarize yourself with the content.
4. Arrange to have the projector and screen or video equipment in the classroom and set up on the day scheduled for showing the film. Be sure to arrange for someone to run the projector if you do not know how. Check to see that the projector is operating properly before class starts.
5. Be sure all students can see the screen. The room should be dark enough to produce a quality picture. Good acoustics are also important. Sometimes a special room or the auditorium can be scheduled for showing a movie.
6. Prepare the students for the presentation. A list of major points or questions to answer, or a guide to the lesson is often helpful. Hand it out to the class before the showing.
7. Note-taking is difficult in a darkened room and should not be expected or encouraged while the projector is running.
8. Use the equipment properly. Turn off the projector when it is not in use. Handle film with care. Touch it only along the margins so you don't smudge it with fingerprints.

---

[6]Schuller, ''Using Instructional Resources and Technology.''

9. View a film without interruption, if possible. Save questions and comments for a summary discussion. Show filmstrips and filmslides frame by frame at a reasonable pace. Skip over or omit unnecessary ones.

10. If commentary is needed during the movie, either stop the projector or reduce the volume, but do this as little as possible. Allow time for discussion after the movie.

11. When showing filmstrips with written captions, call on volunteers to read them or summarize detailed captions. (Do not call on non-volunteers, because it may be embarrassing for them if the captions are difficult to read.)

12. Allow time for discussion after the film.

13. Be sure to put the film back properly into its container.

14. Disconnect all wires. Store equipment in appropriate place at the end of the lesson or day.

Overhead Projector

The **overhead projector** projects images of transparencies on a screen, wall, or chalkboard. The transparency is placed on the glass on top of the projector. Light from the lamp located in the projector produces an image that is reflected onto a viewing surface in back of the operator. The teacher can face the class while using it. Since the room does not need to be dark, students can take notes. The machine is lightweight and portable. Because the overhead projector is so convenient to use, it has become standard equipment in many classrooms and has replaced the chalkboard and opaque projector in many of their functions.[7]

Commercially prepared transparencies for the overhead projector are available for several subject areas. These materials can also be prepared by the teacher. The transparencies can be prepared before the class (which is best if materials are long or complex), or they can be made during a discussion and also changed as necessary to elaborate on a point. The teacher can point out various details on the projected image with a grease pencil while still facing the students.

Handmade transparencies are usually made of plastic and drawn with a felt pen or grease pencil. To prevent smudging, start coloring in the center of the transparency and work toward the edges. Typed materials can be added with the use of a thermofax machine.

New overhead projectors have an extra feature or attachment to add motion and speed to special transparencies so that various moving elements can be shown.

---

[7] Kenneth Henson, *Teaching Methods for Secondary and Middle Schools* (New York: Longman, 1987); Naylor and Diem, *Elementary and Middle School Social Studies.*

Guidelines for Using Overhead Projectors

1. Keep the materials up to date.
2. Arrange ahead of time to have the projector and other necessary materials available when you need them. Arrange to have someone in the room who knows how to operate the projector if you do not know how.
3. Preview the materials or prepare them before class begins.
4. Handle overhead transparencies with care; don't smudge them, get fingerprints on them, or let the colors from the grease pens run together before drying.
5. Label materials properly for filing and reshowing.
6. Be sure the materials are appropriate for the students' interests and maturity level and that they fulfill your instructional objective.
7. Be sure all students can see the surface on which the material is projected. Focus the materials properly.
8. Arrange the materials in sequence with the lesson.
9. Explain and discuss each of the projected materials.
10. Shut off the machine when it is not in use during discussions.

TELEVISION

Recent evidence makes it clear that television has become "a second school system." Children under 5 years old watch television an average of 24 hours a week, or about one-fifth of their waking hours. By the time a child graduates from high school, he or she will have spent 15,000 to 20,000 hours in front of the screen as compared to 11,000 to 12,000 hours in school.[8] Before children reach 18, they will have seen 350,000 commercials "urging them to want, want, want."[9]

Rather than viewing television as a second school system, Neil Postman views it and other mass media (radio, comic books, movies) as the "first curriculum" because they appear to be affecting the way children develop learning skills and acquire knowledge and understanding.[10] According to Postman and others, television's curriculum is designed largely to maintain interest; the

---

[8]Aimee Dorr, *Television and Children* (Newbury Park, Calif.: Sage, 1986); John I. Goodlad, *A Place Called School* (New York: McGraw-Hill, 1984); and Kathy A. Kreudl, Kathryn Lasky, and Robert Dawson, "How Television Affects Adolescents," *Educational Horizons*, Spring 1989, pp. 88–91.

[9]Evelyn Kaye, *The Family Guide to Children's Television* (New York: Pantheon, 1974), p. 7. Also see Stuart Oskamp, *Television as a Social Issue* (Newbury Park, Calif.: Sage, 1987).

[10]Neil Postman, *Teaching as a Conserving Activity* (New York: Delacorte, 1979).

Figure 8.1 Good teaching involves the use of different kinds of audio-visual aids. (Photo © Richard Wood 1986/Picture Cube)

school's curriculum is supposed to have other purposes, such as mastery of thinking skills. In addition, watching television requires little effort and few skills; children do not have to think about or solve problems.[11] Rather, they become accustomed to rapidly changing stimuli, quick answers, and "escapist" fantasies, not to mention overdoses of violent and sexual behaviors on the screen. See Tips for Teachers 8.1. In this connection, the Parent Teacher Association (PTA), consisting of more than 6.2 million members, has lobbied for years (and with some success) to curtail violent and sexual scenes on television, especially during prime time (7 to 10 PM).[12]

The research suggests that selected programs for preschool and primary grade children such as "Sesame Street" and "Electric Company" are associated with improved cooperative behavior and cognitive skills. However, most of the data suggest that for upper elementary and secondary school students, watching television more than 5 hours a day is associated with lowered achievement in reading and mathematics.[13] Because of television's impact on acculturation and socialization of children and youth and its influence on all of society, educators cannot ignore this medium. They must find ways to reverse the trend toward lower achievement resulting from too much time spent watching badly produced commercial television, and they must find ways to incorporate the medium into the school curriculum.

Two types of television programming can be employed in schools. **Educational television** refers to programs produced for broadcast on commercial

---

[11] Neal J. Gordon, "Television and Learning," in H. J. Walberg, ed., *Educational Environment and Effects* (Berkeley, Calif.: McCutchan, 1979), pp. 57–65; Robert Hornik, "Out of School Television and Schooling: Hypotheses and Methods," *Review of Educational Research,* Summer 1981, pp. 193–214.

[12] Nancy L. Cecil, "Help Children Become More Critical TV Watchers," *PTA Today,* April 1988, pp. 12–14; Joan M. Bergstran, "Help Your Child Find Great Alternatives to Television," *PTA Today,* April 1988, pp. 15–17.

[13] Hersholt C. Waxman and Herbert J. Walberg, "Teaching and Productivity," *Education and Urban Society,* February 1986, pp. 211–220.

Tips for Teachers 8.1

The Television Test: How Addicted Are You?

Television is a powerful medium; it lures, distracts, and mesmerizes. It can make students unresourceful, lazy, and overly dependent for entertainment. It can and often does interfere with school work. Students need to think about the number of hours they spend watching television. Here is a test designed to make students aware of their viewing habits. (You may also wish to take the test!)

1. Figure out the average number of hours you watch TV each day. Write that number here: _____

2. Would you rather watch TV than spend time with your family? Yes [ ] No [ ]

3. If a program you liked was on TV but a friend called for you to go outside and play, would you stay home and watch TV alone [ ] or go out and play [ ]?

4. When you spend time with friends, do you always [ ], sometimes [ ], or never [ ] watch TV?

5. Do you automatically turn on the TV set when you get home? Yes [ ] No [ ]

6. Do you automatically turn on the TV set when you have nothing to do? Yes [ ] No [ ]

7. Do you watch anything that's on [ ] or only the programs you have chosen to watch ahead of time [ ]?

8. Would you rather give up your father/mother/best friend or your TV set for a month? Dad/Mom/Friend [ ] TV [ ]

9. Do you spend more time watching TV than you do on other things you enjoy (like sports or hobbies)? Yes [ ] No [ ]

10. When you have the TV on, do you always [ ], sometimes [ ], never [ ] do other things?

11. School's cancelled for the rest of the day. What would you do? Read [ ] Play with friends [ ] Go to the movies [ ] Go to a park [ ] Enjoy a sport [ ] Work on a hobby [ ] Spend time with your family [ ] Watch TV [ ]

12. Could you live without television? Yes [ ] No [ ]

What's the score?

1. If you filled in: 0–1 hours, score 2; 1–2, 5; 2–3, 10; 3–4, 15; 4–6, 20; 6–7, 25; 7 +, 30. score: _____

2. Score 10 if you check yes, 0 for no. score: _____

3. Score 10 for staying in, 0 for going out. score: _____

continued

4. Score 10 for always, 5 for sometimes, 0 for never. score: _____

5. Score 10 for yes, 0 for no. score: _____

6. Score 10 for yes, 0 for no. score: _____

7. Score 20 for watching anything, score 5 for planning ahead. score: _____

8. Score 25 for Dad/Mom/Friend, 0 for TV score: _____

9. Score 15 for yes, 0 for no. score: _____

10. Score 5 for always, 10 for sometimes, 15 for never. score: _____

11. Score 15 for TV, 0 for anything else. score: _____

12. Score 0 for yes, 25 for no. score: _____

Add up your score and write the TOTAL here: _____ If you scored between **2 and 10,** you have little trouble managing your TV viewing time. You are not addicted to the tube and do not let it interfere with your life. You probably choose your programs carefully and don't sit through whatever happens to be on. If you scored between **10 and 30,** you might be OK. It depends on where you scored: If all 30 points went to the number of hours you watch TV, or if you traded Dad, Mom, or best friend for your TV set, you might be missing out a lot on life (not to mention being in trouble with your folks). If you scored between **30 and 75,** you're a borderline addict, and may not have your viewing under control. If you scored **over 75**, you might want to take a closer look at the way TV uses your time. It may not matter to you what you are watching as long as you *are* watching, which is exactly what broadcasters want you to do. If you got the top score **(185),** there may be poltergeists in your TV set. But it isn't too late: You can exorcise them by thinking more carefully about what you are watching, why you are watching, and what you are missing.

Source: Don Kaplan, *Children and Media* (New York: Instructors Books, 1986).

or public television stations that are intended to inform and develop understanding. Students watch these programs at home. **Instructional television** refers to programs produced by schools to teach specific skills and subject matter and for viewing in school. Many commercial and public television stations produce programs that fit educational goals and objectives. In particular, public television, which is broadcasted in many large cities, has real educational worth that has not been fully utilized by teachers. Many school systems rely on local television stations to provide most of the programming. Some large or innovative school systems and universities produce their own programs and have their own stations. Master teachers teach large numbers of classes simultaneously by means of television.

In order to guide students in selecting programs, some schools and districts form a committee consisting of teachers and administrators to obtain listing information in advance and to recommend programs. If there is no such committee, individual teachers can do the same job. The weekly schedule is published in local newspapers and magazines, and the three major networks (ABC, CBS, NBC) will supply outlines, suggestions, and schedules for several weeks in advance.

Recent developments in program recording and replaying suggest imaginative uses for television. For example, programs can be recorded on videotape so that they may be played back to the class immediately for further discussion, played back later at a more convenient time, or saved to show to another group the following year. Transcripts of programs are kept in stock in network libraries for loan or rental, making it possible to view a program at any suitable time so long as the school has playback capabilities.

Television has the potential for adding to students' knowledge. Students can learn about current events and scientific advances, be exposed to dramatic and musical performances, become better acquainted with leading figures in the worlds of the arts, science, politics, and business. When used properly, this instructional aid can stimulate discussion and further study of the topic. It can bring the specialist and the expert teacher to class in front of hundreds of students at once, or thousands of students over time if taped and played again. Schools that cannot offer specialized subject matter can use television as a means of providing instruction through prerecorded programs.

Guidelines for Using Television

1. Select programs to coincide with the learners' level of interest and maturity and with instructional objectives. Consider the educational significance, quality, content, writing, and production.
2. Make sure the classroom or media center is suitable for viewing the program. Check the lights and shades, acoustic arrangements, seating facilities, and placement of the television.
3. The classroom television set should have at least a 21-inch screen. It should be placed so that all students can see it well. It should not be less than 5 feet or more than 30 feet away from any student. It should be placed slightly above the height of the heads of seated students, or about 5 to 7 feet from the floor.
4. Lights should be left on if students are to take notes. If they are not expected to take notes, the lights may be dimmed somewhat for improved viewing.
5. There should be no glare or reflected light on the screen. Keep the television away from windows and mirrors and change the location

of light fixtures as necessary. If the source of reflected light cannot be changed, either tilt the set downward or tape cardboard blinders to the set.

6. Before a program is viewed, give students any necessary background data and tell them what to expect. You may want to hand out question sheets that focus on major points. These are especially helpful if students are assigned to watch a program at home.

7. Avoid using the program as a lecturing device or a substitute for instruction. Integrate it into the lesson and discussion.

8. Keep questions and comments during the program to a minimum, or ask students to save them until the end of the program.

9. After the program, hold a discussion to analyze the main points.

10. The ideal program lasts no longer than two-thirds of the subject period so there is time for introduction and summary.

11. By using videotapes, programs can be fit into the daily class schedule. If a school system operates a network, it can play programs to fit class schedules.

12. When assigning programs for homework, make sure all students have access to a television set. Arrangements (such as a buddy system) should be made for those who do not.[14]

COMPUTERS

Computer technology for school purposes has been available since the 1950s, but it is in the last few years that computers have begun to have a major impact on classrooms and schools. Teachers are waking up to the fact that computers are here to stay and can be effective tools of instruction. In 1980 some 50,000 microcomputers were used in 15 percent of the nation's schools; by 1985 the numbers reached 500,000 in 92 percent of all public schools. It is expected that in 1990 there will be more than two million computers in use in nearly 99 percent of the schools.[15] It is envisioned that most high schools will soon be offering students an average of 30 minutes per day at a computer terminal. Many elementary schools and most middle grade and junior high schools already have students learning on computers once or twice a week. Some 50,000 or more teachers are expected to be teaching computer technology as their main subject between 1990 and 1995.[16] What actually happens will depend to

---

[14] Ornstein et al., *The Paraprofessional's Handbook.*

[15] Gary L. Donhardt, "Microcomputers in Education: Elements of a Computer-Based Curriculum," *Educational Technology,* April 1984, pp. 30–32; Arthur S. Melmed, "Information Technology for U.S. Schools," *Phi Delta Kappan,* January 1982, pp. 308–311; and *The Condition of Education 1987* (Washington, D.C.: U.S. Government Printing Office, 1987), Tables 258–259, p. 314.

[16] Donhardt, "Microcomputers in Education"; Peter Smith and Samuel Dunn, "Human and Quality Considerations in High Tech Education," *Educational Technology,* February 1987, pp. 35–39.

Figure 8.2 Computers have become powerful tools of instruction and will play an increasingly important role in the future of the students' education. (Photo © Spencer Grant/Picture Cube)

a large extent on the money available for the purchase of computers, the software available for student use, and the way computers are adopted into the curriculum.

In integrating computers into instructional methods, teachers should consider the following questions.

1. What are the objectives of using computers in schools?
2. Should they be restricted to students who have particular abilities? To particular grade levels? To particular subjects?
3. Should they be used to teach about computing and programming or to teach other subjects?
4. Should students be charged user fees for computers?
5. Who will train teachers in computer use?
6. Should the classroom be reorganized to have computers at every desk or should a computer center or laboratory be set up?[17]

---

[17] Allan C. Ornstein and Daniel U. Levine, *Introduction to the Foundations of Education*, 3rd ed. (Boston: Houghton Mifflin, 1985).

The Role of Computers

Decker Walker maintains that few people really know how to use computers well for educational purposes.[18] Seymour Papert, the inventor of Logo and author of *Mindstorm*, argues that the computer is a medium of expression and should be used to build a sense of inquiry, to "mess about," to explore, and to improve thinking skills.[19] He also argues that the main impact of computers on learning will not come about through teaching students practical applications such as data processing and filing; the real impact will only come when students are taught how to program, because programming requires that they think logically and solve problems. When they learn how to program, "the world is open for very wonderful things to happen."[20]

We are in the midst of an "information explosion," the generation and availability of an ever-increasing quantity of information through the use of the computer. People can participate in this explosion at three or four levels of **computer knowledge**: (1) *computer literacy*, general knowledge of what computers are used for and some general experience in using them; (2) *computer competency*, ability to use the computer as a tool for particular purposes; and (3) *computer expertise*, knowledge of how computers work and how to program them.[21] A new, fourth level is a *computer hacker*, who is more than an expert—he or she spends days and even nights working on games or problems, transmitting messages across the country or across oceans, devising ingenious games and software to sell, and/or swapping new software among fellow hackers. In general, the hacker is freewheeling and addictive to the computer ferment.

As educators, we should aim at making our students computer-literate at an early age and view computer literacy as "a fourth R" or a fundamental skill. Several questions arise, however. How computer-competent are teachers? Should every teacher be computer-competent? Should every teacher be at least computer-literate? Should we expect only a few teachers in each school to have the skills to teach students how to use the computer? Should only a few teachers have the skills to use the computer as an instructional aid?

A teacher can become computer-literate in a workshop that meets for a few practice sessions. The time spent in training is not critical to the teacher's ability to use the computer as an integral part of the teaching day; the key

---

[18]Decker F. Walker, "Reflections on the Educational Potential and Limitations of Microcomputers," *Phi Delta Kappan*, October 1983, pp. 103–107.

[19]Seymour Papert, "Computer Criticism vs. Technocentric Thinking," *Educational Researcher*, January/February 1987, pp. 22–30.

[20]Charlotte Cox, "An Interview with Seymour Papert," *Curriculum Review*, January–February 1987, pp. 14–18.

[21]Allan C. Ornstein, "Emerging Curriculum Trends: An Agenda for the Future," *National Association of Secondary School Principals*, February 1989, pp. 37–48; Judith A. Turner, "Ohio State Eyes Computer Literacy," *Chronical of Higher Education*, January 11, 1984, pp. 1, 14.

Professional Viewpoint

The Pencil Makes the Point

Since the late 1950s, computer-literate educators have been enthusiastically promoting the use of computer technology in education. Until recently, that advocacy has involved solutions to either nonexistent or noncompelling problems. However, the advent of the microcomputer and the national focus on growing educational issues could foster the linking of technology-related solutions to compelling problems. Among these challenges are growing illiteracy; the need for education reform and restructure; and the challenge of teaching in the information age.

Having made the connection between a possible solution and a recognizable problem has, however, in turn generated still another difficulty—implementing a computer-based solution. There are on the average approximately 30 students sharing each computer in the country's elementary and secondary schools. If those computers were pencils, one would hardly consider the "bi-functional" pencil a viable student writing instrument. The multi-functional computer with a student-to-computer ratio of 30:1 could certainly be predicted to be equally ineffective in producing a national impact.

With the total number of computers in the elementary/secondary schools being about two million and the aggregate teacher population numbering about two and one-half million, perhaps it would have been more rational first to address teacher needs as these relate to teaching in the information age.

Few would dispute that computers through networks provide access to information, to computing, and most certainly to people. But today, only one in five faculty actually uses computers in the teaching process. The remainder, either because of personal choice or the lack of access to computers, deny their students the benefits derived from information searches, interactive computing, and the elimination of teacher isolation through computer conferencing.

With pencils in the hands of virtually all students and teachers, the author of this text has chosen not to dedicate a segment to "pencil technology." I hope that practical thinking and logical implementation of computer technology will lead on similar terms to the demise of "pencil technology" as well.

Harvey S. Long, Ph.D.
Education Industry Consultant, IBM

factor is the attitude of the teacher. If the teacher is hesitant about using the computer, many children will pick up on this attitude. If the teacher is enthusiastic, children will learn more eagerly and more easily. According to one educator, a 15-hour workshop laboratory experience reduces teaching anxiety (fear of helplessness in dealing with computers) from above average to below average anxiety (3.04 to 1.75 out of 5) and increases interest in computers from (1.96 to 4.08).[22]

Computer Programming

Because so much software with programs in so many subject areas and grade levels is now available, it is not essential for teachers to know how to program. Furthermore, a mass of educational software is now available from many companies to allow teachers to construct their own lessons without knowing a computer language. But the ability to program is still a valuable skill to acquire. It gives teachers facility in using computers and makes it easier for them to plan lessons and individualize instruction.

Programming is an active mental endeavor, and it fosters critical thinking, rational thinking, and problem-solving skills. Programmers must break down complex problems into subproblems and then develop procedural instructors.[23] One research study found that programming is the only subject in the whole curriculum that succeeds in teaching students about things as a process, that writing and debugging a program forces the programmer to think logically and carefully about the subject.[24] An analysis of the program can also tell the user about the quality of the thinking that went into the solution. According to these results, students and teachers should be encouraged to learn how to program.

On the other hand, there is also research that suggests that there is no "convincing relationship between learning to program and learning to think."[25] Some studies suggest that computer programming "promises more than it has

---

[22] Ann D. Thompson, "Helping Preservice Teachers Learn Computers," *Journal of Teacher Education*, May–June 1985, pp. 52–54.

[23] Willis J. Horak and Edward B. Brown, "Using Computers to Develop Mathematical and Scientific Thinking Strategies," in Fifth Annual Microcomputers in Education Conference, *Tomorrow's Technology* (New York: Computer Science Press, 1984), pp. 163–167; Marcia C. Linn, "The Cognitive Consequences of Programming Instruction in Classrooms," *Educational Researcher*, May 1985, pp. 14–16, 25; and David Moursund, "Problem Solving: A Computer Educator's Perspective," *Computing Teacher*, February 1985, pp. 3–5.

[24] Arthur Luehrmann, "Adopting Microcomputers in Ways That Will and Won't Work," *Peabody Journal of Education*, Winter 1985, pp. 42–56; Luehrmann, "Why Teach Programming? Two Good Reasons," *Electronic Learning*, May–June 1985, pp. 14–18.

[25] Richard E. Mayer, "*Automaticity and Its Implications for Instructional Design*," paper presented at the annual meeting of the American Educational Research Association, San Francisco, April 1986.

delivered" and that there are "no intellectual benefits" or measurable thinking skills produced by teaching how to program.[26]

Advocates counter these criticisms by arguing that the amount and quality of computer instruction varies from study to study, that different students respond differently to different learning environments, and that student groups are often not controlled properly. They further argue that when students master programming, it becomes possible for teachers to teach in different ways, ways that indirectly foster achievement in children. The point is also made that it is what students do with programming that counts, and it is not important to test its direct effects.[27] An analogy to learning how to read is made; what is learned as a result of learning how to read is more important than just learning how to read.

According to researchers, Logo is the programming language commonly used for elementary school children because of its simplicity and engaging stimuli. BASIC tends to be used most by middle grade and high school students because the educational market is dominated by Apple, which uses BASIC as a standard feature with most of its computer models.[28] Pascal requires more stringent thinking and therefore is not used in most schools; it encourages students to organize their thinking into modulars or groups of directions rather than linear commands or long strings. COBOL and FORTRAN are even more complex; moreover, they are not yet available on microcomputers, which is the common equipment in schools. The newer languages are limited because there are few people qualified to teach them, and few teachers have learned them.[29] Table 8.1 summarizes the advantages and disadvantages of various program languages.

James Muller, the president of Young People's Logo Association, asserts that "youngsters are far more at home with computer technology than are the adults attempting to teach them computer literacy." Most teachers teach Logo and BASIC programming the same way they teach French, Spanish, English, and other subjects. They teach students "to memorize the commands, to practice them, to test their knowledge, . . . and then move on to more advanced

---

[26]David L. Lillie, Gary B. Stuck, and Wallace H. Hannum, *Computers and Effective Instruction* (New York: Longman, 1989); Richard E. Mayer, ed., *Teaching and Learning: Computer Programming* (Hillsdale, N.J.: Erlbaum, 1988).

[27]Jodi Bonner, "Computer Courseware: Frame Based on Intelligence," *Educational Technology,* March 1987, pp. 30–33; Cox, "An Interview with Seymour Papert"; and James E. Eisele, *Instructional Computing: What's New in Computing?" Educational Technology,* August 1985, pp. 24–26.

[28]Douglas Clements, "Logo Programming: Can it Change How Children Think?" *Electronic Learning,* January 1985, pp. 28, 74–75; Luehrmann, "Why Teach Programming?"

[29]Gary Bitter et al., "Pascal: The New Word on High School Computers," *Curriculum Review,* May–June 1986, pp. 27–30; Allan C. Ornstein, "Curriculum Computer Technology," *National Association of Secondary School Principals* (in print 1990).

Table 8.1   ADVANTAGES AND DISADVANTAGES OF SELECTED PROGRAM
LANGUAGES

Language	Advantages	Disadvantages
Pascal	Promotes logical thinking Familiarity with it makes it easier to learn other languages Designed to teach problem-solving concepts Widely used in both business and universities Designed to exploit advantages of other languages	Compiled rather than interpreted language Necessary to buy a Pascal package for each microcomputer
BASIC	Inexpensive Standard on most microcomputers Easy to learn Used by many students at home Probably learned in elementary school	Lengthy program necessary to solve complex problems Not considered a structured language Poor programming habits likely to develop
Logo	Suitable for elementary as well as older students Visually engaging	Limited in scope Not application-oriented
True BASIC, BASIC C, and others	General purpose languages Sophisticated data flow structures Rich set of operators Structured languages	Supported by only a few systems Not easy for beginners to learn
FORTRAN and COBOL	Good for business (COBOL) or scientific (FORTRAN) uses	Application specific Difficult for beginners to learn Not structured languages

Source: Adapted from Gary Bitter, "Pascal: The New Word on High School Computers," *Curriculum Review*, May-June 1986, p. 28.

procedures."[30] Many students have never learned Logo or BASIC per se, but rather use them "as merely another learning tool to accomplish their goal." In an age of computer technology, programming isn't something you just learn; it is something you learn with. You don't teach programming by rote proce-

---

[30]James H. Muller, "Learning Must Be More Than Computer Literacy," *National Association of Secondary School Principals*, April 1986, p. 37.

dures; rather you teach the children to think, observe, analyze, plan, hypothesize, and test strategies.

Computer Software

Instructional software offerings have gradually improved in quality and variety and are available for all subject areas and grade levels. No longer do they cover only isolated topics or provide practice in one or two skills; current software presents whole units and courses of instruction.[31]

However, there is still a good deal of criticism about the quality of the software. Recent studies reported that only 5 percent of software are rated "exemplary," and less than 25 percent met minimum state standards in California.[32] A Canadian research team was able to recommend only one out of ten software products previewed for use in the province of Alberta.[33] Another group concluded that only 5 percent of the software it studied was exemplary in terms of content, 5 percent in terms of instructional presentation, 12 percent in terms of documentation, and 9 percent in terms of technical adequacy. Although fewer programs were classified as "deficient" in these four areas compared to earlier studies, the percentages still ranged from 9 to 29 percent. About a third of the programs were classified as "acceptable" or "desirable" in terms of content, instruction, documentation, and technical adequacy.[34] The most common explanation for the poor ratings in these studies has been that most software is written either by persons with expertise in computers but not in education or by persons with expertise in educational theory but not in computers.

Probably the most frequent criticism of software is the predominance of drill and tutorial programs. This is changing now, as more simulations and **interactive systems** are being introduced. Whereas the early software consisted of sequenced questions with specific answers, the new software permits a variety of student responses with branching to appropriate levels of instruction based on the student's response. If students fail to master a task or concept, the new drill and tutorial software breaks down the concept using analogies, examples, and suggestions rather than presenting a sequenced repetition of the subject matter.[35] Not only do graphics and sound enhance the overall appeal

---

[31] Pamela McCorduck and Avery Russell, "Computers in Schools," *Principal*, November 1986, pp. 16–21; Sherry Trimble, "Is Second Generation Software Any Better?" *National Association of Secondary School Principals*, April 1986, pp. 32–35.

[32] "Software for Schools," *Technological Horizons in Education Journal*, February 1989, pp. 15–16; "What's in the Educational Software Pool?" *Microgram*, March 1985, pp. 1–4.

[33] *Computer Courseware Evaluations* (Edmonton, Alberta: Alberta Education Province, 1985).

[34] Curt Dudley-Marling and Ronald D. Owston, "The State of Educational Software: A Criterion Based Evaluation," *Educational Technology*, March 1987, pp. 25–29.

[35] Bonner, "Computer Courseware: Frame-Based on Intelligence"; Stellan Ohlsson, "Computer Simulation and its Impact on Educational Practice," *Educational Research*, 1, 1988, pp. 5–34.

of the software, but the new simulations also permit students to experience something closer to real-life situations. Students can conduct experiments; experience past events, current happenings, or future possibilities; and consider "what if" problems through simulations. Through interactive participation the new programs can promote logical thinking, hypothesizing, and problem-solving strategies, since the learner gets immediate feedback and the opportunity to analyze and pursue responses. Computerized simulations should soon interact in several ways with the learner, including tutoring systems, cognitive diagnosis, problem-solving tasks, experimental tasks, and predictive reasoning.

There is a small but growing number of technically sound programs that integrate high-level thinking skills through pattern-recognition, problem-solving, decision making, and game-playing skills. Some educators refer to this software as "mindware." Examples are *Ace Detective* by Mindplay, *Balance of Power* by Mindscape, *Design Your Own Train* by Abracadata, *Pipeline* by Learning Technologies, and *Science Toolkit* by Broderbund.[36]

In selecting, evaluating, or purchasing software, teachers need to consider in general how well the program sustains student interest and, most important, how well students receive and process information. More specifically, teachers need to focus on (1) how well the software appeals to both the eyes and the mind and how well visual and textual data are integrated; (2) how well the software helps students select and organize concepts and analyze and evaluate relationships; and (3) how well the software promotes subjective, divergent, and creative thinking.[37] Of almost equal importance is whether the software makes the best use of hardware capabilities, how free the system is of errors, and to what extent the instructional program content coincides with the teacher's instructional objectives. See Tips for Teachers 8.2.

Guidelines for Using Computers and Computer Software

1. A company that produces, distributes, or sells computers or computer materials should be willing to provide a number of services: (a) installation assistance as part of the purchase, not as an add-on cost; (b) user training as part of the computer purchase (the more complicated the computer hardware or software, the more important the user training); (c) a toll-free or local number to call for answers to questions and solutions to problems; and (d) updates to the software for little or no extra charge.

---

[36]David Harte, "Purchasing Mindware," *Media and Methods*, March–April 1988, p. 22; Howard N. Sloane et al., *Evaluating Educational Software: A Guide for Teachers* (Englewood Cliffs, N.J.: Prentice-Hall, 1989).

[37]Harte, "Purchasing Mindware."

Tips for Teachers 8.2

Evaluating Computer Software

Future teachers will be expected to know not only something about how to use computers in the classroom, but also how to evaluate software. Several characteristics contribute to quality and usability. In many ways, the evaluation of computer software is like the evaluation of any other instructional material, whether it is a textbook, film, or television program.

1. *Content.* The program should be current and accurate. There should be no spelling or grammatical errors. Terminology and subject matter should be compatible with student achievement level, students' learning experiences, and course objectives.
2. *Educational quality.* The presentation of material should be compatible with what we know about learning. The material should be well sequenced, it should build on prior learning, feedback should be provided promptly, and there should be time for review.
3. *Directions.* Clear, concise, and well-organized directions about use should be given within the program itself or as a supplement. The directions must match the skills and developmental levels of the students.
4. *User interaction.* Students should be able to control the pace of the program. The program should encourage students to answer or respond to the questions or problems. The best programs are user-friendly, that is, easy to use, helpful, and stimulating.
5. *Data flexibility.* The computer's ability to handle data quickly and easily makes it possible for software to include *branching.* In branching the answer to one question determines what material will come next. It is valuable for promoting individualized learning.
6. *Graphics and sound.* Graphics and sound should be designed to highlight data, elaborate on explanations, and emphasize causal relationships. It should be possible to turn off the sound, if the users want to do so.
7. *Tracking and monitoring.* Parts of the program (or another program) should record scores and indicate problems or types of answers the students handle well or poorly. Access to this data should have security provisions, such as a secret password, to protect confidential information.
8. *Evaluation.* Does the program fit the curriculum? Is it compatible with available computer equipment in the school? Is it mistake-free? Is it easy to use? How does it deal with incorrect student responses? Does it promote student interaction? Is it too short or

continued

too long? What is the cost? How does it compare to other software packages?

Source: Adapted from Carol A. Doll, "Software Purchasing Strategies," *Media and Methods*, March–April 1988, pp. 19–23.

2. The use of the computer in the classroom should correspond with the school's goals.

3. If only one computer is available for class use, you will have to devise large-group instruction or divide the class into smaller groups that take turns at the computer. You will need several computers to permit several students to work on the program at the same time.

4. A group of teachers or curriculum specialists should preview software before it is purchased by the school. Individual teachers should preview material before using it in class.

5. Decide on what you want to do with the computer. Do you want to use it for practice and drill, problem solving, tutorial activities, simulations, games?

6. Establish criteria for use based on the objectives of your subject and the abilities and needs of your students.

7. The software should be suitable for your instructional grouping (individual, small group, or large group).

8. The software should be easy to use. The screen format should be clear. The instructions should be easy to follow. The software should have a complete menu (index or contents) for quick reference, a help section, and illustrations of input screen and output formats.

9. The software should be sound in terms of instructional and learning theory. It should motivate students more than conventional methods because of its cost. It should be designed to foster students' critical thinking, problem-solving strategies, and creativity. It should be accurate, up to date, and clearly organized.

10. The software should be capable of being integrated with other software and with traditional materials into a comprehensive curriculum and instructional package.

11. You should know what supporting materials are available that can interface with your computer hardware and software.

12. You should know how to use both floppy and hard disks. Hard disks hold more data and access it more rapidly; however, floppy discs cost less and have sufficient storage capacity for educational exercises.

13. Software should provide user feedback on the display about what part of the process is taking place and whether it is proceeding normally. The user should be able to correct simple problems.

14. Periodically, review and evaluate the software for quality and variety on a team basis. Be prepared to recommend supplementary course materials.[38]

TELECOMMUNICATION SYSTEMS

Telecommunication refers to information exchange between two or more locations connected by electronic media, including television, radio, and telephone. Several hundred educational organizations (mostly large universities and state agencies and a few school systems) lease or own their own telecommunication system. About 50 percent own their system, 45 percent lease, and 5 percent operate a combined leased-owned system. Owned systems operate through television or radio broadcast systems; leased or leased-owned systems operate through telephone wires.[39]

Satellite Dishes

Schools now can select television programs specifically developed for educational purposes and have the programs beamed into the classroom by satellite. Schools can subscribe to various program series, for example, 24 one-hour, commercial-free programs on how to improve writing or reading. The major producer of television programs for classroom use via satellite is the Agency for Instructional Television, a nonprofit American-Canadian organization. Regularly scheduled commercial satellite service can include educational programs for the home, but this will happen only if educators call for it and use it when available.

Teleconferences

It is possible for people in different locations, even across state and national boundaries, to communicate and interact through television connections. Such conferences are widely used in business, government, and to a lesser extent, universities. Teleconferencing is just appearing in a few school systems, as an experiment, on the secondary level. Groups of students can meet with teachers and other resource people through the television screen. The participants can watch, listen, interrupt, ask questions, make decisions, as if they were across the table. It is a wonderful way for students to speak to an expert or com-

---

[38] Chase W. Crawford, "Administrative Uses of Microcomputers, Part III: Evaluation and Selection," *National Association of Secondary School Principals*, May 1985; Ornstein, "Curriculum Computer Technology."

[39] Jerold Grubel, W. Neal Robinson, and Susan Rutledge, "Interstate Educational Telecommunication Systems: A National Survey," *Educational Technology*, April 1981, pp. 33–36; Dietrich Meutsch, "Information Transfer by Television," paper presented at the annual meeting of the American Educational Research Association, New Orleans, April 1988.

municate with their peers almost anywhere in the world. It is also an excellent way for small, rural schools to have students meet with other teachers, especially if the schools lack specialized personnel (for example, a physics teacher).

Teletext Systems

Teletext systems are one-way systems in which information is sent to receivers through television broadcast. Receivers view what is sent, but there is no interaction and no sound transmission. Teletext information systems permit the viewer to receive news headlines, government reports, and various kinds of primary data. Such systems are currently used in business, medicine, research, and government.

Educators will need to design teletext systems that can be used to advantage by students. For example, large information-based industries, such as publishing and newspaper companies or libraries and universities, might compile current information from various sources (books, reports, journals, newspapers) in electronic "bins."[40] By pressing the appropriate button, a user of the data bin from anywhere around the country could have selected information delivered electronically.

Telewriting

Telewriting operates through telephone lines. The visual is sent over a telephone line, and the audio is sent in conjunction through another telephone line. The telewriting device is sometimes called an electronic chalkboard, although an overhead projector is used to enlarge the visual images for viewers.[41] The fact that an oral presentation can accompany and explain the visual presentation makes the system more appealing for teachers. As with teletext, however, there is no two-way communication between sender and receiver; the device is useful for older students to receive information, but it does have limitations as an instructional tool since it does not permit two-way communication.

Telepicturephones

The Telepicturephone is an offshoot of the telewriting system. It allows a person to send images from one monitor to another over the telephone lines. By focusing a camera on a person or document and pressing a button, the sender can transmit a picture to another unit in 8 to 30 seconds. An ordinary phone is plugged into a machine similar to a television set with an attached camera; two-way voice communication through that phone is temporarily

---

[40]"An Electronic McGraw-Hill," *Newsweek*, December 10, 1984, p. 69; Marjorie Ferguson, *New Communication Technologies and the Public Interest* (Newbury, Calif.: Sage, 1986).

[41]Kirk and Gustafson, *Instructional Technology*.

interrupted when the picture is sent. Pictures can be stored for recall later, but prints of the pictures cannot be made.[42] For purposes of learning, older students (at least at the middle or junior high school level) can use this two-way audio and one-way video phone as a supplement to the typical classroom instruction both in school and at home.

As an offshoot of this picturephone system, it is possible for two distant schools (or colleges) to install a microwave transmission system that links the two points within a 200-mile range. The audio hookup is made with the telephone line and the visual is delivered through the television. This long-distance learning is achieved without being charged long-distance rates.

Telecourses

A few large universities are beginning to produce telecourse materials for local and national use. For an investment of $75,000 to $150,000, an institution can put into operation a studio with sufficient equipment, subject experts, and telecommunication personnel to produce and market materials that can be used in the home as long as the user has a VCR and a television set. To recover costs, the university must produce several telecourses, use them for several years, and/or market them to other institutions.[43]

Local school districts have the opportunity to work with a local or regional university to develop telecourse materials. At the secondary level the materials can be used at home by students, since older students can work independently. At the elementary level they are better used in whole-group instruction in the school so teachers can provide necessary monitoring and feedback.

Charges for the telecourses vary, depending on whether the material has already been produced (and only needs to be modified) or has to be produced from the start. Charges might be as low as $500 to $5,000 to a school district for a set of tapes and the right to use them for a given period. Another method of payment might be on a per-student basis, almost like a user fee. See Tips for Teachers 8.3.

Guidelines for Using Telecommunications

Although there are many different telecommunication systems, some general guidelines apply to all of them.

---

[42] "Compact, Affordable Picture Phones May Revive Once-Heralded Technology," *Wall Street Journal*, November 16, 1985, p. 23.

[43] John W. McCutcheon and James Swartz, "Planning for Cablecast Telecourses," *Technological Horizons in Education*, September 1987, pp. 98–100.

Tips for Teachers 8.3

Evaluating Telecourses

There may be telecourses available that suit your lesson, unit, or course objectives. Some telecourses require a great deal of teacher feedback and others very little. Start compiling a list of telematerials that coincide with your subject and grade level. Evaluation criteria should include the following.

1. Is the telecourse designed for a lesson, unit, or course?
2. Is the telecourse available for review?
3. Is the content presented in a varied and interesting format that takes full advantage of television's visual potential?
4. Does the telecourse include support materials such as transparencies, handouts, or test banks?
5. Can the telecourse be used in conjunction with the text being used or with existing classroom materials?
6. Is the content accurate and current?
7. What is the cost to purchase or use the material?
8. Will the producer permit making multiple copies of the telematerials?
9. What do other adopters say about the effectiveness of the telematerials?
10. Have the materials been pretested?

Source: Adapted from John W. McCutcheon and James Swartz, "Planning for Cablecast Telecourses," *Technological Horizons in Education,* September 1987, p. 99.

1. Decide just what you want the system to do. Decide on objectives and the instructional use of the system (practice, tutoring, demonstrations, explanations, problem solving).
2. Consider use of the system in relation to the abilities, needs, and interests of your students.
3. Find out what systems are available and how they work.
4. If programs are already available, preview them. Find out what supporting materials and equipment are necessary, suitable, and available.
5. Be sure that the system is easy to use and that the instructions are easy to follow for students and for you.

6. Be sure the system is manageable—that is, that not only will you know how to use it, but also you will be able to to supervise students at the same time they use it.
7. Find out what services and support the supplier will provide.
8. Consider both the cost and the reputation of the company who will install and repair the equipment.

VIDEOSYSTEMS

Video technology has made available another valuable tool for instruction. There are several different **videosystems** that make it possible for various audiovisual experiences to be produced, stored, and retrieved as needed. They permit the teacher and student to produce and create their own materials and to use audiovisual systems in numerous ways and in a variety of learning situations.

Teachers must plan how to integrate the new video technology into the curriculum. They also need to "train children to become critical video consumers who are literate in 'reading' images."[44] On their own or through in-service training, teachers should investigate new methods to heighten awareness of how visual images affect us as individuals and as a society and how students can enhance their esthetic and thinking skills related to our television and video-dominated culture.[45] In 1985 the number of videos rented from video stores surpassed the total number of books checked out of libraries.[46] The hope is that students will start checking out video documentations—not only video movies and games—with gentle encouragement from teachers.

Videotapes

Videotapes have many applications for instruction. They can demonstrate, explain, record, and replay data. They can be used in classrooms, libraries, resource centers, and homes.

Recent advances have made video recording and playback equipment lightweight, portable, and relatively inexpensive. The teacher and students can record various events and play back the recording in class through a VCR system attached to a television. Interviews, community meetings, special events, and students' projects can be recorded. Students can produce videos based on their own stories or research.

---

[44]Dennis M. Adams and Mary Hamm, "Teaching Students Critical Viewing Skills," *Curriculum Review*, January–February 1987, pp. 29–30.

[45]Dennis M. Adams and Mary Hamm, *Electronic Learning: A Practical Guide to Activities, Issues, and Trends in Educational Technology* (Springfield, Il.: Thomas, 1988).

[46]Dennis M. Adams and Mary Hamm, "Changing Gateways to Knowledge: New Media Symbol Systems," *Tech Trends*, January 1988, pp. 2–23.

Figure 8.3 Videos can be used for instructions in libraries, resource centers, homes, and classrooms. (Photo © Donald Dietz/Stock, Boston)

Some large school districts now produce their own videos through recording departments and also distribute them to surrounding school systems. Students never have to miss a lesson, since the video can be stored and played back at a convenient time.

Videocassettes

Videocassettes are even easier than tapes to collect, store, and reuse as needed because they are extremely lightweight and small. Considering the low cost of equipment needed to record and play back the cassette, its potential is enormous.

There are also now many catalogs that list hundreds of commercially produced videos on educational subjects. There are even video "magalogs" (hybrids of magazines and catalogs) that are available at newsstands and libraries. Public libraries today rent or lend videocassettes, and school libraries are beginning to develop a sizable collection of titles.

In theory, one might argue that now there is little reason for students to come to class to listen to a teacher. All they have to do is ask the school or college to send them a videocassette, or check the library shelves, or go to the media store. The point is, however, that these products should not be marketed as teacher substitutes, but as electronic tools to empower teachers to facilitate teaching and to empower students to facilitate learning.

Videodisks

Most videos are recorded on tapes or cassettes. Recordings are also made on videodisks, which resemble long-playing records, but have a larger storage capacity and are not subject to damage while in use. Videodisks, usually made of metal, contain digitized information that is read by laser beams. The picture resolution and tuning is finer than that of magnetic tape, and the quality doesn't deteriorate with time. The disadvantages of videodisks are that they are more expensive, they can be made only by professionals, and they cannot be erased or edited.

Videodisks are coming to the classroom, despite the cost. Among the most interesting ones are (1) the *Knowledge Disc*, a disk-based encyclopedia with 32,000 entries and 9 million words (the equivalent of a 20-volume encyclopedia) on a single disk; (2) *Bioscience*, with 6,000 still images of animals and plants that can be used with daily biology and general science lesson plans; and (3) *History Disquiz*, containing 45 important newsreel film clips and several thousand "trivia" questions about them.[47]

Interactive videodisks, to be used in conjunction with a computer, are being made. Realistic situations, simulations, and action-reaction situations can be presented as part of a training or learning program. Interactive vidoes have enormous teaching-learning potential—permitting students to receive and respond to a video program, to react accordingly, and to obtain information aboout the probable outcomes of their behavior (if the situation had been real). The program can tell the viewer he or she is wrong or right, present the viewer with options, and show the outcome of these options. The program can be used for individual instruction or small group instruction. See Tips for Teachers 8.4.

Videoprinters

The videoprinter attaches to the television and produces a postcard-size color print of almost anything you can see on the screen almost instantly. This includes not only regular broadcast television, but also teletext, videotape, videodisk, or anything transmitted through television. Pictures can be made at the rate of one a minute of such things as maps, weather forecast data for detailed study, or snapshots from student-made videotapes. Whatever material needs to be further explained can be printed and stored for future use.

Video Games

Video games are interactive; a microcomputer is programmed to respond to a player's move with a move of its own. All serious video game players play for mastery, but most video games are sufficiently difficult that novice players (including most students) are lucky if they can play more than two or three minutes on the first few tries.[48] Although this billion-dollar-a-year game in-

---

[47] Royal Van Horn, "Isn't It About Time for Videodiscs to Come to School?" *PTA Today*, April 1988, pp. 22–25.

[48] Nancy R. Needham, "Thirty Billion Quarters Can't Be Wrong—Or Can They?" *Today's Education*, Annual 1982–1983, pp. 53–55.

Tips for Teachers 8.4

Using Videos in the Classroom

Fueled by the same consumer demand influencing the computer revolution, schools are integrating the VCR into the curriculum as a major choice in educational technology. The VCR has emerged as an instructional aid so rapidly that most authorities have been caught off guard with little discussion in the textbook literature. As a teacher, you need to consider the powerful role that videos will play in your classroom. Consider these tips as basic for integrating videos into your instructional practices.

I. *Preview* the video you are considering.

II. *Ask* yourself the following questions about the video:
1. Is it interesting?
2. Is the technical quality good?
3. Does it have appropriate content?
4. Can I, as teacher, use this video effectively?
5. Does it generate student activities or discussion?

III. *Select* the parts that fit your objectives. The VCR permits easy and effective editing of what is to be shown so that you can use only the parts you need.

IV. *Plan* how the video will be used in the actual lesson or class activity:
1. to introduce new materials.
2. to review prior learning.
3. to support ideas or concepts.
4. to enrich the viewer's world.
5. to explore feelings of subjects and viewers.
6. to clarify special points.
7. to reinforce key concepts.

V. *Prepare* the students. Tell them
1. what to expect, how to assess what they see.
2. what you expect them to get out of the activity.
3. what to watch for or what to take down in the notes.
4. what you will do after the viewing of the video.

VI. *Stop* and *explain* if necessary. Ask questions, make comments, or emphasize points of special importance. (Fast forward through parts that are not useful in the lesson.)

VII. *Follow up* by summarizing the video, reminding students of the planned expectations, and generating discussion with questions and comments.

continued

VIII. *Evaluate* the video to determine if you want to use it again.
1. Do you need to modify or edit it?
2. Do you need better equipment?
3. What better follow-up activities can you use next time?

Source: Adapted from David G. Guelette, "A Better Way to Use Television in Our Classroom," *Tech Trends*, January 1988, pp. 28–29.

dustry has been criticized, mainly because the sound and light displays provide an escapist reaction, some observers believe the effects can be positive. (Although not games, music videos are another problem, due to the proliferation of sex and violence found in them, and very few educators support their use.[49]) Practice in eye-hand coordination and manual dexterity are obvious benefits. Also, educational material in video game format could be a pedagogical device—livening up practice and drill, teaching reading, writing, and other learning skills, and solving math and science problems.

Guidelines for Using Videosystems

1. Be sure the use of videosystems is compatible with and leads to attainment of course objectives.
2. Preview the most promising systems and programs. Evaluate the video, just as you analyze textbook content. Is the video content educational, accurate, presented clearly, free from bias?
3. Find out what services and support the supplier of equipment and materials will provide.
4. Find out what supporting equipment and materials are needed and available.
5. Monitor student responses in interactive programs for purposes of diagnosis and evaluation.
6. Observe the students and try to notice emotional response and development of decision-making ability.
7. Be clear on the place for learning—classroom, library, resource center, home, etc. Be sure the video accomplishes your instructional purpose: practice and drill, tutoring, simulation, problem solving.

---

[49]Jennifer Norwood, "Music Videos—Have They Gone Too Far?" *PTA Today*, April 1988, pp. 26–28.

8. Be sure the video is suitable for the instructional grouping pattern (individualized, small group, whole group) you plan to use.

THEORY INTO PRACTICE

As educators, we must note that electronic media are increasingly supplementing, even replacing, traditional printed material in school and flooding our homes. Understanding and applying the processes and symbol systems of these new devices is essential for students and teachers alike if they are to learn from and have control over this new electronic technology.

The potential for learning is immense. The new electronic devices promote individualized learning and react flexibly to student responses. Correct answers can be acknowledged promptly; incorrect responses can be handled by giving the student a second chance, easier questions or problems, or a review of the program, or by showing them correct answers. A student's response to a question can determine what will be presented next. The new tools also allow teachers the time to analyze the thinking process of students, to free them from just reacting in terms of right or wrong.

As computers take their place in the classroom, as television and videos become more interactive, and as teledevices provide instant information, students have more tools for thinking and learning, and teachers have broadened abilities to invigorate their teaching and instructional processes. The new technology gives students more control over their learning and teachers more knowledge and options to guide the process of teaching.

In order to use these technologies effectively in the classroom, it is worthwhile to remember some general guidelines for operation. The guidelines below review the points we have made in regard to all the equipment and special media discussed in this chapter.

1. Familiarize yourself with the special materials and equipment available in the classroom or center you are assigned to.
2. Find out what special materials and equipment are available elsewhere in the school and what check-out procedures apply to their use.
3. Learn how to operate the equipment you plan to use.
4. Preview special materials and evaluate their suitability for the lesson you have in mind.
5. Order the special materials, allowing enough time for delivery by the scheduled date.
6. Review the materials again, if you have time, before using them.
7. Prepare a standby set of plans in case the equipment breaks down or something else goes wrong.
8. Set up the equipment before class begins.
9. Avoid using too many different types of materials in one class period.
10. Return the equipment to the proper storage place when you are finished with it. Report all defective equipment and materials.

SUMMARY

1. Basic guidelines related to using instructional technology include (a) selecting equipment suitable to objectives, (b) learning how to operate the equipment, and (c) previewing the materials.

2. Visual images increase effectiveness of presentation of materials. Visual images can be incorporated into a presentation through the use of chalkboards and display boards; films, filmstrips, and filmslides; and overhead projectors.

3. Two types of television programming for use in schools are educational television (informative programs produced by commercial and public television stations) and instructional television (programs produced by educators for specific teaching purposes).

4. Teachers and students can participate in these levels of computer use: computer literacy, computer competency, and computer expertise. All students should be at least computer-literate.

5. The quality and variety of computer software has improved in recent years. The most challenging and interesting uses of computer-based instruction are in the growing number of simulations and interactive systems.

6. Various telecommunication systems include satellite dishes, teleconferences, teletext systems, telewriting, telepicturephones, and telecourses.

7. Videosystems include videotapes, videocassettes, videodisks, and video printers. The use of video games for educational purposes is controversial, but they can be used to liven up instruction.

QUESTIONS TO CONSIDER

1. Do you agree that the chalkboard is still a valuable instructional aid? Explain.

2. What are five suggestions for using overhead projectors?

3. Some educators feel computers will revolutionize education. Do you agree? Explain.

4. What are three important factors to consider in choosing appropriate videosystems?

5. How can teachers encourage students to change their television and video viewing habits from movies to documentaries, from entertainment to education?

THINGS TO DO

1. Select one of the instructional aids discussed in this chapter. Do an oral report on its advantages and disadvantages.

2. Project a filmstrip or filmslide on a screen or light-colored curtain. Determine the minimum size of projector that all students in the room can see.

3. Write on a transparency with a variety of appropriate pencils and in a variety of sizes. Project the transparency to determine the best size, color, and type of markers for good visibility.

4. Invite an expert on computers to discuss with the class how to use them in instruction and how to teach computer literacy.

5. Check nearby colleges or local cable operators to find what telecourses are available in your local community.

RECOMMENDED READINGS

Cuban, Larry. *Teachers and Teaching: The Classroom Use of Technology Since 1920.* New York: Teachers College Press, Columbia University, 1986. A compact book on the history of education technology—and why for many years teachers have not accepted machines in the classroom.

Kinzer, Charles, Robert D. Sherwood, and John D. Bransford. *Computer Strategies for Education.* Columbus, Ohio: Merrill, 1986. General information about microcomputers and computer languages for educational purposes.

Mayer, Richard E., ed. *Teaching and Learning: Computer Programming.* Hillsdale, N.J.: Erlbaum, 1988. A collection of works describing how to teach students to use computers productively and what effect computer programming has on students.

Nickerson, Raymond S., and Philip P. Zodhiates, eds. *Technology and Education in the Year 2020.* Hillsdale, N.J.: Erlbaum, 1988. An analysis of how technology may influence elementary and secondary education in the future.

Oskamp, Stuart. *Television as a Social Issue.* Newbury Park, Calif.: Sage, 1987. Social issues relating to television viewing—violence, stereotyping of women and minorities, sex, and the potential of quality or prosocial programs.

Skinner, B. F. *The Technology of Teaching.* New York: Appleton-Century-Crofts, 1968. A classic text on the art of teaching and the science of learning involving various technological tools of the first half of the twentieth century.

Sloane, Howard N., et al. *Evaluating Educational Software: A Guide for Teachers.* Englewood Cliffs, N.J.: Prentice-Hall, 1989. How to find and evaluate well-designed, instructionally sound, and technically reliable software for classroom use.

KEY TERMS

Chalkboard	Instructional television
Display board	Computer knowledge
Film	Computer programming
Filmstrip	Interactive systems
Filmslide	Telecommunication systems
Overhead projector	Videosystems
Educational television	

Chapter
9

Grouping for Instruction

FOCUSING QUESTIONS

1. When is it appropriate to use whole-group, small-group, and individual instruction?

2. What are the advantages and disadvantages of large-group instruction?

3. On what basis may students be organized into small groups?

4. What procedures should teachers follow in organizing small groups for instruction?

5. What methods can be used to provide individualized instruction?

6. What methods are recommended for using adaptive instruction? mastery instruction?

7. How can computers be used for individualized instruction?

8. How can teachers enhance the study skills of students, particularly in the areas of homework, studying, and note taking?

*T*he most common means of organizing students for instruction is to group 25 to 30 students according to age and grade level, and sometimes ability, and assign them to a specific classroom and teacher. When most instruction occurs in this setting, it is called a **self-contained classroom.** At the elementary school level a teacher is assigned to the class for the whole day. Students may travel as a class to another class one or two periods a day to receive special instruction (for example, in remedial reading, music, or physical education), or other teachers may visit the class to provide special instruction.

At the secondary level the self-contained classroom is modified by what is commonly called **departmentalization.** Students are assigned to a different teacher for each subject and may have six or seven different teachers each day. Departmentalization usually begins at the sixth, seventh, or eighth grade—depending on the school district.

There are three basic ways of grouping for instruction: (1) *whole-group instruction*, sometimes called large-group instruction, in which the entire class is taught as a group, (2) *small-group instruction*, in which the large group is broken up into subgroups according to ability, interest, project, or other criterion, and (3) *individualized instruction*, in which the individual student works alone or with another person on an individualized task or assignment. Different groupings require different physical settings, so we will take a look at some designs for seating arrangement, and then look at characteristics of instruction for each grouping.

CLASSROOM SEATING ARRANGEMENTS

In a classic study on teaching, Adams and Biddle found that, for the most part, what takes place in the classroom requires the attention of all the students. Teachers tend to stay in front of the classroom more than 85 percent of the time when teaching the whole class, but they change their location on the average once every 30 seconds. Elementary teachers tend to move around through the aisles more than secondary teachers.[1]

Adams and Biddle further found that student participation is restricted by the environment or physical setting itself in ways that neither the teacher nor students seem to be aware of. It appeared to them that students who sit in the center of the room are the most active learners, or what they called "responders." The verbal interaction is so concentrated in this area of the classroom and in a line directly up the center of the room, where the teacher is in front most of the time, that they coined the term "action zone" to refer to this area (Figure 9.1).

---

[1]Raymond S. Adams and Bruce J. Biddle, *Realities of Teaching* (New York: Holt, Rinehart and Winston, 1970).

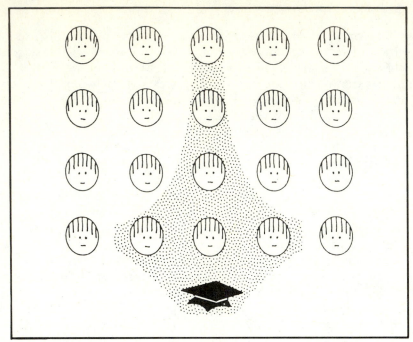

Front

Figure 9.1 Classroom action zone.

Teachers who are student-centered, indirect, and warm or friendly, as opposed to being subject-centered, direct, and businesslike, tend to reject the traditional **formal seating pattern** of rows of students directly facing the teacher at the front of the classroom. Formal seating patterns tend to reduce student-to-student eye contact and student interaction and to increase teacher control and student passivity. Student-centered teachers tend to favor **informal seating patterns,** such as rectangular (seminar), circular, and horseshoe (U-shaped) patterns, in which students face each other as well as the teacher (Figure 9.2).

What usually results when elementary students face each other is less time on tasks and more inappropriate behavior by students who lack inner control.[2] At higher grade levels, or when being on task requires greater student discussion, the informal patterns are likely to be more effective. However, at all levels there is greater potential for discipline problems with nontraditional

---

[2] Saul Axelrod et al., "Comparison of Two Common Classroom Seating Arrangements," *Academic Therapy,* September 1979, pp. 29–36; Valerie Caproni et al., "Seating Position, Instructor's Eye Contact Availability, and Student Participation," *Journal of Social Psychology,* December 1977, pp. 315–316. Also see Carolyn M. Evertson et al., *Classroom Management for Elementary Teachers,* 2nd ed. (Englewood Cliffs, N.J.: Prentice-Hall, 1989).

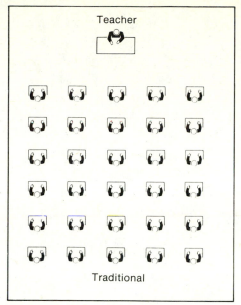

Traditional

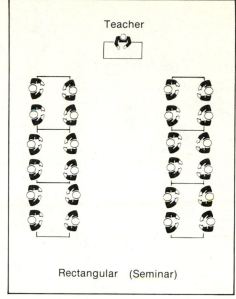

Rectangular   (Seminar)

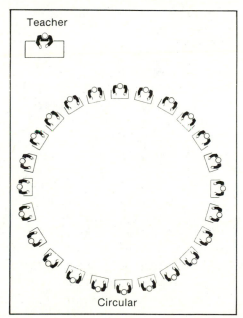

Circular

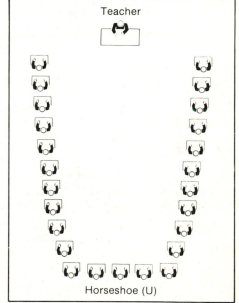

Horseshoe (U)

The teacher's desk is at the corner to avoid neck strain among students in the front of the classroom.

Figure 9.2 Four seating patterns.

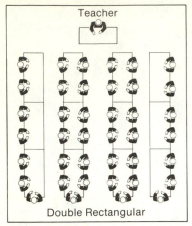

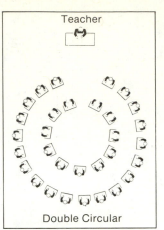

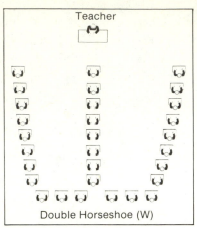

Double Rectangular	Double Circular	Double Horseshoe (W)
Having rows of students separated by tables prevents students' from sitting too close to each other and reduces potential discipline problems.	Space is provided for teacher to move around and into smaller circle.	If space permits seating may be arranged to form a double U instead of a W.

Figure 9.3 Three modified seating patterns.

seating, and insecure teachers and those who are not good managers should keep to more traditional seating until they gain more experience.

Special Classroom Designs   The rectangular, circular, and horseshoe arrangements in Figure 9.2 assume no more than 20 to 25 students. Double rectangular, double circular, and double horseshoe (W-shaped) arrangements are needed to accommodate more than 25 students (Figure 9.3).

An **open classroom** seating arrangement is appropriate for elementary, middle grade, and junior high school students (Figure 9.4). The many shelves, tables, and work areas allow for small-group and individualized instruction. The formal rows of fixed desks of the traditional classroom are gone. The desks are arranged in groups or clusters and can be moved. The open classroom increases student interaction and gives students the opportunity to move around and engage in different learning activities in different settings.

George Musgrave distinguishes between *home-based seating* and *special formations* designed for particular activities.[3] The classroom designs in Figures 9.2, 9.3, and 9.4 are home-based; those in Figures 9.5 and 9.6 are special formations.

These special seating arrangements enhance student interaction in large groups, cooperative learning arrangements, and small groups, for students help one another and share materials. The designs on the left side of Figure 9.5 and on the right side of Figure 9.6 work well for presenting instructional content,

---

[3]George R. Musgrave, *Individualized Instruction: Teaching Strategies Focus on the Learner* (Boston: Allyn and Bacon, 1975).

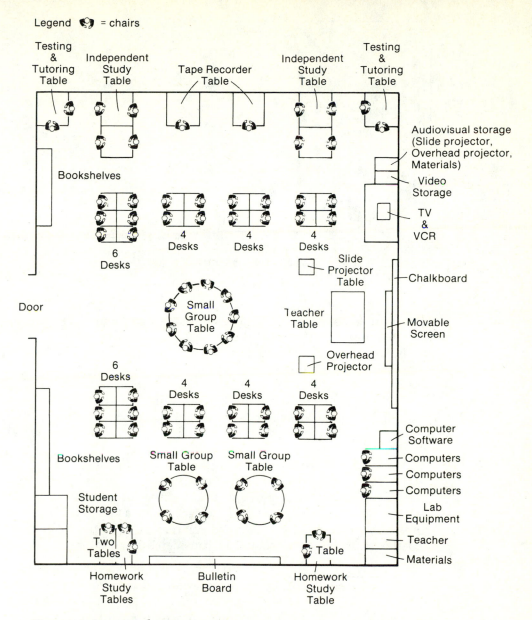

Figure 9.4 An open classroom seating pattern.

and enhance student interaction during debates, forums, or exhibits. The designs on the right side of Figure 9.5 and on the left side of Figure 9.6 facilitate buzz sessions and special interest activities. These special formations are not as open as the one in Figure 9.4. The arrangements in Figure 9.4 are well suited to elementary students and, to a lesser extent, middle grade and junior high

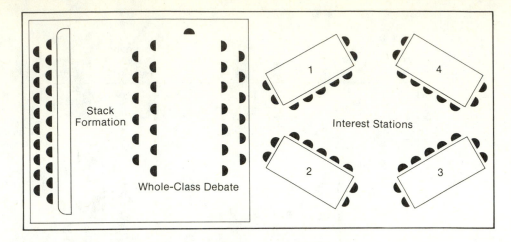

Figure 9.5 Special formation arrangements.
Source: George R. Musgrave, *Individualized Instruction: Teaching Strategies Focusing on the Learner* (Boston: Allyn and Bacon, 1975), 48, 63, 65.

school students; those in Figures 9.5 and 9.6 are better suited to junior and senior high school groups.

Because of increased student interaction, discipline problems may arise with these special seating arrangements, unless the teacher has good managerial skill. However, all these designs allow the teacher flexibility in activities. They function for small groups, create feelings of group cohesion and cooperation, and also allow the teacher to present a demonstration, ask the class to brainstorm a problem or debate an issue, or use audiovisual materials.

Factors to Consider in Classroom Designs   Classroom design will be determined by the size of the room, the number of students in the class, the size and shape of tables and chairs, the amount of movable furniture, the location of fixed features such as doors, windows, closets, and chalkboard, the audiovisual equipment to be used, the school's practice, and the teacher's approach and experience. Eight factors should be considered in arranging the classroom.

1. *Fixed features.* The teacher cannot change the "givens" of a room and must take into account the location of doors, windows, closets, electric outlets, and so forth. For example, seats should not be too close to doors or closets. Electric equipment needs to be near an outlet, and wires should not run across the center of the room. (If they must, they should be taped to the floor.)
2. *Traffic areas.* High traffic areas, such as supply areas, closets, and space near the pencil sharpener and wastebasket, need to be open and easily accessible. The teacher's desk should be located in a low traffic area.
3. *Work areas.* Work areas and study areas should be private and quiet, preferably placed in the corner or rear of the room, away from traffic lanes and noisy areas.

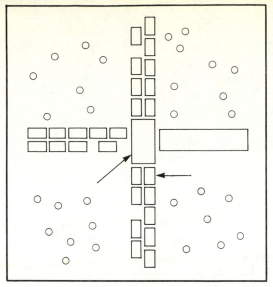

This "cross plan" creates more floor space. The open areas can be used for different activities.

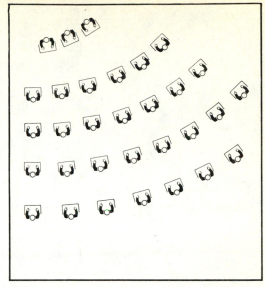

The class directs its attention to two or three people in front of the group. This arrangement can be used to prepare for a lesson or to summarize and evaluate a recently completed activity.

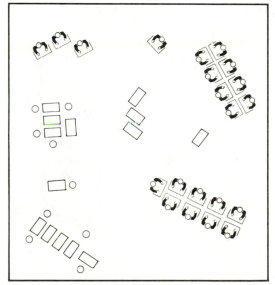

This arrangement allows pupils to work in small groups and move freely from one work area to another.

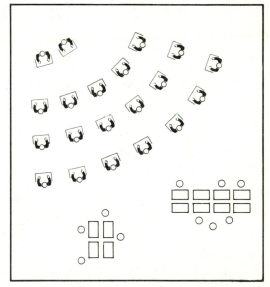

This plan provides for a large-group activity, while two smaller groups work on projects elsewhere in the room. To minimize distractions, children in the large group face away from the small-group areas.

Figure 9.6 Additional special formation arrangements.
Source: Robert E. Reys and Thomas R. Post, *The Mathematics Laboratory: Theory into Practice* (Boston: Prindle, Weber, and Schmidt), p. 59.

4. *Furniture and equipment.* The room, furniture, and equipment should be kept clean and in repair so that they can be used. Desks and chairs may be old, but they should be clean and smooth (make the appropriate requisition to the janitorial department or supervisor), and graphics and doodling should be discouraged immediately. The equipment should be stored in a designated space.

5. *Instructional materials.* All materials and equipment should be easily accessible so activities can begin and end promptly and clean up time can be minimized. Props and equipment that are not stored in closets should be kept in dead spaces away from traffic.

6. *Visibility.* The teacher should be able to see all students from any part of the room to reduce managerial problems and enhance instructional supervision. Students should be able to see the teacher, chalkboard, projected images, and demonstrations without having to move their desks and without straining their necks.

7. *Flexibility.* The classroom design should be flexible enough so that it can be modified to meet the requirements of different activities and different groupings for instruction.[4]

As long as the furniture is not bolted to the floor, the teacher can make changes in room design. Elementary teachers will need to be more flexible, since they are teaching several subjects; moreover, they can be more flexible, since they rarely share the room with other teachers. The room is theirs to set up learning areas, interest areas, work and study areas for reading, mathematics, science, arts and crafts. At the secondary level, where teachers teach one subject and other teachers share the room, the possibilities are reduced, but the room can still be divided into areas for small groups, audiovisual activities, projects, and independent study. Cooperation among the teachers who share the room is needed.

Only through experience and time will teachers learn if a given arrangement suits their teaching style and the needs of their students. It may take several tries and continual revision to have a classroom design in which students work efficiently, materials and equipment are used to their best advantage, unnecessary equipment is removed, and the teacher finds it easy to instruct and to supervise the students.

WHOLE-GROUP INSTRUCTION

Whole-group instruction is the most traditional and common form of classroom organization. Teachers generally gear their teaching to the "mythical" average student on the assumption that this level of presentation will meet

---

[4]Edmund T. Emmer et al., *Classroom Management for Secondary Teachers,* 2nd ed. (Englewood Cliffs, N.J.: Prentice-Hall, 1989); Vincent R. Ruggiero, *Teaching Thinking Across the Curriculum* (New York: Harper & Row, 1988).

Figure 9.1 Traditional classroom settings are often characterized by the centrality of the teacher and stationary desks and tables. (Photo © Roger Malloch/Magnum)

the needs of the greatest number of students. A common block of content (in any subject) is taught on the assumption that large-group instruction is the most effective and convenient format for teaching it.[5]

In the large group the teacher lectures, explains, and demonstrates on a topic, asks and answers questions in front of the entire class, provides the same practice and drill exercises to the entire class, works on the same problems, and employs the same materials. Instruction is directed toward the whole group, but the teacher may ask specific students to answer questions, monitor specific students as they carry out the assigned activities, and work with students on an individual basis.

Whole groups can be an economical and efficient way of teaching. The method is especially convenient for teaching the same skills or subject to the entire class, making assignments, administering tests, setting group expectations, and making announcements. Bringing members of a class together for certain activities strengthens the feeling of belonging to a large group and can help establish a sense of community and class spirit. The whole group learns to cooperate by working with and sharing available resources, setting up rules

[5]Hilda Taba, *Teacher's Handbook for Elementary School Studies* (Reading, Mass.: Addison-Wesley, 1967); Louis E. Raths et al., *Teaching for Thinking: Theory, Strategies, and Activities for the Classroom* (New York: Teachers College Press, Columbia University, 1986).

and regulations for the learning environment, and exchanging ideas.[6] Finally, this method of grouping students is most effective for directing and managing large numbers of students.

The critics of whole-group instruction contend that it fails to meet the needs and interests of individual students. Teachers who use this method tend to look upon students as a homogeneous group with common abilities, interests, styles of learning, and motivation. Instruction is geared to a hypothetical average student, and all students are expected to learn and perform within narrow limits. Students are evaluated, instructional methods and materials are selected, and learning is paced on the basis of the group average.[7] High-achieving students eventually become bored, and low-achieving students eventually become frustrated. The uniqueness of each student is often lost in the large group. Extroverted students tend to monopolize the teacher's time, and passive students usually are not heard from or do not receive necessary attention. Finally, students sometimes act out their behavioral problems in the safety of numbers.

Although a good teacher can compensate for these problems, it is best not to use the whole group as the only grouping for instruction. Different grouping is essential for variety, motivation, and flexibility in teaching and learning.

SMALL-GROUP INSTRUCTION

Dividing students into small groups seems to provide an opportunity for students to become more actively engaged in learning and for teachers to monitor student progress better. Between five and eight students seems to be an optimal number to ensure successful small-group activity. When there are fewer than five, especially in a group discussion, students tend to pair off rather than interact as a group.[8]

Small-group instruction works best in rooms with movable furniture, but it can also be used in classrooms with fixed furniture. Small groupings can enhance student cooperation and social skills. Appropriate group experiences foster the development of democratic values, cultural pluralism, and appreciation for differences among people. Small-group instruction can provide in-

---

[6]David W. Johnson, *Reaching Out: Interpersonal Effectiveness and Self-Actualization*, 3rd ed. (Englewood Cliffs, N.J.: Prentice-Hall, 1986); George J. Posner and Alan N. Rudnitsky, *Course Design: A Guide to Curriculum Development for Teachers*, 3rd ed. (New York: Longman, 1986).

[7]Jeannie Oakes, "Tracking, Inequality, and the Rhetoric of Reform," *Journal of Education*, Summer 1986, pp. 60–80; Kimberly Trimble and Robert L. Sinclair, "*Ability Grouping and Differing Conditions for Learners*," paper presented at the annual meeting of the American Educational Research Association, San Francisco, April 1986.

[8]Robert E. Slavin, "Student Teams and Comparison among Equals: Effects on Academic Performance and Student Attitudes," *Journal of Educational Psychology*, August 1978, pp. 532–538; Noreen M. Webb, "Verbal Interaction and Learning in Peer-Directed Groups," *Theory into Teaching*, Winter 1985, pp. 32–39.

teresting challenges, permit students to progress at their own pace, provide a psychologically safe situation in which to master the material, and encourage them to contribute to class activities.

Dividing the class into small groups helps the teacher monitor work and assess progress through questioning, discussions, and checking workbook exercises and quizzes geared for the particular group. Small groups also give the teacher a chance to introduce new skills at a level suited to a particular group. Because the number of students assigned to each group is often determined by their progress, the group size will vary. Students may move from group to group if their progress exceeds or falls below that of their assigned group. In effect, the teacher is using grouping to restructure a heterogeneously grouped class into several homogeneous subgroups.

Small groups are typically used in elementary school reading and mathematics. The teacher divides the class into two or three groups, depending on the number of students, their range of ability, and the number of groups the teacher is able to handle. The teacher usually works with one group at a time, while the other students do seatwork or independent work.

The use of small groups can be extended beyond the typical grouping in elementary reading and mathematics to all grade levels and subjects. There are seven logical criteria on which small grouping can be based.

1. _Ability_. Grouping by ability reduces the problems of heterogeneity in the classroom.
2. _Interest_. Students have some choice in group membership based on special interests in a particular subject matter or activity.
3. _Skill_. The teacher forms groups in order to develop different skills in students or to have them learn to work with different types of materials.
4. _Viewpoint_. Students have some choice in forming groups based on feelings about a controversial issue.
5. _Activity or project_. The teacher forms groups to perform a specific assignment.
6. _Integration_. The teacher forms groups considering race, ethnicity, religion, or sex to enhance human relations.
7. _Arbitrary_. Groupings are made at random or on the basis of alphabetical order, location in the room, or some other method not related to student or work characteristics.[9]

David Berliner contends that teachers who engage in small-group instruction seem to attend to five strategies of teaching: (1) _compensation_, favoring the shy, quiet, or low-achieving student, (2) _strategic leniency_, ignoring some inappropriate behaviors of students, (3) _proper sharing_, enlisting some students

---

[9] Association of Teachers of Social Studies in the City of New York, _A Handbook for the Teaching of Social Studies_, 4th ed. (Boston: Allyn and Bacon, 1977); Allan C. Ornstein, Harriet Talmage, and Anne W. Juhasz, _The Paraprofessional's Handbook_ (Belmont, Calif.: Fearon, 1975).

Figure 9.2 Small group instructions plays an important factor in enhancing the teaching-learning process. (Photo © Steve Takasuno/ Picture Cube)

to aid in sharing homework or tutoring responsibility, (4) *progressive sharing*, compensating for the problems of low-ability students, and (5) *suppressing emotions*, limiting their emotions or feelings because they feel they are inappropriate or may lead to management problems. Thus, the apparently simple task of organizing small groups involves numerous complex decisions and strategies.[10]

Regardless of the basis of the grouping, assignments should be specific enough and within the range of the students' abilities and interests so the group can work on its own without teacher support. This permits the teacher to single out one group for attention or to help individuals by explaining, questioning, redirecting, and encouraging.

Ability Grouping

The most common means of dealing with heterogeneity is to assign students to classes and programs according to ability. In high schools students may be tracked into college preparatory, vocational or technical, and general programs. In many middle and junior high schools, students are sometimes assigned to a class by ability and stay with that class as it moves from teacher to teacher. In a few cases, and more often in elementary schools, students are assigned to a class on the basis of a special characteristic, such as being gifted, handicapped,

---

[10]David C. Berliner, ''Laboratory Setting and the Study of Teacher Education,'' *Journal of Teacher Education*, November–December 1985, pp. 2–8.

or bilingual. Elementary schools may use several types of **ability grouping.** In addition to the types used in the secondary schools, they may assign students to a heterogeneous class and then regroup them homogeneously by ability in selected areas, such as reading and mathematics.

Despite widespread criticism of **between-class ability grouping** (separate classes for students of different abilities), teachers overwhelmingly support the idea because of the ease in teaching a homogeneous group. The primary criticism is that separating students into high- and low-achieving groups fosters corresponding expectations among teachers and students (self-fulfilling prophecies), and encourages tracked classes.[11] Some researchers have found that high-ability students benefit from such grouping, but this does not compensate for the losses for students in low-ability groups. When Slavin weighed the outcomes of all students (high and low) in ability-grouped classes, "the effects . . . cluster closely around zero."[12] However, instruction in mixed-ability, untracked classes more closely resembles instruction in high-achieving and middle-track classes than instruction in low-track classes,[13] so the mixed-ability grouping tends to benefit low-ability students.

Within-class ability grouping, on the other hand, has been assessed as effective for all students. Moreover, students in heterogeneous classes who are regrouped homogeneously learn more than students in classes that do not use such grouping. This is especially true in reading and mathematics, for which within-class grouping is common, as well as for low-achieving students.[14]

The research data suggest that a small number of within-class groups (two or three) is better than a large number, permitting more monitoring by and feedback from the teacher and less seatwork time and transition time.[15] For

---

[11] Thomas L. Good, "Two Decades of Research on Teacher Expectations: Findings and Future Directions," *Journal of Teacher Education*, July–August 1987, pp. 32–47; Thomas L. Good and Hermine H. Marshall, "Do Students Learn More in Heterogeneous or Homogeneous Groups?" in P. L. Peterson, L. C. Wilkerson, and M. Hallinan, eds., *The Social Context of Instruction* (New York: Academic Press, 1984), pp. 15–38; and Oakes, "Tracking, Inequality and the Rhetoric of Reform."

[12] Robert E. Slavin, "Grouping for Instruction in the Elementary School," *Educational Psychologist*, Spring 1987, p. 112.

[13] John I. Goodlad, *A Place Called School* (New York: McGraw-Hill, 1984); Jeannie Oakes, *Keeping Track: How Schools Structure Inequality* (New Haven, Conn.: Yale University Press, 1985).

[14] Jeannie Oakes, "Tracking in Secondary Schools: A Contextual Perspective," *Educational Psychologist*, Spring 1987, pp. 129–153; Robert E. Slavin and Nancy L. Karweit, "Effects of Whole-Class, Ability Grouped and Individualized Instruction on Mathematics Achievement," *American Educational Research Journal*, Fall 1985, pp. 351–367. Also see Robert E. Slavin, Nancy L. Karweit, and Nancy A. Madden, *Effective Programs for Students at Risk* (Needham Heights, Mass.: Allyn and Bacon, 1989).

[15] Hilda Borko and Jerome Niles, "Teachers' Strategies for Forming Reading Groups," paper presented at the annual meeting of the American Educational Research Association, New Orleans, April 1984; and Elfrieda Heibert, "An Examination of Ability Grouping in Reading Instruction," *Reading Research Quarterly*, Winter 1983, pp. 231–255; and Peter Winograd and Scott G. Paris, "A Cognitive and Motivational Agenda for Reading Instruction," *Educational Leadership*, December–January 1989, pp. 30-35.

Professional Viewpoint

On Being "Dumb"

I am writing as a parent and not in my usual role as professor.

It was two years ago when the standardized reading test, administered in the beginning of the term, sealed John's fate. The results revealed that his reading grade declined from 1 year above level, the previous school year, to 1.2 years below level. He was shunted into the "slow" reading group by Mrs. Smith, his fourth-grade teacher, and was assigned three times a week to a special reading teacher, Mrs. Jones, who thrived on Prussian rules of order and drill activities.

The boy who had only a few months ago during the summer read for enjoyment the abridged versions (100–150 pages) of *Treasure Island*, *Robinson Crusoe*, *Swiss Family Robinson*, and *Dr. Jekyll and Mr. Hyde*, was now unable to answer questions about "Tony's visit to the Zoo" and unable to do his homework. The reading teacher's phone call at home confirmed his lack of comprehension and inability to keep up with the class.

A new nailbiting habit, repeated outbursts at the dinner table, fights with his brother and sister, and frequent remarks about his new reading group and "dumbness"—all in six weeks—prompted me to make an appointment with the school principal, the popular Mr. Green, who knew every child in school by name and whose office magazine rack contained the latest issues of *Educational Leadership*, *National Elementary Principal*, *Phi Delta Kappan*, and *Reading Teacher*.

When I mentioned John's behavior at home, the principal suggested further testing. "No," I responded. "If you test a child long enough, the school will find more things wrong with him and slap more labels on him." When I elaborated on my child's summer reading habits, Mr. Green pointed to recent research which concluded that poor readers don't understand what they read. Somewhat frustrated, I asserted: "Only a fool or nitwit would read a book for ½ to 1 hour before bedtime each evening and then, after finishing the book, want to read another book."

The principal was flexible, but did not give ground easily. He alluded to John's age—that he was the youngest person in his class—and then reviewed Piaget's development stages of growth. I responded with the principles of test reliability and boring methods of instruction. A compromise was eventually reached. My wife and I would make an appointment with the school social worker, so she could assess family conditions, and John would be retested.

After three additional weeks of school bureaucracy, the principal called

continued

with good news: John's retest score was .75 year above grade level. In order to preserve the reading teacher's ego, however, he suggested that the program transfer take place in January, when the semester ended.

John is in the sixth grade, today, still bored with his school reading assignments, but reading Dick Gregory, John Steinbeck, Jack London, and Pearl Buck for his own pleasure. It's sad to think what might have happened to my son had I not intervened. But what about all the children who don't have fathers sitting at the dinner table, or checking homework, much less a parent with the knowledge to challenge the system? Armed with test data and reading labels, Mrs. Smith and Mrs. Jones had boxed a nine-year-old child into a no-win, no-escape situation—in which he could not fend or cope with by himself. The school, with its professional jargon, had labeled and grouped a bright child so that he no longer wanted to learn and no longer felt he could learn. His means of expression was rebellion—stupidity in class and anger at home. In only *a few weeks*, the classroom's ability group coupled with the teacher's self-fulfilling prophecy had overshadowed the child's past performance and behavior.

My son had all the advantages: high SES, two educated parents, bright peer group, and a top-rated school—yet he could not cope with these new labels. Think of all the millions of students who don't have these advantages, in fact, who by chance are classified into the other side of the socioeconomic and school continuum. Then think of their test scores, their stupidity in school, and anger inside and outside of school. Ask yourself, as an educator, who is responsible; then ask yourself what you intend to do that is different from what Smith, Jones, and Green did.

Since the story is true and John still attends the same school system, I am signing with warm regards and as,

Professor Anonymous
Heartland University

example, in a class of three ability groups students spend approximately two-thirds of the time doing seatwork without direct supervision, but with four groups they spend three-quarters of the class time doing seatwork without the teacher's monitoring their work. See Tips for Teachers 9.1.

When within-class ability groups are formed, students proceed at different paces on different materials. The tasks and assignments tend to be more flexible than those in between-class groups. Teachers also tend to try to increase the tempo of instruction and the amount of time for instruction in low-achieving

---

Tips for Teachers 9.1

Components of Direct Instruction

Most teachers rely on whole-group instruction, and evidence suggests that for teaching low-achieving and at-risk students in this type of setting, a high-structured approach is the most effective method. This approach, today, is often called "direct" instruction or "explicit" instruction. The major aspects of direct instruction are listed below. (Note, however, this approach is not suitable for high-achieving or independent learners who prefer a low-structured and flexible situation so they can utilize their initiative.)

1. Begin a lesson with a short statement of goals.
2. Begin with a short review of previous, prerequisite learning.
3. Present new material in small steps, with student practice after each step.
4. Give clear and detailed instructions and explanations.
5. Provide a high level of active practice for all students.
6. Guide students during initial practice.
7. Ask a large number of questions, check for student understanding, and obtain responses from all students.
8. Provide systematic feedback and corrections.
9. Obtain a student success rate of 80 percent or higher during initial practice.
10. Provide explicit instruction for seatwork exercises, and, where possible, monitor and help students during seatwork.
11. Provide for spaced review and testing.

Source: Barak Rosenshine, "Explicit Teaching and Teacher Training," *Journal of Teacher Education*, May–June 1987, p. 34.

---

within-class groups to bring students closer to the class mean.[16] There is less stigma for low-ability groups in within-class grouping than in between-class grouping, since grouping is only for part of the day and the class is integrated

---

[16]Benjamin S. Bloom, "The 2 Sigma Problem: The Search for Methods of Instruction as Effective as One-to-One Tutoring," *Educational Researcher*, June 1984, pp. 4–16; Brian Rowan and Andrew W. Miracle, "Systems of Ability Grouping and the Stratification of Achievement in Elementary Schools," *Sociology of Education*, July 1983, pp. 133–144; and Joseph S. Yarworth, Timothy L. Schwambach, and Robert F. Nicely, "Organizing for Results in Elementary and Middle School Mathematics," *Educational Leadership*, October 1988, pp. 61–67.

the rest of the time. In addition, regrouping plans tend to be more flexible than in between-class groups, because moving students from group to group is less disruptive within a class than between classes.

Guidelines for Ability Grouping Instruction

Slavin and Karweit have developed a step-by-step procedure for teaching elementary and middle grade classes in mathematics, which can also be utilized for reading groups.[17] The program, called Ability-Grouped Active Teaching (AGAT), uses two ability groups rather than the typical three, to increase the amount of time the teacher can spend with each group. Studies have found that students gained approximately one grade equivalent more with the AGAT program than with large-group instruction. The procedures are as follows.

1. *Assign* students to one of two groups—the top 60 percent to the high-middle teaching group and the remaining 40 percent to the low teaching group.
2. *Pace* the lesson and teach at a level according to the abilities of each group. The low ability group, for example, may require twice as much time to cover the same material.
3. *Quiz* students frequently. Give a pretest to determine their initial ability and then quizzes about once a week to determine if they are learning the material and if the pace of the lesson should be adjusted.
4. *Prepare* separate lessons for each group. The lessons should include (a) starter problems every day, which should last about 3 minutes (or up to 5 to 8 minutes); (b) instructional materials such as pictures, graphs, and illustrations; (c) practice problems or seatwork activities for about half the class period; (d) homework every day except perhaps Friday, and (e) quizzes at least once a week.
5. *Arrange seating* so that groups are separate during group work but students are in a mixed arrangement for the rest of the day.
6. *Schedule activities* to make the best use of teacher and student time (or time on task), and be sure activities are clear to students and consistent each class period.[18]

---

[17]Robert E. Slavin and Nancy L. Karweit, *Ability-Grouped Active Teaching (AGAT): Teacher's Manual* (Baltimore: Center for Social Organization of Schools, Johns Hopkins University, 1982); Slavin and Karweit, "Effects of Whole Class, Ability Grouped, and Individualized Instruction on Mathematics Achievement."

[18]Ibid.

Peer Tutoring

Peer tutoring, also called *pairing students,* is the assignment of students to help one another on a one-to-one basis or in small groups in a variety of situations. According to Ornstein, there are three types of pairing students: (1) Students may tutor others *within* the same class; (2) older students may tutor students in lower grades outside of class; (3) two students may work together and help each other as equals with learning activities.[19] The purpose of the first two types is to pair a student who needs assistance with a tutor on a one-to-one basis, although small groups of two or three tutees and one tutor can also be formed. The third type of pairing students, also called *peer-pairing,* is more then tutoring. More than two students working together as equals is sometimes called *cooperative learning.*

Of all three pairing arrangements, peer tutoring within the same class is the most common. A student who has completed a lesson and has shown understanding of the material is paired with a student who needs help. The research suggests that because students are less threatened by peers, they are more willing to ask fellow students questions that they fear the teacher might consider "silly." In addition, they are less afraid that fellow students might criticize them for being unable to understand an idea or problem after a second or third explanation.[20] It has also been found that a student can usually explain a concept in language that another student can grasp; unfamilar vocabulary is cut to a minimum, and sometimes a few choice slang terms can make a difficult concept comprehensible. Also, because the faster student has just learned the concept, he may be more aware than the teacher of what is giving the slower student difficulty. Peer tutors benefit from the relationship; their own understanding is reinforced by explaining the idea or problem, and their social skills are enhanced.[21] The teacher benefits by having additional time to work with students who have more severe learning problems.

Donald and Roger Johnson find these advantages of peer tutoring.

1. Peer tutors are often effective in teaching students who do not respond well to adults.
2. Peer tutoring can develop a bond of friendship between the tutor and tutee, which is important for integrating slow learners into the group.
3. Peer tutoring allows the teacher to teach a large group of students, but still gives slow learners the individual attention they need.
4. Tutors benefit by learning to teach, a general skill that can be useful in an adult society.[22]

---

[19] Ornstein, Talmage, and Juhasz, *The Paraprofessional's Handbook.*

[20] Robert E. Slavin, *Cooperative Learning* (New York: Longman, 1983).

[21] Russel Ames and Carole Ames, *Research on Motivation in Education* (Orlando, Fla.: Academic Press, 1984); Penelope L. Peterson et al., "Ability X Treatment and Children's Learning in Large-Group and Small-Group Approaches," *American Educational Research Journal,* Winter 1981, pp. 453–473.

[22] David W. Johnson and Roger T. Johnson, *Learning Together and Alone,* 2nd ed. (Englewood Cliffs, N.J.: Prentice-Hall, 1987).

The help that one student gives another can be *explanatory* or *terminal.* Explanatory help consists of step-by-step accounts of how to do something. Terminal help consists of correcting an error or giving the correct answer without explaining how to obtain the answer or solve the problem. Most studies of explanatory and terminal help conclude that giving explanations aids the tutor in learning the material, whereas giving terminal help does not.[23] In giving explanations the tutor clarifies the material in her own mind, may see new relationships, and builds a better grasp of the material. Giving terminal help involves little restructuring of concepts.[24]

Not surprisingly, receiving explanations is correlated with achievement. Students who receive terminal help or receive no help tend to learn less than students who receive explanatory help.[25] The benefit of receiving explanations seems to be that it fills in incomplete understanding of the material and corrects misunderstandings; it also increases effort and motivation to learn. Receiving terminal help or receiving no help is frustrating and causes students to lose interest in learning.

Benjamin Bloom argues that tutoring (with preferably a 1:1 student-student ratio, but no more than 3:1) is the most effective method of grouping for instruction compared to conventional methods (30:1 student-teacher ratio) and even mastery learning methods (which he helped develop) when the mastery methods are used in a class of about 30 students. Bloom found that as many as 90 percent of the tutored students and 70 percent of the mastery learning students attained a level of increased achievement reached by only 20 percent of the students with conventional instruction over a three-week period.[26] Figure 9.7 compares achievement with conventional, mastery, and tutor instruction.

Nancy Madden agrees with one-to-one tutoring, especially for elementary school students, and adds three more dimensions: It is most effective when (1) tutors are teachers, (2) tutees spend most of the day in heterogeneous classes, and (3) tutors work with the same students for a minimum of eight weeks to ensure continuity.[27] Madden adds, during whole-group reading instruction, the tutors should serve as additional reading teachers to reduce student-teacher

---

[23] Susan R. Swing and Penelope L. Peterson, "The Relationship of Student Ability and Small-Group Interaction to Student Achievement," *American Educational Research Journal,* Summer 1982, pp. 259–274; Noreen M. Webb, "Predicting Learning from Student Interaction: Defining the Interaction Variables," *Educational Psychologist,* Spring 1983, pp. 33–41.

[24] John A. Bargh and Yaacov Schul, "On the Cognitive Benefits of Teaching," *Journal of Educational Psychology,* October 1980, pp. 593–604; Webb, "Verbal Interaction and Learning in Peer-Directed Groups."

[25] Swing and Peterson, "The Relationship of Student Ability and Small-Group Interaction to Student Achievement"; Penelope L. Peterson et al., "Merging the Process-Product and the Sociolinguistic Paradigms: Research on Small Group Processes," in Peterson, Wilkerson, and Hallinan, eds., *The Social Context of Instruction,* pp. 126–152.

[26] Benjamin S. Bloom, "Helping All Children Learn in Elementary School—and Beyond," *Principal,* March 1988, pp. 12–17; Bloom, "The 2 Sigma Problem: Search for Methods of Group Instruction as Effective as One-to-One Tutoring."

[27] Nancy A. Madden et al., "Restructuring the Urban Elementary School," *Educational Leadership,* February 1989, pp. 14-18.

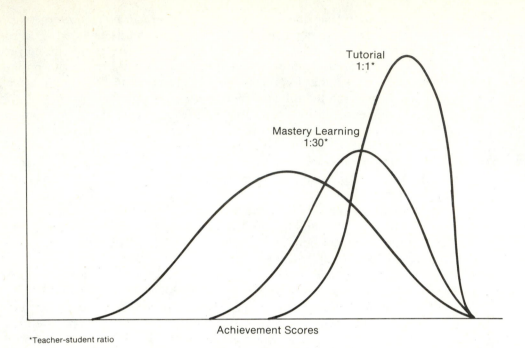

*Teacher-student ratio

Figure 9.7 Achievement distribution for students with conventional, mastery learning, and tutor instruction. Source: Benjamin S. Bloom, "The 2 Sigma Problem: The Search for Methods of Group Instruction as Effective as One-to-One Tutoring." *Educational Researcher*, June–July, 1989, p.5.

ratios to no more than 15 to 1. (Where all the money will come from to implement this program on a large scale is another issue.) Tutoring programs that seem most effective, both for tutors and tutees, have the following characteristics: (1) formal organization with procedural rules established by the teacher, (2) instruction in basic skills and content, (3) explanatory rather than terminal help given, (4) no more than three tutees per tutor and ideally one tutee per tutor, and (5) short duration, about four weeks.[28] (This last point contradicts Madden's eight-week recommendation.) When a tutorial program with these features is combined with regular classroom instruction, "the students being tutored not only learned more than they did without tutoring, they also developed a more positive attitude about what they were studying." In addition, the "tutors learned more than students who did not tutor."[29]

[28]Peter A. Cohen, James A. Kulik, and Chen-Lin C. Kulik, "Educational Outcomes of Tutoring: A Meta-Analysis of Findings," *American Educational Research Journal*, Summer 1982, pp. 237–248; Linda Devin-Sheehan, Robert S. Feldman, and Vernon I. Allen, "Research on Children Tutoring Children: A Critical Review," *Review of Educational Research*, Summer 1976, pp. 355–385.

[29]*What Works: Research about Teaching and Learning* (Washington, D.C.: U.S. Government Printing Office, 1986), p. 36.

Guidelines for Peer Tutoring

Peer tutoring, like ability grouping, can be effective if implemented properly, but it takes substantial time and effort to get off to a good start. Following are some suggestions for effective peer tutoring.

1. The teacher assesses students' needs. Needs may be mainly academic (for example, specific students may need remedial instruction in specific subjects). Needs may be social (another goal of tutoring is to enhance peer group relations or cross-cultural relations).
2. The teacher creates the expectation that everyone can learn from one another through verbalization and modeling.
3. Specific class time is set aside for tutoring.
4. The teacher provides directions for each tutor about time schedules and exactly what to do (for example, "Read the sentence to the group and get at least two students to identify the adjectives and nouns").
5. No tutor should work with the same students for more than a month at a time. This will prevent the tutor's assuming the role of substitute teacher, limit extended mismatching, and prevent boredom.
6. Tutors should not administer tests to tutees. One reason for peer tutoring is to develop a nonthreatening relationship, and testing may defeat this purpose.
7. Shy students should be assigned to work with cooperative, friendly tutors.
8. The teacher must be sure students understand their respective roles. He or she should select a student and demonstrate tutoring to the class. The teacher should model appropriate tutor behavior, provide examples of what is to be achieved, and show how it is to be achieved.
9. Pairing of good friends is unwise because they tend to drift from cognitive tasks into social interaction.
10. It is the teacher's job to plan tutoring arrangements well so that tutors understand and use a mix of materials, media, and activities (for example, one week doing review and drill in the workbooks, the next week doing library research, the next week writing and discussing stories).
11. Parents should be informed about the organization, purpose, and procedures of the tutoring program.
12. Parents can help in developing the classroom and schoolwide tutoring programs, collecting resources, gaining community support, assessing student needs, matching and assigning students, and helping tutors and tutees.[30]

---

[30] Thomas L. Good and Jere E. Brophy, *Looking into Classrooms*, 4th ed (New York: Harper & Row, 1988); Michael Webb and Wendy Schwartz, "Children Helping Children: A Good Way to Learn," *PTA Today*, October 1988, pp. 16–17.

Cooperative Learning

Grouping students to work together instead of competing is becoming a more and more accepted practice by teachers. In the traditional classroom structure, students compete for teacher recognition and grades. The same students tend to be "winners" and "losers" over the years. High-achieving students continually receive rewards and are motivated to learn, and low-achieving students continually experience failure (or near-failure) and frustration. Reducing competition and increasing cooperation among students may diminish hostility, prejudice, and patterns of failure among many students.

This does not mean that competition has no place in the classroom or school. Even the advocates of cooperation feel that competition under the right conditions and with evenly matched individuals or groups can be a source of motivation, excitement, fun, and improved performance—for example, in simple drill activities, speed tasks, low-anxiety games and psychomotor activities, and athletics.[31]

According to a review of the research, cooperation among participants helps build (1) positive and coherent personal identity, (2) self-actualization and mental health, (3) knowledge and trust of others, (4) communication, (5) acceptance and support of others, (6) wholesome relationships, and (7) reduction of conflicts. The data also suggest that cooperation and group learning are considerably more effective in fostering these social and interpersonal skills than competitive or individualistic efforts.[32]

In **cooperative learning,** students divide the work among themselves, help one another (especially the slow members), praise and criticize one another's efforts and contributions, and receive a group performance score. Of all the cooperative learning arrangements, the two developed by Slavin are most popular: student team achievement divisions (STAD) and team-assisted instruction (TAI). Both arrangements have been found to increase student achievement, given the proper implementation. In STAD, teams of four or five members (preferably four, which contradicts an earlier statement that groups of four tend to pair off) are balanced by ability, gender, and ethnicity. Students are ranked by previous test scores or grades and divided into thirds or quarters. Each team consists of one student from each of the thirds or quarters of the class ranking, with extra middle-ranked students becoming the fourth or fifth members. STAD involves five basic steps.

1. The teacher presents the *lesson to the whole group* in one or two class periods.

[31] David W. Johnson and Frank P. Johnson, *Joining Together: Group Theory and Group Skills,* 2nd ed. (Englewood Cliffs, N.J.: Prentice-Hall, 1982); Robert E. Slavin, *Student Team Learning* (Washington, D.C.: National Education Association, 1983).

[32] David W. Johnson and Roger T. Johnson, *Cooperative Learning* (New Brighton, Mass.: Interaction Books, 1984); D. Johnson, *Reaching Out: Interpersonal Effectiveness and Self-Actualization,* 3rd ed. (Englewood Cliffs, N.J.: Prentice-Hall, 1986).

2. *Team study* follows for one or two class periods. Students who have already mastered the material help slower teammates with it. Drill is stressed, although students can engage in discussion and questioning. In a group of four students only two copies of the work sheets and answer sheets are given to each team to encourage team interaction and support. Students can work alone, if they prefer, or in pairs or threes. The team is not finished with the assignment until all members can score 100 percent on a practice quiz. Students are supposed to give one another explanations, not just check answer sheets and supply answers. The teacher moves around the room to monitor the teams' activities, and provides additional assistance.

3. *Class quizzes* are given frequently to see if students have learned the material while in the group. Students return to their assigned seats or move their desks apart for quizzes. The student scores are averaged into a team score, so that group members are more likely to help each other. Quizzes are scored in terms of progress so that slow-performing groups have the opportunity to gain recognition. The teacher grades the quizzes promptly, or students may exchange test papers for faster feedback.

4. *Recognition* is given teams for high average scores or improvement scores. Recognition can be given through bulletin boards, certificates, class newsletters, and letters to parents. Individuals are also recognized for good performance to maintain motivation, but a balance between individual reward and team accomplishment must be found. Giving too many individual rewards heightens competition and reduces co-operation.

5. *Teams are changed* every five or six weeks to give students an opportunity to work with other students and to give members of low-scoring teams a new chance.[33]

The steps involved in *team-assisted instruction* (TAI) are similar to those in STAD, but there is more emphasis on diagnosing through pre- and post-testing and on mastery of skills through practice. Instead of first studying the material together and then checking understanding through practice quizzes in teams, students first work on their own skill sheets and then have their team members check their answers and provide assistance. Not until a student gets 80 percent or higher on the practice quiz is he or she certified by the team to take the final test. Teams are given achievement and improvements scores and recognized as in STAD, but in addition they are labeled "super teams" (high performing), "great teams" (moderate performing), or "good teams" (minimum passing grade). Each day the teacher works for about 5 to 15 minutes (based on a 45-minute lesson) with two or three groups who are at about the

---

[33] Robert E. Slavin, *Student Team Learning* (Washington, D.C.: National Education Association, 1983); Slavin, *School and Classroom Organization* (Hillsdale, N.J.: Erlbaum, 1988).

same point in the curriculum. The other teams work on their own during this time.[34]

The emphasis of TAI is on teaching basic skills more through a type of mastery learning than through direct instruction. The approach is designed for the elementary and junior high school, not the senior high school, and has been successfully implemented in teaching reading and mathematics. In some comparisons to students in traditional classes in mathematics, for example, TAI students have tended to show nearly twice as much progress in learning over the same period of time.[35] One of the most important factors related to achievement, however, is that group goals be balanced with individual accountability and recognition; group goals alone have minimal achievement effects.[36]

A cooperative learning approach designed for junior high and senior high school students is called the **jigsaw classroom.** It is an old idea with a new name. Students work together in a small group on a specific academic task, assignment, or project.[37] They depend on each other for resources, information, and study assignments. It is an excellent method not only for reducing classroom competition and increasing cooperation, but also for reducing classroom or student prejudices, if any exist, and improving human relations.

While the teacher instructs the rest of the class, one group works in a study area on a special task. Students share materials, help one another, and evaluate each other's ideas and assignments. Each group meets once a week for half of or a whole period. Groups can also meet outside of class, say in the library, before school, or at someone's home after school. The group is required to finish its task in a specified period of time, and, depending on the task, they may report their results to the whole class or turn in the finished product to the teacher. Students are evaluated on an individual and group basis. New groups are formed when new assignments are given by the teacher. Groups are formed according to interests, but are mixed according to ability, gender, and ethnicity, thus promoting concepts of democracy and integration.

---

[34] Robert E. Slavin, "Student Teams and Comparison among Equals," *Journal of Educational Psychology,* August 1978, pp. 532–538; Slavin, "Student Teams and Achievement Division," *Journal of Research and Development in Education,* Fall 1978, pp. 38–49; and Slavin, *Using Student Teams,* 3rd ed. (Baltimore: Center for Research on Elementary and Middle Schools, Johns Hopkins University, 1986).

[35] Thomas L. Good, Douglas A. Grouws, and Howard Ebmeier, *Active Math Teaching* (New York: Longman, 1983); Robert E. Slavin, "Team Assisted Individualization: Combining Cooperative Learning and Individualized Instruction in Mathematics," in R. E. Slavin, ed., *Learning to Cooperate, Cooperating to Learn* (New York: Plenum, 1985), pp. 177–209.

[36] Robert E. Slavin, "Cooperative Learning and Student Achievement," *Educational Leadership,* October 1988, pp. 31–33.

[37] Elliot Aronson et al., *The Jigsaw Classroom* (Beverly Hills, Calif.: Sage, 1978).

Guidelines for Cooperative Learning

In addition to the general steps for STAD and TAI already mentioned, some specific strategies for cooperative approaches have been developed by David and Roger Johnson in several texts. A number of these strategies are presented below.

1. *Arrange the classroom to promote cooperative goals.* Students will need to work in clusters, and seating arrangements should reflect this need. Provide sufficient space and study areas for students to share; position media equipment in a way that students have easy access as a group.
2. *Present the objectives as group objectives.* The group and not the individual is the focus. Gear the reward structure to achieving group objectives.
3. *Communicate intentions and expectations.* Students need to understand what is being attempted. They should know what to expect from the teacher and from each student in the group and what the teacher expects them to accomplish.
4. *Encourage a division of labor where appropriate.* Students should understand their roles and responsibilities. This will take time and practice.
5. *Encourage students to share ideas, materials, and resources.* Students should look to each other and not the teacher. The teacher may act as a catalyst in making suggestions, but not be the major source of ideas.
6. *Supply a variety of materials.* Since the sharing of materials is essential to the group, sufficient quantities and variety are needed. If materials are insufficient, the group may bog down and perhaps become disruptive.
7. *Encourage students to communicate their ideas clearly.* Verbal messages should be clear and concise. Verbal and nonverbal messages should be congruent with each other.
8. *Encourage supportive behavior and point out rejecting or hostile behavior.* Behaviors such as silence, ridicule, personal criticism, one-upmanship, and superficial acceptance of an idea should be discussed and stopped since they hinder cooperation and productive group behavior.
9. *Provide appropriate cues and signals.* Point out when the noise level is too high (""Things are getting a little too boisterous"). Direct the group's attention to individual problems and encourage students to use the group ("Check with the group"; "Would you please add this problem to the group's agenda?").

10. *Monitor the group.* Check progress of individuals in a group and of the group as a whole. Explain and discuss problems, assist, and give praise as appropriate.

11. *Evaluate the individual and group.* In evaluation focus on the group and its progress. Evaluate the individual in the context of the group's effort and achievement. Provide prompt feedback.

12. *Reward the group for successful completion of its task.* After evaluation, recognition and rewards should be given on a group basis so that individuals come to realize that they benefit from each other's work and will help each other succeed.[38]

In a supplementary review of cooperative learning, the Johnsons point out that each lesson in cooperative learning should include five basic elements: (1) *positive interdependence*—students must feel they are responsible for their own learning and other members of the group; (2) *face-to-face interaction*—students must have the opportunity to explain what they are learning to each other; (3) *individual accountability*—each student must be held accountable for mastery of the assigned work; (4) *social skills*—each student must communicate effectively, maintain respect among group members, and work together to resolve conflicts; and (5) *group processing*—groups must be assessed to see how well they are working together and how they can improve.[39]

Group Activities

In various kinds of group activities the teacher's role moves from engineer or director to facilitator or resource person, and many leadership functions transfer from the teacher to the students. Although there is no clear research showing that the group techniques below correlate with student achievement, it is assumed that under appropriate circumstances instruction in these groups can be as effective as or more effective than relying on the teacher as the major source of learning. It is also assumed that many kinds of group activities (1) help teachers deal with differences among learners, (2) provide opportunity for students to plan and develop special projects on which groups can work together, and (3) increase student interaction and socialization. In short, they achieve social and emotional as well as cognitive purposes.

There are many ways for teachers to arrange activity in groups. Different group arrangements, also called group projects, result in different roles and responsibilities for the students and teacher. Listed below are 15 possible group projects.

1. *A committee* is a small group working together in a common venture for a given period of time. Using committees succeeds to the extent that

---

[38]David W. Johnson and Roger T. Johnson, *Learning Together and Alone* (Englewood Cliffs, N.J.: Prentice-Hall, 1975); D. Johnson, *Reaching Out.*

[39]David W. Johnson and Roger T. Johnson, "Toward a Cooperative Effort," *Educational Leadership,* April 1989, pp. 80–81.

members grow socially in the group process and are able to accomplish cognitive tasks apart from close teacher direction. A committee representative may be chosen to report to the entire class.

2. *Brainstorming* is a technique to elicit large numbers of imaginative ideas or solutions to open-ended problems. Group members are encouraged to expand their thinking beyond the routine sort of suggestions. Everyone's suggestions are accepted without judgment, and only after all the ideas are put before the group do the members begin to focus on a possible solution.

3. *A buzz session* provides an open environment in which group members can discuss their opinions without fear of being "wrong" or being ridiculed for holding an unpopular position. Buzz sessions can also serve to clarify a position or bring new information before the group to correct misconceptions.

4. *The debate and panel* are more structured in format than some of the other small-group activities. In a debate, two positions on a controversial issue are presented formally; each debater is given a certain amount of time to state a position, to respond to questions from others in the group, and to pose questions. The panel is used to present information on an issue and, if possible, to arrive at group consensus. Several students (three to eight) may sit on a panel. Each panel member may make an opening statement, but there are no debates among panel members.

5. *A symposium* is not as structured as a debate and not as relaxed as the give-and-take exchange of a panel. The symposium is appropriate for airing topics that divide into clear-cut categories or viewpoints. Participants are expected to represent a particular position and try to convince others, but the method of interaction is more spontaneous and no one is timed as in a debate.

6. *Role playing and improvization* are techniques for stepping outside of one's own role and feelings and placing oneself in another's situation. Role playing also serves as a technique for exploring intergroup attitudes and values.

7. *Fish bowl* is a technique in which group members give their full attention to what one individual wants to express. The whole group sits in a circle. Two chairs are placed in the center of the circle. A member who wants to express a point of view does so while sitting in one of the chairs. Any other member who wants to discuss the view takes the other chair, and the two converse while the others listen. To get into the discussion, students must wait for one chair to be vacated.

8. *A critiquing session* is the examination of members' work by the group. The group offers constructive comments and suggestions about ways to improve the work.

9. *Round table* is a quiet, informal group, usually four or five students, who sit around a table conversing either among themselves (similar to a buzz session) or with an audience (similar to a forum).

10. *A forum* is a panel approach in which members interact with an audience.

11. *Jury trial* is a technique in which the class simulates a court room. It is excellent for evaluating issues.

12. *Majority-rule decision making* is a technique for arriving at an agree-

ment or selecting an individual for a task when members of the group hold different opinions. It involves discussion, working out compromises, and making conclusions or decisions based on the wishes of the majority.

13. *Consensus decision making* requires group members to agree. Consensus requires the views of all members of the group be considered, since the group must arrive at a conclusion or agree on a plan of action.

14. *A composite report* synthesizes and summarizes the views or information of all members of a group. Rather than a series of reports by individual members, one report is presented in written or oral form to the class or teacher.

15. *An agenda* is a formal method for organizing a group task. Students or the teacher can plan the agenda, and members of the group must keep to it.[40]

Using group techniques in flexible and imaginative ways can have important instructional advantages. They give students some control over their own personal adjustment as well as over their cognitive learning. They allow the teacher to plan different lessons to meet the needs and interests of different groups. They permit the teacher to vary instructional methods, to plan interesting and active (as opposed to passive) activities, and to supplement the lecture, questioning, practice and drill methods.

The key to the success of group projects is the way the teacher organizes them. Flexible space and furniture undoubtedly make them easier, but furniture is not the critical factor. All of the group techniques, if planned and implemented properly, tend to promote five group-oriented characteristics in the classroom: (1) task structures that lend themselves to cooperation among group members, (2) a chance for students to work at their own pace, but think in terms of group goals, (3) the development of social and interpersonal skills among participants—students learn to communicate with and trust one another, (4) a reward structure based on the performance of the group (which encourages helping behaviors), and (5) a variety of team-building strategies—students learn to work together, appreciate individual diversities, and capitalize on individual strengths (see Tips for Teachers 9.2).

Based on a five-year longitudinal study, Daniel Solomon lists five major behaviors that should evolve with an effective group project.

1. *Cooperative activities* in which students work on learning tasks or play together.
2. *Regular participation in helping and sharing activities.*
3. Experiencing the *positive expectations* of others (that is, the group expects members to be considerate, cooperate, take responsibility, help, and share).
4. Role playing and other activities designed to enhance children's *understanding of other people's needs, intentions, and perspectives.*

---

[40]Ornstein, Talmage, and Juhasz, *The Paraprofessional's Handbook*; Leonard H. Clark and Irving S. Starr, *Secondary and Middle School Teaching Methods*, 5th ed (New York: Macmillan, 1986); and Donald P. Kauchak and Paul D. Eggen, *Learning and Teaching* (Needham Heights, Mass.: Allyn and Bacon, 1989).

Tips for Teachers 9.2

Basic Rules of Group Participation For Students To Remember

In order for students to benefit from a group exercise, they must learn to participate in a way that adds to other students' ideas while confirming their feelings of competence. Students can learn to value differing views as opportunities for learning, not to fear or reject them as personal attacks, so long as every group member learns some basic rules of group participation.

1. I am critical of ideas, not people.
2. I focus on making the best decision possible, not on "winning."
3. I encourage everyone to participate and master all of the relevant information.
4. I listen to everyone's ideas, even if I do not agree.
5. I restate what someone has said if it is not clear.
6. I first bring out all the ideas and facts supporting both sides and then try to put them together in a way that makes sense.
7. I try to understand both sides of the issue.
8. I change my mind when the evidence clearly indicates that I should do so.

Source: David W. Johnson and Roger T. Johnson, "Critical Thinking Through Structured Controversy," *Educational Leadership*, May 1988, p. 63.

---

5. *Positive discipline*, which includes the development and clear communication of rules and norms that emphasize the individual's rights and responsibilities with respect to others.[41]

David Johnson points out that when students work on group projects, they must learn to disclose their attitudes and behaviors in an honest way (1) by giving and receiving supporting feedback, (2) by focusing on specific problems, not personalities, (3) by providing feedback that the receiver can understand, and (4) by providing feedback on actions that the receiver can change.[42] In this way, mutual trust and communication is improved. Basically, the giving and receiving of feedback in this way requires courage, understanding, and respect

---

[41] Daniel Solomon et al., "A Program to Promote Interpersonal Consideration and Cooperation in Children," in Slavin, ed., *Learning to Cooperate, Cooperating to Learn*, pp. 7–8; Solomon et al., "Promoting Prosocial Behaviors in Schools: An Intervention Report of a Five-year Longitudinal Intervention Program," paper presented at the annual meeting of the American Educational Research Association, San Francisco, April 1986.

[42] Johnson, *Reaching Out.*

for others and oneself. The teacher should stress that honesty and support are important and can be used to improve or hinder people's attitudes and actions, and therefore they should not be taken lightly.

Guidelines for Group Activities

Students can be assigned to group projects by interest, ability, friendship, or personality. The teacher must know the students and the objectives for using small groups before establishing the groups. If the objective is to get the job done expeditiously, the teacher should assign a strong leader to each group, rely on high-achieving students to lead the activities, avoid known personality conflicts, and limit the group size to five. If the objective is more interpersonal than cognitive, the students may be grouped according to their diversities rather than similarities and the group might be larger.

In order to organize such group activities, the following recommendations should be considered. They are basically sequential, although each recommendation should be used only if it coincides with your circumstances and teaching style.

1. Decide on the group project selectively to enhance objectives and outcomes.
2. Consider social and cognitive purposes (intermixing students by ability, matching students and topics, blending personalities, promoting social or racial integration) and potential managerial problems when assigning members to groups.
3. Solicit volunteers for membership in group projects, reserving the right to decide final membership.
4. Go over directions for carrying out each phase of the group activity in writing or orally to the point of redundancy.
5. Explain the role of participants, the way they are to interact, and whatever problems might occur. Define roles, interactions, and problems through examples and preliminary simulations.
6. Be sure that individuals can function socially, emotionally, and intellectually in their roles as members of a particular group.
7. Allot class time for groups to organize, plan, and develop some of their projects or assignments, with supervision as needed.
8. Be sure a group is able to function effectively and do a good job before asking it to perform for the class.
9. Allow group members to decide on the nature of the class presentation, within general rules that have been established.
10. Do not allow any individual to dominate the activities or responsibilities of the group. All members of the group should participate,

within the limits of their abilities, and assume responsibility for the success of the project.

11. Evaluate the completed group project with the students. Discuss problems and decisions participants had to face and the strategies chosen by each participant. Note recommendations and revisions that should be implemented with the next group project.

12. Do not direct a class into a group project unless you are willing to work harder than you would in large-group instruction. The process of organizing and supervising group projects from behind the scenes of the classroom is almost always more taxing than the process of direct teaching in the foreground of the classroom.[43]

INDIVIDUALIZED INSTRUCTION

In the past three decades several systematic programs for **individualized instruction** have been advanced. Although the approaches vary somewhat, all the programs seem to attempt to maximize individual learning by (1) diagnosing the student's entry achievement levels or learning deficiencies, (2) providing a one-to-one teacher-to-student or machine-to-student relationship, (3) introducing sequenced and structured instructional materials, frequently accompanied by practice and drill, and (4) permitting students to proceed at their own rate. Most of the approaches combine behavioral and cognitive psychology, although the behaviorist component seems more in evidence because of the stress on instructional objectives and drill exercises, small instructional units and sequenced materials, evaluation of instruction in terms of changes in learning or progress, and reinstruction based on post-test evaluations.

Early Individualized Programs

One of the early programs for individualized instruction was the Project on Individually Prescribed Instruction (IPI), developed at the University of Pittsburgh in the late 1950s and early 1960s. For every student an individual plan was prepared for each skill or subject based on a diagnosis of the student's proficiency levels. Learning tasks were individualized, and the student's progress was continually evaluated.[44]

The Program for Learning in Accordance with Needs (PLAN), developed in the 1960s and 1970s, relies on instructional objectives and two-week modules arranged according to the student's level of achievement. Instructional

---

[43]Gail M. Inlow, *Maturity in High School Teaching*, 2nd ed. (Englewood Cliffs, N.J.: Prentice-Hall, 1970); George W. Maxim, *Social Studies and the Elementary School Child*, 2nd ed. (Columbus, Ohio: Merrill, 1983); and Ornstein, Talmage, and Juhasz, *The Paraprofessional's Handbook*.

[44]Robert Glaser and Lauren B. Resnik, "Instructional Psychology," *Annual Review of Psychology*, 23, 1972, pp. 207–276. Also see Robert Glaser, ed., *Advances in Instructional Psychology* (Hillsdale, N.J.: Erlbaum, 1978).

Figure 9.3 "Messing around" and working independently are characteristic of open and flexible classrooms. (Photo © Ned Haines/Photo Researchers)

materials are ungraded, and alternative sets of materials are available for each unit of instruction.[45]

Individually Guided Education (IGE) is a total educational system developed at the University of Wisconsin and introduced in several thousand schools. Planned variations are made in what and how each student learns. The program includes individual objectives, one-to-one relationships with teachers or tutors, diagnostic testing, independent study, small-group instruction, and large-group instruction.[46]

A more behaviorist and teacher-directed approach is the Personalized System of Instruction (PSI), sometimes called the Keller plan after its originator. It was developed initially for high school and college students. PSI makes use of study guides (which break the course down into small units with specific objectives); individuals progress through the units as fast or slow as they wish,

[45] John C. Flanagan, "Program for Learning in Accordance with Needs," paper presented at the annual meeting of the American Educational Research Association, Chicago, February 1968.

[46] Herbert J. Klausmeier and Richard E. Ripple, *Learning and Human Abilities*, 3rd ed. (New York: Harper & Row, 1971).

master units (80 percent or better) before proceeding to the next unit, and act as proctors (high-achieving students assisting others).[47]

Field testing of these individualized instruction programs has generally been positive. Some reports on IPI, PLAN, IGE, and PSI have shown significant gains in student achievement, especially with low-achieving students, since they seem to prefer a structured approach to learning.[48] Of the four programs, IPI and IGE were the most widely used and seemed to report the most consistent rise in student test scores.[49] Nevertheless, individualized plans are expensive to implement, and most schools today continue to employ group methods of instruction, partially out of habit and because it is easier for teachers.

Independent Study

Although the idea dates back to the 1920s and 1930s, independent study is still practiced today because of its application in a variety of instructional settings (including outside the classroom). **Independent study** involves work conducted by the student on a topic using school or nonschool resources under the direction of the teacher. It was introduced in the 1960s as part of **flexible module scheduling** (dividing the class day or schedule into small time units to enhance flexibility) and **nongraded education** (advancement of students in each skill area or subject at their own rate so they may be at one level of learning in mathematics and another in reading).[50]

Independent study has been used by curriculum and instructional experts particularly in connection with the "self-directed learner," the student who has developed the desire to learn and the study skills needed for pursuing independent study. Although independent study is most applicable at the secondary school level, because students have mastered certain basic skills, elementary school students can be moved from dependence on the teacher toward self-directed learning related to their specific abilities, needs, and interests. In general, independence in performing academic tasks or projects is an extension of having learned how to learn; it requires curiosity, interest, and independent reading and study skills. See Tips for Teachers 9.3.

Although many schools say they make independent study available, it often means different things to different educators. It might mean working in various

---

[47] Fred S. Keller, "Good-bye Teacher," *Journal of Applied Behavioral Analysis*, April 1968, pp. 79–84.

[48] Margaret C. Wang and Herbert J. Walberg, eds., *Adapting Instruction to Individual Differences* (Berkeley, Calif.: McCutchan, 1985). Also see N. L. Gage and David C. Berliner, *Educational Psychology*, 4th ed. (Boston: Houghton Mifflin, 1988).

[49] Herbert Klausmeier, *Learning and Teaching Concepts* (New York: Academic Press, 1980); Deborah B. Strother, "Adapting Instruction to Individual Needs," *Phi Delta Kappan*, December 1985, pp. 308–311.

[50] B. Frank Brown, *The Non-graded High School* (Englewood Cliffs, N.J.: Prentice-Hall, 1963); J. Lloyd Trump and Dorsey Baynham, *Focus on Change* (Chicago: Rand McNally, 1961).

Tips for Teachers 9.3

Cultivating Independent Learning

Based on 20 years of working with teachers, Harold and Joan Herber have developed the following list of important elements in planning for independent instructional activities.

1. *Preparation* that helps students get ready for the activity.
2. *Guidance* that shows students how to apply appropriate study skills.
3. *Independence* that helps students learn from their study or reading.
4. *Instruction* that enhances independence:
   a. *Defining*, or fine-tuning what has been learned, when students meet with other students or the teacher to discuss what they are studying.
   b. *Extending*, or applying what they are learning, when students meet with other students or the teacher.
   c. *Sharing*, or communicating what is being learned and helping other students to define and extend their learning.

Source: Adapted from Harold L. Herber and Joan Nelson-Herber, "Helping Students Become Independent Learners," *Journal of Reading*, April 1987, pp. 584–588.

work areas or resource centers, such as in libraries, in labs, or on computers for portions of the day, or it might mean being assigned to a cafeteria or auditorium when other students are not using the facility and working on homework. Despite this confusion, a review of the research shows that students in traditional classes in English and history do just as well as students engaged in independent study the first year. It is not until the second or third years, as students and teachers become better acquainted with the approach, that students in independent study show significant differences in achievement.[51] As students gain more experience in independent study programs, they tend to show higher creative scores, more satisfaction with school, better study habits and library skills, more individual resourcefulness, and less group dependence in school compared to students not involved in independent study.[52]

---

[51] Don H. Richardson, "Independent Study: What Difference Does It Make?" *National Association of Secondary School Principals*, September 1967, pp. 53–62.

[52] William M. Alexander and William I. Burke, "Independent Study in Secondary Schools," *Interchange*, 3, 1972, pp. 101–113; Harold L. Herber and Joan Nelson-Herber, "Helping Students Become Independent Learners," *Educational Digest*, December 1987, pp. 12–15; and Selma Wasserman, "Reflections on Measuring Thinking, While Listening to Mozart's *Jupiter* Symphony," *Phi Delta Kappan*, January 1989, pp. 365–370.

Guidelines for Independent Study

Basic requirements for an independent study program include (1) a clear set of objectives for students to follow, (2) a variety of materials and resources for students to use, (3) outlining of methods or steps for students to follow to carry out tasks and assignments, (4) checks by the teacher at intervals to assess progress and problems, (5) discussion of problems that a student has encountered or is likely to encounter on the basis of other students' experience, (6) schedules to allow for individual research or study, and (7) interest-area arrangements in class and outside of class (library, computer lab, etc.). Some educators also advocate a "contract" between the teacher and each student on what is to be learned or demonstrated during independent study.

Trump and Miller make the following recommendations for a successful program.

1. Independent study may be an individual activity or involve a small group of students with similar needs or interests.
2. Independent study can take several different forms and be used in several different skill areas or subjects.
3. At the high school level students should spend as much as 12 hours of the usual 30 hours per school week in independent study. (No corresponding provision is discussed at the elementary school level.)
4. The cooperation of teachers, supervisors, counselors, and resource personnel is needed for a full program.
5. The use of five school locations or interests areas is recommended: (a) libraries, (b) resource centers, (c) small-group conferences, (d) relaxation rooms, and (e) restriction zones (usually called study halls).
6. Out-of-school study is recommended, such as work involving industrial sites, social and community agencies, government agencies, museums, and local businesses.[53]

Adaptive Instruction

Two individualized instructional programs, adaptive instruction and mastery learning, have stood the test of time and are still used in many schools today. Developed and refined during the past three decades, both programs recognize that students differ at any given point not only in learning capacity, but also in the degree to which they are able to understand the instruction and move to the next task or topic. Both programs attempt to adapt instruction to the individual, not the group or some hypothetical average.

Adaptive instruction, sometimes called adaptive education, grew out of

---

[53]J. Lloyd Trump and Delmas F. Miller, *Secondary School Curriculum Improvement*, 3rd ed. (Boston: Allyn & Bacon, 1979).

the University of Pittsburgh's IPI. Under this program adaptions occur on two levels: (1) developing the abilities and learning skills of the student and (2) altering the instructional environment to correspond to the individual's abilities and learning skills.[54]

The first level is achieved by determining in what way and to what extent the students' basic cognitive structure needs to be developed. This includes techniques they use for processing information, their skills for learning how to learn, their interests, attitudes, and behavior in class—all of which affect learning. Adaptations are made on the basis of an initial and then periodic diagnosis of the students' competence and also on the assumptions that academic performance can be influenced by what the school does, particularly by the quality and quantity of instruction, and that in no way are students fixed in one track.

The second level is achieved by flexibility in instruction to meet the needs and abilities of each child in the classroom. Instruction is individualized in several ways—for example, varying the amount of time allowed for different students to learn each skill, topic, or subject; establishing different goals for different students rather than uniform goals; grouping students according to abilities, needs, tasks; adjusting tasks and assignments to coincide with patterns of learning, problems, talents, aptitudes, interests; and providing different curriculum content and choices for students.

The research in general indicates that students who are taught by teachers who adapt instruction to their needs, especially low-achieving or mildly handicapped students, learn more than students in traditional classes or in large-group instruction. High-achieving students are capable of learning more than less able students in the same class without this approach; however, both groups are capable of learning more when instructional methods, materials, and assignments mesh with their abilities.[55] A quantitative synthesis of 38 studies and 7,200 students over a 10-year period indicates that adaptive instruction in various grade levels and content areas (although 21 of these studies involved math or reading) has a strong influence (.45 or nearly a half a standard deviation) on student achievement. Students in adaptive programs score on average at the 67th percentile, while students not in such programs (the control group) scored at the 50th percentile.[56]

---

[54] Robert Glaser, *Adaptive Education: Individual Diversity and Learning* (New York: Holt, Rinehart and Winston, 1977); Lauren B. Resnick and Robert Glaser, *The Nature of Intelligence* (Hillsdale, N.J.: Erlbaum, 1976); and Margaret C. Wang, *The Rationale and Design of the Self Schedule System* (Pittsburgh: University of Pittsburgh, Learning Research and Development Center, 1974).

[55] Sandra Cohen and Laurie Debettencourt, "Teaching Children To Be Independent Learners: A Step by Step Strategy," *Focus on Exceptional Children*, 3, 1983, pp. 1–12; Margaret C. Wang and Herbert J. Walberg; "Adaptive Instruction and Classroom Time," *American Educational Research Journal*, Winter 1983, pp. 601–626.

[56] Hersholt C. Waxman et al., "Synthesis of Research on the Effects of Adaptive Instruction," *Educational Leadership*, September 1985, pp. 26–29.

Professional Viewpoint

Adapting Instruction to Student's Needs

I started my career as a remedial reading teacher in a junior high school. My seventh grade remedial reading group (a group of failing, disinterested, disruptive, turned-off boys) had a new young science teacher who they liked very much. To please him, they wanted to do well on the upcoming science test. They asked me to forego my planned remedial reading instruction and help them prepare for a science test. Since I knew very little about the seventh grade science curriculum, we simply used their science textbook. We took the vocabulary words at the end of the chapter, put them on the board, defined them, and analyzed the root words, prefixes, and suffixes. We looked at the charts and pictures in the chapters and the students explained them to me. We took the topic sentences in the book and turned each into a question, and the students read and discussed the material to answer each question.

The happy result was that my remedial reading group did very well on the science test, much better than the other students who were not in remedial reading. In fact, the other students complained to the principal that it wasn't fair because my students had this extra instruction and were prompted on the answers to the questions.

What elements did these naive lessons have from the perspective of today's educational theory and effective teaching practices? The elements probably included high motivation, active and purposeful learning, self-involvement, and cognitive learning strategies.

Janet W. Lerner
Professor of Special Education
Northeastern Illinois State University

Guidelines for Adaptive Instruction

Patterns of adaptation are numerous, but the overall emphasis should be on matching the student's abilities and needs with various instructional paths. Robert Glaser outlines seven basic characteristics of adaptive instruction.

1. *Time, materials, and resources are flexible.* Time in school is made flexible to accommodate different styles and rates of learning. Materials and resources are varied and used in context with the students' needs and abilities. Module materials, with various entry points and options for students to choose, skip, or go back to certain items, are made available.

2. *The curriculum provides sequence, structure, and multiple options for learning.* The subject matter is sequenced and structured so that skills or concepts build upon one another; prerequisite content is defined and mastered before moving to a more advanced level of learning. The curriculum permits movement in several directions to facilitate instruction that best suits the individual. Students can slow down and review or move more rapidly through a defined sequence of the curriculum, depending on their abilities and needs.

3. *There is open display of and access to instructional materials and media equipment.* Various learning environments are created by organizing and modifying the arrangement of the classroom. There is a place for browsing through books and materials, for reading, for studying or doing quiet work, for reviewing or tutoring, and for engaging in independent work. Seats and desks are changed, depending on the materials and activities that are being stressed.

4. *Tests provide information for teachers to make decisions.* Performance is measured at several points, including before instruction. The function of tests is not so much to compare students (norm reference) as to assess initial abilities and progress (criterion reference). Tests are used primarily for diagnostic reasons, not for grading.

5. *Teaching students how to learn is emphasized.* Students are taught "management" skills that allow them to assess instructional materials and media for their own purposes and use them wisely, and to search out information that will help them learn. They learn to assess their own performance and behavior, to learn from past experiences, and to plan future activities. They learn to take greater responsibility in their own learning and thus come to understand their own learning and cognitive strategies. Students learn study skills, homework skills, concentration skills, test-taking skills, and problem-solving skills.

6. *The role of the student is expanded.* Students who work at their own pace have a chance to choose their materials and activities. Students help one another to achieve individual and group goals. Students are able to move about, talk quietly with one another, and make decisions about what they will learn by themselves and in conjunction with the classmates and teacher. The learner takes on added responsibilities about his or her own education.

7. *The role of the teacher as instructor is expanded.* Teachers learn to use their particular strengths in different ways to help students learn. Teachers direct, guide, and encourage students on a one-to-one basis. They learn new pedagogical, monitoring, and tutoring skills that are

involved in organizing and running a classroom in which instruction is individualized. They move about the classroom providing appropriate assistance, attention, correction, direction, and praise for specific students. They learn to identify students who need support and feedback to accomplish a task and those who can work on their own with little assistance.[57]

Mastery Instruction

Mastery instruction is a desired educational goal for all grade levels and subjects. The approach being used most widely in the public schools is Learning for Mastery (LPM), often referred to as **mastery learning.** It was associated originally with John Carroll and later with James Block and Benjamin Bloom. Their mastery learning ideas have gained supporters particularly in urban school districts, where there is an obvious need to improve academic performance among inner-city students.

Carroll maintained that if students are normally distributed by ability or aptitude for some academic subject and are provided appropriate instruction tailored to their individual characteristics, the majority should achieve mastery of the subject and learning should be dramatically improved. He also held that if a student does not spend sufficient time to learn a task, he or she will not master it. However, students vary in the amount of time they need to complete a task. Nearly all students (assuming no major learning disability) can achieve average outcomes if given sufficient time.[58]

Carroll and, later, Robert Slavin distinguish between time needed to learn (based on student characteristics such as aptitude) and time available for learning (under the teacher's control). High-achieving students need less time than low-achieving students to learn the same material. Group instruction, large or small, rarely accommodates varying learner characteristics or considers the time needed to learn. The teacher has the ability to vary instructional time for different individuals or groups of students with mastery instruction, especially for low-achieving students who usually need additional time.[59]

Block and Bloom argue that 90 percent of the public school students can learn much of the curriculum at the same level of mastery, with the slower 20 percent of students in this 90 percent needing 10 to 20 percent more time than the faster 20 percent.[60] Although slower students require a longer period

---

[57] Glaser, *Adaptive Education.*

[58] John B. Carroll, "A Model of School Learning," *Teacher's College Record*, May 1963, pp. 723–733.

[59] John B. Carroll, "The Carroll Model: A 25-Year Retrospective and Prospective View," *Educational Researcher*, January-February 1989, pp. 26–31; Robert E. Slavin, "Mastery Learning Reconsidered," *Review of Educational Research*, Summer 1987, pp. 175–214.

[60] James H. Block, *Mastery Learning: Theory and Practice* (New York: Holt, Rinehart and Winston, 1971); Benjamin S. Bloom, *Human Characteristics and School Learning* (New York: McGraw-Hill, 1976); and Bloom, *All Our Children Learning* (New York: McGraw-Hill, 1981).

of time to learn the same materials, they can succeed if their initial level of knowledge is correctly diagnosed, and if they are taught with appropriate methods and materials in a sequential manner beginning at their initial competency level.

To accomplish this goal, criterion-reference tests must be used to determine whether a student possesses skills required for success in each step in the learning sequence. Also, small units of instruction must be used. An entire course such as third-grade mathematics or seventh-grade social studies is too complex to be studied in large units. Instead it should be broken down into smaller pieces following some of the principles of programmed instruction.

A substantial body of data indicates that mastery learning can result in large learning gains for students. One observer, for example, has reviewed more than a hundred studies on mastery learning and concludes that the results "indicate that mastery strategies do indeed have moderate to strong effects on student learning when compared to conventional methods of instruction."[61] Similarly, in a review of more than 25 studies, Block and Burns found that 61 percent of the mastery-taught students scored significantly higher on achievement test than nonmastery-taught students.[62] In studies of entire school districts the results show that mastery approaches are successful in teaching basic skills, such as reading and mathematics, that form the basis for later learning; moreover, inner-city students profit more from this approach than from traditional groupings for instruction.[63]

The favorable findings do not mean that all the important questions have been answered or that mastery strategies do not have critics. Educators do not know, for example, how well differing mastery approaches can work for high-order learning and affective learning or for different types of students (high-achieving, middle-class students, and ethnic groups other than black and Hispanic). Moreover, we are unsure to what extent teachers are teaching the tests to their students in order to avoid blame, since the assumption is that students can master the material.[64] And since most teachers rely on criterion-reference

---

[61] Robert B. Burns, "Mastery Learning: Does it Work?" *Educational Leadership*, November 1979, p. 112.

[62] James H. Block and Robert B. Burns, "Mastery Learning," in L. S. Shulman, ed., *Review of Research in Education*, vol. 4 (Itasca, Ill.: Peacock, 1976), pp. 118–146. Also see James H. Block, Helen E. Efthim, and Robert B. Burns, *Building Effective Mastery Learning Schools* (New York: Longman, 1989).

[63] Daniel U. Levine and Eugene E. Eubanks, "A First Look at Effective School Projects in Milwaukee and New York," *Phi Delta Kappan*, June 1983, pp. 697–702; Levine, "Achievement Gains in Self-Contained Chapter I Classes in Kansas City," *Educational Leadership*, March 1987, pp. 22–23; and Robert E. Slavin and Nancy A. Madden, "What Works for Students at Risk: A Research Synthesis," *Educational Leadership*, February 1989, pp. 4-13.

[64] Allan C. Ornstein, "Emphasis on Student Outcomes Focuses Attention on Quality of Instruction," *National Association of Secondary School Principals*, January 1987, pp. 88–95; Grant Wiggins, "Teaching to the (Authentic) Test," *Educational Leadership*, April 1989, pp. 41–47.

or teacher-made tests to provide evidence of mastery, there is a question of the reliability and validity of the criteria used in determining mastery; different teachers may reach different conclusions about what students know by using a different criterion for testing.[65]

Other critics claim that basic skills— reading, writing, and mathematics —are being broken down into discrete tasks that students master, but the students still do not acquire the actual skill—they cannot read, write, or compute any better. Students may show gains in small skill items, but this does not necessarily prove learning.[66] What happened to the notions of wholeness and the importance of concepts and problem-solving skills? "It is quite possible," adds Walter Doyle, "for a teacher to achieve high work involvement and student productivity by simplifying task demands to the point that students learn very little."[67]

Traditionally, teachers have held time constant so that individual differences were reflected in achievement differences. A mastery learning situation, which varies time among students, will narrow achievement differences among students in favor of those who need extra time at the expense of other students.[68] Also, in a situation in which high-achieving students must wait for slow students to catch up, and high achievers must wait for the teacher's attention because the teacher spends an inordinate amount of time with low achievers so they can gain mastery, the high achievers are being discriminated against; they will become bored, and their learning outcomes will probably suffer.

These criticisms do not nullify the importance of mastery learning or other direct instructional approaches. However, questions arise whether any instructional approach that breaks learning into tiny, sequenced items has desirable end results with any students, especially high-achieving, talented, or creative students; whether all students need so much practice to master fundamental skills and tasks; and whether it can be considered acceptable to vary instructional time to the disadvantage of higher achievers.

---

[65] Lorin W. Anderson, "Values, Evidence, and Mastery Learning," *Review of Educational Research*, Summer 1987, pp. 215–223; Thomas R. Guskey, "Rethinking Mastery Learning Reconsidered," *Review of Educational Research*, Summer 1987, pp. 225–229.

[66] Linda Darling-Hammond, "Mad-Hatter Tests of Good Teaching," *New York Times*, January 8, 1984, sec. 12, p. 57; Ornstein, "Emphasis on Student Outcomes."

[67] Walter Doyle, "Effective Teaching and the Concept of the Master Teacher," *Elementary School Journal*, September 1985, p. 31.

[68] Marshal Arlin, "Time, Equality, and Mastery Learning," *Review of Educational Research*, Spring 1984, pp. 65–86; Arlin, "Time Variability in Mastery Learning," *American Educational Research Journal*, Spring 1984, pp. 103–120.

Guidelines for Implementing Mastery Instruction

Mastery instruction is not easy to implement. The teacher must adapt the instruction to the student, rather than the student adapting to the instruction. The teacher must continually monitor each student's work, provide a variety of instructional materials and activities, determine what skills and tasks each student has mastered, and provide immediate feedback—not an easy task in a class of 25 or more students. As more studies on mastery learning are conducted in various settings, educators will discover whether these problems and questions can be resolved.

Table 9.1 lists suggestions for using mastery instruction by Hyman and Cohen, who have summarized the mastery approaches adopted in more than 3,000 schools, and by Carroll and then Block and Anderson, who promoted and developed mastery learning. In all three approaches it is clear that mastery learning requires careful teacher planning and organization. It requires extensive diagnostic criterion-reference testing. It is necessary to determine different standards for mastery for each class depending on the students' abilities. Teach-

---

Table 9.1   SUGGESTIONS FOR MASTERY LEARNING

Hyman and Cohen

1. Define instructional objectives behaviorally so the teacher and learner know exactly where they are and what they must accomplish.
2. Teach the behavior (or skill) sought in the objective directly rather than "building" to or around it.
3. Provide immediate feedback to all learner responses.
4. Set the level of instruction so that students are maximally successful (80–90 percent correct).
5. Divide instruction into small, self-contained and sequenced modules.
6. Control the stimulus (materials, media, activities) so the teacher knows exactly what the learner is responding to.
7. Provide positive feedback to reinforce the learners "critical response" (the response that corresponds to the instructional stimulus precisely defined by the instructional objective).

Carroll

1. Specify what is to be learned.
2. Motivate pupils to learn it.
3. Provide instructional materials.
4. Present materials at a rate appropriate for different pupils.
5. Monitor students' progress.
6. Diagnose difficulties and provide remediation.
7. Give praise and encouragement for good performance.
8. Maintain a high rate of learning over a period of time.

Table 9.1   CONTINUED

Block and Anderson

1. Inform students about the features of the model including what they are expected to learn, how they will be graded, and that extra time will be allowed if needed.

2. Teach the lesson relying on large-group or whole-group instruction.

3. Give a "formative" quiz on a no-fault basis to assess student progress; students can check their own papers or switch papers.

4. Based on the results, divide the class into a "mastery" group and "nonmastery" group; 90 percent is considered mastery.

5. Give "enrichment" to mastery group—group projects, independent study, etc.

6. Give "corrective" instruction to nonmastery group—small study groups consisting of two or three students, individual tutoring, alternative instructional materials, rereading materials, practice and drill, etc.

7. The amount of time and support the teacher spends with each group will depend on their size; however, the teacher should spend more time with the students of the "nonmastery" group.

8. Give a "summative" or final quiz on the unit or topic; students who achieved mastery on the "formative" quiz do not need to take this quiz.

9. At least 75 percent of the students should have achieved mastery by the summative test.

10. If not, repeat the procedures starting with "corrective" instruction to "summative" test.

Source: Adapted from Joan S. Hyman and S. Alan Cohen. "Learning for Mastery: Ten Conclusions After 15 Years and 3,000 Schools," *Educational Leadership*, November 1979, pp. 104–109; John B. Carroll "On Learning from Being Told," *Educational Psychologist*, Winter 1968, pp. 5–10; and James H. Block and Lorin W. Anderson, *Mastery Learning in Classroom Instruction* (New York: Macmillan, 1975).

ers have to devise alternative assignments (remedial, corrective, or enrichment) for different students at different stages and at least two forms of tests to measure changes in learning. Teachers must cope with individual rates of learning and vary content coverage and time. You can be sure that it takes a master teacher who is willing to work hard to implement mastery instruction successfully.

Computerized Instruction

Patrick Suppes, an innovator in computer use in schools, coined the term **computer-assisted instruction** (CAI). Suppes defined three levels of CAI: practice and drill, tutoring, and dialogue.[69] At the simplest level, students work through drills in spelling, reading, foreign languages, simple computations, and so forth. At the second level, the computer acts as a tutor, taking over the function of presenting new concepts. As soon as the student manifests a clear understanding, he or she moves to the next exercise. The third and highest

---

[69] Patrick Suppes, "Computer Technology and the Future of Education," *Phi Delta Kappan*, April 1968, pp. 420–423.

level, dialogue, involves a sophisticated interaction between the student and the computer. The student can not only give responses but also ask new questions, and the computer will react appropriately. Computers that can conduct a true dialogue with students are still in the developmental stage, but many educators expect them to reach the mass market in the 1990s.

Other educators tend to envision the role of the computer in terms of three types of application: tool application, computer-assisted instruction, and computer-managed instruction.

Tool application is the use of computers by the student to aid in accomplishing some task, for example, using word processing to write a report or solving mathematical problems. The use of the computer is a personal decision on the part of the students and not originated or requested by the teacher.

Computer-assisted instruction is the use of the computer by the student to facilitate learning. This type of application involves tutoring and practice and drill programs and is appropriate when subject matter needs to be mastered or for practice of critical skills before advancing to higher levels of learning. It coincides with Suppes's first and second levels of computerized instruction.

Computer-managed instruction is the use of the computer by the teacher and school for the systematic control and organization of aspects of instruction including testing, diagnostics data, learning prescriptions, and record keeping. If programmed properly, and if the computer has sufficient memory and storage capacity, the computer can monitor, test, prescribe programs for, and keep the records for more than 100,000 students throughout a school district.[70]

Most instructional use of computers is one of the first two types of application. Increasingly, however, teachers of students with handicaps or learning disabilities are using the third type to monitor, test, prescribe instruction for, and store information on each student they teach. In fact, the procedure is often part of the individualized education program (IEP) developed by the special educators.[71] For slow students and students with disabilities, computer-managed instruction can help the teacher diagnose the students' difficulties, analyze instructional techniques, and replace ineffective techniques with alternative strategies. For average and rapid learners, it offers increased capacities for self-teaching, problem-solving, and independent instruction.

Summaries of the research on computer-assisted instruction suggest that it is effective as a *supplement* to regular instruction. At higher grade levels, particularly college, it can be used effectively as a *replacement* for regular

---

[70]John C. Cook, "Creating a Statewide Computer Education Network," *Education Digest,* October 1985, pp. 36–39; Alan M. Holmeister, "The Special Educator in the Information Age," *Peabody Journal of Education,* Fall 1984, pp. 5–21; and Allan C. Ornstein, "Curriculum Computer Technology," *National Association of Secondary School Principals* (in print 1990).

[71]Tom V. Hanley, "CAI in Special Education: Research Directions," *Peabody Journal of Education,* Fall 1984, pp. 22–39; Holmeister, "The Special Educator in the Information Age"; and Richard J. Shavelson and Gavriel Salomon, "Information Technology: Toll and Teacher of the Mind," *Educational Researcher,* May 1985, pp. 4–5.

instruction.[72] CAI has been shown to be effective for short-term achievement gain (quizzes and examinations), but not for long-term gains (retention).[73] Some studies show that low-achieving students make significant gains in reading and math skills with 10 to 20 minutes daily of CAI that emphasizes practice and drill.[74] However, others show no significant differences in achievement between CAI and non-CAI students, suggesting that CAI is not uniformly effective, and the teacher or instructor may be a crucial variable.

Given the computer craze, an additional word of caution is needed. In computerized instruction students interact with machines and materials that have no emotional and affective components. Critics contend that substituting a machine for a human teacher leaves students with no true guidance and with too little personal interaction. Ralph Tyler concludes that the use of computers in education is based on two faulty assumptions: "that teaching is mostly, if not solely, presenting materials to students [and] that teaching is primarily a technical activity, whereas, in fact, it is a human service."[76] Actually, the computer is only as good as the person (teacher or student) who is using it and the person who wrote the software that accompanies it; the key to successful computer use is still the human factor.

Guidelines for Using Computers in Classrooms

Unquestionably, computers are here to stay. Questions arise, however. How computer-competent are teachers? Are the research findings on computerized

---

[72] James A. Kulik, Chen-Lin C. Kulik, and Peter A. Cohen, "Effectiveness of Computer-Based College Teaching," *Review of Educational Research*, Winter 1980, pp. 525–544; David W. Miller, "The Great American History Machine," *Academic Computing*, October 1988, pp. 28; 43–47, 50–55.

[73] Judith Edwards et al., "How Effective is CAI? A Review of the Research," *Educational Leadership*, November 1975, pp 147–153; James A. Kulik, Robert L. Bangert, and George Williams, "Effects of Computer-Based Teaching on Secondary School Students," *Journal of Educational Psychology*, February 1983, pp. 19–26; and Peter Smith and Samuel Dunn, "Human Quality Considerations in High Tech Education," *Educational Technology*, February 1987, pp. 35–39.

[74] Richard E. Clark, "Reconsidering Research on Learning from Media," *Review of Educational Research*, Winter 1983, pp. 445–459; Paul A. McDermott and Marley W. Watkins, "Computerized vs. Conventional Remedial Instruction for Learning Disabled Pupils," *Journal of Special Education*, Spring 1983, pp. 81–88. Also see "CAD Software: Packages Flex New Muscles," *Technological Horizons in Education Journal*, February 1989, pp. 18–20.

[75] Marcia C. Linn, "The Cognitive Consequences of Programming Instruction in Classrooms," *Educational Researcher*, May 1985, pp. 14–16, 25–29; Terian Tyre and Julie S. Vargas, "Instructional Design Flaws in Computer-Assisted Instruction," *Phi Delta Kappan*, June 1986, pp. 738–744.

[76] Ralph W. Tyler, "Utilization of Technological Media, Devices, and Systems in School," *Educational Technology*, January 1980, pp. 13–14.

instruction mixed because teacher competency is mixed? Should every teacher have facility in computer application and for what type of application? Is there an appropriate grade level to introduce computerized instruction? Should computers be taught as a separate subject, as part of mathematics, or as part of several subjects? Should computers be used only in a computer laboratory or should they be installed in classrooms as part of the daily teaching learning process? These are issues for which it is hard for educators to agree on the answers. Below are specific procedures on which educators can usually find agreement.

I. *Integrate computer use with underlying instruction.*
   1. Match computer application with objectives of the course.
   2. Match computer application with specific unit and lesson plans.
   3. Include a computer-based testing system that measures students' abilities, including test-retest (pre- and posttests).
   4. Use a program that can manage large amounts of student data, including daily attendance, student grades on homework and quizzes, and standardized test data.

II. *Keep apprised of the software available to meet your student needs.*
   1. If possible, obtain a preview copy from the company.
   2. Examine advertisements in computer magazines; read software reviews published in computer magazines.
   3. Solicit recommendations from teachers who are using computers.
   4. Be sure the word processing commands coincide with those of the school's computer.
   5. Look for software that has several different ways of teaching the same concept while offering different levels of difficulty. (This gives the student the opportunity to learn at his or her own pace.)
   6. Ensure that the software can identify individual learning problems and automatically provide a tutorial set of exercises.
   7. The software should be able to distinguish between a user's typing mistakes and basic errors in understanding the material.
   8. The software should have a branching function, so that if the student is having difficulty with a specific task or problem, the program can offer remedial exercise or alternative ways for learning the material.

III. *What schools can do to enhance computer use among students.*
   1. Schools should make sure students have adequate access to computers. Students who have computers at home are more likely to be interested in school computers and have extra time at home to practice their computer skills. Students who do not have computers at home are at a disadvantage in school and need extra computer time in school.
   2. Schools need to provide students with opportunities for extracurricular computer experiences before and after school.

Professional Viewpoint

Improving Instruction

For the past twenty years, I and others from around the world have been attempting to implement an unusually effective set of instructional techniques commonly called "mastery learning." This experience has left three lasting impressions about the fundamental instructional improvement efforts. One is that university or college experts rarely make a difference in these efforts. Another is that research data rarely make a difference either. The third is that what does make a difference is educators' basic beliefs about humans' capacities to learn. Depending on these beliefs, educators then select data and the experts who have generated these data to support their belief system.

While the importance of educators' beliefs in instructional improvement efforts cannot be denied, what has been denied has been explicit concern with these beliefs in most teacher and administrator instructional leadership programs. Program after program has tended to focus on the skills side of teaching rather than the belief one. The result has been instructional leaders often more versed in technique than in vision.

I believe more attention ought to be paid in instructional improvement efforts to educators' basic beliefs about most students' capacities to learn excellently, swiftly, and self-confidently. Such attention would highlight the often ignored ethical side of instructional leadership. It would also dramatize the delicate, but necessary, relationship between ethical and technical leadership in effective instruction.

James H. Block
Professor of Education
University of California-Santa Barbara

3. Schools should establish computer clubs and closely monitor them to ensure they do not become monopolized by students who are computer-proficient.
4. Schools should restructure courses in computers (or in specific subjects) so all students become computer-literate.
5. Since many classrooms do not have computers, or have only one or two, the schools should provide computer labs or classrooms that can house 15 to 30 students at one time.

STUDY STRATEGIES

Regardless of the method of grouping, students must learn to study on their own. Whether the student is working in class or at home, in math or in English, the development of certain study skills and practices makes learning easier. With proper study habits, students achieve more and teachers seem more effective. The study strategies examined below are homework skills, studying skills, and note taking.

Homework Skills

The amount of **homework** performed by the individual student is related to academic learning performance. In the international educational achievement tests, conducted in 19 countries including the United States and involving 133,000 elementary and secondary schools, the number of hours of homework per week was significantly related to achievement.[77] According to Herb Walberg, graded homework or homework commented upon can raise a typical student from the 50th to the 70th percentile in cognitive performance. Graded homework has nearly three times more effect on student outcomes than nongraded homework does.[78] In all of these studies, however, the data is correlational—that is, the variables may occur together but that does not necessarily indicate which variable is cause and which is effect. It is possible that students who get higher grades do more homework, not that doing homework causes higher grades. It is also possible that high-achieving students do more homework because of intrinsic motivation or the belief that homework pleases the teacher and results in higher grades.

The reasons students fail to complete homework assignments are unclear. According to one expert, most schools do not have a clear homework policy and teachers of different secondary school subjects rarely coordinate homework assignments in terms of length, difficulty, or context.[79] The result is that in one night students may have little or no homework and the next night too much, resulting in stress or frustration.[80] Not only can excessive homework interfere with the student's social and personal development, but also the wrong homework (too easy or too difficult) can hinder the student's optimal cognitive growth. For example, routine drill is boring and counterproductive for high-achieving students, and problem-solving and divergent questions,

---

[77] Torsten Husén, "An International Research Venture in Retrospect: The IEA Surveys," *Comparative Education Review*, October 1979, pp. 371–385.

[78] Herbert J. Walberg, Rosanne A. Paschal, and Thomas Weinstein, "Homework's Powerful Effects on Learning," *Educational Leadership*, April 1985, pp. 76–79.

[79] J. Michael Palardy, "The Effect of Homework Policies on Student Achievement," *National Association of Secondary School Principals*, April 1988, pp. 14–17.

[80] Harris Cooper, *Homework* (New York: Longman, 1989); Ronald T. LaConte, *Homework as a Learning Experience* (Washington, D.C.: National Education Association, 1981).

without assistance and monitoring from the teacher, can cause many other students to give up.

Reviews of the literature suggest that in more than 50 percent of the cases all students in a class are given the same assignment, as if all of them have the same abilities or are learning at the same rate. Individual abilities, interests, and learning styles are rarely considered.[81] Most important, teachers rarely correct, grade, and return homework on a regular basis. In more than two-thirds of the cases teachers do not provide feedback to students about homework, even though the data strongly suggest that student achievement is correlated with graded homework at all grade levels[82]—especially after grade 6 or 7, when the homework becomes more difficult and feedback from the teacher is more important.

From the beginning of the year, teachers need to be clear on homework assignments, be sure students have prerequisite skills, vary the types of assignments, individualize them, and explain, collect and check the homework. Some experienced teachers contend that homework should not be assigned until the third grade, others say that it can be introduced as early as the first grade for practice and drill, and still others say that it can be introduced in the first or second grade as an enjoyable assignment, say reading, with the assistance of parents.

Another problem exists with students who can do the assigned work, but who not finish it or turn it in; the reasons must be investigated. Recent data on sixth-grade students show that the five most prominent disturbances of studying and doing homework at home are the phone, television, family members (walking in and out of the room, parents asking questions, siblings teasing), general noise (vacuum cleaner, washing machine, doorbell), and the radio, stereo, or tape recorder. Other problems include insufficient sleep, pets, background conversations, and siblings who are crying.[83] In related studies it has been found that the most positive influence on the amount of time spent on homework is the parent, and the most negative are television and the lack of a quiet place for studying.[84]

---

[81] Kenneth Dunn and Rita Dunn, "Dispelling Outmoded Beliefs about Student Learning," *Educational Leadership*, March 1987, pp. 55–62; Palardy, "The Effect of Homework Policies on Student Achievement."

[82] P. M. Marshall, "Homework and Social Facilitation Theory in Teaching Elementary School Mathematics," unpublished doctoral dissertation, Stanford University, School of Education, 1982; and Gary Natriello and Edward McDill, "Performance Standards, Student Effort on Homework, and Academic Achievement," *Sociology of Education*, January 1986, pp. 18–31.

[83] Ron Benson, "Helping Pupils Overcome Homework Distractions," *Clearing House*, April 1988, pp. 370–372.

[84] Timothy Z. Keith et al., "Parent Involvement, Homework and TV Time: Direct and Indirect Effects on High School Achievement," *Journal of Educational Psychology*, October 1986, pp. 373–380; Dennis E. McGuire and John S. Lyons, "A Transcontextual Model for Intervention with Problems of School Achievement," *American Journal of Family Therapy*, Fall 1985, pp. 37–45.

Guidelines for Assigning Homework

In assigning homework, the following suggestions are worthwhile to consider.

1. The school district may have a policy on homework that the teacher should follow or at least consider.
2. Experienced teachers or supervisors can be asked about the type and amount of homework to assign.
3. Homework should be assigned regularly. The amount should increase with the student's grade level.
4. Homework should be relevant to the subject matter, interesting (if possible), and consonant with students' abilities and needs.
5. Homework can be used to reinforce the present day's lesson or prepare for the next day's lesson.
6. Homework can be used to introduce new skills or concepts for older students; it can also be used to teach students to be independent learners.
7. Homework should periodically incorporate available materials and media at home: books, magazines, newspapers, television.
8. Students should not be permitted to do homework (assigned for home or after school) in class, especially when the teacher is engaged in instructing the class.
9. Teachers should grade homework and provide appropriate comments. It is better to require less homework and check and return it, or at least review it in class, than to assign homework that will not be graded and returned.
10. Teachers should review homework in class the next day, and discuss problems or questions that students may have had.
11. Teachers can discuss the previous day's homework during the lesson as part of a warm-up exercise or review exercise. They may discuss the next day's homework (such as problems that may be encountered, new concepts, etc.) after the summary or as a closing activity of the lesson.
12. Parents should be informed about their children's homework and how they may help them with it. Homework should be the responsibility of the student. If parents have to do more than occasionally explain or review the homework, then the homework assignment is inappropriate.
13. Reasons students do not do, turn in, or complete the homework must be explored. Is it a poor home situation, pressures of a part-time job, competing after-school or out-of-school activities, poor study skills, or inappropriate assignments?
14. Homework should not be used as a punishment. The purpose of homework is to facilitate learning, not to control students. Assigning homework as punishment connotes loss of control and mismatching

the student's misbehavior with the teacher's controlling (managerial) behavior.

Study Skills

Study skills include various linguistic and verbal activities such as listening, reading, library skills, and reference skills for all grade levels, and note taking and research skills for older students. In general, good study skills will mean the ability to learn and make use of what one is reading or studying—to understand information and to engage in independent learning without immediate feedback from the teacher.

In an analysis of 69 students, Van Rossum and Schenk divided the students into two groups: *surface-level* studiers, who attempt to memorize content so they can reproduce it in another context (for example, a test), and *deep-level* studiers, who develop insights and understand how to use the material. Surface-level studiers view learning in terms of knowledge and facts. They become flustered easily when they are unable to perform work or process information and are significantly more nervous in taking tests than deep-level studiers. Deep-level studiers interpret data and filter it through a generalized schema.[85]

Sound study skills involve adjusting practices to (1) difficulty of the materials, (2) time available for studying, (3) what is already known about the material, (4) purpose and importance of the assignment, and (5) standards to be met.[86] Good studiers (1) space learning and review sessions on an assignment over time and rarely cram or study the same topic continuously, (2) identify the main idea in new information and connect new content or material to what they already know, (3) draw inferences about the significance of the new information, and (4) appraise their own progress and whether their study methods are working.[87] Good studiers are well organized, and use their time well, and have heightened awareness of what is entailed in their assignments. They are motivated and have positive self-concepts about school achievement. Finally, they read with understanding, retain what they study, and have well-developed note taking, listening, reading, and writing skills.[88]

---

[85] E. J. Van Rossum and Simone Schenk, "The Relationship Between Learning Conception, Study Strategy, and Learning Outcome," *British Journal of Educational Psychology,* February 1984, pp. 73–83. Also see Ray Hembree, "Correlates, Causes, Effects, and Treatment of Test Anxiety," *Review of Educational Research,* Spring 1988, pp. 47–78.

[86] Franz E. Weinert and Rainer H. Kluwe, eds., *What Works: Research about Teaching and Learning: Metacognition, Motivation, and Understanding* (Hillsdale, N.J.: Erlbaum, 1987).

[87] John D. Bransford, *Human Cognition: Learning, Understanding, and Remembering* (Belmont, Calif.: Wadsworth, 1980); Stephen D. Brookfield, *Developing Critical Thinkers* (San Francisco: Jossey-Bass, 1987).

[88] Barry F. Beyer, *Practical Strategies for the Teaching of Thinking* (Needham Heights, Mass.: Allyn and Bacon, 1987); Bernice J. Bragstad and Sharyn M. Stumpf, *A Guidebook for Teaching Study Skills and Motivation,* 2nd ed. (Needham Heights, Mass.: Allyn and Bacon, 1988).

Models for Studying   One of the best-known models for studying is called *SQ3R* (survey, question, read, recite, and review). It was developed by Francis Robinson and modified into a fuller system, *SQ4R* (with a fourth R for *reflect*), by Thomas and Robinson.[89] Although many educators have advocated the use of this procedure, the research indicates its effects are small or neutral. The steps in 3Q3R and 4Q4R are listed below.

1. *Survey* the material to get an idea of the general organization and topics. Skim headings, subheadings, diagrams, and highlighted words.
2. *Question* the material as you read it. Turn the headings into questions to consider.
3. *Read* the material to answer the questions you posed.
4. *Reflect* (in SQ4R) on the material and relate it to previous knowledge or information. Relate topics and headings to ideas and theories you already know.
5. *Recite* the information by asking and answering questions. Use topics, readings, notes, underlined phrases, and other text aids to formulate questions and answers.
6. *Review* the material or reread it. Ask yourself questions and complete practice exercises.

Another model for studying is *comprehension monitoring*. This model lists four monitoring strategies to improve understanding: summarizing, questioning, clarifying, and predicting.[90] *Murder* is still another model that identifies six focusing strategies to improve recall and retrieval: (1) Getting the proper *Mood* for learning by relaxing and focusing on the task, (2) *Understanding* the conditions and details of the task, (3) *Recalling* information relevant to the task through analysis and summary, (4) *Detecting* errors and omissions in the analysis or summary (without getting bogged down by difficult terms or unfamiliar material), (5) *Elaborating* main points, and (6) *Reviewing* the material and elaborating information by relating it to previous knowledge.[91] The murder model is primarily used for high school and college students. Both of these study models have been shown to be moderately successful.

[89]Francis P. Robinson, *Effective Study*, 2nd ed. (New York: Harper & Row, 1970); Ellen J. Thomas and Alan H. Robinson, *Improving Reading in Every Class* (Boston: Allyn and Bacon, 1971).

[90]Ann L. Brown, *"Learners' Characteristics and Scientific Texts,"* paper presented at the annual meeting of the American Educational Research Association, New Orleans, April 1984; Mary J. Gray, "Comprehension Monitoring: What the Teacher Should Know," *Clearing House*, September 1987, pp. 38–41.

[91]Donald F. Dansereau, "Learning Strategy Research," in J. Segal, S. Chipman and R. Glaser, eds., *Thinking and Learning Skills* (Hillsdale, N.J.: Erlbaum, 1985), pp. 209–239; Velma I. Hythecker, Donald F. Dansereau, and Thomas Rocklin, "An Analysis of the Process Influencing the Structured Dyadic Learning Environment," *Educational Psychologist*, Winter 1988, pp. 23–37.

Guidelines for Study Skills

Every student develops his or her own study strategies over the years. Some people summarize what they read in notes, others make comments in the margins of the text, and still others underline key passages. Some people can skim materials effectively, and others must read every word to understand the information.

For the elementary and secondary student, Gage and Berliner have listed some general behavioral guidelines for students to follow.

    I. Avoidance of delay
       1. Plan carefully.
       2. Avoid hurrying.
       3. Avoid procrastination.
       4. Correct errors on returned homework or papers.
       5. Study at least one hour per day after school.
       6. Keep up with your assignments; do the required work regularly each day.
   II. Teacher approval
       1. Talk to the teacher about school work, especially about school problems.
       2. Ask the teacher for explanations or assistance when appropriate, especially when unclear about the task or assignment.
  III. Acceptance of tasks
       1. Try to become motivated.
       2. Avoid excessive commitments to extracurricular or nonacademic activities.
  IV. Work methods
       1. Work hard.
       2. Be neat and organized.
       3. Avoid interruptions while studying.
       4. Periodically review all assignments.
       5. Get sufficient rest.
       6. Read school guides for written assignments.
       7. Copy the teacher's notes from the blackboard.
       8. Keep the radio, phonograph, and television off while studying.
       9. Check over answers before turning in homework or a test paper.
     10. Study alone, if you are able, rather than with others (the latter leads to socialization and time wasting).[92]

---

[92] N. L. Gage and David C. Berliner, *Educational Psychology*, 4th ed. (Boston: Houghton Mifflin, 1988). Also see William F. Brown and Wayne H. Holtzman, *Survey of Study Habits and Attitudes* (New York: Psychological Corporation, 1967).

Note Taking

Note taking is an important study strategy that can be practiced in all subjects, starting around the fifth or sixth grade. Notes can be based on written or oral sources. In all cases, students need to be taught to record important information in their class and study work.

Research on the function or worth of note taking is mixed. Some data show a positive correlation between effective note taking and student achievement, others find no effect, and a few show a negative correlation.[93] The mixed results seem to relate to how students use their notes. When students take notes, a *product* function, but do not review them, the effect is almost zero. When students take notes and study them, a *process* function, the results are usually positive.[94] But this information is incomplete, because it fails to specify why some students take notes and do not use them to study. Moreover, the results do not indicate a cause-effect relationship; there is the possibility that students who are high achieving to begin with take more notes and use them, and low-achieving students take fewer notes and use them less or not at all.

The quality of note taking is influenced mainly by three factors: (1) *note taker's background knowledge* of the subject, his or her ability to integrate new information into prior knowledge, to select factual data and process them into generalized connections or subject matter information[95]; (2) *note taker's cognitive capabilities*, attention to important ideas, verbal ability, and ability to process information rapidly and accurately[96]; and (3) *note taker's memory*, ability to search memory to determine if the data are important to note, the number of pieces of information that can be processed in working memory (active consciousness), and capacity for transferring information from short-term to long-term memory (permanent storage).

Students who are less able to integrate information in working memory and select information from long-term memory possess fewer anchors or hooks

---

[93] Kenneth A. Kiewra, "Investigating Notetaking and Review," *Educational Psychologist*, Winter 1985, pp. 23–32; Claire E. Weinstein and Richard E. Mayer, "The Teaching of Learning Strategies," in M. C. Wittrock, ed., *Handbook of Research on Teaching*, 3rd ed. (New York: Macmillan, 1986), pp. 315–327.

[94] Francis J. DiVesta and G. Susan Gray, "Listening and Notetaking," *Journal of Educational Psychology*, June 1973, pp. 278–287; Kenneth A. Kiewra, "Cognitive Aspects of Autonomous Notetaking," *Educational Psychologist*, Winter 1988, pp. 39–56.

[95] Thomas H. Anderson and Bonnie B. Armbruster, "Reader and Text Study Strategies," in W. Otto and S. White, eds., *Reading Expository Material* (New York: Academic Press, 1984), pp. 219–242; Jerrold E. Barnett and Donald Freud, "Prior Knowledge and the Generative Theory of Notetaking," paper presented at the annual meeting of the American Educational Research Association, Chicago, April 1985.

[96] Ann L. Brown, "Knowing When, Where and How to Remember," in R. Glaser, ed., *Advances in Instructional Psychology* (Hillsdale, N.J.: Erlbaum, 1978), pp. 77–165; Ann L. Brown and Joseph C. Campione, "Modifying Intelligence or Modifying Cognitive Skills," in D. K. Detterman and R. J. Sternberg, eds., *How and How Much Can Intelligence Be Increased* (Norwood, N.J.: Ablex, 1982), pp. 215–229.

to process new information, record fewer notes, and use fewer main ideas and subordinate ideas when taking notes. It is questionable whether students' memory can be improved by what the teacher does; rather, it is possible for teachers to help students organize new information and to use anchors in processing and recalling data. Also, two researchers suggest that computer-assisted instruction, because of its practice and drill format, can possibly play a role in facilitating memory of academic data.[97]

Richard Mayer lists four encoding processes involved in teaching and learning that apply to note taking: (1) *selection*—the learner (note taker) pays attention to certain information and transfers it into working memory; (2) *acquisition*—the learner transfers the information from working memory to long-term memory; (3) *construction*—the learner builds connections between the new information and working memory; the connections lead to the development of an outline or schema organization; and (4) *integration*—the learner transfers prior knowledge to working memory, then connects new information with prior knowledge.[98] The ability to select, acquire, construct, and integrate new information with old information in the form of notes results in the ability to generalize and apply the incoming information in other situations including tests.

Note-Taking Methods   There is no one method that is better than any other. A good deal depends on the student's age or cognitive stage, cognitive processes, ability to read and process information, ability to write and organize information.

Thomas Devine examines four basic forms of note taking: (1) underlining, (2) marginal notes, (3) outlining, and (4) summarizing.[99] Underlining, which is quite common, seems to be the least effective approach, because it is passive. Students tend to underline too much, focusing on many bits of information (names, dates) and not absorbing or processing the information. Devine recommends marginal notes, coupled with outlining important concepts and words in separate notes. He also recommends various coding systems, including using different colors for main ideas, subordinate ideas, and supporting data, or using different symbols such as circles around key terms, arrows to show relationships between ideas, boxes to show connecting ideas, stars to indicate importance of ideas, and question marks to indicate ideas that need to be clarified.

Although these methods are more active than mere underlining, they suggest a sophisticated and older learner, someone who has background knowledge

---

[97] Douglas H. Clements and Bonnie K. Nastasi, "Social and Cognitive Interactions in Educational Computer Environments," *American Educational Research Journal*, Spring 1988, pp. 87–106.

[98] Richard E. Mayer, "Aids to Text Comprehension," *Educational Psychologist*, Winter 1984, pp. 30–42; Richard E. Mayer and Linda K. Cook, "Effects of Shadowing on Prose Comprehension and Problem Solving," *Memory and Cognition*, January 1981, pp. 101–109. Also see Weinstein and Mayer, "The Teaching of Learning Strategies."

[99] Thomas G. Devine, *Teaching Studying Skills: A Guide for Teachers*, 2nd ed. (Boston: Allyn and Bacon, 1988).

of the subject and is highly motivated. Also, since most grade school students must return their texts at the end of the term, they have to rely on outlining and summarizing in a notebook.

The point is that whatever the method, students should learn to organize and take notes systematically. Strategies for organizing notes fall under the following categories: (1) *factual note taking*, sometimes called selection strategies, which emphasizes recording information, including names, dates, and terms; (2) *target note taking*, sometimes called specific strategies, in which notes are selected on the basis of an anticipated set of learning outcomes or test expectancies; (3) *concept note taking*, sometimes called internal strategies, in which notes follow relationships indicated in the text, such as main headings and subheadings or main topics and subtopics; and (4) *integrative note taking*, sometimes called elaboration strategies, which involves connecting new information with prior knowledge and processing information beyond the chapter or text.

According to researchers, a strong relationship exists between the last two strategies and students' good performance on tests; at best only a moderate or small relationship exists between the first two strategies and performance.[100] The data, therefore, support the notion that generalized approaches to note taking are more effective than specific approaches. Concept note taking and integrative note taking are the approaches that teachers should encourage students to develop and use in class and at home.

Guidelines for Notetaking

Students take notes most often in two situations: when they outline or summarize from the text, and when they copy from the chalkboard. (Note taking based on lectures or explanations—without the chalkboard—should not be required for students before tenth or eleventh grade, and only with high-achieving students.) The teacher should teach students the following note-taking practices.

1. Distinguish between main ideas (information) and subordinate ideas (information). Organize subordinate ideas with a corresponding main idea.[101]

---

[100] Anderson and Armbruster, "Reader and Text Study Strategies"; Brown and Campione, "Modifying Intelligence or Modifying Cognitive Skills"; and Kiewra, "Cognitive Aspects of Autonomous Notetaking."

[101] Carol A. Carrier and Amy Titus, "Effects of Notetaking, Pretraining and Test Mode Expectations on Learning from Lectures," *American Educational Research Journal*, Winter 1981, pp. 385–397.

2. Condense or shorten important new information. Use your own words.
3. Use an outline form, with main headings and two or three subheadings. Do not use more subheadings to avoid confusion or trivial outlining.
4. Avoid random or verbatim notes. Integrate new information with old information.
5. Pay attention to text structures such as headings and subheadings.[102] Organize notes around text generalizations or main ideas.
6. Record some examples to support generalizations or main ideas.
7. Organize notes into a hierarchy of information. Create a diagram or chart to show relationships.
8. Place information in groups or patterns (chronological order, reasons for and against, comparisons, cause-effect).[103]

The above guidelines pertain mainly to note taking from a text. When the teacher outlines material on the chalkboard, students should be expected to copy the notes.

1. Students should be expected to copy a moderate amount of notes from the chalkboard starting at the fifth or sixth grades. The amount and complexity of the notes can increase with the students' grade level. (Note taking from text, without the presence of the teacher, can begin in the sixth or seventh grade.)
2. Note-taking capabilities and limitations are related to the amount of knowledge the student brings to the situation. Knowledge and note-taking skills interact.
3. Low-achieving students should be given fewer notes to copy, since they cannot process information quickly and pay attention to the class discussion at the same time.
4. Low-achieving students should be given notes to copy from the chalkboard in whole sentences; otherwise, they will rarely process or understand information effectively when reviewing notes.
5. Notes on the blackboard should be organized into main ideas and subordinate ideas. Low-achieving students can profit from no more than three or four subordinate ideas per main idea and no more than three or four main ideas per class lesson. Age is also a factor.
6. High-achieving students can process more information. They can profit from notes that deal with main ideas, subordinate ideas, and subsubordinate ideas.
7. High-achieving students can be taught to fill in information pertaining to the class discussion that is not listed on the blackboard.

---

[102] Mayer, "Aids to Text Comprehension."

[103] Devine, *Teaching Study Skills*; Weinstein and Mayer, "The Teaching of Learning Strategies."

THEORY INTO PRACTICE

Just as it is important to use different instructional methods and materials, it is important to mix instructional groupings to meet classroom conditions and student characteristics and to provide variety. No one grouping approach is appropriate for every circumstance. A mixture of large-group, small-group, and individualized instruction should be used. Here we provide a few commonsense methods for large-group, small-group, and individualized instruction.

For Whole-Group Instruction

1. Make the classroom attractive and safe. Consider flexible spacing and furnishings.
2. Consider the physical conditions of the classroom when arranging desks and tables.
3. Allow for the physical and psychological needs of the students. Some students will have to sit close to the chalkboard for vision reasons; some students will have to be separated because they are too friendly or disruptive.
4. Involve all students in the instructional activities. Avoid emphasizing teacher-student interaction on one side or in the middle of the room.
5. Encourage dialogues among students. Avoid monologues by the teacher or extended dialogues between the teacher and one student.
6. Arrange instructional materials and media equipment so that all students can readily see and participate in the activities.
7. Direct and monitor classroom activities.
8. Make smooth transitions from large-group activities to either small-group or individualized instruction. Maintain a brisk pace when making transitions.

For Small-Group Instruction

1. Make sure students know what to do and how to proceed. Be sure they understand the objectives or tasks and when they have achieved them.
2. Make sure students are aware of their responsibilities while working in small groups.
3. Enhance communication and minimize conflicts by discussing appropriate behavior for individuals within groups.
4. When organizing groups, consider the abilities and needs of the students. Mix groups by ethnicity, social class, and sex for purposes of integration; mix groups by ability so they are relatively equal on a cognitive basis.
5. Take into account special learning and behavior problems. Separate students who do not work well together.
6. Direct learning experiences toward the efforts of the smaller groups.

The teacher is no longer the director of activities and the source of knowledge, but a facilitator and resource person.

7. Permit students to work at their own pace within their respective groups. Permit the entire group to work at its own pace.

8. For high-achieving students and those who can work by themselves, give them latitude and encourage a sense of independence and resourcefulness. For low-achieving students and those who need extra encouragement or assistance, provide the necessary support and feedback. Try to improve their sense of self-esteem and achievement.

9. Monitor the work of each group. Make comments, ask questions, and assist the group as necessary.

10. Conduct periodic probes. Stop the lesson and bring everyone to attention to discuss common problems or errors experienced by two or more groups.

11. Provide knowledge of group results by emphasizing the positive. Provide immediate feedback and group rewards for achievement.

12. Provide smooth transitions from small-group activities to either large-group or individualized instruction. Maintain the momentum of the lesson when making transitions.

For Individualized Instruction

1. Make sure students know what to do and how to proceed. Objectives, tasks, and achievement levels should be stated.

2. Make sure students understand their responsibilities when working on individual assignments or independent study.

3. Select diverse materials and media based on individual needs and abilities. Explain the various materials and media available and where they may be found. Permit students latitude in selecting instructional tools.

4. Arrange instructional materials in small, sequenced units to enhance correct responses from students, especially low-achieving students.

5. Permit student to work at their own pace.

6. Monitor and check for understanding. Permit independent work after students indicate understanding of the main skills or concepts of the lesson.

7. Provide enrichment activities for high-achieving students; give them more latitude in selecting materials and activities. Provide corrective activities for low-achieving students; give them more assistance and encouragement.

8. Evaluate student work and provide immediate feedback, if possible.

9. Assess for the purpose of guiding, modifying instruction, and measuring progress; do not compare or rank students.

10. Provide smooth transitions from individualized instruction to either large-group or small-group instruction. Maintain the pace of the lesson when making transitions. Avoid abrupt transitions.

Study Strategies

Too many teachers make the false assumption that their students have already developed good study habits. A sequence of lessons early in the term should be devoted to helping students to improve homework skills, study skills, and note taking; these lessons should be continued from one grade level to the next. The following strategies should be included in the lessons.

1. Define the specific study strategies.
2. Select a few examples of the strategies to elaborate.
3. Correct imperfect examples of the skills strategies.
4. Execute the strategies with appropriate work and explanations of how and why students did what they did to execute the strategies.
5. Provide practice, especially with less informed students, on how to execute the strategies, for example, by writing a set a directions or drawing a diagram.
6. Train students to read textbook paragraphs and place them in outline form with main and subordinate ideas.
7. Have students listen to class discussion to discern main ideas.
8. List main and subordinate ideas in mixed order and have students arrange them in the right order.

The curriculum often does not allow teachers adequate time to teach these skills, especially at the secondary level. Some students, mostly high achievers, are able to acquire study strategies, and the ones that do acquire these skills do so by accident or as part of their larger cognitive abilities. Most students don't acquire these strategies on their own and their academic achievement suffers. Every teacher, from the third grade on, needs to set aside time to develop and review study habits, skills appropriate for their respective grade level or subject. The amount of training needed in these skills for students will vary by grade and subject; high-achieving students will need less information and training by the time they reach high school.

SUMMARY

1. Instruction may take place in large-group, small-group, and individual settings. The teacher is responsible for varying these three groupings according to the needs of the students and the objectives of the lesson.

2. Classroom seating arrangements include traditional, rectangular, circular, horseshoe, and various special formations designed to meet special activities.

3. Large-group or whole-group instruction is the most common form of classroom organization, suitable for the teacher when lecturing and explaining, questioning, and providing practice and drill.

4. Whole-group instruction tends to be geared to the average learner, and the students are expected to perform within a narrow range.

5. Small groups give the teacher flexibility in instruction and an opportunity to introduce skills and tasks at the level suited to a particular group of students.

6. There are several methods for organizing students in small groups, including grouping by ability, peer tutoring, cooperative learning, and group activities. Small-group activities are best achieved when group size is limited to five to eight students per group.

7. Individualized instruction permits the student to work alone at his or her own pace and level over short or long periods of time. Individualized instruction permits the teacher to adapt instruction to the abilities, needs, and interests of the learner.

8. Programs for individualized study developed in the past include Individually Prescribed Instruction, Individually Guided Education, Program for Learning in Accordance with Needs, and Personalized System of Instruction. Current types of individualized instruction include independent study, adaptive instruction, mastery instruction, and computer-assisted instruction.

9. Study strategies include homework skills, study skills and note-taking skills. Students need more practice in these skill areas than most teachers might expect.

QUESTIONS TO CONSIDER

1. What type of seating arrangements do you prefer during large-group instruction? What does this say about your teaching approach?

2. Which small-group instructional methods do you prefer? Why?

3. Which individualized instructional methods do you prefer? Why?

4. What are three advantages and three disadvantages of mastery learning?

5. In what ways can teachers of various grade levels or subjects work together to develop homework skills? Study skills? Note-taking skills?

THINGS TO DO

1. Discuss the advantages and disadvantages of three seating arrangements for the subject level and grade level you wish to teach.

2. Defend or criticize the nature of competitive and cooperative classrooms. Be sure to describe the advantages of each, whatever your overall preference. How would you change the reward structures in school?

3. Observe a tutoring program for students in a local school. Report back to the class on the merits of the program.

4. Discuss your views about computerized instruction. Describe how you expect to use computers for instructional purposes.

5. What study strategies can you recommend that work for you and might work for others?

RECOMMENDED READINGS

Anderson, Lorin W., and John B. Carroll, eds. *Perspectives on School Learning.* Hillsdale, N. J.: Erlbaum, 1985. Selected writings on cognitive learning, individual instruction, and learning for mastery.

Bloom, Benjamin S. *Human Characteristics and School Learning.* New York: McGraw-Hill, 1976. Emphasis on individual instruction and school learning, with methods of changing the level of learning and rate of learning through mastery approaches.

Bragstad, Bernice J., and Sharyn M. Stumpf. *A Guidebook for Teaching Study Skills and Motivation,* 2nd ed. Needham Heights, Mass.: Allyn and Bacon, 1988. Research-based strategies and activities for helping students develop homework and study skills.

Fenstermacher, Gary D., and John I. Goodlad. *Individual Differences and the Common Curriculum,* Eighty-second Yearbook of the National Society for the Study of Education, Part I. Chicago: University of Chicago Press, 1983. Several chapters written by well-known authorities on individualized instruction and learning; easy to read and yet grounded in research.

Glaser, Robert. *Adaptive Education: Individual Diversity and Learning.* New York: Holt, Rinehart and Winston, 1977. Compact description of various conditions and characteristics of instruction that can be adapted to the individual student.

Johnson, David W., et al. *Circles of Learning: Cooperation in the Classroom.* Alexandria, Va.: Association for Supervision and Curriculum Development, 1984. One of many books authored by Johnson that focuses on the need for cooperative learning through various small-group methods.

Lillie, David L., Wallace H. Hannum, and Gary B. Stuck. *Computers and Effective Instruction.* New York: Longman, 1989. Various methods of using computers and software in classrooms.

KEY TERMS

Self-contained classroom
Departmentalization
Formal seating pattern
Informal seating pattern
Open classroom
Whole-group instruction
Small-group instruction
Ability grouping
Between-class ability grouping
Within-class ability grouping
Peer tutoring
Cooperative learning

Jigsaw classroom
Individualized instruction
Independent study
Flexible module scheduling
Nongraded education
Adaptive instruction
Mastery learning
Computer-assisted instruction
Homework skills
Study skills
Note taking skills

Chapter 10

Instructional Planning

FOCUSING QUESTIONS

1. How do teachers plan for instruction? At what levels do they plan?

2. How do teachers map a course of study?

3. What are the main components of a unit plan?

4. What are the main components of a lesson plan?

5. What components would be stressed in a mastery lesson plan? Creativity lesson plan?

6. How do unit and lesson plans facilitate teaching and instruction?

*E*ffective planning is based on knowledge of (1) the general goals of the school, (2) the objectives of the course or subject, (3) students' abilities, aptitudes, needs, and interests, (4) content to be included and appropriate units into which the subject can be divided, and (5) techniques of short-range instruction or lesson planning.

Although planning is the shared responsibility of administrators, supervisors, and teachers, the individual teacher must modify any plan and originate his or her own plans for instruction in the classroom.

HOW TEACHERS PLAN

Teacher planning is a form of decision making. Planning a course, unit, or lesson involves decisions in two areas: (1) *subject matter knowledge*, concerning organization and presentation of content, knowledge of student understanding of content, and knowledge of how to teach the content, and (2) *action system knowledge*, concerning teaching activities such as diagnosing, grouping, managing, and evaluating students and implementing instructional activities and learning experiences.[1]

Both kinds of knowledge are needed for effective planning for instruction. Most teachers have knowledge of subject matter, but lack expertise in various aspects of action system knowledge. Shavelson and Stern found that while various planning models are included in teacher training (mostly based on subject matter knowledge), the models are not always used by teachers once they begin planning in schools. "Obviously, there is a mismatch between the demands of classroom instruction and the prescriptive planning model."[2] According to Good and Brophy, this mismatch occurs because teachers are easily "overwhelmed by the rapid pace" of the classroom "and become simply *reactive* to classroom events."[3]

According to John Zahorik, who sampled some 200 teachers, most teachers do not engage in rational planning or make use of objectives. They tend to emphasize content, materials, resources, and learning activities.[4] In a study of

---

[1] Pamela L. Grossman and Anna E. Richert, "Unacknowledged Knowledge Growth," *Teaching and Teacher Education* (no. 4, 1988), pp. 53–62. Gaea Leinhardt and David Smith, "Expertise in Mathematics Instruction: Subject Matter Knowledge," paper presented at the annual meeting of the American Educational Research Association, New Orleans, April 1984.

[2] Richard Shavelson and Paula Stern, "Research on Teachers' Pedagogical Thoughts, Judgments, Decisions, and Behavior," *Review of Educational Research*, Winter 1984, p. 477.

[3] Thomas L. Good and Jere E. Brophy, *Educational Psychology: A Realistic Approach*, 4th ed. (New York: Longman, 1988), p. 25.

[4] John A. Zahorik, "Teachers' Planning Models," *Educational Leadership*, November 1975, pp. 134–139.

Figure 10.1 The age of students is an important factor to consider in planning and teaching the lesson. (Photo © Elizabeth Crews)

experienced teachers, Penelope Peterson also found that teachers emphasize subject matter knowledge or content and instructional activities when planning a daily lesson. Of five planning categories, they spend the least time on planning objectives.[5]

According to Gail McCutcheon, when plans are required by supervisors, teachers tend to turn in "a shorthand description" of what they plan to do in class. They "[list] objectives for a lesson in their plan books only if requested to do so by the principal." In the teachers' view, objectives are implicit in the content and activities of the lesson and need not be shown. For many teachers, "planning serves as a memory jogger, a list of things to be sure to accomplish."[6] Because of this view, most teachers do not value the use of objectives or of detailed or elaborated plans. Although researchers tend to see logic in planned lessons, Elliot Eisner points out that most of what happens in the classroom cannot be observed, measured, or preplanned, and much of teaching is based on impulse and imagination, and cannot be preplanned.[7]

Planning By Level of Instruction

Teachers engage in five levels of planning: yearly, term, unit, weekly, and daily. Planning at each level involves a set of goals, sources of information,

---

[5] Penelope L. Peterson, Christopher W. Marx, and Ronald M. Clark, "Teacher Planning, Teacher Behavior, and Student Achievement," *American Educational Research Journal*, Summer 1978, pp. 417–432.

[6] Gail McCutcheon, "How Do Elementary School Teachers Plan?" *Elementary School Journal*, September 1980, pp. 4–23.

[7] Elliot W. Eisner, *The Educational Imagination*, 2nd ed. (New York: Macmillan, 1985).

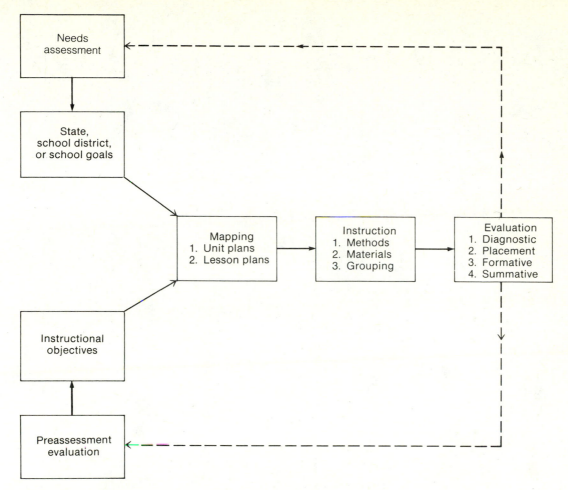

Figure 10.1 Instructional planning sequence.

forms or outlines, and criteria for judging the effectiveness of planning (Table 10.1).

One researcher points out that middle-grade teachers rely most heavily on: (1) previous success and failures, (2) district curriculum guides, (3) textbook content, (4) student interest, (5) classroom management factors, (6) school calendar, and (7) prior experience when they plan at the yearly or term levels. At the unit, weekly, and daily levels, they are mostly influenced by: (1) availability of materials, (2) student interest, (3) schedule interruptions, (4) school calendar, (5) district curriculum guides, (6) textbook content, (7) classroom management, (8) classroom activity flow, and (9) prior experience.[8] According

---

[8]Deborah S. Brown, "Twelve Middle School Teachers' Planning," *Elementary School Journal*, September 1988, pp. 69-87.

Table 10.1 LEVELS OF TEACHER PLANNING

Level	Goals of planning	Sources of information	Form of plan	Criteria for judging effectiveness of planning
Yearly planning	1. Establishing general content (fairly general and framed by district curriculum objectives) 2. Establishing basic curriculum sequence 3. Ordering and reserving materials	1. Students (general information about numbers and returning students) 2. Resources available 3. Curriculum guidelines (district objectives) 4. Experience with specific curricula and materials	1. General outlines listing basic content and possible ideas in each subject are a (spiral notebook used for each subject)	1. Comprehensiveness of plans 2. Fit with own goals and district objectives
Term planning	1. Detailing of content to be covered in next three months 2. Establishing a weekly schedule for term that conforms to goals and emphases for the term	1. Direct contact with students 2. Time constraints set by school schedule 3. Resources available	1. Elaboration of outlines constructed for yearly planning 2. A weekly schedule outline specifying activities and times	1. Outlines—comprehensiveness, completeness, and specificity of elaborations
Unit planning	1. Developing a sequence of well-organized learning experiences 2. Presenting comprehensive, integrated and meaningful content at an appropriate level	1. Students' abilities, interests, etc. 2. Materials, length of lessons, set-up time, demand, format 3. District objectives 4. Facilities available for activities	1. Lists or outlines of activities and content 2. Lists of sequenced activities 3. Notes in plan book	1. Organization, sequence, balance, and flow of outlines 2. Fit with yearly and term goals 3. Fit with anticipated student interest and involvement
Weekly planning	1. Laying out the week's activities within the framework of the weekly schedule 2. Adjusting schedule for interruptions and special needs 3. Maintaining continuity and regularity of activities	1. Students' performance in preceding days and weeks 2. Scheduled school interruptions (for example, assemblies, holidays) 3. Materials, aides, and other resources	1. Names and times of activities in plan book 2. Day divided into four instructional blocks modified by schedule	1. Completeness of plans 2. Degree to which weekly schedule has been followed 3. Flexibility of plans to allow for special time constraints or interruptions 4. Fit with goals
Daily planning	1. Setting up and arranging classroom for next day 2. Specifying activity components not yet decided upon 3. Fitting daily schedule to last-minute intrusions 4. Preparing students for day's activities	1. Instructions in materials to be used 2. Set-up time required for activities 3. Assessment of class "disposition" at start of day 4. Continued interest, involvement, and enthusiasm	1. Schedule for day written on the chalkboard and discussed with students 2. Preparation and arrangement of materials and facilities in the room	1. Completion of last-minute preparations and decisions about content, materials, etc. 2. Involvement, enthusiasm, and interest communicated by students

Source: Robert J. Yinger, "A Study of Teaching Planning," *Elementary School Journal,* January 1980, pp. 114–115.

to Robert Yinger, planning is perceived as rational, logical, and structured, and as being reinforced by a number of instructional and managerial routines. By the middle of the school year about 85 percent of the instructional activities are routinized.[9] In planning teachers use instructual routines for questioning, monitoring, and managing students, as well as for coordinating classroom activities.

But the teacher needs to consider variety and flexibility in planning, as well as structure and routine, to take into account the students' differing developmental needs and interests. Some students, especially high achievers, divergent thinkers, and independent learners, learn more in nonstructured and independent situations, whereas many low achievers, convergent thinkers, and dependent learners prefer highly structured and directed environments.[10]

Mental versus Formal Planning

McCutcheon maintains that the most valuable form of teacher planning at the classroom level is "the reflective thinking that many teachers engage in before writing a unit or lesson plan, or while teaching a lesson."[11] Often the exact weekly or daily lesson plan is sketchily outlined. Much of what happens is a reflection of what happened in other years when a similar lesson was taught. It develops as the teaching-learning process unfolds and as teachers and students interact in the classroom. Many actions related to planning cannot be predetermined in a classroom of 30 students or more who are rapidly interacting with their teacher.

Mental planning is the teacher's spontaneous response to events in the classroom; the teacher considers situations and responds intuitively. (Of course, that intuition must be well grounded in subject matter and action system knowledge.) Mental planning is a part of teaching that is crucial for effectiveness, but it cannot be easily observed, recorded, or detailed. Therefore, it often goes unnoticed and unmentioned as part of the planning process. Mental planning suggests that instruction (or teaching) is an art that cannot be planned in advance—that a theory of teaching or a principles (or methods) approach to teaching cannot easily be determined or agreed upon. But mental planning is a practical, common, and effective method of instructional planning.

Formal planning is what most educators and researchers recognize as a legitimate and necessary instructional activity. Perhaps it is examined so often

---

[9]Robert J. Yinger, "A Study of Teacher Planning," *Elementary School Journal,* January 1980, pp. 107–127.

[10]Stephen F. Foster, "Ten Principles of Learning Revised in Accordance with Cognitive Psychology," *Educational Psychologist,* Summer 1986, pp. 235–243; N. L. Gage and Margaret C. Needels, "Process-Product Research on Teaching: A Review of the Criticisms," *Elementary School Journal,* January 1989, pp. 253–300; and Richard E. Snow, "Individual Differences and the Design of Educational Programs," *American Psychologist,* October 1986, pp. 1029–1039.

[11]McCutcheon, "How Do Elementary School Teachers Plan?" p. 7.

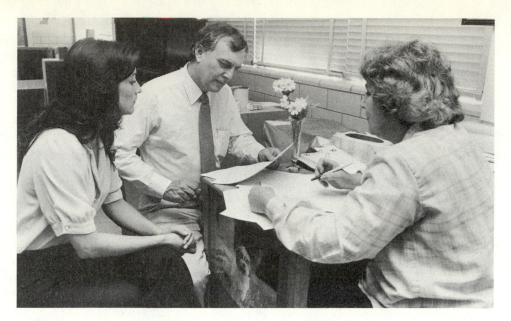

Figure 10.2 Good planning at the subject or grade level involves communication with colleagues. (Photo © Meri Houtchens-Kitchens/Picture Cube)

simply because it can be prescribed, categorized, and classified. Formal planning is structured and task oriented; it suggests that teaching and instruction can be taught as part of teacher training and staff development.

Course Plans: Mapping

A long-range teacher guide is usually called a *map* or *course of study*. In large school districts the map is often prepared by a committee of experts. In small school districts the teachers, working as a group or as individuals, may develop their own map, within limits defined by state guidelines. As a teacher plans a map, he or she must consider: (1) needs assessment data, if available, by the school or district,(2) goals of the school (or school district), (3) preassessment or placement evaluation data of the students, such as reading tests, aptitude tests, self-report inventories, observational reports, and (4) instructional objectives of the course according to district or state guidelines and grade level or departmental publications.[12] See Figure 10.1.

Mapping identifies and details the content, concepts, skills, and sometimes, values to be taught for the entire course. Performing this task places the teacher in a better position to do unit and lesson planning. The mapping

---

[12]Walter Dick and Robert A. Reiser, *Planning Effective Instruction* (Englewood Cliffs, N.J.: Prentice-Hall, 1989); Bruce W. Tuckman, *Evaluating Instructional Programs*, 2nd ed. (Boston: Allyn and Bacon, 1985).

process also helps connect the goals and objectives of the course. It helps teachers to view the course as a whole and to see the relationship of content, concepts, and skills being stressed.[13] Mapping requires that the teacher know, before the term or school year begins, what the important content areas, concepts, and skills of the course are.

In general, the map or course of study provides a total view of the entire term's or year's work without specifying sequences or relationships of tasks. As an example, the map in Table 10.2 identifies the major content, concepts, skills, and values for any subject or grade level.

Guidelines for Mapping

Here are a few recommendations for the map or course level of planning.

1. Be sure you understand the rationale for the course in the context of the goals of the school or district.
2. Be sure you understand the objectives of the course, according to state or district guidelines.
3. Clarify the focus of the course. Should it be designed to stress subject matter, learner needs, or societal needs?
4. Determine if there is a special need (special audience, special instructional program) for the course.
5. Identify the important components: content, concepts, skills, values.
6. Examine the components to see if they (a) meet the important objectives of the course, (b) foster critical or high-order thinking, (c) match student abilities, according to data obtained from preplanning evaluation, (d) stimulate student interest, (e) are realistic in terms of school time allotted to the course and school resources, and (f) are balanced in terms of sequence (vertically) and scope (horizontally related.)
7. Decide on important components so that they can be used as a framework for your unit planning.
8. Show the map to an experienced colleague or supervisor. Revise it in light of the feedback received.
9. As you use the map, evaluate, modify, and improve it. Note components that should be (a) added to cover gaps, (b) eliminated to avoid redundancy, trivia, and unnecessary complications, or (c) changed to avoid unanticipated negative effects and to provide better guidance for you and the students.

---

[13]George J. Posner and Alan N. Rudnitsky, *Course Design: A Guide to Curriculum Development for Teachers,* 2nd ed. (New York: Longman, 1986); Jon Wiles and Joseph C. Bondi, *Curriculum Development: A Guide to Practice,* 3rd ed. (Columbus, Ohio: Merrill, 1989).

Table 10.2   MAPPING: IDENTIFYING MAJOR CONTENT, CONCEPTS, SKILLS, AND VALUES

Content areas*	Concepts (major ideas of the course)
1. According to headings (such as chapters or topics in the text)	1. Classifying information with a focus
2. According to similarities and differences (such as communities, cities, states, nations, and continents)	2. Grouping information with a focus
	3. Categorizing information with implicit relationships
3. According to "what" or "who" relationships (such as Matisse, Picasso, and Miro)	4. Categorizing information with explicit relationships
4. According to a system of classification (such as animals, foods, chemicals, governments)	5. Comparing information with a focus
	6. Comparing information with qualifications
5. According to "why" or explanation of phenomena (such as what if questions, possibilities, probabilities, and projections)	7. Explaining (interpreting) information by logical relationships
	8. Explaining (interpreting) information by separating relevant from irrelevant information
6. According to "how" (such as working out problems of weight, volume, density, motion)	9. Organizing information based on principles, formulas, or cause-effect relationships
	10. Assimilating new information with old information based on principles, formulas, or cause-effect relationships
	11. Applying principles, formulas, or cause-effect relationships to explain new information
	12. Applying principles, formulas, or cause-effect relationships to predict trends, events, or measurements

Basic academic skills	Learning skills

1. Speaking
    Listening
    Debating
    Rethinking
    Concluding
	1. Note taking
	    Outlining main ideas only
	    Outlining main and subordinate ideas
	    Classifying information
	    Grouping information
	    Outlining from chalkboard
	    Outlining from text

2. Reading
    Vocabulary
    Skimming
    Comprehension
    Interpreting pictures and graphs
	2. Homework
	    Routine homework
	    Problem-solving homework
	    Independent work
	    Reporting
	    Special projects (library, laboratory)
	    Group assignments

3. Writing
    Essay
    Reporting
    Creative	

Table 10.2 CONTINUED

Basic academic skills	Learning skills
4. Computer Skills 　Practice and drill 　Using or transferring information 　Writing ideas or stories 　Reporting 　Problem solving 　Simulations 　Programming	3. Studying 　Copying from text 　Underlining text 　Notes on text margins 　Studying alone 　Studying in groups 　Reviewing while reading assignments 　Reviewing for quizzes or tests

Higher-cognitive functioning	Values
1. Using facts 2. Analyzing 3. Synthesizing 4. Inferring 5. Drawing conclusions 6. Evaluating 7. Problem solving 8. Predicting	1. Affirming one's identity 2. Affirming one's group 3. Listening to others 4. Appreciating others 5. Working with others 6. Choosing friends 7. Making choices 8. Being responsible for one's actions 9. Understanding legal issues 10. Understanding moral and ethical issues

*Content areas can be based on the units of the course. Units should be organized around the content items listed. The five content areas and twelve concepts suggest a hierarchy based on difficulty and sophistication in thinking. There seems to be a correlation with content 1 and concept 1; content 2 and concepts 2–4; content 3 with concepts 5–6; content 4 with concepts 7–8; content 5 with concepts 9–10; and content 6 with concepts 11–12. No proof of the correlation has been established.

Strategic Planning

Teachers can make good use of collaborative or joint planning in preparing unit and lesson plans. The object of **strategic planning** is to help teachers in planning together and sharing their teaching experiences.

It is important that teachers design unit and lesson plans, or any other instructional activity, to help students learn content and process information. The idea is to blend content with principles of thinking. The teacher continually asks himself or herself what the students' capabilities are and when to incorporate what instructional techniques. The goal of strategic planning is to enable students to integrate and apply new learning at the lesson plan stage, and to enable teachers to check and clarify various points within the planning stage. The teacher regularly revises the unit and lesson plan according to student outcomes.

Professional Viewpoint

On "Teaching Formulas"

What are principles of teaching and learning? They are propositions or "rules of thumb" about teaching and learning that can be used to form a theory or theories of teaching, and/or to guide educational practice. Principles of teaching are derived from principles of learning and motivation, based on psychological theory and research in educational psychology, largely research on learning from teaching. They have a "scientific basis." Are these formulas to be applied to all teaching situations by all teachers? No! Teaching by formula would be no better than using a five-step procedure for creative thinking. Principles of teaching and learning provide a core repertoire of pedagogical or instructional knowledge on which to base practice. Teachers must carefully temper and polish this knowledge in their own classrooms as they gain a special kind of "pedagogical intelligence." For the novice, such principles can be essential confidence aids—a kind of defense against feelings of incompetence and ineptitude. They provide a sense of the structure of the subject matter of teaching and its powerful and generative ideas. Teachers in training must systematically reflect on these ideas in light of their own and others' experiences with the craft.

Lyn Corno
Associate Professor of Education
and Psychology
Teachers College, Columbia University

Six steps in strategic planning are outlined. They deal with content, cognitive processes, and student characteristics.

1. Establish the content prior to the unit or lesson plan.
2. Outline the basic organization of information that will facilitate student learning; consider how the text and other instructional materials are organized.
3. Decide on expected outcomes.
4. Anticipate prior knowledge students possess about the topic, problem, or organizational frames that will be examined; link present content to students' prior knowledge.
5. Check the text and other instructional materials to determine if vocabulary and other written features will pose reading problems.

6. Anticipate what learning strategies students will use to learn the material; sequence instruction to coincide with these strategies.[14]

UNIT PLANS

A **unit plan** is a blueprint to clarify what content will be taught by what learning experiences during a specific period of time. It is a segment of the map or course of study. One reason for developing unit plans is related to the theory that learning by wholes is more effective than piece-by-piece learning. Another is the need for teachers to plan experiences in advance to meet the different kinds of objectives. Advance planning at the unit plan level requires teachers to survey the entire subject and enables them to be more effective in designing and structuring the instructional process. The overall view it provides helps them anticipate problems that may arise, especially in terms of prerequisite content, concepts, and skills.

Components of the Unit Plan

The unit plan consists of six basic components. They are objectives, content, skills, activities, resources and materials, and evaluation (Table 10.3). All should be considered in planning a unit, although in some cases skills and materials do not always have to be specified.

Objectives   Objectives can be behavioral or nonbehavioral (topics, problems, questions). Most teachers today rely on behavioral objectives partly because of recent emphasis on them in the professional literature. The method you use as the core of your plan will depend on your approach and the schools' approach to planning units.

Content   The scope of the content should be outlined. The content often includes three major catagories: knowledge, skills, and values.[15] The development of skills is usually more important at the elementary school level and with teachers who emphasize behaviorist or mastery learning. Knowledge is more important at the secondary school level and with teachers who emphasize cognitive or inductive learning. Valuing is more a reflection of the individual teacher and school than the specific grade level.

---

[14] Beau F. Jones et al., *Strategic Teaching and Learning: Cognitive Instruction in the Content Areas* (Alexandria, Va.: Association for Supervision and Curriculum Development, 1987); Donald M. Ogle, "Implementing Strategic Teaching," *Educational Leadership*, December–January 1989, pp. 47–48, 57–60.

[15] Ronald C. Doll, *Curriculum Improvement: Decision Making and Process*, 7th ed. (Boston: Allyn and Bacon, 1989); Ralph W. Tyler, *Basic Principles of Curriculum and Instruction* (Chicago: University of Chicago Press, 1949).

Table 10.3   UNIT PLAN COMPONENTS

1. Objectives
   General objectives and specific objectives.
   Behavioral objectives or nonbehavioral objectives (topics, problems, questions)
2. Content
   Knowledge (concepts, problem solving, critical thinking)
   Skills (cognitive, affective, psychomotor)
   Values
3. Skills
   Work habits
   Discussion and specific communication skills
   Reading skills
   Writing skills
   Note-taking skills
   Dictionary skills
   Reference skills (table of contents, glossary, index, card catalog)
   Library skills
   Reporting and research skills
   Computer skills
   Interpreting skills (maps, charts, tables, graphs, legends)
   Inquiry skills (problem solving, experimenting, hypothesizing)
   Social skills (respecting rules, accepting criticism, poise and maturity, peer acceptance)
   Cooperative and competitive skills (leadership, self-concept, participation in group)
4. Learning activities
   Lectures and explanations
   Practice and drill
   Grouping activities (buzz sessions, panels, debates, forums)
   Role playing, simulations, dramatizations
   Research, writing projects (stories, biographies, logs)
   Experiments
   Field trips
   Reviews
5. Resources and Materials
   Written materials (books, pamphlets, magazines, newspapers)
   Audiovisual materials (films, records, slides, television, video tapes)
   Programmed or computer materials
   Models, replicas, charts, graphs, specimens
6. Evaluation procedures
   Demonstrations, exhibits, debates
   Reviews, summaries
   Quizzes, examinations
   Reteaching
   Remediation
   Special training

Skills   A list of cognitive and social skills to be developed is sometimes optional. The skills should be based on the content to be taught but sometimes may be listed as separate from the content. Important basic skills to develop include critical reading, skimming and scanning, reading graphic materials (maps, diagrams, charts, tables), library skills, composition and reporting skills, note taking, homework skills, study skills, social and interpersonal skills, discussion and speaking skills, cooperative and competitive skills, and leadership skills.

Learning Activities   Learning activities, sometimes called *student activities*, should be based on implementing objectives and students' needs and interests. Only special activities, such as guest speakers, field trips, debates and buzz sessions, research reports, projects, experiments, and summative examinations, need be listed. The recurring or common activities can be shown as part of the daily lesson plan.

Resources and Materials   The purpose of including resources and materials in the plan is to guide the teacher in assembling the reading material, library and research materials, and audiovisual equipment needed to carry out instruction. This list at the unit plan level should include only essential resources and materials. A list of resources is often covered in a listing of learning activities and so is sometimes considered an optional element in a unit plan.

Evaluation Procedures   The major evaluation procedures and culminating activities should be included. These include formative and summative evaluations: student exhibits and demonstrations, summary debates and discussions, quizzes and examinations, reteaching, remedial work, and special tutoring or training. Evaluation can be conducted by students or the teacher or both. The intent is to appraise whether the objectives have been achieved and to obtain information for improving the unit plan. See Tips for Teachers 10.1.

Tips for Teachers 10.1

Organizing and Implementing Unit Plans: A Model

The Muhlenberg, Pennsylvania, school district has devised a diagnostic and prescriptive model for organizing and implementing unit plans in the classroom. The emphasis is on integrating the written unit plan with teaching, testing, and student grouping. It seems to combine the ideas of mastery learning with cooperative learning.

continued

1. Review with class the required objectives for the unit.
2. Pretest students on terminal behaviors for the unit. Establish criterion for mastery (80 or 90 percent).
3. Score and record pretest results.
4. Prepare to teach each objective of the unit; objectives may correspond to lessons.
5. Conduct a brief (about 5 minutes) overview of each objective for the day.
6. Group students into three groups based on pretest data.
    a. Group I contains students who did not demonstrate mastery (less than 50 percent); daily lesson activities need to be teacher-centered.
    b. Group II contains students who have readiness for mastery (50 to 75 percent); daily lesson activities should be a mix of teacher- and learner-centered.
    c. Group III contains students who have demonstrated mastery (75 percent or higher); daily lesson activities should be learner-centered.
7. Bring class together each day (lesson) for summary and review or closing activity.
8. As groups I and II demonstrate mastery of the objective, proceed to next objective; learning is self-paced.
9. If a group has not demonstrated mastery of the objective, continue the lesson the next day.
10. Move students into different groups as they master the objectives.
11. When the basic group has mastered all the objectives of the unit, review the unit with the whole class.
12. Post-test all students on terminal behaviors of unit.
13. If remediation is indicated for some students, note it for further "review days" and move to the new unit.
14. If mastery is demonstrated, move to a new unit.

Source: Adapted from Joseph S. Yarworth, Timothy L. Schwambach, and Robert F. Nicely, "Organization for Results in Elementary and Middle School Mathematics," *Educational Leadership*, October 1988, pp. 61–64.

Approaches to Unit Planning

The teacher might check with his or her supervisor before planning a unit. Some school districts have a preferred approach for developing units, and others permit more latitude for their teachers. Some supervisors require teachers to submit units for final approval, while other supervisors give more professional authority to teachers. Below are two basic approaches to unit planning that teachers may wish to consider.

Taxonomic Approach   Table 10.4 illustrates a unit plan based on the taxonomy of educational objectives. The objectives are divided into three domains of learning: cognitive processes, attitudes and values, and psychomotor skills. The unit plan states a daily problem that leads to the objectives and shows corresponding activities and materials and resources. Evaluation is not listed separately, but is blended as part of the activities suggested for the ninth and tenth lessons. The approach combines both behaviorist and cognitive developmental theory.

Topic Approach   Table 10.5 illustrates the topic approach. The unit plan is organized by topics and objectives. Objectives introduce the lesson, but the topics serve as the major basis for outlining the unit. The objectives coincide with the recommendation that content focus on concepts, skills, and values. Note that the objectives (related to knowledge, skills, and values) do not build upon one another (they are somewhat independent) nor are they divided into general and specific. The topics are arranged in the order in which they will be treated, suggesting that they correspond to the table of contents of a textbook. Indeed, it is appropriate to follow a text, as long as it is well planned and the teacher knows when to modify or supplement the text with related activities and materials.

The topics also represent daily lesson plans. The activities listed are nonrecurring, special activities; repeated activities can be listed at the lesson plan level. The activities are listed in the order in which they will occur, but there is not one particular activity listed for each topic (as in Table 10.4). The evaluation component is separate and includes formative and summative tests, discussion, and feedback.

Guidelines for Developing Unit Plans

The number of units and the time allotted and emphasis for each unit are matters of judgment, although experts tend to recommend about 15 to 30 units for a year's course and about 5 to 10 lessons per unit.[16] Consideration is usually given to the organization of the textbook, the emphasis suggested by state and

---

[16] M. Sierra Goethals and Rose A. Howard, *Handbook of Skills Essential to Beginning Teachers* (Lanham, Md.: University Press of America, 1985); Edward L. Meyen, *Developing Instructional Units*, 3rd ed. (Dubuque, Iowa: Brown, 1980); and William J. Stewart, *Transforming Traditional Unit Teaching* (Boston: American Press, 1982).

Table 10.4 UNIT PLAN FOR ENVIRONMENTAL SCIENCE

Problem	Cognitive processes	Attitudes and values	Psychomotor skills	Learning activities	Resources and materials
1. Identifying an environment	To identify environments based on physical and biological characteristics	To explore social and scientific issues; to ask questions		Class discussion	Filmstrip
2. Comparing environments	To recognize different environments	To discuss alternative viewpoints; to debate responsibility for health and welfare of others	To use tools that call for fine adjustment and discrimination	Debates	Pictures, replicas, models
3. Taking a field trip to compare environments	To compare environments based on physical and biological characteristics	To formulate new ideas about natural resources	To visualize different environments; to listen to tour guides present relevant information	Field trip to museum	Tape recorder
4. Other ways to compare environments	To distinguish environments based on physical and biological characteristics	To ask questions; to compare alternative viewpoints	To manipulate laboratory equipment	Experiment (see text)	Plants, rocks, soil
5. Summarizing differences between environments	To judge different environments	To discuss balance and theorize ideas		Class discussion	Visiting expert

6. Exploring the limits of environmental change	To deduce that environments change and still conserve their identity and that they lose identity when their capacity to change is exceeded	To ask questions; to define limits of biological and environmental systems	To handle plants, rocks, soil	Class discussion	Graphs, maps, showing weather, volcanoes, mountains, rivers
7. Understanding the consequences of changing environment	To appraise the results of changing environments	To seek alternative viewpoints; to revise ideas	To use equipment that requires fine adjustments	Student interviews	Old "timers" in community, old newspapers
8. Implementing a plan to improve the school environment	To recognize that environments can change and improve	To demonstrate responsibility for health and welfare of others	To use and care for tools and equipment	Brainstorming sessions	Visiting administrator
9. Surveying world environments that have changed	To detect how world environments have changed and assumed new identities	To demonstrate the need to use natural resources wisely; to organize a plan that contributes to the conservation of natural resources		Oral reports judged by students	Technical journals, library materials
10. Summarizing and evaluating	To demonstrate proficiency in facts, concepts, and principles of subject matter	To argue, appraise, and judge in terms of scientific standards		Unit examination	

Source: Adapted from Rita Peterson et al., *Science and Society: A Source Book for Elementary and Junior High School Teachers* (Columbus, Ohio: Merrill, 1984), pp. 166–167.

Table 10.5   UNIT PLAN FOR AMERICAN HISTORY

Objectives

I. Knowledge
 1. To recognize that the U.S. Constitution is rooted in English law
 2. To identify the causes and events leading to the forming of the U.S. Constitution
 3. To argue the advantages and limitations of the U.S. Constitution
 4. To illustrate how amendments are enacted

II. Skills
 1. To expand vocabulary proficiency
 2. To improve research skills
 3. To improve oral reporting skills
 4. To expand reading habits to include historical events and people
 5. To develop debating techniques

III. Values
 1. To develop an understanding that freedom is based on laws
 2. To recognize the obligations of freedom (among free people)
 3. To appreciate how rights are protected
 4. To develop a more positive attitude toward minorities
 5. To develop a more positive attitude toward classmates

Topics

I. Historical background of the Constitution
 1. English common law
 2. Magna Carta
 3. Mayflower Compact
 4. Colonial freedom
 5. Taxation without representation
 6. Boston Tea Party
 7. First and second Constitutional Congress
 8. Declaration of Independence
 9. Age of Enlightenment and America

II. Bill of Rights and the Constitution
 1. Constitutional Convention
 2. Framing of the Constitution
 3. Bill of Rights
    a. Reasons
    b. Specific freedoms
 4. Powers reserved to the states
 5. Important amendments
    a. Thirteenth, Fourteenth, Fifteenth (slavery, due process, voting rights)
    b. Nineteenth (women's suffrage)
    c. Twentieth (progressive tax)
    d. Twenty-second (two-term limit to presidency)
    e. Others

Evaluation

 1. Short quiz for I.1–9
 2. Graded reports with specific feedback for each student; half a lesson
 3. Discussion of students' role as citizens in a free society; compare rights and responsibilities of American citizens with rights and responsibilities of students; a full lesson or one day
 4. Unit test; review I.1–9; II,1–5

Table 10.5 CONTINUED

Activities

1. Filmstrip introducing part I
2. List of major points to be discussed in part I
3. Homework—reading list for each topic or lesson (I, 1–9; II, 1–5)
4. Television program on "American Freedom" and discussion after I.9
5. Field trip to historical museum as culminating activity for I and introduction to II
6. Topics and reports for outside reading, with two-day discussion of reports after II.3
7. Two-day debate (with four teams): "What's wrong with our Constitution?" "What's right with our Constitution?" after II.5

Source: Adapted from Gail M. Inlow, *Maturity in High School Teaching,* 2nd ed. (Englewood Cliffs, N.J.: Prentice-Hall, 1970), pp. 110–112. Parts of the topics are based on Inlow, remaining segments are mainly the author's.

school district curriculum guides, and the special abilities, needs, and interests of the students. Also, according to test specialists, there is an increasing tendency for teachers to plan units around national, state, and school district testing programs, what is sometimes called "focused" instruction or "high-stake" evaluation.[17]

Having already outlined the basic components of the unit plan, we now provide suggestions that deal with some of the details. These suggestions are applicable for all subjects and grade levels.

1. Develop the unit plan with a particular class or group of students in mind.
2. Indicate the subject, grade level, and length of time to teach the unit.
3. Outline the unit around a general theme or idea (the unit title).
4. Identify the general objectives, problems, or topics of the unit. Each objective, problem, or topic should correspond to a lesson plan (to be discussed below).
5. Include one or more of the following: (a) content and activities, (b) cognitive processes and skills, (c) psychomotor skills, (d) attitudes and values.
6. Match objectives (problems or topics) with content and activities, and possibly processes and skills.
7. Identify methods for evaluating the outcomes of the unit. Possibly include a pretest and posttest to determine learning outcomes or improvement in learning.
8. Include resources (materials and media) needed to supplement the text.

[17] W. James Popham, "Can High-Stakes Tests Be Developed at the Local Level?" *National Association of Secondary School Principals,* February 1987, pp. 77–84; Herbert C. Rudman, "Classroom Instruction and Tests," *National Association of Secondary School Principals,* February 1987, pp. 3–22.

9. Plan an effective way of introducing the unit, possibly an overview exercise, problem, or recent event.
10. Classify the unit, if possible, according to different levels of problem solving, creative work, or achievement.
11. Design parts of the unit for low-achieving, average-achieving, and high-achieving students.
12. Plan the unit so it is vertically related to other parts of the course subject and, if possible, horizontally related to other subjects.
13. Develop the unit to include the life experiences of the students or out-of-school activities such as field trips, or work in the library or community.
14. Duplicate the unit plan for the students so they can follow it.
15. Periodically modify and update the unit plan for subsequent use.

LESSON PLANS

A **lesson plan** sets forth the proposed program, or instructional activities, for each day; it is sometimes referred to as a *daily plan*. In general, the lesson plan should be planned around the fixed periods (usually 35 to 50 minutes) of the typical school schedule, allowing adequate time for teachers or students to arrive (if they are changing classrooms) and to leave at the end of the period. Shorter blocks of time may be allowed for younger students or for those whose attention span is limited. Good timing or scheduling is an aid to good instruction and good classroom management.

Although special school activities may require shortened or lengthened periods, most lessons should be planned for full periods. Sometimes students need more or less time to finish an activity or assignment, and teachers need to learn how to be flexible in adjusting timing. As teachers develop their planning and pacing skills, they learn to plan better schedules in advance and to plan supplementary activities and materials for use or elimination as the need arises, to maintain a good pace. Additional activities might include performing a committee function, completing a research assignment, finishing a workbook assignment, illustrating a composition or report, working on a study activity, performing an honor or extra credit assignment, or tutoring another student. Additional materials might include pictures, charts, and models to further demonstrate a major point in the lesson, review exercises for practice and drill, and a list of summary questions to review major points of the lesson.

To avoid omissions, underemphasis, or overemphasis, the teacher needs to consider his or her style of teaching and the students' abilities and interests. The teacher should review the progress of each day's lesson and periodically take notes on important student responses to different methods, media, and activities—to reuse with another class or at another time. Inexperienced teachers need to plan the lessons in detail, follow the plan, and refer to it frequently. As they grow in experience and confidence, they become able to plan with

Figure 10.3 Schools provide different opportunities for teachers to discuss their lesson plans with colleagues and supervisors. (Photo © Laimute E. Druskis/Taurus)

less detail and rely more on their spontaneous responses to what happens in the classroom as the teaching-learning process unfolds.

Lesson Plans by Authorities

Many current authorities who write about what a lesson plan should contain write from the point of view of direct instructional methods, that is, a view of the classroom in which teaching is teacher-directed, methods and materials are sequenced, content is extensive and focused, students are provided with practice as the teacher checks or monitors the work, and the teacher provides evaluation of performance. The objectives are clearly stated in the beginning of the lesson, and a review either proceeds or follows the statement of objectives. Learning takes place in an academic, subject-centered environment. There is little mention or concern about student needs or interests; emphasis is on student abilities and achievement.

The authors listed in Table 10.6 all exhibit this direct, step-by-step approach to learning. The categories or components are lined up within the table to show similiarities among approaches. All lesson plan components and classroom events are controlled by the teacher, no provision is made for student choice or planning, and the classroom is highly structured and businesslike. Most important, the emphasis is on knowledge, skills, and tasks, as well as practice, review, and testing; very few, if any, of their prescriptions seem directed to problem solving, critical thinking, or creativity, much less personal, social, or moral development.

Although the authorities listed in the table might not admit it or agree, their approaches apply mainly to the teaching of basic skills and basic subjects

Table 10.6 LESSON PLAN COMPONENTS BY AUTHORITIES

Mastery learning (Hunter)	Instructional design (Gagné)	Lesson planning (Slavin)	Instructional behaviors (Good and Grouws, Good and Brophy)
1. *Review.* Focus on previous lesson; ask students to review questions orally or in writing; ask students to summarize main points.		1. *State learning objectives.* Explain what students are expected to learn; provide background information.	1. *Review.* Review concepts and skills related to homework; provide review exercises.
2. *Anticipatory set.* Focus students' attention on lesson to be presented; stimulate interest in new material.	1. *Gain attention.* Alert students to what to expect; get students started on a routine or warm-up drill.	2. *Review prerequisites.* Have students recall major points of previous lesson.	
3. *Objective.* State explicitly what will be learned; state rationale or how it will be useful.	2. *Inform learner of objective.* Activate the learners' motivation by informing them of the objective to be achieved.		
	3. *Recall prior knowledge.* Remind students of previously learned knowledge or concepts germane to new material; recall relevant prerequisites.		
4. *Input.* Identify needed knowledge and skills for learning new lesson; present material in logical and sequenced steps.	4. *Present the stimulus material.* Present new knowledge or skills; indicate distinctive properties of the concepts to be learned.	3. *Present new material.* Teach the lesson; present new information; provide examples; illustrate concepts.	2. *Development.* Promote student understanding of new material; provide examples, explanations, demonstrations.
5. *Modeling.* Provide several examples or demonstrations throughout the lesson.	5. *Provide learning guidance.* Elaborate on directions, provide assistance; integrate new information with previous (long-term memory) information.	4. *Conduct learning probes.* Pose questions to assess student understanding, provide "corrective instruction" or assistance when necessary.	3. *Assess student comprehension.* Ask questions; provide controlled practice.
6. *Check for understanding.* Monitor students' work before they become involved in lesson activities; check to see they understand the directions or tasks.	6. *Elicit performance.* Suggest, do not specify, methods for performing tasks or problems; provide cues or directions, not answers; students are to provide answers.		
7. *Guided practice.* Periodically ask student questions or problems and check their answers. The same type of monitoring and response formats are involved in checking for understanding as in guided practice.	7. *Provide feedback.* Reinforce learning by checking students' work and providing frequent feedback, especially during the acquisition stage of the new material. Use feedback to adapt instruction to individual students.		

Table 10.6 CONTINUED

Mastery learning (Hunter)	Instructional design (Gagné)	Lesson planning (Slavin)	Instructional behaviors (Good and Grouws, Good and Brophy)
8. *Independent practice.* Assign independent work or practice when it is reasonably sure that students can work on their own with minimal effort.		5. *Provide independent practice.* Give students practice exercises or problems; permit students to apply new information on their own.	4. *Seatwork.* Provide uninterrupted seatwork; get everyone involved; sustain momentum.
	8. *Assess performance.* Inform students of their performance in terms of outcomes; establish an "expectancy" level.	6. *Assess performance and provide feedback.* Review independent practice; provide feedback; reteach whatever is necessary.	5. *Accountability.* Check the students' work.
	9. *Ensure retention and transfer.* Utilize various instructional techniques to ensure retention (outline, classify information, use tables, charts, and diagrams). Enhance transfer of learning by providing a variety of cues, practice situations, and interlinking concepts.	7. *Provide practice and review.* Assign homework; review material in next lesson; integrate material in later lessons.	6. *Homework.* Assign homework regularly; provide review problems.
			7. *Special reviews.* Provide weekly reviews (exercises, quizzes) each Monday to enhance and maintain learning; provide monthly reviews every fourth Monday to further enhance and maintain learning.

such as reading, mathematics, and foreign language, where practice and drill are often recommended. They are not as effective, if they can be used at all, in teaching inquiry or discovery learning or creative thinking. Nevertheless, since the approaches do receive much attention in the professional literature and since they are applicable in more than one teaching area, they should be read. Later, we will present a less direct approach, along with sample lesson plans, that provides teachers with greater flexibility in teaching.

Teaching Techniques The authorities listed in Table 10.6, as well as other advocates of direct instruction, emphasize structured and sequenced strategies for enhancing student understanding while presenting and teaching from the lesson plan. Barak Rosenshine, for example, refers to **teaching functions**—that is, *checking* procedures to ensure full student comprehension. Throughout the lesson the teacher engages in a series of functions to check student understanding.

I. To check previous work
  1. Asking questions or problems about concepts or skills.
  2. Administering a short quiz on previous lessons or homework.
  3. Having students correct their own quizzes or homework.
  4. Organizing small student groups to review previous lessons or homework.
  5. Encouraging students to prepare questions about previous lessons or homework to ask each other or the teacher.
  6. Having students prepare a written summary of previous lessons.
  7. Reteaching and providing additional practice.
II. To check current work
  1. Asking students several questions concerning the main points of the new material.
  2. Calling on nonvolunteers.
  3. Asking students to summarize main points on paper or at the chalkboard.
  4. Having students write answers on paper and then check answers with a neighbor.
  5. Discussing main points of the lesson in small groups and preparing a summary for presentation to the class.
  6. Providing sufficient practice exercises, monitoring for understanding, and providing feedback.
  7. Reteaching when necessary.
  8. Providing additional successful repetitions.[18]

Emmer and Evertson present five categories of *clarifying* techniques. Their suggestions pertain to both elementary and secondary school in all subjects.

I. Communicate lesson objectives
  1. State the objectives at the beginning of the lesson.
  2. Explain to students what they will be accountable for knowing or doing.
  3. Emphasize major ideas as they are presented.
  4. Review the objectives or major points at the end of the lesson.
II. Present information systematically
  1. Outline the lesson in an easy-to-follow sequence.
  2. Stick to the topic.
  3. Summarize previous points; make transitions between major ideas or concepts.
  4. Provide step-by-step directions when necessary.

---

[18] Barak V. Rosenshine, "Teaching Functions in Instructional Programs," *Elementary School Journal*, March 1983, pp. 335–351; Barak V. Rosenshine and Robert Stevens, "Teaching Functions," in M. C. Wittrock, ed., *Handbook of Research on Teaching*, 3rd ed. (New York: Macmillan, 1986), pp. 376–391.

   5. Check for understanding at intervals before proceeding to next major idea or concept.
   6. Maintain an appropriate pace.
III. Avoid vagueness
   1. Provide concrete examples to explain and reinforce information.
   2. Use appropriate vocabulary.
   3. Be specific and precise; refer to concrete objects, events.
IV. Check for understanding
   1. Ask questions or obtain work samples before proceeding.
   2. Have students summarize main points to show understanding.
   3. Call on slower students and nonvolunteers.
   4. Reteach necessary parts.
 V. Provide practice and feedback
   1. Provide adequate practice of objectives to be mastered.
   2. Reinforce learning with review assignments.
   3. Check work on a regular basis.
   4. Reexplain and reteach when appropriate.[19]

Components of the Lesson Plan

There is no one ideal format to follow for a lesson plan. Teachers should modify the suggestions of methods experts and learning theorists to coincide with their teaching style and the suggestions of their school or district. For example, the New York City school system recommends that beginning teachers include the following seven components in a lesson plan.

1. Specific *objectives* of the lesson
2. Appropriate *motivation* to capture the students' interest and maintain it throughout the lesson
3. *Development* or *outline* of a lesson (sometimes referred to as content or activities)
4. Varied *methods,* including drill, questions, and demonstrations, designed to keep the lesson on track
5. Varied *materials and media* to supplement and clarify content
6. Medial and final *summaries*
7. Provision for an *assignment* or *homework*[20]

This list of components can serve as a logical framework for constructing a lesson plan. The teacher can vary how much time he or she spends on each

---

[19] Edmund T. Emmer et al., *Classroom Management for Secondary Teachers,* 2nd ed. (Englewood Cliffs, N.J.: Prentice-Hall, 1989); Carolyn M. Evertson et al., *Classroom Management for Elementary Teachers,* 2nd ed. (Englewood Cliffs, N.J.: Prentice-Hall, 1989).

[20] *Getting Started in the Elementary School: A Manual for New Teachers,* rev. ed. (New York: Board of Education of the City of New York, 1986); *Getting Started in the Secondary School: A Manual for New Teachers,* rev. ed. (New York: Board of Education of the City of New York, 1986).

Tips for Teachers 10.2

Monitoring The Lesson Plan

One school district in Aurora, Colorado has devised a procedure for monitoring the lesson plan, that is, seeing if the curriculum is being implemented at the classroom level. Events in the classroom are identified as green or red flags, with green signifying effective strategies and red signifying ineffective strategies. The teacher can use this list for self-evaluation, or students, colleagues, or supervisors can use it to provide feedback to the teacher.

GREEN FLAGS

1. Heterogeneous classes with groups within
2. Student interest and teacher enthusiasm
3. Recognizing that students may change in skills
4. Integration of problem solving
5. Students applying [content] to real-life situations
6. Use of manipulatives
7. Enrichment activities available to students

RED FLAGS

1. All students in the class doing the same assignments
2. No or excessive homework
3. Students grouped homogeneously
4. Excessive or no purpose for chalkboard work
5. Teacher grading papers while students do homework or students doing homework on own; homework consisting of an excessive number of similar problems
6. Students repeating operations they have mastered
7. Class bogged down on "mastery" of specific operations
8. No diagnostic testing
9. Lack of variety of strategies and class activities
10. Too much or too little [explanation and] demonstration
11. Students not understanding purposes of their homework
12. Rigidity of [student] groupings—no fluidity of movement to allow for weaknesses, strengths, or ability
13. [Lack of] checking for understanding
14. Overemphasis on "drill and practice"
15. Never any use of [supplementary materials or media]

Source: Tom Maglaras and Deborah Lynch, "Monitoring the Curriculum: From Plan to Action," *Educational Leadership,* October 1988, p. 59.

component, how much detail is included in each, and which components are included. With experience the teacher discovers the most useful components to include and the amount of detail needed in the plan as a whole. See Tips for Teachers 10.2.

Objectives   The first questions a teacher considers when sorting out the content he or she plans to teach are: What do I plan to teach? What do I want the students to learn from the lesson that will be worthwhile? The answers to these questions are the objectives; they form the backbone of the lesson. Motivation, methods, and materials are organized to achieve the objectives. Establishing objectives ensures against aimlessness.

Objectives may be phrased as statements or questions. (Most people think they can only be written as statements.) The question form may encourage students to think. Regardless of how they are phrased, they should be written on the chalkboard or on a printed handout for students to see. Here are some examples of objectives for a lesson plan, written first as a statement and then as a question.

1a. To compare the prices of agricultural goods and industrial goods during the depression
1b. Why did the prices of agricultural goods decline more than the prices of industrial goods during the depression?
2a. To recognize that the production of oil in the Middle East affects economic conditions in the United States
2b. How does the production of oil in the Middle East affect economic conditions in the United States?
3a. To recognize that the skin protects people from diseases.
3b. How does our skin protect us from diseases?

The major objective of a lesson may have ancillary (secondary) objectives. Ancillary objectives divide the lesson into segments and highlight or supplement important ideas. Below is an example of a lesson objective with two ancillary objectives (expressed as statements and then questions).

1a. *Lesson objective:* To explain the causes of World War I *Ancillary objectives:* To compare nationalism, colonialism, and militarism; to distinguish between propaganda and facts
1b. *Lesson objective:* What were the causes of World War I? *Ancillary objectives:* How are nationalism, colonialism, and militarism related? How can we distinguish between propaganda and facts?

Motivation   Motivational devices or activities arouse and maintain interest in the content to be taught. Fewer motivational devices are needed for students who are intrinsically motivated, that is, are motivated to learn to satisfy some inner need or interest, than for students who are extrinsically motivated, that is, require incentives or reinforcers for learning. Lesson planning and instruction must seek to enhance both forms of motivation.

1. *Intrinsic motivation.* **Intrinsic motivation** involves sustaining or in-

creasing the interest students already have in a topic or task. The teacher selects and organizes the lesson so that it will (a) whet students' appetite at the beginning of the lesson; (b) maintain student curiosity and involvement in the work by using surprise, doubt, and perplexity; novel as well as familiar materials; interesting and varied methods; (c) provide active and manipulative opportunities; (d) permit students autonomy in organizing their time and effort; and (e) provide choices or alternatives to meet requirements of the lesson. Some activities and materials than can be used to enhance intrinsic motivation are:

1. *Challenging statements.* Nuclear power plants are unnecessary and potentially dangerous.
2. *Pictures and cartoons.* How does this picture illustrate the American public's feelings toward Japanese-made automobiles?
3. *Personal experiences.* What type of clothing is best to wear during freezing weather?
4. *Problems.* What metals conduct heat well? Why?
5. *Exploratory and creative activities.* I need three volunteers to come to the chalkboard to fill in the blanks of the puzzle, while the rest of you do it in your seats.
6. *Charts, tables, graphs, maps.* From a study of the chart, what characteristics do all these animals have in common?
7. *Anecdotes and stories.* How does the paragraph I have just read convey the author's feelings about the South?
8. *Contests and games.* Let's see how well you remember yesterday's homework. We will organize five teams by rows. In your notebooks, list eight different string instruments. You will have two minutes. We will average the scores. The winning row, with the highest average score, will receive extra credit.

2. *Extrinsic motivation.* **Extrinsic motivation** focuses on cognitive strategies. Activities that enhance success and reduce failure increase motivation. High-achieving students will persist longer than low-achieving students, even when experiencing failure, so incentives for learning are more important for average- and low-achieving students.[21] They are important for all students when the subject matter or content is uninteresting or difficult.[22]

Nine basic principles can be used by teachers for enhancing extrinsic motivation.

---

[21] Bernice J. Bragstad and Sharyn M. Stumpf, *A Guide for Teaching Study Skills and Motivation*, 2nd ed. (Needham Heights, Mass.: Allyn and Bacon, 1987); Franz E. Weinert and Rainer H. Kluwe, *Metacognition, Motivation and Understanding* (Hillsdale, N.J.: Erlbaum, 1986).

[22] Ellis D. Evans, "The Effects of Achievement Motivation and Ability upon Discovery Learning and Accompanying Incidental Learning under Two Conditions of Incentive Set," *Journal of Educational Research*, January 1967, pp. 195–200; Eva Sivan, "Motivation in Social Constructionist Theory," *Educational Psychologist*, Summer 1986, pp 209–233.

1. *Clear directions and expectations.* Students must know exactly what they are expected to do and how they will be evaluated.
2. *Time on task.* Keep students on task. The amount of time allocated to a particular topic or task varies considerably from school to school and from teacher to teacher. Time on task, student motivation, and student achievement are related.
3. *Cognitive match.* Student motivation is highest when students work on tasks or problems appropriate to their achievement levels. When they are confused or when the work is above their abilities, they resist or give up. When it is below their abilities, they seek other interests or move through the lesson as fast as possible.
4. *Prompt feedback.* Feedback on student performance should be constructive and prompt. A long delay between behavior (or performance) and results diminishes the relationship between them.
5. *Relate past learning with present learning.* Use reinforcers to strengthen previous learned content.
6. *Frequent rewards.* No matter how powerful a reward, it may have little impact if it is provided infrequently. Small, frequent rewards are more effective than large, infrequent ones.
7. *Praise.* Verbal praise ("Good," "Great," "Fine work") is a powerful motivating device.
8. *High expectations.* Students who are expected to learn will learn more and be motivated to learn more than students who are not expected to learn.
9. *Value of rewards.* Motivation is partially based on the value an individual places on success, as well as the individual's estimate of the possibility of success. Thus, incentives used for students should have value for them.[23]

Development   The **development,** sometimes called the *outline,* can be expressed as topics and subtopics, a series of broad or pivotal questions, or a list of activities (methods and materials). Most secondary teachers rely on topics or questions, and most elementary teachers refer to activities.

Emphasis on topics, concepts, or skills indicates a content orientation in teaching approach. Emphasis on activities has a more sociopsychological orientation; there is more stress on student needs and interests. For example, outlining the problems of the ozone layer on the chalkboard is content-oriented. Interviewing someone about the ozone layer is an activity that encompasses a wide range of social stimuli.

1. *Content.* Several criteria have been proposed for selecting and organizing

[23]N. L. Gage and David C. Berliner, *Educational Psychology,* 4th ed. (Boston: Houghton Mifflin, 1988); Robert E. Slavin, *Educational Psychology: Theory into Practice,* 2nd ed. (Englewood Cliffs, N.J.: Prentice-Hall, 1988); and Carole Ames and Russell Ames, *Research on Motivation in Education,* vol. 2 (New York: Academic Press, 1984).

appropriate content and experiences in the development section. The following are criteria for *content* developed by Ornstein and Hunkins.

1. *Validity.* The content selected should be verifiable, not misleading or false.
2. *Significance.* The content needs to be constantly reviewed so that worthwhile content—basic ideas, information, principles of the subject—is taught, and lessons do not become cluttered by masses of more trivial content now available through the "information explosion."
3. *Balance.* The content should promote macro and micro knowledge; students should experience the broad sweep of content, and they should have the opportunity to dig deep.
4. *Self-sufficiency.* The content should help students learn how to learn; it should help them gain maximum sufficiency in the most economic manner.
5. *Interest.* Content is best learned when it is interesting to the student. Some progressive educators urge that the child should be the focus of the teaching and learning process.
6. *Utility.* The content should be useful or practical in some situation outside the lesson, either to further other learning or in everyday experiences. How usefulness is defined depends on whether a teacher is subject-centered or student-centered, but most teachers would agree that useful content enhances the human potential of the learner.
7. *Learnability.* It should be within the capacity of the students to learn the content. There should be a cognitive match between the students' aptitudes and the subject (and between their abilities and academic tasks).
8. *Feasibility.* The teacher needs to consider the time needed, resources and materials available, curriculum guides, state and national tests, existing legislation, and the political climate of the community. There are limitations on what can be planned and taught.[24]

2. *Experiences.* Ronald Doll has raised several questions useful in developing appropriate learning activities, which he refers to as *experiences.* This term connotes a larger concept, including classroom and school activities, as well as out-of-school and community activities.

1. Can the experiences profit the [pupils] we teach?
2. Do the experiences help to meet the needs of our pupils?
3. Are our pupils likely to be interested in the experiences?
4. Do the experiences encourage pupils to inquire further?
5. Do the experiences seem real?
6. How do the experiences accord with the life patterns of our pupils?
7. How contemporary are some of the major experiences?

---

[24] Allan C. Ornstein and Francis P. Hunkins, *Curriculum: Foundations, Principles, and Issues* (Englewood Cliffs, N.J.: Prentice-Hall 1988).

Professional Viewpoint

Integrating Real-Life Experiences

I have been teaching for more than 60 years. In every one of my classes I have found some students who have difficulty in learning what I had hoped the class would help them learn. At first, I thought these students were unable to learn and that they would never be successful in their schoolwork. But then, I noticed that many of them were learning to play games, to deliver newspapers, to plan for field trips, and to learn to carry out many other activities.

I asked several students, "Why are you so good at learning things outside of school and seem to have difficulty with school work and with your homework?" Some said, "The things we learn outside of school are *real*, while school work is dull and *not* real." Some others said, "The things we do outside of school are our jobs. In school we are doing your job."

From these experiences, I began to realize that I must give my students responsibility for jobs in school, on the playground, and in the neighborhood. Then, when they accepted these responsibilities, I helped them learn to meet these responsibilities successfully. Now, I try to find out from my students what they are trying to do, and then help them to learn how to use reading, mathematics, literature, science, art, and music by doing well in activities they believe to be important. As students understand that they need to learn what schools are expected to teach, I become their helper, not their slave driver. Then teaching becomes fun for me.

Ralph W. Tyler
Director Emeritus
Center for Advanced Study
    in the Behavioral Sciences,
Palo Alto, Calif.

   8. How fundamental to mastery of total learning content are they?
   9. Do the experiences provide for attainment of a range of objectives?
   10. Do the experiences provide opportunities for both broad study and deep study?[25]

Methods Relying on the same methods day after day would be boring, even for adults. Different procedures sustain motivation throughout the lesson. Although many different procedures can be employed in a lesson, four basic

---

[25]Doll, *Curriculum Improvement: Decision Making and Process,* p. 150.

methods are (1) practice and drill, (2) questioning, (3) explanations and lectures, and (4) demonstrations and experiments. Depending on the type of lesson—as well as the students, subject, and grade level—these instructional methods should be used in varying degrees. We have already discussed these methods at length (Chapter 6), but we will review them here in a different mode.

1. *Practice/Drill.* There is general agreement that students need *practice* exercises to help them transfer new information into long-term memory and integrate new and old learning. Practice problems may come from workbooks, textbooks, and teacher-made materials. Practice, in the form of seatwork, can be helpful for students if it is given for limited time periods (no more than ten minutes per class session), the instructions for it are clear, and it is integrated into the lesson (not assigned to fill time or to maintain order). *Drill* can be helpful for basic skills, such as reading, mathematics, and language, and in lower grades and with low-achieving students who need more practice to learn new skills or integrate information.

Robert Slavin is a strong advocate of incorporating practice and drill as a major component of the lesson plan. He recommends six steps for enhancing what he calls *"independent practice."*

1. *Be sure students can do the work.* Do not assign the work until you are sure students understand or can do almost all items on the practice or worksheet. A high success rate on practice items is important for student learning.

2. *Assign short independent practice.* Implement short practice sessions at one sitting; otherwise, the result becomes neutral or negative. The trouble is that many teachers assign long practice sessions.

3. *Give clear instructions.* If instructions are unclear, the practice session will be confusing or wasteful. In lower grades, it is sometimes necessary to elaborate on instructions and give examples.

4. *Get students started.* Once students start, it is best to avoid interrupting them. See to it that the students are working before attending to problems of individual students.

5. *Monitor the work.* Circulate around the room to help students or to resolve questions.

6. *Collect and assess work.* A problem with seatwork is that many students see little need to do it since it has no bearing on grades. Students should know that the practice work will be collected and graded; moreover, immediate feedback should be provided.[26]

A short drill provides a quick and efficient way for teachers to check on the effectiveness of instruction before moving to the next stage or level in the lesson. It is well suited for mastery and direct methods of lesson planning, and

---

[26]Slavin, *Educational Psychology: Theory into Teaching.*

especially for low-achieving students.[27] Following are some drill techniques that can be used in your lesson planning.

1. Ask pupils to repeat answers.
2. List facts or concepts to be remembered.
3. Identify characteristics or attributes of the content.
4. Review answers to questions.
5. State answers in different ways.
6. Have volunteers answer a number of questions and discuss answers.
7. Give a short quiz and have students grade papers.
8. Assign exercises from the workbook or text.
9. Monitor seatwork and provide immediate feedback.
10. Discuss or review common problems, as revealed by a short quiz or monitoring of the seatwork.

2. *Questioning.* Teachers should include four to six broad *questions* that serve the dual purpose of stimulating discussion among students and outlining the major topics or parts of the lesson. Teachers who emphasize critical thinking or problem solving tend to rely on questions to stimulate the lesson. Such questions should:

1. Be simple and direct.
2. Encourage critical thought.
3. Be aimed at eliciting broad answers, not memory or factual information.
4. Be asked in an order that corresponds to the content of the lesson.
5. Build on each other, that is, be sequential.
6. Challenge students, yet not be above the level of the class.
7. Be framed to meet the needs and interests of the students.
8. Vary in difficulty and abstractness to encourage participation by different students.[28]

Good questioning, according to Jerome Bruner, leads to higher modes of learning. In answering a thought-provoking question, a high-achieving student limits it, analyzes parts of it, reformulates it, and decides on the best methods to use for answering.[29] Thought-provoking questions usually ask how and why,

---

[27]John V. Hamby, "How to Get an 'A' on Your Dropout Prevention Report Card," *Educational Leadership*, February 1989, pp. 21-28; Gavriel Salomon and David N. Perkins, "Rocky Road to Transfer: Rethinking Mechanisms of a Neglected Phenomenon," *Educational Psychologist*, Spring 1989, pp. 113–142.

[28]J. T. Dillon, *Questioning and Teaching: A Manual of Practice* (New York: Teachers College Press, Columbia University, 1988); Francis P. Hunkins, *Teaching Thinking Through Questioning* (Needham Heights, Mass.: Gordon Publishers, 1989).

[29]Jerome S. Bruner, *Toward a Theory of Instruction* (Cambridge, Mass.: Harvard University Press, 1966).

not when, where, who, or what, unless introduced by a provocative comment. Questions that call for a yes-or-no answer do not promote discussion or stimulate critical thinking or problem solving strategies. Examples of thought questions are:

1. The temperature was identical on Thursday and today, yet today we feel warmer. What accounts for this difference?
2. How can we determine whether the author is serious or poking fun?
3. How did the concept of Manifest Destiny lead to our Latin American colonial policy during the nineteenth century?
4. Why are Japan and Korea outproducing Americans in manufacturing goods?

3. *Lectures/Explanations.* Teachers are often required to give *lectures* and *explanations* to emphasize an important point, to fill in content gaps in the workbook or textbook, or to elaborate on a specific content area. Short explanations may be embedded in the lesson plan without writing or noting it.

In planning an explanation or short lecture, the teacher should keep in mind the following characteristics.

I. Continuity
  1. *Sequence of discourse.* The lesson should follow a planned sequence, with few diversions or tangential discussions. Explanations should be included at proper places to maintain the sequence of the lesson.
  2. *Fluency.* The teacher should speak in clear, concise, complete grammatical sentences.
II. Simplicity
  1. *Visual aids.* Pictures, tables, charts, models, and computer graphics or videos can be used to enhance verbal explanations.
  2. *Vocabulary.* The teacher should use the students' normal vocabulary for effective explanations. Technical or new terms pertaining to the content should be introduced and clearly defined during the explanation.
III. Explicitness
  1. *Inclusion of elements.* The major ideas of the lesson should be elaborated with specific descriptions or examples.
  2. *Explicit explanations.* Causal and logical relationships should be made explicit.[30]

4. *Demonstrations/Experiments.* Demonstrations and experiments play an important role in *inductive inquiry.* They are ideal for creative and discovery methods of lesson planning, whereby the teacher and students integrate the

---

[30]Elizabeth Perrott, *Effective Teaching: A Practical Guide to Improving Your Teaching* (New York: Longman, 1982).

subject matter by collecting data, observing, measuring, identifying, and examining causal relationships.

Young students and low-achieving students will need more instruction and feedback from the teacher. Older and high-achieving students work more independently and participate more in demonstrations and experiments because they are more able to handle quantities of information, reorganize it into new forms, and transfer it to new learning situations.[31] In either case the recommendations below ensure the effectiveness of the demonstration and experiment.

1. Plan and prepare for the demonstration (or experiment). Make certain that all materials needed are available when you begin. Practice the demonstration (if conducted for the first time) before the lesson to see what problems may arise.
2. Present the demonstration in context with what students have already learned or as a stimulus for searching for new knowledge.
3. Make provisions for full participation of the students.
4. Maintain control over the materials or equipment to the extent the students are unable to work on their own.
5. Pose both close-ended and open-ended questions according to students' capacity for deductive and inductive responses. ("What is happening to the object?" is a close-ended question; "What can you generalize from . . . ?" is open-ended.)
6. Encourage students to ask questions as they arise.
7. Encourage students to make observations first and then to make inferences and generalizations. Encourage them to look for and express new information and insights.
8. Allocate sufficient time so that (a) the demonstration can be completed, (b) students can discuss what they have observed, (c) students can reach conclusions and apply principles they have learned, (d) students can take notes or write up the demonstration, and (e) materials can be collected and stored away.

Materials and Media   Media and materials, sometimes referred to as resources or instructional aids, facilitate understanding and foster learning by clarifying verbal abstractions and arousing interest in the lesson. Many materials and media are available (Table 10.7). The teacher's selection should depend on the objectives and content of the lesson plan; the age, abilities, and interests of the students; the teacher's ability to use the resources; the availability of the materials and equipment; and the classroom time available. The materials and media should be:

---

[31]Ruth Gardner and Patricia A. Alexander, "Metacognition: Answered and Unanswered Questions," *Educational Psychologist*, Spring 1989, pp.143-158; Velma I. Hythecher, Donald F. Dansereau, and Thomas R. Rocklin, "An Analysis of the Process Influencing the Structured Dyadic Learning Environment," *Educational Psychologist*, Winter 1988, pp. 23–38.

1. Accurate and up-to-date.
2. Large enough to be seen by all the students.
3. Ready for use (check in advance of the lesson).
4. Interesting and varied.
5. Suited for developing the objective(s) of the lesson.
6. Properly displayed and used throughout the lesson.

Many lessons fail because materials or media that were needed were inadequate, unavailable, or inappropriate for the level of the students. If students need to bring special materials for a task or project, they should be told far in advance so that they may obtain them. The teacher should be sure that necessary equipment is available, scheduled in advance, set up on the appropriate day, and in working order.

Summaries   Teachers cannot assume that learning is taking place in the class as a whole (or even with the majority) just because some students give correct answers to their questions or because they have presented well-organized explanations and demonstrations. Some students may have been daydreaming

Table 10.7   MATERIALS AND MEDIA FOR LESSON PLAN USE

Input suggestions			Output suggestions		
View/Observe	Read	Listen	Make/Construct	Verbalize	Write
Visuals	*Materials*	*Media*	*Materials*	*Verbalizations*	*Written Perfor-*
Bulletin boards	Books	Radio	Dioramas	Oral reports	*mance*
Banners	Comic books	Records	Collages	Panels	Themes
Posters	Pamphlets	TV	Scrolls	Debates	Research
Transparencies	Posters	*Verbalizations*	Sand paintings	Discussions	papers
Slides	Newspapers	Speeches	Diaries	Brainstorming	Reports
Films/filmstrips	Bulletin boards	Lectures	Pictographs	Oral questions	Workbook
Flashcards	Flashcards	Debates	Maps	and answers	answers
TV	Reports	Discussions	Models	*Solve*	Blackboard
Graphs	Wall graffiti	Dramatic/	Timelines	Puzzles	problems
Community	Letters	interpretive	Paintings	Mazes	Poems, essays,
Events	*Smell/Taste/*	readings	Food	Problems	etc.
Field trips	*Touch*	Interviews	Clothing	Equations	*Perform*
Dramatic	Objects	*Try/Do/Use*	Bulletin boards	Games	Simulations
presenta-	Textures	Games	Banners	Riddles	Role plays
tions	Food	Experiments	Graphs		Sociodramas
	Temperatures	Exercises	Word wall		Concerts
	Chemicals	Manipulative	Drawings		Pantomimes
		materials	*Presentations*		Interpretive
			Films		readings
			Filmstrips		Dramas
			Tapes		

Source: Carol Barber, *Mastery Learning Training Manual* (Price, Utah: Southeastern Education Service Center, 1985), p. 1.

or even confused while other students answered questions and while the demonstrations took place. To ensure understanding of the lesson and to determine whether the objectives of the lesson have been achieved, teachers should include one or more of the following types of summaries.

There should be a short *review* of each lesson in which the lesson as a whole and important or confusing parts are summarized. A short review can take the following forms:

1. Pose several thought-provoking questions that summarize previous learning (or previous day's homework).
2. Ask for a comparison of what has already been learned with what is being learned.
3. Ask a student to summarize the main ideas of the lesson. Have other students make modifications and additions.
4. Assign review questions (on the chalkboard or in the workbook or textbook).
5. Administer a short quiz.

During the lesson at some point when a major concept or idea has been examined, it is advisable to present a **medial summary**—a series of pivotal questions or a problem that will bring together the information that has been discussed. Medial summaries slow down the lesson; however, they are important for low-achieving and young students who need more time to comprehend new information and more links with prior knowledge. A **final summary** is needed to clinch the basic ideas or concepts of the lesson. If you realize that it is impossible to teach all you planned, then end the lesson at some logical point and provide a summary of the content you have covered. Each lesson should be concluded by a summary activity, not by the bell.

Following are *chalkboard activities* that can be used as summaries.

1. Refer to the outline on the chalkboard that has been developed during the lesson. Erase all but the headings. Have students supply the details.
2. Ask two or three students to go to the chalkboard and have them list or identify people, places, or outcomes.
3. Ask two or three students to go to the chalkboard and have them each solve a problem that reviews what has been learned. Discuss steps of the problems.

Following are types of *thought questions* that can be used as summaries.

1. Who can review the four steps in . . . ?
2. Who can solve the following problem: . . . ?
3. In light of what we have learned, who can describe the best method for . . . ?
4. Based on what we have learned, who can discuss the causes for . . . ?
5. Would you recommend this story to others? Why? Why not?
6. What would happen if . . . ?

The following *activities* are suited for summaries.

1. Ask students to interpret a cartoon, map, or model related to the lesson.
2. Ask students to draw a diagram or chart labeling the major parts or areas that have been discussed.
3. Have one or two students give an oral report.
4. Have a few students debate the issues or conclusions.
5. Have students make predictions based on the data or problems that have been discussed.

Assignments   The work that students are requested to do at home should furnish them with the content (knowledge, skills, and tasks) needed to participate in the next day's lesson. Following are some characteristics of effective assignments.

1. The homework should be interesting.
2. Attention should be directed to definite concepts or problems.
3. Questions should be framed so as to provide background information necessary to answer the teacher's questions on the following day.
4. Homework should periodically incorporate previously taught content to reinforce learning.
5. The assignment should provide opportunities for students to grow in written (or symbolic) expression, reading, or important skills related to the subject.
6. Provision should be made for individual differences. There should be minimum assignments for all students with enrichment levels for high-achieving students.
7. The new assignment can be copied or given at the beginning or end of the period, but any discussion should be at the end and grow out the lesson in a logical manner.
8. Homework should be explained, and practice or examples given if necessary. Problems that may arise when doing the homework should be briefly examined in class at the end of the period.
9. Assignments should not be dictated, because of the time dictation takes and the errors students make in recording oral assignments. Either the homework should be written on and copied from the chalkboard at the beginning of the period while the teacher engages in administrative or clerical tasks, or it should be duplicated and handed out on a weekly basis (for younger students) or monthly basis (for older students).
10. The length of the assignment will vary by grade level and subject. It is generally thought that homework in grades 1 to 3 should not exceed 15 to 30 minutes per day; grades 4 to 6, 45 minutes, grades 7 to 9, 15 to 30 minutes per subject, and grades 10 to 12, 20 to 45 minutes per subject.[32] Lengthy assignments discourage students, especially slow students, and create anxiety and stress.

---

[32] J. Michael Palardy, "The Effect of Homework on Student Achievement," *National School Administrators*, April 1988, pp. 14–17; Deborah B. Strother, "Homework: Too Much, Just Right, or Not Enough," *Phi Delta Kappan*, February 1984, pp. 423–426. Most of these grade categories and homework time are the authors'.

Professional Viewpoint

Lesson Plans and the Professional

Should teachers be required to prepare lockstep lesson plans? Of course, teachers need to plan, and most of them do. But does each teacher have to do the same amount of planning and use the same format? Do all the plans have to be inspected on the same morning? Do some teachers plan better in their heads than on paper? More important, what are the plans for? They are supposed to help teachers focus and improve their instruction. But now, in many schools, teachers are not given a satisfactory rating, no matter how good they are as teachers, unless they have complied with the ritualistic planbook requirements. This is clear management incompetence. Would anybody rate Pavarotti a poor opera singer because he fails to fill out bureaucratic forms telling management how he intends to approach each aria?

This reminds me of the morning some 35 years ago when I appeared for the examination to become a New York City public school teacher. After we had assembled in the school cafeteria, someone appeared, blew a whistle, and ordered us to form a double line. We were then marched down a hall and told to form a single line to move to various classrooms in which we would take the test. Throughout this march, we continued to receive instructions. "Keep in single file." "Hurry up." "No talking." It was clear from the start that we were back in school. Even though we had gone to college and received our degrees, we were being treated very much like children again.

Rigid requirements for lesson plans are like that. They treat educated adults, veteran teachers among them, like children, requiring them to jump to a whistle and "keep in single file." Even after we have solved the problem of providing adequate financial rewards, we are not going to get good teachers or keep them so long as school management rewards blind obedience to authority above creativity and excellence.

Professionalism for teachers will come only through hard work. This will mean not only questioning outmoded practices but also offering better alternatives that serve the interest of student success, rather than bureaucratic convenience.

Albert Shanker, President
American Federation of Teachers

11. For variety, assignments might include: (a) notebook and textbook assignments, (b) working on projects, (c) writing letters, articles, or reports, (d) analyzing television programs, (e) reading related books and articles, (f) interviewing people and visiting places in the community, and (g) conducting or summarizing an experiment or being involved in a hands-on activity.

12. Homework should be monitored for completion and accuracy, and students should receive timely, specific, and constructive feedback. Where performance is poor, teachers should provide not only feedback and additional time for review, but also additional assignments designed to ensure mastery of content.

13. It is important for the school to have a coordinated homework/tutoring program for students who need assistance—and the assistance should be provided on a daily basis, if necessary. Provisions must be made for students who do not understand the daily assignment; otherwise frustration and lack of interest take over and interfere with learning.

SAMPLE LESSON PLANS

Five sample lesson plans are included to illustrate how the various components of the lesson can be used. Explanations accompanying each plan give some sense of what the teacher is trying to achieve. The lesson plans are written for different grade levels and subjects, but the lesson types can be used for all students regardless of age, ability, or subject matter.

The first three samples are lesson plans for structured approaches. The remaining two are plans for more divergent and flexible approaches. The words in italics coincide with the previously discussed components of a lesson plan; they serve as anchors or highlight the major ideas of the lessons.

Flexible Grouping Lesson Plan (Table 10.8)

1. *The lesson topic* is derived from the unit plan on vocabulary.
2. The *primary objective* is to teach the meaning of 10 new words. The two *secondary objectives* accomplish the primary objective and enhance dictionary and writing skills.
3. The teacher immediately starts the lesson with a *review* of the previous homework. The class as a whole discusses the homework.
4. Only *materials* specific to the lesson are noted in the lesson plan.
5. The teacher uses the term *activities* to outline the development or outline, since the focus of attention is on classroom activities.
6. The class is divided into *two groups* for the activities. Group I is slower or lower achieving than group II.
7. Both groups do similar *seatwork*. Group I is given the extra step of alphabetizing for extra practice in the process. Group II understands the need for alphabetical order in searching through the dictionary, so

Table 10.8   FLEXIBLE GROUPING LESSON PLAN

Grade: 5–7
Lesson Topic: Vocabulary
Objective: To define 10 new words.
  1. To deduce the meaning of the words using a dictionary
  2. To write the meaning of the new words in a sentence
Review: Both groups (10 minutes)
  1. Correct homework, workbook, pp. 36–39.
  2. Focus on questions, p. 39.
Materials: Dictionaries, logs, supplementary books.
Development:

Group I: Activities	Group II: Activities
Seatwork (15 minutes)	Seatwork (15 minutes)
1. Alphabetize the following 10 words: explicit, implicit, appropriate, inappropriate, potential, encounter, diminish, enhance, master, alligator.	1. Find each of the following 10 words in the dictionary: explicit, implicit, appropriate, inappropriate, potential, encounter, diminish, enhance, master, alligator (same words for both groups).
2. Find each new word in the dictionary.	2. Write a definition for each new word.
3. Write a definition for each new word.	3. Divide each new word into syllables.
Medial summary (15 minutes)	Independent work (15 minutes)
1. Teach new words; students give examples and discuss meaning of new words.	1. Continue reading supplementary books.
	2. Underline at least five new words in the pages you read.
	3. Find their meaning in the dictionary.
Independent work: (10 minutes)	Final summary (10 minutes)
1. Get up to date with logs.	1. Discuss the 10 assigned words plus the 5 words students have chosen in their independent reading.
2. Include the 10 new words in logs.	
Homework: Both groups	
1. Continue with logs.	
2. Write each new word in an original sentence.	

this step is omitted. Group II is given another, more difficult task of dividing words into syllables to make up for the one task that was omitted. The teacher monitors the seatwork of the students and helps anyone with individual problems.

8. After seatwork, the two groups engage in different activities. The teacher works with one group while the other is involved in independent work. For group I the teacher provides a *medial summary* for feedback, review, and assessment. (Prompt and varied feedback and review are needed for the slower group.) Group II engages in *independent work*, having selected their own books to read for enjoyment. The teacher

then works with group II in a *summary* activity, connecting the original objective with the students' independent work, while group I does its independent assignment. Group I has 5 minutes less independent work and 5 minutes more teacher-directed summary work because these students need more teacher time, are less able to work independently of the teacher, and are likely to have more problems that need to be discussed.

9. The whole class receives the same *homework* assignment. Group I is permitted to start the homework in class so the assignment at home does not overwhelm them. The lesson for the day is integrated into the homework in both the logs and the writing assignment.

Thinking Skills Lesson Plan (Table 10.9)

1. The *lesson topic* can be part of a separate unit on critical thinking skills, or it can serve as an introductory lesson for a unit in almost any subject.

2. There is only one *objective*. It pertains to classifying—a critical thinking skill.

3. The *motivation* assumes a certain amount of abstract thinking on the part of the students. It is verbal as opposed to visual or auditory. The first question is divergent and open ended. The second question is more convergent and focused. The short exercise provides students with a challenge, introduces them to the main part of the lesson, and shows how they handle certain information before the lesson. Some words (*elephant, donkey, Lincoln*, etc.) can be categorized into various groups, and *table* does not belong in any category. (It serves as irrelevant information to see how students handle it.)

4. The *development* is a set of *procedures* or operations to teach students how to classify information. The *pivotal questions* are to be introduced at different stages of the lesson. They stimulate discussion, clarify points, and check understanding. They are divergent in nature and provide students with latitude in the way they can answer; the teacher must listen carefully to the responses, since the answers are not necessarily right or wrong, but involve, in part, viewpoints and subjectivity.

5. The *summary* is a series of important or key questions that lead to a discussion and elaboration of what has been taught. The length of the summary discussion is based on the time permitted. Question 1 is vague, and students may not respond, or may respond in a way that the teacher does not expect. Questions 2 and 3 are more focused. Question 4 leads to a good overview and reinforcement exercise. (The teacher may or may not have time to use it.)

6. The *homework* is based on the lesson and leads to the next step or slightly more advanced aspect of classifying.

Table 10.9   THINKING SKILLS LESSON PLAN

Grade: 6–12
Lesson Topic: Classifying information
Objective: To arrange information into groups on the basis of similar or common attributes
Motivation:
1. Why should we learn to classify information into categories or groups?
2. Into what groups would you classify the following information: Kennedy, table, elephant, Lincoln, Roosevelt, Chicago, Nixon, Boston, Bush, donkey and San Francisco?

Development:

Pivotal Questions

1. Procedures. Discuss at least three reasons for classifying information.

1a. When do you classify information? Why?
1b. What happens to information that is not organized? Why?

2. Skim text (pp. 48–55) to get an idea of important items or ideas that might be classified.

3. Agree on categories (groups or labels) to be used in classifying information in text.

3a. What advantages are there to the categories?
3b. What are their unifying attributes?
3c. What other categories could we have used? Explain.

4. Focus on three practice items in the text and agree on related categories for purpose of ensuring understanding.

5. Read carefully the same pages and place selected items into appropriate categories.

5. Why raise your hand if you are stuck on a particular item?

6. Discuss similar or common attributes.

6a. Why did you identify these items with those categories?
6b. Why did you choose these common attributes as a category to classify the items?
6c. What other common attributes might you have chosen?

7. Modify (change, subtract, or add) categories, if necessary.

7a. Why did you change these categories?
7b. What can we do with the items that fit into more than one category? Which items fit into more than one category?

8. Repeat procedures using other important items; read pp. 56–63.

8. What categories did you select? Why?

9. Combine categories or subdivide into smaller categories.

9a. Why did you reclassify (add or subdivide) these categories?
9b. What should we do with the leftover items? Which ones are left over?

Summary:
1. What important things have you learned about classifying information?
2. What are different ways of classifying information?
3. When is it appropriate to subdivide categories?
4. Look at the chalkboard (text). Who wishes to categorize these five new items into one of the categories we have already established?

Homework:
1. Read Chapter 7.
2. Classify important information into pro/con categories listed on p. 68.

Mastery Learning Lesson Plan (Table 10.10)

1. Subtraction as a *lesson topic* is introduced in the second grade in most school districts and continued in the third grade.
2. The *objective* is written in terms of a performance level.
3. Mastery learning lessons entail a good deal of *review*.
4. The *motivation* is in the form of two separate problems that involve real-life experiences and interests.
5. Only unusual *materials* are listed. Popsicle sticks, baseball cards, or any other items easy to count can be used in lieu of checkers.
6. The *development* is in the form of problems and related activities. The problems, involving one- and two-digit numbers, coincide with the worksheet the students are up to. The teacher explains each problem and then introduces the related activity. While students work on the activity, the teacher moves around the room and monitors their work. The problems get progressively more difficult. Each item that is missed by even a small percentage of students must be further explained, since the work builds on previous learning.
7. The teacher provides additional *practice* before asking students to complete the worksheet on their own. Only volunteers are called on because the work is new. Three items are explained. The teacher moves around the room monitoring the students' work and providing additional help when necessary.
8. As a *summary* all items are discussed. All items missed by students, especially those that are missed by 20 percent or more, are discussed in greater detail. Individuals' scores on the worksheet determine how much practice is needed the next day in the form of review.
9. The *homework* is related to the lesson; it is assigned and explained. The next day it will be reviewed.

Inquiry-Discovery Lesson Plan (Table 10.11)

1. The *lesson topic* is derived from the unit on energy and environment.
2. The two *objectives* are written as questions to stimulate curiosity and indicate problems students are to solve.
3. The *materials* needed are supplementary readings that examine efficiency and cost of various forms of insulation.
4. The *development* of the lesson consists of two sections corresponding to the two objectives. Each section contains a problem and related problems. The problems serve as motivating devices, since students are challenged to investigate answers and make decisions about ranking. Thus the component on motivation is unnecessary.
5. Each problem includes a *medial summary*; a student works out a problem at the chalkboard while the other students do the same at their seats. The whole class discusses the problems during the *medial summaries,* which replace the usual final summary. The *related prob-*

Table 10.10 MASTERY LEARNING LESSON PLAN

Grade: 2–3

Lesson Topic: Subtraction

Objective: Students will perform the worksheet items on subtraction (worksheet 12), with at least 80 percent accuracy after the lesson.

Review: Review yesterday's homework on subtraction.

Motivation:

1. There are 25 students in the class, as you know. We are planning to go to a movie next Friday afternoon. Three of you—Joel, Jason, and Stacey—have soccer practice and will not attend the movie. How many tickets should we buy?
2. We are going to plan a Halloween party in class. Each of you may have one dessert choice with your milk. Most of us enjoy chocolate-chip cookies, but some might prefer vanilla-cream cookies. Let's see how many prefer vanilla-cream cookies. (Show of hands. Good.) Ten of you prefer the vanilla-cream cookies. Who can tell the class how many chocolate-chip cookies we will need for the party?

Materials: Overhead projector, checkers (pass out to students)

Development:

Problems	Activities
1. With overhead projector explain how to solve $11-5$, $11-7$.	1a. At their desks students use the checkers and perform $12-2$, $12-5$, $12-8$.
	1b. Students record work (and answers) in their notebooks.
	1c. Discuss all items missed by more than 10 percent of the students.
2. With overhead projector explain $20-5$, $20-10$.	2a. At their desks students use the checkers and perform $21-3$, $21-5$, $21-7$.
	2b. Repeat 1b.
	2c. Repeat 1c.
3. With overhead projector explain $22-6$, $22-10$, $22-15$.	3a. At their desks students use the checkers and perform $23-5$, $23-8$, $23-12$, $23-20$.
	3b. Repeat 1b.
	3c. Repeat 1c.

Practice:

1. Hand out worksheet 12
2. Call on volunteer to do first sample item in worksheet.
3. Call on second and third volunteers to do next two sample items.
4. Have students complete remaining worksheet on their own at their own pace.

Summary (Evaluation):

1. With overhead projector show correct answers for all the items.
2. Ask students how many got each item right.
3. Discuss all the items, but emphasize items that 20 percent or more missed.
4. Have students score their own papers and turn them in.

Homework:

1. Distribute homework or explain new worksheet that is to be answered.
2. Review assignment next day.
3. Reteach problem items (items that 20 percent or more missed during previous lesson).

Table 10.11 INQUIRY-DISCOVERY LESSON PLAN

Grades: 9–12
Lesson Topic: Energy conservation
Objectives:
1. How can (heating) energy be conserved at home?
2. How can (gasoline) energy be saved in driving?
Materials: Supplementary readings on insulation
Development:

Conserving Energy in Home Heating

1. Problem: Investigate the best ways to save energy in the house, and rank them. Assume a 1,200-foot house, no insulation in ceiling or walls, no storm windows (15 windows), and poor weatherstripping around windows and doors (2 doors).

Rank	Item	Gallons of oil saved (average temperature 30°F over 8 months)
2	Add storm windows	290
1	Add 3 inches of fiberglass insulation to ceiling	1,044
4	Close drapes	58
3	Renew weatherstripping	203

2. Medial summary: Discuss reasons for ranking and best insulators.
3. Related problems (questions): (a) Discuss costs for each insulating item. (b) Compare the cost and energy saved. (c) Determine payback period.

Conserving Gasoline in Driving

1. Problem: Investigate the best ways to save energy while driving and assume a car that gets 10 miles per gallon (mpg) and is driven 15,000 miles per year.

Rank	Item	Gallons of gas saved
4	Drive only 12,000 miles	300
2	Buy a compact car (30 mpg) and drive 15,000 miles	1,000
1	Buy a compact car (30 mpg) and drive 12,000 miles	1,100
3	Buy a standard car (20 mpg) and drive 15,000 miles	750

2. Medial summary: Investigate actual savings for each item by assuming the cost of gasoline at $1.10 per gallon.
3. Related problems (questions): (a) Discuss factors influencing energy used—amount of driving, driving speed (wind resistance), efficiency of car. (b) Discuss need to travel less than 55 mph. (c) Discuss ways to improve efficiency of car.

Homework:
1. Select 10 electrical appliances at home.
2. Determine wattage for each appliance.
3. Determine annual usage of each appliance (consult with parents).
4. Be prepared to discuss the wattage and kilowatt use of your appliances.

Source: The two tables on oil and gas are adapted from Alfred E. Friedl, *Teaching Science to Children: An Integrated Approach* (New York: Random House, 1986), pp. 298–299; the other components are the author's ideas.

lems are written as statements, but could be rewritten as *questions* ("What is the cost for each insulating item?"). The time devoted to the related problems will depend on the time required for students to work out the two major problems and discuss them in the medial summaries.

6. The *homework* is a series of investigative activities. These activities set the stage for another set of related problems to be worked out in class the next day.

Creativity Lesson Plan (Table 10.12)

1. The *lesson topic* provides an opportunity for students to create or develop their own project, based on key geographical terms they have learned.
2. The *objectives* focus on understanding terms that describe and distinguish special features considered essential to geographical education. Students move from understanding geographical concepts to applying them in class.
3. The *review* component of the lesson may also be considered an introductory activity. The activity provides background information for the main part or development of the lesson.
4. Different *materials* are displayed, available for research, and distributed to students for use.
5. The *development* employs cooperative learning. Rules in working together need to be briefly discussed. The number of land and water terms should depend on the students' grade level. The naming of features on the island can be optional, based on time considerations, but it provides a way of relating the content of the lesson to the experiences of the students. Activity 4 can be introduced as a bonus.
6. The *summary* component is achieved in part through cooperative learning as students discuss the groups projects. Provision is made for supplementary discussion and review of hypothetical cities if the lesson is finished with time remaining. This activity can also be assigned as part of the homework.
7. The *homework* is an extension of the class activity. It tests further understanding of the subject and critical thinking. The last two homework problems are geared for advanced students.

Table 10.12   CREATIVITY LESSON PLAN

Grade: 6–12
Lesson Topic: Creating an island
Objectives:
1. To understand that all places on earth have special features that distinguish them from other places.
2. To become familiar with terms that identify landforms and bodies of water.
3. To apply terms for geographical landforms and bodies of water to an original student project.

Review/Introductory Activity (10 minutes):
1. Students use atlases and maps to review land and water terms.
2. Students create a glossary of important geographical land and water terms in the form of a three-column chart giving terms (basin, bay, canyon, cape, cove, delta, gulf, hill, inlet, island, lake, mountain, peninsula, plateau, river, sea, valley), definitions, and examples (Florida is a peninsula).

Materials: Atlases, wall maps, textbooks, glossary, large pieces of drawing paper or poster board, felt pens or markers.

Development (Activities):
1. The class is divided into groups of four (or five). Group members are to work cooperatively to plan and draw an imaginary island.
2. Each island should feature at least 10 (or 15 depending on grade level and previous related lessons) of the following geographical forms: basin, bay, canyon, cape, cove, etc.
3. Students are to give all features on the island names of their choice. The names are to be related to one theme, for example, Computer Island, Bytes Bay, and Microchip Mountain.
4. Students who finish early are to include map features (depending on the grade level) such as latitude, longitude, elevation key, scale.

Summary (10–15 minutes):
1. Each group shows its completed map to the class. Students discuss each group's portrayal of the geographical terms.
2. If time permits, students are to place five fictitious towns on each island and discuss the locations of towns, reasons for their choice, best locations.

Homework:
1. Determine the island's climate and natural resources based on latitude and longitude coordinates given by the teacher.
2. Discuss where most of the island's population would most likely live, given the island's configuration and natural resources.
3. Discuss possible environmental problems that might develop as a result of using the available resources (only for upper grade levels).
4. Discuss possible trade problems that might develop as a result of using available resources (only for upper grade levels).

Source: Adapted from "Geography Lesson Plan," *National Geographical Society Update*, Fall 1987, pp. 9–10. All the ideas have been restructured to coincide with the author's lesson plan components.

Guidelines for Implementing Lesson Plans

You will need to consider several factors as you begin to move from planning to performance. Even after you have had some experience, it is wise to review the following factors to ensure your success in the execution of the lesson plan: student differences, length of period, flexibility, student participation, student understanding, and evaluation.

1. *Student Differences.* Individual and group differences must be considered as you plan your lesson and then teach it. Teachers need to make provisions for student differences in ability, age, background, and reading level.

2. *Length of Period.* One of the major problems beginning teachers have is planning a lesson that will coincide with time allotted (the 30, 40, or 50 minutes of each period). New teachers must learn to pace themselves, not to plan too much (and have to end abruptly) or too little (and have nothing planned for the last 5 or 10 minutes of the period).

If during a lesson a teacher realizes too little has been planned, he or she can:

1. Pose additional questions to explore various facets of the content.
2. Drill the students on the major points of the lesson.
3. Set up a short panel in which students take a position on the issues or topics discussed.
4. Spend additional time on the new assignment, discussing problems that may arise and going over sample questions.

If during a lesson the teacher realizes too much has been planned, he or she should:

1. Select a major subheading or breakpoint in the development to end the lesson.
2. End the lesson with a brief summary.
3. Conclude the lesson the next day by including in the new lesson the content that was not covered the previous period.

3. *Flexibility.* The teacher must be flexible, that is, prepared to develop a lesson along a path different from the one set down in the plan. Student reactions may make it necessary or desirable to elaborate on something included in the plan, or to pursue something unexpected that arises as the lesson proceeds. Although effective teachers tend to encourage on-task behavior and discourage off-task behavior, they are willing to make corrections and take advantage of unforeseen developments. The basis for the change is more intuitive than objective, more unplanned than preplanned.

4. *Student Participation.* Teachers must encourage the participation of the greatest number of students in each lesson. They should not permit a few students to dominate the lesson and should draw nonvolunteers into the lesson. They should not talk too much or dominate the lesson with teacher-directed

activities. The need is to encourage student participation, student-to-student interaction, and increased performance among shy students, low-achieving students, and students on the sides and in the rear rows (as opposed to students in the middle or front of the room).

5. *Student Understanding.* There is often a gap between what students understand and what teachers think they understand. Part of the reason for this gap has to do with the rapidity of the teaching process—so much happens at once that the teacher is unaware of everything that goes on in the classroom. Following are suggestions to increase student understanding as you teach the lesson.

1. Insist that students respond to the questions put to them. Students who do not know answers or have trouble in understanding the lesson tend to mumble or speak too quietly to be heard clearly, try to change the subject, or ask another question instead of responding to the original question. These are some of the strategies students adopt to outwit teachers.[33]

2. If a student answer lacks detail, does not cover the major aspects of the problem, or is partially or totally incorrect, (a) probe the student by rephrasing or simplifying the question, using another question to lead the student toward the desired answer, or providing additional information, or (b) call on another student to help the first student.

3. If, after calling on a few students, you are unable to obtain the desired response, you may have to reteach parts of the lesson. Although this is not planned, you cannot ignore that several students are having problems understanding the lesson.

4. Prepare students for demonstrations and experiments, ask questions during these activities, and follow up with written exercises in which students analyze or synthesize what they observed or performed.

5. Include practice, review, or applications in every lesson. The amount of time you spend on these activities will depend on the students' abilities. Low-achieving and younger students need more practice, review, and concrete application.

6. Be sure to include medial and final summaries. Low-achieving and younger students need more medial summaries than high-achieving students.

6. *Evaluation.* The lesson plan must be evaluated so that it can be modified and improved. At the end of a lesson, the teacher should have a clear idea about how the students reacted and whether they understood and enjoyed the lesson. To appraise your lesson plan, ask yourself the following questions.

---

[33]John Holt, *How Children Fail* (New York: Pitman, 1964).

[34]John P. Richards, "Homework," in H. Mitzel, ed., *Encyclopedia of Educational Research*, 5th ed. (New York: Free Press, 1982), pp. 831–834.

1. Was the instruction congruent with the objectives?
2. Were the students motivated throughout the lesson?
3. What parts of the lesson were boring, confusing, or inappropriate? How can these parts be improved?
4. Do I need to spend more time reviewing parts of the lesson?
5. Were the questions appropriate? Which ones came up that were not planned and can be used in the future?
6. What problems arose? How can I correct them?
7. What other activities can be used to improve the planning?
8. Was there sufficient time to complete the lesson?
9. What did I fail to accomplish in the lesson?
10. Should certain parts of the lesson be omitted, condensed, or elaborated on?

A good teacher, no matter how experienced, is a critic of his or her lesson and seeks new ways for improving the teaching-learning situation. The teacher takes time for self reflection and self analysis. The teacher is aware of what is happening during the lesson and intuitively judges what is worthwhile and what needs to be modified for the next time the lesson plan is used. See Tips for Teachers 10.3.

Tips for Teachers 10.3

Organizing and Implementing Lesson Plans: A Checklist

The teacher should always look for ways to improve the lesson plan. Below are 25 research-based tips that correlate with student achievement; as many as possible (not necessarily all in one lesson) should be incorporated into portions of the lesson plan. Although most of the statements seem to be based on a mastery approach, the checklist can be used for most types of teaching.

1. Plan lesson toward stated objectives or topics of the unit plan.
2. Require academic focus of students.
3. Follow the plan. Keep to a schedule, start the lesson on time, and be aware of time.
4. Provide a review of previous lesson or integrate previous lesson with new lesson.
5. Indicate to students the objectives of the lesson; explain what is to be accomplished.
6. Utilize whole, flexible, and small groups and independent study.
7. Present lesson with enthusiasm; motivate students.
8. Present lesson at appropriate pace, not too slow or too fast.

continued

9. Explain things clearly. Be sure students understand what to do and how to do it.
10. Give students a chance to think about what is being taught.
11. Try to find out when students don't understand.
12. Provide sufficient time for practice.
13. Ask frequent questions; be sure they are challenging and relevant.
14. Answer student questions or have other students answer them.
15. Provide explanations, demonstrations, or experiments.
16. Elaborate on difficult points of the lesson; give details, provide examples.
17. Show how students are to do classwork.
18. Choose activities that are interesting and promote success.
19. Make smooth transitions between activities.
20. Incorporate supplementary materials and media.
21. Summarize the lesson.
22. Schedule seatwork; monitor and assess student work.
23. Give homework, provide examples of how to do homework, and collect and check homework.
24. Evaluate lesson plan after teaching.
25. Be open to feedback and modification; listen to students, colleagues, supervisors, and other observers.

Source: Adapted from James H. Block, Helene E. Efthim, and Robert B. Burns, *Building Effective Mastery Learning Schools* (New York: Longman, 1989); Carolyn M. Evertson et al., *Classroom Management for Elementary Teachers*, 2nd ed. (Englewood Cliffs, N.J.: Prentice-Hall, 1989).

THEORY INTO PRACTICE

As you prepare your unit and lesson plans, you should be aware of common mistakes. The idea is to minimize them by following guidelines that have proved to be practical, by discussing plans with your colleagues or supervisor, and by practicing.

Below is a list of suggestions that apply to all levels of unit planning and can be adapted to accommodate your school's requirements and your teaching style and instructional approach.

1. Ask your principal or supervisor for curriculum plans pertaining to your subject and grade level to guide your planning.
2. Ask your colleagues or supervisor for a file of unit plans to guide your planning.
3. Check the instructor's manual of the textbook or workbook, if you are using one; many have excellent examples of unit plans.

4. Consider vertical (different grades, same subject) and horizontal (same grade, different subjects) relationships of subject matter in formulating your unit plans. Be sure you understand the relationship between new information and prior knowledge.

5. Consider students' abilities, needs, and interests as you plan your unit.

6. Decide on objectives and related content for the various units of the subject.

7. After objectives and content have been established, sequence the units.

8. Determine the order of the content by considering cognitive processes (skills, concepts, problems) and affective processes (attitudes, feelings, values) involved. Developmental theories, mastery learning, or task analysis can be used to determine the order of the units.

9. Consider appropriate time allocation for each unit. Most units will take one to three weeks to complete.

10. Investigate resource materials and media available in your district and school; incorporate appropriate materials and media.

11. Provide opportunities for student practice and review.

12. Provide opportunities for evaluation (not necessarily testing or marks in early grades).

13. Ask your colleagues or supervisor for feedback after you implement your unit plan; discuss questions, problems, and proposed modifications.

14. Rewrite or at least modify your unit plan whenever you teach the same subject and grade level; the world changes, classes change, and students differ.

15. Be patient. Do not expect immediate results. Practice will not make you perfect, but it will make you a better teacher.

Table 10.13 presents a series of questions to be used when you plan your lessons to avoid common mistakes.

SUMMARY

1. Teachers plan at five different levels: yearly, term, unit, weekly, and daily.

2. Mapping takes place at different subject and grade levels; it helps clarify what content, skills, and values you wish to teach.

3. Strategic planning helps teachers plan together, share ideas about unit plans and lesson plans—and reflect on their experiences.

4. The basic components of a unit plan are: objectives, content, skills, activities, resources, and evaluation.

5. Two types of unit plans are the taxonomic approach and the topic approach.

Table 10.13   QUESTIONS TO CONSIDER TO AVOID COMMON MISTAKES IN UNIT AND LESSON PLANNING

Batchelder

1. Have you considered the course study and grade requirements?
2. Did you consider the abilities and interests of the students?
3. Have you considered the knowledge already possessed by students?
4. Have you selected appropriate objectives?
5. Did you tie the lesson with previous lessons?
6. Did you include the best illustrative materials available?
7. Are crucial or pivotal questions included?
8. Are your instructional methods appropriate?
9. Are the materials in the textbook appropriate?
10. Have you considered supplementary materials in the library?
11. Are your activities logically developed (in terms of your content)?
12. Have you anticipated equipment needs?
13. Have you provided adequate summaries?
14. Did you include an appropriate assignment?
15. Did you include a method for evaluating the results of the lesson?
16. Is your plan flexible enough to permit students to follow their own interests?
17. Have you budgeted time to coincide with the various phases of the lesson?

Clark & Starr

1. Are the objectives clear and concise?
2. Are the objectives attainable?
3. Have you included test items to see whether the objectives have been achieved?
4. Are your procedures outlined to meet the objectives?
5. Are your procedures detailed enough so that another person would know what you intend to do? Can a substitute teacher follow your lesson plan?
6. Are your procedures likely to encourage learning? Are they interesting? Boring?
7. Do your activities allow for differences in student abilities, interests, and learning styles?
8. Are your materials and equipment readily available?
9. Would you enjoy the lesson as a student?
10. Would you learn from the lesson plan if you were a student?

Orlich

1. Did the lesson originate from your unit plan?
2. Do your objectives stem from the goals of the subject?
3. Are your objectives clear in terms of the knowledge and skills you wish to stress?
4. Have you included a rationale or justification for the lesson?
5. Is your content arranged in the order you intend to teach it?
6. Are your instructional methods clear?
7. Are your materials ordered in advance so they are ready for use?
8. Do you provide for summative evaluation? Can you determine if your outcomes were achieved?

Source: Adapted from Howard T. Batchelder, Maurice McGlasson, and Raleigh Schorling, *Student Teaching in Secondary Schools,* (New York: McGraw-Hill, 1964); pp. 129–130; Leonard H. Clark and Irving S. Starr, *Secondary and Middle School Teaching Methods,* 5th ed. (New York: Macmillan, 1985), pp. 185–186; and Donald C. Orlich et al., *Teaching Strategies: A Guide to Better Instruction,* 2nd ed. (Lexington, Mass.: D.C. Heath, 1985), pp. 131–143.

6. The basic components of a lesson plan are objectives, motivation, development, methods, materials and media, summaries, and homework.

7. Five lesson plans were discussed: flexible grouping, thinking skills, mastery learning, inquiry-discovery, and creativity.

QUESTIONS TO CONSIDER

1. Why do educators advise planning in cooperation with students? Why do many teachers ignore student input when planning?

2. What are the criteria for a good unit plan?

3. According to what approach do you think a unit for your subject or grade could best be planned? Why?

4. Which are the most essential components to consider when planning a lesson? Why?

5. Which instructional methods do you plan to stress in your lesson plans? Why?

THINGS TO DO

1. Prepare a map or course of study for your subject and grade level.

2. Speak to an experienced teacher. Ask the teacher to provide you with a series of unit plans for the subject or grade level you plan to teach. Examine the major components in class.

3. Select one of the above units and list the activities and resources that could be incorporated into it.

4. Plan a lesson in your subject and grade level; then teach it according to the specifications listed. What were the good parts of the lesson? What were the unsatisfactory parts?

5. List some common mistakes in lesson planning. Ask experienced teachers: What are ways for preventing some of these mistakes?

RECOMMENDED READINGS

Beyer, Barry K. *Practical Strategies for the Teaching of Thinking*. Needham Heights, Mass.: Allyn and Bacon, 1987. How teaching skills can be planned and taught in most classrooms K–12, including sample exercises and lesson plans.

Block, James H., Helene E. Efthim, and Robert B. Burns. *Building Effective Mastery Learning Schools*. New York: Longman, 1989. A mastery approach to teaching and learning, including how to plan unit plans and lesson plans for mastery.

Gagné, Robert M., Leslie J. Briggs, and Walter W. Wager. *Principles of Instructional Design*, 3rd ed. New York: Holt, Rinehart and Winston, 1988. Methods and steps in planning for instruction, starting with performance objectives and ending with student performance.

Goethals, M. Sierra, and Rose A. Howard. *Handbook of Skills Essential to Beginning Teachers.* Lanham, Md.: University Press of America, 1985. A step-by-step approach to lesson planning and teaching, with numerous exercises related to planning and performance.

Good, Thomas L., and Jere E. Brophy. *Looking in Classrooms*, 4th ed. New York: Harper & Row, 1988. A research-oriented book on several aspects of teaching including lesson planning.

Kindsvatter, Richard, William Wilen, and Margaret Ishler. *Dynamics of Effective Teaching.* New York: Longman, 1988. An up-to-date introduction to the principles of classroom instruction and planning, with numerous instruments for evaluating instruction and planning.

Posner, George J., and Alan N. Rudnitsky. *Course Design: A Guide to Curriculum Development for Teachers*, 3rd ed. New York: Longman, 1986. Numerous examples of course planning, unit planning, and lesson planning.

KEY TERMS

Mental planning	Teaching functions
Formal planning	Intrinsic motivation
Mapping	Extrinsic motivation
Strategic planning	Development
Unit plan	Medial summary
Lesson plan	Final summary

Chapter
11

The Effective Teacher

FOCUSING QUESTIONS

1. Do teachers have an effect on student outcomes?
2. What is the difference between teacher processes and teacher products?
3. Are different teacher strategies effective with different types of students?
4. How can the interaction between the teacher and students in the classroom be measured?
5. What are the characteristics of a good teacher?
6. What is the difference between teacher characteristics and teacher competencies?
7. Can we determine teacher effectiveness?

*T*o help you appreciate the research findings in this chapter, you might try this exercise. Make a list of teachers you have had about whom you have pleasant memories. List those teachers in whose classes you were not happy. What do you remember about attitudes and behaviors about both type teachers? As you read this chapter, think about how the attitudes and behaviors of the teachers on the two lists correspond to research findings and information about effective and ineffective teachers.

We will present first an overview of the research on effective teaching and then five basic aspects of teachers: teacher style, teacher interactions, teacher characteristics, teacher competencies, and teacher effects. In the early stages of research, up to the mid-1970s, theorists were concerned with **teacher processes,** that is, teacher behaviors, or the teaching that was going on in the classroom. The attempt to define and explain good teaching focused on teacher styles, teacher interactions, and teacher characteristics. More recently, researchers have become concerned with **teacher products**, that is, student outcomes. The assessment of products focuses on teacher competencies and teacher effects.

REVIEW OF THE RESEARCH ON TEACHING

Over the years thousands of studies have been conducted to identify the behaviors of successful and unsuccessful teachers. However, teaching is a complex act; what works in some situations with some students may not work in different school settings with different subjects, students, and goals. There will always be teachers who break many of the rules of procedures and methods and yet are profoundly successful. There will always be teachers who follow the rules and are unsuccessful.

Some educational researchers maintain that we cannot distinguish between "good" and "poor" or "effective" and "ineffective" teachers, that no one knows for sure or agrees what the competent teacher is, that few authorities can "define, prepare for, or measure teacher competence."[1] They point out that disagreement over terms, problems in measurement, and the complexity of the teaching act are major reasons for the negligible results in judging teacher behavior. The result is that "much of the data have been confusing, contradictory, or confirmations of common sense (i.e., a cheerful teacher is a good teacher), and that so-called acceptable findings have often been repudiated."[2] The more complex or unpredictable one views teaching as being, the more one

---

[1]Bruce J. Biddle and William J. Ellena, "The Integration of Teacher Effectiveness," in B. J. Biddle and W. J. Ellena, eds., *Contemporary Research on Teacher Effectiveness* (New York: Holt, Rinehart and Winston, 1964), p. 3.

[2]Allan C. Ornstein, "Teacher Effectiveness Research: Some Ideas and Issues," *Education and Urban Society*, February 1986, p. 168. Also see Philip W. Jackson, *The Practice of Teaching* (New York: Teachers College Press, Columbia University, 1986).

is compelled toward concluding that it is difficult to agree upon generalizations about successful teaching.[3]

Other researchers assert that appropriate teaching behaviors can be defined (and learned by teachers), that good or effective teachers can be distinguished from poor or ineffective teachers, and that the magnitude of the effect of these differences on students can be determined.[4] They conclude that the kinds of questions teachers ask, the ways they respond to students, their expectations of and attitudes toward students, their classroom management techniques, their teaching methods, and their general teaching behaviors (sometimes referred to as "classroom climate") all make a difference. However, in some cases the positive effects of teachers upon student performance may be masked or washed out by the relative negative effects of other teachers in the same school.[5] The teacher may not be the only variable, or even the major one, in the teaching-learning equation, but they do make a difference, either a positive one or a negative one as a group and as individuals.

If teachers do not make a difference, then the profession has problems. If teachers do not make a difference, the notions of teacher evaluation, teacher accountability, and teacher performance are nonworkable; sound educational policy cannot be formulated, and there is little hope for many students, and there is little value in trying to learn how to teach. However, even if we are convinced that teachers have an effect, it is still true that we are unable to assess with confidence the influence a teacher has on student performance or behavior because the learning variables are numerous and the teaching interactions and relationships are complex.

Empirical findings are needed if we are to establish realistic expectations concerning teacher effects. In the meantime, we must find strength and confidence in the belief that we can, and often do, make a difference with our students. You may not be successful with all of your students all the time, but as long as you give your best, you will have served well your students, yourself, your colleagues, and your profession. Most of you will succeed— through experience, self-reflection, and productive supervision. See Tips for Teachers 11.1.

---

[3]Homer Coker, Donald M. Medley, and Robert S. Soar, "How Valid Are Expert Opinions about Effective Teachers?" *Phi Delta Kappan*, October 1980, pp. 131–134, 149; Lee S. Schulman, "A Union of Insufficiencies: Strategies for Teacher Assessment," *Educational Leadership*, November 1988, pp. 35-41; and Robert S. Soar, Donald M. Medley, and Homer Coker, "Teacher Evaluation: A Critique of Currently Used Methods," *Phi Delta Kappan*, December 1983, pp. 239–246.

[4]Jere E. Brophy, "Classroom Management Techniques," *Education and Urban Society*, February 1986, pp. 182–194; Carolyn M. Evertson et al., "Making a Difference in Education Quality Through Teacher Education," *Journal of Teacher Education*, May–June 1985, pp. 2–12; N. L. Gage, "What Do We Know about Teaching Effectiveness?," *Phi Delta Kappan*, October 1984, pp. 87–90; and Nancy L. Zimpher, "A Design for the Professional Development of Teacher Leaders," *Journal of Teacher Education*, January–February, 1988, pp. 53–61.

[5]Thomas L. Good, Bruce J. Biddle, and Jere E. Brophy, *Teachers Make a Difference* (New York: Holt, Rinehart and Winston, 1975); Allan C. Ornstein, "Theoretic Issues Related to Teaching," *Education and Urban Society*, November 1989, pp. 96–105.

Tips for Teachers 11.1

Observing Other Teachers to Improve Teaching Practices

The statement "Teachers are born, not made" fails to take into account the wealth of knowledge we have about good teaching and how children learn. Teachers can supplement their pedagogical knowledge and practices by observing other good teachers. Assuming that your school has a policy of observations or your supervisor can make arrangements with experienced teachers, you will be able to see how other teachers organize their classrooms. The next step is to ask yourself which of their practices are compatible with your approach to teaching and which might you be able to use. The questions below indicate some of the things to look for when you are observing.

STUDENT-TEACHER INTERACTION

1. What evidence was there that the teacher truly understood the needs of the students?
2. What techniques were used to encourage students' respect for each others' turn to talk?
3. How did the teacher react to students who interrupted the class routine?
4. What student behaviors in class were acceptable and unacceptable?
5. How did the teacher motivate students?
6. How did the teacher encourage student discussion?
7. In what way did the teacher see things from the students' point of view?
8. In what way did the teacher provide and use students' curiosity?
9. What evidence was there that the teacher responded to students' individual differences?
10. What evidence was there that the teacher responded to students' affective development?

TEACHING-LEARNING PROCESSES

1. Which instructional methods interested the students?
2. How did the teacher provide for transitions between instructional activities?
3. Which instructional materials (or media) interested students?
4. What practical life experiences (or activities) were used by the teacher to integrate concepts being learned?
5. How did the teacher minimize student frustration or confusion concerning the skills or concepts being taught?

continued

6. How did the teacher promote a positive learning environment?
7. In what way did the teacher encourage creative, imaginative work from students?
8. What instructional methods were used to make students think about ideas, opinions, or answers?
9. How did the teacher arrange the groups? What social factors were evident within the groups?
10. How did the teacher encourage independent (or individualized) student learning?
11. What methods reflected sound knowledge of subject matter?
12. How did the teacher integrate the subject matter with other subjects?

CLASSROOM ENVIRONMENT

1. How did the teacher utilize classroom space effectively?
2. How were the desks and chairs arranged? Why?
3. In what ways was the classroom esthetically pleasant?
4. How did the teacher utilize classroom equipment effectively?
5. What did you like and dislike about the physical environment of the classroom?

TEACHER STYLES

Teaching style is viewed as a broad dimension or personality type that encompasses teacher stance, pattern of behavior, mode of performance, and attitude toward self and others. Penelope Peterson defines teacher style in terms of how teachers utilize space in the classroom, their choice of instructional activities and materials, and their method of student grouping.[6] Donald Medley refers to teacher style as a dimension of classroom climate.[7] Still others describe teacher style as an *expressive* aspect of teaching (characterizing the emotional relationship between students and teachers, such as warm or businesslike) and as an *instrumental* aspect (how teachers carry out the task of instruction, organize learning, and set classroom standards).[8]

---

[6]Penelope L. Peterson, "Direct Instruction Reconsidered," in P. L. Peterson and H. J. Walberg, eds., *Research on Teaching: Concepts, Findings, and Implications* (Berkeley, Calif.: McCutchan, 1979), pp. 57–69.

[7]Donald M. Medley, "The Effectiveness of Teachers," in Peterson and Walberg, eds., *Research on Teaching: Concepts, Findings, and Implications*, pp. 11–27.

[8]Allan C. Ornstein and Harry L. Miller, *Looking into Teaching* (Chicago: Rand McNally, 1980).

Professional Viewpoint

The Science and Art of Teaching

Teaching is both a science and an art. The science is based on psychological research that identifies cause–effect relationships between teaching and learning. The art is how those relationships are implemented in successful and artistic teaching.

All excellent teaching does not look the same but it does contain the same basic psychological elements: In the same way, the Taj Mahal and the Lincoln Memorial are very different in appearance but they both commemorate a person, are made of marble, and follow the same principles of aesthetics and engineering.

Teaching in kindergarten or calculus, literature or auto shop manifests the same elements of instructional effectiveness. Teachers need to learn the science of pedagogy so they, in their own classrooms with their own personalities, can implement it artistically.

Teaching excellence is not a genetically endowed power but a result of rigorous study and inspired performance.

Madeline Hunter
Professor of Education
Univesity of California-Los Angeles

Regardless of which definition of teacher style you prefer, the notion of stability or pattern is central. Certain behaviors and methods are stable over time, even with different students and different classroom situations. There is a purpose, rationale—a predictable teacher pattern even in different classroom contexts. Aspects of teaching style dictated by personality can be modified by early experiences and perceptions and by appropriate training as a beginning teacher. As years pass, a teacher style becomes more ingrained and it takes a more powerful set of stimuli and more intense feedback to make changes. If you watch different teachers at work, including your college professors, you can sense that each one has a style of his own for teaching, for structuring the classroom and delivering the lesson.

Descriptive Models of Teaching Styles

Many educators have delineated various teaching styles in descriptive and colorful terms. Herbert Thelen attempts to compare teaching styles with characteristics of societal positions or with what appear to be roles associated with other occupations. Frank Riessman's eight teaching styles describe personality

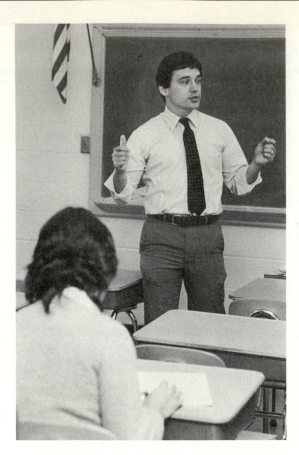

Figure 11.1 A business-like, firm approach is one of many styles of teaching. (Photo © J.B. Berndt 1982/ Picture Cube)

types; they were originally based on observations of effective teachers of inner-city students, but they can be used for all teachers. Louis Rubin, more recently, defines six kinds of teaching styles related to the act of teaching. These descriptions of teaching styles are summarized in Table 11.1.

The models by Thelen, Riessman, and Rubin are not research-based, but you may find these educators quite insightful about the qualities of an effective teacher and how these qualities relate to classroom teaching. Each style results in different teaching techniques and methods. As long as positive results are obtained, and as long as the teacher feels at ease with a particular style, it is important to follow personal preferences.

There are many other teacher styles. Teachers must develop their own style and teaching techniques based on their own physical and mental characteristics. Teachers must feel at ease in the classroom; if they are not genuinely themselves, students see through them and label them as "phony." The social, psychological, and educational climate in the classroom and school also has something to do with determining teaching style. Nonetheless, no one should be locked into a recommended style, regardless of conventional wisdom, contemporary history, or popular opinion. Teacher style is a matter of choice

Table 11.1   DESCRIPTIONS OF TEACHING STYLES

Thelen (1954)

1. *Socratic.* The image is a wise, somewhat crusty teacher who purposely gets into arguments with students over the subject matter through artful questioning.
2. *Town-Meeting.* Teachers who adapt this style use a great deal of discussion and play a moderator role that enables students to work out answers to problems by themselves.
3. *Apprenticeship.* This person serves as a role model toward learning, as well as occupational outlook, perhaps even toward general life.
4. *Boss-Employee.* This teacher asserts his or her own authority and provides rewards and punishments to see that the work is done.
5. *Good-Old Team Person.* The image is one of a group of players listening to the coach working as a team.

Riessman (1967)

1. *Compulsive Type.* This teacher is fussy, teaches things over and over, and is concerned with functional order and structure.
2. *Boomer.* This teacher shouts out in a loud, strong voice: "You're going to learn"; there is no nonsense in the classroom.
3. *Maverick.* Everybody loves this teacher, except perhaps the principal. She raises difficult questions and present ideas that disturb.
4. *Coach.* This teacher is informal, earthy, and maybe an athlete; he is physically expressive in conducting the class.
5. *Quiet One.* Sincere, calm, but definite, this teacher commands both respect and attention.
6. *Entertainer.* This teacher is free enough to joke and laugh with the students.
7. *Secular.* This person is relaxed and informal with children; she will have lunch with them, or play ball with them.
8. *Academic.* The teacher is interested in knowledge and in the substance of ideas.

Rubin (1985)

1. *Explanatory.* The teacher is in command of the subject matter and explains particular aspects of the lesson.
2. *Inspiratory.* The teacher is stimulating and exhibits emotional involvement in teaching.
3. *Informative.* The teacher presents information through verbal statements. The student is expected to listen and follow the instructions of the teacher.
4. *Corrective.* The teacher provides feedback to the student—analyzing the work, diagnosing for errors, and presenting corrective advice.
5. *Interactive.* Through dialogue and questioning, the teacher facilitates the development of students' ideas.
6. *Programmatic.* The teacher guides the students' activities and facilitates self instruction and independent learning.

Source: Adapted from Frank Riessman, "Teachers of the Poor: A Five Point Plan," *Journal of Teacher Education,* Fall 1967, pp. 326–336; Louis Rubin, *Artistry in Teaching* (New York: Random House, 1985); and Herbert A. Thelen, *Dynamics of Groups at Work* (Chicago: University of Chicago Press, 1954).

and comfort, and what works with one teacher may not work with another teacher. Similarly, operational definitions of good teachers and good teaching styles vary among and within school districts. There is no ideal teacher type or teacher style—and no educational institution (school or college) should impose one on its staff or faculty.

Research on Teacher Styles

Lippitt and White laid the groundwork for a more formal classification of what a teacher does in the classroom. Initially, they developed an instrument for describing the "social atmosphere" of children's clubs and for quantifying the effects of group and individual behavior. The results have been generalized in numerous research studies and textbooks on teaching. The classic study used classifications of authoritarian, democratic, and laissez-faire styles.[9]

The *authoritarian* teacher directs all the activities of the program. This style shares some characteristics with what is now called the *direct teacher*. The *democratic* teacher encourages group participation and is willing to let students share in the decision-making process. This behavior is typical of what is now called the *indirect teacher*. The *laissez-faire* teacher (now often considered to be an unorganized or ineffective teacher) provides no (or few) goals and directions for group or individual behavior.

Investigations based on Lippitt and White found that children taught by the authoritarian teacher failed to initiate activity and became dependent upon the teacher; some of the authoritarian groups exhibited aggressive and rebellious behavior toward the leader. The democratic teacher generated a friendly and cooperative group atmosphere; students' output was the highest in this group and the students carried through work assignments without the aid of the teacher for periods of time. The laissez-faire style of leadership generated confusion and minimal student productivity.

The authoritarian-democratic-laissez-faire constructs led to hundreds of empirical studies that concentrated on the same or similar teacher categories, such as (1) direct vs. indirect teaching; (2) dominative-integrative teaching; (3) teacher-centered, student-centered, and problem-centered teaching; and (4) inclusive-conjunctive-preclusive teaching.[10]

One of the most ambitious research studies on teacher styles was conducted by Ned Flanders and his associates between 1954 and 1970. Flanders focused on developing an instrument for quantifying verbal communication

---

[9] Ronald Lippitt and Ralph K. White, "The Social Climate of Children's Groups," in R. G. Barker, J. S. Kounin, and H. F. Wright, eds., *Child Behavior and Development* (New York: McGraw-Hill, 1943), pp. 485–508. Also see Kurt Lewin, Ronald Lippitt, and Ralph K. White, "Patterns of Aggressive Behavior in Experimentally Created Social Climates," *Journal of Social Psychology*, May 1939, pp. 271–299.

[10] Allan C. Ornstein, "Research on Teaching: Trends and Policies," *High School Journal*, December–January 1986, pp. 160–170.

Professional Viewpoint

Teaching Styles

I have found it convenient and useful to characterize teaching by the style of three of the best teachers I ever had: (1) Maggie Didactics, a strict votary of constant and often nauseating drill on basic ingredients of teaching French and German to high schoolers; (2) Edgar Heuristics, a professor of philosophy whose classes were brilliant adaptations of the Socratic dialogue, and (3) Fanny Philetics, a charming sixth-grade teacher whose many early adolescent pupils would labor gladly at any school task to gain her approval and affection.

Most of Maggie's pupils disliked her, but in 20 years none of them failed a college board examination in French or German. Some students were annoyed by the skirmishes of intellect and wit that Edgar Heuristics staged in the classroom, but many of his pupils became distinguished scholars. Fanny Philetics' classes were not well-organized, but many of her pupils achieved remarkable scholastic results to merit her approval.

In 12 years of schooling, one hopes that pupils would encounter a fair proportion of teachers who would elicit their enthusiastic efforts. As for teachers, they too might hope that over the years they would encounter a fair share of pupils for whom their style of teaching would qualify them as "the best teacher I ever had."

Until such happy coincidences can be "planned," pupils and teachers will have to learn to adjust to a variety of styles—the mark of the good student and the good teacher.

Harry S. Broudy
Emeritus Professor of Philosophy of Education
University of Illinois-Urbana

---

in the classroom.[11] Every three seconds observers sorted teacher talk into one of four categories of *indirect* behavior or one of three categories of *direct* behavior. Student talk was categorized as response or initiation and there was a final category representing silence or when the observer could not determine who was talking. The ten categories are shown in Table 11.2.

---

[11] Ned A. Flanders, *Teacher Influence, Pupil Attitudes, and Achievement* (Washington, D.C.: U.S. Government Printing Office, 1965); Flanders, *Analyzing Teaching Behavior* (Reading, Mass.: Addison-Wesley, 1970).

Table 11.2   FLANDERS' CLASSROOM INTERACTION ANALYSIS SCALE

Teacher talk		Student talk	Silence
Indirect behavior	Direct behavior		
1. *Accepts feeling:* Accepts and clarifies the tone of feeling of the students in an unthreatening manner. Feelings may be positive or negative. Predicting or recalling feelings are included. 2. *Praises or encourages:* Praises or encourages student action or behavior. Jokes that release tension, but not at the expense of another individual; nodding head or saying "Um hm?" or "Go on" are included. 3. *Accepts and uses ideas of student:* Clarifying, building ideas suggested by a student. As teacher brings more of his own ideas into play, shift to category 5. 4. *Asks questions:* Asking a question about content or procedure with the intent that a student will answer.	5. *Lecturing:* Giving facts or opinions about content or procedure; expressing his own ideas, asking rhetorical questions. 6. *Giving directions:* Directions, commands, or orders with which students are expected to comply. 7. *Criticizing or justifying authority:* Statements intended to change student behavior from unacceptable to acceptable pattern; bawling someone out; stating why the teacher is doing what he is doing; extreme self-reference.	8. *Response:* Talk by students in response to teacher. Teacher initiates the contact or solicits student statement. 9. *Initiation:* Talk initiated by students. If "calling on" student is only to indicate who may talk next; observer must decide whether student wanted to talk.	10. *Silence or confusion:* Pauses, short periods of silence, and periods of confusion in which communication cannot be understood by the observer.

Source: Ned A. Flanders, *Teacher Influence, Pupil Attitudes, and Achievement* (Washington, D.C.: U.S. Government Printing Office, 1965), p. 20.

Flanders' indirect teacher tended to overlap with Lippitt and White's democratic teaching style, and the direct teacher tended to exhibit behaviors similar to their authoritarian teacher. Flanders found that students in the indirect classrooms learned more and exhibited more constructive and independent attitudes than students in the direct classrooms. All types of students in all types of subject classes learned more working with the indirect (more flexible) teachers. In an interesting side note, Flanders found that as much as 80 percent of the classroom time is generally consumed in teacher talk. We will return to this point later.

The following questions, developed by Amidon and Flanders, represent a possible direction for organizing and analyzing observations.

1. What is the relationship of teacher talk to student talk? This can be answered by comparing the total number of observations in categories 1 to 7 with categories 8 and 9.
2. Is the teacher more direct or indirect? This can be answered by comparing categories 1 to 4 (indirect) with categories 5 to 7 (direct).
3. How much class time does the teacher spend lecturing? This can be answered by comparing category 5 with the total number of observations in categories 1 to 4 and 6 to 7.
4. Does the teacher ask divergent or convergent questions? This can be answered by comparing category 4 to categories 8 and 9.[12]

The data obtained from this system do not show when, why, or in what context teacher-student talk occurs, only how often particular types of interaction occur. Nonetheless, it is considered a useful device for making teachers aware of their interaction behaviors in the classroom.

The Flanders system can be used to examine teacher-student verbal behaviors in any classroom, regardless of grade level or subject. Someone can observe the verbal behavior of a prospective, beginning, or even experienced teacher and show how direct or indirect the teacher is. (Most prospective and beginning teachers tend to exhibit direct behavior, since they talk too much. Professors, also, usually lecture and thus exhibit many direct behaviors while teaching.)

Teachable Groups

The analysis of teaching styles eventually leads to two questions: Is student learning affected by the teachers' use of different approaches or styles? Are different teaching strategies effective for different students? Assuming the answer is "yes" in both cases, the aim is to match the appropriate teacher style and strategies with the appropriate group of students in order to achieve the best teaching-learning situation.

Herbert Thelen calls this the proper "fit." He states that teachers recognize four kinds of students: good, bad, indifferent, and maladjusted. Each teacher places different students in these categories, and teachable students for one teacher may be quite different for another. The proper fit between teacher and students results in the best kind of classroom or best group—what is defined as the **teachable group.** He contends that homogeneous grouping is essential for a group to become more "teachable." A teacher in such a group accom-

---

[12]Edmund J. Amidon and Ned A. Flanders, *The Role of the Teacher in the Classroom* (St. Paul, Minn.: Amidon & Associates, 1971). Also see Robert F. McNergney and Carol A. Carrier, *Teacher Development* (New York: Macmillan, 1981).

plishes more with students than in groups in which the range of ability and behavior is wide; moreover, it is easier to fit students and teachers together to achieve the best combinations. Any grouping that does not attempt to match students and teachers can have only "accidental success."[13]

Of special interest to the concept of teaching style is the classic work of Heil and Washburne. On the basis of observing fifth- and sixth-grade classrooms in New York City, students were divided into four categories: (1) *conformers*, characterized by high academic standards, high social orientation, and control over impulses; (2) *opposers*, characterized by conflict with authority, hostile or pessimistic tone, intolerance toward disappointment, easy frustration; (3) *waverers*, characterized by anxiety, ambivalence, fear, and indecision; and (4) *strivers*, characterized by marked drive for recognition, especially in school achievement and exhibitionistic activities. The teachers were divided into three personality types: *turbulent* (sloppy, inconsistent, impatient), *controlling* (orderly, businesslike, organized, yet sensitive to students' feelings), and *fearful* (anxious, dependent on approval from students and supervisors, unable to bring structure and order to their teaching task).[14]

Neither the striving nor the conforming students were affected by the teacher type, but teaching type made a difference in achievement for the opposers and waverers (behaviors exhibited by many problem and at-risk children). For opposers and waverers, the controlling teachers were the most effective. The turbulent teachers were less successful in teaching opposers, who evidenced the highest intolerance toward ambiguity. The fearful teachers were the least effective with all kinds of students, but especially with the opposers and waverers. Heil's findings, though apparently inconclusive, are consistent with the idea of grouping students according to cognitive and sociopsychological characteristics and "matching" them with teaching styles (and the belief that teachable students for one teacher may be quite different for another). This would lead to the formation of teachable groups.

Other researchers have addressed the problem of teachable groups and point out that effective teachers vary for students with different learning characteristics and socioeconomic backgrounds, as well as for different grade levels and subjects. For example, Donald Medley presents one of the most comprehensive reviews of 289 teacher process and product studies.[15] He concludes that effective teachers behave differently with different types of students. As shown in Table 11.3, the most effective teachers of low socioeconomic status elementary school students (1) spend less time discussing matters unrelated to lesson

[13]Herbert A. Thelen, *Classroom Grouping for Teachability* (New York: Wiley, 1967).

[14]Louis M. Heil and Carlton Washburne, "Brooklyn College Research on Teacher Effectiveness," *Journal of Educational Research*, May 1962, pp. 347–351.

[15]Donald M. Medley, *Teacher Competence and Teacher Effectiveness: A Review of Process-Product Research* (Washington, D.C.: American Association of Colleges for Teacher Education, 1977); Medley, "The Effectiveness of Teachers," in Peterson and Walberg, eds., *Research on Teaching: Concepts, Findings, and Implications*, pp. 11–27.

Table 11.3 EFFECTIVE AND INEFFECTIVE BEHAVIORS IN TEACHING LOW-INCOME STUDENTS IN THE ELEMENTARY GRADES

Teaching function	Effective behaviors	Ineffective behaviors
Maintenance of learning environment	Less deviant, disruptive pupil behavior	More deviant, disruptive pupil behavior
	Fewer teacher rebukes	More teacher rebukes
	Less criticism	More criticism
	Less time spent on classroom management	More time spent on classroom management
	More praise, positive motivation	Less praise, positive interaction
Use of pupil time	More class time spent in task-related "academic" activities	Less class time spent in task-related "academic" activities
	More time spent working with large groups or whole class	Less time spent working with large groups or whole class
	Less time spent working with small groups	More time spent working with small groups
	Small groups of pupils work independently less of the time	Small groups of pupils work independently more of the time
	Less independent seatwork	More dependent seatwork
Method of instruction	More "low-level" questions	Fewer "low-level" questions
	Fewer "high-level" questions	More "high-level" questions
	Less likely to amplify, discuss, or use pupil answers	More likely to amplify, discuss, or use pupil answers
	Fewer pupil-initiated question and comments	More pupil-initiated questions and comments
	Less feedback on pupil questions	More feedback on pupil questions
	More attention to pupils when they are working independently	Less attention to pupils when they are working independently

Source: Adapted from Donald M. Medley, *Teacher Competence and Teacher Effectiveness* (Washington, D.C.: American Association of Colleges for Teacher Education, 1977), pp. 11–24, 65.

content, (2) present structured and sequential learning activities, (3) permit little time on independent and small group work, (4) initiate low-level and narrowly defined questions and are less likely to amplify or discuss student answers, (5) spend little time on and discourage student-initiated questions and comments, (6) provide less feedback on student-initiated questions, (7) engage in fewer teacher rebukes, and (8) spend less time on discipline matters. The type of instruction, type of questions, and management techniques tend to be opposite for middle-class students.

Three things are important to note from Medley's review. First, his notion of changing teaching strategies for different students is similar to Heil's "match" between teacher and student types and Thelen's "fit" between teachers and students to establish teachable groups. Teachable students for one teacher may be quite different for another, not all students are easy to teach or even teachable under normal conditions, some good teachers cannot successfully teach some types of problem students, and different students need different teaching techniques.

Second, his description of effective teaching behaviors for low socioeconomic students does not resemble the current progressive model of instruction. The least effective teachers are those who ask the most high-level and fewest low-level questions, whose students ask more questions and get more feedback, and who amplify or discuss student-initiated comments. Teachers who use more low-level questions and fewer high-level ones, whose students initiate fewer questions and who tend not to discuss what students say are the most effective. Unquestionably, Medley's ideas are threatening and open to criticism, since they can lead to tracking students by ability and restricting low socioeconomic status students to limited cognitive experiences.[16]

Finally, Medley's ideas appear to be very much in line with teaching approaches and methods that have been identified by current researchers as highly successful with low-achieving students, both at the elementary and secondary grade levels: basic skill, drill, time on task, feedback, competency and mastery learning approaches; they coincide with instruction labeled "direct" and "explicit." Such teacher styles tend to be in line with the Brophy, Doyle, Evertson, Good, and Rosenshine models (discussed below in this chapter), but in opposition to a good deal of traditional and conventional wisdom that favors a warmer, more humanistic teacher (especially at the elementary school level).

TEACHER INTERACTION

An approach to the study of teacher behavior is based on systematic observation of **teacher-student interaction** in the classroom, as, for example, in the work of Flanders, which we have already described. The analysis of interaction often deals with a specific teacher behavior and a series of these behaviors constituting a larger behavior, described and recorded by an abstract unit of measurement that may vary in size and time (for example, every three seconds a recording is made).

Verbal Communication

In a classic study of teacher-student interaction, Arno Bellack analyzed the linguistic behavior of teachers and students in the classroom.[17] Classroom

---

[16]Allan C. Ornstein, "How Good Are Teachers in Affecting Student Outcomes?" *National Association of Secondary School Principals*, December 1982, pp. 61–70; Ornstein, "A Difference Teachers Make," *Educational Forum*, Fall 1984, pp. 109–118.

[17]Arno A. Bellack et al., *The Language of the Classroom* (New York: Teachers College Press, Columbia University, 1966).

activities are carried out in large part by verbal interaction between students and teachers; few classroom activities can be carried out without the use of language. The research, therefore, focused on language as the main instrument of communication in teaching. Four basic verbal behaviors or "moves" were labeled.

1. *Structuring moves* serve the function of focusing attention on subject matter or classroom procedures and beginning interaction between students and teachers. They set the context for subsequent behavior. For example, beginning a class by announcing the topic to be discussed is a structuring move.
2. *Soliciting moves* are designed to elicit a verbal or physical response. For example, the teacher asks a question about the topic with the hope of encouraging a response from the students.
3. *Responding moves* occur in relation to and after the soliciting behaviors. Their ideal function is to fulfill the expectations of the soliciting behaviors.
4. *Reacting* moves are sometimes occasioned by one or more of the above behaviors, but are not directly elicited by them. Reacting behaviors serve to modify, clarify, or judge the structuring, soliciting, or responding behavior.[18]

According to Bellack, these pedagogical moves occur in combinations he called "teaching cycles." A cycle usually begins with a structuring or soliciting move by the teacher, both of which are initiative behaviors, continues with a responding move from a student, and ends with some kind of reacting move by the teacher. In most cases the cycle begins and ends with the teacher. The investigators' analysis of the classroom also produced several insights.

1. Teachers dominate verbal activities. The teacher-student ratio in words spoken is 3:1. (This evidence corresponds with Flanders' finding that teachers' talk is 80 percent of classroom activity.)
2. Teacher and student moves are clearly defined. The teacher engages in structuring, soliciting, and reacting behaviors, while the student is usually limited to responding. (This also corresponds with Flanders' finding that most teachers dominate classrooms in such a way as to make students dependent.)
3. Teachers initiate about 85 percent of the cycles. The basic unit of verbal interaction is the soliciting-responding pattern. Verbal interchanges occur at a rate of slightly less than 2 cycles per minute.
4. In approximately two-thirds of the behaviors and three-fourths of the verbal interplay, talk is content-oriented.
5. About 60 percent of the total discourse is fact-oriented.

[18]Ibid.

In summary, the data suggest that the classroom is teacher-dominated, subject-centered, and fact-oriented. The students' primary responsibility seems to be to respond to the teacher's soliciting behaviors. (As a teacher, you should want to break this cycle of teaching.)

In another study Smith and Meux focused on the linguistic behavior of the teacher.[19] It was divided into "episodes" and "monologues." The **teacher episode** is defined as one or more verbal exchanges between two or more speakers. Questions by the teacher and answers by the students constitute the most common episode. The **teacher monologue** consists of a solo performance by a speaker addressing the group; the teacher who gives directions or a command is engaged in a monologue. Effective teachers tend to engage in episodes. The ideal episode seems to be an exchange in which several speakers respond to an original question or statement. Thus the most effective linguistic behavior is not teacher to student or student to teacher, but teacher to several students.

A series of episodes or monologues form a "cycle" that includes one or more of several verbal entries (that is, questions or statements that initiate the exchange):

1. *Defining* entries are concerned with how words are used to refer to objects: "What does the word . . . mean?"
2. *Describing* entries ask for an explanation or description about something: "What did John find out?"
3. *Designating* entries identify something by name: "What mountain range did we see in the film?"
4. *Stating* entries involve statements of issues, proofs, rules, theories, conclusions, beliefs, and so on: "What is the plot of the story?"
5. *Reporting* entries ask for a summary or a report on a book or document: "Can you summarize the major points of the book?"
6. *Substituting* entries require the performance of a symbolic operation, usually of mathematic or scientific value: "Who can write the equation on the chalkboard?"
7. *Evaluating* entries ask for judgment or estimate of worth of something: "Would you like to assess the validity of the argument?"
8. *Opinioning* entries ask for a conclusion, affirmation, or denial based upon evidence: "How do you feel President Bush will be judged by historians?"[20]

Nonverbal Communication

According to Miles Patterson, nonverbal behavior in the classroom serves five teacher functions: (1) *providing information,* or elaborating upon a verbal state-

---

[19]Othaniel Smith and Milton Meux, *A Study of the Logic of Teaching,* 2nd ed. (Urbana, Ill.: University of Illinois Press, 1970).

[20]Ibid.

ment; (2) *regulating interactions*, such as pointing to someone; (3) *expressing intimacy or liking*, such as smiling or touching a student on the shoulder; (4) *exercising social control*, reinforcing a classroom rule, say, by proximity or distance, and (5) *facilitating goals*, as when demonstrating a skill that requires motor activity or gesturing.[21] These categories are not mutually exclusive; there is some overlap, and nonverbal cues may serve more than one function depending on how they are used.

Although the teaching-learning process is ordinarily associated with verbal interaction, **nonverbal communication** operates as a silent language that influences the process. What makes the study of nonverbal communication so important and perhaps fascinating is that some researchers contend that it comprises about 65 percent of the social meaning of the classroom communication system.[22] As the old saying goes, "Action speaks louder than words."

In a recent study of 225 teachers (and school principals) in 45 schools, Stephens and Valentine observed 10 specific nonverbal behaviors: (1) smiles or frowns, (2) eye contact, (3) head nods, (4) gestures, (5) dress, (6) interaction distance, (7) touch, (8) body movement, (9) posture, and (10) seating arrangements.[23] In general, the first four behaviors are easily interpreted by the observer; some smiles, eye contact, head nods, and gestures are expected, but too many make students suspicious or uneasy. Dress is a matter of professional code and expectation. Distance, touch, body movement, posture, and seating are open to more interpretation, are likely to have personal meaning between communicators, and are based on personalities and social relationships.[24] Different types of these five behaviors, especially distance, touch, and body movement, can be taken as indications of the degree of formality in the relationship between the communicators, from intimate to personal to social to public. Teachers should maintain a social or public relationship—that is, a formal relationship—with their students. Behaviors that are appropriate to or could be interpreted as indicating intimate and personal relations should be avoided.

When the teacher's verbal and nonverbal cues contradict one another, according to Charles Galloway, the students tend to read the nonverbal cues as a true reflection of the teacher's real feelings. Galloway developed global guidelines for observing nonverbal communication of teachers, which he referred to as the "silent behavior of space, time, and body."[25]

---

[21] Miles L. Patterson, *Nonverbal Behavior: A Functional Perspective* (New York: Springer, 1983).

[22] Aron W. Siegman and Stanley Feldstein, eds., *Nonverbal Behavior and Communication* (Hillsdale, N.J.: Erlbaum, 1978).

[23] Pat Stephens and Jerry Valentine, "Assessing Principal Nonverbal Communication," *Educational Research Quarterly*, Winter 1986, pp. 60–68.

[24] Ibid.

[25] Charles M. Galloway, "Nonverbal Communication," *Theory into Practice*, December 1968, pp. 172–175; Galloway, "Nonverbal Behavior and Teacher Student Relationships: An Intercultural Perspective," in A. Wolfgang, ed., *Nonverbal Behavior: Perspectives, Applications, Intercultural Insights* (Toronto: Hogrefe, 1984), pp. 411–430.

1. *Space.* A teacher's use of space conveys meaning to students. For example, teachers who spend most of their time by the chalkboard or at their desk may convey insecurity, a reluctance to venture into student territory.
2. *Time.* How teachers utilize classroom time is an indication of how they value certain instructional activities. The elementary teacher who devotes a great deal of time to reading but little to mathematics is conveying a message to the students.
3. *Body maneuvers.* Nonverbal cues are used by teachers to control students. The raised eyebrow, the pointed finger, the silent stare all communicate meaning.

As shown in Table 11.4, Galloway suggests that various nonverbal behaviors of the teacher can be viewed as encouraging or restricting. By their facial expressions, gestures, and body movements, teachers affect student participation and performance in the classroom. The concept of encouraging versus restricting behavior can help in analyzing interactions. In referring to the table, we might ask the following questions:

Table 11.4 ENCOURAGING AND RESTRICTING TEACHER NONVERBAL BEHAVIORS

Encouraging behaviors	Restricting behaviors
Facial expression connotes enjoyment or satisfaction.	Teacher avoids eye contact, communicating inattention, disinterest, or unwillingness to listen.
Facial expression implies understanding or acceptance of student's need or problem.	Facial expression implies that he or she is unenthusiastic, condescending, impatient, or unsympathetic.
Teacher maintains eye contact, indicating patience, attention, and willingness to listen.	Teacher scowls, frowns, sneers.
Teacher moves toward students.	Teacher slouches or stands in a way that suggests disinterest or absorption in own work or thought.
Teacher pats student on back.	
Teacher uses gesture that indicates student is on the right track.	Teacher uses gestures or facial expressions to indicate that students stop, e.g., hand up, waving, angry look.
Teacher stands or sits in a way that suggests alertness or readiness to respond to student.	Teacher pokes, slaps, grabs student.
Voice intonation or inflection suggests approval or support.	Teacher uses vocal utterance to indicate that students are to stop talking or one that interrupts, e.g., "shhh," "ugh."
Teacher utters approval or suggests that student go on, e.g., "um-hm."	Voice intonation or inflection suggests antagonism, irritability, depreciation, or discouragement.
Teacher displays understanding, compassion, supportiveness by laughing.	

Source: Adapted from Charles M. Galloway, *Silent Language in the Classroom* (Bloomington, Ind.: Phi Delta Kappan Foundation, 1976); Galloway, "Nonverbal Behavior and Teacher Student Relationships," in A. Wolfgang, ed., *Nonverbal Behavior: Perspectives, Applications, Intercultural Insights* (Toronto: Hogrefe, 1984), pp. 411–430. Also based on conversations with Galloway, September 18, 1987.

1. How much time does the teacher spend on encouraging versus restricting behavior?
2. When (and why) does the teacher use encouraging and restricting cues?
3. Does the teacher's nonverbal behavior reveal his or her true feelings?
4. Is the teacher's verbal behavior (questions, directions, responses) accompanied by nonverbal cues?
5. Does the teacher's verbal behavior coincide with his or her nonverbal behavior?
6. To what extent do indirect and direct teachers, as defined by Flanders and Rosenshine, exhibit encouraging and restricting nonverbal behavior, as defined by Galloway?

The related concept of attentive and inattentive nonverbal behavior by students is also important in analyzing teacher-student interactions. See Tips for Teachers 11.2.

Students also exhibit nonverbal behavior that influences teachers' impressions, attitudes, reciprocal behavior, expectations, and existing and future student-teacher interactions. Nonverbal communication of students has been organized by researchers into four different categories.

1. *Location/proximity.* Where a student chooses to sit at the beginning of the year, assuming choice is available, influences the teacher's impression of how likable, initiating, and responsive the student is.
2. *Attentiveness.* Nonverbal behaviors such as erect posture, eye contact, and smiling communicate attention and are related to positive evaluations of the student's competence, learning, and attitude.
3. *Disruptive behaviors.* The absence of eye contact and verbal responsiveness is associated with negative teacher impressions. Rejecting help from the teacher and responding to teacher initiatives with negative nonverbal behaviors indicate disinterest or dislike to many teachers, and teachers often respond in kind with negative nonverbal behavior.
4. *Timing.* Students who make requests at inappropriate times are perceived negatively by teachers. Students who respond quickly to teacher requests appear to be perceived more positively by their teacher. "Successful interrupters" pick the best time to engage in mischief or deviant behavior, that is, when the teacher is engaged in an activity; "unsuccessful interrupters" get caught because their timing is wrong.[26]

Teacher Expectations

Teachers communicate their expectations of students through verbal and nonverbal cues. It is well established that these expectations affect the interaction

---

[26] Walter Doyle, "Classroom Organization and Management," in M. C. Wittrock, ed., *Handbook of Research on Teaching*, 3rd ed. (New York: Macmillan, 1986) pp. 392–431; Thomas L. Good and Jere E. Brophy, *Educational Psychology: A Realistic Approach*, 3rd ed. (New York: Longman, 1986).

Tips For Teachers 11.2

Inattentive and Attentive Nonverbal Behaviors

The teacher should look for nonverbal student behavior to determine whether the student is attentive (or engaged in an appropriate activity) or inattentive (not engaged). This awareness on the part of the teacher should take place regardless of the classroom activity. Below are cues that are useful in recognizing attentiveness and inattentiveness.

INATTENTIVE BEHAVIORS

1. Moving around the room without permission or at an inappropriate time
2. Reading a book or doing homework during class discussion
3. Doodling with a pencil; drawing instead of doing the assigned activity
4. Laying head on desk
5. Gazing out the window or at someone in the hallway
6. Staring fixedly at an object not related to a class activity
7. Sitting with elbows on desk or hands underneath thighs
8. Poking or annoying a classmate
9. Being unprepared (no pencil, pen, notebook)
10. Tipping the chair back and forth

ATTENTIVE BEHAVIORS

1. Raising a hand to volunteer a response
2. Maintaining eye contact with the teacher
3. Working on the assigned activity; academically engaged
4. Turning around to listen to a student who is speaking
5. Engaging in some task during a free activity or independent study period
6. Being prepared (with pencil, pen, notebook)
7. Alert, energetic, positive facial expressions
8. Nonjerky movement in seat, quiet sitting in front of classroom

Source: Adapted from Thomas L. Good and Jere E. Brophy, *Looking in Classrooms,* 4th ed. (New York: Harper & Row, 1988), pp. 89–90. About half of the inattentive and attentive behaviors are based on Good and Brophy; the remaining items are the author's.

Figure 11.2 Teachers' expectations toward students affect student learning. (Photo © Jeffry W. Myers/Stock, Boston)

between teachers and students and, eventually, the performance of students. In many cases teacher expectations become **self-fulfilling prophecies;** that is, if the teacher expects students to be slow or exhibit deviant behavior, he or she treats them accordingly, and in response they adopt such behaviors.

The research on teacher expectations is rooted in the legal briefs and arguments of Kenneth Clark prepared during his fight for desegregated schools in the 1950s and in his subsequent description of the problem in New York City's Harlem schools.[27] He pointed out that prophesying low achievement for black students not only provides teachers with an excuse for their students' failure, but also communicates a sense of inevitable failure to the students.

Clark's thesis was given empirical support a few years later by Rosenthal and Jacobsen's *Pygmalion in the Classroom*, a study of students in the San Francisco schools.[28] After controlling for the ability of students, teachers were told that there was reason to expect that certain students would perform better, and the expectancy was fulfilled. However, confidence in *Pygmalion* diminished when Robert Thorndike, one of the most respected measurement experts, pointed out that there were several flaws in the methodology and that the tests were unreliable.[29]

---

[27] Kenneth B. Clark, *Dark Ghetto* (New York: Harper & Row, 1965).

[28] Robert Rosenthal and Lenore Jacobson, *Pygmalion in the Classroom* (New York: Holt, Rinehart and Winston, 1968).

[29] Robert Thorndike, "Review of *Pygmalion in the Classroom*," *American Educational Research Journal*, November 1968, pp. 708–711.

Interest in teacher expectations and the self-fulfilling prophecy reappeared in the 1970s and 1980s. Cooper and then Good and Brophy outlined how teachers communicate expectations to students and in turn influence student behavior.

1. The teacher expects specific achievement and behavior from particular students.
2. Because of these different expectations, the teacher behaves differently toward various students.
3. This interaction suggests to students what achievement and behavior the teacher expects from them, which affects their self-concepts, motivation, and performance.
4. If the teacher's interaction is consistent over time, it will shape the students' achievement and behavior. High expectations for students will influence achievement at high levels, and low expectations will produce lower achievement.
5. With time, student achievement and behavior will conform more and more to the original expectations of the teacher.[30]

Brophy and Good's model in particular shows that many teachers vary sharply in their interaction with high- and low-achievers (Table 11.5). The two researchers contend that it is not necessary for the teacher to engage in all the behaviors listed in the table to have an impact. For example, if a teacher assigns low achievers considerably less content than they can handle, that factor alone will inhibit their learning.

The most effective teacher is realistic about the differences between high and low achievers. The teacher who develops a rigid or sterotyped perception of students is likely to have a harmful effect on them. The teacher who understands that differences exist and adapts realistic methods and content accordingly will have the most positive effect on students.

TEACHER CHARACTERISTICS

In the reams of research published on teacher behavior, the greatest amount concerns **teacher characteristics.** The problem is that researchers disagree on which teacher characteristics constitute successful teaching, on how to categorize characteristics, and on how to define them. In addition researchers use a variety of terms to name what they are trying to describe, such as "teacher

---

[30]Jere E. Brophy and Thomas L. Good, *Teacher-Student Relationships* (New York: Holt, Rinehart and Winston, 1974); Harris M. Cooper, "Pygmalion Grows Up: A Model for Teacher Expectation Communication and Performance Influence," *Review of Educational Research,* Summer 1979, pp. 389–410; Cooper and Good, *Pygmalion Grows Up* (New York: Longman, 1983); and Thomas L. Good and Rhona G. Weinstein, "Teacher Expectations: A Framework for Exploring Classrooms" in K. Kepler-Zumwalt, ed., *Improving Teaching* (Alexandria, Va.: Association for Supervision and Curriculum Development, 1986), pp. 63–85.

Table 11.5   TEACHER BEHAVIOR WITH LOW ACHIEVERS AND HIGH ACHIEVERS

1. *Waiting less time for low achievers to answer questions.* Teachers often give high-achieving students more time to respond than low-achieving students.

2. *Interrupting low achievers more often.* Teachers interrupt low achievers more often than high achievers when they make reading mistakes and/or are unable to sustain a discussion about the content or lesson.

3. *Giving answers to low achievers.* Teachers more frequently respond to incorrect responses of low achievers by giving them the answer or calling on another student to answer the question than they do with high achievers.

4. *Rewarding inappropriate behavior.* Teachers at times praise inappropriate responses of low achievers, which serves to dramatize the weakness of such students.

5. *Criticizing low achievers more often and praising them less often.* Some teachers criticize low achievers more than high achievers, a practice that is likely to reduce initiative and risk-taking behavior. Moreover, low achievers seem less likely to be praised, even when they get the correct answer.

6. *Not confirming responses of low achievers.* Teachers sometimes respond to answers from low achievers with indifference. Even if the answers are correct, they call on other students to respond without confirming answers, a practice that is likely to sow seeds of doubt concerning the adequacy of their response.

7. *Paying less attention to low achievers.* Teachers simply pay less attention to low achievers. For example, they smile more frequently and maintain more eye contact with high achievers, give briefer and less informative feedback to low achievers' questions, and are less likely to follow through on time-consuming instructional methods with low achievers.

8. *Calling on low achievers less often.* Teachers seem inclined to call on high achievers more often than low achievers.

9. *Using different interaction patterns.* Contact patterns between teachers and students are different for high and low achievers. Public response patterns dominate in interaction with high achievers, but low achievers have more private contacts with teachers. For low achievers, private conferences may be a sign of inadequacy.

10. *Seating lows further from the teacher.* Teachers often place low achievers in locations that are more distant from them.

11. *Demanding less from lows.* Teachers are more likely to demand little from and give up on low achievers and let them know it. Teachers demand more work from high achievers and ask more high-level questions.

12. *Administering different tests and grades.* Teachers often give low achievers less demanding tests and assignments. They are more likely to give high achievers the benefit of the doubt in borderline cases involving grades.

Source: Adapted from Thomas L. Good, ''Two Decades of Research on Teacher Expectations: Findings and Future Directions,'' *Journal of Teacher Education*, July–August 1987, pp. 32–47; Good and Brophy, *Educational Psychology: A Realistic Approach*, pp. 490–492.

traits,'' ''teacher personality,'' ''teacher performance,'' ''teacher outcomes.''[31] Descriptors or characteristics have different meanings to different people, and even when similar descriptors are used, categories have dissimilar meanings.

[31]Biddle, ''The Integration of Teacher Effectiveness Research''; N. L. Gage and David C. Berliner, ''Nurturing the Critical, Practical, and Artistic Thinking of Teachers,'' *Phi Delta Kappan*, November 1989, pp. 212–214.

Professional Viewpoint

The Teacher with Wisdom

There is a sense in which the following aphorism is true: The dumber the teacher, the better the student. What is meant by this is that a teacher's knowledge can often be an obstacle to learning. If teachers know a great deal and spend most of the time telling what they know, students are often intimidated, rendered passive, and made entirely dependent on the source of knowledge. But this is not what most good teachers want to accomplish. What is required of teachers is to be restrained and to be sparing in how they employ their knowledge in a classroom. This is not to argue that teachers should, in fact, be ignorant. It is to say that they may use ignorance as a means of inviting students to participate actively in the quest for knowledge. For if students believe that everything is known and the teacher knows it, the students must remain outsiders to the "great conversation."

Of course, if the teacher is truly a learned person then there is no need for him or her to feign ignorance. A learned person knows how ignorant he is and, in teaching, simply gives more prominence and emphasis to what he does not know than to what he does. Moreover, truly learned teachers are never frightened or defensive about making what is not known the focus of their lessons.

Neil Postman
Professor of Communication
New York University

Warm behavior for one investigator often means something different for another; effects of such behavior may be seen differently. Further, it can be assumed that a warm teacher would have a different effect on students according to age, sex, achievement level, socioeconomic class, ethnic group, subject, and classroom context.[32]

These differences tend to operate for every teacher characteristic and to affect every study on teacher behavior. Although a list of teacher characteristics may be suitable for a particular study, the characteristics (as well as the results) cannot always be compared with another study. The fact is, they often are compared, integrated, and built upon each other to form a theory or viewpoint about which teacher characteristics are most effective.

---

[32] Allan C. Ornstein, "Do Teachers Make a Difference?" *Childhood Education*, May–June, 1983, pp. 342–351; Ornstein, "Teacher Effectiveness Research"; and Soar, Medley, and Coker, "Teacher Evaluation: A Critique of Currently Used Methods."

Table 11.6   BARR'S CHARACTERISTICS IMPORTANT FOR SUCCESSFUL TEACHING

1. *Resourcefulness.* Originality, creativeness, initiative, imagination, adventurousness, progressiveness.
2. *Intelligence.* Foresight, intellectual acuity, understanding, mental ability, intellectual capacity, common sense.
3. *Emotional stability.* Poise, self-control, steadfastness, sobriety, dignity, nonneuroticism, emotional maturity, adjustment, constancy, loyalty, easy-going realism in facing life, not excitable, stable, integrated character.
4. *Considerateness.* Appreciativeness, kindliness, friendliness, courteousness, sympathy, tact, good-naturedness, helpfulness, patience, politeness, thoughtfulness, tolerance.
5. *Buoyancy.* Optimism, enthusiasm, cheerfulness, gregariousness, fluency, talkativeness, sense of humor, pleasantness, carefreeness, vivaciousness, alertness, animation, idealism, articulativeness, expressiveness, wit.
6. *Ojectivity.* Fairness, impartiality, open-mindedness, freedom from prejudice, sense of evidence.
7. *Drive.* Physical vigor, energy perseverance, ambition, industry, endurance, motivation, purposefulness, speediness, zealousness, quickness.
8. *Dominance.* Self-confidence, forcefulness, decisiveness, courageousness, independence, insensitiveness to social approval, self-sufficiency, determination, thick-skinnedness, self-reliance, self-assertiveness.
9. *Attractiveness.* Dress, physique, freedom from physical defects, personal magnetism, neatness, cleanliness, posture, personal charm, appearance.
10. *Refinement.* Good taste, modesty, morality, conventionality, culture, polish, well-readness.
11. *Cooperativeness.* Friendliness, easy-goingness, geniality, generosity, adaptability, flexibility, responsiveness, trustfulness, warm-heartedness, unselfishness, charitableness.
12. *Reliability.* Accuracy, dependability, honesty, punctuality, responsibility, conscientiousness, painstakingness, trustworthiness, consistency, sincerity.

Source: A. S. Barr, "Characteristics of Successful Teachers," *Phi Delta Kappan*, March 1958, pp. 282–283.

Nonetheless, many researchers feel that certain teacher characteristics can be defined, validated, and generalized from one study to another, that recommendations can be made from the generalizations, and that the recommendations can be used in a practical way.

Research on Teacher Characteristics

Although researchers have named literally thousands of teacher characteristics over the years, A. S. Barr organized recommended behaviors into a manageable list.[33] Reviewing some 50 years of research, he listed and defined 12 successful characteristics (Table 11.6). Other authorities have made other summaries of teacher characteristics, but Barr's work is considered most comprehensive.

While Barr presents an overview of hundreds of studies of teacher characteristics, the single most comprehensive study was conducted by David

---

[33] A. S. Barr, "Characteristics of Successful Teachers," *Phi Delta Kappan*, March 1958, pp. 282–284.

Ryans.[34] More than 6,000 teachers in 1,700 schools were involved in the study over a six-year period. The objective was to identify through observations and self-ratings the most desirable teacher characteristics. Respondents were asked to identify and describe a teaching act that they felt made a difference between success or failure. These critical behaviors were reduced to the list of 25 effective behaviors and 25 ineffective behaviors (Table 11.7). The lists, combined with Barr's recommendations, serve as good guidelines for beginning and even experienced teachers. The teacher should examine them in terms of his or her own personality and perceptions of good teaching.

Ryans went on to develop a bipolar list of 18 teacher characteristics (for example, original vs. conventional, patient vs. impatient, hostile vs. warm). Respondents were asked to identify the approximate position of teachers for each pair of characteristics on a seven-point scale. (A seven-point scale makes it easier for raters to avoid mid-point responses and nonpositions.)

The 18 teacher characteristics were defined in detail and further grouped into three "patterns" of successful vs. unsuccessful teachers:

1. *Pattern X:* understanding, friendly, responsive, versus aloof, egocentric
2. *Pattern Y:* responsible, businesslike, systematic, versus evading, unplanned, slipshod
3. *Pattern Z:* stimulating, imaginative, original, versus dull, routine

These three primary teacher patterns were the major qualities singled out for further attention. Elementary teachers scored higher than secondary teachers on the scales of understanding and friendly classroom behavior (Pattern X). Differences between women and men teachers were insignificant in the elementary schools, but in the secondary schools women consistently scored higher in Pattern X and in stimulating and imaginative classroom behavior (Pattern Z), and men tended to exhibit businesslike and systematic behaviors (Pattern Y). Younger teachers (under 45 years) scored higher than older teachers in patterns X and Z; older teachers scored higher in pattern Y.

A similar but more recent list of teacher characteristics was compiled by Bruce Tuckman, who has developed a feedback system for stimulating change in teacher behavior.[35] His instrument contains 28 bipolar items on which teachers are also rated on a seven-point scale (Table 11.8).

The characteristics cluster into four teacher "dimensions," similar to Ryans's patterns.

1. *Creative.* The creative teacher is imaginative, experimenting, and original; the noncreative teacher is routine, exacting, and cautious.
2. *Dynamic.* The dynamic teacher is outgoing, energetic, and extroverted; the nondynamic teacher is passive, withdrawn, and submissive.

---

[34] David G. Ryans, *Characteristics of Teachers* (Washington, D.C.: American Council of Education, 1960).

[35] Bruce W. Tuckman, "Feedback and the Change Process," *Phi Delta Kappan* (January 1986), pp. 341–344; Tuckman, *Evaluating Instructional Programs*, 2nd ed. (Boston: Allyn and Bacon, 1985).

Table 11.7   RYANS' CRITICAL TEACHER BEHAVIORS

Effective behaviors	Ineffective behaviors
1. Alert, appears enthusiastic.	1. Is apathetic, dull, appears bored.
2. Appears interested in pupils and classroom activities.	2. Appears uninterested in pupils and classroom activities.
3. Cheerful, optimistic.	3. Is depressed, pessimistic; appears unhappy.
4. Self-controlled, not easily upset.	4. Loses temper, is easily upset.
5. Likes fun, has a sense of humor.	5. Is overly serious, too occupied for humor.
6. Recognizes and admits own mistakes.	6. Is unaware of, or fails to admit, own mistakes.
7. Is fair, impartial, and objective in treatment of pupils.	7. Is unfair or partial in dealing with pupils.
8. Is patient.	8. Is impatient.
9. Shows understanding and sympathy in working with pupils.	9. Is short with pupils, uses sarcastic remarks, or in other ways shows lack of sympathy with pupils.
10. Is friendly and courteous in relations with pupils.	10. Is aloof and removed in relations with pupils.
11. Helps pupils with personal as well as educational problems.	11. Seems unaware of pupils' personal needs and problems.
12. Commends effort and gives praise for work well done.	12. Does not commend pupils, is disapproving, hypercritical.
13. Accepts pupils' efforts as sincere.	13. Is suspicious of pupils' motives.
14. Anticipates reactions of others in social situations.	14. Does not anticipate reactions of others in social situations.
15. Encourages pupils to try to do their best.	15. Makes no effort to encourage pupils to try to do their best.
16. Classroom procedure is planned and well organized.	16. Classroom procedure is without plan, disorganized.
17. Classroom procedure is flexible within over-all plan.	17. Shows extreme rigidity of procedure, inability to depart from plan.
18. Anticipates individual needs.	18. Fails to provide for individual differences and needs of pupils.
19. Stimulates pupils through interesting and original materials and techniques.	19. Uninteresting materials and teaching techniques used.
20. Conducts clear, practical demonstrations and explanations.	20. Demonstrations and explanations are not clear and are poorly conducted.
21. Is clear and thorough in giving directions.	21. Directions are incomplete, vague.
22. Encourages pupils to work through their own problems and evaluate their accomplishments.	22. Fails to give pupils opportunity to work out own problems or evaluate their own work.
23. Disciplines in quiet, dignified, and positive manner.	23. Reprimands at length, ridicules, resorts to cruel or meaningless form of correction.
24. Gives help willingly.	24. Fails to give help or gives it grudgingly.
25. Foresees and attempts to resolve potential difficulties.	25. Is unable to foresee and resolve potential difficulties.

Source: David G. Ryans, *Characteristics of Teachers* (Washington, D.C.: American Council on Education, 1960), p. 82.

Table 11.8   TUCKMAN'S TEACHER CHARACTERISTICS

1.	Original	_ _ _ _ _ _ _	Conventional
2.	Patient	_ _ _ _ _ _ _	Impatient
3.	Cold	_ _ _ _ _ _ _	Warm
4.	Hostile	_ _ _ _ _ _ _	Amiable
5.	Creative	_ _ _ _ _ _ _	Routinized
6.	Inhibited	_ _ _ _ _ _ _	Uninhibited
7.	Iconoclastic	_ _ _ _ _ _ _	Ritualimental
8.	Gentle	_ _ _ _ _ _ _	Organized
9.	Unfair	_ _ _ _ _ _ _	Sociable
10.	Capricious	_ _ _ _ _ _ _	Uncertain
11.	Cautious	_ _ _ _ _ _ _	Outspoken
12.	Disorganized	_ _ _ _ _ _ _	Exactiistic
13.	Unfriendly	_ _ _ _ _ _ _	Harsh
14.	Resourceful	_ _ _ _ _ _ _	Fair
15.	Reserved	_ _ _ _ _ _ _	Purposeful
16.	Imaginative	_ _ _ _ _ _ _	Experng
17.	Erratic	_ _ _ _ _ _ _	Systematic
18.	Aggressive	_ _ _ _ _ _ _	Passive
19.	Accepting	_ _ _ _ _ _ _	Critical
20.	Quiet	_ _ _ _ _ _ _	Bubbly
21.	Outgoing	_ _ _ _ _ _ _	Withdrawn
22.	In control	_ _ _ _ _ _ _	On the run
23.	Flighty	_ _ _ _ _ _ _	Conscientious
24.	Dominant	_ _ _ _ _ _ _	Submissive
25.	Observant	_ _ _ _ _ _ _	Preoccupied
26.	Introverted	_ _ _ _ _ _ _	Extroverted
27.	Assertive	_ _ _ _ _ _ _	Soft-spoken
28.	Timid	_ _ _ _ _ _ _	Adventurous

Source: Bruce W. Tuckman, "Feedback and the Change Process," *Phi Delta Kappan*, January 1976, p. 342. Also see Tuckman, *Evaluating Instructional Programs*, 2nd ed. (Boston: Allyn and Bacon, 1985, p. 95.

3. *Organized.* The organized teacher is purposeful, resourceful, and in control; the disorganized teacher is capricious, erratic, and flighty.
4. *Warm.* The warm teacher is sociable, amiable, and patient; the cold teacher is unfriendly, hostile, and impatient.

TEACHER COMPETENCIES

Because of the problem with lack of agreement in defining teacher characteristics, Medley and others recommend more precise terms, what they call **teacher competencies.**[36] These competencies may or may not stem from broad teacher

[36]Donald M. Medley, Homer Coker, and Robert S. Soar, *Management-Based Evaluation of Teacher Performance* (New York: Longman, 1984), p. 58.

characteristics, but they are "specific items of behavior" that can be defined with care necessary for inclusion in a manual of instruction or in a teacher-appraisal system.

The University of Toledo and the Salt Lake City school district have developed reliable lists of competencies. The 49 Toledo competencies were designed to measure five broad areas of behaviors (called topics) that student teachers should be expected to exhibit (Table 11.9). They reflect some 2,000 behavioral objectives on which the instrument was developed; they can apply to all preservice teachers K–12, and they can be used to assist beginning teachers as well. The Salt Lake City list contains 24 competencies in four broad categories (Table 11.10). The instrument was developed by administrators and

Table 11.9   UNIVERSITY OF TOLEDO COMPETENCY INDICATORS

Topic: Planning, teaching materials/equipment and evaluation

1. Plans units of instruction.
2. Plans instruction at a variety of cognitive levels.
3. Can state pupil outcomes and/or student course objectives in behavioral terms (behavioral objectives).
4. Has realistic expectations for the learning process and student readiness for learning.
5. Gathers, organizes, and evaluates pertinent information about students for effective instruction.
6. Identifies and evaluates learning problems of students in content area being taught.
7. Keeps informed of current professional/subject area literature and curricular learning materials/resources available.
8. Knows how to select (or construct), organize and use appropriate instructional materials and equipment to faciliate learning activities.
9. Uses criteria and effective procedures for determining pupil achievement of learning objectives.
10. Selects/develops appropriate assessment techniques and instruments for instructional activities.
11. Collects, quantifies, and interprets data from appropriate assessment instruments.
12. Maintains evaluation records.
13. Engages in professional development by obtaining and analyzing evaluative information concerning the effectiveness of instruction.
14. Uses information about the effectiveness of instruction to revise it, with possible curriculum modifications.
15. Relates to accountability issues concerning responsibilities to students, parents, and the instructional process.

Topic: Instructional strategies, techniques, and/or methods

16. Uses a variety of instructional strategies.
17. Uses convergent and divergent inquiry strategies.
18. Develops and demonstrates problem solving skills.
19. Establishes transitions and sequences in instruction which are varied.
20. Modifies instructional activities to accommodate identified learner needs.
21. Demonstrates ability to work with individuals, small groups and large groups.
22. Structures the use of time to facilitate student learning.

Table 11.9 CONTINUED

23. Uses a variety of resources and materials.
24. Provides learning experiences which enable students to transfer principles and generalizations to situations outside of school.
25. Provides assignments/learning opportunities interesting and appropriate to different ability levels of pupils.
26. Demonstrates knowledge in the subject areas.
27. Demonstrates self-direction and conveys the impression of knowing what to do and how to do it.
28. Works effectively as a member of an instructional team.
29. Uses acceptable written and oral expression with learners.
30. Adjusts components of the physical/learning environment over which the teacher has control to facilitate learning.

Topic: Communication with learners

31. Provides group communication (cooperation, interaction, learning from others).
32. Uses a variety of functional verbal and non-verbal communication skills with students.
33. Gives clear directions and explanations.
34. Motivates students to ask questions.
35. Uses questions that lead students to analyze, synthesize and think critically.
36. Accepts varied student viewpoints and/or asks students to extend or elaborate answers or ideas.
37. Demonstrates proper listening skills.
38. Provides feedback to learners on their cognitive performance.
39. Expresses a positive personal attitude toward the teaching profession.

Topic: Learner reinforcement-involvement

40. Maintains an environment in which students are actively involved, working on-task.
41. Implements an effective classroom management system for positive student behavior (discipline).
42. Uses positive reinforcement patterns with students.
43. Assists students in discovering and correcting errors and inaccuracies.
44. Develops student feedback, evaluation skills and student self-evaluation.

Topic: Professional standards

45. Accepts responsibility, is dependable.
46. Evidences cooperation with others (teachers, administrators, support staff, parents, etc.) in planning and teaching.
47. Acts as an appropriate model in terms of ethics, attitudes and values.
48. Attends teacher and other professional meetings.
49. Understands and follows school law, policies, and procedures and their effects on teachers, and teaching, including professional conduct standards.

Source: Thomas Gibney and William Wiersma, ''Using Profile Analysis for Student Teacher Evaluation,'' *Journal of Teacher Education*, May–June 1986, p. 43.

Table 11.10   SALT LAKE CITY SCHOOL DISTRICT COMPETENCY INDICATORS

1. Determines standards of expected student performance
   a. Preassessment (diagnosis)
   b. Competencies expected at a given level
   c. Determines individual needs
   d. Expected goals for student achievement
   e. Evaluation of goals
2. Provides learning environment
   a. Availability of resource personnel
   b. Availability of variety of resource materials
   c. Physical organization and learning process
   d. Positive attitude toward students
   e. Exhibits an attitude that all students can learn
   f. Teacher shows enthusiasm and commitment for the subject taught
   g. Student behavior demonstrates acceptance of learning experience
3. Demonstrates appropriate student control
   a. Evidence that student knows what to do
   b. Evidence that student is working at task
   c. Demonstrates fairness, acceptance, respect, and flexibility.
   d. Appropriate control in difficult situations.
   e. Anticipate and avoid crisis
4. Demonstrates appropriate strategies for teaching
   a. Demonstrates techniques that are appropriate to different levels of learning
   b. Adjusts techniques to different learning styles
   c. Uses variety of techniques to teach specific skill or concept
   d. Gives directions that are clear, concise, and appropriate to the student learning level
   e. Establishes two-way communication with students and utilizes feedback to determine teaching strategies
   f. Demonstrates a purpose has been determined for the instruction
   g. Exhibits evidence of effective planning

Source: A Continuing Written Agreement . . . Between the Board of Education of Salt Lake City . . . and Salt Lake Teachers Association, 1988–89. Salt Lake City, UT.: Salt Lake Teachers Association, 1988), pp. 36–37.

teachers of the school district and therefore is valid for that particular school setting. It is used chiefly for purposes of remediation and improvement and is applicable to teachers of all grades and subjects.

Both sets of competencies deal mainly with what the teacher is doing while teaching. Both sets deal with specific behaviors as opposed to broad characteristics or teaching patterns. Because the competencies are more specific, long lists are needed to get an idea of the teacher's performance. The longer the list, however, the greater the chance that the competencies will overlap and cluster in other broad categories, which brings us back to many teacher characteristic inventories.

Because such long lists of competencies can be generated, it is important to determine which competencies school principals believe to be significant,

Table 11.11   PRINCIPALS' RANKING OF EFFECTIVE TEACHER COMPETENCIES

Rank of importance	Competency	Definition
1	Task orientation	The extent to which the classroom is businesslike, the students spend their time on academic subjects, and the teacher presents clear goals to the students
2	Enthusiam and interest	The amount of the teacher's vigor, power, and involvement
3	Direct instruction	The extent to which the teacher sets and articulates the learning goals, actively assesses student progress, and frequently makes class presentations illustrating how to do assigned work
4	Pacing	The extent to which the level of difficulty and the pace of the lesson is appropriate for the students' ability and interest
5	Feedback	The extent to which the teacher provides the students with positive and negative feedback
6	Management	The extent to which the teacher is able to conduct the class without instruction being interrupted
7	Questioning	The extent to which the teacher asks questions at different levels and adjusts them appropriately in the classroom
8	Instructional time	The allocation of a period of time for a lesson adequate to cover the material yet flexible enough to allow for the unexpected
9	Variability	The amount of flexibility or adaptability of teaching methods; the amount of extra material in the classroom
10	Structuring	The extent to which the teacher directs instruction
11	Opportunity to learn criterion material	The extent to which criterion material is covered in class

Source: John H. Arnn and John N. Mangieri, "Effective Leadership for Effective Schools: A Survey of Principal Attitudes," *National Association of Secondary School Principals,* February 1988, p. 4.

since they invariably play a role in developing teacher evaluation plans, in observing and judging teachers (usually at the elementary and junior high level), and in assigning supervisors to evaluate teachers' performance (usually at the high school level). In a nationwide study of 202 secondary schools selected for special recognition for effectiveness in educating their students (conducted under the aegis of the U.S. Department of Education), principals were asked to identify and rank the competencies they emphasized with teachers.[37] The top 11 competencies are presented in Table 11.11.

---

[37]John W. Arnn and John N. Mangieri, "Effective Leadership for Effective Schools: A Survey of Principal Attitudes," *National Association of Secondary School Principals,* February 1988, pp: 1–7.

The five competencies most important for principals—task orientation, enthusiasm and interest, direct instruction, pacing, and feedback—emphasize the "active" dimension of teaching and businesslike behaviors. Principals of effective schools expect their teachers to teach and in a way that can be observed and measured. One might assume, however, that elementary principals might have emphasized fewer task-oriented, explicit behaviors and more socially oriented and humanistic behaviors.

In general, most measurements of teacher competence focus on minimal competencies. According to Arthur Wise, school districts and administrators that evaluate competencies of teachers spend "little time evaluating teachers who appear to be competent"; therefore, competent teachers often are not threatened by the process nor do they consider it useful. "Rather they criticize evaluations for providing too few observations and evaluators for making [too few] comments . . . [that] relate specifically to . . . their particular teaching assignment." This does not mean that teacher competency instruments are invalid or unreliable measures; rather, their present utility is linked to identifying teacher incompetence. In some school districts, for example, "the absence of minimal teaching competence, especially the inability to manage the classroom, triggers remediation, probation, or intervention."[38]

A further word of caution is needed. Many school districts (even entire states such as Florida and North Carolina) have developed a specific list of teacher competencies as a basis for appraisal and merit pay plans. Teachers who do not exhibit explicit behaviors are often penalized, labeled as "marginal" or "below standard," and in some cases they may lose their jobs. According to critics, these lists of competencies tend to reflect a narrow and behaviorist view of a "good" teacher and to ignore humanistic or affective behaviors that also contribute to good teaching.[39]

Nevertheless, the national movement for reform in education, coupled with the influence of the behaviorist movement in psychology, has pushed for an appraisal system based on specific teacher competencies. When used for such purposes, multiple observations are required. If inferences or decisions about teaching competencies are to be the grounds for personnel decisions, then adequate sampling of teacher performance is necessary (especially in an era of litigation).

Wise maintains that successful appraisal of competencies requires four factors: (1) *commitment*—top level leadership must approve of the evaluation process and allocate institutional resources for it; (2) *evaluator competence*—the evaluator (or user) must have the expertise to perform the task of observation (or analysis); (3) *collaboration*—administrators, supervisors, and teachers must develop a common understanding of the goals and processes involved;

---

[38] Arthur F. Wise et al., "Teacher Evaluation: A Study of Effective Practices," *Elementary School Journal,* September 1985, p. 94.

[39] Allan C. Ornstein, "For Teachers, About Teachers," *Peabody Journal of Education* (in print 1990); Ornstein, "Theoretical Issues Related to Teaching."

and (4) *compatibility*—there must be joint decision making, agreed-upon support systems, and agreement between evaluation goals and processes and school or district goals and processes.[40]

Successful appraisal also requires a degree of willingness to give the teacher being appraised the benefit of doubt and a chance to remediate before being terminated. It also calls for an open mind so that other competencies not listed can be incorporated into the appraisal system. It also calls for commonsense —that there is more than one preferred model that connotes teacher competency.

Guidelines for Evaluating Teacher Characteristics and Competencies

---

Having to be evaluated in terms of characteristics or competencies can generate marked anxiety in beginning teachers. They need extra counseling and support to reduce their fears and to make them aware that a teacher's probationary period involves evaluation as a guide to improvement. One researcher suggests seven means of support that should be made available to beginning teachers who must be evaluated for minimal teacher competencies.

1. *System information.* Providing information related to procedures, guidelines, and expectations of the school district.
2. *Resources and materials.* Disseminating materials that explain the rationale of the process.
3. *Instructional information.* Giving information about recommended teaching and instructional methods.
4. *Emotional support.* Offering support by colleagues and supervisors through conferences and by sharing experiences.
5. *Classroom management suggestions.* Providing ideas and guidance on effective management.
6. *Classroom environment suggestions.* Providing ideas and guidance on arranging and organizing the physical setting of the classroom.
7. *Demonstration teaching.* Permitting new teachers to observe experienced teachers and to discuss competencies in a follow-up conference.[41]

---

[40] Wise et al., ''Teacher Evaluation: A Study of Effective Practices''; Arthur E. Wise, Linda Darling-Hammond, and Barnett Berry, *Effective Teacher Selection: From Recruitment to Retention* (Santa Monica, Calif.: Rand Corporation, 1987).

[41] Sandra J. Odell, ''Induction Support of New Teachers: A Functional Approach,'' *Journal of Teacher Education,* January–February 1986, pp. 26–29.

The model developed by Ben Harris provides a method for improving teaching by analyzing classroom behavior. It requires teachers and supervisors to agree upon behaviors that will be observed and analyzed, and upon the importance of those behaviors.

1. Establish criteria that indicate positive teacher characteristics or competencies.
2. Observe the teacher three separate times by three different "sources," that is, professionals (colleague, supervisor, principal).
3. Rate the teacher on the agreed-upon criteria.
4. Compare the perceptions or analysis of the three observers.
   a. All agree behaviors are clearly demonstrated.
   b. All agree behaviors are not demonstrated.
   c. Two out of three agree behaviors are demonstrated.
   d. Two out of three agree behaviors are not demonstrated.
5. Generate four types of diagnoses.
   a. *Accomplishments*—areas where all three sources (observers) agree that characteristics or competencies are clearly demonstrated.
   b. *Need for improvement*—areas where all three sources agree that characteristics or competencies are not demonstrated.
   c. *Uncertainty* (need attention)—areas where sources disagree or question.
   d. *Refine/upgrade*—areas where sources agree that refinement or upgrading is required.[42]

TEACHER EFFECTS

Teacher behavior research has shown that teacher behaviors, as well as specific teaching principles and methods, make a difference with regard to student outcomes. Rosenshine and Furst analyzed some 42 correlational studies in their often quoted review of **process-product research.** They concluded that there were 11 teacher processes (behaviors or variables) strongly and consistently related to products (outcomes or student achievement). The first five teacher processes showed the strongest correlation to positive outcomes.

1. *Clarity* of teacher's presentation and ability to organize classroom activities
2. *Variability* of media, materials, and activities used by the teacher
3. *Enthusiasm,* defined in terms of the teacher's movement, voice inflection, and the like
4. *Task orientation* or businesslike teacher behaviors, structured routines, and an academic focus

[42]Ben M. Harris, *Developmental Teacher Evaluation* (Boston: Allyn and Bacon, 1986); Harris, *In-Service Education for Staff Development* (Boston: Needham Heights, Mass.: Allyn and Bacon, 1989).

5. *Student opportunity to learn*, that is, the teacher's coverage of the material or content in class on which students are later tested[43]

The six remaining processes were classified as promising: use of student ideas, justified criticism, use of structuring comments, appropriate questions in terms of lower and higher cognitive level, probing or encouraging student elaboration, and challenging instructional materials.

With the Rosenshine and Furst review, it appeared that research on teaching had begun to provide objective information about what teachers do, how it relates or contributes to student learning, and how it can be measured. As critics pointed out, however, the studies cited in their review and even their own analysis were marked by serious technical problems and made prescriptions based on such evidence hazardous.[44]

Rosenshine himself later revised his conclusions; subsequent analysis showed that only two behaviors or processes consistently correlated with student achievement: (1) task orientation (later referred to as *direct instruction)* and (2) opportunity to learn (later referred to as *academic time, academic engaged time,* and *content covered)*. On a third behavior, clarity, he wavered, pointing out that it seemed to be a correlate of student achievement for students above the fifth grade. The other eight processes appeared to be less important and varied in importance not only according to grade level, but also according to subject matter, instructional groups and activities, and students' social class and abilities.[45] Nevertheless, the original review remains a valuable study on how teacher processes relate to student products.

The Gage Model

Nate Gage recently analyzed 49 process-product studies. He identified four clusters of behaviors that show a strong relationship to student outcomes: (1) *teacher indirectness*, the willingness to accept student ideas and feelings and the ability to provide a healthy emotional climate; (2) *teacher praise*, support and encouragement, use of humor to release tensions (but not at the expense of others), and attention to students' needs; (3) *teacher acceptance*, clarifying,

[43]Barak V. Rosenshine and Norma F. Furst, "Research in Teacher Performance Criteria," in B. O. Smith, ed., *Research on Teacher Education* (Englewood Cliffs, N.J.: Prentice-Hall, 1971), pp.37-72; Rosenshine and Furst, "The Use of Direct Observation to Study Teaching," in R. M. Travers, ed., *Second Handbook of Research on Teaching* (Chicago: Rand McNally, 1973), pp. 122–183. Note that the first five processes also appear in Arnn and Mangieri's list of competencies (Table 11.11), but in different order of importance.

[44]Robert W. Heath and Mark A. Nielson, "The Research Bias for Performance Based Teacher Education," *Review of Educational Research*, Fall 1974, pp. 463–484; Ornstein, "How Good Are Teachers in Affecting Student Outcomes?"

[45]Barak V. Rosenshine, "Content, Time and Direct Instruction," in Peterson and Walberg, eds., *Research on Teaching: Concepts, Findings, and Implications*, pp. 28–56.

building, and developing students' ideas; and (4) *teacher criticism*, reprimanding students and justifying authority. The relationship between the last cluster and outcome was negative; where criticism occurred, student achievement was low.[46] In effect, the four clusters suggest the traditional notion of a democratic or warm teacher (nothing more than what has been emphasized for several decades).

From the evidence on teacher effects upon student achievement in reading and mathematics in the elementary grades, Gage presents successful teaching principles and methods that seem relevant for other grades as well. These strategies are summarized below. Bear in mind that they are commonsense strategies, they apply to many grade levels, and most experienced teachers are familiar with them. Nonetheless, they provide guidelines for education students or beginning teachers who say, "Just tell me how to teach."

1. Teachers should have a system of rules that allow students to attend to their personal and procedural needs without having to check with the teacher.

2. A teacher should move around the room, monitoring students' seatwork and communicating an awareness of their behavior while also attending to their academic needs.

3. To ensure productive independent work by students, teachers should be sure that the assignments are interesting and worthwhile, yet still easy enough to be completed by each student without teacher direction.

4. Teachers should keep to a minimum such activities as giving directions and organizing the class for instruction. Teachers can do this by writing the daily schedule on the board and establishing general procedures so students know where to go and what to do.

5. In selecting students to respond to questions, teachers should call on volunteers and nonvolunteers by name before asking questions to give all students a chance to answer and to alert the student to be called upon.

6. Teachers should always aim at getting less academically oriented students to give some kind of response to a question. Rephrasing, giving clues, or asking leading questions can be useful techniques for bringing forth some answer from a silent student, one who says "I don't know," or one who answers incorrectly.

7. During reading group instruction, teachers should give a maximum amount of brief feedback and provide fast-paced activities of the "drill" type.[47]

---

[46] N. L. Gage, *The Scientific Basis of the Art of Teaching* (New York: Teachers College Press, Columbia University, 1978).

[47] *Ibid.* The author disagrees with item 5; see chapter 6 on questioning.

The Good and Brophy Model

For the last 15 years Good and Brophy have identified several factors related to effective teaching and student learning. They are basically principles of teaching, but not teacher behaviors or characteristics. In this connection, the researchers contend that teachers today are looking more for principles of teaching than for prescriptions.

1. *Clarity* about instructional goals (objectives).
2. Knowledge about *content* and ways for teaching it.
3. *Variety* in the use of teaching methods and media.
4. *"With-it-ness,"* awareness of what is going on, alertness in monitoring classroom activities.
5. *"Overlapping,"* sustaining an activity while doing something else at the same time.
6. *"Smoothness,"* sustaining proper lesson pacing and group momentum, not dwelling on minor points or wasting time dealing with individuals, and focusing on all the students.
7. *Seatwork* instructions and management that initiate and focus on productive task engagement.
8. Holding students *accountable* for learning; accepting responsibility for student learning.
9. *Realistic expectations* in line with student abilities and behaviors.
10. *Realistic praise*, not praise for its own sake.
11. *Flexibility* in planning and adapting classroom activities.
12. *Task orientation* and businesslike behavior in the teacher.
13. *Monitoring* of students' understanding; providing appropriate feedback, giving praise, asking questions.
14. Providing student *opportunity to learn* what is to be tested.
15. Making comments that help *structure learning* of knowledge and concepts for students; helping students learn how to learn.[48]

The fact that many of these behaviors are classroom management techniques and structured learning strategies, rooted in Kounin's model of classroom management and discipline, suggests that good discipline is a prerequisite for good teaching.

The Evertson and Emmer Model

The Evertson and Emmer model is similar to the Good and Brophy model (in fact, Evertson has written several texts and articles with Brophy). The models

---

[48] Thomas L. Good and Jere E. Brophy, *Looking in Classrooms*, 4th ed. (New York: Harper & Row, 1988); Good and Brophy, "Teacher Behavior and Student Achievement," in M. C. Wittrock, ed., *Handbook of Research on Teaching*, 3rd ed. (New York: Macmillan, 1986), pp. 328–375. Also see Andrew C. Porter and Jere Brophy, "Synthesis of Research on Good Teaching," *Educational Leadership*, May 1988, pp. 74–85.

are similar in three ways: (1) teacher effectiveness is associated with specific teaching principles and methods; (2) organization and management of instructional activities are stressed, and (3) their findings and conclusions are based primarily on process-product studies. A good deal of the work is based on the time when Evertson, Emmer and Brophy were colleagues at the University of Texas at Austin. (They all went their separate ways by the mid-1980s.) Their work also is based on nearly 15 years of collaborative research.

Nine basic teaching principles represent the core of Evertson's work with Emmer and, to a lesser extent, with Brophy. Effectiveness is identified in terms of raising student achievement scores.

1. *Rules and procedures.* Rules and procedures are established and enforced and students are monitored for compliance.
2. *Consistency.* Similar expectations are maintained for activities and behavior at all times for all students. Inconsistency causes confusion in students about what is acceptable.
3. *Prompt management of inappropriate behavior.* Inappropriate behavior is attended to quickly to stop it and prevent its spread.
4. *Checking student work.* All student work, including seatwork, homework, and papers, is corrected, errors are discussed, and feedback is provided promptly.
5. *Interactive teaching.* This takes several forms and includes presenting and explaining new materials, question sessions, discussions, checking for student understanding, actively moving among students to correct work, providing feedback, and, if necessary, reteaching materials.
6. *Academic instruction,* sometimes referred to as "academic learning time" or "academic engaged time." Attention is focused on the management of student work.
7. *Pacing.* Information is presented at a rate appropriate to the students' ability to comprehend it, not too rapidly or too slowly.
8. *Transitions.* Transitions from one activity to another are made rapidly, with minimum confusion about what to do next.
9. *Clarity.* Lessons are presented logically and sequentially. Clarity is enhanced by the use of instructional objectives and adequate illustrations and by keeping in touch with students.[49]

---

[49]Edmund T. Emmer, Carolyn M. Evertson, and Jere E. Brophy, "Stability of Teacher Effects in Junior High Classrooms," *American Educational Research Journal,* Winter 1979, pp. 71–75; Emmer et al., *Classroom Management for Secondary Schools,* 2nd ed. (Englewood Cliffs, N.J.: Prentice-Hall, 1989); Evertson, "Do Teachers Make a Difference?" *Education and Urban Society,* February 1986, pp. 195–210; Evertson and Emmer, "Effective Management at the Beginning of the School Year in Junior High Classes," *Journal of Educational Psychology,* August 1982, pp. 485–498; and Evertson et al., *Classroom Management for Elementary Teachers,* 2nd ed.(Englewood Cliffs, N.J.: Prentice-Hall, 1989).

Principles of Instruction

From the integration of research on how young children learn, Linda Anderson and her colleagues (Evertson and Brophy) have developed an instructional model consisting of 22 specific principles. The model was based on process-product studies on teaching reading to primary grade students in whole group instruction. However, the researchers contend that the principles are curriculum-neutral and apply across subject matter. The principles, listed in Table 11.12, correlate with student achievement and provide guidelines for organizing, managing, and instructing classroom groups as a whole. They make it possible for the teacher to provide as much individual attention as possible in a group setting. By and large, the 22 principles coincide with direct instruction and mastering learning.

Table 11.12   PRINCIPLES OF INSTRUCTION AND THE EFFECTIVE TEACHER

I. *Obtaining group attention*
   1. *Getting started.* The lesson should start quickly; use standard and predictable signals to get the attention of the class.
   2. *Seating.* Seat the class so you can work with the whole group and individuals at the same time.

II. *Introducing the lesson*
   3. *Overview.* Provide an overview of the lesson to prepare students for the remaining presentation.
   4. *New learning.* Present new words, skills, and tasks in the beginning of the lesson so they can be used and integrated into the instructional activities.
   5. *Practice.* Provide practice in new skills and tasks until they are understood. Phase in new learning gradually while old learning is being mastered.
   6. *Work assignments.* Be sure students know what to do and how to do it. Before asking them to work independently, have them explain or demonstrate how the activities will be accomplished.

III. *Ensuring everyone's attention*
   7. *Monitoring.* Move around the room and check everyone's work during the lesson; provide feedback.
   8. *Ordered turns.* Adopt a pattern or style of selecting students to read or answer questions; students should know when to expect their turn, thus reducing their anxiety about being called to recite.
   9. *Alertness.* Keep students alert between turns by occasionally questioning a student about a previous response from another student.
  10. *Minimize call outs.* Don't allow call outs; emphasize that everyone must wait his or her turn.

IV. *Meeting individual needs within the group*
  11. *Differences in learning.* Be aware of different rates of learning; consider when the group as a whole can or cannot move on to the next part of the lesson.
  12. *Needed assistance.* Provide extra help when necessary, stay after class or the next day before class begins.
  13. *Models.* Use students who have mastered the content as models for others.
  14. *Tutorial assistance.* If one or more students still have difficulty mastering the content, provide tutorial assistance.

V. *Teacher questions and student responses*

   15. *Academic focus.* Concentrate questions on academic content; minimize questions that deal with personal experiences.

   16. *Wait for answers.* After asking a question, wait for the students to answer. Some students need extra time to think. Do not continue to wait if the student seems confused or embarrassed.

   17. *Provide the answer if necessary.* When a student is unable to respond to a question, call on another student or give the answer, especially if the question deals with factual knowledge.

   18. *Explain and elaborate if necessary.* If a question requires thinking, explain the steps involved in answering the question. If the student is unable to respond to a question or is incorrect, rephrase the question or provide clues.

   19. *Acknowledge correct answers.* Acknowledge correct responses; make sure everyone hears and understands the answer.

   20. *Follow-up questions.* Occasionally use follow-up questions to the same student (or to another student) to help integrate information or extend ideas to a logical conclusion.

VI. *Praise and criticism*

   21. *Praise in moderation.* Provide moderate praise for specific achievements and behaviors. Recognize effort and creative thinking, even if the answer is wrong.

   22. *Avoid criticism.* Use correction, not criticism; specify correct or desirable alternatives.

Source: Adapted from Linda M. Anderson, Carolyn M. Evertson, and Jere E. Brophy, "An Experimental Study of Effective Teaching in First-Grade Reading Groups," *Elementary School Journal,* March 1979, pp. 193–223; Anderson, Evertson and Brophy, *Principles of Small Group Instruction in Elementary Reading.* Paper no. 58 (East Lansing, Mich.: Institute for Research on Teaching, Michigan State University, 1982). Also see Jere E. Brophy and Thomas L. Good, "Teacher Behavior and Student Achievement," in W. C. Wittrock, ed., *Handbook of Research on Teaching,* 3rd ed. (New York: Macmillan, 1986), p. 346.

The Master Teacher

The national interest in education reform and excellence in teaching has focused considerable attention on teachers and the notion of the "master teacher." The instructional principles suggested by Anderson, the direct behaviors suggested by Medley, and the Good, Brophy, and Evertson models correspond with Walter Doyle's task-oriented and business-like description of a master teacher. Such teachers "focus on academic goals, are careful and explicit in structuring activities . . ., promote high levels of student academic involvement and content coverage, furnish opportunities for controlled practice with feedback, hold students accountable for work, . . . have expectations that they will be successful in helping students learn, [and are] active in explaining concepts and procedures, promoting meaning and purpose for academic work, and monitoring comprehension."[50]

---

[50] Walter Doyle, "Effective Teaching and the Concept of Master Teacher," *Elementary School Journal,* September 1985, p. 30.

Figure 11.3 Each of us may be lucky enough to have a couple of great teachers; this teacher was *Teacher of the Year.* (Photo © Paul Hosefros/NYT Pictures)

When 641 elementary and secondary teachers were asked to "rate criteria for recognition of a master teacher," they listed in rank order: (1) knowledge of subject matter, (2) encourages student achievement through positive reinforcement, (3) uses a variety of strategies and materials to meet the needs of all students, (4) maintains an organized and disciplined classroom, (5) stimulates students' active participation in classroom activities, (6) maximizes student instruction time, (7) has high expectations of student performance, and (8) frequently monitors student progress and provides feedback regarding performance.[51]

Although the sample of teachers was predominately female (71 percent), so that it can be argued that the recommended behaviors reflect female norms, it must be noted that the teaching profession is predominately female (67 percent, according to NEA survey data). Most important, the teachers were experienced (77 percent had been teaching for at least 11 years) and their rank order list of criteria corresponds closely to the principals' rank order list (see Table 11.11) and to Doyle's notion of a master teacher. The teachers emphasize academic focus, high expectations, organized classrooms, and variety in strategies and methods. They stress task orientation (although not as much as the principals do), enthusiasm and interest, direct instruction, and feedback. Finally, both teachers and principals consider working with and responding to students to be important.

---

[51]Jann E. Azumi and James L. Lerman, "Selecting and Rewarding Master Teachers," *Elementary School Journal*, November 1987, p. 197.

Professional Viewpoint

Be a Great Teacher!

There are far too few great teachers and society desperately needs them. Great teachers are great artists. Teaching is perhaps the greatest of the arts because the medium is the human mind and spirit.

My experience and research have made me aware of the importance of falling in love with what you are going to do—a dream, an image of the future. Positive images of the future are a powerful and magnetic force. These images of the future draw us on and energize us, giving us the courage and will to take important initiatives and move forward to new solutions and achievements. To dream and to plan, to be curious about the future and to wonder how much of it can be influenced by our efforts are important aspects of our being human.

There is considerable evidence that our future image is a powerful motivating force and determines what we are motivated to learn and achieve. In fact, a person's image of the future may be a better predictor of future attainment than his past performances.

I would encourage you to begin developing a future image of yourself as a great teacher—a new, positive, compelling and exciting image. Then, fall in love with this image—your unique future image! You *can* become a great teacher—and that is a great thing.

E. Paul Torrance
Distinguished Professor Emeritus of Psychology
University of Georgia

Cautions and Criticisms

Although the notions of teacher competencies and teacher effectiveness are often identified as something new in research efforts to identify good teaching, they are nothing more than a combination of teaching principles and methods that good teachers have been using for many years prior to this recent wave of research. What these product-oriented researchers have accomplished is to summarize what we have known for a long time, but often passed on in the form of "tips for teachers" or practical suggestions (and were once criticized by researchers as being recipe oriented). These researchers confirm the basic principles and methods of experienced teachers; however, they give credibility to the teachers' practices by correlating their behaviors (processes) to student achievement (products). But, the researchers do dispel the notion that teachers have little or no measurable effect on student achievement.

However, there is some danger in the new research. The conclusions overwhelmingly portray the effective teacher as task-oriented, organized, and structured (nothing more than Ryan's Pattern Y teacher). But the teacher competency and teacher effectiveness models tend to overlook the friendly, warm, and democratic teacher; the creative teacher who is stimulating and imaginative; the dramatic teacher who bubbles with energy and enthusiasm; the philosophical teacher who encourages students to play with ideas and concepts; and the problem-solving teacher who requires that students think out the answers. In the new researchers' desire to identify and prescribe behaviors that are measurable and quantifiable, they overlook the emotional, qualitative, and interpretive descriptions of classrooms, and the joys of teaching. Most of their research has been conducted at the elementary grade levels, where one would expect more social, psychological, and humanistic factors to be observed, recorded, and recommended as effective. A good portion of their work also deals with low achievers and at-risk students—perhaps the reason why many of their generalizations or principles coincide with classroom management and structured and controlling techniques.

Maxine Greene asserts that a good deal of teaching is not subject to empirical inquiry or correlates of student achievement. For Greene, good teaching and learning involve values, experiences, insights, imagination and appreciation—the "stuff" that cannot be easily observed or measured. For her, teaching and learning are an existential encounter, a general philosophical process involving ideas and creative inquiries, which cannot be easily quantified.[52]

Elliot Eisner is concerned that what is not measurable goes unnoticed in a product-oriented teaching model. By breaking down the teaching act into dimensions and competencies and criteria that can be defined operationally and quantified, educators overlook the hard-to-measure aspects of teaching, the personal, humanistic, and playful aspects of teaching.[53] To say that excellence in teaching requires measurable behaviors and outcomes is to miss a substantial part of teaching—what some educators refer to as artistry, drama, tones, and flavor.[54]

Gerald Unks is also concerned that the teacher effectiveness models are too behaviorist and product-oriented. Teacher behaviors that correlate with measurable outcomes often lead to rote learning, "learning bits" and not wholes, memorization, drill, and automatic responses. This current teaching-learning set treats the "mind as a jug" to be filled up with facts that will later be funneled out in a test.[55] The new models also seem to miss moral and ethical outcomes, as well as social, personal, and self-actualizing factors related to

[52] Maxine Greene, "Philosophy and Teaching," in Wittrock, ed., *Handbook of Research on Teaching*, pp. 479–500; Greene, *The Dialectic of Teaching* (New York: Teachers College, Columbia University Press, 1988).

[53] Elliot W. Eisner, *The Educational Imagination*, 2nd ed. (New York: Macmillan, 1985).

[54] Ornstein, "Theoretical Issues Related to Teaching."

[55] Gerald Unks, "Product-Oriented Teaching: A Reappraisal," *Education and Urban Society*, February 1986, pp. 242–254.

learning and life—in effect, the affective domain of learning and the psychology of being human. In their attempt to observe and measure what teachers do, and detail whether students improve their performance on reading or math tests, these models ignore the learner's imagination, fantasy, and intuitive thinking—their dreams, hopes, and aspirations, and how teachers impact on these hard to define but very important aspects of the students' life. The chief variable of this current research is cognitive performance; if there is a secondary variable, it is student control. Learning experiences that deal with character, spiritual outlook, and philosophy are absent.

The new and popular teacher competency and teacher effectiveness models lock us into a narrow mold that misses many nuances of teaching. Many of these prescriptions (which the models call principles) themselves are old ideas bottled under new labels such as "withitness," "smoothness," "clarity," etc. They seem to confirm what effective teachers have been doing for many years, but the confirmation is needed so that beginning teachers have a better yardstick or starting point.

Finally, the new models of research on teaching are just beginning to pay closer attention to the content component of teaching and learning. In the past there has been little mention by these researchers of the subject knowledge of the teacher, how it relates to student understanding, how it is taught, and how it can be integrated with the principles and methods they recommend. And they still pay little attention to the thought processes of learning, especially critical thinking, problem solving, creativity, and other forms of high-level cognition. By increasing the teacher's ability to teach students how to learn, and by increasing the students' repertoire of tactics for learning, we can increase student achievement and learning beyond the classroom.

Thus the research on teacher effectiveness in the 1990s should be expanded to include more humanistic and affective principles, more emphasis on content or subject matter, and more emphasis on learning how to learn, or learning strategies. (See Tips for Teachers 11.3)

Tips for Teachers 11.3

Reaching and Teaching Students

Most of the research on teacher competencies and teacher effectiveness stresses direct and explicit instructional techniques and overlooks attitudinal and motivational factors related to learning. The current principles of teaching tend to emphasize structure, sequence, seatwork, practice, monitoring, and feedback. Below are some methods that deal with the human side of teaching children and youth. They have proven to be successful and complement and fill a void in the recent research on teaching, they have special meaning for teaching at-risk students.

continued

ACHIEVEMENT

1. Focus on teaching basic skills as well as higher cognitive functioning levels based on knowledge of the skills.
2. Develop individualization and self-pacing, as well as mastery approaches to learning.
3. Recognize absolute achievement as well as individual improvement by expanding achievement awards, sending letters to parents, and notifying school officials.
4. Involve parents in their children's learning, especially in early grades.
5. Develop a peer tutoring program using classmates or upper-grade students.

ATTITUDE

1. Provide support, encouragement, and realistic praise.
2. Recognize good work, and provide confirmation of success.
3. Develop a class philosophy that each student is worthwhile and can learn.
4. Help students build self-esteem, a sense of responsibility, and self-respect.
5. Help students clarify values, deal with personal choices, and realize responsibility for themselves and for learning.
6. Hold "rap" sessions with students; listen to what they have to say, permit them to get to know one another, and express individual perspectives.
7. Involve students in school services and extracurricular activities to build self-confidence and group identification.
8. Invite successful people to act as models and to talk to students in class.
9. Enforce classroom rules; instill a sense of pride in the students and the classroom.
10. Involve students in real-life situations; encourage them to deal with personal issues.
11. Use community resources by bringing people into the schools and by taking students on field trips.
12. Supply career education and information about jobs starting at an early grade level; provide work-related experiences in higher grades.

Source: Adapted from John V. Hamby, "How to Get an 'A' on Your Dropout Prevention Report Card," *Educational Leadership*, February 1989, pp. 21–28; Bettie B. Youngs, "The Phoenix Curriculum," *Educational Leadership*, February 1989, p. 24.

THEORY INTO PRACTICE

It is obvious that certain behaviors contribute to good teaching. Although there is little agreement on exactly what traits or qualities are most important, the discussion of various teacher styles, interactions, characteristics, competencies, and effects should help you understand why some teachers are successful and others are not, why some appear to act effortlessly the classroom and others consider teaching a chore.

While our discussion and analysis provides a vocabulary and system for identifying teacher behaviors in the classroom and gives you insight into good teaching, there is a danger that it may lead to becoming too rigid in your view of teaching. Following only the research can lead to too much emphasis on labels—on being an "indirect" or "direct" teacher, a "democratic" or "businesslike" teacher—while other behaviors are ignored. To be sure, there is a certain amount of insight and intuitive judgment involved in good teaching, as well as humanism and common-sense—all which cannot be easily measured or prescribed in advance.

Past assessment of teaching has been conducted through various measurement instruments: personality tests, attitudinal scales, observation, rating scales, checklists, bipolar descriptors, self-reports, close-ended and open-ended statements. Evaluation has been conducted by students, peers, supervisors, administrators, parents, and researchers. The results of teaching have been studied in terms of student achievement, adjustment, behavior, attitudes, creativity, and college admissions.

Much anxiety is associated with being observed and rated. However, you should learn to appreciate the benefits of appropriate, honest, and realistic feedback: (1) to learn what your mistakes are so you can correct them (and that as a new teacher you are expected to make mistakes), (2) to adopt successful teacher behaviors that fit your personality, and (3) to improve your overall effectiveness as a teacher.

Most teacher evaluation processes do not address the question of how to change teacher behavior. The developers of evaluation instruments assume that once they have discovered what ought to be done, teachers will naturally do what is expected. If our purpose is to change or improve the practices of teachers, then it is necessary to come to grips with teachers' beliefs and attitudes and with their concepts of "good" or "effective."

In providing feedback and evaluation to teachers many factors need to be considered so the advice or information does not fall on deaf ears. Teachers appreciate feedback processes, whereby they can improve their teaching, so long as the processes are honest and fair and are professionally planned and administered. Duke and Stiggins have developed a list of factors to consider, which has been approved by the American Association of School Administrators, the National Association of Elementary School Principals, the National Association of Secondary School Principals, and the National Education Association.

1. Amount of feedback to give at one time, since too much can be overwhelming and too little can have minimal effect.
2. Level of formality, including the place or setting.
3. Communicating ideas and suggestions that will make sense to the teacher and be relevant to his or her problems.
4. Specificity of information, what specific behaviors and actions can help the teacher.
5. Frequency of feedback to ensure continued growth.
6. Whether to provide descriptive information on teaching (or performance) or evaluative judgments regarding teaching (or performance).
7. Timing of feedback to have maximum impact.
8. Relevancy of feedback with regard to agreed-upon teaching or performance standards.[56]

In one or more of your education course sequence you should have some practice in teaching during which you are observed and appraised by your classmates. Your classmates can learn from your strengths and limitations, and you can learn from theirs. You need to explore and analyze through live demonstrations, simulations, and videotapes different teacher styles, teacher-student interactions, teacher characteristics, and teacher competencies. You need to model effective teachers. You should see the relationship of teaching to specific principles and methods taught in this course and others. You need to clarify and integrate the ideas and concepts presented in this chapter with your own teaching personality and philosophy. Through your willingness and ability to learn, to change, and to improve, you will grow as a teacher and person.

SUMMARY

1. Research on teacher behavior has looked at teacher styles, teacher-student interactions, teacher characteristics, teacher competencies, and teacher effects.

2. Although much remains to be learned about successful teaching, research has identified some teacher behaviors that seem to be effective and influence student performance.

3. Recent research on effective teaching has shifted from the process of teaching to the products of teaching.

4. The classic, important research on teaching, prior to the 1970s, was the work of A. S. Barr, Arno Bellack, Ned Flanders, and David Ryans. These researchers focused on teacher styles, teacher-student interactions, and teacher characteristics—that is, the process, what was happening in the classroom or the behavior of the teacher.

---

[56]Daniel L. Duke and Richard J. Stiggins, *Teacher Evaluation: Five Keys to Growth* (Washington, D.C.: National Education Association, 1986).

5. Recent research on teaching tends to emphasize classroom management and explicit, organized, and businesslike teaching.

6. The more recent research on teaching effectiveness is based on the work of Jere Brophy, Walter Doyle, Carolyn Evertson, N. L. Gage, Thomas Good, Donald Medley, Barak Rosenshine, and Arthur Wise. Their research tends to focus on the products or outcomes of teaching.

QUESTIONS TO CONSIDER

1. Do teachers make a difference in student outcomes? If you say yes, to what extent? If your answer is no, why?

2. How would you describe your teaching style in the terms used by Riessman, Rubin, Anderson, and Lippitt?

3. How would you use the Flanders interaction analysis scale to provide feedback for a beginning teacher?

4. What teacher competencies listed in the tables of this chapter seem most important to you? Why?

5. What behaviors listed by Brophy and Good as well as Evertson and Emmer coincide with your own teacher style? What behaviors seem to conflict with your teacher style?

THINGS TO DO

1. Evaluate the behaviors Medley labels as "effective" for low-income students. Discuss in class whether these behaviors make sense for low-income students of different sex, age, and achievement scores.

2. Volunteer to teach a lesson in class for about ten minutes. Use a simplified version of the Flanders interaction analysis scale (direct vs. indirect) or Bellack's verbal behaviors (structuring, soliciting, responding, reacting). Note whether there is agreement among class members in categorizing your teacher behavior.

3. Observe two or three professors while they teach and take note of the amount of time they talk compared to student talk. Use every 3 seconds as a time interval to calculate the ratio of teacher to student talk. Report to the class.

4. Recall three or four of your favorite teachers. Compare their teacher characteristics, as you remember, with the list of successful characteristics compiled by Barr. Which characteristic on Barr's list do you think they possess?

5. Interview several experienced teachers concerning the recommended teacher principles and methods of Rosenshine, Gage, Brophy, and Evertson. Do the teachers support or reject the recommendations? What reservations do teachers bring up? What do they like about the recommendations?

RECOMMENDED READINGS

DeRoche, Edward F. *An Administrator's Guide for Evaluating Programs and Personnel*, 2nd ed. Boston: Allyn and Bacon, 1987. A complete, practical guide for evaluating teachers with more than 20 ready-to-use teacher instruments and inventories.

Flanders, Ned A. *Analyzing Teaching Behavior*. Reading, Mass.: Addison-Wesley, 1970. Description of the chain of classroom events, interaction of teacher and students, and activities for helping the teacher organize his or her behavior in the classroom.

Gage, Nathaniel L. *The Scientific Basis of the Art of Teaching*. New York: Teachers College Press, Columbia University, 1978. A discussion of teacher effectiveness studies, successful teaching strategies, and the notion of teaching as a "practical" art with a scientific basis.

Good, Thomas L., and Jere E. Brophy. *Looking in Classrooms*, 4th ed. New York: Harper & Row, 1988. An important book that helped move the field from the study of teacher processes to teacher products, and a convincing argument that teachers do make a difference.

Joyce, Bruce, and Marsha Weil. *Models of Teaching*, 2nd ed. Englewood Cliffs, N.J.: Prentice-Hall, 1986. A book that combines theory with practice and examines various cognitive and behavioral teaching models.

Medley, Donald M., Homer Coker, and Robert S. Soar. *Measurement-Based Evaluation of Teacher Performance*. New York: Longman, 1984. A theoretical book on evaluating teachers, with emphasis on measurement problems and methods.

Rosenholtz, Susan J. *Teachers' Workplace*. New York: Longman, 1989. Quantitative and qualitative data on differences in teacher effectiveness.

KEY TERMS

Teacher processes

Teacher products

Teaching style

Teachable groups

Teacher-student interaction

Teacher episode

Teacher monologue

Nonverbal communication

Self-fulfilling prophecy

Teacher characteristics

Teacher competencies

Process-product research

Chapter 12

Professional Growth

FOCUSING QUESTIONS

1. What are some methods for improving the support and learning opportunities for teachers during the first few years of their teaching career?

2. How can students' evaluation of their teachers be implemented?

3. How does self-evaluation improve a person's capabilities as a teacher? What methods of self-evaluation might a teacher use?

4. How do peer evaluation and supervisory evaluation contribute to evaluating teachers?

5. What sources and products can supply information to be used for teacher evaluation and growth?

6. How do professional organizations serve teachers?

You can always improve your teaching. The extent of improvement is related to how much improvement you think you need and how hard you work at it. Beginning teachers in particular should expect to encounter some problems and frustrations, but they should also learn from their experiences and improve their technical skills over time.

If you hope to be an effective teacher who enjoys his or her work, not only will you need to be well prepared for each day's lessons, but also you will need to possess a variety of skills in working with people—with students, colleagues, supervisors, and parents. You will need to have a general education, knowledge of the subject you teach, and training in teaching your grade level and type of student. The preceding chapters in this book dealt with methods of teaching. This final chapter is intended to help you grow as a teacher.

HELPING THE BEGINNING TEACHER

What are the general needs of the beginning teacher? Most schools plan for teacher orientation, but in spite of efforts to help teachers succeed, many still encounter adjustment problems. A review of the research on problems of beginning teachers shows that feelings of isolation, poor understanding of what is expected of them, work load and extra assignments that they were unprepared to handle, lack of supplies, materials, or equipment, poor physical facilities and lack of support or help from experienced teachers or supervisors contribute to their feelings of frustration and failure.[1]

Problems of Education Students and Beginning Teachers

Frances Fuller suggests a progression in the type of concerns teachers have. Education students are characterized by "nonconcern"; student teachers are characterized by "increased concern"; beginning teachers are preoccupied with "survival concerns"; and experienced teachers focus on the tasks and problems of teachers (they have gotten past initial survival and are more involved with "self" concerns).[2]

A number of factors may contribute to the increasing concerns and anxieties of student teachers about the difficulty of teaching, including the fact that most people do have concerns of the unknown when they are about to

---

[1]Jerry A. Ligon, "Four Ways to Reduce Worry for New Teachers," *American School Board Journal*, March 1988, p. 50; Simon Veenman, "Perceived Problems of Beginning Teachers," *Review of Educational Research*, Summer 1984, pp. 143–178.

[2]Frances F. Fuller, "Concerns for Teachers: A Developmental Conceptualization," *American Educational Research Journal*, March 1969, pp. 207–226.

Table 12.1   PERCEIVED PROBLEMS OF BEGINNING TEACHERS AND EDUCATION
STUDENTS

Ranking of first-year teachers	Questionnaire item	Ranking of education students	Mean score difference in perceived difficulty*
1	Dealing with work load	1	− .49
2	Improving academic performance of low-achieving students	3	− .62
3	Adapting curriculum and instruction to needs of slow learners	5	− .68
4	Teaching students from different cultures and backgrounds	21	−1.17
5	Figuring out why students are having difficulties with assignments	6	− .61
6	Responding effectively to student misbehavior	11	− .61
7	Maintaining discipline	11	− .87
8	Dealing with insufficient materials and supplies	2	− .43
9	Dealing with a lack of supplementary and enriching materials	4	− .47
10	Planning lessons and units	14	− .81

*All differences in the degree of difficulty are significant at the .0001 level; they reflect differences in difficulty between beginning teachers (always ranked more difficult) and education students.

Source: Adapted from Carol S. Weinstein, "Preservice Teachers' Expectations About the First Year of Teaching," Teaching and Teacher Education, (no. 1, 1988), p. 35.

embark on a new job (especially their first job). However, the content of introductory teacher education courses does not seem to prepare teachers for the realities of the job. Another factor may be that age and optimism may be inversely related. It takes a few years of seasoning to face reality, and college students at the prestudent teaching level tend to have confidence in their own abilities and to believe they are better equipped than others (older people) to be teachers. What young student cannot, after all, reasonably criticize many former teachers and say, "I can do a better job"?

In a recent study, beginning teachers and education students were asked to rank problems they expected.[3] The problems perceived by the teachers as the ten most important are listed in Table 12.1. Although there is some agreement between the groups in the ranking of important problems, there is significant disagreement on the perceived difficulty of the problems. First-year teachers consistently rank the items as more difficult than education students, and that difference is noted in Column 3 by the minus sign. For problems

---

[3]Carol S. Weinstein, "Preservice Teachers' Expectations about the First Year of Teaching," Teaching and Teacher Education, 1, 1988, pp. 31–40.

teachers considered less important (not shown on the table), there seems to be strong agreement in the ranking. The less important items dealt with getting along with colleagues, following school policies, being accepted by students, dealing with administrative constraints, and knowledge of subject matter. However, the mean scores in perceived difficulty show that beginning teachers also view the less important problems more seriously.

Numerous reports over the last several years document the shock for the new teacher that accompanies the realities of the school and classroom.[4] Organized programs and internal support systems for beginning teachers are scarce. Mentor relations between experienced and beginning teachers and support from colleagues for continued learning and professional development are still exceptions, not the rule.[5]

Without question, there is recognition that the **induction period,** the first two or three years of teaching, is critical in developing teachers' capabilities, and that beginning teachers should not be left alone to sink or swim. Several state education agencies have recently developed internship programs for new teachers, while other states have increased staff development activities.[6] However, it is the internal support systems and strategies that the schools adopt, that is, the daily support activities and continual teaching opportunities, that are most important for the professional development of new teachers.

Common causes of failure of new teachers need to be identified and addressed. One school administrator has identified six general causes of failure that the schools should rectify.

1. *Assignment to difficult classes.* "Good" courses and "good" students are assigned to teachers on the basis of seniority; beginning teachers are given the "dregs" or "leftovers" to teach. A better balance is required (actually the opposite assignments) to permit beginning teachers to survive and learn from their mistakes in the classroom.

2. *Isolation of classrooms from colleagues and supervisors.* The classrooms furthest from the central office are usually assigned to beginning teachers. Isolating the new teacher from experienced teachers con-

[4]Judith E. Lanier and Judith W. Little, "Research on Teacher Education," in M. C. Wittrock, ed., *Handbook of Research on Teaching,* 3rd ed. (New York: Macmillan, 1986), pp. 527–569; Ronald N. Marso and Fred L. Pigge, "Differences between Self-Perceived Job Expectations and Job Realities of Beginning Teachers," *Journal of Teacher Education,* November–December 1987, pp. 53–56; and Terry M. Wildman and Jerry A. Niles, "Essentials of Professional Growth," *Educational Leadership,* February 1987, pp. 4–10.

[5]Gene I. Maeroff, *The Empowerment of Teachers* (New York: Teachers College Press, Columbia University, 1988); Donald C. Orlich, *Staff Development: Enhancing Human Development* (Boston: Allyn and Bacon, 1989).

[6]Carolyn M. Evertson, "Do Teachers Make a Difference?" *Education and Urban Society,* February 1986, pp. 195–210; Joseph R. Jenkins and Linda M. Jenkins, "Making Peer Tutoring Work," *Educational Leadership,* March 1987, pp. 64–68; and Patricia Raney and Pam Robbins, "Professional Growth and Support through Peer Coaching," *Educational Leadership,* May 1989, pp. 35–36.

tributes to failure. Beginning teachers need to be assigned to rooms near the main office and near experienced teachers to encourage daily communication.

3. *Poor physical facilities.* Classrooms, room fixtures, and equipment are usually assigned on the basis of seniority. Providing the leftovers to new teachers is damaging to morale. A more equitable assignment of facilities is needed.

4. *Burdensome extra class assignments.* Extra class duties are cited as a source of ill feelings more than any other item. New teachers are often assigned burdensome or tough assignments that they were unprepared for and did not expect as teachers, such as yard patrol, hall patrol, cafeteria patrol, or study hall duties. Furthermore, the afternoon and evening assignments for which teachers are paid extra usually go to senior teachers. Assignments given to beginning teachers should not be so burdensome that they affect the quality of their teaching; also, the assignments with pay should be awarded on a merit basis.

5. *Lack of understanding of the school's expectations.* School officials should clarify the school's goals and priorities and the responsibilities of teachers early in the first term. Administrators do provide orientation and written guides about roles and responsibilities, but the problem seems to be the dearth of continuing communication and reinforcement as the teacher progresses through various stages of role acquisition.

Professional Viewpoint

Helping the Beginning Teacher

How we induct and support our "brightest and best" teaching candidates directly impacts the quality and effectiveness of the professionals who will shape our future generations. If we are committed to making significant improvements in the design and delivery of the instruction we provide for our students in the 21st century, we must also be committed to cultivating carefully the talented beginning teachers we hire.

Imagine yourself having just graduated from an accredited university with a teaching degree and landing your first teaching job. Regardless of the adequacy of your pre-service preparation program, you are now about to make the transition from theory into practice, from the hypothetical arena into the reality of a classroom, and from the role of student into the role of teacher. The moment you are presented the keys to your classroom and the roster of your students, you realize you are "in charge" and "on your own." During this introductory time frame, and consistently during your first year

continued

of teaching, the support and council of colleagues at your school are extremely valuable.

Beginning teacher programs should be designed as an integral component to supplement all first-year teaching experiences. They should include realistic induction/orientation activities for new teachers as well as a comprehensive networking/support system. Beginning teachers need opportunities to examine educational structures that allow teachers to apply, refine, expand, and uphold profession standards of practice. They must be invited to participate actively in the school's unique educational culture.

Teacher isolation must be overcome so that staff members have regular opportunities to discuss problems of practice, are involved in the evaluation of practice, and are involved in decision making about policies and practices that have an impact on the school. A cluster of peer teachers rather than just one should have responsibility for collegially designing induction experiences and supporting beginning teachers.

In order for there to be ongoing professional development for teachers, there must be an environment that encourages creativity and innovation, as well as a means for client-oriented accountability. Time must be provided to review professional practice (peer assistance), and to debrief with colleagues. Constructive feedback and developmental/planning sessions are essential to the success of the beginning teacher.

There is no one best system by which all beginning teachers may gain access to the collegial support and assistance of peers to ensure a successful first year, however, by placing a priority on the time and resources needed to implement a comprehensive induction and assistance program, the chances of grooming an effective career teacher who will grow into a new breed of professional educator will certainly be enhanced.

> Joseph A. Fernandez
> Superintendent of Schools
> New York City

6. *Inadequate supervision.* Most problems of beginning teachers could be either prevented or curtailed with proper supervision. Supervision often consists of only two or three formal visits a year to the classroom and possibly a few informal contacts and one or two meetings. The need is for increased supervisory contact, both formal and informal, so that assistance is provided regularly in the early stages of the teacher's career.[7]

---

[7]William H. Kurtz, "How the Principal Can Help Beginning Teachers," *National Association of Secondary School Principals*, January 1983, pp. 42–45.

Support from Colleagues for Beginning Teachers

In general, having to learn by trial and error without support and supervision has been the most common problem faced by new teachers. Expecting teachers to function without support is based on the false assumptions that (1) teachers are well prepared for their initial classroom and school experiences, (2) teachers can develop professional expertise on their own, and (3) teaching can be mastered in a relatively short period of time. Researchers find that there is little attempt to lighten the class load and limit extra class assignments to make the beginning teacher's job easier. In the few schools that do limit these activities, teachers have reported that they have had the opportunity to "learn to teach."[8]

Studies of elementary and secondary schools have shown that teachers expect to learn from one another when the school provides opportunities for teachers (1) to talk routinely to one another about teaching, (2) to be observed regularly in the classroom, and (3) to participate in planning and preparation.[9] Teachers who are given opportunity to (1) develop and implement curriculum ideas, (2) join study groups about implementing classroom practices, or (3) experiment in new skills and training feel more confident in their individual and collective ability to perform their work.[10]

According to Joyce and Showers, an experienced teacher who acts as a **peer coach** or **resource teacher** for an inexperienced teacher performs five functions: (1) *companionship*, discussing ideas, problems, and successes; (2) *technical feedback*, especially related to lesson planning and classroom observations; (3) *analysis of application*, integrating what happens or what works as part of the beginning teacher's repertoire; (4) *adaptation*, helping the beginning teacher adapt to particular situations; and (5) *personal facilitation*, helping the teacher feel good about himself or herself after trying new strategies.[11] See Tips for Teachers 12.1.

Similar data have been reported by Neubert and Bratton, involving visiting

---

[8]Judith E. Lanier and Joseph Featherstone, "A New Commitment to Teacher Education," *Educational Leadership*, November 1988, pp. 18–22; Phillip C. Schlechty, "A School District Revises the Functions and Rewards of Teaching," paper presented at the annual meeting of the American Educational Research Association, 1984; and Deborah B. Strother, "Peer Coaching for Teachers: Opening Classroom Doors," *Phi Delta Kappan*, June 1989, pp. 824-827.

[9]Judith W. Little, *School Success and Staff Development* (Boulder, Colo.: Center for Action Research, 1981); Little, "District Policy Choices and Teacher Professional Development Opportunities," paper presented at the annual conference of the American Educational Research Association, New Orleans, April 1988.

[10]Thomas D. Bird, "Early Implementation of the California Mentor Teacher Program," paper presented at the annual meeting of the American Educational Research Association, San Francisco, April 1986. Aurora Chase and Pat Wolfe, "Off to a Good Start in Peer Coaching," *Educational Leadership*, May 1989, pp. 37-38.

[11]Bruce Joyce and Beverly Showers, *Power in Staff Development Through Research in Training* (Alexandria, Va.: Association for Supervision and Curriculum Development, 1983); Joyce and Showers, *Student Achievement Through Staff Development* (New York: Longman, 1988).

Tips for Teachers 12.1

Questions for a Conference with a Cooperating Teacher or Coach

Most experienced teachers are sympathetic to the problems of student teachers and beginning teachers, and are willing to provide assistance. Below are 21 questions developed by George Posner that a student teacher might want to ask a cooperating teacher, or a beginning teacher might want to ask a peer coach or colleague.

1. I've noticed some special areas in your room. (*Specify one of them.*) What do you and the students do in this area? Who gets to use it? How are they selected? (*Repeat for each area.*)

2. Did you arrange the room this way? (*If no*) Who did? (*If yes*) What were you trying to do with this arrangement? How long has it been this way?

3. Did you put up the posters, pictures, exhibits, etc., on the walls and bulletin boards? (*If no*) Who did? (*If yes*) What was the purpose? When did you put them up? (*May be different for each poster.*)

4. I've been looking through the textbook. How was it selected and by whom? How do you like it? What are its strengths? Weaknesses? Is it successful with some kids but not with others? (*Repeat this set of questions for each text.*)

5. I also looked over the worksheets and quizzes you've been using. Did you write them? (*If no*) Where did you get them? (*If yes*) When did you make them up? Did you base them on anything in particular? Are you happy with them?

6. I enjoyed the lesson(s) that I observed. When I compared your lesson plan with the actual lesson, I noticed that you did not follow your plan precisely. (*This question is used only if you noticed some discrepancies.*) What caused you to modify your plan?

7. What rules do you expect students in your class to follow? (*Probe: rules for waiting their turn to speak and to receive help, rules for moving around the classroom, leaving the classroom, being on time, what to do when finished working, working together, resolving conflicts among students, homework, forms to follow, procedures for work, language, noises, who may speak, etc.*) Does the school have rules or regulations with which you disagree? (*If yes*) Why do you disagree? Do you follow them anyway? Which rules are the most important to you? How do you handle infractions? Do some students break rules more than others? Tell me about those kids.

8. Do parents ever visit the classroom? (*If no*) Would you like them to? (*If yes*) Are you pleased that they do? How can parents be of

continued

most help to you as a teacher? How can they hinder you? Should parents be involved in selection of school books? What about in hiring teachers?

9. Does the school or the district have a curriculum? Are you expected to follow it? Do you? Did you have any say in it? Do you ever depart from it?

10. Do your students' interests affect your teaching methods? (*If yes*) In what ways? What about the content, do their interests affect it? Do they have any say in what they study? (*If yes*) In what ways?

11. What sorts of students do you teach? Are there different groups? Could you describe the groups? Do you devote more time to certain students? Do you expect all of them to assume the same degree of responsibility for their learning? Do you use different criteria to evaluate different students? Do you find the diversity among them to be a major problem?

12. How friendly are you with the children? Do you tell them much about yourself? What do you think is the proper role for a teacher?

13. Do you try to develop a sense of competition in your class? How important is cooperation among students? What do you use to motivate the kids? (*Probe: grades, interest and curiosity, comparison of one child's work with another's, fear.*)

14. Do you ever let the kids know your political views? Do you think that the schools are doing a pretty good job or do they need to change drastically? Are you trying to help kids fit into the society as it is, or would you like to equip them to reform society?

15. How important are the *3 Rs* to you? What about the children's emotional needs, are they important? What about things like problem-solving skills and creativity—are they important? What is the relative importance of these various goals?

16. Do you ever try to relate one subject matter (e.g., science) with another that you or another teacher teaches? Or do you think that different subject matters should be treated separately?

17. Most people have days in their work when they go home feeling especially good because the day and its activities were particularly rewarding. What makes a good day in teaching for you?

18. How do you tell how well you are doing as a teacher? That is, what things provide you with evidence that you're doing a good job?

19. Suppose you accidently happened to overhear a group of your former students discussing you as a teacher. What kinds of things would you like to hear them saying?

20. Why did you ask to help a student teacher/beginning teacher?

21. What do you expect from me?

Source: George J. Posner, *Field Experience: A Guide to Reflective Teaching,* 2nd ed. (New York: Longman, 1989), pp. 54–55.

resource teachers in Maryland school districts who, rather than observe class-room teachers, teach alongside them. Five characteristics of the resource teach-ers that promote an effective coaching relationship are: (1) *knowledge*—more knowledge about teaching methods than the classroom teacher; (2) *credibility*—demonstrated success in the classroom; (3) *support*—a mix of honest praise and constructive criticism; (4) *facilitation*—recommending and encouraging rather than dictating, assisting rather than dominating in the classroom, and (5) *availability*—accessible to the classroom teacher for plan-ning, team teaching, and conferences.[12]

Guidelines for Improving Support for Beginning Teachers

Whatever the existing provisions for the induction period for entry teachers, there is the need to improve provisions for their continued professional de-velopment, to make their job easier, to make them feel more confident in the classroom and school, to reduce the isolation of their work settings, and to enhance interaction with colleagues. Below are some recommendations for achieving these goals.

1. Schedule beginning teacher orientation in addition to regular teacher orientation. Beginning teachers need to attend both sessions.
2. Appoint someone to help beginning teachers set up their rooms.
3. Provide beginning teachers with a proper mix of courses, students, and facilities (not all leftovers). If possible, lighten their load for the first year.
4. Assign extra class duties of moderate difficulty and requiring mod-erate amounts of time, duties that will not become too demanding for the beginning teacher.
5. Pair beginning teachers with master teachers to meet regularly to identify general problems before they become serious.
6. Provide for coaching groups, tutor groups, or collaborative problem-solving groups for all beginning teachers to attend. Encourage begin-ning teachers to teach each other.
7. Provide for joint planning, team teaching, committee assignments, and other cooperative arrangements between new and experienced teachers.
8. Issue newsletters that report on accomplishments of all teachers, especially beginning teachers.
9. Schedule reinforcing events, involving beginning and experienced teachers, such as tutor-tutoree luncheons, parties, and awards.

---

[12] Gloria A. Neubert and Elizabeth C. Bratton, ''Team Coaching: Staff Development Side by Side,'' *Educational Leadership*, February 1987, pp. 29–32.

10. Provide regular (say, twice monthly) meetings between the beginning teacher and supervisor to identify problems as soon as possible and to make recommendations for improvement.
11. Plan special and continuous in-service activities with topics directly related to the needs and interests of beginning teachers. Eventually, integrate beginning staff development activities with regular staff development activities.
12. Carry on regular evaluation of beginning teachers; evaluate strengths and weaknesses, present new information, demonstrate new skills, and provide opportunities for practice and feedback.[13]

STUDENT EVALUATION

Teachers can learn a lot from student evaluations. In trying to analyze their own effectiveness and ways to improve, it may be difficult for teachers to recognize mistakes. Colleagues and supervisors are usually present in the classroom only briefly and infrequently, but students observe the teacher all day every day. Teachers receive student feedback continually as soon as they enter the classroom, regardless of how and what they teach and how and what the students learn. Student feedback is both overt and covert, ranging from facial expressions and gestures to focused attention or disruptive behavior. Moreover, the students' feelings and attitudes affect the quality of the teaching and the teacher's products.

Honest evaluation and feedback can be obtained from students through questionnaires and rating forms that are filled out anonymously. Some teachers develop their own forms, which are probably not the most reliable and valid instruments, but suffice if the teacher is uncomfortable or dissatisfied with prepared forms. In constructing a form, researchers agree that the teacher should focus on eight areas: (1) objectives, (2) content, (3) method, (4) materials, (5) homework, (6) classroom management, (7) tests and evaluation, and (8) behavior or interaction with students.[14] The easiest rating method is a five-point rating scale from "strongly agree" to "strongly disagree" or from "very good" to "very poor." It is not so much the content of the instrument or the point scale as the acceptance of student evaluation by the teacher that is important for professional growth and development.

For the teacher who wishes to use an evaluation instrument with more

---

[13]Bruce Joyce and Renee T. Clift, "The Phoenix Agenda: Essential Reform in Teacher Education," *Educational Researcher*, April 1984, pp. 5–18; Kurtz, "How the Principal Can Help Beginning Teachers"; and Jenkins and Jenkins, "Making Peer Tutoring Work."

[14]Milbrey W. McLaughlin and R. Scott Pfeifer, *"Teacher Evaluation: Improvement, Accountability, and Effective Learning,* (New York: Teachers College Press, Columbia University, 1988); Donald M. Medley, Homer Coker, and Robert S. Soar, *Measurment-Based Evaluation of Teacher Performance* (New York: Longman, 1984).

reliability and validity, there are many sources. A supervisor or principal will probably recommend an instrument used by the school or school district. One instrument designed by the state of Florida (and now used in parts of Colorado and Washington) has been tested for reliability in grades K–12; the coefficients from many pilot tests range from .79 to .98. The instrument comprises a formative scale (designed to identify problems) and a summative scale (which shows positive relationships between instrument rating scores and student achievement).[15] A section of the Florida performance measurement instrument is shown in Table 12.2. Although originally designed for supervisors to rate teachers, it can also be used by many different groups of raters, including secondary school students, to rate teachers. The instrument focuses on 4 of the 6 teacher domains or clusters and 21 bi-polar items of teacher behavior identified over 50 years of teacher behavior research.[16] The measurement procedure is based on recording the actual frequency of each behavior. However, when used by raters such as students at the end of school term, the measurement procedure should involve estimating behavior on a seven-point scale (to prevent mid-range scores), with a high effectiveness rating equivalent to "very often" and a low rating equivalent to "rarely."

Many teachers will use more than one type of evaluation, both informal and formal, throughout the year. The formal evaluation is one of the best instruments to use because of its consistency in format and ease of interpretation. The most important thing to keep in mind is that all raters and ratings are imperfect, but the data suggest that students actually make the best raters in terms of reliability and validity. Since they see the teachers in different situations over an extended period of time, they cannot be fooled or misled by a single day's performance as a formal observer might be.[17]

Student ratings will probably never become institutionalized as long as teachers have some say in the evaluation process. To the extent that teachers feel insecure about their own teaching, they are likely to oppose such ratings. But this is not an instrument that teachers should be required to use. Rather, it is an instrument that can and should be used by teachers who wish to improve their teaching through realistic evaluation, and whose personal and professional self-concepts are positive enough to risk feedback from their students.

[15]B. O. Smith, Donovan Peterson, and Theodore Micceri, "Evaluation and Professional Improvement Aspects of the Florida Performance Measurement System," *Educational Leadership*, April 1987, pp. 16–19.

[16]Donovan Peterson et al., "Evaluation of a Teacher's Classroom Performance: Using the Florida Performance Measurement System," *Teaching and Teacher Education*, no. 4 1986, pp. 309–314. The other two teacher domains deal with planning and testing. Since they are difficult to observe they are not part of this instrument but can be used for rating purposes.

[17]N. L. Gage, "What Do We Know about Teaching Effectiveness?" *Phi Delta Kappan*, October 1984, pp. 87–90; Allan C. Ornstein, "Can We Define a Good Teacher?" *Peabody Journal of Education*, April 1976, pp. 201–207; and Ornstein, "Teacher Effectiveness Research: Some Ideas and Issues," *Education and Urban Society*, February 1986, pp. 168–175.

Table 12.2 FLORIDA PERFORMANCE MEASUREMENT SYSTEM

	Total freq.	Frequency	Frequency	Total freq.	
					Domain: Instructional organization and development
1. Begins instruction promptly					1. Delays
2. Handles materials in an orderly manner					2. Does not organize or handle materials systematically
3. Orients students to classwork/maintains academic focus					3. Allows talk/activity unrelated to subject
4. Conducts beginning/ending review					4.[a]
5. Questions: academic comprehension/lesson development a. single factual (domain 5.0) b. requires analysis/reasons					5a. Allows unison response b. Poses multiple questions asked as one c. Poses nonacademic questions/nonacademic procedural questions
6. Recognizes response/amplifies/gives correct feedback					6. Ignores student or response/expresses sarcasm, disgust, harshness
7. Gives specific academic praise					7. Uses general, nonspecific praise
8. Provides for practice					8. Extends discourse, changes topic with no practice
9. Gives directions/assigns/checks comprehension of homework, seatwork assignments/gives feedback					9. Gives inadequate directions on homework/no feedback
10. Circulates and assists students					10. Remains at desk/circulates inadequately

Domain: Presentation of subject matter

11. Treats concepts—definition/attributes/examples/nonexamples	11. Gives definition or examples only
12. Discusses cause-effect/uses linking words/applies law or principle	12. Discusses either cause or effect only/uses no linking word(s)
13. States and applies academic rule	13. Does not state or does not apply academic rule
14. Develops criteria and evidence for value judgment	14. States value judgment with no criteria or evidence

Domain: Communication: verbal and nonverbal

15. Emphasizes important points	15.[a]
16. Expresses enthusiasm verbally/challenges students	16.[a]
17.[a]	17. Uses vague/scrambled discourse
18.[a]	18. Uses loud-grating, high pitched, monotone, inaudible talk
19. Uses body behavior that shows interest—smiles, gestures	19. Frowns, deadpan or lethargic

Domain: Management of student conduct

20. Stops misconduct	20. Delays desist/doesn't stop misconduct/desists punitively
21. Maintains instructional momentum	21. Loses momentum—fragments nonacademic directions, overdwells

Note: [a] No item listed.
Source: "Florida Performance Measurement System," rev. ed. (Tampa, Fla.: University of South Florida, Teacher Evaluation Assessment Center, 1987).

Guidelines for Implementing Student Evaluations

In using student evaluations it is important to clarify (1) the policy for their use—for example, whether the results will be seen by supervisors, whether teachers will discuss the results with the students, whether the results will be used officially for evaluating teachers, and (2) standards to ensure reliability and validity—for example, appropriate conditions, clear directions, suitable questions.

Lawrence Kult recommends the following procedures for having the students do the evaluations.

1. An informative discussion in class should precede the actual evaluation, preferably just before it. The reasons for the evaluation and the type of questions to expect should be discussed. The positive effect that the evaluation can have for both students and teacher should be stressed. All questions by the students should be answered by the teacher.
2. All evaluations should be anonymous, and students must be assured that in no way will their grades be affected by the evaluations.
3. Sufficient time should be given to students to complete the evaluation.
4. The completed evaluations should be collected in such a way that a particular evaluation form cannot be identified with a student.
5. Any problems that surfaced during the evaluation should be discussed after the completion of the evaluation to improve the next one.
6. To alleviate some of the pressure concerning the evaluation, the students may be permitted to converse among themselves for a few minutes following the completion of the evaluation.
7. Positive acknowledgment of the students' participation should be made by the teacher after the completion of the evaluation.[18]

The assumption is that most teachers, if they are candid with themselves, will find that student evaluations parallel most of their own beliefs concerning their strong and weak teaching points. In some cases, they will gain knowledge about their teaching and instruction. The interpretation of the results should be performed with the idea of gaining personal insight. Negative comments should be read as guides for making corrections in the future, not as personal attacks that must be repudiated. The results will have more meaning if they are reviewed more than once, and they should be saved to compare with results on the next evaluation to see if changes have been made. The whole process will probably have a more beneficial effect on the professional growth of the teacher if the evaluations are optional and not required to be turned over to a supervisor.

---

[18]Lawrence E. Kult, "Using Teacher Evaluation by Students," *Clearing House,* September 1975, pp. 11–13.

The student evaluations are extremely important for learning how students react to a teacher's approach and methods and how they feel about their relationship with the teacher. Evaluations can enhance rapport and understanding between teacher and students as long as they are used properly. If teachers are chastised or penalized as a result, if teachers are required to administer evaluations, or if teachers do not take the results seriously and act on them, then little self-improvement will result. Teachers who are committed to self-improvement will administer and interpret student evaluation forms.

SELF-EVALUATION

Teaching presents ample opportunities for self-evaluation. The teacher who does a good job, and knows it, has the satisfaction of seeing students grow, feeling their respect and affection, and obtaining the recognition of colleagues, parents, and the community.

Self-evaluation by the teacher can contribute to professional growth. This idea is a logical outgrowth of modern belief in the value of teacher-supervisor cooperation. If teacher evaluations are accepted as an integral part of an effective supervisory situation for professional development, then teachers should be involved in the clarification and continual appraisal of their goals and effectiveness.

According to Good and Brophy, teachers "seek opportunities to evaluate and improve their teaching, if acceptable and useful methods are available." The trouble is, these researchers continue, teachers have not been encouraged or taught to engage in self-criticism, to recognize weaknesses, and to "link criticisms with constructive plans designed to improve ... skills."[19] Bruce Tuckman concludes that teachers are willing to engage in and even welcome self-evaluation as long as it is conducted in an appropriate manner, they participate in the planning stages, and they have some assurance of how the results will be used.[20]

Recent data also indicate that teachers favor self-evaluation over evaluation by students, peers, and supervisors. Teachers rated as "good" by supervisors picked self-evaluation as their first choice among instruments to use in judging their own effectiveness (selected by 37 percent of more than 2,700 teachers surveyed). Objective evaluations by students and reactions of other teachers familiar with their work were second (19 percent) and third (16 percent) choices for assessing their own performance. Furthermore, as many as 52 percent of teachers assert that it is *relatively easy* to know when one is teaching effectively.[21]

---

[19] Thomas L. Good and Jere E. Brophy, *Looking in Classrooms*, 4th ed. (New York: Harper & Row, 1988), pp. 526–527.

[20] Bruce W. Tuckman, *Evaluating Instructional Programs*, 2nd ed. (Boston: Allyn and Bacon, 1985).

[21] Robert B. Kottkamp, Eugene F. Provenzo, and Marilyn M. Cohn, "Stability and Change in a Profession: Two Decades of Teacher Attitudes, 1964–1984," *Phi Delta Kappan*, April 1986, pp. 559–566.

There are basically two forms of self-evaluation. First, teachers can rate themselves on their *teaching methods* at the classroom level. This type of evaluation form can be developed by the teacher, a group of teachers, the school district, or by researchers. The eight areas of behavior, previously discussed under student evaluation or the instrument used in Florida (page 586), or any other instrument the teacher is comfortable with, can be modified for the purpose of self-evaluation.

Second, teachers can rate themselves on their *professional responsibilities* at the school and community level. According to two administrators, this form might include (1) classroom techniques, (2) contractual responsibilities, (3) service to school, and (4) professional development.[22] To this list might be added (5) relations with students, (6) relations with colleagues, (7) relations with parents, and (8) service to the community.

The evaluation instrument used by the Chicago public school system combines both teaching and professional elements of evaluation (Table 12.3). It assumes that teachers are responsible not only for good instruction, competence in subject matter, and positive teacher-student relationships (parts I and II of the evaluation form), but also for good community relations and professional and personal growth (parts III and IV). The school principal is required to use the form in evaluating teachers, and the Chicago handbook for teachers suggests that teachers themselves use it as a guide for self-improvement.

Guidelines for Self-Evaluation

Self-evaluation can serve as the initial step in an ongoing attempt to improve teaching and instructional procedures. A *forced-choice instrument* (with three or five choices per item) or an open-ended technique with minimal boundaries or guides to choose from might be used. A written self-evaluation can be used to describe almost any aspect of teaching and instruction, with freedom to focus on any item perceived as important. Regardless of which method is used, the following suggestions are worth noting.

1. The value of self-evaluations is dependent upon how they are used.
2. The teacher's ability to assess his or her weaknesses and strengths is important for self-improvement. This ability can be enhanced through good relations and communication between the teacher and supervisor.
3. Self-evaluation of overall teaching competence used for personnel (or salary) decisions entails many problems, most notably credibility.

---

[22] Eileen Pembroke and Edmund R. Goedert, "What Is the Key to Developing an Effective Teacher Evaluation System?" *National Association of Secondary School Principals*, December 1982, pp. 29–37.

Table 12.3   SELECTED CRITERIA FROM THE CHICAGO PUBLIC SCHOOL SYSTEM'S FORM FOR EVALUATING TEACHERS

I. Instruction
  A. Instructional planning
    1. Provides written lesson plans and preparation in accordance with the objectives of the instructional program
    2. Periodically evaluates pupils' progress and keeps up-to-date records of pupils' achievement
  B. Instructional methods
    1. Draws from the range of instructional materials available in the school
    2. Exhibits willingness to participate in the development and implementation of new ideas and teaching techniques
  C. Competency in subject matter taught or services provided
    1. Exhibits and applies knowledge of the curriculum content related to subject area and instructional level
    2. Shows evidence of student performance and progress

II. School environment
  A. School-wide environment
    1. Carries out daily routines and administrative requests
    2. Complies with the policies, rules, and regulations of the school system and of the building
  B. Classroom management
    1. Establishes and maintains reasonable rules of conduct within the classroom
    2. Maintains attendance books, seating chart(s), and grade books accurately
  C. Teacher-pupil relationships
    1. Encourages student growth in self-discipline and positive self-concept
    2. Exhibits an understanding and respect for students as individuals

III. Community relationships
    1. Uses appropriate resources available in the community
    2. Communicates the academic progress, attendance, and conduct of students to their parents
    3. Endeavors to understand the life styles and values of the school community

IV. Professional and personal standards
  A. Professional responsibilities
    1. Is punctual and regular in attendance to school and duty assignments
    2. Participates in in-service meetings and uses information and materials provided
    3. Makes proper use of professional preparation periods
  B. Personal qualities
    1. Presents an appearance that does not adversely affect the student's ability to learn
    2. Demonstrates proper diction and grammatical usage when addressing students

Note: The actual evaluation form lists 33 items. Provision is made for school principals to add other criteria during the school year as long as teachers are informed about all criteria on which they will be judged.

Source: Adapted from *Teacher Evaluation Plan and Handbook of Procedures* (Chicago: Office of Superintendent, Chicago Public Schools, 1988), pp. 7–9.

4. Self-evaluation for self-improvement is more acceptable than judgments of worth for supervisory decisions.

5. If growth contracts are used in a school, self-evaluations may be used as part of the contract or formal evaluation process.

6. Self-ratings should be compared with student ratings if the same items are included in the forms. Discrepancies between the ratings should be interpreted or analyzed.

7. Self-evaluations can be better utilized by discussing them with colleagues or staff members in charge of staff development.

8. Self-evaluations can be used as a starting point for the formal evaluation of the teacher by the supervisor.

9. Teachers wishing to focus on specific behaviors or instructional activities should videotape a particular lesson in conjunction with the self-evaluation of that lesson.

PEER EVALUATION AND ASSISTANCE

No matter how successful individuals are as student teachers and how good their preservice training is, they can benefit from the advice and assistance of experienced colleagues. Talking to other teachers gives people the chance to sound out ideas and pick up information. Write two educators, "Self-confidence is often developed through the reactions of fellow teachers. Thus, to create a healthy and productive teaching environment, there must be opportunities and a willingness to share information and ideas."[23]

Unquestionably, new teachers need the feedback and encouragement experienced teachers can provide. The exchange of ideas can take place in school and out, such as sharing a ride to a local meeting. Most important, experienced teachers must be willing to open their classrooms to new teachers. Because of the desire for autonomy in their classrooms that most teachers develop, there is "seldom as much communication or visitation between classrooms as there should be."[24] In some studies as many as 45 percent of the teachers report no contact with other teachers during the school day, and another 32 percent report having infrequent contact with other teachers.[25]

Whether observing other teachers is done on an informal or formal basis, permission should be granted by the teacher to be observed and by the supervisor or administrator in charge of the new teacher's professional development. The new teachers should look for techniques of teaching and lesson planning that they were not aware of, that concide with their teaching style, and that

[23]Shirley F. Heck and C. Ray Williams, *The Complex Roles of the Teacher* (New York: Teachers College Press, Columbia University, 1984), p. 17.

[24]Ibid., p. 19.

[25]*What Works: Research about Teaching and Learning* (Washington, D.C.: U.S. Department of Education, 1986).

Professional Viewpoint

Enhancing Teacher Professionalism

Teacher professionalism demands:

- Reform of *teacher education* so that prospective teachers are well-educated and knowledgeable about teaching. Increasingly, this preparation is seen as requiring a four-year liberal-arts education, a fifth year of graduate-level professional and pedagogical preparation, and a yearlong supervised internship school.
- Reform of *teacher licensing* so that prospective teachers must demonstrate that they have acquired the knowledge and developed the skills necessary to practice independently. Increasingly, licensing is seen as requiring the creation of state professional practices boards to establish and enforce meaningful standards for entry to teaching.
- Reform of *schools* so that they can accommodate the professional practice of teaching. Increasingly, this change is seen as requiring teacher participation in school planning and decision making.
- Reform of *teacher organizations* to balance their union and professional functions. Increasingly, this reform is seen as requiring the National Education Association (NEA) and American Federation of Teachers (AFT) to collaborate with states and school districts to establish workable procedures for evaluating and improving teacher performance.
- Reform of *testing practices* so that student assessment encourages good educational results and professional teaching practices. Increasingly, these practices are seen as requiring essay examinations and the evaluation of student projects and products, with teachers involved in developing outcome criteria and grading beyond their own classrooms.

Taken together, these reforms would begin to ensure every child access to good educational practices and ultimately good educational results.

Arthur E. Wise
Director of the Center for the
    Study of the Teaching Profession
The RAND Corporation

Figure 12.1 Peer interaction and feedback are essential for the teachers' professional growth. (Photo © Mimi Forsyth/Monkmeyer)

are an improvement over what they are doing. A short follow-up conference to go over specific points should be scheduled either the same day or the next day while the observation is fresh.

It is perhaps more beneficial for new teachers to ask one or more experienced teachers to observe them teach. The observers should have teaching assignments (by subject or grade level) similar to those of the new teachers, and some experience as observers. Untrained observers, for example, often focus on the teacher and not on the students, so they miss clues and behaviors that indicate degree of student interest and involvement and aspects of student-teacher interaction. New teachers need to have self-confidence to be willing to be observed, but they do have a lot to gain from informed comments about their teaching and lesson planning.

Schools often schedule **staff development** or in-service time for teachers to work in small groups with other teachers. In elementary schools teachers are often divided into groups by grade level. In secondary schools they may be divided by subject. In these small in-service groups teachers may discuss specific or general aspects of teaching and instruction, focus on students who have learning or behavioral problems, or work on curriculum development. The members of the group may observe each other regularly.

Joyce and Showers, who have studied staff development programs, describe **mentor programs,** which should involve the following activities: (1) discussion of the theory and practice of teaching strategies and methods, (2) modeling or demonstration of teaching strategies, (3) practice in simulated and real class-

---

Tips for Teachers 12.2

Professional Interaction in Staff Development Programs

In various staff development programs, exchanging ideas and asking teachers to examine what they observed or did in the classroom makes them feel less isolated and more confident about their teaching. Questions designed to promote professional dialogue and reflective thinking in such programs include:

1. What do you remember about the classroom situation?
2. What do you recall were your thoughts at the time?
3. What seemed to be the most important issue in the situation?
4. What alternatives did you consider?
5. Why did you select the action you did?
6. Did it turn out to be the right choice? How did you know it was the right choice?
7. What was inappropriate about the other alternatives in this situation?
8. What might have happened if you had chosen another alternative? Take one alternative and describe specifically what you anticipate might have happened.
9. How did you know this might happen?
10. What knowledge did you use in making this decision?
11. What is another situation that this one was like?
12. What percentage of this decision was based on intuition and what percentage on knowledge?
13. How would you act in a similar situation in the future?
14. What might you change?
15. What did you learn from this situation that you can transfer from intuition to knowledge for the future?

Source: Adapted from Joellen P. Killion and Cynthia R. Harrison, "Evaluating Training Programs: Three Critical Elements for Success," *Journal of Staff Development*, Winter 1988, p. 36.

---

rooms, (4) feedback about performance, and (5) coaching on problems and transferring new skills to the classroom.[26]

Such structured in-service programs encourage professional exchanges and mentor relations that can help teachers develop teaching and instructional

---

[26]Joyce and Showers, *Student Achievement Through Staff Development.*

skills. These small groups should emphasize self-improvement, be voluntary, and be conducted without the presence of a supervisor. As Good and Brophy assert, "sharing information and the search for new alternatives" mean more when people want to participate than when they have to do so.[27] Similarly, discussion is more open without the presence of a supervisor; the members of the group are more likely to say what they want and help each other in the way they want, not to say and do what they think the supervisor wants. See Tips for Teachers 12.2.

Based on studies of New York City teachers who assumed diverse staff development roles, Ellen Saxl and her colleagues developed 18 key skills for teachers who assist other teachers in school-site activities; they are listed in Table 12.4. Their data suggest that teachers can make a significant contribution as either part-time or full-time mentors or staff developers, and that ongoing training and support for the mentors are a vital part of the process.[28]

The mentor program of the Toledo schools has gained national recognition as a model of peer evaluation of and assistance to beginning teachers during an induction period, and of peer assistance to experienced teachers. The model is different from others because it is a full peer review system. Experienced teachers determine whether a beginning teacher (or intern) becomes a full-fledged teacher.[29] The assumption is that new teachers lack practical experience and that experienced teachers have a legitimate professional role in screening and assisting new entrants. The experienced teachers tend to emphasize the same skills that were previously emphasized by supervisors and principals in their evaluation of new teachers, but too often the supervisory group lacked time to provide ongoing assistance. Teachers who are not new entrants but who never mastered basic teaching techniques or have trouble managing students are also assigned to the program.

Under the Toledo mentor program, a new teacher and an experienced teacher are matched on the basis of subject or grade level. The evaluation of the beginning teacher is a continuing process involving detailed observations and analysis of the novice's teaching behaviors and instructional methods. The experienced teacher may point out a deficiency, suggest a new teaching method, or demonstrate a sample lesson. The program has the blessing of the local teachers' union and school administrators and is bound to spread as the idea of peer evaluation and mentor assistance programs become incorporated as part of the reform of teacher education.

---

[27] Good and Brophy, *Looking into Teaching*, p. 557.

[28] Ellen R. Saxl, Ann Lieberman, and Matthew B. Miles, "Help Is at Hand: New Leadership for Teachers as Staff Developers," *Journal of Staff Development*, Spring 1987, pp. 7–11; Saxl, Miles, and Lieberman, *Professional Assister Training* (Alexandria, Va.: Association for Supervision and Curriculum Development, 1988).

[29] Personal letter to author from Albert Shanker, president of the American Federation of Teachers, June 21, 1988.

Table 12.4   KEY SKILLS FOR STAFF DEVELOPERS

Skill	Examples
1. *Interpersonal ease.* Relating to and directing others.	Very open person; nice manner; has always been able to deal with staff; knows when to stroke, when to hold back, when to assert; knows "which buttons to push"; gives individuals time to vent feelings, lets them know her interest in them; can talk to anyone.
2. *Group functioning.* Understanding group dynamics, able to facilitate team work.	Has ability to get a group moving; started with nothing and then made us come together as a united body; good group facilitator; lets the discussion flow.
3. *Training/doing workshops.* Directing instruction, teaching adults in systematic way.	Gave workshops on how to develop plans; taught us consensus method with 5 group game; prepares a great deal and enjoys it; has the right chemistry and can impart knowledge at the peer level.
4. *Educational general (master teacher).* Wide educational experience, able to impart skills to others.	Excellent teaching skills; taught most grades, grade leader work, resource teacher; has done staff development with teachers; was always assisting, supporting, being resource person to teachers; a real master teacher; much teacher training work.
5. *Educational content.* Knowledge of school subject matter.	Demonstrating expertise in a subject area; showed parents the value of play and trips in subject area; knows a great deal about teaching; what she doesn't know she finds out.
6. *Administrative/organizational.* Defining and structuring work, activities, time.	Highly organized, has everything prepared in advance; could take an idea and turn it into a program; good at prioritizing, scheduling; knows how to set things up.
7. *Initiative-taking.* Starting or pushing activities, moving directly toward action.	Assertive, clear sense of what he wanted to do; ability to poke and prod where needed to get things done; had to assert myself so he didn't step on me.
8. *Trust/rapport-building.* Developing a sense of safety, openness, reduced threat on part of clients; good relationship-building.	In 2 weeks he had gained confidence of staff; had to become one of the gang, eat lunch with them; a skilled seducer (knows how to get people to ask for help); "I have not repeated what they said so trust was built"; did not threaten staff; was so open and understanding that I stopped feeling uneasy.
9. *Support.* Providing nurturant relationship, positive affective relationship.	Able to accept harsh things teachers say, "It's OK, everyone has these feelings"; a certain compassion for others; always patient, never critical, very enthusiastic.
10. *Confrontation.* Direct expression of negative information, without generating negative affect.	Can challenge in a positive way; will lay it on the line about what works and what won't; is talkative and factual; can point out things and get away with being blunt; able to tell people they were wrong, and they accept it.

Table 12.4   CONTINUED

Skills	Examples
11. *Conflict mediation.* Resolving or improving situations where multiple incompatible interests are in play.	Effected a compromise between upper and lower grade teachers on use of a checklist; spoke to the chair about his autocratic behavior and things have been considerably better; able to mediate with the principal to soften her attitude; can handle people who are terribly angry, unreasonable; keeps cool.
12. *Collaboration.* Creating relationships where influence is mutually shared.	Deals on same level we do, puts in his ideas; leads and directs us, but as peers; doesn't judge us or put us down; has ideas of her own, but flexible enough to maintain the teachers' way of doing things too.
13. *Confidence-building.* Strengthening client's sense of efficacy, belief in self.	She makes all feel confident and competent; doesn't patronize; "You can do it"; has a way of drawing out teachers' ideas; injects a great deal, but you feel powerful; makes people feel great about themselves; like a shot of adrenaline boosting your ego, talents, and professional expertise.
14. *Diagnosing individuals.* Forming a valid picture of the needs/problems of an individual teacher or administrator as a basis for action.	Realizes that when a teacher says she has the worst class, that means "I need help"; has an ability to focus in on problems; picks up the real message; sensitive, looks at teacher priorities first; knows when an off-hand joke is a signal for help.
15. *Diagnosing organizations.* Forming a valid picture of the needs/problems of the school organization as a basis for action.	Analyzes situation, recognizes problems, jumps ahead of where you are to where you want to go; anticipates problems schools face when students enter the program; helped us know where we should be going; helped team look at the data in the assessment package.
16. *Managing/controlling.* Orchestrating the improvement process; coordinating activities, time, and people; direct influence on others.	Prepared materials and coordinated our contact with administration and district; is a task master and keeps the process going; makes people do things rather than doing them himself.
17. *Resource-bringing.* Locating and providing information, materials, practices, equipment useful to clients.	He uses his network to get us supplies; brings ideas that she has seen work elsewhere; had the newest research methods, articles, and ideas and waters them down for our needs.
18. *Demonstrating.* Modeling new behavior in classrooms or meetings.	Willing to go into classrooms and take risks; modeling; showed the chair by his own behavior how to be more open.

Source: Ellen R. Saxl, Ann Lieberman, and Matthew B. Miles, "Help Is at Hand: New Knowledge for Teachers as Staff Developers," *Journal of Staff Development,* Spring 1987, p. 9.

> ## Guidelines for Peer Evaluation and Assistance

In all the methods of peer evaluation, there is opportunity for feedback. In order to effect change, feedback must be handled properly. Bruce Tuckman offers 12 rules for implementing effective feedback for purposes of improving teaching.

1. Feedback must be specific and involve concrete behaviors and activities.
2. Feedback must be clear and describe how one appears to behave.
3. The feedback source must be reputable and believable.
4. Feedback must be in terms that the teacher understands and relates to.
5. The feedback recipient must have an understanding of an acceptable standard so the discrepancy between what is and what should be is clear.
6. The feedback recipient must know the expectations of others so he or she can meet them.
7. The feedback recipient must be personally committed to change.
8. The feedback recipient's commitment to change must be public.
9. The feedback process must create some tension.
10. The feedback recipient needs support from others; the receptivity to change must involve low risk.
11. Models for change and self-improvement must be provided.
12. Both the feedback recipient and the feedback giver must accept and use feedback in a constructive way that contributes to each other's professional growth.[30]

SUPERVISORY EVALUATION AND ASSISTANCE

Beginning teachers should welcome supervision as a means to develop professionally. In most schools the purpose of supervisory observation and conferences is to increase morale and effective teaching.

Teacher-supervisor interaction, often referred to as **clinical supervision,** follows a similar pattern in many schools. Members of the supervisory and administrative staff meet with new teachers at the beginning of the school year to acquaint them with school policies and programs. As the school year gets under way, a grade-level or subject-related supervisor helps the novice plan lessons, suggests appropriate materials and media, and provides curriculum suggestions. Ideally, he or she informally visits the class for short periods

---

[30]Bruce W. Tuckman, "Feedback and the Change Process," *Phi Delta Kappan,* January 1976, pp. 341–344; Tuckman, *Evaluating Instructional Programs.*

Figure 12.2 A supervisor's leadership style and techniques sets the tone for the way teachers can improve. (Photo © Miriam Reinhart/Photo Researchers)

of time to learn about the new teacher's style, abilities, and needs. Later, at the teacher's invitation or by mutual agreement, the supervisor observes a complete lesson. Such a visit is often formally planned in conjunction with a **pre-observation conference** to talk over the plans for the lesson and a **post-observation conference** to discuss the observation and evaluation of the lesson.

This three-step process (pre-observation conference, observation, and post-observation conference) has been enlarged to eight "phases" by Morris Cogan, a major theorist in the area of supervision of teachers: (1) establishing the teacher-supervisor relationship, (2) planning the lesson with the teacher, (3) planning the strategy of observation, (4) observing instruction, (5) analyzing the teaching-learning process, (6) planning the strategy of the conference, (7) the conference, and (8) renewed planning.[31]

Robert Goldhammer, a student of Cogan, developed a similar model consisting of five "stages": (1) pre-observation conference, (2) observation, (3) analysis and strategy, (4) supervision conference, and (5) post-conference analysis.

---

[31] Morris Cogan, *Clinical Supervision* (Boston: Houghton Mifflin, 1973).

In both of these models the teacher's behavior and techniques are observed, analyzed, and interpreted, and decisions are made in order to improve the teacher's effectiveness.[32]

According to Ben Harris, the teacher can learn to assume increasing responsibilities for each step in the process. As the teacher learns to analyze and interpret observational data and confronts his or her own concerns and needs, he or she should become less dependent on the supervisor and more capable of self-analysis.[33]

Supervisory evaluation involves judgments about the teacher and can put teachers on the defensive. Albert Shanker questions the value of "having a supervisor sit in the back of the classroom, watch a lesson, write an evaluation, and then meet with [the teacher] to discuss the evaluation." He believes the practice is "ineffective" but that supervisors stick to the practice "because everybody else does it."[34] Experienced teachers are often uncomfortable with the idea that the supervisor is seeing only a fragment of a lesson or only one or two lessons and that their techniques and methods may be misinterpreted.

Obviously, several observations and conferences are needed before any formal judgment is made about a teacher's performance. However, even one or two observations by a skilled supervisor can be helpful to the teacher, especially for the new teacher who lacks practical experience in the classroom. There is also evidence, according to both Brookover and Wise, that beginning (and experienced) teachers value supervisory feedback and appreciate supervisors' and principals' input in diagnosing, prescribing, and recommending teaching strategies and skills. The input helps teachers learn to teach and to understand the expectations of the school district. The latter is considered important in view of the fact that the turnover among new teachers (those with less than three years of experience) may be as high as 40 percent.[35]

Some researchers distinguish between *peer coaching* (already discussed) and **technical coaching,** or supervisor-teacher evaluation. Technical coaching includes supervisory evaluations; it assists teachers in developing new teaching strategies and skills and helps them attain new knowledge about the strategies for longer periods than peer coaching. But it has a price: It tends to inhibit professional dialogue and peer exchange, and teachers often focus on the presence or absence of a particular behavior or item on an evaluation form that may have little value for an individual teacher or for students.

---

[32] Robert Goldhammer et al., *Clinical Supervision: Special Methods for the Supervison of Teachers,* 2nd ed. (New York: Holt, Rinehart, 1980).

[33] Ben M. Harris, *Supervisory Behavior in Education,* 3rd ed. (Englewood Cliffs, N.J.: Prentice-Hall, 1985); Harris, *In-Service Education for Staff Development* (Needham Heights, Mass.: Allyn and Bacon, 1989).

[34] Albert Shanker, "The Revolution That's Overdue," *Phi Delta Kappan,* January 1985, p. 314.

[35] Wilbur B. Brookover et al., *Creating Effective Schools: An Inservice Program for Enhancing School Learning Climate and Achievement* (Holmes Beach, Fla.: Learning Publications, 1982); Arthur E. Wise et al., *Effective Teacher Selection: From Recruitment to Retention* (Santa Monica, Calif.: Rand Corporation, 1987).

Table 12.5 CHARACTERISTICS OF AN EFFECTIVE SUPERVISORY EVALUATION SYSTEM

---

1. *All participants accept the validity of the system.* The supervisor and teachers must believe that the evaluation methods and procedures employed will accurately reflect the teachers' performance.

2. *All participants thoroughly understand the mechanics of the system.* This includes frequency of evaluation, forms, methods of data collection, timeliness, purpose of conferences, relation of process to personnel decisions, and rebuttal and appeal procedures.

3. *Teachers know that the performance criteria have a clear, consistent rationale.* They understand where the criteria came from, why they are important, and what standards or outcomes are being compared.

4. *Supervisors are properly trained in using the system.* The supervisor needs technical skills (data collection, methods of observation, data analysis) and personal skills (communicating, conferencing, changing teacher behavior).

5. *Evaluation results in distinctions of level of performance.* Effective methods distinguish among above standard, standard, and below standard performance, telling teachers how they rate.

6. *There is a distinction between formative evaluation during the growth period and summative evaluation for final determinations.* The distinction is valuable, especially for teachers in a remedial track, to reduce anxiety about formative evaluation and allow teachers in the development period to make better use of it.

7. *A variety of sources of evaluation are used.* Although supervisory evaluation is an accepted practice, other methods of assessing performance are also included.

8. *Evaluation is a district priority.* The system must be formal and tie into district goals. It should be emphasized that the system is designed to meet the needs of professional growth and accountability.

Source: Adapted from David T. Conley, ''Critical Attributes of Effective Evaluation Systems,'' *Educational Leadership,* April 1987, pp. 60–64.

The supervisor-teacher system, however, assumes that objective feedback and evaluation, given in a nonthreatening and constructive climate, can improve teaching. According to two supervisors, the key to developing an effective supervisor-teacher evaluation system is that it must:

1. Be accepted as fair and objective by teachers.
2. Be related to the requirements of the job and needs of the school.
3. Specify the factors and behaviors on which the teacher will be judged.
4. Reliably measure teacher performance and indicate how the measurement will be performed.
5. Clearly communicate the expectations for performance to the teacher.
6. Provide for teacher development as part of the system.[36]

Table 12.5 summarizes the major characteristics of a supervisory evaluation system that achieves maximum teacher growth and accountability. Both

---

[36] Robert J. Garmston, ''How Administrators Support Peer Coaching,'' *Educational Leadership,* February 1987, pp. 34–36; Pembroke and Goedert, ''What Is the Key to Developing an Effective Teacher Evaluation System?''

teachers and supervisors understand the mechanics of the system, accept its purpose and utility, and recognize it as only one method for evaluation.

Guidelines for Supervisory Evaluation and Assistance

Procedures for the pre-observation, observation, and post-observation of supervisory evaluation are interrelated. During the pre-observation conference, the teacher and supervisor get to know each other and build mutual trust and respect. According to Harris, pre-observation preparations should include:

1. Identifying and accepting the purpose of observation.
2. Setting the time of the observation.
3. Selecting and agreeing on an instrument or method for observation.
4. Reviewing observation procedures.
5. Reassuring the teacher.
6. Deciding on follow-up activities.[37]

During the observation the supervisor should pay attention to specific behaviors and teacher-student interactions. The observation should be objective and free of any prejudgments about the teacher. Eight suggestions for the overall observation process are made by John Robinson.

1. Analysis of the classroom observation should be written in a report by the supervisor and include comments on actual events, an overall evaluation of the lesson, and recommendations for improving instruction.
2. Supervisors should make an effort to observe classes more often than they do at the present. (On the average teachers are only observed twice during a school year.)
3. Supervisors should announce in advance when they intend to visit the teacher. (Many teachers claim their observations are unannounced.)
4. The pre-observation conference should be emphasized as an integral and necessary part of the observation report.
5. Observations should be planned with the goal of effecting long-range improvement of instruction in a few basic but important areas.
6. The observation report should concentrate on major points, both favorable and unfavorable. Minor recommendations should be made in the post-observation conference and should not be part of the report.
7. The report should be sent to the teacher before the post-observation conference.
8. School districts should offer an in-service course in observation and

---

[37]Harris, *Supervisory Behavior in Education.*

feedback methods. (Supervisors report they receive little help from their district in these supervisory functions.)[38]

The post-observation conference is essential for analyzing the lesson and the teacher's behavior in general. Agreements reached during the pre-observation conference about what is to be observed should be helpful in focusing the post-observation discussion. The observer should also bring up any specific problem or recurring behavior that came to his or her attention (for example, the teacher repeatedly calls the name of the student before asking a question; the teacher repeatedly turns his or her back to the class when writing on the chalkboard). According to Lovell and Wiles, analysis of behavior should include the following:

1. Compare anticipated (ideal) teacher and student behavior with actual behavior.
2. Identify consequences of discrepancies between anticipated and actual behavior.
3. Decide on what should be done about the discrepancies between anticipated and actual behavior.
4. Compare projected (ideal) use of materials, media, equipment, physical space, and social environment with actual use; identify consequences of discrepancies and make recommendations for future use.
5. Compare desired learning outcomes with actual learning outcomes (as observed during the lesson) and make recommendations to improve learning outcomes in the future.[39]

As the teacher receives feedback on his or her behavior, tension and anxiety are likely. A solid base of mutual trust and respect must exist for maximum benefit to be derived from these supervisory-teacher functions.

ALTERNATIVE FORMS OF EVALUATION

Some school districts have been experimenting with other forms of evaluation or with eliminating evaluation entirely. Since there is a lack of agreement on what constitutes "effective teaching" and since the instruments involve problems of reliability and validity, other efforts have been advised with the idea of promoting professional growth.

Artifacts of Teaching

Samples or **artifacts of teaching** are sources of data for teacher evaluation and growth. Rarely considered as a source of feedback or information, teachers

---

[38] John J. Robinson, "The Observation Report—A Help or a Nuisance?" *National Association of Secondary School Principals,* March 1978, pp. 22–26.

[39] John T. Lovell and Kimball Wiles, *Supervision for Better Schools,* 5th ed. (Englewood Cliffs, N.J.: Prentice-Hall, 1983).

should recognize that these products offer prime examples of their workmanship and are representative of their performance. They can serve as excellent alternative sources for evaluating teachers.

1. *Lesson plans and unit plans.* Examination of lesson plans and unit plans should indicate whether the curriculum or course syllabus is being taught, whether the teacher's pace and focus is correct, how individual student differences are provided for, whether the instructional objectives are clear, activities appropriate, and whether study and homework exercises are adequate.

2. *Tests.* Do quizzes and examinations reflect the important objectives and learning outcomes? Are the directions clear? Are the test questions appropriately written? Is there a good mix of different types of questions?

3. *Laboratory and special projects.* These handouts should be examined for clarity, spelling, punctuation, and appropriateness. They should coincide with the important objectives and content of the course and serve to motivate students and enrich their learning experiences.

4. *Materials and media.* The quality and appropriateness of materials and media and the way they are incorporated into the instructional process partially reveal the teacher's knowledge, skills, and effort for facilitating student learning.

5. *Reading lists and bibliographies.* These lists should accommodate varied student abilities, needs, and interests.

6. *Student outcomes.* Samples of student work and test results indicate students' mastery of skills and subject matter. They provide feedback for teachers and provide a basis on which to judge whether the teacher has achieved his or her own objectives as well as the standards set by the school.[40]

These artifacts (when several, not just one or two are considered) are sources of valid and valuable data that can be used by the teacher for self-examination. They can also be used by supervisors as a supplement to the formal evaluation process. One advantage of these artifacts is that they can be collected quickly and examined with a colleague or supervisor to provide objective feedback and recommendations for improvement. Another is that they enable the teacher to look at his or her teaching and instructional skills over an extended period of time, even the entire school year (or longer), as opposed to a one-time rating or classroom observation. Also, since the teacher selects the artifacts, he or she may feel more at ease and more willing to examine the data than when evaluation is based on formal rating scales or observations where the teacher has less input and control. Finally most colleagues and supervisors do not have enough time for thorough classroom observations and pre- and post-observation conferences, and examining the artifacts is much less time-consuming.

---

[40]John G. Savage, "Teacher Evaluation Without Classroom Observation," *National Association of Secondary School Principals*, December 1982, pp. 41–45.

New Staff Development Programs

Some school districts are experimenting with eliminating formal teacher evaluations on the assumption that staff development programs can be sufficient to improve teaching and instruction. It can also be tried in places where the majority of teachers are tenured and expect little supervisory or administrative assistance and in school districts that have a strong sense of collegiality and professionalism and feel that less supervision and good in-service programs would best serve teacher growth.

For example, the Valley Stream, New York suburban school district has designed a five-year staff development program that eliminates supervisory observations of teachers. The following resources are used: (1) consultants, (2) professional materials, including videotapes, journals, and books, (3) experts within the system such as experienced teachers, principals, district directors, and department heads, (4) professional networks such as educational associations, research agencies, and teaching laboratories, (5) staff development programs from commercial or professional groups, (6) statewide and regional education agencies, and (7) colleges and universities. The format includes (1) summer workshops, (2) summer projects, (3) conference attendance (local, state, and national), (4) teacher centers, (5) faculty meetings (school and district), (6) in-service days and administrative days, (7) inter-visitations, (8) after-school seminars and workshops, and (9) university courses.[41] Demonstrations, coaching, and feedback are provided, and the sessions are spaced over the entire school year. Most of the in-service activities take place on school grounds or school district grounds. There is an attempt to integrate new research and theories about teaching and learning with practical application in the classroom.

PROFESSIONAL ASSOCIATIONS AND ACTIVITIES

Membership in professional organizations and participation in meetings, research, and advanced study can contribute to professional growth and help improve conditions for teachers.

Teacher Associations

There are two major teacher associations, the American Federation of Teachers (AFT) and the National Education Association (NEA). In most school districts teachers vote on which of the two associations all of them will join. In some school districts, the choice of joining or not joining a local chapter of the AFT or a state affiliate of the NEA is left to the individual. If you have a choice, you should not be rushed into making a decision. Keep in mind, however, that

---

[41] Glen Grube, Henry G. Crain, and Timothy M. Melchior," Taking Risks to Improve Instruction," *Educational Leadership*, October 1988, pp. 17-21.

Figure 12.3 Keeping up with the professional literature and enrolling in professional course work are important for developing and maintaining teacher effectiveness. (Photo © Frank Siteman/Taurus)

both organizations have helped improve salaries, benefits, and working conditions for teachers and that you should probably join one of them. At present nearly 85 percent of public school teachers belong to either the AFT or the NEA.[42]

The AFT has approximately 750,000 members, organized in 2,200 locals mainly in cities. Included in the membership are some 550,000 teachers, 100,000 municipal workers and nurses who are not teachers, 75,000 college teachers, and 25,000 auxiliary staff (secretaries, paraprofessionals, cafeteria workers, etc.).[43] By 1995 the AFT membership is expected to reach 950,000. See Table 12.6. The AFT publishes a monthly newspaper, *American Teacher;* a professional magazine, *Changing Education;* and a yearly policy statement, *Consortium Yearbook.* It requires members to join the local, state, and national organizations simultaneously. The AFT has not been involved in publishing research. It focuses on issues of conditions of employment and professional status.

The NEA has a membership of more than 1.9 million, including 35,000 students, 100,000 retired members, 50,000 auxiliary staff, 50,000 college professors, 200,000 professional support staff (guidance counselors, librarians, administrators), and nearly 1.5 million classroom teachers, more than half the nation's 2.4 million public school teachers.[44] This figure is expected to grow, as shown in Table 12.6.

---

[42] Allan C. Ornstein and Daniel U. Levine, *Introduction to the Foundations of Education,* 4th ed. (Boston: Houghton Mifflin, 1989).

[43] Telephone conversation with Robert Porter, Secretary-Treasurer of the American Federation of Teachers, March 7, 1989.

[44] *NEA Handbook, 1989–1990* (Washington, D.C.: National Education Association, 1990); telephone conversation with Margaret Jones, Director of Research, National Education Association, February 17, 1989.

Table 12.6   MEMBERSHIP IN
AFT AND NEA

Year	AFT	NEA
1857*		43
1870		170
1880		354
1890		5,474
1900		2,322
1910		6,909
1916*	1,500	12,500
1920	10,000	22,850
1930	7,000	216,188
1940	30,000	203,429
1950	41,000	453,797
1960	59,000	713,994
1970	205,000	1,100,00
1980	550,000	1,650,000
1985	600,000	1,700,000
1990†	750,000	1,900,000
1995†	950,000	2,100,000

*Year organization was founded.

†Estimated membership.

Source: Allan C. Ornstein and Daniel U. Levine, *Introduction to the Foundations of Education*, 4th ed. (Boston: Houghton Mifflin, 1989), p. 61.

Disproportionately suburban and rural, the membership is served by a large network of affiliates in every state, Puerto Rico, and the District of Columbia. There are more than 12,000 local affiliate groups, but unlike the AFT (where the local affiliate is powerful), most of the power is derived from the state affiliates. In terms of numbers the NEA represents the second largest lobby force in the country, trailing only behind the Teamsters.

The NEA publishes the *NEA Research Bulletin* and several research reports and opinion surveys about teachers each year. Its major publication is *Today's Education,* now an annual publication, with a supplementary monthly newspaper.

Although the two organizations occasionally take different positions on educational matters and battle over membership, "no raid" efforts have been discussed at the state level. Most important, both organizations seek to improve the status of the teaching profession, agree on many issues concerning teachers and schools, and sometimes join forces on policy matters. Merger

---

Professional Viewpoint

Becoming a Professional

As teachers consider strategies to realize more effective practice, I urge consideration of active involvement in organized associations, including unions. When I began my career, more than twenty years ago, I was too soon aware that the reality of the classroom was far short of the ideal. I'm talking about basics, like textbooks and equipment. I also remember how little power the individual teacher had regarding solutions to these matters. My decision to become active in Association work was driven by my beliefs that teachers have a responsibility to speak out on issues that have an impact on their ability to teach well, and that the union is an appropriate organization for that purpose.

I have been proud of the courage and determination with which the members of the National Education Association have attacked some of the most critical problems of effective practice. We have helped the public become better informed about violence and drugs in the nation's schools; we have devoted our own dues money to support research conducted by teachers on matters such as dropout prevention, instructional technology, and restructuring schools; we have credentialing. Through collective action, professional responsibility and generosity, the NEA will create an educators' foundation, the National Foundation for the Improvement of Education (NFIE), which is one of the largest grant-giving foundations in America. We also encourage our members to be good citizens, through well-informed political action and community involvement.

The problems of adequate instructional supplies which prompted my personal involvement in Association work have not been fully resolved, but I continue to find professional fulfillment in our efforts. As a professional we can do no less.

Mary Hatwood Futrell
President 1983–1989
National Education Association

---

talks have begun to sound serious in more than 15 states in recent years, and to be sure, there are immense political and economic advantages to be gained from the formation of a united "super" teacher organization.[45]

---

[45] Allan C. Ornstein, "The Changing Status of the Teaching Profession," *Urban Education*, October 1988, pp. 261–279.

Professional Organizations

At the working level of the classroom, the professional organization of greatest academic benefit to a teacher (and education student) is usually one that focuses on his or her major field. Each professional association provides a meeting ground for teachers of similar interests. The activities of these professional organizations usually consist of regional and national meetings and publication of a monthly or quarterly journal that describes accepted curriculum and teaching practices.

Some organizations are *subject-centered*. Others focus on the needs and rights of special *students*, and are organized to ensure that these children and youth are served by well-prepared school personnel and to improve specialized teaching techniques. Table 12.7 lists 15 major teaching organizations that focus on specific subject matter and 15 on specific types of students.

Still another type of professional organization cuts across subjects and student types. These organizations tend to highlight innovative teaching and instructional practices in general. They describe, in their journals, new trends and policies that affect the entire field of education, have a wide range of membership including teachers, administrators, and professors, and work for the advancement of the teaching profession in general.

Perhaps the best known organization of this type is Phi Delta Kappa, which includes 585 local and 7 regional chapters in the United States and Canada and 8 international chapters. As of 1990, it had approximately 135,000 members, with no distinctions made among graduate students, administrators, and grade school and college-level teachers. Originally open only to men, it opened its membership to women in 1974. The purpose of the organization is to promote quality and equality of education, with particular emphasis on public education. Members receive *Phi Delta Kappan*, a highly respected journal published 10 times a year, and the fraternity newsletter. Paperback publications of interest are available at reduced rates for members.

Professional Activities

If you are to continue to do a good job teaching, you must keep up with your subject and the latest teaching and instructional trends in your specialization. Without continued updating, one's teaching becomes dated and dry. To keep abreast of developments in your field you will need to do three things: (1) read professional books and journals, (2) attend professional conferences, at least one or two a year, and (3) enroll in advanced courses in conjunction with a university-sponsored program or a school district in-service program. All three activities will help you keep up on changes in methods and materials, teaching and learning theories, and current experimentation.

Readings   Almost any professional organization you join should have a monthly or quarterly journal. The journal that will have the most immediate value for you is the one that focuses on your subject and grade level. For example, reading teachers might subscribe to the *Journal of Reading, Reading Teacher*, or *Read-*

Table 12.7 PROFESSIONAL TEACHING ORGANIZATIONS

Specialization by subject

1. American Alliance for Health, Physical Education, Recreation and Dance
2. American Council on the Teaching of Foreign Languages
3. American Industrial Arts Association
4. American School Health Association
5. American Vocational Association
6. Association for Education in Journalism
7. International Reading Association
8. Modern Language Association
9. Music Teachers National Association
10. National Art Education Association
11. National Business Education Association
12. National Council for the Social Studies
13. National Council of Teachers of English
14. National Council of Teachers of Mathematics
15. National Science Teachers Association

Specialization by type of student

1. American Association for Gifted Children
2. American Association of Workers for the Blind
3. American Association for Asian Studies
4. American Montessori Society
5. American Speech-Language-Hearing Association
6. Association for Childhood Education International
7. Association for Children with Learning Disabilities
8. Convention of American Instructors of the Deaf
9. Council for Exceptional Children
10. National Association for Bilingual Children
11. National Association for Creative Children and Adults
12. National Association for the Education of Young Children
13. National Rehabilitation Association
14. National Scholarship Service and Fund for Negro Students
15. Rural Education Association

Source: Allan C. Ornstein and Daniel U. Levine, *Introduction to the Foundations of Education*, 4th ed. (Boston: Houghton Mifflin, 1989), pp. 71–72.

ing Today. Math teachers might want to subscribe to the *Arithmetic Teacher* or *Mathematics Teacher,* and social studies teachers would do well to read *Social Education* and *Social Science Quarterly.* For those teachers who are more tuned to their grade level, elementary school teachers might subscribe to *Childhood Education* or *Young Education,* and high school teachers might want *Clearing House* or *High School Journal.*

There are many professional journals in education (more than 100 are available), and the need is to pick and choose wisely because of time and the cost of subscriptions. The answers to two questions can help determine your

Professional Viewpoint

Professional Associations and NCATE

National Council for Accreditation of Teacher Education, the recognized accrediting body for the preparation of school personnel, brings together 21 major professional organizations interested in quality preparation of school personnel. Among these 21 are representatives of most of the significant specialized professional organizations among which are: American Association of Colleges for Teacher Education; American Federation of Teachers; American Library Association; Association for Supervision and Curriculum Development; Council for Exceptional Children; International Reading Association; International Technology Education Association; National Association for the Education of Young Children; National Council for the Social Studies; National Council of Teachers of English; National Council of Teachers of Mathematics; National Education Association; National Middle School Association; National School Boards Association; National Science Teachers Association.

These organizations work effectively as a coalition in NCATE to see that program-specific guidelines drive and influence the quality of preparation programs in our nation's schools. Currently, a process exists as part of the NCATE redesign of 1986, which was created to allow systematically for each of these specialty organizations to critique the subject-specific training program that exists at each institution. This critique and the information derived from it helps the NCATE Board of Examiners when they visit a campus, as well as when they make a recommendation to the Unit Accreditation Board. What this does for the professional is to assure that not only the institution from which one graduates, but also the specific school preparation program has been judged at a level of quality. The influence of these special professional organizations is important, not only with regard to accreditation with NCATE, but also their interest in state licensure and forms of state and national certification. The meshing of the role of these specialty organizations with the importance of the two teachers unions, the AFT and the NEA, overall, in all of their concern for quality preparation of candidates to work in our schools is the important role of national accreditation.

Richard C. Kunkel
Executive Director
National Council for Accreditation
of Teacher Education

reading and subscription focus: Do I want practical advice and easy-to-read articles or theoretical and in-depth reading? Do I want to focus on subject or grade level issues or do I want a broad discussion of education issues?

Meetings   The two major teacher organizations—American Federation of Teachers and National Education Association—meet annually in different cities. If you become a member of one of these organizations, it would be beneficial to be an active participant and attend the annual meeting. The various subject-related associations and specialized student associations also have conferences. Keep an eye on your local colleges and universities; their departments or schools of education often sponsor professional meetings and short seminars that are excellent for updating your knowledge about teaching and for meeting other professionals in the local area. State departments of education and local school districts frequently organize in-service workshops and one- or two-day conferences on timely educational topics and teaching techniques.

The idea is to choose wisely which meetings and conferences best serve your professional needs and interests and to organize your schedule so you can attend them. Become acquainted with the scheduling and travel policy of your school district. If the meetings take place during the school calendar, you will need special permission to attend. Some school districts allow travel reimbursement for certain meetings. Local meetings sponsored by colleges or universities, state departments, regional education agencies, or local school districts often convene after school hours or on weekends. These sessions are easier to attend in terms of scheduling, time, and cost.

Course Work   You should take advantage of university course work and programs that lead to a graduate degree and state certification in a field of study. You may also attend summer sessions, workshops, special institutes, and in-service courses conducted by a local university or the school district.

Check to see whether special stipends, scholarships, or grants are available. Several states offer monetary incentives for enrolling in programs in special fields, especially science education, math education, and special education. Many school districts offer partial or full reimbursement for graduate work.

Although many of the recent reports on excellence in education recommend reducing the role of teacher training institutions in the preparation and certification of teachers by limiting the number of professional educational courses, others, such as the Carnegie Report and the National Commission on Excellence in Education, call for increased professional education and field experiences. Reports by the Education Commission of the States, the National Governor's Association, and the Holmes group call for a fifth-year (not a five-year) program, where education courses are offered after the student receives a bachelor's degree.[46] Perhaps the most consistent recommendation is for closer

---

[46] *Report Card on School Reform* (Princeton, N.J.: Carnegie Foundation for the Advancement of Teaching, 1988); *Tomorrow's Teachers: A Report of the Holmes Group* (East Lansing, Mich.: The Holmes Group, 1986). Also see Mary H. Futrell, "Standards for the Teaching Profession: A Call for Collaborative Action," *Peabody Journal of Education* (in print 1990).

cooperation between schools and universities in offering preservice and in-service education of teachers.

Researcher-Teacher Collaboration

Increasingly, university researchers are joining with schools in an effort to deal with a range of educational problems. The action research model of the 1950s encouraged cooperative study of problems by practitioners and researchers. In the 1980s Gary Griffin and Ann Lieberman developed three models for **collaborative research centers,** which they termed Interactive Research and Development in Schooling (IR&DS), involving (1) single school districts, (2) state regional agencies, and (3) teacher centers sponsored by the AFT.[47]

The collaborative research model has spread because of the belief that through cooperative problem solving researchers can get a better grasp of practitioners' problems and develop strategies that improve teaching and benefit teachers and schools.[48] In fact, a large portion of the new research on teacher effectiveness is derived from such cooperative efforts. The new collaborative centers (sometimes called R&D education centers or laboratory research centers) tend to focus less on theory and what researchers want to study and more on practical and enduring problems of teachers.

Decisions regarding research questions, data collection, and reporting are jointly determined by the university and the school. Collaboration between teachers and researchers is stressed, and both groups work together to improve the theory and practice of education. Researchers are learning to respect teachers and to conduct research of practical value, and teachers are learning to appreciate the work of researchers and to do research.[49]

PROFESSIONALISM AND EMPLOYMENT OPPORTUNITIES

Procedures and criteria for hiring new teachers are not standardized. Thus, new graduates and teachers looking to change school districts do not have a clear picture of how to present themselves and what qualities to stress.

According to school administrators, the credential file and interview are

---

[47]Gary A. Griffin, Ann Lieberman, and Joann Jacullo-Noto, *Interactive Research and Development in Schooling* (Austin: University of Texas at Austin, Research and Development Center for Teacher Education, 1983). Also see Gary A. Griffin, ed., *Staff Development*, Eighty-second Yearbook of the National Society for the Study of Education (Chicago: University of Chicago Press, 1983); Ann Lieberman, ed. *Rethinking School Improvement* (New York: Teachers College Press, Columbia University, 1986).

[48]Kenneth A Sirotnik and John I. Goodlad, eds., *School-University Partnerships in Action* (New York: Teachers College Press, Columbia University, 1988).

[49]Christopher M. Clark, "Teacher Preparation: Contributions of Research on Teacher Thinking," *Educational Researcher*, March 1988, pp. 5–12; Ornstein, "The Changing Status of the Teaching Profession."

most important. The credential file often determines whether a candidate will make it to the interview, and the interview often determines whether the candidate will get the job.[50]

Key items in a credential file are letters of reference and the resume. General letters rarely convey fitness for a specific position; they send a vague message, and the employer perceives that the candidate is applying to many school districts. Targeting is important; letters should communicate qualifications in ways that relate directly to the needs of a particular school.[51] The resume should detail education, employment, and skills related to the position.

More than 85 percent of the principals responding to a survey saw the interview as a very important factor in teacher selection.[52] Questions in an interview can be divided into four types:

1. *Questions designed to help relax candidates*, for example, asking applicants how they liked their student teaching experience or previous teaching experience.
2. *Questions designed to assist candidates to express themselves openly*, for example, asking applicants about their philosophy of classroom management or special interests or talents
3. *Questions designed to evaluate candidates' competence*, for example, asking questions related to specific problems or actions rather than philosophy, such as how they would handle the gifted learner, the slow learner.
4. *Questions designed to evaluate candidates' enthusiasm about teaching*, for example, asking about specific activities to make the classroom an exciting place for students, and asking why candidates became teachers.[53]

In most cases the principal and three to five school people participate in the interview. Although some interviewers ask superficial questions and are influenced by the physical characteristics and personality of the applicant, most interviewers structure the interview around certain questions and emphasize the responses of the candidate. See Tips for Teachers 12.3.

In a survey of 271 elementary and secondary principals, it was found that the five most important variables in reviewing a candidate's *application* were: (1) correct spelling and punctuation in the candidate's application letter, (2)

[50]Robert J. Olney, "How Employers View Resumes," *Journal of College Placement*, Spring 1982, pp. 64–67; Jo Roberts, "How to Make the Most of Teacher Interviews," *National Association of Secondary School Principals*, December 1987, pp. 103–108.

[51]Herman Holtz, *Beyond the Resume* (New York: McGraw-Hill, 1984); Dick Viering, "How to Survive the Paper Screening in a Job Search," *National Association of Secondary School Principals*, December 1987, pp. 109–114.

[52]James A. Vornberg and Kelsey Liles, "Taking Inventory of Your Interviewing Techniques," *National Association of Secondary School Principals*, January 1983, pp. 88–91.

[53]Ibid.

Tips for Teachers 12.3

Questions Interviewers Ask Teacher Candidates

Applying for a teacher's job? Here are some questions written by an administrator for administrators to ask young teachers being interviewed for a job. Although not all these questions will be asked or will be asked in this exact form during your interview, anticipating these types of questions should help you to prepare. Good luck.

1. *Philosophy of education.* In your opinion, what are the purposes of public education?
2. *Age/grade level suitability.* What do you see as the main differences between the needs of elementary and middle level students, and middle level and high school students?
3. *Subject matter competence.* What would you say are the comparative strengths and weaknesses of the _____ book series?
4. *Discipline and class management.* Have you found that any one form of disciplinary action is more effective than any other?
5. *Lesson planning skills.* What variety of teaching techniques would you plan to use in the classroom and in what situations?
6. *Flexibility within ability levels.* What special talents or abilities are needed to help a slow learner?
7. *Adaptability to administrative decisions.* What would be your attitude and reaction to an administrative decision with which you do not wholeheartedly agree?
8. *Expected relationship with peers.* How do you feel you will go about fitting into an established teaching staff that has had little turnover?
9. *Extracurricular interests.* Which activities would you be willing and able to direct if the opportunity should arise?
10. *Plans for professional improvement.* Where do you hope to be as an educator in approximately 10 years?

Source: Thomas P. Kopetskie, "An Administrator's Guide to Hiring the Right Person," *National Association of Secondary School Principals*, January 1983, p. 14.

letters of recommendation from those who were familiar with the candidate's work with children, (3) letters of recommendation from administrators, (4) neatness of materials, and (5) evaluation of student teaching from the cooperating teacher.[54] Most interesting, academic work (grade point average, honors

---

[54] Joseph A. Braun et al., "A Survey of Hiring Practices in Selected School Districts," *Journal of Teacher Education*, March–April 1987, pp. 45–49.

Table 12.8   RANK ORDER OF VARIABLES IN CONSIDERING A CANDIDATE'S
APPLICATION

Variable	Mean*
Correct spelling, punctuation, and English usage	5.52
Letters of recommendation from those who have seen candidate work with children	5.33
Letters of recommendation from adminstrators	5.26
Neatness of materials, e.g., quality of reproduction	5.13
Evaluation from cooperating teacher of student teaching	5.03
Previous employment experience	4.99
Typed vs. untyped materials	4.80
Closed or confidential letters of recommendation	4.54
Candidates' narrative statement	4.28
Substitute teaching experience	4.27
Evaluation from university supervisor of student teaching experience	4.15
Extracurricular activities	4.13
Grade point average	4.01
Honors, awards, scholarships	3.86
Work as aide	3.80
Letters of reference from personal contact	3.11
Institution certifying candidate	3.09
Age	2.76
Military experience	2.15

*Mean based on ratings of 271 principals on a scale from 6 for most important to 1 for least important.

Source: Joseph A. Braun et al., ''A Survey of Hiring Practices in Selected School Districts,'' *Journal of Teacher Education*, March–April 1987, p. 46.

and awards) did not rank high. Table 12.7 presents 19 of the most important items in rank order with mean scores. The variables considered most important about the candidate *interview* were, in rank order, (1) honesty of responses, (2) interpersonal skills, (3) use of oral English, (4) personal appearance, (5) anticipated ability to adjust to the community, and (6) sophistication of responses.[55]

THEORY INTO PRACTICE

Ralph Tyler points out that we are now learning that most professionals reach their peak performance by their seventh year of practice, and then performance begins to decline. (If the number who express fatigue, show stress symptoms, or drop out is any indication, the peak may be earlier.) In order to prevent this decline, teachers need challenging and practical in-service programs. Each school has to concentrate on a few of its most serious problems and then develop in-service programs to meet these problems. In-service programs can be vastly

[55]Ibid.

improved if the staffs of teacher education institutions and school districts work together to identify and focus on serious problems.[56]

If you expect to be an effective teacher, you will need to be able to cope with frustrations and problems that arise on the job. Regardless of the amount of satisfaction you obtain from teaching, there will be dissatisfying aspects of the job. What follows is a list of **mental health strategies** that are a mix of common sense and psychology for self-understanding. They were developed to help you deal with problems or dissatisfactions that may arise on the job.

1. *Develop self-awareness.* The better you understand yourself, the less likely you are to be overwhelmed by events or feel out of control.
2. *Evaluate dissatisfactions.* If you are dissatisfied with aspects of teaching, try to deal with parts of the problem that can be remedied. Don't give up.
3. *Expose yourself to new professional experiences.* Broaden your professional experiences. Volunteer for workshops and exchange teaching. Devote time to study and travel.
4. *Reevaluate total load.* Maintain a balance between work and social activities. Try to reduce work tension. Too much work leads to undue pressure and too little work leads to boredom.
5. *Study someone else with similar problems.* It helps to assess people with similar problems to see what they are doing wrong to avoid making the same mistakes.
6. *Evaluate personal problems.* Evaluate what problems affect your job performance. How serious are they? How widespread are they? What can be done to improve the situation? Try to confront, not avoid, the source of the problems. Try to deal with one problem at a time.
7. *Look for help on specific questions.* Often teacher dissatisfaction pertains to a specific problem, for example, the inability to maintain discipline. Consulting with an experienced colleague or supervisor sometimes helps.
8. *Talk to friends.* Talking to friends about a problem often clarifies the problem and sometimes, even what can be done to help alleviate it.
9. *Get professional help.* When friends or family cannot help with your problems, it is wise to seek professional help.
10. *Participate in group discussions.* Since many problems of teachers are similar, pool ideas and experiences. Even the "gripe" session in the teachers' lounge has benefits in expressing one's dissatisfactions and learning that others have similar problems.
11. *Develop supplementary areas.* Participate in various community and social activities to broaden your experiences and to maintain a healthy outlook on life.

---

[56]Ralph W. Tyler, "What We've Learned from Past Studies of Teacher Education," *Phi Delta Kappan*, June 1985, pp. 682–684; personal conversation by author with Ralph Tyler, July 6, 1989.

12. *Recognize new possibilities in teaching.* Many teachers have remedied dissatisfaction by discovering new teaching responsibilities, such as work on workshops, experimental programs, and staff development projects.

13. *Don't take out your frustrations in class.* Don't vent your dissatisfactions on your students. It solves nothing and adds to your teaching problems.

14. *Be willing to admit failure.* In extreme cases it is best to withdraw from the school or profession if you find that teaching in the present situation has too many problems or that you simply don't enjoy teaching.[57]

Your ability to learn from experience and to grow professionally and personally depends in large part on your capacity to face, analyze, and deal constructively with the realities of your life and work conditions. Ten strategies for understanding yourself in relation to the realities of your school situation are listed below.

1. *Strengths and weaknesses.* The ability to make realistic self-estimates is crucial, given the fact that your students and colleagues will observe and make judgments about your behavior, attitude, and abilities. Learn to see yourself as others see you and to compensate for or modify areas that need to be improved.

2. *Ability to make use of resources.* As a teacher you will come across many different texts, tests, materials, and people. You will need to make judgments about their value and how to best utilize these resources for your growth.

3. *Social and personal skills.* You will need to understand the attitudes and feelings of your students, colleagues, and supervisors, how to adapt to and interact with different persons, how to learn from them, and how to work cooperatively with them.

4. *Ability to function in a bureaucratic setting.* Schools are bureaucracies, and you must learn the rules and regulations, as well as the norms and behaviors of the school. As a teacher, you are an employee of an organization that has certain expectations of you and all employees.

5. *Forms, reports, and records.* Schools expect teachers to complete a host of forms, reports, and records accurately and on time. The quicker you become familiar with this work, the smoother it will be for you. At first the various forms, reports, and records may seem burdensome, yet neither you, your supervisors, nor the school can function without them.

---

[57] The first 12 items are derived from Fritz Redl and William W. Wattenberg, *Mental Hygiene in Teaching,* 2nd ed. (New York: Harcourt Brace 1959). The last two are derived from Robert F. Biehler and Jack Snowman, *Psychology Applied to Teaching,* 6th ed. (Boston: Houghton Mifflin, 1990).

6. *Ability to make choices.* You will need to understand and apply the decision-making process purposefully and logically. Learn to be consistent and rational when making a choice. Think about the impact your decisions have on others in the school.

7. *Understanding your roles as a teacher.* The teacher's role goes far beyond teaching a group of students in class. Teaching occurs in a particular social context, and much of what you do and are expected to do is influenced by this context. Different students, supervisors, administrators, parents, and community members expect different things from you. You must expect to perform varied roles depending on the realities, demands, and expectations of a school's culture.

8. *Know how to organize your time.* There are only so many hours in a day, and many demands and expectations are imposed on you as a person and professional. You will need to make good use of time, to set priorities, to plan, and to get your work done.

9. *Separate your job from your personal life.* Never let the teaching job (or any job) overwhelm you to the point that it interferes with your personal life. There are times when you may have to spend a few extra hours in school helping students or working with colleagues, and there are times when you will have to spend extra afterschool hours grading papers and tests, preparing lessons, and performing clerical tasks, but for your own mental health be sure you have time left for your private, family, and social life.

10. *Develop a professional identity.* Professional identity involves an understanding of the relation between your professional training and professional roles; knowledge of yourself and how others perceive you, your teaching style and capabilities, the teaching styles and capabilities of your colleagues, your expectations as a teacher, and the expectations of your supervisor or administrators; and the ability to select and evaluate future career plans.

As we conclude this chapter, it is important to note that teaching can be difficult and rewarding. Few roles are more exciting and important than teaching. When competent teachers work with young children, there is rarely a dull moment. Through their students, teachers can contribute to the shaping and growth of the community and the nation; the teachers' impact is long term —and we are unable to determine where the influence ceases. Teaching is a proud profession, and professional growth and development are an important part of the life of a teacher. Take the job seriously, and work at improving your skills and abilities as a teacher.

SUMMARY

1. Beginning teachers need support and assistance to ease into their position and improve their instructional skills.

2. To become a master of the trade, you will need to continually improve your teaching abilities. People closely associated with your teaching and instruction, including students, peers, and supervisors, are best able to provide feedback and evaluation. Several procedures for utilizing the ratings and observations of these three groups have been outlined.

3. Research suggests that student raters of teachers are more reliable and valid than other raters, since students see teachers over an extended period in various situations.

4. Teachers favor self-evaluation over all other forms of evaluation, including student, peer, and supervisory evaluation.

5. Supplementary sources for evaluating teachers include lesson and unit plans, special projects, instructional materials and media, reading lists, and student work and test outcomes.

6. There are hundreds of education associations for teachers to join; the two largest ones and the ones that have probably done the most to improve teacher salaries and working conditions are the American Federation of Teachers and the National Education Association.

7. Several other opportunities exist to help teachers grow as professionals, including reading the professional literature, attending conferences, taking courses, and collaborating with researchers.

8. When pursuing a job, it is important to realize that letters of reference and the resume are key items that school officials look at. These items help you get to the interview in which interpersonal and communication skills are important factors for being hired.

QUESTIONS TO CONSIDER

1. Why should you begin now to consider ways for improving your skills as a teacher?

2. What are some ways for coping with problems or concerns related to the job of teaching?

3. Which of your experiences as a preservice teacher do you think will help you as a beginning teacher?

4. Of the following evaluation alternatives—student, peer, self, and supervisory—which would you prefer as a beginning teacher? Why? As an experienced teacher? Why?

5. Name two or three professional organizations you expect to join as a teacher. How do you expect to benefit from membership in these organizations?

THINGS TO DO

1. Survey the class on the basic adjustment problems of new teachers. Rank order them. Discuss in class how problems considered important (top 5) can be remedied.

2. Study the important evaluation techniques of teaching. If your professor permits, select one instrument and evaluate his or her performance.

3. Have a class member teach a sample lesson in his or her subject or grade level. Evaluate the lesson in terms of instructional methods, use of media, and organization of subject matter.

4. Invite a representative of the AFT and NEA to your class to discuss the organizations.

5. The text lists several professional organizations and several professional journals. Identify the ones that offer potential for your professional development. Explain the reasons to the class.

RECOMMENDED READINGS

Bolin, Frances S., and Judith M. Falk, eds. *Teacher Renewal: Professional Issues and Personal Choice.* New York: Teachers College Press, Columbia University, 1986. A plan to engage teachers in professional policies and issues affecting their careers.

Jackson, Philip W. *The Practice of Teaching.* New York: Teachers College Press, Columbia University, 1986. The complexity of teaching and the uncertainties teachers face in classrooms and schools.

Kowalski, Theodore, Roy A. Weaver, and Kenneth T. Henson, *Case Studies of Teaching,* New York: Longman, 1989. Thirty-six case studies of first-year teachers, providing an analysis of common experiences faced by new teachers.

McNergney, Robert, ed. *Guide to Classroom Teaching.* Needham Heights, Mass.: Allyn and Bacon, 1989. An outline of the methods and skills of teaching and an understanding of the roles and responsibilities of teachers.

Rubin, Louis J. *Artistry in Teaching.* New York: Random House, 1985. Aimed at trainers of teachers and teachers in training who believe that teaching is more art than science and that prescriptive practices cannot really be taught in advance.

Ryan, Kevin. *Biting the Apple: Accounts of First Year Teachers.* New York: Longman, 1980. Experiences of several beginning teachers to help others explore their feelings about teaching and give them an idea of what to expect.

Tom, Alan R. *How Should Teachers Be Educated?* Bloomington, Ind.: Phi Delta Kappa, 1987. An overview and analysis of several reports calling for major reforms and restructuring of teacher education.

KEY TERMS

Induction period

Peer coach

Resource teacher

Staff development

Mentor program

Clinical supervision

Pre-observation conference

Post-observation conference

Technical coaching

Artifacts of teaching

Collaborative research centers

Mental health strategies

NAME INDEX

SUBJECT INDEX

628